Linux Networking Cookbook™

Carla Schroder

O'REILLY®

Beijing · Cambridge · Farnham · Köln · Paris · Sebastopol · Taipei · Tokyo

Linux Networking Cookbook™
by Carla Schroder

Copyright © 2008 O'Reilly Media, Inc. All rights reserved.
Printed in the United States of America.

Published by O'Reilly Media, Inc., 1005 Gravenstein Highway North, Sebastopol, CA 95472.

O'Reilly books may be purchased for educational, business, or sales promotional use. Online editions are also available for most titles (*safari.oreilly.com*). For more information, contact our corporate/institutional sales department: (800) 998-9938 or *corporate@oreilly.com*.

Editor: Mike Loukides	**Indexer:** John Bickelhaupt
Production Editor: Sumita Mukherji	**Cover Designer:** Karen Montgomery
Copyeditor: Derek Di Matteo	**Interior Designer:** David Futato
Proofreader: Sumita Mukherji	**Illustrator:** Jessamyn Read

Printing History:

November 2007:   First Edition.

QA
76.774
.L46
S33
2008

Nutshell Handbook, the Nutshell Handbook logo, and the O'Reilly logo are registered trademarks of O'Reilly Media, Inc. The *Cookbook* series designations, *Linux Networking Cookbook*, the image of a female blacksmith, and related trade dress are trademarks of O'Reilly Media, Inc.

Java™ is a trademark of Sun Microsystems, Inc. .NET is a registered trademark of Microsoft Corporation.

Many of the designations used by manufacturers and sellers to distinguish their products are claimed as trademarks. Where those designations appear in this book, and O'Reilly Media, Inc. was aware of a trademark claim, the designations have been printed in caps or initial caps.

While every precaution has been taken in the preparation of this book, the publisher and author assume no responsibility for errors or omissions, or for damages resulting from the use of the information contained herein.

 This book uses RepKover™, a durable and flexible lay-flat binding.

ISBN-10: 0-596-10248-8
ISBN-13: 978-0-596-10248-7
[M]

To Terry Hanson—thank you!
You make it all worthwhile.

Table of Contents

Preface . . . . **xv**

1. Introduction to Linux Networking **1**
    1.0 Introduction   1

2. Building a Linux Gateway on a Single-Board Computer **12**
    2.0 Introduction   12
    2.1 Getting Acquainted with the Soekris 4521   14
    2.2 Configuring Multiple Minicom Profiles   17
    2.3 Installing Pyramid Linux on a Compact Flash Card   17
    2.4 Network Installation of Pyramid on Debian   19
    2.5 Network Installation of Pyramid on Fedora   21
    2.6 Booting Pyramid Linux   24
    2.7 Finding and Editing Pyramid Files   26
    2.8 Hardening Pyramid   27
    2.9 Getting and Installing the Latest Pyramid Build   28
    2.10 Adding Additional Software to Pyramid Linux   28
    2.11 Adding New Hardware Drivers   32
    2.12 Customizing the Pyramid Kernel   33
    2.13 Updating the Soekris comBIOS   34

3. Building a Linux Firewall **36**
    3.0 Introduction   36
    3.1 Assembling a Linux Firewall Box   44
    3.2 Configuring Network Interface Cards on Debian   45
    3.3 Configuring Network Interface Cards on Fedora   48
    3.4 Identifying Which NIC Is Which   50

3.5   Building an Internet-Connection Sharing Firewall on a Dynamic
        WAN IP Address   51

3.6   Building an Internet-Connection Sharing Firewall on a Static
        WAN IP Address   56

3.7   Displaying the Status of Your Firewall   57

3.8   Turning an iptables Firewall Off   58

3.9   Starting iptables at Boot, and Manually Bringing Your Firewall
        Up and Down   59

3.10 Testing Your Firewall   62

3.11 Configuring the Firewall for Remote SSH Administration   65

3.12 Allowing Remote SSH Through a NAT Firewall   66

3.13 Getting Multiple SSH Host Keys Past NAT   68

3.14 Running Public Services on Private IP Addresses   69

3.15 Setting Up a Single-Host Firewall   71

3.16 Setting Up a Server Firewall   76

3.17 Configuring iptables Logging   79

3.18 Writing Egress Rules   80

4. **Building a Linux Wireless Access Point** **82**

4.0   Introduction   82

4.1   Building a Linux Wireless Access Point   86

4.2   Bridging Wireless to Wired   87

4.3   Setting Up Name Services   90

4.4   Setting Static IP Addresses from the DHCP Server   93

4.5   Configuring Linux and Windows Static DHCP Clients   94

4.6   Adding Mail Servers to dnsmasq   96

4.7   Making WPA2-Personal Almost As Good As WPA-Enterprise   97

4.8   Enterprise Authentication with a RADIUS Server   100

4.9   Configuring Your Wireless Access Point to Use FreeRADIUS   104

4.10 Authenticating Clients to FreeRADIUS   106

4.11 Connecting to the Internet and Firewalling   107

4.12 Using Routing Instead of Bridging   108

4.13 Probing Your Wireless Interface Card   113

4.14 Changing the Pyramid Router's Hostname   114

4.15 Turning Off Antenna Diversity   115

4.16 Managing dnsmasq's DNS Cache   117

4.17 Managing Windows' DNS Caches   120

4.18 Updating the Time at Boot   121

5. Building a VoIP Server with Asterisk **123**

    5.0 Introduction 123

    5.1 Installing Asterisk from Source Code 127

    5.2 Installing Asterisk on Debian 131

    5.3 Starting and Stopping Asterisk 132

    5.4 Testing the Asterisk Server 135

    5.5 Adding Phone Extensions to Asterisk and Making Calls 136

    5.6 Setting Up Softphones 143

    5.7 Getting Real VoIP with Free World Dialup 146

    5.8 Connecting Your Asterisk PBX to Analog Phone Lines 148

    5.9 Creating a Digital Receptionist 151

    5.10 Recording Custom Prompts 153

    5.11 Maintaining a Message of the Day 156

    5.12 Transferring Calls 158

    5.13 Routing Calls to Groups of Phones 158

    5.14 Parking Calls 159

    5.15 Customizing Hold Music 161

    5.16 Playing MP3 Sound Files on Asterisk 161

    5.17 Delivering Voicemail Broadcasts 162

    5.18 Conferencing with Asterisk 163

    5.19 Monitoring Conferences 165

    5.20 Getting SIP Traffic Through iptables NAT Firewalls 166

    5.21 Getting IAX Traffic Through iptables NAT Firewalls 168

    5.22 Using AsteriskNOW, "Asterisk in 30 Minutes" 168

    5.23 Installing and Removing Packages on AsteriskNOW 170

    5.24 Connecting Road Warriors and Remote Users 171

6. Routing with Linux **173**

    6.0 Introduction 173

    6.1 Calculating Subnets with ipcalc 176

    6.2 Setting a Default Gateway 178

    6.3 Setting Up a Simple Local Router 180

    6.4 Configuring Simplest Internet Connection Sharing 183

    6.5 Configuring Static Routing Across Subnets 185

    6.6 Making Static Routes Persistent 186

    6.7 Using RIP Dynamic Routing on Debian 187

    6.8 Using RIP Dynamic Routing on Fedora 191

    6.9 Using Quagga's Command Line 192

6.10 Logging In to Quagga Daemons Remotely   194
6.11 Running Quagga Daemons from the Command Line   195
6.12 Monitoring RIPD   197
6.13 Blackholing Routes with Zebra   198
6.14 Using OSPF for Simple Dynamic Routing   199
6.15 Adding a Bit of Security to RIP and OSPF   201
6.16 Monitoring OSPFD   202

7. Secure Remote Administration with SSH **204**
7.0 Introduction   204
7.1 Starting and Stopping OpenSSH   207
7.2 Creating Strong Passphrases   208
7.3 Setting Up Host Keys for Simplest Authentication   209
7.4 Generating and Copying SSH Keys   211
7.5 Using Public-Key Authentication to Protect System Passwords 213
7.6 Managing Multiple Identity Keys   214
7.7 Hardening OpenSSH   215
7.8 Changing a Passphrase   216
7.9 Retrieving a Key Fingerprint   217
7.10 Checking Configuration Syntax   218
7.11 Using OpenSSH Client Configuration Files for Easier Logins 218
7.12 Tunneling X Windows Securely over SSH   220
7.13 Executing Commands Without Opening a Remote Shell   221
7.14 Using Comments to Label Keys   222
7.15 Using DenyHosts to Foil SSH Attacks   223
7.16 Creating a DenyHosts Startup File   225
7.17 Mounting Entire Remote Filesystems with sshfs   226

8. Using Cross-Platform Remote Graphical Desktops **228**
8.0 Introduction   228
8.1 Connecting Linux to Windows via rdesktop   230
8.2 Generating and Managing FreeNX SSH Keys   233
8.3 Using FreeNX to Run Linux from Windows   233
8.4 Using FreeNX to Run Linux from Solaris, Mac OS X, or Linux   238
8.5 Managing FreeNX Users   239
8.6 Watching Nxclient Users from the FreeNX Server   240
8.7 Starting and Stopping the FreeNX Server   241

8.8 Configuring a Custom Desktop   242

8.9 Creating Additional Nxclient Sessions   244

8.10 Enabling File and Printer Sharing, and Multimedia in Nxclient   246

8.11 Preventing Password-Saving in Nxclient   246

8.12 Troubleshooting FreeNX   247

8.13 Using VNC to Control Windows from Linux   248

8.14 Using VNC to Control Windows and Linux at the Same Time   250

8.15 Using VNC for Remote Linux-to-Linux Administration   252

8.16 Displaying the Same Windows Desktop to Multiple Remote Users   254

8.17 Changing the Linux VNC Server Password   256

8.18 Customizing the Remote VNC Desktop   257

8.19 Setting the Remote VNC Desktop Size   258

8.20 Connecting VNC to an Existing X Session   259

8.21 Securely Tunneling x11vnc over SSH   261

8.22 Tunneling TightVNC Between Linux and Windows   262

**9. Building Secure Cross-Platform Virtual Private Networks
with OpenVPN** **265**

9.0 Introduction   265

9.1 Setting Up a Safe OpenVPN Test Lab   267

9.2 Starting and Testing OpenVPN   270

9.3 Testing Encryption with Static Keys   272

9.4 Connecting a Remote Linux Client Using Static Keys   274

9.5 Creating Your Own PKI for OpenVPN   276

9.6 Configuring the OpenVPN Server for Multiple Clients   279

9.7 Configuring OpenVPN to Start at Boot   281

9.8 Revoking Certificates   282

9.9 Setting Up the OpenVPN Server in Bridge Mode   284

9.10 Running OpenVPN As a Nonprivileged User   285

9.11 Connecting Windows Clients   286

10. Building a Linux PPTP VPN Server **287**

10.0 Introduction   287

10.1 Installing Poptop on Debian Linux   290

10.2 Patching the Debian Kernel for MPPE Support   291

10.3 Installing Poptop on Fedora Linux   293

10.4 Patching the Fedora Kernel for MPPE Support   294

10.5 Setting Up a Standalone PPTP VPN Server   295

10.6 Adding Your Poptop Server to Active Directory 298
10.7 Connecting Linux Clients to a PPTP Server 299
10.8 Getting PPTP Through an iptables Firewall 300
10.9 Monitoring Your PPTP Server 301
10.10 Troubleshooting PPTP 302

11. Single Sign-on with Samba for Mixed Linux/Windows LANs **305**
11.0 Introduction 305
11.1 Verifying That All the Pieces Are in Place 307
11.2 Compiling Samba from Source Code 310
11.3 Starting and Stopping Samba 312
11.4 Using Samba As a Primary Domain Controller 313
11.5 Migrating to a Samba Primary Domain Controller from an
     NT4 PDC 317
11.6 Joining Linux to an Active Directory Domain 319
11.7 Connecting Windows 95/98/ME to a Samba Domain 323
11.8 Connecting Windows NT4 to a Samba Domain 324
11.9 Connecting Windows NT/2000 to a Samba Domain 325
11.10 Connecting Windows XP to a Samba Domain 325
11.11 Connecting Linux Clients to a Samba Domain with
      Command-Line Programs 326
11.12 Connecting Linux Clients to a Samba Domain with
      Graphical Programs 330

12. Centralized Network Directory with OpenLDAP **332**
12.0 Introduction 332
12.1 Installing OpenLDAP on Debian 339
12.2 Installing OpenLDAP on Fedora 341
12.3 Configuring and Testing the OpenLDAP Server 341
12.4 Creating a New Database on Fedora 344
12.5 Adding More Users to Your Directory 348
12.6 Correcting Directory Entries 350
12.7 Connecting to a Remote OpenLDAP Server 352
12.8 Finding Things in Your OpenLDAP Directory 352
12.9 Indexing Your Database 354
12.10 Managing Your Directory with Graphical Interfaces 356
12.11 Configuring the Berkeley DB 358
12.12 Configuring OpenLDAP Logging 363

12.13 Backing Up and Restoring Your Directory   364
12.14 Refining Access Controls   366
12.15 Changing Passwords   370

13. Network Monitoring with Nagios **371**
13.0 Introduction   371
13.1 Installing Nagios from Sources   372
13.2 Configuring Apache for Nagios   376
13.3 Organizing Nagios' Configuration Files Sanely   378
13.4 Configuring Nagios to Monitor Localhost   380
13.5 Configuring CGI Permissions for Full Nagios Web Access   389
13.6 Starting Nagios at Boot   390
13.7 Adding More Nagios Users   391
13.8 Speed Up Nagios with check_icmp   392
13.9 Monitoring SSHD   393
13.10 Monitoring a Web Server   397
13.11 Monitoring a Mail Server   400
13.12 Using Servicegroups to Group Related Services   402
13.13 Monitoring Name Services   403
13.14 Setting Up Secure Remote Nagios Administration with OpenSSH   405
13.15 Setting Up Secure Remote Nagios Administration with OpenSSL   406

14. Network Monitoring with MRTG **408**
14.0 Introduction   408
14.1 Installing MRTG   409
14.2 Configuring SNMP on Debian   410
14.3 Configuring SNMP on Fedora   413
14.4 Configuring Your HTTP Service for MRTG   413
14.5 Configuring and Starting MRTG on Debian   415
14.6 Configuring and Starting MRTG on Fedora   418
14.7 Monitoring Active CPU Load   419
14.8 Monitoring CPU User and Idle Times   422
14.9 Monitoring Physical Memory   424
14.10 Monitoring Swap Space and Memory   425
14.11 Monitoring Disk Usage   426
14.12 Monitoring TCP Connections   428
14.13 Finding and Testing MIBs and OIDs   429
14.14 Testing Remote SNMP Queries   430

	14.15	Monitoring Remote Hosts	432
	14.16	Creating Multiple MRTG Index Pages	433
	14.17	Running MRTG As a Daemon	434

15. Getting Acquainted with IPv6 .... **437**
	15.0	Introduction	437
	15.1	Testing Your Linux System for IPv6 Support	442
	15.2	Pinging Link Local IPv6 Hosts	443
	15.3	Setting Unique Local Unicast Addresses on Interfaces	445
	15.4	Using SSH with IPv6	446
	15.5	Copying Files over IPv6 with scp	447
	15.6	Autoconfiguration with IPv6	448
	15.7	Calculating IPv6 Addresses	449
	15.8	Using IPv6 over the Internet	450

16. Setting Up Hands-Free Network Installations of New Systems **452**
	16.0	Introduction	452
	16.1	Creating Network Installation Boot Media for Fedora Linux	453
	16.2	Network Installation of Fedora Using Network Boot Media	455
	16.3	Setting Up an HTTP-Based Fedora Installation Server	457
	16.4	Setting Up an FTP-Based Fedora Installation Server	458
	16.5	Creating a Customized Fedora Linux Installation	461
	16.6	Using a Kickstart File for a Hands-off Fedora Linux Installation	463
	16.7	Fedora Network Installation via PXE Netboot	464
	16.8	Network Installation of a Debian System	466
	16.9	Building a Complete Debian Mirror with apt-mirror	468
	16.10	Building a Partial Debian Mirror with apt-proxy	470
	16.11	Configuring Client PCs to Use Your Local Debian Mirror	471
	16.12	Setting Up a Debian PXE Netboot Server	472
	16.13	Installing New Systems from Your Local Debian Mirror	474
	16.14	Automating Debian Installations with Preseed Files	475

17. Linux Server Administration via Serial Console **478**
	17.0	Introduction	478
	17.1	Preparing a Server for Serial Console Administration	479
	17.2	Configuring a Headless Server with LILO	483
	17.3	Configuring a Headless Server with GRUB	485
	17.4	Booting to Text Mode on Debian	487

17.5   Setting Up the Serial Console   489

17.6   Configuring Your Server for Dial-in Administration   492

17.7   Dialing In to the Server   495

17.8   Adding Security   496

17.9   Configuring Logging   497

17.10 Uploading Files to the Server   498

18. Running a Linux Dial-Up Server **501**

18.0   Introduction   501

18.1   Configuring a Single Dial-Up Account with WvDial   501

18.2   Configuring Multiple Accounts in WvDial   504

18.3   Configuring Dial-Up Permissions for Nonroot Users   505

18.4   Creating WvDial Accounts for Nonroot Users   507

18.5   Sharing a Dial-Up Internet Account   508

18.6   Setting Up Dial-on-Demand   509

18.7   Scheduling Dial-Up Availability with cron   510

18.8   Dialing over Voicemail Stutter Tones   512

18.9   Overriding Call Waiting   512

18.10 Leaving the Password Out of the Configuration File   513

18.11 Creating a Separate pppd Logfile   514

19. Troubleshooting Networks **515**

19.0   Introduction   515

19.1   Building a Network Diagnostic and Repair Laptop   516

19.2   Testing Connectivity with ping   519

19.3   Profiling Your Network with FPing and Nmap   521

19.4   Finding Duplicate IP Addresses with arping   523

19.5   Testing HTTP Throughput and Latency with httping   525

19.6   Using traceroute, tcptraceroute, and mtr to Pinpoint Network
       Problems   527

19.7   Using tcpdump to Capture and Analyze Traffic   529

19.8   Capturing TCP Flags with tcpdump   533

19.9   Measuring Throughput, Jitter, and Packet Loss with iperf   535

19.10 Using ngrep for Advanced Packet Sniffing   538

19.11 Using ntop for Colorful and Quick Network Monitoring   540

19.12 Troubleshooting DNS Servers   542

19.13 Troubleshooting DNS Clients   545

19.14 Troubleshooting SMTP Servers   546

19.15 Troubleshooting a POP3, POP3s, or IMAP Server   549
19.16 Creating SSL Keys for Your Syslog-ng Server on Debian   551
19.17 Creating SSL Keys for Your Syslog-ng Server on Fedora   557
19.18 Setting Up stunnel for Syslog-ng   558
19.19 Building a Syslog Server   560

A. Essential References **563**

B. Glossary of Networking Terms **566**

C. Linux Kernel Building Reference **590**

Index **599**

Preface

So there you are, staring at your computer and wondering why your Internet connection is running slower than slow, and wishing you knew enough to penetrate the endless runaround you get from your service provider. Or, you're the Lone IT Staffer in a small business who got the job because you know the difference between a switch and hub, and now you're supposed to have all the answers. Or, you're really interested in networking, and want to learn more and make it your profession. Or, you are already knowledgeable, and you simply have a few gaps you need to fill. But you're finding out that computer networking is a subject with reams and reams of reference material that is not always organized in a coherent, useful order, and it takes an awful lot of reading just to figure out which button to push.

To make things even more interesting, you need to integrate Linux and Windows hosts. If you want to pick up a book that lays out the steps for specific tasks, that explains clearly the necessary commands and configurations, and does not tax your patience with endless ramblings and meanderings into theory and obscure RFCs, this is the book for you.

Audience

Ideally, you will have some Linux experience. You should know how to install and remove programs, navigate the filesystem, manage file permissions, and user and group creation. You should have some exposure to TCP/IP and Ethernet basics, IPv4 and IPv6, LAN, WAN, subnet, router, firewall, gateway, switch, hub, and cabling. If you are starting from scratch, there are any number of introductory books to get you up to speed on the basics.

If you don't already have basic Linux experience, I recommend getting the *Linux Cookbook* (O'Reilly). The *Linux Cookbook* (which I authored) was designed as a companion book to this one. It covers installing and removing software, user account management, cross-platform file and printer sharing, cross-platform user authentication, running servers (e.g., mail, web, DNS), backup and recovery, system rescue and repair, hardware discovery, configuring X Windows, remote administration, and lots more good stuff.

The home/SOHO user also will find some useful chapters in this book, and anyone who wants to learn Linux networking will be able to do everything in this book with a couple of ordinary PCs and inexpensive networking hardware.

Contents of This Book

This book is broken into 19 chapters and 3 appendixes:

Chapter 1, *Introduction to Linux Networking*
>   This is your high-level view of computer networking, covering cabling, routing and switching, interfaces, the different types of Internet services, and the fundamentals of network architecture and performance.

Chapter 2, *Building a Linux Gateway on a Single-Board Computer*
>   In which we are introduced to the fascinating and adaptable world of Linux on routerboards, such as those made by Soekris and PC Engines, and how Linux on one of these little boards gives you more power and flexibility than commercial gear costing many times as much.

Chapter 3, *Building a Linux Firewall*
>   Learn to use Linux's powerful *iptables* packet filter to protect your network, with complete recipes for border firewalls, single-host firewalls, getting services through NAT (Network Address Translation), blocking external access to internal services, secure remote access through your firewall, and how to safely test new firewalls before deploying them on production systems.

Chapter 4, *Building a Linux Wireless Access Point*
>   You can use Linux and a routerboard (or any ordinary PC hardware) to build a secure, powerful, fully featured wireless access point customized to meet your needs, including state-of-the-art authentication and encryption, name services, and routing and bridging.

Chapter 5, *Building a VoIP Server with Asterisk*
>   This chapter digs into the very guts of the revolutionary and popular Asterisk VoIP server. Sure, these days, everyone has pretty point-and-click GUIs for managing their iPBX systems, but you still need to understand what's under the hood. This chapter shows you how to install Asterisk and configure Asterisk

from scratch: how to create user's extensions and voicemail, manage custom greetings and messages, do broadcast voicemails, provision phones, set up a digital receptionist, do PSTN (Public Switched Telephone Network) integration, do pure VoIP, manage road warriors, and more.

Chapter 6, *Routing with Linux*

Linux's networking stack is a powerhouse, and it includes advanced routing capabilities. Here be recipes for building Linux-based routers, calculating subnets (accurately and without pain), blackholing unwelcome visitors, using static and dynamic routing, and for monitoring your hard-working little routers.

Chapter 7, *Secure Remote Administration with SSH*

OpenSSH is an amazing and endlessly useful implementation of the very secure SSH protocol. It supports traditional password-based logins, password-less public-key-based logins, and securely carries traffic over untrusted networks. You'll learn how to do all of this, plus how to safely log in to your systems remotely, and how to harden and protect OpenSSH itself.

Chapter 8, *Using Cross-Platform Remote Graphical Desktops*

OpenSSH is slick and quick, and offers both text console and a secure X Windows tunnel for running graphical applications. There are several excellent programs (FreeNX, rdesktop, and VNC) that offer a complementary set of capabilities, such as remote helpdesk, your choice of remote desktops, and Linux as a Windows terminal server client. You can control multiple computers from a single keyboard and monitor, and even conduct a class where multiple users view or participate in the same remote session.

Chapter 9, *Building Secure Cross-Platform Virtual Private Networks with OpenVPN*

Everyone seems to want a secure, user-friendly VPN (Virtual Private Network). But there is a lot of confusion over what a VPN really is, and a lot of commercial products that are not true VPNs at all, but merely SSL portals to a limited number of services. OpenVPN is a true SSL-based VPN that requires all endpoints to be trusted, and that uses advanced methods for securing the connection and keeping it securely encrypted. OpenVPN includes clients for Linux, Solaris, Mac OS X, OpenBSD, FreeBSD, and NetBSD, so it's your one-stop VPN shop. You'll learn how to create and manage your own PKI (Public Key Infrastructure), which is crucial for painless OpenVPN administration. And, you'll learn how to safely test OpenVPN, how to set up the server, and how to connect clients.

Chapter 10, *Building a Linux PPTP VPN Server*

This chapter covers building and configuring a Linux PPTP VPN server for Windows and Linux clients; how to patch Windows clients so they have the necessary encryption support, how to integrate with Active Directory, and how to get PPTP through an *iptables* firewall.

Chapter 11, *Single Sign-on with Samba for Mixed Linux/Windows LANs*

Using Samba as a Windows NT4-style domain controller gives you a flexible, reliable, inexpensive mechanism for authenticating your network clients. You'll learn how to migrate from a Windows domain controller to Samba on Linux, how to migrate Windows user accounts to Samba, integrate Linux clients with Active Directory, and how to connect clients.

Chapter 12, *Centralized Network Directory with OpenLDAP*

An LDAP directory is an excellent mechanism on which to base your network directory services. This chapter shows how to build an OpenLDAP directory from scratch, how to test it, how to make changes, how to find things, how to speed up lookups with smart indexing, and how to tune it for maximum performance.

Chapter 13, *Network Monitoring with Nagios*

Nagios is a great network monitoring system that makes clever use of standard Linux commands to monitor services and hosts, and to alert you when there are problems. Status reports are displayed in nice colorful graphs on HTML pages that can be viewed on any Web browser. Learn to monitor basic system health, and common servers like DNS, Web, and mail servers, and how to perform secure remote Nagios administration.

Chapter 14, *Network Monitoring with MRTG*

MRTG is an SNMP-aware network monitor, so theoretically it can be adapted to monitor any SNMP-enabled device or service. Learn how to monitor hardware and services, and how to find the necessary SNMP information to create custom monitors.

Chapter 15, *Getting Acquainted with IPv6*

Ready or not, IPv6 is coming, and it will eventually supplant IPv4. Get ahead of the curve by running IPv6 on your own network and over the Internet; learn why those very long IPv6 addresses are actually simpler to manage than IPv4 addresses; learn how to use SSH over IPv6, and how to auto-configure clients without DHCP.

Chapter 16, *Setting Up Hands-Free Network Installations of New Systems*

Fedora Linux and all of its relatives (Red Hat, CentOS, Mandriva, PC Linux OS, and so forth), and Debian Linux and all of its descendants (Ubuntu, Mepis, Knoppix, etc.) include utilities for creating and cloning customized installations, and for provisioning new systems over the network. So, you can plug-in a PC, and within a few minutes have a complete new installation all ready to go. This chapter describes how to use ordinary installation ISO images for network installations of Fedora, and how to create and maintain complete local Debian mirrors efficiently.

Chapter 17, *Linux Server Administration via Serial Console*

When Ethernet goes haywire, the serial console will save the day, both locally and remotely; plus, routers and managed switches are often administered via the serial console. Learn how to set up any Linux computer to accept serial connections, and how to use any Linux, Mac OS X, or Windows PC as a serial terminal. You'll also learn how to do dial-up server administration, and how to upload files over your serial link.

Chapter 18, *Running a Linux Dial-Up Server*

Even in these modern times, dial-up networking is still important; we're a long way from universal broadband. Set up Internet-connection sharing over dial-up, dial-on-demand, use *cron* to schedule dialup sessions, and set up multiple dial-up accounts.

Chapter 19, *Troubleshooting Networks*

Linux contains a wealth of power tools for diagnosing and fixing network problems. You'll learn the deep dark secrets of *ping*, how to use *tcpdump* and Wireshark to eavesdrop on your own wires, how to troubleshoot the name and mail server, how to discover all the hosts on your network, how to track problems down to their sources, and how to set up a secure central logging server. You'll learn a number of lesser-known but powerful utilities such as *fping*, *httping*, *arping*, and *mtr*, and how to transform an ordinary old laptop into your indispensible portable network diagnostic-and-fixit tool.

Appendix A, *Essential References*

Computer networking is a large and complex subject, so here is a list of books and other references that tell you what you need to know.

Appendix B, *Glossary of Networking Terms*

Don't know what it means? Look it up here.

Appendix C, *Linux Kernel Building Reference*

As the Linux kernel continues to expand in size and functionality, it often makes sense to build your own kernel with all the unnecessary bits stripped out. Learn the Fedora way, the Debian way, and the vanilla way of building a custom kernel.

What Is Included

This book covers both old standbys and newfangled technologies. The old-time stuff includes system administration via serial console, dial-up networking, building an Internet gateway, VLANs, various methods of secure remote access, routing, and traffic control. Newfangled technologies include building your own iPBX with Asterisk, wireless connectivity, cross-platform remote graphical desktops, hands-free network installation of new systems, single sign-on for mixed Linux and Windows LANs, and IPv6 basics. And, there are chapters on monitoring, alerting, and troubleshooting.

Which Linux Distributions Are Used in the Book

There are literally hundreds, if not thousands of Linux distributions: live distributions on all kinds of bootable media, from business-card CDs to USB keys to CDs to DVDs; large general-purpose distributions; tiny specialized distributions for firewalls, routers, and old PCs; multimedia distributions; scientific distributions; cluster distributions; distributions that run Windows applications; and super-secure distributions. There is no way to even begin to cover all of these; fortunately for frazzled authors, the Linux world can be roughly divided into two camps: Red Hat Linux and Debian Linux. Both are fundamental, influential distributions that have spawned the majority of derivatives and clones.

In this book, the Red Hat world is represented by Fedora Linux, the free community-driven distribution sponsored by Red Hat. Fedora is free of cost, the core distribution contains only Free Software, and it has a more rapid release cycle than Red Hat Enterprise Linux (RHEL). RHEL is on an 18-month release cycle, is designed to be stable and predictable, and has no packaged free-of-cost version, though plenty of free clones abound. The clones are built from the RHEL SRPMs, with the Red Hat trademarks removed. Some RHEL-based distributions include CentOS, White Box Linux, Lineox, White Box Enterprise Linux, Tao Linux, and Pie Box Linux.

Additionally, there are a number of Red Hat derivatives to choose from, like Mandriva and PCLinuxOS. The recipes for Fedora should work for all of these, though you might find some small differences in filenames, file locations, and package names.

Debian-based distributions are multiplying even as we speak: Ubuntu, Kubuntu, Edubuntu, Xandros, Mepis, Knoppix, Kanotix, and Linspire, to name but a few. While all of these have their own enhancements and modifications, package management with *aptitude* or Synaptic works the same on all of them.

Novell/SUSE is RPM-based like Red Hat, but has always gone its own way. Gentoo and Slackware occupy their own unique niches. I'm not even going to try to include all of these, so users of these distributions are on their own. Fortunately, each of these is very well-documented and have active, helpful user communities, and they're not that different from their many cousins.

Downloads and Feedback

Doubtless this book, despite the heroic efforts of me and the fabulous O'Reilly team, contains flaws, errors, and omissions. Please email your feedback and suggestions to *netcookbook@bratgrrl.com*, so we can make the second edition even better. Be sure to visit *http://www.oreilly.com/catalog/9780596102487* for errata, updates, and to download the scripts used in the book.

Conventions

Italic

> Used for pathnames, filenames, program names, Internet addresses, such as domain names and URLs, and new terms where they are defined.

`Constant Width`

> Used for output from programs, and names and keywords in examples.

`Constant Width Italic`

> Used for replaceable parameters or optional elements when showing a command's syntax.

`Constant Width Bold`

> Used for commands that should be typed verbatim, and for emphasis within program code and configuration files.

Unix/Linux commands that can be typed by a regular user are preceded with a regular prompt, ending with $. Commands that must be typed as *root* are preceded with a "root" prompt, ending with a #. In real life, it is better to use the *sudo* command wherever possible to avoid logging in as *root*. Both kinds of prompts indicate the username, the current host, and the current working directory (for example: `root@xena:/var/llibtftpboot #`).

This icon signifies a tip, suggestion, or general note.

This icon indicates a warning or caution.

Using Code Examples

This book is here to help you get your job done. In general, you may use the code in this book in your programs and documentation. You do not need to contact us for permission unless you're reproducing a significant portion of the code. For example, writing a program that uses several chunks of code from this book does not require permission. Selling or distributing a CD-ROM of examples from O'Reilly books *does* require permission. Answering a question by citing this book and quoting example code does not require permission. Incorporating a significant amount of example code from this book into your product's documentation *does* require permission.

We appreciate, but do not require, attribution. An attribution usually includes the title, author, publisher, and ISBN. For example: "*Linux Networking Cookbook*, by Carla Schroder. Copyright 2008 O'Reilly Media, Inc., 978-0-596-10248-7."

If you feel your use of code examples falls outside fair use or the permission given above, feel free to contact us at *permissions@oreilly.com*.

Comments and Questions

Please address comments and questions concerning this book to the publisher:

O'Reilly Media, Inc.
1005 Gravenstein Highway North
Sebastopol, CA 95472
800-998-9938 (in the United States or Canada)
707-829-0515 (international or local)
707-829-0104 (fax)

We have a web page for this book, where we list errata, examples, and any additional information. You can access this page at:

http://www.oreilly.com/catalog/9780596102487

To comment or ask technical questions about this book, send email to:

bookquestions@oreilly.com

For more information about our books, conferences, Resource Centers, and the O'Reilly Network, see the web site:

http://www.oreilly.com

Safari® Books Online

 When you see a Safari® Books Online icon on the cover of your favorite technology book, that means the book is available online through the O'Reilly Network Safari Bookshelf.

Safari offers a solution that's better than e-books. It's a virtual library that lets you easily search thousands of top tech books, cut and paste code samples, download chapters, and find quick answers when you need the most accurate, current information. Try it for free at *http://safari.oreilly.com*.

Acknowledgments

Writing a book like this is a massive team effort. Special thanks go to my editor, Mike Loukides. It takes unrelenting patience, tact, good taste, persistence, and an amazing assortment of geek skills to shepherd a book like this to completion. Well done and thank you. Also thanks to:

James Lopeman
Dana Sibera
Kristian Kielhofner
Ed Sawicki
Dana Sibera
Gerald Carter
Michell Murrain
Jamesha Fisher
Carol Williams
Rudy Zijlstra
Maria Blackmore
Meredydd Luff
Devdas Bhagat
Akkana Peck
Valorie Henson
Jennifer Scalf
Sander Marechal
Mary Gardiner
Conor Daly
Alvin Goats
Dragan Stanojević -Nevidljvl

## CHAPTER 1

Introduction to Linux Networking

1.0   Introduction

Computer networking is all about making computers talk to each other. It is simple to say, but complex to implement. In this Introduction, we'll take a bird's-eye view of Ethernet networking with Linux, and take a look at the various pieces that make it all work: routers, firewalls, switches, cabling, interface hardware, and different types of WAN and Internet services.

A network, whether it is a LAN or WAN, can be thought of as having two parts: computers, and everything that goes between the computers. This book focuses on connectivity: firewalls, wireless access points, secure remote administration, remote helpdesk, remote access for users, virtual private networks, authentication, system and network monitoring, and the rapidly growing new world of Voice over IP services.

We'll cover tasks like networking Linux and Unix boxes, integrating Windows hosts, routing, user identification and authentication, sharing an Internet connection, connecting branch offices, name services, wired and wireless connectivity, security, monitoring, and troubleshooting.

Connecting to the Internet

One of the biggest problems for the network administrator is connecting safely to the Internet. What sort of protection do you need? Do you need expensive commercial routers and firewalls? How do you physically connect your LAN to the Internet?

Here are the answers to the first two questions: at a minimum, you need a firewall and a router, and no, you do not need expensive commercial devices. Linux on ordinary PC hardware gives you all the power and flexibility you need for most home and business users.

The answer to the last question depends on the type of Internet service. Cable and DSL are simple—a cable or DSL line connects to an inexpensive broadband modem, which you connect to your Linux firewall/gateway, which connects to your LAN switch, as Figure 1-1 shows.

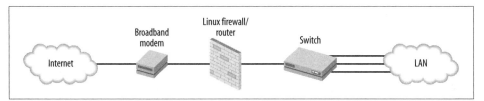

Figure 1-1. Broadband Internet connected to a small LAN

In this introduction, I'm going to refer to the interface between your LAN and outside networks as the *gateway*. At a bare minimum, this gateway is a router. It might be a dedicated router that does nothing else. You might add a firewall. You might want other services like name services, a VPN portal, wireless access point, or remote administration. It is tempting to load it up with all manner of services simply because you can, but from security and ease-of-administration perspectives, it is best to keep your Internet gateway as simple as possible. Don't load it up with web, mail, FTP, or authentication servers. Keep it lean, mean, and as locked-down as possible.

If you are thinking of upgrading to a high-bandwidth dedicated line, a T1 line is the next step up. Prices are competitive with business DSL, but you'll need specialized interface hardware that costs a lot more than a DSL modem. Put a PCI T1 interface inside your Linux gateway box to get the most flexibility and control. These come in many configurations, such as multiple ports, and support data and voice protocols, so you can tailor it to suit your needs exactly.

If you prefer a commercial router, look for bundled deals from your service provider that include a router for free. If you can't get a deal on a nice router, check out the abundant secondhand router market. Look for a router with a T1 WAN interface card and a Channel Service Unit/Data Service Unit (CSU/DSU). Don't expect much from a low-end router—your Linux box with its own T1 interface has a lot more horsepower and customizability.

A typical T1 setup looks like Figure 1-2.

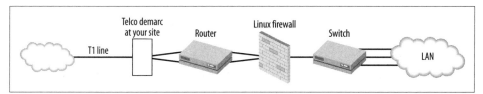

Figure 1-2. Connecting to a T1 line

Beyond T1, the sky's the limit on service options and pricing. Higher-end services require different types of hardware LAN interfaces. A good service provider will tell you what you need, and provide optional on-site services. Don't be too proud to hire help—telecommunications is part engineering and part voodoo, especially because we started pushing data packets over voice lines.

Overview of Internet Service Options

The hardworking network administrator has a plethora of choices for Internet connectivity, if you are in the right location. A wise (though under-used) tactic is to investigate the available voice and data services when shopping for an office location. Moving into a space that is already wired for the services you want saves money and aggravation. Otherwise, you may find yourself stuck with nothing but dial-up or ISDN, or exotic, overpriced, over-provisioned services you don't want.

Cable, DSL, and Dial-Up

Cable, DSL, and dial-up are unregulated services. These are the lowest-cost and most widely available.

Cable

Cable Internet is usually bundled with television services, though some providers offer Internet-only service. Cable's primary attraction is delivering higher download speeds than DSL. Many providers do not allow running public services, and even block common ports like 22, 25, 80, and 110. Some vendors are notorious for unreliable service, with frequent outages and long downtimes. However, some cable providers are good and will treat you well, so don't be shy about shopping around. Beware restrictive terms of service; some providers try to charge per-client LAN fees, which is as silly as charging per-user fees for tap water.

DSL

DSL providers are usually more business-friendly. Some DSL providers offer business DSL accounts with SLAs, and with bandwidth and uptime guarantees. DSL isn't suitable for mission-critical services because it's not quite reliable enough for these, but it's fine for users who can tolerate occasional downtimes.

DSL runs over ordinary copper telephone lines, so anyone with a regular landline is a potential DSL customer. It is also possible to get a DSL line without telephone service, though this is usually expensive. DSL is limited by distance; you have to be within 18,000 wire-feet of a repeater, though this distance varies a lot between providers, and is affected by the physical quality of the line. Residential accounts are often restricted to shorter distances than business accounts, presumably to limit support costs.

With DSL, you're probably stuck with a single telco, but you should have a choice of ISP.

DSL comes in two primary flavors: symmetric digital subscriber line (SDSL) and asymmetric digital subscriber line (ADSL). SDSL speeds are the same upstream and downstream, up to a maximum of 3 Mbps. ADSL downstream speeds go as high as 9 Mbps, but upstream maxes out at 896 Mbps. ADSL2+, the newest standard, can deliver 24 Mbps downstream, if you can find a provider. Keep in mind that no one ever achieves the full speeds; these are theoretical upper limits.

Longer distances means less bandwidth. If you're within 5,000 feet you're golden, assuming the telco's wires are healthy. 10,000 is still good. The reliability limit of the connection is around 18,000 feet—just maintaining connectivity is iffy at this distance.

Dial-up

Good old dial-up networking still has its place, though its most obvious limitation is bandwidth. It's unlikely you'll get more than 48 Kbps. However, dial-up has its place as a backup when your broadband fails, and may be useful as a quick, cheap WAN—you can dial in directly to one of your remote servers, for example, and do a batch file transfer or some emergency system administration, or set it up as a VPN for your users.

Cable, DSL, and dial-up gotchas

One thing to watch out for is silly platform limitations—some ISPs, even in these modern times, are notorious for supporting only Microsoft Windows. Of course, for ace network administrators, this is just a trivial annoyance because we do not need their lackluster support for client-side issues. Still, you must make sure your Linux box can connect at all, as a significant number of ISPs still use Microsoft-only networking software. Exhibit A is AOL, which supports only Windows and Mac, and replaces the Windows networking stack with its own proprietary networking software. This causes no end of fun when you try to change to a different ISP—it won't work until you reinstall Windows networking, which sometimes works, or reinstall Windows, which definitely works, and is almost as much fun as it sounds.

Regulated Broadband Services

Regulated services include broadband networking over copper telephone lines and fiber optic cable. These are supposed to be more reliable because the network operators are supposed to monitor the lines and fix connectivity problems without customer intervention. When there is a major service interruption, such as a widespread power outage, regulated services should be restored first. As always in the real world, it depends on the quality of your service provider.

T1, T3, E-1, E-3, DS1, and DS3 run over copper lines. T1/T3 and DS1/DS3 are the same things. These are symmetrical (same bandwidth upstream and downstream) dedicated lines. Because it's an unshared line, even a T1 handles a lot of traffic satisfactorily. OC-3–OC-255 run over fiber optic cable; these are the super-high capacity lines that backbone providers use. Table 1-1 shows a sampling of the many available choices, including European standards (prefixed with an E).

Table 1-1. Regulated broadband service offerings

Service type	Speed
T1/DS1	1.544 Mbps
T3/DS3	43.232 Mbps
OC-3	155 Mbps
OC-12	622 Mbps
OC-48	2.5 Gbps
OC-192	9.6 Gbps
OC-255	13.21 Gbps
E-1	2.048 Mbps
E-2	8.448 Mbps
E-3	34.368 Mbps

Other common options are frame relay and fractional services, like fractional T1, fractional T3, and fractional OC-3. Frame relay is used point-to-point, for example, between two branch offices. It's shared bandwidth, and used to be a way to save money when a dedicated T1 was too expensive. These days, it's usually not priced low enough to make it worthwhile, and the hardware to interface with frame relay is expensive. DSL or T1 is usually a better deal.

Fractional T1 is still an option for users on a budget, though DSL is often a good lower-cost alternative. When you need more than a single T1, bonding two T1 lines costs less than the equivalent fractional T3 because the T3 interface hardware costs a mint. Linux can handle the bonding, if your interface hardware and service provider support it. When you think you need more than two T1s, it's time to consult with your friendly service provider for your best options.

Always read the fine print, and make sure all fees are spelled out. The circuit itself is often a separate charge, and there may be setup fees. If you're searching online for providers and information, beware of brokers. There are good ones, but as a general rule, you're better off dealing directly with a service provider.

Private Networks

As more service providers lay their own fiber optic networks, you'll find interesting options like Fast Ethernet WAN, even Gigabyte Ethernet WAN, and also high-speed wireless services. Again, these depend on being in the right location. The nice part about these private services is they bypass the Internet, which eliminates all sorts of potential trouble spots.

Latency, Bandwidth, and Throughput

When discussing network speeds, there is often confusion between bandwidth, latency, and throughput. *Broadband* means fat pipe, not necessarily a fast pipe. As us folks out here in the sticks say, "Bandwidth is capacity, and latency is response time. Bandwidth is the diameter of your irrigation line. Latency is waiting for the water to come out."

Throughput is the amount of data transferred per unit of time, like 100 Kbps. So, you could say throughput is the intersection of bandwidth and latency.

Many factors affect latency, such as server speed, network congestion, and inherent limitations in circuits. The *ping* command can measure latency in transit time roundtrip:

```
$ ping oreilly.com
PING oreilly.com (208.201.239.37) 56(84) bytes of data.
64 bytes from www.oreillynet.com (208.201.239.37): icmp_seq=2 ttl=45 time=489 ms
64 bytes from www.oreillynet.com (208.201.239.37): icmp_seq=3 ttl=45 time=116 ms
```

Compare this to LAN speeds:

```
$ ping windbag
PING localhost.localdomain (127.0.0.1) 56(84) bytes of data.
64 bytes from localhost.localdomain (127.0.0.1): icmp_seq=1 ttl=64 time=0.040 ms
64 bytes from localhost.localdomain (127.0.0.1): icmp_seq=2 ttl=64 time=0.039 ms
```

It doesn't get any faster than pinging localhost. The latency in an Ethernet interface is around 0.3 milliseconds (ms). DSL and cable are around 20 ms. T1/T3 have a latency of about 4 ms. Satellite is the highest, as much as two seconds. That much latency breaks IP. Satellite providers play a lot of fancy proxying tricks to get latency down to a workable level.

Hardware Options for Your Linux Firewall/Gateway

There are a lot of hardware choices for your gateway box. Linux supports more hardware platforms than any other operating system, so you don't have to stick with x86. Debian in particular supports a large number of hardware architectures: Alpha, ARM, HPPA, i386, ia64, m68k, MIPS, MIPSEL, PowerPC, SPARC, and s/390, so you can use whatever you like. (If you build one on an s/390, please send photos to *carla@bratgrrl.com*!)

Of course, you have the option of purchasing a commercial appliance. These range from little SOHO devices like the Linksys, Netgear, and SMC broadband routers for sharing a DSL or cable Internet line for under $100, to rackmount units that end up costing several thousand dollars for software licenses and subscriptions. A growing number of these are Linux-based, so your Linux skills will serve you well.

But, it's not necessary to go this route—you can get unlimited flexibility, and possibly save money by purchasing the bare hardware, or reusing old hardware, and installing your own favorite Linux distribution on it.

There are many choices for form factor and hardware types: small embedded boards like Soekris and PC Engines, Mini-ITX, microATX, blade, rackmount, and more. The smaller units use less power, take up less space, and are fanless for peace and quiet. Larger devices are more configurable and handle bigger loads.

A plain old desktop PC makes a perfectly good gateway box, and is a good way to keep obsolete PCs out of landfills. Even old 486s can do the job for up to a hundred or so users if they are just sharing an Internet connection and not running public services. Repurposed PCs may be a bit questionable for reliability just from being old, and you may not be able to get replacement parts, so if you're nervous about their reliability, they still work great for training and testing. An excellent use for one of these is as a fully provisioned backup box—if your main one fails, plug in the backup for minimal downtime.

High-End Enterprise Routers

When do you need an elite, hideously expensive, top-of-the-line Cisco or Juniper router? To quote networking guru Ed Sawicki: "You don't need more performance than what you need." Unless you're an ISP handling multimegabyte routing tables, need the fastest possible performance, highest throughput, good vendor support, and highest reliability, you don't need these superpowered beasts.

The highest-end routers use specialized hardware. They are designed to move the maximum number of packets per second. They have more and fatter data buses, multiple CPUs, and TCAM memory.

TCAM is *Ternary Content Addressable Memory*. This is very different from ordinary system RAM. TCAM is several times faster than the fastest system RAM, and many times more expensive. You won't find TCAM in lower-cost devices, nor will you find software that can shovel packets as fast as TCAM.

Not-So-High-End Commercial Routers

The mid-range commercial routers use hardware comparable to ordinary PC hardware. However, their operating systems can make a significant performance difference. Routers that use a real-time operating system, like the Cisco IOS, perform better under heavy loads than Linux-based routers, because no matter how hard some folks try to make Linux a real-time operating system, it isn't one.

But, for the average business user this is not an issue because you have an ISP to do the heavy lifting. Your needs are sharing your Internet connection, splitting a T1 line for voice and data, connecting to some branch offices, offsite backups, or a data center. Linux on commodity hardware will handle these jobs just fine for a fraction of the cost.

Switches

Switches are the workhorses of networking. Collision domains are so last millennium; a cheap way to instantly improve LAN performance is to replace any lingering hubs with switches. Once you do this, you have a switched LAN. As fiber optic lines are becoming more common, look for cabling compatibility in switches. (And routers and NICs, too.)

Switches come in many flavors: dumb switches that simply move packets, smart switches, and managed switches. These are marketing terms, and therefore imprecise, but usually, smart switches are managed switches with fewer features and lower price tags. Higher-end features have a way of falling into lower-priced devices over time, so it no longer costs a scary amount to buy managed or smart switches with useful feature sets. There are all kinds of features getting crammed into switches these days, so here is a list of some that I think are good to have.

Management port

Because switches forward traffic directly to the intended hosts, instead of promiscuously spewing them to anyone who cares to capture them, you can't sniff a switched network from anywhere on a subnet like you could in the olden hub days. So, you need a switch that supports port mirroring, or, as Cisco calls it, SPAN. (An alternative is to use the *arpspoof* utility—use it carefully!)

Serial port

Most managed switches are configured via Ethernet with nice web interfaces. This is good. But still, there may be times when you want to get to a command line or do some troubleshooting, and this is when a serial port will save the day.

MDI/MDI-X (Medium Dependent Interfaces)

This is pretty much standard—it means no more hassles with crossover cables, because now switches can auto-magically connect to other switches without needing special uplink ports or the exactly correct crossover or straight-through cables.

Lots of blinky lights

Full banks of LEDs can't be beat for giving a fast picture of whether things are working.

Jumbo frames

This is a nice feature on gigabit switches, if it is supported across your network. Standard frames are 1,500 bytes, which is fine for Fast Ethernet. Some Gigabit devices support 9,000 byte frames.

Port trunking

This means combining several switch ports to create a fatter pipeline. You can connect a switch to a switch, or a switch to a server if it has a NIC that supports link aggregation.

VLANs

This is a feature that will have you wondering why you didn't use it sooner. *Virtual LANs* (VLANs) are logical subnets. They make it easy and flexible to organize your LAN logically, instead of having to rearrange hardware.

QoS

Quality of Service, or traffic prioritization, allows you to give high priority to traffic that requires low latency and high throughput (e.g., voice traffic), and low priority to web-surfin' slackers.

Per-port access controls

Another tool to help prevent intruders and snoopy personnel from wandering into places they don't belong.

Network Interface Cards (NICs)

With Linux, it's unlikely you'll run into driver hassles with PCI and PCI-Express NICs; most chipsets are well-supported. New motherboards commonly have 10/100/1000 Ethernet onboard. Just like everything else, NICs are getting crammed with nice features, like wake-on-LAN, netboot, QoS, and jumbo frame support.

USB NICs, both wired and wireless, are good for laptops, or when you don't feel like opening the box to install a PCI card. But beware driver hassles; a lot of them don't have Linux drivers.

Server NICs come with nice features like link aggregation, multiple ports, and fiber Gigabit.

Gigabit Ethernet Gotchas

As Gigabit Ethernet becomes more common, it's important to recognize the potential choke points in your network. Now we're at the point where networking gear has outstripped PC capabilities, like hard drive speeds, I/O, and especially bus speeds.

The PCI bus is a shared bus, so more devices result in slower performance. Table 1-2 shows how PCI has evolved.

Table 1-2. Evolution of PCI

Bits	MHz	Speed
32	33	132 Mbps
64	33	264 Mbps
64	66	512 Mbps
64	133	1 Gbps

PCI-Express is different from the old PCI, and will probably replace both PCI and AGP. It is backward-compatible, so you won't have to chuck all of your old stuff. PCI-E uses a point-to-point switching connection, instead of a shared bus. Devices talk directly to each other over a dedicated circuit. A device that needs more bandwidth gets more circuits, so you'll see slots of different sizes on motherboards, like PCI-Express 2x, 4x, 8x, and 16x. PCI-E x16 can theoretically move 8 Gbps.

USB 1.1 tops out at 11 Mbps, and you'll be lucky to get more than 6–8 Mbps. USB 2.0 is rated at 480 Mbps, which is fine for both Fast and Gigabit wired Ethernet. You won't get full Gigabit speeds, but it will still be faster than Fast Ethernet.

32-bit Cardbus adapters give better performance on laptops than the old 16-bit PCMCIA, with a data transfer speed of up to 132 Mbps.

Cabling

Ordinary four-twisted-pair Cat5 should carry you into Gigabit Ethernet comfortably, though Cat5e is better. Chances are your Cat5 is really Cat5e, anyway; read the cable markings to find out. Watch out for cheapie Cat5 that has only two twisted pairs.

Cat6 twisted-pair cabling, the next generation of Ethernet cabling, is a heavier gauge (23 instead of Cat5's 24), meets more stringent specifications for crosstalk and noise, and it always has four pairs of wires.

Wireless Networking

Wireless networking gear continues to be a source of aggravation for admins of mixed LANs, which is practically all of them. Shop carefully, because a lot of devices are unnecessarily Windows-dependent. Wireless gear is going to be a moving target for awhile, and bleeding-edge uncomfortable. Go for reliability and security over promises of raw blazing speeds. As far as security goes, *Wired Equivalent Privacy* (WEP) is not suitable for the enterprise. WEP is far too weak. *Wi-Fi Protected Access* (WPA) implementations are all over the map, but WPA2 seems to be fairly sane, so when you purchase wireless gear, make sure it supports WPA2. Also, make sure it is Wi-Fi Certified, as this ensures interoperability between different brands.

Whatever you do, don't run naked unprotected wireless. Unless you enjoy having your network compromised.

## CHAPTER 2

Building a Linux Gateway on a Single-Board Computer

2.0   Introduction

Linux lends itself so readily to hacking on old hardware we often forget it is not always the best hardware to use. While it is good to keep old PCs out of landfills, there are disadvantages to using them as routers and firewalls. They're big, they use a lot of power, and they're noisy, unless you have something of sufficient vintage to run fanless. Old hardware is that much closer to failure, and what do you do if parts fail? Even if you can find new parts, are they worth replacing?

Single-board computers (SBCs), like those made by Soekris Engineering (*http://www.soekris.com*) and PC Engines (*http://www.pcengines.ch/wrap.htm*) are great for routers, firewalls, and wireless access points. They're small, quiet, low-power, and sturdy. You'll find information on single-board computers and other small form-factor computers at the LinuxDevices.com Single Board Computer (SBC) Quick Reference Guide (*http://www.linuxdevices.com/articles/AT2614444132.html*).

This chapter will show you how to install and configure Pyramid Linux (*http://metrix.net/*) on a Soekris 4521 board. There are many small distributions designed to power routers and firewalls; see Chapter 3 for more information on these, and to learn how to build an Internet-connection sharing firewall.

Despite their small size, the Soekris and PC Engines boards are versatile. PC Engines' and similar boards all operate in pretty much the same fashion, so what you learn here applies to all of them. A cool-sounding shortcut for these boards is to call them *routerboards*.

You might look at the specs of our little 4521 and turn your nose up in scorn:

- 133 MHz AMD ElanSC520 CPU
- 64 MB SDRAM, soldered on board
- 1 Mb BIOS/BOOT Flash
- Two 10/100 Ethernet ports

- CompactFLASH Type I/II socket, 8 MB Flash to 4 GB Microdrive
- 1 DB9 Serial port
- Power, Activity, Error LEDs
- Mini-PCI type III socket
- 2 PC-Card/Cardbus slots
- 8 bit general purpose I/O 14-pins header
- Board size 9.2" x 5.7"
- Option for 5V supply using internal connector
- Power over Ethernet
- Operating temperature 0–60°C

You'll find more raw horsepower in a low-end video card. But don't let the numbers fool you. Combined with a specialized Linux, BSD, or any embedded operating system, these little devices are tough, efficient workhorses that beat the pants off comparable (and usually overpriced and inflexible) commercial routers. You get complete control and customizability, and you don't have to worry about nonsense like hardcoded misconfigurations or secret backdoors that are known to everyone but the end user. These little boards can handle fairly hostile environments, and with the right kind of enclosures can go outside.

The 4521 can handle up to five network interfaces: two PCMCIA, two Ethernet, and one wireless in the mini-PCI slot. Six, if you count the serial interface. So, with this one little board, you could build a router, firewall, and wireless access point, and throw in some DMZs as well. All of these kinds of boards come in a variety of configurations.

You probably won't see throughput greater than 17 Mbps with the Soekris 45xx boards. The 48xx and PC Engines WRAP boards have more powerful CPUs and more RAM, so you'll see speeds up to 50 Mbps. This is far faster than most users' Internet pipelines. Obviously, if you are fortunate enough to have an Ethernet WAN or other super high-speed services, you'll need a firewall with a lot more horsepower. As a general rule, a 45xx set up as a firewall and router will handle around 50 users, though of course this varies according to how hard your users hammer the little guy.

Required Hardware

In addition the board itself, you'll need a Compact Flash card or microdrive for the operating system, and a reader/writer on a separate PC to install the OS on your CF or microdrive. Or, you may install the operating system from a PXE boot server instead of using a CF writer. Also required are a power supply and a null-modem DB9 serial cable. A case is optional.

Complete bundles including an operating system are available from several vendors, such as Metrix.net (*http://metrix.net*) and Netgate.com (*http://netgate.com/*).

Software

Your operating system size is limited by the size of your CF card or microdrive. The CPU and RAM are soldered to the board, and are not expandable, so the operating system must be lean and efficient. In this chapter, we'll go for the tiny gusto and use a little 64 MB CF card, so we'll need a suitably wizened operating system. Pyramid Linux fits nicely. The stock image occupies a 60 MB partition, and uses about 49 MB. It uses stock Ubuntu packages, so even though it does not come with any package management tools, you can still add or remove programs.

What to Do with Old PCs?

Old PCs are still valuable as thin clients, test labs, and drop-in replacement boxes. Keep some around configured and ready to substitute for a fried router, firewall, or server.

2.1   Getting Acquainted with the Soekris 4521

Problem

You're not familiar with these little boards, and aren't sure where to start. How do you talk to it? What do you do with it?

Solution

It's easy. You will need:

- PC running Linux
- Null-modem serial cable
- Minicom installed on the Linux PC

Configure Minicom, connect the two machines, power up the Soekris, and you're ready.

Here are all the steps in detail. First, find out what physical serial ports your Linux box has:

```
$ setserial -g /dev/ttyS[0123]
/dev/ttyS0, UART: 16550A, Port: 0x03f8, IRQ: 4
/dev/ttyS1, UART: unknown, Port: 0x02f8, IRQ: 3
/dev/ttyS2, UART: unknown, Port: 0x03e8, IRQ: 4
/dev/ttyS3, UART: unknown, Port: 0x02e8, IRQ: 3
```

This PC has only one, which is the one with a UART value. If you have more than one, it will probably take a bit of trial and error to figure out which one is connected to the Soekris board.

Now, set up Minicom:

```
# minicom -s
------[configuration]-------
| Filenames and paths
| File transfer protocols
| Serial port setup
| Modem and dialing
| Screen and keyboard
| Save setup as dfl
| Save setup as..
| Exit
| Exit from Minicom
---------------------------
```

Select "Serial port setup." Your settings should look just like this, except you need to enter your own serial port address. Soekris boards default to "Bps/Par/Bits 19200 8N1," no flow control:

```
--------------------------------------------
| A -    Serial Device     : /dev/ttyS0
| B - Lockfile Location    : /var/lock
| C -    Callin Program    :
| D -  Callout Program     :
| E -      Bps/Par/Bits    : 19200 8N1
| F - Hardware Flow Control : No
| G - Software Flow Control : No
|
|    Change which setting?
--------------------------------------------
```

Next, select the "Modem and dialing" option, and make sure the "Init string" and "Reset string" settings are blank. Finally, select "Save setup as dfl" to make this the default, and then "Exit." This takes you back to the main Minicom screen:

```
Welcome to minicom 2.1

OPTIONS: History Buffer, F-key Macros, Search History Buffer, I18n
Compiled on Nov  5 2005, 15:45:44.

Press CTRL-A Z for help on special keys
Now power up the Soekris, and you'll see something like this:
comBIOS ver. 1.15  20021013  Copyright (C) 2000-2002 Soekris Engineering.

net45xx

0064 Mbyte Memory                    CPU 80486 133 Mhz

PXE-M00: BootManage UNDI, PXE-2.0 (build 082)
```

```
Slot   Vend Dev  ClassRev Cmd  Stat CL LT HT  Base1     Base2     Int
--------------------------------------------------------------------
0:00:0 1022 3000 06000000 0006 2280 00 00 00  00000000  00000000  00
0:16:0 168C 0013 02000001 0116 0290 10 3C 00  A0000000  00000000  10
0:17:0 104C AC51 06070000 0107 0210 10 3F 82  A0010000  020000A0  11
0:17:1 104C AC51 06070000 0107 0210 10 3F 82  A0011000  020000A0  11
0:18:0 100B 0020 02000000 0107 0290 00 3F 00  0000E101  A0012000  05
0:19:0 100B 0020 02000000 0107 0290 00 3F 00  0000E201  A0013000  09

4 Seconds to automatic boot.  Press Ctrl-P for entering Monitor.
```

Boot into the comBIOS by pressing Ctrl-P:

```
comBIOS Monitor.   Press ? for help.


>

Go ahead and hit ? to see the Help. You'll get a list of commands:

comBIOS Monitor Commands

boot [drive][:partition] INT19 Boot
reboot                   cold boot
download                 download a file using XMODEM
flashupdate              update flash BIOS with downloaded file
time [HH:MM:SS]          show or set time
date [YYYY/MM/DD]        show or set date
d[b|w|d] [adr]           dump memory (bytes/words/dwords)
e[b|w|d] adr value [...] enter bytes/words/dwords
i[b|w|d] port            input from 8/16/32-bit port
o[b|w|d] port value      output to 8/16/32-bit port
cmosread [adr]           read CMOS RAM data
cmoswrite adr byte [...] write CMOS RAM data
cmoschecksum             update CMOS RAM Checksum
set parameter=value      set system parameter to value
show [parameter]         show one or all system parameters
?/help                   show this help
```

Go ahead and set the time and date. Other than that, there's not much to do until we install the operating system.

If you do not have a CF card installed, a Soekris board will automatically boot to the comBIOS menu.

Discussion

You don't have to use a Linux machine as the serial terminal; using Hyperterminal from a Windows machine works fine, too. Other Unix serial communication programs are *cu*, *tip*, and Kermit. Kermit is fun if you want a versatile program that does everything except cook dinner. Mac OS X users might try Minicom, which is in Darwin Ports, or ZTerm.

See Also

The documentation for your routerboard:

- Soekris Engineering: *http://www.soekris.com*
- PC Engines: *http://www.pcengines.ch/wrap.htm*
- LinuxDevices.com Single Board Computer (SBC) Quick Reference Guide: *http://www.linuxdevices.com/articles/AT2614444132.html*

2.2   Configuring Multiple Minicom Profiles

Problem

You have a laptop set up as a portable serial terminal and all-around networking troubleshooting tool, so you need multiple connection profiles in Minicom to connect to different servers.

Solution

As *root*, set up a new Minicom configuration just like in the previous recipe. Then, instead of selecting "Save as dfl," select "Save as…" and type in the name of your choice, such as *pyramid*. Now, any user can use this configuration with this command:

```
$ minicom pyramid
```

Discussion

Ordinary users cannot change the serial port setup settings in Minicom, except for bits per second, and cannot save configurations.

See Also

- man 1 minicom

2.3   Installing Pyramid Linux on a Compact Flash Card

Problem

There you are with your new single-board computer, and it looks very nice, but you're wondering how to get an operating system on it.

Solution

The two most common methods are via a *Compact Flash* (CF) writer, or bootstrapping the operating system from a PXE boot server. This recipe tells how to install Pyramid Linux using the first method. You need:

- A Compact Flash writer
- The Pyramid Linux *dd* image

The most common CF writers cost around $20 and connect to a USB port. This is the easiest kind to use. Linux automatically recognizes and mounts the device when you plug it in.

A second option is an IDE CF writer. You'll know if you have one of these because they take up an IDE slot on your system and a front drive bay. A system with one of these needs to be booted with the CF card in the reader, or it won't see it.

First, download the latest *dd* image:

```
$ wget http://metrix.net/support/dist/pyramid-1.0b1.img.gz
```

Next, find the */dev* name of your CF card with the `fdisk -l` command. A USB CF writer looks like this:

```
# fdisk -l
   Device Boot      Start        End      Blocks   Id  System
/dev/sdb1            1          977       62512   83  Linux
```

An IDE CF writer looks like this:

```
   Device Boot      Start        End      Blocks   Id  System
/dev/hdc1    *       1          977       62512   83  Linux
```

Copy the image to your CF card with these commands, using your own correct image and */dev* names. Do not use any partition numbers:

```
# gunzip -c pyramid-1.0b1.img.gz | dd of=/dev/sdb bs=16k
3908+0 records in
3908+0 records out
```

And that's all there is to it. Now it's ready to go in your routerboard.

Discussion

This requires a bootable operating system image. You can't just copy files to the Flash card because it needs a boot sector. *dd* does a byte-by-byte copy, including the boot sector, which most other copy commands cannot do. The maintainers of Pyramid thoughtfully provide a complete image, which makes for a simple installation.

See Also

- Pyramid Linux home page: *http://pyramid.metrix.net/*

2.4　Network Installation of Pyramid on Debian

Problem

You would rather install Pyramid Linux via PXE boot because you have several routerboards to install, or you have onboard nonremovable Compact Flash, or you just prefer to do it this way. Your installation server runs Debian.

Solution

No problem, you can do this because the Soekris boards (and PC Engines and all their little cousins) support netbooting. While the HTTP, TFTP, and DHCP services in this recipe can be on different machines, the examples here assume they are all on a single PC. Any PC will do (e.g., a workstation, your special network administrator laptop, anything).

To get started, first download the latest Pyramid *dd* image or tarball from *http://metrix.net/support/dist/* into the directory of your choice:

```
$ wget http://metrix.net/support/dist/pyramid-1.0b2.img.gz
```

Then, you need these services installed:

- DHCPD
- TFTP
- HTTP
- Subversion

You don't need a big old heavyweight HTTP server like Apache. Lighttpd is great for lightweight applications like this. Install them with this command:

```
# apt-get install lighttpd lighttpd-doc tftpd-hpa dhcp3-server subversion
```

Copy this */etc/dhcp3/dhcpd.conf* file exactly:

```
##/etc/dhcp3/dhcpd.conf
  subnet 192.168.200.0 netmask 255.255.255.0 {
  range 192.168.200.100 192.168.200.200;
  allow booting;
  allow bootp;

  next-server 192.168.200.1;
  filename "PXE/pxelinux.0";

  max-lease-time 60;
  default-lease-time 60;
}
```

next-server is the IP address of the boot server; it must be 192.168.200.1.

Next, configure *tftpd* by editing */etc/default/tftpd-hpa* like this:

```
##/etc/default/tftpd-hpa
RUN_DAEMON="yes"
OPTIONS="-a 192.168.200.1:69 -l -s -vv /var/lib/tftpboot/"
```

Change your working directory to */var/lib/tftpboot* and download the PXE environment from Metrix's Subversion repository:

```
root@xena:/var/lib/tftpboot # svn export http://pyramid.metrix.net/svn/PXE
```

This is about a 45 MB download.

Next, inside your *httpd* document root directory, */var/www*, make a symlink to the Pyramid tarball or image you downloaded and name it "os":

```
root@xena:/var/www # ln -s /home/carla/downloads/pyramid-1.0b2.tar.gz os
```

Then, temporarily change the IP address of your installation server with this command:

```
# ifconfig eth0 192.168.200.1  netmask 255.255.255.0 broadcast 192.168.200.255
```

Now, start all these services:

```
# cd /etc/init.d
# dhcp3-server start && lighttpd start && tftpd-hpa start
```

Install the CF card, then connect the serial and Ethernet cables to your Soekris board, and fire up Minicom. It doesn't matter if something is already installed on the CF card. Power up the board, and enter the comBIOS by pressing Ctrl-P when prompted. Then, enter boot F0:

```
comBIOS Monitor.   Press ? for help.
> boot F0
```

You'll see it acquire a DHCP lease, a quick TFTP blink, and then you'll be in the installation menu:

```
Choose from one of the following:
1. Start the automated Pyramid Linux install process via dd image file
2. Start the automated Pyramid Linux install process via fdisk and tarball
3. Boot the Pyramid Linux kernel with a shell prompt
4. Boot the Pebble Linux install process
5. Boot the Pebble Linux kernel with a shell
6. Install the latest snapshot
```

Select either 1 or 2, according to what you downloaded. Go have a nice healthy walk, and in 10 minutes, you'll have a fresh Pyramid installation all ready to go.

Finally, restore your server's IP address with *ifupdown*:

```
# ifdown eth0
# ifup eth0
```

Discussion

A slick way to do this is to put it all on your special netadmin laptop. It's portable, and you can easily isolate it from the other servers on your network. You especially don't want to conflict with any existing DHCP servers. Just connect the routerboard and laptop with a crossover Ethernet cable and null modem cable, and away you go.

If you're using a LAN PC for this, you might want to configure the HTTP, DHCP, and TFTP servers so that they do not automatically start at boot, especially the DHCP server.

Pay close attention to your filepaths; this is the most common source of errors.

You should still have a CF writer handy in case of problems. For example, if a non-Linux operating system is already installed on it, you'll probably have to manually zero out the Master Boot Record (MBR). So, you'll need to be able to mount the card in a CF writer, then use *dd* to erase the MBR. In this example, the Flash card is */dev/hdc*:

```
# dd if=/dev/zero of=/dev/hdc bs=512 count=1
```

Check your HTTP server configuration file for the location of the server's documentation root directory. On Apache, this is the DocumentRoot directive. Currently, you'll find this in */etc/apache2/sites-available/default*. On Lighttpd, look for the server.document-root directive in */etc/lighttpd/lighttpd.conf*.

When your Pyramid image file or tarball is copied to your HTTP root directory, verify that it's in the correct location by going to *http://192.168.200.1/os*. It should try to download the file into your web browser, which will appear as a big gob of binary gibberish.

See Also

- Pyramid Linux home page: *http://pyramid.metrix.net/*
- man 8 tftpd
- man 8 dhcpd
- */usr/share/doc/lighttpd-doc/*

2.5   Network Installation of Pyramid on Fedora

Problem

You would rather install Pyramid Linux via PXE boot because you have several boards to install, or you have onboard Compact Flash, or you just prefer to do it this way. Your installation server runs Fedora Linux.

Solution

No problem, you can do this because the Soekris boards (and PC Engines, and all their little cousins) support netbooting. While the HTTP, TFTP, and DHCP services in this recipe can be on different machines, the examples here assume they are all on a single PC.

To get started, first download the latest Pyramid dd image or tarball from *http://metrix.net/support/dist/* into the directory of your choice:

```
$ wget http://metrix.net/support/dist/pyramid-1.0b2.img.gz
```

Then, you need these services installed:

- DHCPD
- TFTP
- HTTP
- Subversion

You don't need a big old heavyweight HTTP server like Apache. Lighttpd is great for lightweight applications like this. Install the necessary packages with this command:

```
# yum install dhcp lighttpd tftp-server subversion
```

Copy this */etc/dhcpd.conf* file exactly:

```
# dhcpd.conf
  subnet 192.168.200.0 netmask 255.255.255.0 {
  range 192.168.200.100 192.168.200.200;

  allow booting;
  allow bootp;
  next-server 192.168.200.1;
  filename "PXE/pxelinux.0";

  max-lease-time 60;
  default-lease-time 60;
}
```

next-server is the IP address of the boot server; it must be 192.168.200.1.

Next, configure *tftp-server*. All you do is change two lines in */etc/xinetd.d/tftp*. Make sure they look like this:

```
disable = no
server_args = -svv /tftpboot -a 192.168.200.1:69
```

Change your working directory to */tftpboot,* and download the PXE environment from Metrix's Subversion repository:

```
root@penguina:/tftpboot # svn export http://pyramid.metrix.net/svn/PXE
```

This is about a 45 MB download.

Next, in your *httpd* root directory, */srv/www/lighttpd/*, make a symlink to the Pyramid tarball or image you downloaded and name it "os":

```
root@xena:/srv/www/lighttpd# ln -s /home/carla/downloads/pyramid-1.0b2.tar.gz os
```

Then, start all these services:

```
# cd /etc/init.d/
# xinetd start && lighttpd start && dhcpd start
```

Finally, connect the serial and Ethernet cables to your Soekris board, and fire up Minicom. Your CF card must be installed. It doesn't matter if a Linux distribution is already installed on it. Power up the board and enter the comBIOS. Enter boot F0:

```
comBIOS Monitor.    Press ? for help.
> boot F0
```

You'll see it acquire a DHCP lease, a quick TFTP blink, and then you'll be in the installation menu:

```
Choose from one of the following:
1. Start the automated Pyramid Linux install process via dd image file
2. Start the automated Pyramid Linux install process via fdisk and tarball
3. Boot the Pyramid Linux kernel with a shell prompt
4. Boot the Pebble Linux install process
5. Boot the Pebble Linux kernel with a shell
6. Install the latest snapshot
```

Select either 1 or 2, according to what you downloaded. Go have a nice healthy walk, and in a few minutes you'll have a fresh Pyramid installation all ready to go.

Discussion

You should still have a CF writer handy in case of problems. For example, if a non-Linux operating system is already installed on it, you should manually zero out the Master Boot Record (MBR). To do this, use a CF writer to mount the card on a PC, then use *dd* to erase the MBR. In this example, the Flash card is */dev/hdc*:

```
# dd if=/dev/zero of=/dev/hdc bs=512 count=1
```

fdisk -L will tell you the */dev* name of the card.

You can verify that *xinetd* is controlling Lighttpd and listening on port UDP 69 like it's supposed to with this command:

```
# netstat -untap | grep xinetd
udp    0    0 0.0.0.0:69    0.0.0.0.*    4214/xinetd
```

See the Discussion in the previous recipe for more information on the configurations, IP addressing, and verifying that everything is working correctly.

See Also

- Pyramid Linux home page: *http://pyramid.metrix.net/*
- */usr/share/doc/lighttpd*
- man 8 tftpd
- man 8 dhcpd

2.6 Booting Pyramid Linux

Problem

OK, so far so good—you have successfully installed Pyramid Linux on your Compact Flash card and plugged it into your Soekris board. Now, how do you log in to Pyramid and get to work?

Solution

You now have three ways to communicate with your Soekris board: serial link, Ethernet, and Pyramid's Web interface. The default login is *root*, password *root*. Boot up with the serial terminal connected and Minicom running, and you'll see a nice GRUB boot screen:

```
    GNU GRUB  version 0.95  (639K lower / 64512K upper memory)

 +-------------------------------------------------------------+
 | Metrix                                                      |
 | Shell                                                       |
 |                                                             |
 |                                                             |
 |                                                             |
 |                                                             |
 |                                                             |
 |                                                             |
 +-------------------------------------------------------------+
        Use the ^ and v keys to select which entry is highlighted.
        Press enter to boot the selected OS, 'e' to edit the
        commands before booting, or 'c' for a command-line.
```

By default, it will boot to Metrix, which is Pyramid Linux. *Shell* is for fixing filesystem problems—it goes directly to a Bash shell without mounting any filesystems, starting any services, or loading any network drivers.

On the Soekris 4521, eth0 is the Ethernet port immediately to the left of the serial port. Pyramid's default address for eth0 is 192.168.1.1. (If this doesn't work with your LAN addressing, you can easily change it via Minicom.)

SSH is enabled by default, so you can log in over SSH:

```
$ ssh root@192.168.1.1
```

Fire up a web browser on any connected PC, point it to *https://192.168.1.1*, and you'll be greeted by the welcome screen.

Discussion

A common task you'll boot to the Bash shell for is running the filesystem checker. This command turns on verbosity and answers "yes" to all questions:

```
# bash-3.00# /sbin/e2fsck -vy /dev/hda1
```

It's safe to let it go ahead and fix any filesystem problems it finds. Run this when you see this warning at boot: "EXT2-fs warning: mounting unchecked fs, running e2fsck is recommended," or a warning that your filesystem was shut down uncleanly.

The web GUI offers limited functionality; you need the command line for complete control. Figure 2-1 shows the web login screen.

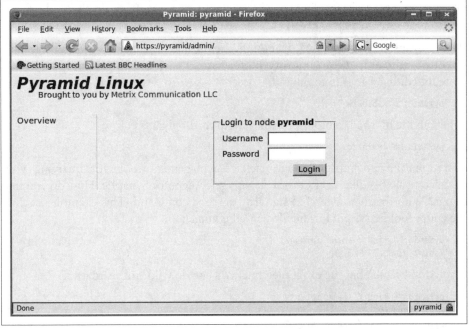

Figure 2-1. Pyramid Linux's web administration panel

From here on out, it's plain old Ubuntu Linux, the same old configuration files and startup scripts.

Pyramid is easily hackable for noncoders because you can grab whatever Ubuntu packages you want and install them. To keep it small, there are none of the usual Ubuntu package-management tools: no *apt*, *apt-get*, nor even *dpkg*. Recipe 2.10 tells how to add software without these.

See Also

- Pyramid Linux home page: *http://pyramid.metrix.net/*

2.7   Finding and Editing Pyramid Files

Problem

The web GUI doesn't do everything you want it to, or you just prefer editing text configuration files. Can you edit Pyramid files directly? How do you search for files without nice package-querying tools?

Solution

Pyramid is just a stripped-down Ubuntu Linux. If you know your way around an Ubuntu or Debian system (Ubuntu is a Debian derivative), Pyramid should be familiar ground.

Pyramid runs entirely in RAM. It mounts the filesystem read-only to extend the life of your Flash card, and to improve performance. To remount the filesystem read/write for editing, run this command:

```
pyramid:~# /sbin/rw
```

When you're finished, remount the filesystem read-only:

```
pyramid:~# /sbin/ro
```

You don't have Ubuntu's usual package-management tools for querying your installed packages, like *dpkg*, *apt-cache*, *apt-get*, Adept, or Synaptic. How do you find things? With that old-fashioned standby, the find command. This example searches the entire root filesystem for the file named *iptunnel*:

```
pyramid:~# find / -name iptunnel
/sbin/iptunnel
```

If you don't remember the exact filename, you can do wildcard searches:

```
pyramid:~# find / -name iptun*
/sbin/iptunnel
pyramid:~# find / -name *ptunn*
/sbin/iptunnel
```

You can start your search in any directory, like so: find /sbin -name pppd. To search the current directory, use a dot:

```
# find . -name foo-config
```

Discussion

If you're horrified at the thought of using the find command because you're used to it taking a long time, don't worry—with less than 50 MB to search, all find searches are quick.

See Also

- man 1 find

2.8   Hardening Pyramid

Problem

You want your little routerboard to be as hardened as you can make it. What steps can you take to make it as secure as possible?

Solution

Your first job is to change *root*'s password to something a little less obvious than "root," the default password. Run these commands:

```
pyramid:~# /sbin/rw
pyramid:~# passwd
```

Then, add an unprivileged user for remote logins over SSH:

```
pyramid:~# useradd -m alrac
pyramid:~# passwd alrac
```

You'll need to set the setuid bit on the su command so that ordinary users can su to *root*:

```
pyramid:~# chmod +s /bin/su
```

Next, harden OpenSSH: disable root logins over SSH, disable password logins, and set up public-key authentication. Chapter 7 tells how to do all this.

Turn off unnecessary services and network interfaces. If you're not going to use the web interface or SSH login, turn them off. SSH is disabled by changing its startup command to a kill command, like this:

```
pyramid:/etc/rc2.d# mv S20ssh K20ssh
```

The web GUI is disabled by commenting out this line in */etc/inittab*:

```
# Lighttpd (with FastCGI, SSL and PHP)
HT:23:respawn:/sbin/lighttpd -f /etc/lighttpd.conf -m /lib -D > /dev/null 2>&1
```

Pay close attention to your application security. Because this is a multihomed device, configure your applications to use only the interfaces they need to, and allow only authorized users. Keep your user accounts tidy, and don't leave unused ones lying around. Use good strong passwords, written down and stored in a safe place.

Run Netstat locally and Nmap remotely to see what services are listening, and to see what the outside world sees.

When you're finished, don't forget to run /sbin/ro to set the filesystem back to read-only.

Discussion

That's right, the same old basic steps for any Linux. They work.

See Also

- Chapter 7, "Starting and Stopping Linux," in *Linux Cookbook*, by Carla Schroder (O'Reilly) to learn how to manage services
- Chapter 8, "Managing Users and Groups," in *Linux Cookbook*
- Chapter 17, "Remote Access," in *Linux Cookbook*

2.9 Getting and Installing the Latest Pyramid Build

Problem

You want to try out the latest Pyramid build from Metrix's Subversion repository, instead of the official stable release. It has some features you want, or you want to contribute to the project by testing new builds.

Solution

You'll need a PXE boot installation server to make this work. Use the *pyramid-export.sh* script available from *http://pyramid.metrix.net/trac/wiki/GettingPyramid* to download the latest build and roll it into a tarball. Then, copy the tarball to your HTTP document root directory, and run the PXE boot installation in the usual way.

Discussion

It's about a 100 MB download, and Subversion can be slow, so don't be in a hurry.

See Also

- Recipe 2.4
- Recipe 2.5
- Pyramid Linux home page: *http://pyramid.metrix.net/*

2.10 Adding Additional Software to Pyramid Linux

Problem

Pyramid doesn't come with everything you want; how can you add more software? It doesn't have any of the usual Ubuntu package management tools, nor any package management tools at all, so you're at a bit of a loss.

Solution

The process is a bit fiddly, but not that bad. You can add user-space applications, kernel modules, and even customized kernels. You need an Ubuntu liveCD and a PC to run it on. You don't need to install it to a hard drive; just boot it up on any PC, and then copy off any files you want. I know in Recipe 2.8 I said to disable root logins over SSH, but for this task, you need to re-enable them, because the Ubuntu liveCD does not include an SSH server.

Suppose you want to install the Fortune program. Fortune displays a random fortune every time you run it, like this:

```
$ fortune
You will gain money by a fattening action.
```

Fortune comes with a number of different fortune databases, and you can easily create your own custom fortunes. It's a nice way to display a different Message of the Day every time users log in.

First boot up the Ubuntu liveCD. Then, find out what packages you need with the *dpkg* command:

```
ubuntu@ubuntu:~$ dpkg -l| grep fortune
ii  fortune-mod  1.99.1-3  provides fortune cookies on demand
ii  fortunes-min 1.99.1-3  Data files containing fortune cookies
```

Next, find out what files are in the Fortune packages:

```
ubuntu@ubuntu:~$ dpkg -L fortune-mod
/.
/usr
/usr/games
/usr/games/fortune
/usr/bin
/usr/bin/strfile
/usr/bin/unstr
/usr/share
/usr/share/man
/usr/share/man/man6
/usr/share/man/man6/fortune.6.gz
/usr/share/man/man1
/usr/share/man/man1/strfile.1.gz
/usr/share/doc
/usr/share/doc/fortune-mod
/usr/share/doc/fortune-mod/README.Debian
/usr/share/doc/fortune-mod/copyright
/usr/share/doc/fortune-mod/changelog.gz
/usr/share/doc/fortune-mod/README.gz
/usr/share/doc/fortune-mod/changelog.Debian.gz
/usr/share/menu
/usr/share/menu/fortune-mod
/usr/share/man/man1/unstr.1.gz
```

The only files you need are the executables and any libraries they depend on. Don't bother with manpages because Pyramid Linux has no manpage viewer. You may omit all documentation and example files to save space.

For the Fortune program, all you need are *fortune*, *strfile*, and *unstr*. How do you know? Because they are in */usr/bin*. Anything in a */bin* or */sbin* directory is an executable. Use the *du* command to see how big they are:

```
ubuntu@ubuntu:~$ du - /usr/games/fortune
21k     /usr/games/fortune
```

The others are equally dinky, so there is no problem finding room on our little 60 MB Pyramid image.

We also need to know how much space the Fortune databases require. They are all in a single directory, which is convenient:

```
ubuntu@ubuntu:~$ du -sh /usr/share/games/fortunes
127k    /usr/share/games/fortunes
```

OK, now you know what files to copy. Next, configure the network card on Ubuntu, using an address suitable for your own LAN addressing scheme:

```
ubuntu@ubuntu:~$ sudo ifconfig eth0 192.168.1.100  netmask 255.255.255.0 broadcast
192.168.1.255
```

Then, log in to Pyramid, and make the Pyramid filesystem writable:

```
ubuntu@ubuntu:~$ ssh root@pyramid
The authenticity of host '192.168.1.1 (192.168.1.1)' can't be established.
RSA key fingerprint is 6b:4a:6b:3c:5e:35:34:b2:99:34:ea:9d:dc:b8:b1:d7.
Are you sure you want to continue connecting (yes/no)? yes
Warning: Permanently added '192.168.1.1' (RSA) to the list of known hosts.
root@192.168.1.1's password:
pyramid:~# /sbin/rw
```

Now, you can copy files to Pyramid with the *scp* command. Open a second terminal on Ubuntu, and run the *scp* command. Ubuntu does not come with an SSH server, so you cannot log in to Ubuntu from Pyramid. This example copies the files to the */sbin* directory on Pyramid:

```
ubuntu@ubuntu:~$ scp /usr/games/fortune /usr/bin/strfile /usr/bin/unstr root@192.168.
1.1:/sbin/
root@192.168.1.1's password:
fortune     100%   18KB  17.8KB/s   00:00
strfile     100%   11KB  11.4KB/s   00:00
unstr       100% 5596    5.5KB/s   00:00
```

Mind your slashes and colons. Now, try running Fortune on Pyramid:

```
pyramid:~# fortune
fortune: error while loading shared libraries: librecode.so.0: cannot open shared
object file: No such file or directory
```

This tells you that you need *librecode.so.0*. Find it with the *locate* command on Ubuntu, then copy it over:

```
ubuntu@ubuntu:~$ locate librecode.so.0
/usr/lib/librecode.so.0.0.0
/usr/lib/librecode.so.0
ubuntu@ubuntu:~$ scp /usr/lib/librecode.so.0 root@192.168.1.1:/usr/lib/
```

Try it again:

```
pyramid:~# fortune
question = ( to ) ? be : ! be;
           -- Wm. Shakespeare
```

Remember to run /sbin/ro on Pyramid when you're finished.

Discussion

Pyramid is mostly unmodified Ubuntu binaries, so sticking with Ubuntu binaries and source files is the safest and easiest method for modifying it. As long as your Ubuntu CD is the same release as your Pyramid installation (Breezy, Dapper, and so forth) you shouldn't experience any compatibility problems.

You can copy applications and they will work. All you need are all the relevant binaries or scripts, and whatever libraries the applications depend on.

Run df -h / to see how much available space you have on Pyramid.

You can use *ldd* to see what libraries your application depends on before you start copying files:

```
$ ldd /usr/games/fortune
        linux-gate.so.1 =>  (0xffffe000)
        librecode.so.0 => /usr/lib/librecode.so.0 (0xb7df7000)
        libc.so.6 => /lib/tls/i686/cmov/libc.so.6 (0xb7cc8000)
        /lib/ld-linux.so.2 (0xb7f42000)
```

To see a new fortune every time you log in, place the Fortune command in your personal *~/.bash_profile*, or the systemwide */etc/profile,* like this:

```
fortune
```

That's right, a single word on a line by itself. You may modify this with any of the Fortune command's options.

See Also

- man 6 fortune
- Tips and Tricks For Hardworking Admins:

  http://www.enterprisenetworkingplanet.com/netsysm/article.php/10954_3551926_2 (which includes a Fortune How-To)

2.11   Adding New Hardware Drivers

Problem

You are using a network interface card (NIC) that is not supported in Pyramid, and you want to install the driver.

Solution

You'll need a loadable kernel module. The easy way is to boot up an Ubuntu liveCD, find a module in */lib/modules/[kernel-version]/kernel/drivers/net*, and copy it to the same directory on Pyramid:

```
ubuntu@ubuntu:~$ scp /lib/modules/2.6.15-26-386/kernel/drivers/net \ root@192.168.1.
1:/lib/modules/2.6.15.8-metrix/kernel/drivers/net/
```

Then, on Pyramid, run:

```
pyramid:~# update-modules
```

To immediately load the module for testing use *modprobe*, like this example using the fake *nicdriver.ko* module:

```
pyramid:~# modprobe nicdriver
```

Don't use the file extension, just the module name. To load it automatically at boot, place the module in */etc/modules* with a comment telling what NIC it belongs to:

```
#driver for Foo wireless pcmcia
nicdriver
```

Discussion

What if Ubuntu does not include the module? If it's a Linux kernel module, you'll have to build it from Ubuntu sources, then copy it to Pyramid. Use Ubuntu kernel sources. If it's a vendor module, follow their instructions for installation. But your best option is to use an NIC that is well-supported in the Linux kernel.

See Also

- man 8 modprobe
- man 8 lsmod
- man 5 modules
- Appendix C
- Chapter 10, "Patching, Customizing, and Upgrading Kernels," in *Linux Cookbook*, by Carla Schroder (O'Reilly)

2.12   Customizing the Pyramid Kernel

Problem

You want to compile a custom kernel with everything built-in instead of hassling with kernel modules. Your little routerboard runs only a limited set of hardware, and it's not something you're going to be updating or modifying a lot. Additionally, this will save a fair amount of storage space on your Compact Flash card.

Solution

No problem. You need a build environment on a PC, with kernel sources and build tools. Build your kernel there, then copy it to your Pyramid board. Use Ubuntu kernel sources with Ubuntu patches. Fetch Ubuntu kernel sources and build tools with this command:

```
$ sudo apt-get install linux-source linux-kernel-devel
```

That should get you everything you need.

If you want to start with the existing Pyramid kernel configuration, copy the */proc/config.gz* file to your build machine:

```
pyramid:/# scp /proc/config.gz carla@192.168.1.10:downloads/
```

Unpack it using gunzip:

```
$ gunzip config.gz
```

Now you can build a new custom kernel and drop it into place on Pyramid. Remember to update */boot/grub/menu.lst* with the new kernel name.

Discussion

Pyramid consists of mostly unmodified Ubuntu binaries, so sticking with Ubuntu binaries and source files is the safest and easiest method for modifying it. As long as your Ubuntu CD is the same release as your Pyramid installation (Breezy, Dapper, and so forth), you shouldn't experience any compatibility problems.

To see how much space */lib/modules* occupies, use the du command:

```
pyramid:/# du --si -c /lib/modules/2.6.17.8-metrix
...
6.3M    /lib/modules/2.6.17.8-metrix
6.3M    total
```

The kernel itself will occupy around 1 MB.

Typically, these little boards are "set it and forget it," so they are good candidates for statically compiled kernels.

See Also

- Chapter 10, "Patching, Customizing, and Upgrading Kernels," in *Linux Cookbook*, by Carla Schroder (O'Reilly)

2.13 Updating the Soekris comBIOS

Problem

The comBIOS on your Soekris board is old, so you have downloaded a newer version. How do you install it? Is it safe? Will you turn your routerboard into a high-tech doorstop?

Solution

Relax, it's fast and easy. The only risk is if the power fails during the actual installation; if that happens, your board could indeed be rendered useless. The installation takes a few seconds, so the risk is minute.

First, download the updated comBIOS to your PC from *http://www.soekris.com/ downloads.htm*.

Then, upload the file over the serial link to the Soekris board. To do this, enter the comBIOS by pressing Ctrl-P before Pyramid boots. Next, at the BIOS command line, enter the download - command (that's download, space, hyphen). Then, hit Enter.

Next, press Ctrl-A, S (that's Ctrl-A, release, S, release) to bring up Minicom's download menu. Select Xmodem from the list of protocols. Navigate to the upgrade file by using the spacebar to select any directories you want to change to, and then the file itself. (Sometimes it takes a couple of spacebar hits to change to a new directory.) The file is small, but it takes a couple of minutes to upload. You'll see something like Figure 2-2.

When the file is finished downloading, and you are back at the BIOS command prompt, type flashupdate:

```
> flashupdate
.Erasing Flash.... Programming Flash........ Verifying Flash.... Done.

>
```

Reboot, and that's all there is to it.

Discussion

You're using both comBIOS and Minicom commands to perform the upload. Press Ctrl-A, Z at any time for Minicom help.

If you get a "Failure executing protocol" error, you need to install *lrzsz* on the PC that you're running Minicom from.

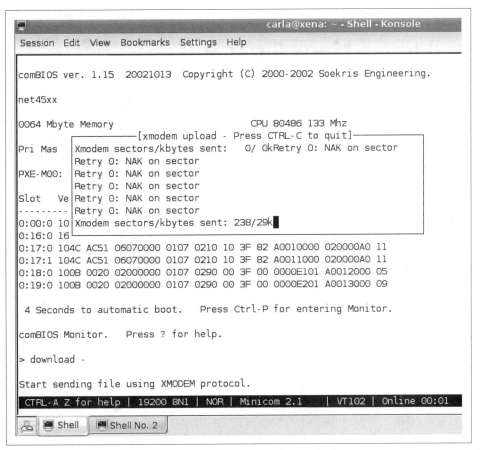

Figure 2-2. Downloading a file using the Xmodem protocol on Minicom

If you are too slow, you'll get a bunch of "Retry 0: NAK on sector" errors, and it will time out. It's rather impatient, so don't dink around.

Read the changelog at *http://www.soekris.com/downloads.htm* for useful information.

See Also

- man 1 minicom

CHAPTER 3
Building a Linux Firewall

3.0   Introduction

In this chapter, you'll learn how to build a Linux *iptables* firewall from scratch. While the recipes are aimed at DSL and cable Internet users, they also work for T1/E1 customers. In fact, a Linux box with a T1 interface card is a great alternative to expensive commercial routers. If you're a normal business user and not an ISP that needs Buick-sized routers handling routing tables with hundreds of thousands of entries, then Linux on good-quality x86 hardware will serve your needs just fine.

A Linux border firewall can provide security and share an Internet connection for a whole LAN, which can contain Linux, Windows, Mac, and other PCs. A host firewall protects a single PC. There are a multitude of hardware choices for your firewall box, from small single-board computers, to recycled old PCs, to rackmount units. Any Linux distribution contains everything you need to build a sophisticated, configurable, reliable firewall on any hardware.

Definitions and roles get a bit blurry, as an *iptables* firewall does both packet filtering and routing. You could call it a filtering router.

iptables is the key to making everything work. Having a solid understanding of how *iptables* works and how to write custom rules will give you mighty network guru powers. Please study Oskar Andreasson's Iptables Tutorial (*http://iptables-tutorial. frozentux.net/*) and Craig Hunt's *TCP/IP Network Administration* (O'Reilly) to get a deeper understanding of how *iptables* and TCP/IP work. Another excellent resource is the Netfilter FAQ (*http://www.iptables.org/documentation/index.html*). At the least, you should know what headers IP, TCP, UDP, and ICMP packets contain, and the section "Traversing Of Tables and Chains" in the Iptables Tutorial is especially helpful for understanding how packets move through *iptables*. If you don't understand these things, *iptables* will always be mysterious.

Firewalls and routers are often combined on the same device, which is often called an *Internet gateway*. Strictly speaking, a gateway moves traffic between networks that use different protocols, such as NETBEUI and TCP/IP, which is not something we see much anymore. These days, it means any network devices that connect networks.

Routers forward traffic between networks. You always need a router between your LAN and other networks. You may also add intrusion detection, traffic control, proxies, secure remote access, DNS/DHCP, and any other services you want, though in my opinion, it's better to limit your firewall to routing, firewalling, and traffic control. Other services should sit on separate boxes behind your Internet firewall, though of course this is up to you. In small shops, it's not uncommon for a single box to host a multitude of services. The risks are that any successful intruder will have a feast of yummy services to exploit, or you may simply overload the box to the point that performance suffers.

Any computer or network device that is exposed to untrusted networks is called a *bastion host*. Obviously, bastion hosts have special needs—they must be well-hardened, not share authentication services with your LAN hosts, and must have strict access controls.

Separating Private and Public

If you are going to run Internet-accessible services, you need to isolate your public servers from your private LAN. If you are sharing a single Internet connection, the simplest way is to build a tri-homed (three network interfaces) Linux router; one NIC connects to the Internet, the second one connects to your LAN, and the third one connects to your demilitarized zone (DMZ). A *demilitarized zone* is a neutral zone between two opposing groups. In computer terms, it's a separate subnet where you segegrate your public servers from your private LAN hosts, and your DMZ hosts are treated as only slightly less untrustworthy than the big bad Internet.

Simply placing your public servers on a different subnet adds a useful layer of protection. DMZ hosts are not able to initiate connections back into the private network without being explicitly allowed to do so. If a DMZ server is compromised, an attacker should not find a path into your private network.

It doesn't matter if your DMZ hosts have public or private IP addresses. Never run public services from inside your LAN. The last thing you want to do is introduce a big fat Internet hole into your LAN.

If your servers have public routable IP addresses, then you may elect to connect them directly to the Internet or on a separate Internet connection. Host firewalls are useful for restricting traffic to the server and blocking the zillions of automated attacks that infest the Internet. A nice thing is a standalone firewall in front of your public servers to filter out unwanted traffic before it hits them.

Windows Security

While firewalls are useful, remember to give a lot of attention to your application-level and OS security. Some admins recommend configuring your servers as though you have no firewall, and that is a good strategy. Linux and Unix servers can be hardened to the point where they really don't need a firewall. Windows systems are impossible to harden to this degree. Nor is a firewall a cure-all. A nice strong *iptables* firewall is a good umbrella to place over Windows hosts, but a firewall will not protect them from email-borne malware, infected web sites, or the increasing hordes of spyware, adware, Trojan horses, and rootkits that come in legitimate commercial software products, or the inability of commercial security products to detect all the bad stuff.

Iptables and NAT, SNAT, and DNAT

Our Linux-based *iptables* firewall is going to perform several jobs:

- Packet filtering
- Routing
- Network Address Translation (NAT)

Packet filtering is an extremely powerful, flexible mechanism that lets us perform all manner of mojo even on encrypted transmissions because TCP/IP packet headers are not encrypted. *iptables* rules filter on addresses, protocols, port numbers, and every other part of a TCP/IP packet header; it does not perform any sort of data inspection or filtering.

Having routing built-in a nice convenience that lets you pack a lot of functionality into a single device and into a few *iptables* rules.

NAT is the magic that lets you share a single public IP address with a whole private subnet, and to run public servers with private nonroutable addresses. Suppose you have a typical low-cost DSL Internet account. You have only a single public IP address, and a LAN of 25 workstations, laptops, and servers, protected by a nice *iptables* NAT firewall. Your entire network will appear to the outside world as a single computer. (Canny network gurus can penetrate NAT firewalls, but it isn't easy.) Source NAT (SNAT) rewrites the source addresses of all outgoing packets to the firewall address.

It works the other way as well. While having public routable IP addresses is desirable for public services, like web and mail servers, you can get by on the cheap without them and run public servers on private addresses. Destination NAT (DNAT) rewrites the destination address, which is the firewall address, to the real server addresses, then *iptables* forwards incoming traffic to these servers.

Someday, when IPv6 is widely implemented, we can say good-bye to NAT, except for those times when we really want it. It is useful for stretching the limited pool of

IPv4 addresses, and unintentionally provides some security benefits. But, it also creates a host of routing problems. Protocols that have to traverse NAT, like FTP, IRC, SMTP, and HTTP have all kinds of ingenious hacks built into them to make it possible. Peer protocols like BitTorrent, instant messaging, and session initiation protocol (SIP) are especially challenging to get through NAT.

iptables and TCP/IP Headers

iptables reads the fields in packet headers, but not the data payload, so it's no good for content filtering.

When you're studying the different protocols, you'll run into conflicting terminology. To be strictly correct, IP and UDP move datagrams, TCP exchanges segments, and ICMP packets are messages. In the context of *iptables*, most admins just say "packets," though you run the risk of annoying pedantic network engineers. The important part is understanding that every data transmission is broken into a series of packets that travel independently over the network, often taking different routes. Then, when they arrive at their destination, the TCP protocol reassembles them in the correct order. Each packet contains in its headers all the information necessary for routers to forward it to its destination. IP and UDP are unreliable protocols because they do not have delivery confirmations, but this makes them very fast. TCP takes care of delivery confirmations, sequence numbers, and error-checking, so it incurs a bit of overhead, but gains reliability. TCP/IP together are extremely reliable.

If you have any questions about connecting to the Internet or networking hardware basics, read the Introduction to this book.

When Is a Firewall Needed?

Do you even need a firewall? Short answer: if you connect to other networks, yes. Ubuntu Linux, for one famous example, does not include a firewall configurator during installation because it installs with no running services. No services means no points of attack. But, I think this is missing an important point: things change, mistakes happen, and layered defenses are a standard best practice. Why let your hosts be pummeled and your LAN congested by outside attacks, even if they are futile? Head all that junk off at your firewall. Even public services benefit from being firewalled. For example, there's no need to subject your web server to the endless SSH attacks and MS SQL Server worms infesting the Internet, so you can block everything but port TCP 80. The same goes for all of your hosts: reduce the load and potential compromises by diverting unwanted traffic before it hits them.

You can take this a step further and fine-tune exactly where you allow incoming traffic to come from. SSH is the poster child for this—if you're not expecting legitimate connection attempts from far-flung lands, write rules to allow only the address ranges or specific addresses that you know are legitimate, and bitbucket the rest.

iptables Overview

iptables is part of the Netfilter project. Netfilter is a set of Linux kernel hooks that communicate with the network stack. *iptables* is a command and the table structure that contains the rulesets that control the packet filtering.

iptables is complex. It filters packets by the fields in IP, TCP, UDP, and ICMP packet headers. A number of different actions can be taken on each packet, so the key to *iptables* happiness is simplicity. Start with the minimum necessary to get the job done, then add rules as you need them. It's not necessary to build vast *iptables* edifices, and in fact, it's a bad idea, as it makes it difficult to maintain, and will hurt performance.

iptables Policies and Rules

Policies are the default actions applied to packets that do not match any rules. There are three built-in tables: filter, NAT, and mangle. You will use the filter table the most, the NAT table a little, and the mangle table perhaps not at all (it is for advanced packet manipulation). Each table contains a number of built-in chains. You may also create custom chains. A *chain* is a list of rules that defines the actions applied to packets. Rules end with a target specification that tells what to do with the packet. This is done with the jump (-j) command, like this simple example that permits all loopback traffic with the ACCEPT target:

```
iptables -A INPUT -i lo -j ACCEPT
```

Once a packet reaches the ACCEPT target, that is the end of the road, and it does not traverse any more chains. Rules can be run from the command line or put in a script. This is what each part of this rule means:

- iptables = The *iptables* command
- No table is specified, so the default filter table is used
- -A INPUT = Append this rule to the built-in INPUT chain
- -i lo = Apply this rule to packets going to interface lo
- -j ACCEPT = Jump to the built-in ACCEPT chain, which moves packets to their final destinations

iptables does stateful packet inspection, which is done via its connection tracking mechanism. In other words, it knows if a packet is attempting to start a new connection or if it belongs to an existing one. Seeing packets in context is very powerful, and makes it possible to do a lot of work with a few rules. If you are running no public services, you can then easily block all outside attempts to create a connection, because they have no legitimate reason to try to connect to you. When you do run services such as SSH, FTP, or a web or mail server, *iptables* can allow only traffic targeted for the services you are running, and reject all the rest. You might block all outgoing traffic initiated from your servers because they're only supposed to respond to connection attempts from the outside, not initiate them. These things would be difficult to do without stateful packet inspection.

iptables is extensible with the addition of custom kernel modules, so *iptables* features vary by Linux distribution and user modifications. To see what your installation supports, check your */boot/config-** file. If you're not thrilled by the notion of managing a bunch of kernel modules (and *iptables* can use quite a few), build a custom kernel with the *iptables* functions you want built-in.

Tables Overview

There are three tables in *iptables*. Any rules or custom chains that you create will go into one of these tables. The filter table is the default, and is the one you'll use the most. You can think of it as the firewalling portion of *iptables*. The filter table contains these built-in chains:

INPUT
   Processes incoming packets

FORWARD
   Processes packets routed through the host

OUTPUT
   Processes outgoing packets

The NAT table is used only to change the packet's Source Address field or Destination Address field. If you have a single public, routable IP address in front of a LAN that uses private addresses, which is common, NAT translates the source IP addresses on outgoing packets to the public address. It doesn't matter if you have a hundred hosts sharing the connection—it will appear that all your traffic is coming from a single host. Conversely, you may use it to enable access to public services with private IPs. The NAT table has these built-in chains:

PREROUTING
   Alters incoming packets before routing

OUTPUT
   Alters locally-generated packets before routing

POSTROUTING
   Alters packets after routing

The mangle table lets you alter packet headers as you like. This has a host of uses that we will not cover in this book, but here are a few ideas for inspiration:

- Change the TOS field of packets for QoS (there are now better ways for managing QoS, but there it is)
- MARKing packets to collect statistics for filtering, logging, or routing
- Limit packet rate

It has these built-in chains:

PREROUTING
> Alters incoming packets before routing

OUTPUT
> Alters locally generated packets before routing

INPUT
> Alters packets destined for the local machine

FORWARD
> Processes packets routed through the host

POSTROUTING
> Alters packets on their way out, after routing

Packets coming into your network must first pass through the mangle table, then the NAT table, and finally, the filter table.

User-defined chains can improve performance because packets traverse your rules and chains in the order they are listed. Defining your own chains lets you create shortcuts, so packets can jump directly to the chains you want them to traverse, instead of passing through a bunch of irrelevant rules and chains first. Or, you may save some configuration steps by building a custom chain to use over and over.

Specialized Linux Firewall and Routing Distributions

While you can customize any Linux distribution any way you like, there are a number of specialized Linux distributions designed to serve as Internet routers and firewalls. They are stripped-down to the essentials. Some are small enough to fit on a floppy disk. Typically, these include *iptables*, DNS/DHCP servers, secure remote access, intrusion detection, logging, port forwarding, and Internet connection sharing. Here are a few of the more popular ones:

Freesco (http://www.freesco.org/)
> The name means FREE ciSCO. It is a free replacement for commercial routers. It supports up to 10 Ethernet/arcnet/Token Ring/arlan network cards, and up to 10 modems. It is easy to set up, and can be run from a single write-protected diskette, or from a hard drive, if you want additional functionality.

IPCop (http://www.ipcop.org/)
> An excellent prefab Internet gateway. It has a web-based administration interface, supports SSH and console access, and, in addition to the usual gateway services, it supports dial-up networking and DynDNS.

The Sentry Firewall CD (http://www.sentryfirewall.com/)
> Sentry runs from a bootable CD, and stores configuration files on a diskette. Set the diskette to read-only, and recovering from an intrusion is as easy as patching the hole and rebooting.

Pyramid Linux (http://pyramid.metrix.net/)

Pyramid Linux, a descendant of the popular Pebble Linux, is maintained by Metrix Communications, and is based on Ubuntu Linux. It is optimized for wireless access points, and serves equally well as a wired-network firewall. The stock installation occupies under 50 MB, so it's perfect for single-board computers without expandable storage. Because it uses stock Ubuntu packages, you can easily add applications by copying the binaries and any dependent libraries from the Ubuntu liveCD.

Bering uClibc (http://leaf.sourceforge.net/bering-uclibc/)

Bering achieves its small size by using modified libraries. Because it is so customized, you have to rely on the Bering package repositories for additional application. This shouldn't be a problem for most admins, as they offer a large number of additional packages.

Voyage Linux (http://www.voyage.hk/software/voyage.html)

Based on Debian, Voyage can be shrunken to as small as 64 MB, or expanded as desired. Optimized for wireless access points, routers, and firewalls.

Debian Router (http://gate-bunker.p6.msu.ru/~berk/)

This is a work in progress. It is an interesting Debian implementation that takes a slimmed-down, stock Debian, and adapts it to boot from a flash drive and run entirely in memory.

It is equally important to harden your systems, and a great tool for this is Bastille Linux (*http://www.bastille-linux.org/*). Bastille is a set of scripts that walk you through a number of steps to harden your entire system. It is designed to be educational and functional. You can run through it a couple of times without actually changing anything, and it also has an undo feature so that you can practice without running the risk of locking yourself out of your system. It examines almost every aspect of your system, including file permissions, PAM settings, services, and remote access.

Important Disclaimer

I cannot guarantee that the recipes in this chapter are crack-proof, or that they will offer perfect protection. No one can make such a claim. Users clamor for easy, point-and-click security, but there is no such thing. Security is an escalating arms race. The well-armed network administrator studies the relevant RFCs, *iptables* documentation, and keeps up-to-date with important security news (e.g., the security bulletins for their particular Linux distribution, Bugtraq mailing list, *securityfocus.com*, and Bruce Schneier's Crypto-Gram list).

3.1   Assembling a Linux Firewall Box

Problem

You want to build your own Internet firewall box for your cable or DSL Internet line, on ordinary x86 hardware, using your favorite Linux distribution. You want Internet connection sharing and a firewall, and you need to know what hardware components to use. You already have installation disks, or some other method of installing the operating system.

Solution

The Linux distribution you want to use determines your hardware requirements. Some distributions require more horsepower than others, so don't assume you can use some feeble old antique PC without checking. This chapter's Introduction lists a number of specialized firewall distributions.

You'll need these items to build and set up your firewall box:

- A PC with at least two Ethernet interfaces
- A second PC and a crossover cable for testing

You'll connect only the LAN interface until your firewall has been installed and configured.

Go ahead and install your chosen Linux distribution, then follow the recipes in this chapter to configure your network interfaces and firewall.

Install *net-tools* and Nmap because you will use them a lot in this chapter. They should also be installed on a second PC for testing. Debian users will also need to install the *ifrename* package.

Discussion

Repurposing old PCs saves money and keeps them out of landfills. They can be customized any way you like. They also make dandy test-and-practice boxes. The drawbacks are size, noise, power consumption, and the fact that they may not be reliable, just from being old.

An excellent alternative to an old PC is a single-board computer like the PC Engine WRAP boards or Soekris boards. These cost between $150 and $400, depending on which features and accessories you get. They use little power, are small and silent, and very sturdy. (See Chapter 2 to learn how to use one of these.)

WRAP and Soekris boards come in several different configurations. You'll need a minimum of two Ethernet ports. You'll need three if you plan to run servers inside a DMZ. Two Ethernet ports plus two PCMCIA slots and a mini-PCI slot will give you the flexibility to mix-and-match wired and wireless in a number of different ways.

An inexpensive but powerful option is the Linksys WRT54G and its cousins, such as the Buffalo WHR series, the ASUS WL-500 boxes, and other similar products. These are little four-port broadband router and wireless access points targeted at home DSL or cable users. You can find these for well under $100, and even under $50. They're not so hot with their stock firmwares, but when you turborcharge them with the OpenWRT or DD-WRT firmwares, they perform like $500 commercial routers.

Cabling

Youngsters may not remember the olden days before auto-detecting MDI/MDI-X (medium-dependent interface/crossover ports) on Ethernet switches, and even some network interface cards, though these are rare. Back in the bad old days, network admins had to deal with two types of Ethernet cabling: straight cables and crossover cables. Straight cables connected PCs to hubs and switches, and crossover cables were for PC-to-PC and hub-to-hub or switch-to-switch connections. In these modern times, we still need crossover cables for PC-to-PC connections (with rare exceptions), but most hubs and switches can use either one.

Network interfaces

Ordinary Fast Ethernet interfaces are easiest, both PCI and onboard. You may use ISA NICs, if that's all you have. But that puts a greater load on the CPU, and the ISA bus is very slow, around 8 Mb per second. This is still faster than the typical cable or DSL Internet line, so use it as your WAN interface. (Yes, you can find 100BaseTX ISA network cards, which is silly, because they'll still be limited by the ISA bus speed.)

Don't use wireless interfaces unless you are a wireless guru. Wireless interfaces need special handling, so I recommend sticking with plain old wired Ethernet until you have your firewall running satisfactorily.

See Also

- *Repairing and Upgrading Your PC*, by Robert Bruce Thompson and Barbara Fritchman Thompson (O'Reilly)

3.2   Configuring Network Interface Cards on Debian

Problem

You have installed Debian Linux on your firewall box, so you're ready to configure your network interface cards.

Solution

In Debian, you'll edit */etc/network/interfaces* and */etc/iftab*. */etc/iftab* is part of the *ifrename* package.

First, configure the LAN NIC with a static IP address appropriate for your private addressing scheme. Don't use DHCP to assign the LAN address. Configure the WAN interface with the account information given to you by your ISP. These examples show you how to set a static local IP address and a dynamic external address.

Do not connect the WAN interface yet.

In this example, eth0 is the LAN interface, and eth1 is the WAN interface:

```
##/etc/network/interfaces

# The loopback network interface
auto lo
iface lo inet loopback

#lan interface
auto eth0
iface eth0 inet static
     address 192.168.1.26
     netmask 255.255.255.0
     network 192.168.1.0
     broadcast 192.168.1.255

#wan interface
auto eth1
iface eth1 inet dhcp
```

If your WAN address is a static public routable IP address, configure the WAN interface using the information supplied by your ISP. This should include your ISP's gateway address, and your static IP address and netmask, like this:

```
auto eth1
iface eth1 inet static
       address 1.2.3.4
       netmask 255.255.255.0
       gateway 1.2.3.55
```

Then, add your ISP's DNS servers to */etc/resolv.conf* (don't do this for a DHCP WAN address):

```
##/etc/resolv.conf
nameserver 1.2.3.44
nameserver 1.2.3.45
```

There is one more step just for Debian: nail down the interface names with *ifrename*. First, find the MAC addresses of your interfaces with ifconfig -a:

```
$ ifconfig -a
eth0    Link encap:Ethernet  HWaddr 00:0B:6A:EF:7E:8D
[...]
```

The MAC address is the HWaddr. Enter your two MAC addresses and interface names in */etc/iftab*:

```
##/etc/iftab
eth0 mac 11:22:33:44:55:66
eth1 mac aa:bb:cc:dd:ee:ff
```

If */etc/iftab* does not exist, you must create it.

Discussion

The LAN address of your firewall is the gateway address you'll be setting on all of your LAN PCs, so don't complicate your life by using a dynamically assigned address.

Using *ifrename* is the easiest way to make sure your network cards keep the correct configurations on Debian systems. Usually, interfaces will come up in the same order, and the kernel will assign them the same names, but sometimes this can change (e.g., after a kernel upgrade or adding another network card). Your nice Linux firewall won't work with the network interfaces mixed up, so it is best to nail them down. An additional bonus is you can easily name your interfaces anything you want with *ifrename*. You might give them descriptive names like "lan" and "wan," instead of *eth0* and *eth1*.

Routers typically run headless, without a keyboard or monitor. If your Ethernet-working gets all goofed up, and you cannot log in to your router, the serial console will save the day. See Chapter 17 to learn how to set this up.

Configuration definitions

auto
> Start the NIC when ifup -a is run, typically in boot scripts. Interfaces are brought up in the order they are listed. You may bring interfaces up and down manually with *ifup* and *ifdown*, like ifdown eth0 and ifup eth0.

iface
> Name of the interface.

inet
> The name of the address family; inet = IPv4. Other choices are ipx and inet6.

static
> The name of the method used to configure the interface, either static or dhcp. Other choices are manual, bootp, ppp, and wvdial. manual lets you pass in configurations using scripts, or with the up and down commands. bootp receives configurations from a remote boot server, and ppp and wvdial are for modems.

See Also

- man 5 interfaces
- man 8 ifconfig
- man 8 ifrename
- Chapter 10, "Network Configuration," of the Debian Reference Manual (*http://www.debian.org/doc/manuals/reference/*), available in several languages

3.3 Configuring Network Interface Cards on Fedora

Problem

You have installed Fedora Linux on your firewall box, and now you're ready to give your network interface cards their final, working configurations.

Solution

Fedora gives each network interface a separate configuration file. You'll be editing */etc/sysconfig/network-scripts/ifcfg-eth0* and */etc/sysconfig/network-scripts/ifcfg-eth1*.

First, configure the LAN interface with a static IP address appropriate for your private addressing scheme. Don't use DHCP to assign the LAN address.

Configure the WAN interface with the account information given to you by your ISP.

These examples show how to set a static local IP address and a dynamic external IP address.

Do not connect the WAN interface yet.

In this example, *eth0* is the LAN interface and *eth1* is the WAN interface:

```
##/etc/sysconfig/network-scripts/ifcfg-eth0
#use your own MAC address and LAN addresses
DEVICE=eth0
HWADDR=11:22:33:44:55:66
BOOTPROTO=none
ONBOOT=yes
NETMASK=255.255.255.0
IPADDR=192.168.1.23
NETWORK=192.168.1.0
USERCTL=no

##/etc/sysconfig/network-scripts/ifcfg-eth1
#use your real MAC address
DEVICE=eth1
HWADDR=AA:BB:CC:DD:EE:FF
BOOTPROTO=dhcp
USERCTL=no
```

How do you get the MAC addresses and interface names? Run `ifconfig -a`:

```
$ ifconfig -a
eth0    Link encap:Ethernet   HWaddr 00:0B:6A:EF:7E:8D
[...]
```

And that's all you need to do, because you'll get all your WAN configurations from your ISP's DHCP server.

If your WAN address is a static IP address, configure the WAN NIC the same way as the LAN address using the information supplied by your ISP. This should include your ISP's gateway address, and your static IP address and netmask. Then, add your ISP's DNS servers to */etc/resolv.conf*:

```
##/etc/resolv.conf
nameserver 11.22.33.44
nameserver 11.22.33.45
```

Restart networking or reboot, and you're ready for the next steps.

Discussion

The LAN IP address of your firewall is the gateway address you'll be setting on all of your LAN PCs, so don't complicate your life by using a dynamically assigned address.

Routers typically run headless, without a keyboard or monitor. If your Ethernet-working gets all goofed up, the serial console will save the day. See Chapter 17 to learn how to set this up.

Every Linux distribution comes with a number of graphical network configuration tools. Feel free to use these, though it's always good to understand the underlying text configuration files and scripts.

When you have two NICs on a Linux box, they are usually brought up in the same order on boot, and given the same names (e.g., *eth0*, *eth1*, etc.). But sometimes, the order is reversed, which will render your nice firewall box useless, so binding the device names to their MAC addresses ensures that the configurations always stay put. That's what the DEVICE directive is for.

You can even give your interfaces names of your own choosing, like "lan" and "wan." You may also rename the configuration file to help you remember, like */etc/sysconfig/network-scripts/ifcfg-lan*. You must use "ifcfg" in the filename, or it won't work.

This is what the configuration options mean:

DEVICE

Name of the physical device.

HWADDR

The real MAC address of the NIC. Don't confuse this with MACADDR, because MACADDR assigns a new MAC address, overriding the existing one. Why would you want to change a MAC address? There aren't many legitimate reasons, though it is a good reminder to see how easy it is to spoof a MAC address, and why you should not rely on MAC addresses as secure identifiers.

BOOTPROTO

Boot protocol, which is none, dhcp, or bootp.

ONBOOT

Bring the NIC up at boot, yes or no.

NETMASK

Address mask for your network. Unfortunately, CIDR addressing is not yet supported.

IPADDR

The IP address that you choose for the NIC.

USERCTL

Allow unprivileged users to control the NIC, yes or no.

Broadcast addresses are automatically calculated with *ifcalc*, so it's not necessary to specify them.

See Also

- The Discussion in the previous recipe for more discussion of hardware requirements
- man 8 ifconfig
- Red Hat maintains a complete archive of manuals online at *http://www.redhat.com/docs/manuals/*; look for the Networking chapters in the Reference Guides

3.4   Identifying Which NIC Is Which

Problem

You have successfully installed two NICs in your new soon-to-be Linux firewall, but you realize that you don't know how to tell which physical card is *eth0* and which one is *eth1*.

Solution

The most reliable way is to connect one at a time to another PC and *ping* them from the second PC. Once you know which one is which, label them. Using two different interface cards with different drivers also helps to keep them sorted out, though it's not required.

Discussion

If your needs grow to where you need three or four Ethernet adapters, consider purchasing two- or four-port Ethernet adapters. They are configured and managed in exactly the same way as single-port cards, with the advantages of using fewer PCI slots, and requiring fewer interrupts. They're more expensive because they are designed for server duties, so they are more robust, and come with more features.

Soekris single-board computers can have up to eight 10/100 Ethernet ports.

There is no instant method for identifying which NIC is *eth0* or *eth1* when you install them for the first time, or afterward. It takes just a couple of minutes to do the *ping* test and label them, and it will save many hassles down the road.

USB Ethernet adapters are worth considering if you shop carefully and purchase only models with native Linux drivers. Don't use *ndiswrapper*, which is a Linux wrapper that lets you use the device's binary Windows drivers on Linux. It is difficult to install, difficult to upgrade, and using closed, binary device drivers leaves you at the mercy of the vendor for bugfixes and security patches.

Be sure to get USB 2.0 devices, or you won't see any speed at all, because USB 1.1 supports a maximum line speed of 12 Mbps. Most likely you'll top out at 6–8 Mbps, which in these modern times is slower than slow. USB 2.0 supports a theoretical maximum of 480 Mbps. On an unshared USB 2.0 bus, you should hit data transfer rates of around 320 Mbps or so, or around 40 MBps.

See Also

- man 8 ping
- Chapter 5, "Discovering Hardware from Outside the Box," in *Linux Cookbook*, by Carla Schroder (O'Reilly)

3.5 Building an Internet-Connection Sharing Firewall on a Dynamic WAN IP Address

Problem

Your Linux firewall box is assembled and ready to go to work. But first, you must set up a firewall and Internet connection sharing. You're still on IPv4, and your LAN uses mostly nonroutable private IP addresses, so you want a Network Address Translation (NAT) firewall. You have a dynamically assigned WAN address.

Solution

It's all done with *iptables*.

Don't connect the WAN interface yet. Make sure there are no open ports on your firewall machine. Test this by running *netstat* on the firewall box. This command shows all listening and TCP and UDP sockets and established connections:

```
admin@firewall:~# netstat -untap
```

If you find any open ports, close them. Any services you want to run can be restarted later, but for now, it's safer to shut them off, with one exception: you need a DHCP client running so the WAN interface will work correctly. DHCP clients run by default on all Linux distributions, so you shouldn't have to enable it.

Next, edit */etc/sysctl.conf* so that it has these kernel parameters. The first one is the most important because you must have it to enable sharing your Internet connection:

```
net.ipv4.ip_forward = 1
net.ipv4.icmp_echo_ignore_broadcasts = 1
net.ipv4.tcp_syncookies = 1
net.ipv4.conf.all.accept_source_route = 0
```

Next, copy the following script, call it */usr/local/bin/fw_nat*, and make it read/write/executable for *root* only, mode 0700:

```
#!/bin/sh
##/usr/local/bin/fw_nat
#iptables firewall script for sharing
#broadband Internet, with no public services

#define variables
ipt="/sbin/iptables"
mod="/sbin/modprobe"
LAN_IFACE="eth0"
WAN_IFACE="eth1"

#basic set of kernel modules
$mod ip_tables
$mod ip_conntrack
$mod iptable_filter
$mod iptable_nat
$mod iptable_mangle
$mod ipt_LOG
$mod ipt_limit
$mod ipt_state
$mod ipt_MASQUERADE

#add these for IRC and FTP
$mod ip_nat_ftp
$mod ip_nat_irc
$mod ip_conntrack_ftp
$mod ip_conntrack_irc
```

```
# Flush all active rules and delete all custom chains
$ipt -F
$ipt -t nat -F
$ipt -t mangle -F
$ipt -X
$ipt -t nat -X
$ipt -t mangle -X

#Set default policies
$ipt -P INPUT DROP
$ipt -P FORWARD DROP
$ipt -P OUTPUT ACCEPT
$ipt -t nat -P OUTPUT ACCEPT
$ipt -t nat -P PREROUTING ACCEPT
$ipt -t nat -P POSTROUTING ACCEPT
$ipt -t mangle -P PREROUTING ACCEPT
$ipt -t mangle -P POSTROUTING ACCEPT

#this line is necessary for the loopback interface
#and internal socket-based services to work correctly
$ipt -A INPUT -i lo -j ACCEPT

#Enable IP masquerading
$ipt -t nat -A POSTROUTING -o $WAN_IFACE -j MASQUERADE

#Enable unrestricted outgoing traffic, incoming
#is restricted to locally-initiated sessions only
$ipt -A INPUT -m state --state RELATED,ESTABLISHED -j ACCEPT
$ipt -A FORWARD -i $WAN_IFACE -o $LAN_IFACE -m state --state ESTABLISHED,RELATED -j
ACCEPT
$ipt -A FORWARD -i $LAN_IFACE -o $WAN_IFACE -m state --state NEW,ESTABLISHED,RELATED
-j ACCEPT

# Accept important ICMP messages
$ipt -A INPUT -p icmp --icmp-type echo-request  -j ACCEPT
$ipt -A INPUT -p icmp --icmp-type time-exceeded -j ACCEPT
$ipt -A INPUT -p icmp --icmp-type destination-unreachable -j ACCEPT

#Reject connection attempts not initiated from inside the LAN
$ipt -A INPUT -p tcp --syn -j DROP
```

Now, load the new *sysctl* settings and execute the *fw_nat* script as *root*:

```
# /sbin/sysctl -p
# fw_nat
```

Then, connect the WAN interface to your broadband modem, and bring up the WAN interface:

```
# /sbin/ifup eth1
```

You should see some messages from your DHCP client and see your new address.

Now, connect a second PC to your LAN port, either with a switch or a crossover cable. It needs a static address on the same network as the firewall's LAN port, using the firewall's LAN address as the gateway.

You should be able to web surf, *ping* remote sites, and ping each other. Once everything is working correctly, go to Recipe 3.9 to learn how to start your *iptables* script at boot, and how to stop and restart your firewall.

Discussion

If running /sbin/ifup eth1 gives you this message:

```
ifup: interface eth1 already configured
```

run /sbin/ifdown eth1, then /sbin/ifup eth1.

A typical response to running /sbin/ifup eth1 looks like this:

```
# ifup eth1
Internet Systems Consortium DHCP Client V3.0.2
Copyright 2004 Internet Systems Consortium.
All rights reserved.
For info, please visit http://www.isc.org/products/DHCP
sit0: unknown hardware address type 776
sit0: unknown hardware address type 776
Listening on LPF/eth1/00:01:02:03:04:05
Sending on   LPF/eth1/00:01:02:03:04:05
Sending on   Socket/fallback
DHCPDISCOVER on eth1 to 255.255.255.255 port 67 interval 3
DHCPOFFER from 1.2.3.4
DHCPREQUEST on eth1 to 255.255.255.255 port 67
DHCPACK from 1.2.3.4
bound to 1.2.3.44 -- renewal in 34473 seconds.
```

If none of this happens, make sure your cables are connected correctly. If they are, try rebooting. It's usually quicker than dinking around with the network starting/stopping peculiarities of your particular Linux distribution.

The RELATED,ESTABLISHED rules are examples of the power of stateful packet filtering. *iptables'* connection tracking knows which TCP packets belong to an established connection, so we can lock down incoming traffic tightly and still have unfettered functionality with just a few rules.

The default policies apply when no specific rules apply to a packet. The NAT and mangle tables should default to ACCEPT because packets traverse these tables before the filter table. If your NAT and mangle policies are DROP, you will have to create additional rules to allow packets to reach the filter table.

Setting OUTPUT ACCEPT as the default is somewhat controversial. Some admins advocate locking this down with OUTPUT DROP, and writing allow rules only as needed. If you use OUTPUT ACCEPT, see Recipe 3.18 for some tips on writing egress rules for blocking known bad ports, and for adding some other basic precautions.

iptables does not run as a daemon, but operates at the kernel level. The rules are loaded into memory by the `iptables` command. You may run all the commands in the above script from the command line, which is one way of testing. However, they will not survive a reboot. My preference is to script all rules even for testing; it's easy enough to edit and rerun the script. If things go excessively haywire, run the flush script from Recipe 3.8 to delete all rules and reset everything to ACCEPT. If for some reason that does not work, rebooting will clear out everything, provided you have no firewall scripts that run at boot. Then, you need to reexamine your scripts to figure out what went wrong.

Because *iptables* is implemented in the kernel, stock kernels vary in how many modules are built-in, and how many are loadable modules. Check your */boot/config-** file to see how yours was built. It's unnecessary to include kernel modules in your firewall script that are built-in to the kernel, though it doesn't hurt anything. You may wish to build a custom kernel with all the *iptables* modules you need built-in to save the hassle of managing modules. There are no performance differences either way, it's just a matter of personal preference.

It is common to see kernel parameters set in *iptables* scripts, like this:

```
echo 1 > /proc/sys/net/ipv4/icmp_echo_ignore_broadcasts
echo 0 > /proc/sys/net/ipv4/conf/all/accept_redirects
echo 0 > /proc/sys/net/ipv4/conf/all/accept_source_route
```

I prefer to control these options with *sysctl* because that is what it is designed to do, and I prefer that they operate independently of my *iptables* script. The *echo* commands are nice for command-line testing, as they override configuration files. They won't survive a reboot, so any settings you want to keep permanently should go in */etc/sysctl.conf*.

A common point of confusion is dots and slashes. You may use either, like this:

```
net.ipv4.tcp_syncookies = 1
net/ipv4/tcp_syncookies = 1
```

See Also

- Recipe 3.10
- The Discussion in Recipe 3.15 to learn what the kernel parameters in */etc/sysctl. conf* mean
- *ip-sysctl.txt* in your kernel documentation
- `man 8 iptables`
- Chapter 1, "Overview of TCP/IP," in *TCP/IP Network Administration*, by Craig Hunt (O'Reilly)
- Oskar Andreasson's Iptables Tutorial: *http://iptables-tutorial.frozentux.net/*

3.6 Building an Internet-Connection Sharing Firewall on a Static WAN IP Address

Problem

Your Linux firewall box is assembled and ready to go to work. But first, you must configure a firewall and Internet connection sharing. You're still on IPv4, and your LAN uses mostly nonroutable, private IP addresses, so you want a NAT (Network Address Translation) firewall. You have the type of Internet account that gives you a static, public IP address.

Solution

The *fw_nat* script from the previous recipe needs one line changed. Find:

```
$ipt -t nat -A POSTROUTING  -o $WAN_IFACE -j MASQUERADE
```

and replace it with:

```
$ipt -t nat -A POSTROUTING -o $WAN_IFACE -j SNAT --to-source 1.2.3.4
```

Use your own WAN IP address, of course.

Discussion

Static addresses are good candidates for being put in variables at the beginning of the script, like this:

```
WAN_IP="1.2.3.4"
```

Then, your rule looks like this:

```
$ipt -t nat -A POSTROUTING -o $WAN_IFACE -j SNAT --to-source $WAN_IP
```

You could still use the MASQUERADE target, but that incurs more overhead because it checks which IP address to use for every packet.

Source network address translation (SNAT) rewrites the source address of every packet, leaving your network to the IP address of your firewall box. This is necessary for hosts with private-class addresses to be able to access the Internet.

You can see your NAT-ed addresses with *netstat-nat*:

```
# netstat-nat
Proto NATed Address            Foreign Address                  State
tcp   stinkpad.alrac.net:41435 64.233.163.99:www                ESTABLISHED
tcp   stinkpad.alrac.net:45814 annyadvip3.doubleclick.net:www   TIME_WAIT
tcp   stinkpad.alrac.net:45385 annymdnvip2.2mdn.net:www         TIME_WAIT
tcp   stinkpad.alrac.net:50392 63.87.252.186:www                ESTABLISHED
udp   stinkpad.alrac.net:32795 auth.isp.net:domain              ASSURED
udp   stinkpad.alrac.net:32794 auth.isp.net:domain              ASSURED
```

netstat-nat is not the *netstat* command with a -nat option; it is a separate command.

Use the -n flag to display IP addresses instead of hostnames.

See Also

- man 8 iptables
- man 8 netstat
- Chapter 1, "Overview of TCP/IP," in *TCP/IP Network Administration*, by Craig Hunt (O'Reilly)
- Oskar Andreasson's Iptables Tutorial: *http://iptables-tutorial.frozentux.net/*

3.7   Displaying the Status of Your Firewall

Problem

You want a quick way to check the status of your firewall so you can see if it's up, and what rules are active.

Solution

These *iptables* commands tell all:

```
# /sbin/iptables -t filter -L -v -n --line-numbers
# /sbin/iptables -t nat -L -v -n --line-numbers
# /sbin/iptables -t mangle -L -v -n --line-numbers
```

You need to specify all three tables to see all rules. This is easy to script, like this */usr/local/bin/fw_status script*:

```
#!/bin/sh
##/usr/local/bin/fw_status script
#displays all active rules and chains

#define variables
ipt="/sbin/iptables"

echo "These are the currently active rules, chains, and packet and
bytecounts:"

$ipt -t filter -L -v --line-numbers
$ipt -t nat -L -v --line-numbers
$ipt -t mangle -L -v --line-numbers
```

Make it owned by *root*, mode 0700, and run it whenever you want to see what your firewall is doing:

```
# fw_status
```

Discussion

-L means "list rules," -v is verbose, and --line-numbers makes line numbers. You may wish to use -n to display IP addresses instead of hostnames.

See Also

- man 8 iptables
- Chapter 1, "Overview of TCP/IP," in *TCP/IP Network Administration*, by Craig Hunt (O'Reilly)
- Oskar Andreasson's Iptables Tutorial: *http://iptables-tutorial.frozentux.net/*

3.8 Turning an iptables Firewall Off

Problem

Turning on your firewall is easy, just run the *fw_nat* script. But you also want an easy way to turn it off. This will allow you to quickly determine if a problem is caused by the firewall, and to make and test changes easily.

Solution

Use the following script, which I call */usr/local/bin/fw_flush*. This example deletes all the rules in the filter, NAT, and mangle tables; all chains; and resets all packet and byte counters to zero. It also resets all the default policies to ACCEPT (so that nothing is blocked), and turns off forwarding. It's like having no firewall at all:

```
#!/bin/sh
##/usr/local/bin/fw_flush
#flush script, which deletes all active rules
#and chains, and resets default policies to "accept"
#this is like having no firewall at all

#define variables
ipt="/sbin/iptables"

echo "The firewall is now being shut down. All policies are set to
ACCEPT, all rules and chains are deleted, all counters are set to zero."

#Set default policies to ACCEPT everything
$ipt -P INPUT ACCEPT
$ipt -P FORWARD ACCEPT
$ipt -P OUTPUT ACCEPT
$ipt -t nat -P OUTPUT ACCEPT
$ipt -t nat -P PREROUTING ACCEPT
$ipt -t nat -P POSTROUTING ACCEPT
$ipt -t mangle -P INPUT ACCEPT
$ipt -t mangle -P OUTPUT ACCEPT
$ipt -t mangle -P FORWARD ACCEPT
$ipt -t mangle -P PREROUTING ACCEPT
$ipt -t mangle -P POSTROUTING ACCEPT
```

```
#Zero out all counters
$ipt -Z
$ipt -t nat -Z
$ipt -t mangle -Z

# Flush all rules, delete all chains
$ipt -F
$ipt -X
$ipt -t nat -F
$ipt -t nat -X
$ipt -t mangle -F
$ipt -t mangle -X
```

Remember to make this script owned by *root* only, mode 0700. Run this anytime you want to turn your firewall off:

 # fw_flush
The firewall is now being shut down. All policies are set to ACCEPT, all rules and chains are deleted, all counters are set to zero, and routing is turned off.

This leaves you wide open, so you should not be connected to untrusted networks.

Discussion

iptables is not a daemon, so turning off an *iptables* firewall is complicated. Rules are loaded into memory. If you just flush all the rules, your default policies will still be active, and as the default policy is usually DROP, no traffic will get through. So, the easy way is to use a script like the one in this recipe, which flushes all rules and sets the defaults to ACCEPT.

If you have no firewall scripts activated at boot, rebooting really turns the firewall off—kernel modules are unloaded, and no *iptables* rules of any kind remain in memory.

See Also

- man 8 iptables
- Oskar Andreasson's Iptables Tutorial: *http://iptables-tutorial.frozentux.net/*

3.9   Starting iptables at Boot, and Manually Bringing Your Firewall Up and Down

Problem

Your three new *iptables* scripts (see previous recipes) are tested and ready to be put to work—you have *fw_nat*, a *fw_status* script, and the *fw_flush* script. You want your firewall to start automatically at boot, and you want to start, stop, and check *iptables* status manually like any other service. How do you do this?

Solution

First, get rid of any existing firewall scripts, including any that came with your Linux distribution. On Fedora Linux and all of its relatives, also remove the *iptables-save* and *iptables-restore* scripts to prevent conflicts and accidental changes.

The different Linux distributions manage starting and stopping *iptables* in all sorts of different ways. This *init* script, called *firewall*, is as simple as it gets, and it works on any Linux. It calls the scripts used in the previous three recipes, so be sure you already have those tested and ready to use:

```
#!/bin/sh
##/etc.init.d/firewall
# simple start-stop init script for iptables
# start builds the firewall, stop flushes
# all rules and resets default policies to ACCEPT
# restart runs the start and stop commands
# status displays all active rules, and packet and byte counters
# chkconfig: 2345 01 99

startfile="/usr/local/bin/fw_nat"
stopfile="/usr/local/bin/fw_flush"
statusfile="/usr/local/bin/fw_status"

case "$1" in
  start)
        echo "Starting $startfile: iptables is now starting up"
        /bin/sh $startfile start
        ;;

  stop)
        echo "Stopping $stopfile: iptables is now stopped, all rules and
        chains are flushed, and default policies are set to ACCEPT"
    /bin/sh $stopfile stop
        ;;

  status)
        /bin/sh $statusfile status
        ;;

  restart)
        /bin/sh $stopfile stop
        echo "The firewall has stopped."
        /bin/sh $startfile start
        echo "The firewall has now restarted."
        ;;
esac
```

Put this script in */etc/init.d*, then use your distribution's runlevel manager to start it at boot. On Debian, use the *updated-rc.d* command to start it on runlevels 2, 3, 4, and 5, and stop it on runlevels 0, 1, and 6:

```
# update-rc.d firewall start 01 2 3 4 5 . stop 99 0 1 6 .
```

On Fedora, use *chkconfig*:

```
# chkconfig firewall --add
# chkconfig firewall on
```

Now, you can manage it with the standard *init.d*-style commands:

```
# /etc/init.d/firewall start|stop|status|restart
```

You may also run the scripts individually if you prefer. It's a simple, flexible scheme that is easy to customize.

Discussion

Give */etc/init.d/firewall* the highest priority at startup, and lowest priority for shutdown, because you want it to come up first and shut down last. Theoretically, if networking started first, an attacker could exploit the unprotected milliseconds before the firewall came up.

Keep in mind that you are not starting and stopping a daemon, but loading rules into memory, then flushing rules out of memory and setting a default `ACCEPT` policy. *iptables* works in the kernel—it's not a service.

These scripts should work on any Linux, so you only need to learn one way to manage *iptables*. They are as simple as possible to keep them understandable and maintainable. Ace scripting gurus are welcome to add error and sanity checks, and gussy them up as much as they like.

Every Linux distribution handles *iptables* a bit differently. Fedora and its ilk store the rules in the */etc/sysconfig/iptables* file, which is sourced from the */etc/init.d/iptables* script. The Red Hat manual teaches users to enter their *iptables* commands on the command line, then use the `/sbin/service iptables save` command to write the rules to the */etc/sysconfig/iptables* file. This is a nice way to create, test, and edit new rules if you are proficient enough to create them on the fly.

Debian Sarge has a different way of handling *iptables*. It does not use an */etc/init.d* script anymore, but instead expects the user to control *iptables* with *ifupdown*. This means adding inline directives in */etc/network/interfaces*, or placing scripts in the */etc/network/*.d* directories, and then *iptables* goes up or down with the network interfaces.

See Also

- `man 8 iptables`
- The Red Hat System Administration Manual: *htpps://www.redhat.com/docs/*
- Debian users read */usr/share/doc/iptables/examples/oldinitdscript.gz* and */usr/share/doc/iptables/README.Debian.gz*
- Chapter 1, "Overview of TCP/IP," in *TCP/IP Network Administration*, by Craig Hunt (O'Reilly)
- Oskar Andreasson's Iptables Tutorial: *http://iptables-tutorial.frozentux.net/*

3.10   Testing Your Firewall

Problem

You want to be able to test your Linux firewall from inside your LAN and outside it so you can see your network from both sides of your firewall. You especially want to see your network the same way the big bad outside world sees it. What are some good ways to do this?

Solution

Simply network with a second PC and run your tests. Assume your firewall box is named *firewall*, with a WAN IP address of 172.16.0.10, and your PC is called *testpc* at 192.168.2.10. Connect *testpc* to the WAN port of *firewall* with a crossover cable. Then, give them temporary IP addresses and routes to each other:

```
root@testpc:~# ifconfig eth0 192.168.2.10 netmask 255.255.255.0 up
root@firewall:~# ifconfig eth0 172.16.0.10 netmask 255.255.255.0 up
root@testpc:~# route del default
root@testpc:~# route add -net 172.16.0.0/24  gw 192.168.2.10  eth0
root@firewall:~# route del default
root@firewall:~# route add -net 192.168.2.0/24 gw 172.16.0.10  eth0
```

Run *ping* to confirm connectivity.

Here are some quick tests you can run for debugging your new Linux firewall. These commands, run on *firewall*, show your active *iptables* rules:

```
# /sbin/iptables -t filter -L -v --line-numbers
# /sbin/iptables -t nat -L -v --line-numbers
# /sbin/iptables -t mangle -L -v --line-numbers
```

Nmap is an excellent tool for seeing what your firewall looks like from the outside:

```
root@testpc:~# nmap 172.16.0.10
root@testpc:~# nmap -P0 172.16.0.10
```

Run *netstat* on *firewall* to see what sockets are open and listening for new connections:

```
root@firewall:~# netstat -untap
```

This shows the listening interfaces and port numbers, the program names, and user IDs. The safe thing to do is turn off all services until you are satisfied with your firewall. Then, bring them back up one at a time, testing your rules until everything works right. You really shouldn't be running a lot of services on a firewall anyway—keep it lean and mean.

For more extensive network testing and debugging, see Chapter 19.

Discussion

To get completely outside of your network, get a shell account on a PC on a different network. The remote PC needs to be equipped with Nmap, *ping*, *traceroute*, and text web browsers. If you can't do this, the next best thing is a dial-up Internet account, because this still gets you outside of your local network.

My own preference is to use remote shell accounts kindly provided by friends for external testing, because this is more like a "live fire" exercise, with all the complications that come with connecting over the Internet.

Here are some sample command outputs from testing an *iptables* NAT firewall. This Nmap command run from a remote PC to the WAN IP address shows that *iptables* is blocking all inbound connections except port 80, and that the web server is up and accepting connections:

```
user@remotehost:~$ nmap 1.2.3.4
Starting nmap 3.81 ( http://www.insecure.org/nmap/ ) at 2007-10-01 07:11 = EST
Interesting ports on 1.2.3.4: (The 1662 ports scanned but not shown below are in
state: filtered)
PORT    STATE  SERVICE
80/tcp open http
```

According to Nmap, you should be able to point a web browser to *http://1.2.3.4* and hit a web page. Lynx (or its cousins *links* and *elinks*, or *w3m*) is good over ssh:

```
user@remotehost:~$ lynx 1.2.3.4
```

You cannot tell if the web server is on 1.2.3.4, or is sitting on a separate box somewhere behind the firewall, because to the world, a NAT-ed LAN looks like a single computer. If you do not want to run a web server, this shows you better hunt it down and turn it off.

Running Nmap from a neighboring LAN host on the LAN address shows a different picture:

```
user@lanhost:~# nmap 192.168.1.10
Starting nmap 4.10 ( http://www.insecure.org/nmap/ ) at 2007-10-01 13:51 =
PST
Interesting ports on 192.168.1.10:
(The 1657 ports scanned but not shown below are in state: filtered)
PORT    STATE  SERVICE
22/tcp  open ssh
631/tcp open ipp
MAC Address: 00:01:02:03:04:05 (The Linksys Group)
Nmap finished: 1 IP address (1 host up) scanned in 22.645 seconds
```

So now we see that the SSH daemon and CUPS are running on the firewall. (Look in */etc/services* to see which services are assigned to which ports.) Port 80 is not open, so this means the web server is on a different computer. If we run *netstat* on the firewall itself, we can see which ports are open, and which interfaces they are listening to:

```
admin@firewall:~# netstat -untap
Active Internet connections (servers and established)
Proto Recv-Q Send-Q Local Address Foreign Address  State User   Inode
PID/Program name
tcp   0  0 192.168.1.10:22  0.0.0.0:*   LISTEN    0  44420       12544/sshd
tcp   0  0 0.0.0.0:631      0.0.0.0:*   LISTEN    0  142680   22085/cupsd
```

So we see that the SSH daemon is listening to the LAN IP address on TCP port 22, and the CUPS daemon is listening on all interfaces on TCP 631. TCP port 80 is not open because it is on a different machine.

Now we have a good picture of what is happening on both sides of our firewall.

Application-level security

The *netstat* output illustrates an important point—application security is separate from the border security provided by a firewall. The SSH server has been configured to listen only to the LAN IP address, but *cupsd* is listening to all interfaces. Nmap showed us that the firewall is blocking both of those at the WAN interface. Don't feel too safe with just a firewall; the best practice is to use border *and* application-level security. *iptables* can keep the bad bits out, but if someone succeeds in penetrating your firewall, you don't want them to find a wide-open welcome into your servers.

All Linux services have access controls, and most of them also incorporate various types of authentication controls. This example from */etc/ssh/sshd_config* shows how interface access controls are configured:

```
# What ports, IPs and protocols we listen for
Port 22
# Use these options to restrict which interfaces/protocols
# sshd will bind to
ListenAddress 192.168.1.10
```

OpenSSH also restricts access by host, user, and domain, and gives the choice of several different types of authentication. Security is a many-layered beast—don't rely on a firewall to be your entire security.

See Also

- Chapter 19 goes into detail on network testing and troubleshooting
- Chapter 7
- man 8 netstat
- man 1 nmap
- Chapter 14, "Printing with CUPS," in *Linux Cookbook*, by Carla Schroder (O'Reilly)
- Chapter 17, "Remote Access," in *Linux Cookbook*

3.11   Configuring the Firewall for Remote SSH Administration

Problem

You want to SSH into your firewall to do remote administration. You might want to log in from over the Internet, or you might want to restrict SSH to LAN access only. You also want the option of restricting access to certain specific source IP addresses.

Solution

There are several ways to handle this. SSH has a number of access and authentication controls, so you should configure those first. Then, configure `iptables` to add another layer of access controls.

To restrict SSH access to LAN hosts only, add this rule:

```
$ipt -A INPUT -i $LAN_IFACE -p tcp -s 192.168.1.0/24 --dport 22 --sport \
1024:65535 -m state --state NEW -j ACCEPT
```

Of course, you must use your own LAN address and SSH port. To allow SSH logins via the WAN interface, use this rule:

```
$ipt -A INPUT -p tcp -i $WAN_IFACE --dport 22 --sport 1024:65535 \
-m state --state NEW -j ACCEPT
```

This rule accepts SSH logins on all interfaces:

```
$ipt -A INPUT -p tcp --dport 22 --sport 1024:65535 -m state --state NEW -j ACCEPT
```

Or, you may restrict SSH logins to a specific source IP address:

```
$ipt -A INPUT -p tcp -s 12.34.56.78 --dport 22 --sport 1024:65535 \
 -m state --state NEW -j ACCEPT
```

If there are additional source IP addresses you wish to allow, each one needs its own separate rule.

Discussion

Let's take a look at what these rules do:

`-A INPUT -p tcp ! --syn -m state --state NEW -j DROP`
> A subtle *iptables* gotcha is that the NEW state will allow TCP packets through that do not have the SYN flag set, so we must make sure that only SYN-flagged packets are allowed. SYN is always the first step in initiating a new TCP session, so if it isn't present, we don't want to accept the packet.

`-A INPUT -i $LAN_IFACE -p tcp -s 192.168.1.0/24 --dport 22 --sport 1024:65535 -m state --state NEW -j ACCEPT`
> This accepts new SSH (TCP port 22) connections coming in on the LAN interface and from the local subnet only, from high-numbered ports. Anything originating from a privileged port is suspect.

```
-A INPUT -p tcp -i $WAN_IFACE -p tcp --dport 22 --sport 1024:65535 -m state --state
NEW -j ACCEPT
```
> This rule allows connections coming in on the WAN interface only, so LAN access is not allowed.

```
-A INPUT -p tcp --dport 22 --sport 1024:65535 -m state --state NEW -j ACCEPT
```
> This rule accepts all new SSH connections from any host anywhere. Again, the new connection must come from an unprivileged port.

```
-A INPUT -p tcp -i $WAN_IFACE -s 12.34.56.78 --dport 22 --sport 1024:65535 -m state
--state NEW -j ACCEPT
```
> This rule accepts incoming SSH on the WAN interface only, from the named IP address; all others are dropped.

You don't need to add the RELATED,ESTABLISHED states to the rules because there already is a global rule for this.

See Also

- Chapter 5, "Serverwide Configuration," in *SSH, the Secure Shell: The Definitive Guide*, Second Edition, by Richard E. Silverman and Daniel J. Barrett (O'Reilly)
- Chapter 17, "Remote Access," in *Linux Cookbook*, by Carla Schroder (O'Reilly)
- `man 8 iptables`

3.12   Allowing Remote SSH Through a NAT Firewall

Problem

You want to open up remote SSH administration to your LAN so you can log in remotely and access various random LAN hosts. You have the OpenSSH server running on the machines you want to remotely administer, but there is a problem—they use nonroutable private IPs, so they are all source NAT-ed to the firewall IP address. How do you get past your NAT firewall?

Solution

The simplest method uses any of the SSH rules in the previous recipe (except, of course, the LAN-only rule) without requiring any changes. SSH into your firewall, then SSH from there into whatever LAN hosts you need to get into. Your sessions will look like this example, which demonstrates logging from a remote host into the firewall named *windbag*, and then opening an SSH session from *windbag* to *stinkpad*:

```
carla@remotehost:~$ ssh windbag.foo.net
carla@windbag.foo.net's password:
Linux windbag 2.6.12-10-386 #1 Mon Sep 28 12:13:15 UTC 2007 i686 GNU/Linux
Last login: Mon Aug 21 17:07:24 2007 from foo-29.isp.net
carla@windbag:~$ ssh stinkpad
carla@stinkpad's password:
```

```
Last login: Mon Sep 21 17:08:50 2007 from windbag.foo.net
[carla@stinkpad ~]$
```

Using this method avoids the problem of having to write additional *iptables* rules.

What if you have users who need remote SSH access to their PCs, and you deem them worthy enough to have it? To use the two-step SSH login, they will need user accounts on the firewall, which you may not want to allow. To avoid this, you can set up *port forwarding* directly to LAN hosts. For example, you have *host1* at 192.168.1.21, and *host2* at 192.168.1.22. Your remote users are at 12.34.56.78 and 12.34.56.79. You accept remote SSH logins only from those IP addresses:

```
# allow user@12.34.56.78 to ssh directly to work PC
$ipt -t nat -A PREROUTING -i $WAN_IFACE -s 12.34.56.78 --sport 1024:65535 \
-p tcp --dport 10001 -j DNAT--to-destination 192.168.1.21:22
$ipt -A FORWARD -p tcp -i $WAN_IFACE -o $LAN_IFACE -d 192.168.1.21 \
--dport 22 -j ACCEPT

# allow user@12.34.56.79 to ssh directly to work PC
$ipt -t nat -A PREROUTING -i $WAN_IFACE -s 12.34.56.79 --sport \
1024:65535 -p tcp --dport 10002 -j DNAT --to-destination 192.168.1.22:22
$ipt -A FORWARD -p tcp -i $WAN_IFACE -o $LAN_IFACE -d 192.168.1.22 \
 --dport 22 -j ACCEPT
```

Then, your users simply need to specify the port number and the fully qualified domain name or IP address of the firewall to log in:

```
user@12.34.56.78:~$ ssh windbag.foo.net:10001
```

or:

```
user@12.34.56.79:~$ ssh 1.2.3.4:10002
```

What if you or your users need access to more than one LAN host? See Recipe 3.13.

Discussion

I like the second method because it gives the admin the most control. Handing out user accounts just for remote SSH access on your firewall is a bad idea. You should also configure the excellent access and authentication controls in OpenSSH to further batten the hatches, and consider using public-key authentication instead of system passwords. Your user's source IP addresses are specified in the rules because you do not want to leave LAN hosts open to the entire Internet, and you especially don't want them logging in from public machines in libraries or Internet cafes (keystroke loggers, anyone?).

If your WAN IP address is dynamically assigned, then you're going to collect a lot of host keys because host keys are bound to IP addresses. So, every time the WAN address changes, you'll get a new host key. Dynamic WAN IPs cause all sorts of hassles if you want to do anything other than just have an Internet connection—running services and remote administration is a heck of a lot easier on a static WAN IP address.

See Also

- Chapter 7
- Chapter 17, "Remote Access," in *Linux Cookbook*, by Carla Schroder (O'Reilly)

3.13   Getting Multiple SSH Host Keys Past NAT

Problem

You tried the second method in the previous recipe and it worked like a charm. Until you tried to SSH into a second LAN host, that is. Because the remote SSH client sees only a single IP address for your entire network, it freaks out when you try to log in to a second host, displays this scary warning, and refuses to let you log in:

```
@@@@@@@@@@@@@@@@@@@@@@@@@@@@@@@@@@@@@@@@@@@@@@@@@@@@@@@@@
@ WARNING: REMOTE HOST IDENTIFICATION HAS CHANGED!@
@@@@@@@@@@@@@@@@@@@@@@@@@@@@@@@@@@@@@@@@@@@@@@@@@@@@@@@@@
IT IS POSSIBLE THAT SOMEONE IS DOING SOMETHING NASTY!
```

Every LAN host is going to have a different host key with the same IP address because all outgoing traffic is source NAT-ed to the firewall address, so SSH is going to think you're trying to log in to a single PC that keeps changing the host key. What are you going to do? Deleting the host key every single time doesn't seem very practical, and you don't want to turn off StrictHostKeyChecking.

Solution

Use OpenSSH's elegant mechanism for managing multiple host keys that are bound to the same IP address.

Create a *~/.ssh.config* file on your remote PC. This example manages the host keys for *host1* and *host2*. The Host entry can be anything you like; some sort of descriptive name is good. HostName is either the fully qualified domain name or IP address of the firewall. Port is the port number from the corresponding *iptables* rule, and UserKnownHostsFile is the name of file that you want to store the host key in:

```
Host host1
HostName firewall.domainname.net
Port 10001
UserKnownHostsFile ~/.ssh/host1

Host host2
HostName firewall.domainname.net
Port 10002
UserKnownHostsFile  ~/.ssh/host2
```

Log in from the remote host like this:

```
$ ssh host1
```

At the first login, it will ask you the usual:

```
The authenticity of host 'firewall.domainname.com (1.2.3.4)' can't be
established.
RSA key fingerprint is 00:01:02:03:04:05:00:01:02:03:04:05
Are you sure you want to continue connecting (yes/no)?
```

Type "yes," and it will create *~/.ssh/host1* and copy the host key to it. Do the same for all LAN hosts you want SSH access to, and both you and SSH will be happy and will not generate scary warnings.

Discussion

This works for static and dynamic WAN IP addresses. Dynamic WAN IPs will require a bit of extra work if you're using the IP address as the HostName because, obviously, when the address changes, you'll need to change your remote *~/.ssh.config* HostName setting. One way to avoid this is to register a domain name and use *Dyndns. org*'s dynamic DNS service, which will allow you to use your FQDN instead of the IP address.

Even better, get a static routable public WAN IP address.

Some folks like to disable StrictHostKeyChecking in *~/ssh.conf*, which means disabling an important safety feature.

See Also

- Chapter 7
- Chapter 17, "Remote Access," in *Linux Cookbook*, by Carla Schroder (O'Reilly)

3.14 Running Public Services on Private IP Addresses

Problem

You are running a public server on a private IP address, so it is not directly accessible to the Internet. So, you need to configure your *iptables* firewall to forward traffic to your server.

Solution

First of all, you need to add a third network interface card to your firewall box. We'll call it *eth2*, and assign it a different subnet than the LAN interface. This is very important—do not use the same subnet, or your networking will not work at all.

Let's say the three interfaces have these addresses:

- eth0 192.168.1.10 (LAN)
- eth1 11.22.33.44 (WAN)
- eth2 192.168.2.25 (DMZ)

You have one server in the DMZ with an IP address of 192.168.2.50.

Set up your firewall according to the previous recipes, so you have the four scripts: *fw_flush*, *fw_nat*, *fw_status*, and the firewall *init* script. Add the new interface to *fw_nat*:

```
DMZ_IFACE="eth2"
```

Add FORWARD rules to allow traffic between the DMZ, and your WAN and LAN interfaces:

```
$ipt -A FORWARD -i $LAN_IFACE -o $DMZ_IFACE -m state \
--state NEW,ESTABLISHED,RELATED -j ACCEPT
$ipt -A FORWARD -i $DMZ_IFACE -o $LAN_IFACE -m state \
--state ESTABLISHED,RELATED -j ACCEPT
$ipt -A FORWARD -i $DMZ_IFACE -o $WAN_IFACE -m state \
--state ESTABLISHED,RELATED -j ACCEPT
$ipt -A FORWARD -i $WAN_IFACE -o $DMZ_IFACE -m state \
--state NEW,ESTABLISHED,RELATED -j ACCEPT
```

Now, you need to route incoming HTTP traffic to your server with a PREROUTING rule:

```
$ipt -t nat -A PREROUTING -p tcp -i $WAN_IFACE -d 11.22.33.44 \
--dport 80 -j DNAT --to-destination 192.168.2.50
```

If you are using more than one port on your web server, such as 443 for SSL, or some alternate ports for testing like 8080, you can list them all in one rule with the *multiport* match:

```
$ipt -t nat -A PREROUTING -p tcp -i $WAN_IFACE -d 11.22.33.44 \
-m multiport --dport 80,443,8080 -j DNAT --to-destination 192.168.2.50
```

Other services work in the same way, so all you need to do is substitute their port numbers and addresses.

Discussion

You may use DNAT to send traffic to a different port, like this:

```
$ipt -t nat -A PREROUTING -p tcp -i $WAN_IFACE -d 11.22.33.44 \
--dport 80 -j DNAT --to-destination 192.168.2.50:100
```

Because your web server has a private, nonroutable address, it needs to be rewritten using Destination Network Address Translation (DNAT) to the publicly routable address that the Internet thinks your web server has. Because this is really your router's WAN address, it needs to be rewritten and forwarded to your real server address. Then, on the way out, it needs to rewritten back to the your WAN address. Our SNAT rule takes care of this by rewriting all outgoing packets to the WAN address.

Your LAN hosts will not be able to access your web server because DNAT makes a hash of routing. The easy way to give them access is to have a separate LAN DNS server that uses internal addresses, like our excellent Dnsmasq server in Chapter 4. Another easy way is to have a physically separate DMZ that does not share your

LAN router. The hard way is to write a bunch more *iptables* rules that do more address rewriting, which will drive you nuts, cost you your job, and ruin your life.

See Also

- Chapter 2 explains the need for a DMZ
- `man 8 iptables`
- Oskar Andreasson's Iptables Tutorial: *http://iptables-tutorial.frozentux.net/*. Look for the section on DNAT to learn more about the issues associated with DNAT-ing private addresses
- Chapter 22, "Running an Apache Web Server," in *Linux Cookbook*, by Carla Schroder (O'Reilly)

3.15   Setting Up a Single-Host Firewall

Problem

You want to know how to build a firewall on a Linux computer that is running no public services. Just an ordinary PC that may be directly connected to the Internet, or it may be a laptop that travels a lot. You're careful with your application-level security and internal services, but you wisely believe in layered security and want a firewall.

Solution

You need to create an *iptables* script, and to edit the */etc/sysctl.conf* file.

First, copy this *iptables* script, substituting your own IP addresses and interface names, and make it owned by *root*, mode 0700. In this recipe we'll call it */usr/local/bin/fw_host*:

```
#!/bin/sh
##/usr/local/bin/fw_host
#iptables firewall script for
#a workstation or laptop
#chkconfig: 2345 01 99

#define variables
ipt="/sbin/iptables"
mod="/sbin/modprobe"

#Flush all rules, delete all chains
$ipt -F
$ipt -X
$ipt -t nat -F
$ipt -t nat -X
$ipt -t mangle -F
$ipt -t mangle -X
```

```
#Zero out all counters
$ipt -Z
$ipt -t nat -Z
$ipt -t mangle -Z

#basic set of kernel modules
$mod ip_tables
$mod ip_conntrack
$mod iptable_filter
$mod iptable_nat
$mod iptable_mangle
$mod ipt_LOG
$mod ipt_limit
$mod ipt_state
$mod ipt_MASQUERADE

#optional for irc and ftp
#$mod ip_conntrack_irc
#$mod ip_conntrack_ftp

#Set default policies
#Incoming is deny all,
#outgoing is unrestricted
$ipt -P INPUT DROP
$ipt -P FORWARD DROP
$ipt -P OUTPUT ACCEPT
$ipt -t nat -P OUTPUT ACCEPT
$ipt -t nat -P PREROUTING ACCEPT
$ipt -t nat -P POSTROUTING ACCEPT
$ipt -t mangle -P PREROUTING ACCEPT
$ipt -t mangle -P POSTROUTING ACCEPT

#this line is necessary for the loopback interface
#and internal socket-based services to work correctly
$ipt -A INPUT -i lo -j ACCEPT

#Reject connection attempts not initiated from the host
$ipt -A INPUT -p tcp --syn -j DROP

#Allow return traffic initiated from the host
$ipt -A INPUT -m state --state ESTABLISHED,RELATED -j ACCEPT

# Accept important ICMP packets
$ipt -A INPUT -p icmp --icmp-type echo-request -j ACCEPT
$ipt -A INPUT -p icmp --icmp-type time-exceeded -j ACCEPT
$ipt -A INPUT -p icmp --icmp-type destination-unreachable -j ACCEPT
```

Add this script to your desired runlevels. This command adds it to runlevels 2–5 on Debian:

```
# update-rc.d firewall start 01 2 3 4 5 . stop 99 0 1 6 .
```

On Fedora, use *chkconfig*:

```
# chkconfig firewall --add
# chkconfig firewall on
```

Note that both of these commands turn off the firewall on runlevels 0, 1, and 6. This is a standard practice, as typically networking is also shut down on these runlevels, and only a bare set of services are started.

Now, add these kernel parameters to */etc/sysctl.conf*:

```
net.ipv4.ip_forward = 0
net.ipv4.icmp_echo_ignore_broadcasts = 1
net.ipv4.tcp_syncookies = 1
net.ipv4.conf.all.rp_filter = 1
net.ipv4.conf.all.send_redirects = 0
net.ipv4.conf.all.accept_redirects = 0
net.ipv4.conf.all.accept_source_route = 0
```

If you are using dial-up networking or are on DHCP, add this parameter as well:

```
net.ipv4.conf.all.ip_dynaddr = 1
```

To activate everything without rebooting, run these commands:

```
# firewall_host
# /sbin/sysctl -p
```

And you now have a nice restrictive host firewall. See the previous recipes in this chapter to learn how to start the firewall at boot, manually stop and start it, and display its current status. All you do is follow the recipes, replacing the *fw_nat* script with *fw_host*.

Discussion

You may wish to add rules to allow various peer services such as instant messaging or BitTorrent, or to allow SSH. Use this rule with the appropriate port ranges for the protocol you want to allow incoming client requests from:

```
$ipt -A INPUT -p tcp --destination-port [port range] -j ACCEPT
```

Then, delete this rule:

```
#Reject connection attempts not initiated from the host
$ipt -A INPUT -p tcp --syn -j DROP
```

and add this one:

```
#Drop NEW tcp connections that are not SYN-flagged
$ipt -A INPUT -p tcp ! --syn -m state --state NEW -j DROP
```

To simplify maintaining the script, you may create whatever variables you like in the #define variables section. Commands, network interfaces, and IP addresses are the most common variables used in *iptables* scripts.

Flushing all the rules, deleting all chains, and resetting packet and byte counters to zero ensures that the firewall starts up with a clean slate, and no leftover rules or chains are hanging around to get in the way.

Necessary kernel modules must be loaded. Check your */boot/config-** file to see if your kernel was compiled with them already built-in, or as loadable modules, so you don't try to load modules that aren't needed. It doesn't really hurt anything to load unnecessary modules; it's just a bit of finicky housekeeping.

ip_tables and *iptable_filter* are essential for *iptables* to work at all. The *ip_conntrack_irc* and *ip_conntrack_ftp* modules assist in maintaining IRC and FTP connectivity through a NAT firewall. You can omit these if you don't use IRC or FTP.

The default policies operate on any packets that are not matched by any other rules. In this recipe, we have a "deny all incoming traffic, allow incoming as needed" policy combined with an unrestricted outbound policy.

The loopback interface must not be restricted, or many system functions will break.

The next two rules are where the real action takes place. First of all, because you're not running any public services, there is no reason to accept incoming SYN packets. A SYN packet's only job is to initiate a new TCP session. The next rule ensures that you can initiate and maintain connections, such as web surfing, checking email, SSH sessions, and so forth, but still not allow incoming connection attempts.

While some folks advocate blocking all ICMP packets, it's not a good idea. You need the ones listed in the firewall scripts for network functions to operate correctly.

The */etc/sysctl.conf* directives are important kernel security measures. This is what the kernel parameters in the file mean:

`net.ipv4.ip_forward = 0`
> This box is not a router, so make sure forwarding is turned off.

`net.ipv4.icmp_echo_ignore_broadcasts = 1`
> Don't respond to *ping* broadcasts. Ping broadcasts and multicasts are usually an attack of some kind, like a Smurf attack. You may want to use a *ping* broadcast to see what hosts on your LAN are up, but there are other ways to do this. It is a lot safer to leave this disabled.

`net.ipv4.tcp_syncookies = 1`
> This helps to protect from a syn flood attack. If your computer is flooded with SYN packets from different hosts, the syn backlog queue may overflow. So, this sends out cookies to test the validity of the SYN packets. This is not so useful on a heavily loaded server, and it may even cause problems, so it's better to use it only on workstations and laptops.

`net.ipv4.conf.all.rp_filter = 1`
> This helps to maintain state and protect against source spoofing. It verifies that packets coming in on an interface also go out on the same interface. Obviously, this can confuse multihomed routers, which routinely forward packets from one interface to another, so don't use it on them.

```
net.ipv4.conf.all.send_redirects = 0
```
Only routers need this, so all others can turn it off.

```
net.ipv4.conf.all.accept_redirects = 0
```
ICMP redirects are important to routers, but can create security problems for servers and workstations, so turn it off.

```
net.ipv4.conf.all.accept_source_route = 0
```
Source-routed packets are a security risk because they make it all too easy to spoof trusted addresses. The legitimate uses of source-routed packets are few; they were originally intended as a route debugging tool, but their nefarious uses far outweigh the legitimate uses.

It is common to see kernel parameters set in *iptables* scripts, like this:

```
echo 1 > /proc/sys/net/ipv4/icmp_echo_ignore_broadcasts
echo 0 > /proc/sys/net/ipv4/conf/all/accept_redirects
echo 0 > /proc/sys/net/ipv4/conf/all/accept_source_route
```

I prefer to control these options with *sysctl* because that is what it is designed to do, and I like that they operate independently of my firewall. This is a question of taste; do it however you like.

Using the *echo* commands on the command line overrides configuration files, so they're great for testing. They go away with a reboot, which makes it easy to start over.

A common point of confusion is dots and slashes. You may use either, like this:

```
net.ipv4.tcp_syncookies = 1
net/ipv4/tcp_syncookies = 1
```

See Also

- man 8 sysctl
- man 5 sysctl.conf
- Chapter 7, "Starting and Stopping Linux," in *Linux Cookbook*, by Carla Schroder (O'Reilly) for more information on what each runlevel is for, and how to manage them
- man 8 iptables
- Chapter 1, "Overview of TCP/IP," in *TCP/IP Network Administration* by Craig Hunt (O'Reilly)
- Oskar Andreasson's Ipsysctl Tutorial: *http://ipsysctl-tutorial.frozentux.net/*

3.16   Setting Up a Server Firewall

Problem

You want to implement an *iptables* firewall on a server. You may have an external firewall already, and you want to do the fine-tuning on the server, or you have a server directly connected to the Internet. You pay careful attention to hardening your server, and are confident it could survive without a firewall. This is an extra layer of defense in case of mistakes. You want to drop all traffic that doesn't belong on your server, like all the automated brute-force attacks and worms that pummel the Internet unceasingly.

Solution

This script allows only traffic destined for the correct ports, such as port 80 for a web server, or port 25 for an SMTP server, and so on:

```
#!/bin/sh
##/usr/local/bin/fw_server
#for a server
#chkconfig: 2345 01 99
#define variables
ipt="/sbin/iptables"
mod="/sbin/modprobe"

#Flush all rules, delete all chains
$ipt -F
$ipt -X
$ipt -t nat -F
$ipt -t nat -X
$ipt -t mangle -F
$ipt -t mangle -X

#Zero out all counters
$ipt -Z
$ipt -t nat -Z
$ipt -t mangle -Z

#basic set of kernel modules
$mod ip_tables
$mod ip_conntrack
$mod iptable_filter
$mod iptable_nat
$mod iptable_mangle
$mod ipt_LOG
$mod ipt_limit
$mod ipt_state

#optional for irc and ftp
#$mod ip_conntrack_irc
#$mod ip_conntrack_ftp
```

```
#Set default policies
$ipt -P INPUT DROP
$ipt -P FORWARD DROP
$ipt -P OUTPUT ACCEPT
$ipt -t nat -P OUTPUT ACCEPT
$ipt -t nat -P PREROUTING ACCEPT
$ipt -t nat -P POSTROUTING ACCEPT
$ipt -t mangle -P PREROUTING ACCEPT
$ipt -t mangle -P POSTROUTING ACCEPT

#these lines are necessary for the loopback interface
#and internal socket-based services to work correctly
$ipt -A INPUT -i lo -j ACCEPT

#custom tcp allow chain
$ipt -N ALLOW
$ipt -A ALLOW -p TCP --syn -j ACCEPT
$ipt -A ALLOW -p TCP -m state --state ESTABLISHED,RELATED -j ACCEPT
$ipt -A ALLOW -p TCP -j DROP

#Accept important ICMP packets
$ipt -A INPUT -p icmp --icmp-type echo-request -j ALLOW
$ipt -A INPUT -p icmp --icmp-type time-exceeded -j ALLOW
$ipt -A INPUT -p icmp --icmp-type destination-unreachable -j ALLOW
```

Then, you need to add rules for the specific services you are running. For an FTP server, you need to add the *ip_conntrack_ftp* and *ip_nat_ftp* modules. Next, add these rules to allow incoming connections to your server, and the outgoing responses:

```
#FTP control port
$ipt -A INPUT -p tcp --dport 21 -j ALLOW
#FTP data port
$ipt -A INPUT -p tcp --sport 20 -j ACCEPT
```

Passive FTP transfers are a bit of pain, because they use unpredictable high-numbered ports. You may configure your FTP server to use only a limited range of ports, then specify them in your *iptables* rule:

```
$ipt -A INPUT -p TCP --destination-port 62000:64000 -j ACCEPT
```

SSH looks like this:

```
$ipt -A INPUT -p tcp --dport 22 --sport 1024:65535 -j ALLOW
```

IRC servers need the *ip_conntrack_irc* module, and this rule:

```
$ipt -A INPUT -p tcp --dport 6667 --sport 1024:65535 -j ALLOW
```

This rule is for a web server:

```
$ipt -A INPUT -p tcp --dport 80 --sport 1024:65535 -j ALLOW
```

If you are using multiple ports, such as SSL or a test port, list them all with the multiport match:

```
$ipt -A INPUT -p tcp -m multiport --dport 80,443,8080 --sport 1024:65535 -j ALLOW
```

Email servers can also use single or multiport rules, as these two examples show:

```
$ipt -A INPUT -p tcp --dport 25 --sport 1024:65535 -j ALLOW
$ipt -A INPUT -p tcp -m multiport --dport 25,110,143 --sport 1024:65535 -j ALLOW
```

DNS servers need these rules:

```
$ipt -A INPUT -p udp --dport 53 -j ACCEPT
$ipt -A INPUT -p tcp --dport 53 -j ALLOW
```

If your server needs to perform DNS lookups, add these rules:

```
$ipt -A OUTPUT -p udp --dport 53 -j ACCEPT
$ipt -A OUTPUT -p tcp --dport 53 -j ACCEPT
```

Discussion

The ALLOW chain accepts only TCP packets with the SYN flag set. A subtle *iptables* gotcha is that the NEW state will allow TCP packets through that do not have the SYN flag set, so we must make sure that only SYN-flagged packets are allowed. SYN is always the first step in initiating a new TCP session, so if it isn't present, we don't want to accept the packet.

Opening holes in a host firewall for services is easy, as you're not hassling with NAT or forwarding. Be sure of your port numbers, and whether you need UDP or TCP. Most services have UDP and TCP ports reserved for them, but the majority only need one or the other, so check the documentation of your server to make sure.

Connection requests almost always come from high-numbered source ports (i.e., 1024:65535). Anything from a privileged port is suspect, so you don't want to accept those unless you are certain that your server is supposed to accept them, such as FTP.

Be careful about getting the ACCEPT and ALLOW chains mixed up. Use the ALLOW chain only for filtering incoming SYN packets, which doesn't happen with the FTP data ports or UDP datagrams.

See Also

- man 8 sysctl
- man 5 sysctl.conf
- man 8 iptables
- Chapter 1, "Overview of TCP/IP," in *TCP/IP Network Administration*, by Craig Hunt (O'Reilly)
- Oskar Andreasson's Ipsysctl Tutorial: *http://ipsysctl-tutorial.frozentux.net/*

3.17   Configuring iptables Logging

Problem

You have tested your firewall scripts and everything works, and you understand what all the rules do, and are confident of your firewall-editing skills. Now you want to know how to configure some logfiles to help with debugging and monitoring.

Solution

iptables has a built-in logging target that is applied to individual rules. By default, *iptables* messages are dumped into */var/log/kern.log*. An easy way to see this in action is to log one of the ICMP rules:

```
$ipt -A INPUT -p icmp --icmp-type echo-request -j LOG \
--log-level info --log-prefix "ping "
$ipt -A INPUT -p icmp --icmp-type echo-request -j ACCEPT
```

Ping the host a few times, then read */var/log/kern.log*, or follow along with the *tail* command:

```
$ tail -f /var/log/kern.log
Oct  3 17:36:35 xena kernel: [17213514.504000]ping IN=eth1 OUT= MAC=00:03:6d:00:83:
cf:00:0a:e4:40:8b:fd:08:00 SRC=192.168.1.12 DST=192.168.1.10 LEN=60 TOS=0x00
PREC=0x00 TTL=128 ID=4628 PROTO=ICMP TYPE=8 CODE=0 ID=512 SEQ=1280

Oct  3 17:36:36 xena kernel: [17213515.500000] ping IN=eth1 OUT= MAC=00:03:6d:00:83:
cf:00:0a:e4:40:8b:fd:08:00 SRC=192.168.1.12 DST=192.168.1.10 LEN=60 TOS=0x00
PREC=0x00 TTL=128 ID=4629 PROTO=ICMP TYPE=8 CODE=0 ID=512 SEQ=1536
```

If you create only one rule with a log target, the packets will be logged and dropped, which is a safe way to test a new rule. To shoo the packets along to their final destination, create a second rule. The log target takes all the standard syslog levels: debug, info, notice, warning, err, crit, alert, and emerg.

iptables uses Linux's built-in *syslog*, which is pretty limited. The log target's *--log-prefix* is one way to make *kern.log* more parsable. A better way is to use *syslog-ng*, which is more configurable, and has built-in networking support, so it makes an excellent logging server.

Adding these lines to */etc/syslog-ng/syslog-ng.conf* directs all *iptables* log messages to */var/log/iptables.log*. Note the match on "IPT="; this is what tells *syslog-ng* which messages to put in */var/log/iptables.log*. So, you will need to include IPT in all of your --log-prefix options:

```
destination iptables { file("/var/log/iptables.log"); };
filter f_iptables { match("IPT="); };
log { source(src); filter(f_iptables); destination(iptables); };
```

See Also

- man 8 `syslogd`
- man 5 `syslog.conf`
- man 8 `syslog-ng`
- man 8 `iptables`
- Chapter 1, "Overview of TCP/IP," in *TCP/IP Network Administration*, by Craig Hunt (O'Reilly)
- Oskar Andreasson's Iptables Tutorial: *http://iptables-tutorial.frozentux.net/*

3.18   Writing Egress Rules

Problem

You prefer having an OUTPUT ACCEPT policy, and you want to add some egress filtering rules to block traffic destined for known bad ports from leaving your network. You also want to add some basic precautions, such as not allowing NetBIOS traffic or private addresses to escape your network.

Solution

Here are some example egress filter rules that go with an OUTPUT ACCEPT policy. You could add these to any of the firewall scripts in this chapter.

First, create variables containing your desired port numbers. EVILPORTS are port numbers known to be used by various malware. GOODPORTS are for preventing certain types of LAN traffic from escaping:

```
EVILPORTS="587,666,777,778,1111,1218"
GOODPORTS="23,137,138,139,177"
```

iptables doesn't seem to like lists longer than 15 port numbers.

Now, you can use these in rules like these examples:

```
$ipt -A OUTPUT -i $LAN_IFACE -p --dport $EVILPORTS -j DROP
$ipt -A OUTPUT -i $LAN_IFACE -p --dport $GOODPORTS -j DROP
```

Or, you can specify source addresses instead of the interface name:

```
$ipt -A OUTPUT -s 192.168.2.0/24 -p all --dport $EVILPORTS -j DROP
```

The Discussion goes into more detail on what ports to block.

You can block specific addresses, or entire networks:

```
$ipt -A OUTPUT -i $LAN_IFACE -p -d 11.22.33.44 -j DROP
$ipt -A OUTPUT -i $LAN_IFACE -p -d 22.33.44.55/30 -j DROP
```

RFC 1918 addresses, and broadcast and multicast addresses should not leak out of your network:

```
$ipt -A OUTPUT -s 10.0.0.0/8 -j DROP
$ipt -A OUTPUT -s 172.16.0.0/12 -j DROP
$ipt -A OUTPUT -s 192.168.0.0/16 -j DROP
$ipt -A OUTPUT -s 224.0.0.0/4 -j DROP
$ipt -A OUTPUT -s 240.0.0.0/5 -j DROP
$ipt -A OUTPUT -s 127.0.0.0/8 -j DROP
$ipt -A OUTPUT -s 0.0.0.0/8 -j DROP
$ipt -A OUTPUT -d 255.255.255.255 -j DROP
$ipt -A OUTPUT -s 169.254.0.0/16 -j DROP
$ipt -A OUTPUT -d 224.0.0.0/4 -j DROP
```

Nor should traffic without the correct source address, which is your WAN address:

```
$ipt -A OUTPUT -o $WAN_INTERFACE -s !33.44.55.66 -j DROP
```

Discussion

Blocking potentially dangerous outgoing ports is what good netizens do. If you have infected hosts on your network, you should do your best to prevent them from joining the World Wide Botnet and spreading further contagion.

Deciding which destination ports to block is a moving target. You'll need to figure these out yourself, so check your favorite security sites periodically. A Web search for "dangerous TCP/IP ports" is a good way to start.

Check */etc/services* to decide which local services you want to keep fenced in. Here are explanations for the partial list used for GOODPORTS:

23

> *telnet* client. *telnet* is completely insecure because it transmits entirely in cleartext.

137–139

> Windows NetBIOS and Samba broadcasts go out on these ports.

177

> The X Display Manager Control Protocol (XDMCP) is completely insecure. For remote X sessions, tunnel X over SSH.

While *iptables* is useful for basic protections like these, it is a blunt tool for filtering outgoing traffic. A lot of malware uses ports that are registered for legitimate services, so blocking those ports means no access to those services. *iptables* can't perform any content inspection, and doesn't have access control lists. If you want a lot of control over the traffic leaving your network and what your users can do, consider using a proxy server like Squid.

See Also

- *Squid: The Definitive Guide*, by Duane Wessels (O'Reilly)

## CHAPTER 4

Building a Linux Wireless Access Point

4.0 Introduction

Wireless networking is everywhere. Someday, we'll have built-in wireless receivers in our heads. Meanwhile, times are improving for Linux wireless administrators, if you shop carefully and buy wireless interface cards with good Linux support and WPA2 support. Using well-supported wireless interfaces means you'll be able to dive directly into configuring your network instead of hassling with funky driver problems. This chapter shows how to build a secure, flexible, robust combination wireless access point/router/Internet firewall using Pyramid Linux on a Soekris single-board computer. It supports wireless and wired Linux, Windows, and Mac OS X clients sharing a broadband Internet connection and LAN services. Just one big happy clump of wired and wireless clients together in harmony.

Why go to all this trouble? Because you'll have more control, all the powerful features you could ever want, and save money.

You don't have to have an all-in-one-device. The recipes in this chapter are easy to split apart to make separate devices, such as a dedicated firewall and a separate wireless access point.

I use Pyramid Linux, Soekris or PC Engines WRAP boards, and Atheros wireless interfaces because they are battle-tested and I know they work well. See Chapter 2 to learn how to use these excellent little routerboards.

The example configurations for the different services, such as DHCP, DNS, authentication, *iptables*, and so forth work fine on other Debian Linux-based distributions, and any x86 hardware. Adapting them for other distributions means figuring out different ways of configuring network interface cards; configuring applications like *hostapd*, *dnsmasq*, and *iptables* is pretty much the same everywhere.

Some folks are bit confused as to what "native Linux support" means. It doesn't mean using *ndiswrapper*, which is a Linux wrapper around Windows binary drivers. I wouldn't use it unless I were down to my last dime and couldn't afford to buy an interface card with native Linux support. It's only good on the client side, doesn't support all devices or features, and extracting the Windows binary drivers is a fair bit of work. Even worse, it rewards vendors who don't support Linux customers.

Currently, the Linux-friendliest wireless chipset manufacturers, in varying degrees, are Ralink, Realtek, Atheros, Intel, and Atmel. Then there are reverse-engineered GPL Linux drivers for the popular Broadcom and Intersil Prism chips.

While all of these have open source drivers (*http://opensource.org*), the Atheros chips require a closed binary Hardware Access Layer (HAL) blob in the Linux kernel. Older Intel chips need a proprietary binary regulatory daemon in user-space, but the current generation do not. Ralink and Realtek handle this job in the radio's firmware. Supposedly, this is to meet FCC requirements to prevent users from changing frequencies and channels outside of the allowed range. Putting a closed blob in the kernel makes writing and debugging drivers for Linux more difficult, as key parts of the radio's functions are hidden. Some additional concerns are that the binary blob taints the kernel, a buggy kernel blob can cause a kernel panic, and only the vendor can fix it. Buggy firmware is not as problematic because it just means the device won't work. The issue of the regulatory blob is a moving target and subject to change. (Go to the See Also section for some interesting reading on these issues.)

I use the Wistron CM9 mini-PCI interface (based on the Atheros AR5213) in my wireless access points because it gives full functionality: client, master, ad hoc, raw mode monitoring, WPA/WPA2, and all three WiFi bands (a/b/g) are supported. On the Linux client side, any of the supported wireless interfaces will work fine. Be careful with USB WICs—some work fine on Linux, some don't work at all. Get help from Google and the resources listed at the end of this introduction.

Discovering the chipset in any particular device before purchase is a real pain—most vendors don't volunteer the information, and love to play "change the chipset" without giving you an easy way to find out before making a purchase. To get up and running with the least hassle, consult a hardware vendor that specializes in Linux-supported wireless gear.

An inexpensive but powerhouse alternative to the Soekris and PC Engines router-boards are those little 4-port consumer wireless broadband routers, like the Linksys WRT54G series. There are many similar ones under various brand names, and you'll find some for under $50. You don't get all the nice flexibililty that you get with the bigger routerboards, but they're a heck of a value and make excellent dedicated wireless access points. The key to converting these from mediocre home-user boxes into $500 powerhouses is replacing the firmware with OpenWRT (*http://openwrt.org/*) or DD-WRT (*www.dd-wrt.com/*). These are open source, free-of-cost (though sending a bit of cash their way wouldn't hurt any feelings) firmwares designed especially for these little routers. With the new firmware, you can perform amazing feats of packet filtering, bandwidth-shaping, wireless security, VLANs, name services, and much more.

Security

Security is extra important when you're setting up wireless networking. Your bits are wafting forth into the air, so it's dead easy for random snoops to eavesdrop on your network traffic. Unsecured wireless access points expose you to two different threats:

- LAN intrusions. Your data might get stolen, or your LAN hosts turned into malware-spewing botnets, or used as rogue MP3 and porn servers.

- Loss of bandwidth. It's nice to share, but why allow your network performance to suffer because of some freeloader? Or worse, allow your bandwidth to be used for ill purposes?

If you wish to provide an open access point for anyone to use, do it the smart way. Wall it off securely from your LAN, and limit its bandwidth. One way to do this is to use a second wireless interface, if your routerboard supports it, or a dedicated access point, then use *iptables* to forward traffic from it to your WAN interface and block access to your LAN. Pyramid Linux comes with the WiFiDog captive portal, which you can use to remind your visitors of your generosity. Use the web interface to set it up; it takes just a few mouse clicks.

Encrypting and authenticating your wireless traffic is your number one priority. How do you do this? In the olden days, we had Wired Equivalent Privacy (WEP). Using WEP is barely better than nothing—it is famously weak, and can be cracked in less than 15 minutes with tools that anyone can download, like AirSnort and WEPCrack. Don't use WEP. Upgrade to devices that support Wi-Fi Protected Access (WPA).

There are two flavors of WPA: WPA and WPA2. WPA is an upgrade of WEP; both use RC4 stream encryption. It was designed to be a transitional protocol between WEP and WPA2. WPA is stronger than WEP, but not as strong as WPA2. WPA2 uses a new strong encryption protocol called Counter Mode with CBC-MAC Protocol (CCMP), which is based on Advanced Encryption Standard (AES). WPA2 is the complete implementation of the 802.11i standard. See Matthew Gast's excellent book *802.11 Wireless Networks: The Definitive Guide* (O'Reilly) for more information on these. The short story is that using WPA2 gives the best protection.

Using modern wireless devices that support WPA2 makes it easy to encrypt and authenticate all of your wireless traffic. WPA supports two different types of authentication: WPA-PSK (aka WPA-Personal, which uses preshared keys) and WPA-EAP (aka WPA-Enterprise, which uses the Extensible Authentication Protocol).

WPA-Personal is simple to set up. It depends on a shared key, which is a passphrase, and which must be distributed to all authorized users. There is no built-in automated method to distribute the keys; you have to do it manually, or write a clever script, or use something like *cfengine*. The obvious flaw in this scheme is everyone has the same key, so anytime you need to change the key it has to be changed on all clients. However, there is a way to give users unique keys—use *hostapd*, the host access point daemon. It's part of the HostAP suite of wireless drivers and utilities, and it includes a simple mechanism for managing multiple keys. This is a slick, simple way to implement some good, strong security.

WPA-Enterprise requires an authentication server, most commonly a RADIUS server. It's more work to set up, but once it's up, it's easier to manage users and keys. A RADIUS server is overkill if you're running a single access point, but it's a lifesaver if your network has several points of entry, such as dial-up, a VPN gateway, and multiple wireless access points, because all of them can use a single RADIUS server for authentication and authorization.

HostAP includes an embedded RADIUS server. Other access points can use it just like a standalone RADIUS server.

wpa_supplicant handles the interaction between the client and the server. *wpa_supplicant* is included in virtually all Linux distributions, though it may not be installed by default. Mac OS X and Windows also have supplicants. The word *supplicant* was chosen deliberately, with its connotations of humbly requesting permission to enter your network.

See Also

These articles discuss the "binary blob" issue:

- "OpenBSD: wpi, A Blob Free Intel PRO/Wireless 3945ABG Driver":
    http://kerneltrap.org/node/6650
- "Feature: OpenBSD Works To Open Wireless Chipsets":
    http://kerneltrap.org/node/4118

For building your own wireless access points and getting product information in plain English without marketing guff, check out specialty online retailers like:

- Metrix.net at *http://metrix.net/metrix/* offers customized wireless access points and accessories based on Pyramid Linux, and custom services
- Netgate.com: *http://netgate.com/*
- Mini-box.com: *http://www.mini-box.com/*
- Routerboard.com: *http://www.routerboard.com*
- DamnSmallLinux.org store: *http://www.damnsmalllinux.org/store/*

These sites identify wireless chipsets by brand name and model number:

- MadWifi.org for Atheros devices: *http://madwifi.org/*
- Atheros.com: *http://www.atheros.com/*
- rt2x00 Open Source Project for Ralink devices:
    http://rt2x00.serialmonkey.com/wiki/index.php?title=Main_Page
- FSF-approved wireless interface cards:
    http://www.fsf.org/resources/hw/net/wireless/cards.html

General wireless resources:

- Ralinktech.com: *http://www.ralinktech.com/*
- Linux on Realtek: *http://rtl8181.sourceforge.net/*
- Realtek.com: *http://www.realtek.com.tw/default.aspx*
- FS List of supported wireless cards: *http://www.fsf.org/resources/hw/net/wireless/cards.html*
- Seattle Wireless, a great resource for all things wireless, and especially building community networks: *http://seattlewireless.net/*
- LiveKiosk: *http://www.livekiosk.com*
- Wireless LAN resources for Linux, the gigantic mother lode of information for wireless on Linux: *http://www.hpl.hp.com/personal/Jean_Tourrilhes/Linux/*

4.1 Building a Linux Wireless Access Point

Problem

You don't want to dink around with prefab commercial wireless access points. They're either too simple and too inflexible for your needs, or too expensive and inflexible. So, like a good Linux geek, you want to build your own. You want a nice quiet little compact customizable box, and you want to be able to add or remove features as you need, just like on any Linux computer. For starters, you want everything on a single box: authenticated wireless access point, broadband Internet connection sharing, *iptables* firewall, and name services.

Solution

- Install Pyramid Linux on a Soekris or PC Engines WRAP single-board computer.
- Install an Atheros-based wireless mini-PCI card and connect an external antenna.
- Configure and test LAN connectivity, and DHCP and DNS.
- Keep your router off the Internet until it's properly hardened, firewalled, and tested.
- Add Internet connectivity, and voilà! It is done.

Continue on to the next recipes to learn how to do all of these things.

Discussion

If you prefer separating out your services on different physical boxes, such as wireless access point, firewall, and nameserver, the recipes in this chapter are easy to adapt to do this.

Soekris has two series of routerboards: 45xx and 48xx. Choose whatever model meets your needs. At a minimum, you need 64 MB RAM, a Compact Flash slot, a mini-PCI slot, and two Ethernet ports. More powerful CPUs and more RAM are always nice to have. A second mini-PCI slot lets you add a second wireless interface. PCMCIA slots give you more flexibility because these support both wired and wireless interfaces.

The 45xx boards have 100 or 133 MHz CPUs and 32 to 128 MB SDRAM. The 48xx boards have 233 or 266 MHz processors and 128 to 256 MB SDRAM. You'll see network speeds top out on the 45xx boards around 17 Mbps, and the more powerful 48xx boards will perform at up to 50 Mbps. 17 Mbps is faster than most cable or DSL Internet connections. For ordinary web surfing and email, the 45xx boards are fine. If you're running VoIP services, doing online gaming, serving more than 50 users, or running any peer protocols like BitTorrent, then go for the 48xx boards.

PC Engines WRAP boards are similar to the Soekris boards, and are usually a bit less expensive. Both use Geode CPUs, are about the same size, and similarly featured. Both vendors will customize the boards pretty much however you want.

See Also

- Chapter 2
- Chapter 17
- Soekris.com: *http://www.soekris.com/*
- MadWifi.org: *http://madwifi.org/*

4.2 Bridging Wireless to Wired

Problem

How do you integrate your wired and wireless clients so that they share an Internet connection and LAN services all in one big happy subnet? You know that when you have multiple Ethernet interfaces on the same box they cannot all be on the same subnet, but must all have addresses from separate subnets. You want everyone all in a single subnet, and don't want a lot of administration headaches, so how will you do this?

Solution

Your routerboard needs at least three network interfaces: your Atheros interface, plus two Ethernet interfaces. *ath0* is your wireless interface, *eth0* is the LAN interface, and *eth1* is your WAN interface.

What we will do is build an Ethernet bridge between *ath0* and *eth0*. Copy this example *letc/network/interfaces*, substituting your own LAN addresses and your own ESSID. Remember to run /sbin/rw first to make the Pyramid filesystem writable:

```
pyramid:~# /sbin/rw
pyramid:~# nano /etc/network/interfaces

##/etc/network/interfaces
## wireless bridge configuration
auto lo
iface lo inet loopback

auto br0
iface br0 inet static
        address 192.168.1.50
        network 192.168.1.0
        netmask 255.255.255.0
        broadcast 192.168.1.255
        bridge_ports ath0  eth0
         post-down wlanconfig ath0 destroy
         pre-up wlanconfig ath0 create wlandev wifi0 wlanmode ap
         pre-up iwconfig ath0 essid "alrac-net" channel 01 rate auto
         pre-up ifconfig ath0 up
         pre-up sleep 3
```

You can test this now by networking with some LAN hosts that have static IP addresses. First restart networking on the router:

```
pyramid:~# /etc/init.d/networking restart
```

This creates a wide-open wireless access point. Point your clients to 192.168.1.50 as the default gateway, and you should be able to easily join any wireless clients to your LAN, and *ping* both wired and wireless PCs. When you're finished, remember to return the filesystem to read-only:

```
pyramid:~# /sbin/ro
```

Discussion

This recipe is totally insecure, but it lets you test your bridge and wireless connectivity before adding more services.

Let's review the options used in this configuration:

bridge_ports
> Define the two interfaces to bridge.

post-down wlanconfig ath0 destroy
> This command tears down the access point when the network interfaces go down. *wlanconfig* is part of MadWiFi-ng. Use it to create, destroy, and manage access points. With *wlanconfig*, you can have multiple access points on a single device.

`pre-up wlanconfig ath0 create wlandev wifi0 wlanmode ap`
> *wifi0* is the name the kernel gives to your Atheros interface, which you can see with *dmesg*. Next, *wlanconfig* creates the virtual access point, *ath0*, on top of *wifi0*.

`pre-up iwconfig ath0 essid "alrac-net" channel 01 rate auto`
> Assign the ESSID, channel, and bit-rate. To see the channels, frequencies, and bit-rates supported by your interface card, use this command:
>
> > `pyramid:~# wlanconfig ath0 list chan`

How do you know which channel to use? If you have only one access point, channel 1 should work fine. If you have up to three, try using channels 1, 6, and 11. For more complex networks, please refer to Matthew Gast's excellent book, *802.11 Wireless Networks: The Definitive Guide* (O'Reilly):

`pre-up ifconfig ath0 up`
> Bring up *ath0* before the bridge comes up.

`pre-up sleep 3`
> Brief pause to make sure that everything comes up in order.

You don't have to build the bridge in the traditional way, by configuring eth0 with a zero-IP address, or bringing it up before the bridge is built, because scripts in */etc/network/if-pre-up.d* handle that for you.

I'm sure some of you are wondering about *ebtables*. *ebtables* is like *iptables* for Ethernet bridges. *iptables* cannot filter bridge traffic, but *ebtables* can. There are many ingenious ways to use *ebtables* and Ethernet bridges in your network. In this chapter, I'm leaving *ebtables* out on purpose because we will be running an *iptables* Internet firewall on our access point. *ebtables* is not suitable for an Internet firewall, and trying to use both on the same box is too complicated for this old admin.

See Also

- Pyramid Linux does not include manpages, so you should either install the applications in this chapter on a PC, or rely on Google
- *wlanconfig* is part of MadWiFi-ng
- man 8 brctl for bridge options
- *iwconfig* is part of the wireless-tools package
- man 8 iwconfig
- Pyramid Linux: *http://pyramid.metrix.net/*
- Recipe 3.2
- *802.11 Wireless Networks: The Definitive Guide*, by Matthew Gast (O'Reilly)

4.3 Setting Up Name Services

Problem

Your LAN is going to have a combination of hosts with static IP addresses and DHCP clients that come and go, especially wireless clients. And, you want DHCP clients to automatically be entered into DNS so they can be accessed by hostname just like the hosts with static IP addresses.

Solution

You don't want much. Fortunately, you can have it all. Pyramid comes with *dnsmasq*, which handles DHCP and DNS, and automatically enters DHCP clients into DNS. This requires the clients to send their hostnames when they are requesting a DHCP lease. Windows clients do this by default. Most Linux clients do not, so go to Recipe 4.5 to learn about client configuration.

Now, we'll edit */etc/dnsmasq.conf* on your Pyramid box. First make the filesystem writeable by running /sbin/rw. Copy this example, using your own network name instead of alrac.net, whatever DHCP range you prefer, and your own upstream nameservers:

```
pyramid:~# /sbin/rw
pyramid:~# nano /etc/dnsmasq.conf

domain-needed
bogus-priv
local=/alrac.net/
expand-hosts
domain=alrac.net
interface=br0
listen-address=127.0.0.1

#upstream nameservers
server=22.33.44.2
server=22.33.44.3

dhcp-range=lan,192.168.1.100,192.168.1.200,12h
dhcp-lease-max=100
```

Next, add all of your hosts that already have static IP addresses to */etc/hosts* on your Pyramid box, using only their hostnames and IP addresses. At a minimum, you must have an entry for localhost and your Pyramid router:

```
## /etc/hosts
127.0.0.1        localhost
192.168.1.50     pyramid
192.168.1.10     xena
192.168.1.74     uberpc
```

Restart *dnsmasq*:

```
pyramidwrap:~# killall dnsmasq
```

To test your new nameserver, *ping* your LAN hosts from each other:

```
$ ping pyramid
$ ping xena
$ ping uberpc
```

You should see responses like this:

```
PING pyramid.alrac.net (192.168.1.50) 56(84) bytes of data.
64 bytes from pyramid.alrac.net (192.168.1.50): icmp_seq=1 ttl=64 time=0.483 ms
64 bytes from pyramid.alrac.net (192.168.1.50): icmp_seq=2 ttl=64 time=0.846 ms
```

You should be able to *ping* both wired and wireless clients, and DHCP clients should be entered automatically into the DNS table as well.

Finally, verify that their domain names are correctly assigned by DNS:

```
$ hostname
xena
$ hostname -f
xena.alrac.net
$ dnsdomainname
alrac.net
```

Discussion

Pyramid Linux mounts a number of files into a temporary, writeable filesystem, like */etc/resolv.conf*. You can see which ones they are by looking in */rw*, or running `ls -l /etc` to see which ones are symlinked to */rw*. These are copied over from */ro* on boot. It's designed to keep flash writes down. So, you can either edit */ro*, or make the files in */etc* immutable.

dnsmasq.conf crams a lot of functionality into a few lines, so let's take a closer look:

domain-needed

> Do not forward requests for plain hostnames that do not have dots or domain parts to upstream DNS servers. If the name is not in */etc/hosts* or DHCP, it returns a "not found" answer. This means that incomplete requests (for example, "google" or "oreilly" instead of *google.com* or *oreilly.com*) will be cut off before they leave your network.

bogus-priv

> Short for "bogus private lookups." Any reverse lookups for private IP ranges (such as 192.168.x.x) are not forwarded upstream. If they aren't found in */etc/hosts*, or the DHCP leases file, "no such domain" is the answer. Using domain-needed and bogus-priv are simple options for practicing good Netizenship.

`local=/alrac.net/`

Put your local domain name here so queries for your local domain will only be answered from /etc/hosts and DHCP, and not forwarded upstream. This is a nice bit of magic that lets you choose any domain name for your private network and not have to register it. To make this work right, you also need the expand-hosts and domain options.

`expand-hosts`

This automatically adds the domain name to the hostnames.

`domain=alrac.net`

expand-hosts looks here for the domain name.

`interface`

Define which interface *dnsmasq* should listen to. Use one line per interface, if you have more than one.

`listen-address=127.0.0.1`

This tells *dnsmasq* to also use its own local cache instead of querying the upstream nameservers for every request. This speeds up lookups made from the router, and it also allows the router to use your local DNS. You can verify this by pinging your LAN hosts from the router by their hostnames or FQDNs.

`server`

The server option is used for several different purposes; here, it defines your upstream DNS servers.

`dhcp-range=lan,192.168.1.100,192.168.1.200,12h`

Define your pool of DHCP leases and lease time, and define a network zone called "lan." Using named zones lets you assign servers and routes to groups of clients and different subnets; see Recipe 3.13 to see this in action.

`dhcp-max-lease`

Maximum limit of total DHCP leases. The default is 150. You may have as many as your address range supports.

See Also

- Recipe 4.12 for an example of using named zones
- man 8 dnsmasq contains a wealth of helpful information about all the available command-line options, many of which are also *dnsmasq.conf* options
- *dnsmasq.conf* is also a great help resource
- *dnsmasq* home page is where you'll find mailing list archives and excellent help documents: *http://www.thekelleys.org.uk/dnsmasq/doc.html*
- Chapter 24, "Managing Name Resolution," in *Linux Cookbook*, by Carla Schroder (O'Reilly)

4.4 Setting Static IP Addresses from the DHCP Server

Problem

You want to manage your LAN computers from DHCP instead of configuring them individually, so you don't have to run around tweaking individual computers all the time. You want to assign static and dynamic IP addresses, gateways, and servers all via DHCP.

Solution

dnsmasq does it all. There are a couple of ways to assign static IP addresses from *dnsmasq.conf*. One is to use the client's MAC address as the client identifier, like this:

```
dhcp-host=11:22:33:44:55:66,192.168.1.75
```

My favorite way is to set it by hostname:

```
dhcp-host=penguina,192.168.1.75
```

Make sure you do not have entries for these in */etc/hosts*.

The only client configuration that's necessary is the hostname, and for DHCP clients to send the hostname to the DHCP server when they request a new lease. Once you have that, you can control everything else from the server.

Remember to run `killall dnsmasq` every time you change *dnsmasq.conf*.

There are some tricky bits to client configuration, so see Recipe 4.5 for this.

Discussion

Changes in *dnsmasq.conf* are easy to test. After restarting *dnsmasq*, try the following commands on your Linux clients.

ifupdown stops and restarts interfaces:

```
# ifdown eth0
# ifup eth0
```

Sometimes, that doesn't quite do the job, so you can also try:

```
# /etc/init.d/network restart
# /etc/init.d/networking restart
```

The first one is for Fedora, the second for Debian. You'll see it acquire the address you assigned it from the DHCP server, and it will write the correct DNS server or servers to */etc/resolv.conf*.

If those don't work, reboot.

Find MAC addresses with *ifconfig* for wired NICs, and *iwconfig* for wireless NICs. *ifconfig* sees both, but it doesn't differentiate them. *iwconfig* identifies only wireless interfaces.

When you use the MAC address, don't forget to change the entry in *dnsmasq.conf* if you replace the client's network interface card.

MAC addresses are unique, but hostnames are not, so you have to be careful not to have duplicate hostnames. You can't have duplicate hostnames, anyway.

MAC addresses are ridiculously easy to spoof, so don't think you're adding any security by relying on them as secure, unique identifiers.

See Also

- `man 8 dnsmasq` contains a wealth of helpful information about all the available command-line options, many of which are also *dnsmasq.conf* options
- *dnsmasq.conf* is also a great help resource
- *dnsmasq* home page (*http://www.thekelleys.org.uk/dnsmasq/doc.html*) is where you'll find mailing list archives and excellent help documents
- Chapter 24, "Managing Name Resolution," in *Linux Cookbook*, by Carla Schroder (O'Reilly)

4.5 Configuring Linux and Windows Static DHCP Clients

Problem

What with having both Linux and Windows clients, and various Linux distributions that like to do things their own way, you're a bit befuddled as to how to configure them to have *dnsmasq* give them static IP addresses.

Solution

The key to getting static IP addresses from DHCP is for the clients to send their hostnames to the DHCP server when they request a lease.

Windows 2000, 2003, and XP clients do this automatically. All you do is configure them for DHCP in the usual manner.

First, on all Linux machines, make sure there is nothing in */etc/hosts* other than the localdomain entry.

Most Linux distributions are not configured to send the hostname by default. To fix this, add one line to their DHCP client files. On Debian, this is the */etc/dhcp3/dhclient.conf* file. This example is for the computer named Penguina:

```
send host-name "penguina";
```

You must also enter the hostname in */etc/hostname*:

```
penguina
```

Just the hostname and nothing else. Then, set up the normal DHCP configuration in */etc/network/interfaces*, like this:

```
##/etc/network/interfaces
auto lo
iface lo inet loopback

auto eth0
iface eth0 inet dhcp
```

On Fedora, each interface gets its own DHCP client file, like */etc/dhclient-eth1*. You may need to create this file. This takes the same send host-name "penguina"; entry. Then, add this line to */etc/sysconfig/network-scripts/ifcfg-eth0*:

```
DHCP_HOSTNAME=penguina
```

Make sure the HOSTNAME line in */etc/sysconfig/network* is empty.

The sure way to test your new configurations is to reboot, then run these commands:

```
$ hostname
penguina
$ hostname -f
penguina.alrac.net
$ dnsdomainname
alrac.net
```

Ping will look like this:

```
carla@xena:~$ ping penguina
PING penguina.alrac.net (192.168.1.75) 56(84) bytes of data.
64 bytes from penguina.alrac.net (192.168.1.75): icmp_seq=1 ttl=128 time=8.90 ms
carla@penguina:~$ ping penguina
PING penguina.alrac.net (192.168.1.75) 56(84) bytes of data.
64 bytes from penguina.alrac.net (192.168.1.75): icmp_seq=1 ttl=64 time=0.033 ms
```

Discussion

The most common cause of problems with this is not configuring the hostname correctly. Check all of your pertinent configuration files.

Here is a complete example Fedora configuration for *eth0*:

```
##/etc/sysconfig/network-scripts/ifcfg-eth0
DEVICE=eth0
ONBOOT=yes
BOOTPROTO=dhcp
HWADDR=11.22.33.44.55.66
DHCP_HOSTNAME=penguina
TYPE=wireless
PEERDNS=yes
MODE=managed
RATE=auto
```

Either edit Fedora configuration files directly, or use the graphical network configurator, but don't use both because the graphical tool overwrites your manual edits.

dnsmasq automatically enters DHCP clients into DNS. This is a great convenience, and when you deploy IPv6, it will be more than a convenience—it will be a necessity, unless you're comfortable with remembering and typing those long IPv6 addresses.

dnsmasq combines a lot of complex functions into a short configuration file, and can be used in conjunction with BIND, *djbdns*, MaraDNS, and other nameservers. Use *dnsmasq* for your private LAN services, and one of the others for a public authoritative server. This makes it easy to keep the two completely separate, as they should be. Remember the number one DNS server rule: keep your authoritative and caching servers strictly separated, which means using two physically separate network interfaces and different IP addresses. Authoritative servers do not answer queries for other domains; that is the job of a caching resolver like *dnsmasq*. Maintaining two separate servers might sound like more work, but in practice, it's easier and safer than trying to configure a single server to handle both jobs.

See Also

- man 5 dhclient
- *dnsmasq.conf* is a great help resource
- *dnsmasq* home page (*http://www.thekelleys.org.uk/dnsmasq/doc.html*) is where you'll find mailing list archives and excellent help documents
- Chapter 24, "Managing Name Resolution," in *Linux Cookbook*, by Carla Schroder (O'Reilly)

4.6   Adding Mail Servers to dnsmasq

Problem

You have some local mail servers that you want your LAN hosts to know about. How do you do this with *dnsmasq*?

Solution

dnsmasq has a special record type for mailservers. You need these three lines:

```
mx-host=alrac.net,mail.alrac.net,5
mx-target=mail.alrac.net
localmx
```

The mx-host line needs the domain name, server name, and MX priority. The mx-target line is the server name. localmx means all local machines should use this server.

Discussion

A priority number of 5 means the server is higher priority than servers with larger numbers, typically 10 and then multiples of 10. If you have only one mail server, you should still give it a priority to keep clients happy.

See Also

- man 5 dhclient
- *dnsmasq.conf* is also a great help resource
- *dnsmasq* home page (*http://www.thekelleys.org.uk/dnsmasq/doc.html*) is where you'll find mailing list archives and excellent help documents
- Chapter 24, "Managing Name Resolution," in *Linux Cookbook*, by Carla Schroder (O'Reilly)

4.7 Making WPA2-Personal Almost As Good As WPA-Enterprise

Problem

You're nervous about sitting there with an unsecured wireless access point, and you really want to lock it up before you do anything else. You've made sure that all of your wireless network interfaces support WPA2, so you're ready to go. You don't want to run a RADIUS authentication server, but using the same shared key for all clients doesn't seem very secure. Isn't there some kind of in-between option?

Solution

Yes, there is. Pyramid Linux comes with *hostapd*, which is a user space daemon for access point and authentication servers. This recipe will show you how to assign different pre-shared keys to your clients, instead of everyone using the same one. And, we'll use a nice strong AES-CCMP encryption, instead of the weaker RC4-based ciphers that WPA and WEP use.

First, run /sbin/rw to make the Pyramid filesystem writeable, then create or edit the */etc/hostapd.conf* file:

```
##/etc/hostapd.conf
interface=ath0
bridge=br0
driver=madwifi
debug=0
ssid=alrac-net
macaddr_acl=0
auth_algs=3
```

```
wpa=1
wpa_psk_file=/etc/hostapd_wpa_psk
wpa_key_mgmt=WPA-PSK
wpa_pairwise=CCMP
```

Next, create */etc/hostapd_wpa_psk*, which holds the shared plaintext passphrase:

```
00:00:00:00:00:00 waylongpassword
```

Then, edit */etc/network/interfaces* so that *hostapd* starts when the *br0* interface comes up. Add these lines to the end of your *br0* entry:

```
up hostapd -B /etc/hostapd.conf
post-down killall hostapd
```

Run /sbin/ro, then restart networking:

```
pyramid:~# /etc/init.d/networking restart
```

Now, grab a Linux client PC for testing. On the client, create an */etc/wpa_supplicant.conf* file with these lines, using your own ESSID and super-secret passphrase from */etc/hostapd_wpa_psk*:

```
##/etc/wpa_supplicant.conf
network={
    ssid="alrac-net"
    psk="waylongpassword"
    pairwise=CCMP
    group=CCMP
    key_mgmt=WPA-PSK
}
```

Shut down the client's wireless interface, then test the key exchange:

```
# ifdown ath0
# wpa_supplicant -iath0 -c/etc/wpa_supplicant.conf -Dmadwifi -w
  Trying to associate with 00:ff:4a:1e:a7:7d (SSID='alrac-net' freq=2412 MHz)
  Associated with 00:ff:4a:1e:a7:7d
  WPA: Key negotiation completed with 00:ff:4a:1e:a7:7d [PTK=CCMP GTK=CCMP]
 CTRL-EVENT-CONNECTED - Connection to 00:2b:6f:4d:00:8e
```

This shows a successful key exchange, and it confirms that the CCMP cipher is being used, which you want to see because it is much stronger than the RC4 stream encryption used by WEP. Hit Ctrl-C to end the key exchange test. So, you can add more clients, giving each of them a unique key. All you do is line them up in */etc/hostapd_wpa_psk*, and match their passphrases to their MAC addresses:

```
00:0D:44:00:83:CF    uniquetextpassword
00:22:D6:01:01:E2    anothertextpassword
23:EF:11:00:DD:2E    onemoretextpassword
```

Now, you have a good strong AES-CCMP based encryption, and if one user compromises her key, you don't have to change all of them. Revoking a user's access is as easy as commenting out or deleting their key.

You can make it permanent on the clients by configuring their wireless interfaces to call *wpa_supplicant* when they come up. On Debian, do this:

```
##/etc/network/interfaces
auto ath0
iface ath0 inet dhcp
pre-up wpa_supplicant -iath0 -Dmadwifi -Bw -c/etc/wpa_supplicant/wpa_supplicant.conf
post-down killall -q wpa_supplicant
```

On Fedora, add this line to */etc/sysconfig/network-scripts/ifup-wireless*:

```
wpa_supplicant -ieth0 -c/etc/wpa_supplicant/wpa_supplicant.conf -Dmadwifi -Bw
```

Make sure your filepath to *wpa_supplicant.conf* is correct, that you specify the correct interface with -i, and that you specify the correct driver for your wireless interface with the -D option.

Discussion

When you test the key exchange, you need to specify the driver for your WIC (in the example, it's - Dmadwifi). man 8 wpa_supplicant lists all options. The *wext* driver is a generic Linux kernel driver. You'll see documentation recommending that you use this. It's better to try the driver for your interface first, then give *wext* a try if that causes problems.

The example passphrases are terrible, and should not be used in real life. Make yours the maximum length of 63 characters, no words or names, just random jumbles of letters and numbers. Avoid punctuation marks because some Windows clients don't handle them correctly. There are all kinds of random password generators floating around if you want some help, which a quick web search will find.

Windows XP needs SP2 for WPA support, plus client software that comes with your wireless interfaces. Older Windows may be able to get all the necessary client software with their wireless interfaces. Or maybe not—shop carefully.

It takes some computational power to encrypt a plaintext passphrase, so using plaintext passphrases could slow things down a bit. You can use *wpa_password* to encrypt your passphrases, then copy the encrypted strings into place:

```
$ wpa_passphrase alrac-net w894uiernnfif98389rbbybdbyu8i3yenfig87bfop
network={
        ssid="alrac-net"
        #psk="w894uiernnfif98389rbbybdbyu8i3yenfig87bfop"
        psk=48a37127e92b29df54a6775571768f5790e5df87944c26583e1576b83390c56f
}
```

Now your clients and access point won't have to expend so many CPU cycles on the passphrase. Encrypted keys do not have quotation marks in *wpa_supplicant.conf*; plaintext passphrases do.

In our original example, 00:00:00:00:00:00 means "accept all MAC addresses."

You can see your keys in action with the `iwlist ath0 key` command on the access point and clients.

Your access point supports virtually all clients: Linux, Mac OS X, Windows, Unix, the BSDs…any client with a supplicant and support for the protocols will work.

NetworkManager and Kwlan are good graphical network management tools for Linux clients. NetworkManager is designed for all Linux desktops and window managers, and comes with Gnome; Kwlan is part of KDE. Both support profiles, key management, and easy network switching.

When you're using an Ethernet bridge, make sure that you enter your wireless and bridge interfaces in */etc/hostapd.conf*.

hostapd.conf supports access controls based on MAC addresses. You're welcome to use these; however, I think they're a waste of time because MAC addresses are so easy to spoof your cat can do it.

HostAP was originally a project that supported only Prism wireless chips, but now it supports these drivers:

- Host AP driver for Prism2/2.5/3
- madwifi (Atheros ar521x)
- Prism54.org (Prism GT/Duette/Indigo)
- BSD net80211 layer

See Also

- Pyramid Linux does not include manpages, so you should install the applications in this chapter on a PC to get the manpages, or rely on Google
- *wlanconfig* is part of MadWiFi-ng
- `man 8 wlanconfig`
- The default *hostapd.conf* is full of informative comments
- The default *wpa_supplicant.conf* is helpful
- *802.11 Wireless Networks: The Definitive Guide*, by Matthew Gast (O'Reilly)
- MadWiFi.org: *http://madwifi.org/*

4.8   Enterprise Authentication with a RADIUS Server

Problem

The previous recipe is a slick hack for giving your wireless clients individual keys, but it's still not a proper Public Key Infrastructure (PKI), which is better for larger deployments, and better for security. You have decided it's worth running a standalone RADIUS server for your wireless authentication because it offers more security and more flexibility. You'll be able to use it for all network authentication if you want to, not just wireless, and you can scale up at your own pace. So, how do you use a RADIUS server for wireless authentication?

Solution

Use FreeRADIUS together with OpenSSL. There are four steps to this:

1. Install and configure the FreeRADIUS server
2. Create and distribute OpenSSL server and client certificates
3. Configure your wireless access point
4. Configure client supplicants

Your WAP becomes a Network Access Server (NAS) because it passes along the job of user authentication to the FreeRADIUS server.

To ensure the least hair loss and lowest blood pressure, use your distribution's package manager to install FreeRADIUS. If you prefer a source installation, refer to the *INSTALL* document in the source tarball.

This recipe requires a PKI using Extensible Authentication Protocol-Transport Layer Security (EAP-TLS) authentication, which means the server and client must authenticate to each other with X.509 certificates. So, you'll need:

- Your own certificate authority
- Server private key and CA-signed certificate
- A unique private key and a CA-signed certificate for each client

This is the strongest authentication you can use. See Recipe 9.5 to learn how to do this the easy way, with OpenVPN's excellent helper scripts. If you don't have OpenVPN, you can get the scripts from OpenVPN.net (*http://openvpn.net/*).

There are two things you will do differently. First, use password-protected client certificates:

```
# ./build-key-pass [client hostname]
```

And, you will have to create PK12 certificates for Windows clients:

```
# ./build-key-pkcs12  [client hostname]
```

In this recipe, the certificate authority, private server key, and public server key are kept in */etc/raddb/keys*. This directory should be mode 0750, and owned by *root* and the FreeRADIUS group created by your Linux distribution. On Debian, this is *root: freerad*. On Fedora, *root:radiusd*. You'll be editing these FreeRADIUS files:

/etc/raddb/clients.conf
/etc/raddb/users
/etc/raddb/eap.conf
/etc/raddb/radiusd.conf

Debian users, look in */etc/freeradius* instead of */etc/raddb*.

First, tell FreeRADIUS about your wireless access point or points in *clients.conf*, using one section per WAP. You can start over with a clean new file instead of adding to the default file:

```
##/etc/raddb/clients.conf
client 192.168.1.50 {
        secret = superstrongpassword
        shortname = wap1
        nastype = other
        }
```

Then, make a list of authorized users' login names in the *users* file, and a nice reject message for users who are not in this file. The usernames are the Common Names on their client certificates. Add them to the existing *users* file:

```
##/etc/raddb/users
"alrac sysadmin" Auth-Type := EAP
"terry rockstar" Auth-Type := EAP
"pinball wizard" Auth-Type := EAP

DEFAULT Auth-Type := Reject
        Reply-Message = "I hear you knocking, but you can't come in"
```

Now, create two files containing random data, which EAP needs to do its job. These must be owned by *root* and the FreeRADIUS group, and readable only to the file owners:

```
# openssl dhparam -check -text -5 512 -out /etc/raddb/dh
# dd if=/dev/random of=/etc/raddb/random count=1 bs=128
# chown root:radiusd /etc/raddb/dh
# chown root:radiusd /etc/raddb/random
# chmod 0640  /etc/raddb/dh
# chmod 0640  /etc/raddb/random
```

Make sure you use the correct RADIUS group for your distribution.

eap.conf is where you configure the EAP module. Find and edit these lines in your existing file, using your own filenames:

```
##/etc/raddb/eap.conf
default_eap_type = tls
tls {
    private_key_password = [your password]
    private_key_file = /etc/raddb/keys/xena.crt
    certificate_file = /etc/raddb/keys/xena.key
    CA_file = /etc/raddb/keys/ca.crt

    dh_file = /etc/raddb/keys/dh2048.pem
    random_file = /etc/raddb/keys/random
    fragment_size = 1024
    include_length = yes
}
```

radiusd.conf is huge and replete with helpful comments, so I will show just the bits you may need to change. In the Authorization module, make sure the eap line is uncommented:

```
##/etc/raddb/radiusd.conf
# Authorization. First preprocess (hints and huntgroups files),
authorize {
...
eap
...
}
```

Then, in the Authentication module, make sure the eap line is uncommented:

```
# Authentication.
authenticate {
...
eap
...
}
```

Finally, make sure these lines are uncommented and the correct user and group are entered. These vary, so check your own distribution:

```
user = radiusd
group = radiusd
```

Shut down FreeRADIUS if it is running, then run these commands to test it:

```
# freeradius -X
...
"Ready to process requests"
# radtest test test localhost 0 testing123
```

The first command starts it in debugging mode. The second command sends it a fake authentication test, which should fail. What you want to see is FreeRADIUS responding to the test. Debugging mode emits reams of useful output, so if there are any errors in your configurations, you'll be able to track them down.

Discussion

The trickiest bit is getting your certificates right, but fortunately, the Easy-RSA scripts make the process easy. A good alternative is the excellent graphical PKI manager TinyCA (*http://tinyca.sm-zone.net/*).

A slick FreeRADIUS feature is that you don't need to use a Certification Revocation List (CRL), though nothing's stopping you if you want to because revoking a user is as simple as removing them from the *users* file.

The various Linux distributions handle the FreeRADIUS user and group in different ways. Some use *nobody*. Debian creates a *freerad* user and group. It's important to run FreeRADIUS as an unprivileged user, so make sure that the user and group lines in *radiusd.conf* are configured correctly.

If you have several WAPs, you may control access by subnet instead of individual WAP:

```
##/etc/raddb/clients.conf
client 192.168.0.0/24 {
    secret    = superstrongpassword
    shortname = wap_herd
    nastype   = other
```

This is less secure because it uses the same secret for all access points, but it's easier to manage.

See Also

- man 1 openssl
- man dhparam
- The default *eap.conf, radiusd.conf, clients.conf,* and *users* files are excellent help references
- *RADIUS*, by Jonathan Hassell (O'Reilly) for a good in-depth tour of running a RADIUS server
- The FreeRADIUS Wiki: *http://wiki.freeradius.org/*
- TinyCA (*http://tinyca.sm-zone.net/*) is a nice graphical tool for creating and managing PKIs, and for importing and exporting certificates and keys
- Recipe 9.5

4.9   Configuring Your Wireless Access Point to Use FreeRADIUS

Problem

OK, setting up FreeRADIUS was fun, now what do you do to make your WAP use it?

Solution

Your nice Pyramid Linux-based WAP needs but a few lines in */etc/hostapd.conf*. In this example, the IP address of the FreeRADIUS server is 192.168.1.250:

```
##/etc/hostapd.conf
interface=ath0
bridge=br0
driver=madwifi
debug=0
ssid=alrac-net
ieee8021x=1
```

```
auth_algs=0
eap_server=0
eapol_key_index_workaround=1

own_ip_addr=192.168.1.50
nas_identifier=pyramid.alrac.net
auth_server_addr=192.168.1.250
auth_server_port=1812
auth_server_shared_secret=superstrongpassword

wpa=1
wpa_key_mgmt=WPA-EAP
wpa_pairwise=TKIP
wpa_group_rekey=300
wpa_gmk_rekey=640
```

Edit */etc/network/interfaces* so that *hostapd* starts when your LAN interface comes up. Add these lines to the end of your LAN interface stanza:

```
pre-up hostapd -B /etc/hostapd.conf
post-down killall hostapd
```

Restart networking:

```
pyramid:~# /etc/init.d/networking restart
```

And you're almost there. See the next recipe for client configuration.

Discussion

All the different wireless access points are configured in different ways. The three things common to all of them are:

- FreeRADIUS Server IP Address
- FreeRADIUS Port: 1812 is the default
- FreeRADIUS Key: shared secret

Remember, you don't have to worry about keys and certificates on the access point. It's just a go-between.

See Also

- *RADIUS*, by Jonathan Hassell (O'Reilly) for a good in-depth tour of running a RADIUS server
- The FreeRADIUS Wiki: *http://wiki.freeradius.org/*
- The example *hostapd.conf*

4.10   Authenticating Clients to FreeRADIUS

Problem

Now that you have your access point and FreeRADIUS server ready to go to work, how do your clients talk to it?

Solution

All clients need a copy of *ca.crt*. Mac and Linux clients get their own *[hostname].crt* and *[hostname].key* files. Windows clients use *[hostname].p12*.

Your Windows and Mac clients have built-in graphical tools for importing and managing their certificates, and configuring their supplicants. What do you do on Linux? I haven't found anything that makes the job any easier than editing plain old text files. Go back to Recipe 4.7, and start with the configuration for *etc/wpa_supplicant.conf*. Change it to this:

```
## /etc/wpa_supplicant.conf
network={
    ssid="alrac-net"
    scan_ssid=1
    key_mgmt=WPA-EAP
    pairwise=CCMP TKIP
    group=CCMP TKIP
    eap=TLS
    identity="alice sysadmin"
    ca_cert="/etc/cert/ca.crt"
    client_cert="/etc/cert/stinkpad.crt"
    private_key="/etc/cert/stinkpad.key"
    private_key_passwd="verysuperstrongpassword"
}
```

The value for *identity* comes from *etc/raddb/users* on the FreeRADIUS server. Certificates and keys can be stored anywhere, as long as *wpa_supplicant.conf* is configured correctly to point to them.

Continue with the rest of Recipe 4.7 to test and finish configuring *wpa_supplicant*.

Discussion

Be sure that *.key* files are mode 0400, and owned by your Linux user. *.crt* files are 0644, owned by the user.

You can have multiple entries in *wpa_supplicant.conf* for different networks. Be sure to use the:

```
network{
}
```

format to set them apart.

NetworkManager (*http://www.gnome.org/projects/NetworkManager/*) is the best Linux tool for painlessly managing multiple network profiles. It is bundled with Gnome, and is available for all Linux distributions.

See Also

- man 8 wpa_supplicant
- man 5 wpa_supplicant.conf

4.11   Connecting to the Internet and Firewalling

Problem

It's high time to finish up with these LAN chores and bring the Internet to your LAN. Your wireless is encrypted, your LAN services are working, and your users want Internet. So you're ready to configure your WAN interface and build a nice stout *iptables* firewall.

Solution

Easy as pie. First, configure your WAN interface, then set up an *iptables* firewall. (See Chapter 3 to learn how to do these things.) You'll need to make some simple changes to */usr/local/bin/fw-nat* to enable traffic to flow across your bridge. Add these two lines:

```
$ipt -A INPUT -p ALL -i $LAN_IFACE -s 192.168.1.0/24 -j ACCEPT
$ipt -A FORWARD -p ALL -i $LAN_IFACE -s 192.168.1.0/24 -j ACCEPT
```

Use your own subnet, of course. Then, change the value of LAN_IFACE to br0:

```
LAN_IFACE="br0"
```

Restart and test everything according to Chapter 3, and you are set.

Discussion

Ethernet bridges join subnets into a single broadcast domain, with broadcast traffic going everywhere at once. A bridge is easy to set up and is transparent to your users. Your subnets function as a single network segment, so LAN services work without any additional tweaking, such as network printing, Samba servers, and Network Neighborhood. You can move computers around without having to give them new addresses.

Bridging is inefficient because it generates more broadcast traffic. So, it doesn't scale up very far. An Ethernet bridge operates at the data link layer (layer 2) of the OSI Model. It sees MAC addresses, but not IP addresses. Bridge traffic cannot be filtered with *iptables*; if you want to do this, use *ebtables*, which is designed for bridging firewalls.

Routing gives more control over your network segments; you can filter traffic any way you like. It's more efficient than bridging because it's not spewing broadcasts all over the place. Routing scales up indefinitely, as demonstrated by the existence of the Internet. Its main disadvantage in the LAN is it's a bit more work to implement.

See Recipe 4.12 to learn how to use routing instead of bridging on your wireless access point.

See Also

- Chapter 6

4.12   Using Routing Instead of Bridging

Problem

You would rather use routing between your two LAN segments instead of bridging because it gives better performance and more control. For example, you might set up a separate link just to give Internet access to visitors and easily keep them out of your network. Or, you want some separation and different sets of LAN services for each network segment. You know it's a bit more work to set up, but that doesn't bother you, you just want to know how to make it go.

Solution

The example access point in this chapter has three Ethernet interfaces: *ath0*, *eth0*, and *eth1*. Instead of bridging *ath0* and *eth0* to create the *br0* LAN interface, *ath0* and *eth0* are going to be two separate LAN interfaces, and *eth1* will still be the WAN interface. *iptables* will forward traffic between *ath0* and *eth0*, and *dnsmasq.conf* will need some additional lines to handle the extra subnet.

This recipe assumes you are using either WPA-PSK or WPA-Enterprise with a separate RADIUS server. (See the previous recipes in this chapter to learn how to configure encryption and authentication.) You may create an open access point for testing by commenting out the two lines that control *hostapd*:

```
##/etc/network/interfaces
auto lo
iface lo inet loopback

auto ath0
iface ath0 inet static
        address 192.168.2.50
        network 192.168.2.0
        netmask 255.255.255.0
        broadcast 192.168.2.255
        post-down wlanconfig ath0 destroy
```

```
        pre-up wlanconfig ath0 create wlandev wifi0 wlanmode ap
        pre-up iwconfig ath0 essid "alrac-net" channel 01 rate auto
        pre-up ifconfig ath0 up
        pre-up sleep 3
        up hostapd -B /etc/hostapd.conf
        post-down killall hostapd

auto eth0
iface eth0 inet static
        address 192.168.1.50
        network 192.168.1.0
        netmask 255.255.255.0
        broadcast 192.168.1.255

auto eth1
iface eth1 inet static
        address 12.169.163.241
        gateway 12.169.163.1
        netmask 255.255.255.0

##/etc/dnsmasq.conf
domain-needed
bogus-priv
local=/alrac.net/
expand-hosts
domain=alrac.net
listen-address=127.0.0.1
listen-address=192.168.1.50
listen-address=192.168.2.50
server=12.169.174.2
server=12.169.174.3

dhcp-range=lan,192.168.1.100,192.168.1.200,255.255.255.0,12h
dhcp-range=wifi,192.168.2.100,192.168.2.200,255.255.255.0,12h
dhcp-lease-max=100

#default gateway
dhcp-option=lan,3,192.168.1.50
dhcp-option=wifi,3,192.168.2.50

#DNS server
dhcp-option=lan,6,192.168.1.50
dhcp-option=wifi,6,192.168.2.50

#assign static IP addresses
dhcp-host=stinkpad,192.168.2.74,net:wifi
dhcp-host=penguina,192.168.2.75,net:wifi
dhcp-host=uberpc,192.168.1.76,net:lan
dhcp-host=xena,192.168.1.10,net:lan
```

You'll need to add a batch of *iptables* rules to your firewall script. See the Discussion for a complete example *iptables* firewall script.

Discussion

This *iptables* example forwards all traffic freely between your two LAN segments, and makes name services available to all. This is a liberal configuration with no restrictions.

Remember that broadcast traffic does not cross routes, and some network protocols are nonroutable, such as Samba and other NetBIOS traffic. All routable traffic, such as SSH, *ping*, mail and web servers, and so forth will travel between your subnets with no problems.

By routing between your wired and wireless network segments, your options are legion: limit the services available to either network segment, filter on individual hosts, do some fine-grained traffic shaping—anything you want to do is possible.

dnsmasq.conf uses RFC 2132 numbers to represent servers, so refer to it for a complete list. Some common servers are:

dhcp-option=2,[*offset*]
> Time offset from UTC (Coordinated Universal Time). You'll have to manually adjust this twice per year if you are afflicted with daylight saving time. But at least you'll control everything from the server. For example, pacific standard time is written as dhcp-option=2,-28800, which equals UTC -8 hours.

dhcp-option=3,[*IP address*]
> Send clients the default route. Use this when *dnsmasq* is not on the same box as your router.

dhcp-option=7, [*IP address*]
> Syslog server.

dhcp-option=33, wifi, [*destination IP address, router address*]
> Assign a static route to the "wifi" group. You may list as many routes as you want. Each route is defined by a pair of comma-separated IP addresses.

dhcp-option=40, [*domain*]
> NIS domain name.

dhcp-option=41,[*IP address*]
> NIS domain server.

dhcp-option=42,[*IP address*]
> NTP server.

dhcp-option=69,[*IP address*]
> SMTP server.

dhcp-option=70,[*IP address*]
> POP server.

dhcp-option=72,[*IP address*]
> HTTP server.

Because our LAN routes pass through an *iptables* firewall with a default DROP policy, permitted traffic must be explicitly accepted and forwarded.

If you followed Chapter 3 to build your *iptables* firewall, don't forget you can use /etc/init.d/firewall/stop|start|restart when you're testing new rules.

Here is a complete example */usr/local/bin/fw-nat* that gives the wired and wireless subnets nearly unlimited access to each other:

```
#!/bin/sh
#iptables firewall script for sharing a cable or DSL Internet
#connection, with no public services

#define variables
ipt="/sbin/iptables"
mod="/sbin/modprobe"
LAN_IFACE="eth0"
WAN_IFACE="eth1"
WIFI_IFACE="ath0"

#load kernel modules
$mod ip_tables
$mod iptable_filter
$mod iptable_nat
$mod ip_conntrack
$mod ipt_LOG
$mod ipt_limit
$mod ipt_state
$mod iptable_mangle
$mod ipt_MASQUERADE
$mod ip_nat_ftp
$mod ip_nat_irc
$mod ip_conntrack_ftp
$mod ip_conntrack_irc

# Flush all active rules and delete all custom chains
$ipt -F
$ipt -t nat -F
$ipt -t mangle -F
$ipt -X
$ipt -t nat -X
$ipt -t mangle -X

#Set default policies
$ipt -P INPUT DROP
$ipt -P FORWARD DROP
$ipt -P OUTPUT ACCEPT
$ipt -t nat -P OUTPUT ACCEPT
$ipt -t nat -P PREROUTING ACCEPT
$ipt -t nat -P POSTROUTING ACCEPT
$ipt -t mangle -P PREROUTING ACCEPT
$ipt -t mangle -P POSTROUTING ACCEPT
```

```
#this line is necessary for the loopback interface
#and internal socket-based services to work correctly
$ipt -A INPUT -i lo -j ACCEPT

#Allow incoming SSH from the wired LAN only to the gateway box
$ipt -A INPUT -p tcp -i $LAN_IFACE -s 192.168.1.0/24 --dport 22 \
-m state --state NEW -j ACCEPT

#Enable IP masquerading
$ipt -t nat -A POSTROUTING -o $WAN_IFACE -j SNAT --to-source 12.34.56.789

#Enable unrestricted outgoing traffic, incoming
#is restricted to locally-initiated sessions only
#unrestricted between WIFI and LAN
$ipt -A INPUT -m state --state RELATED,ESTABLISHED -j ACCEPT
$ipt -A FORWARD -i $WAN_IFACE -o $LAN_IFACE -m state --state \
ESTABLISHED,RELATED -j ACCEPT
$ipt -A FORWARD -i $LAN_IFACE -o $WAN_IFACE -m state --state \
NEW,ESTABLISHED,RELATED -j ACCEPT
#$ipt -A FORWARD -i $LAN_IFACE -o $WIFI_IFACE -m state --state \
NEW,ESTABLISHED,RELATED -j ACCEPT
#$ipt -A FORWARD -i $WIFI_IFACE -o $LAN_IFACE -m state --state \
NEW,ESTABLISHED,RELATED -j ACCEPT
#$ipt -A FORWARD -i $WIFI_IFACE -o $WAN_IFACE -m state --state \
NEW,ESTABLISHED,RELATED -j ACCEPT
#$ipt -A FORWARD -i $WAN_IFACE -o $WIFI_IFACE -m state --state \
ESTABLISHED,RELATED -j ACCEPT

#Enable internal DHCP and DNS
$ipt -A INPUT -p udp -i $LAN_IFACE -s 192.168.1.0/24 --dport 53 -j ACCEPT
$ipt -A INPUT -p tcp -i $LAN_IFACE -s 192.168.1.0/24 --dport 53 -j ACCEPT
$ipt -A INPUT -p udp -i $LAN_IFACE  --dport 67  -j ACCEPT
$ipt -A INPUT -p udp -i $WIFI_IFACE -s 192.168.2.0/24 --dport 53 -j ACCEPT
$ipt -A INPUT -p tcp -i $WIFI_IFACE -s 192.168.2.0/24 --dport 53 -j ACCEPT
$ipt -A INPUT -p udp -i $WIFI_IFACE  --dport 67  -j ACCEPT

#allow LAN to access router HTTP server
$ipt -A INPUT -p tcp -i $LAN_IFACE   --dport 443  -j ACCEPT
$ipt -A INPUT -p tcp -i $WIFI_IFACE  --dport 443  -j ACCEPT

# Accept ICMP echo-request and time-exceeded
$ipt -A INPUT -p icmp --icmp-type echo-request  -j ACCEPT
$ipt -A INPUT -p icmp --icmp-type time-exceeded -j ACCEPT
$ipt -A INPUT -p icmp --icmp-type destination-unreachable -j ACCEPT

#Reject connection attempts not initiated from inside the LAN
$ipt -A INPUT -p tcp --syn -j DROP

echo "The firewall has now started up and is faithfully protecting your system"
```

See Also

- Chapter 3
- man 5 dhclient
- *dnsmasq.conf* is a great help resource
- *dnsmasq* home page (*http://www.thekelleys.org.uk/dnsmasq/doc.html*) is where you'll find mailing list archives and excellent help documents
- Chapter 24, "Managing Name Resolution," in *Linux Cookbook*, by Carla Schroder (O'Reilly)

4.13 Probing Your Wireless Interface Card

Problem

Your wireless interface card came in a colorful box and wads of multilanguage documentation. But none of it gives you the technical specs that you really want, such as supported channels, encryption protocols, modes, frequencies—you know, the useful information.

Solution

Both *wlanconfig*, which is part of the MadWiFi driver package, and *iwlist*, which is part of *wireless-tools*, will probe your wireless card and tell you what it can do, like this command that displays what protocols the card supports:

```
pyramid:~# wlanconfig ath0 list caps
ath0=7782e40f<WEP,TKIP,AES,AES_CCM,HOSTAP,TXPMGT,SHSLOT,SHPREAMBLE,\
TKIPMIC,WPA1,WPA2,WME>
```

This means this is a nice modern card that supports all of the important encryption and authentication protocols, and it can serve as an access point.

This command shows all of the channels and frequencies the card supports:

```
pyramid:~# wlanconfig ath0 list chan
```

Find out what kind of keys your card supports:

```
pyramid:~# iwlist ath0 key
```

Which card functions are configurable:

```
pyramid:~# iwlist ath0 event
```

This particular card supports variable transmission power rates:

```
pyramid:~# iwlist ath0 txpower
```

What bit-rates are supported?

```
pyramidwrap:~# iwlist ath0 rate
```

The *iwconfig* command shows the card's current configuration:

```
pyramidwrap:~# iwconfig ath0
```

Discussion

What does this output mean?

```
ath0=7782e40f<WEP,TKIP,AES,AES_CCM,HOSTAP,TXPMGT,SHSLOT,SHPREAMBLE,\
TKIPMIC,WPA1,WPA2,WME>
```

It means this particular card supports WEP encryption, Temporal Key Integrity Protocol (TKIP), Advanced Encryption Standard with Counter Mode with CBC-MAC Protocol (AES and AES_CCM), can function as an Access Point, has variable transmission power, supports TKIP Message Identity Check, WPA/WPA2, frame bursting, and Wireless Media Extensions.

SHSLOT and SHPREAMBLE stand for "short slot" and "short preamble," which have to do with faster transmission speeds. Matthew Gast's *802.11 Wireless Networks: The Definitive Guide* (O'Reilly) tells you all about these.

See Also

- Pyramid Linux does not include manpages, so you should install the applications in this chapter on a PC to obtain them, or rely on Google
- *wlanconfig* is part of MadWiFi-ng
- man 8 iwlist
- man 8 wlanconfig
- *802.11 Wireless Networks: The Definitive Guide*, by Matthew Gast (O'Reilly)

4.14   Changing the Pyramid Router's Hostname

Problem

Pyramid is a nice name, but you really want to change it to something else. You tried editing */etc/hostname*, but the name reset to Pyramid after reboot. Arg! How do you make it what you want?

Solution

The files listed in */etc/rw/* are mounted in a temporary writeable filesystem, and are copied from */etc/ro* at boot. */etc/hostname* is symlinked to */rw/etc/hostname*:

```
pyramid:~# ls -l /etc/hostname
lrwxrwxrwx  1 root root 18 Oct  30 2006 /etc/hostname -> ../rw/etc/hostname
```

So, you can make */etc/hostname* immutable (remove the symlink to */rw/etc/hostname*), or edit */ro/etc/hostname*.

Discussion

The filesystem is set up this way to reduce writes, because Compact Flash supports a limited number of writes.

You can use *find* to see which files in */etc* are symlinks:

```
pyramid:~# find /etc -maxdepth 1 -type l -ls
   6051    0 lrwxrwxrwx  1 root     root       14 Oct  4  2006 /etc/mtab -> ../proc/
mounts
   6052    0 lrwxrwxrwx  1 root     root       21 Oct  4  2006 /etc/resolv.conf -> ../
rw/etc/resolv.conf
   6079    0 lrwxrwxrwx  1 root     root       30 Dec 31  2006 /etc/localtime -> /usr/
share/zoneinfo/US/Pacific
   6081    0 lrwxrwxrwx  1 root     root       18 Oct  4  2006 /etc/hostname -> ../rw/
etc/hostname
   6156    0 lrwxrwxrwx  1 root     root       15 Oct  4  2006 /etc/issue -> ../rw/
etc/issue
   6195    0 lrwxrwxrwx  1 root     root       17 Oct  4  2006 /etc/zebra -> ../usr/
local/etc/
   6227    0 lrwxrwxrwx  1 root     root       16 Oct  4  2006 /etc/resolv -> ../rw/
etc/resolv
   6426    0 lrwxrwxrwx  1 root     root       19 Oct  4  2006 /etc/issue.net -> ../
rw/etc/issue.net
   6427    0 lrwxrwxrwx  1 root     root       17 Oct  4  2006 /etc/adjtime -> ../rw/
etc/adjtime
```

See Also

- man 1 find
- man 1 ls

4.15   Turning Off Antenna Diversity

Problem

Your wireless interface supports using two antennas, but you're using just one. You know that this means half of your broadcast and unicast packets are hitting a dead end, which can hurt performance. How do you send power only to one antenna?

Solution

Set Pyramid's filesystem to read/write, then add the following lines to */etc/sysctl.conf*:

```
dev.wifi0.diversity = 0
dev.wifi0.rxantenna = 1
dev.wifi0.txantenna = 1
```

Then, load the new configuration:

```
pyramid:~# /sbin/sysctl -p
```

If the antenna is connected to the second port, just change 1 to 2 and reload *sysctl*.

Discussion

The Linux kernel sees the wireless interface as *wifi0*, which you can see by running dmesg | grep wifi. The MadWiFi driver creates a virtual interface named ath0.

Using two antennas might improve the quality of your wireless service, or it might not. Only one is used at a time, the one with the stronger signal.

Polarization diversity is when one antenna receives a stronger signal because it is lined up differently than the other one. Spatial diversity refers to distance between two antennas. A few inches might make a difference because of reflections, fading, physical barriers, and interference.

The radio hardware evaluates the signal strength at the beginning of the transmission and compares both antennas. Then, it selects the stronger antenna to receive the rest of the transmission. The only user-configurable options are to turn diversity on or off.

Multiple-input/multiple-output (MIMO) technology promises higher data rates and better performance by using both antennas at the same time. Different vendors mean different things when they say MIMO.

Some are referring to multiple data streams, while others use it to mean plain old channel bonding. The goal is the same: more bandwidth and reliability for delivering video, VoIP, and other high-demand applications.

There is considerable controversy and endless arguments over antenna placement, what kind of antennas to use, and how many. Pointless arguments can be fun; when that gets dull, whip out your 802.11 network analyzer and collect some useful data to help you figure it out.

See Also

- Chapter 16, "802.11 Hardware," in *802.11 Wireless Networks: The Definitive Guide*, Second Edition, by Matthew Gast (O'Reilly)
- Chapter 24, "802.11 Network Analysis," in *802.11 Wireless Networks: The Definitive Guide*, Second Edition

4.16   Managing dnsmasq's DNS Cache

Problem

You know that *dnsmasq* automatically creates a local DNS cache. How do you know it's working? How do you see what's in it, and how do you flush it when you're making changes to DNS and want to be sure it's caching fresh data?

Solution

It's easy to see if it's working. From any Linux client or from your Pyramid server, query any Internet site with the *dig* command twice:

```
$ dig oreilly.com
<snip much output>
;; Query time: 75 msec
;; SERVER: 192.168.1.50#53(192.168.1.50)
$ dig oreilly.com
<snip much output>
;; Query time: 3 msec
;; SERVER: 192.168.1.50#53(192.168.1.50)
```

The second request is answered from your local *dnsmasq* cache, so it is faster. This also verifies that your clients are querying the correct DNS server.

What if you want to flush *dnsmasq*'s cache? Just restart it:

```
pyramid:~# killall dnsmasq
```

dnsmasq is controlled from */etc/inittab*, so it will automatically restart.

To view the contents of the cache, first open */etc/inittab* and comment out the line that starts *dnsmasq*:

```
pyramid:~# /sbin/rw
pyramid:~# nano /etc/inittab
# dnsmasq.  This should always be on.
# DN:23:respawn:/sbin/dnsmasq -k  > /dev/null 2>&1
```

Tell *init* to reread *inittab*, stop the active *dnsmasq* process, then start *dnsmasq* in debugging mode:

```
pyramid:~# telinit q
pyramid:~# killall dnsmasq
pyramid:~# dnsmasq -d
```

This runs it in the foreground, so the next thing you need to do is open a second SSH session, or log in on the serial console, and run this command:

```
pyramid:~# killall -USR1 dnsmasq
```

This dumps the cache contents to your first screen. You should see just your localhosts. This line tells you your cache is empty:

```
dnsmasq: cache size 150, 0/0 cache insertions re-used unexpired cache entries.
```

Start *dnsmasq* again, visit some web sites from client PCs to generate some cache entries, then dump the cache again to see what they look like. You should see a lot more entries now. When you're finished, put */etc/inittab* back the way it was, and rerun `telinit q` and `/sbin/ro`.

Discussion

It's unlikely that you'll ever have to do anything with your *dnsmasq* cache because it's pretty much self-maintaining. There are three options in */etc/dnsmasq.conf* for configuring cache behavior:

`local-ttl`

The default is zero, which means do not cache responses from */etc/hosts* and your DHCP leases. This ensures fresh local data all the time. If your network is stable and doesn't have DHCP clients popping in and out a lot, you can set a Time To Live (TTL) value to speed up local look ups.

`no-negcache`

Do not cache negative responses. Caching negative responses speeds up performance by caching "no such domain" responses, so your clients don't wait for additional lookups to fail. *dnsmasq* handles negative caching well, so you shouldn't disable negative caching unless it causes problems.

`cache-size`

The default is 150 names. The maximum is around 2,000. Because the cache is stored in RAM, having a too large cache will hurt router performance without appreciable gain. 150 is just fine for most sites; I wouldn't go over 300.

You are at the mercy of the administrators of the authoritative servers for domains that you visit. If they make changes to their DNS without setting short TTL values, stale data will be cached all over the Internet until their TTLs expire. It can be helpful to flush your *dnsmasq* cache when you're debugging DNS and trying to figure out if a DNS problem is local or remote.

Here are some examples of the output you'll see. This is an empty cache showing only local DNS:

```
pyramidwrap:~# dnsmasq -d
dnsmasq: started, version 2.23 cachesize 150
dnsmasq: compile time options: IPv6 GNU-getopt ISC-leasefile no-DBus
dnsmasq: DHCP, IP range 192.168.1.100 -- 192.168.1.200, lease time 10h
dnsmasq: using local addresses only for domain alrac.net
dnsmasq: read /etc/hosts - 4 addresses
dnsmasq: reading /etc/resolv.conf
dnsmasq: using nameserver 12.169.174.3#53
dnsmasq: using nameserver 12.169.174.2#53
```

```
dnsmasq: using local addresses only for domain alrac.net
dnsmasq: cache size 150, 0/0 cache insertions re-used unexpired cache entries.
dnsmasq: Host                    Address                       Flags      Expires
dnsmasq: stinkpad.alrac.net      192.168.1.102                 4FRI    H
dnsmasq: localhost               127.0.0.1                     4F I    H
dnsmasq: xena.alrac.net          192.168.1.10                  4FRI    H
dnsmasq: pyramid.alrac.net       192.168.1.50                  4FRI    H
dnsmasq: stinkpad                192.168.1.102                 4F I    H
dnsmasq: xena                    192.168.1.10                  4F I    H
dnsmasq: localhost.alrac.net     127.0.0.1                     4FRI    H
dnsmasq: pyramid                 192.168.1.50                  4F I    H
```

This is a snippet from a populated cache:

```
dnsmasq: cache size 150, 0/178 cache insertions re-used unexpired cache entries.
dnsmasq: Host                    Address           Flags      Expires
dnsmasq: stinkpad.alrac.net      192.168.1.102     4FRI    H
dnsmasq: localhost               127.0.0.1         4F I    H
dnsmasq: i.cnn.net               64.236.16.137     4F         Wed Jan 24 15:36:42
2007
dnsmasq: i.cnn.net               64.236.16.138     4F         Wed Jan 24 15:36:42
2007
dnsmasq: bratgrrl.com            67.43.0.135       4F         Wed Jan 24 17:45:49
2007
dnsmasq: a.tribalfusion.com      204.11.109.63     4F         Wed Jan 24 15:29:08
2007
dnsmasq: a.tribalfusion.com      204.11.109.64     4F         Wed Jan 24 15:29:08
2007
dnsmasq: ad.3ad.doubleclick.net  216.73.87.52      4F         Wed Jan 24 15:27:29
2007
dnsmasq: ads.cnn.com             64.236.22.103     4F         Wed Jan 24 16:21:41
2007
```

Table 4-1 shows what the flags mean.

- Both F and R may be set for names from DHCP or /etc/hosts.

Table 4-1. dnsmasq cache flags and their meanings

Flag	Meaning
4	IPv4 address
6	IPv6 address
C	CNAME
F	Forward (name → address) mapping
R	Reverse (address → name) mapping
I	Immortal (no expiry time)
D	Originates from DHCP
N	Negative (name known not to have address)
X	No such domain (name known not to exist)
H	Originates from /etc/hosts

See Also

- `man 8 dnsmasq` contains a wealth of helpful information about all the available command-line options, many of which are also *dnsmasq.conf* options
- *dnsmasq.conf* is also a great help resource
- *dnsmasq* home page (*http://www.thekelleys.org.uk/dnsmasq/doc.html*) is where you'll find mailing list archives and excellent help documents
- Chapter 24, "Managing Name Resolution," in *Linux Cookbook*, by Carla Schroder (O'Reilly)

4.17 Managing Windows' DNS Caches

Problem

You know that Windows 2000, XP, and 2003 Server include DNS resolver caches by default. Which is a big surprise to most Windows users, who sometimes get stuck with stale data and don't understand why some addresses are not resolving correctly. Most of the time you don't even have to think about it, but when you're making changes, you want to be sure that your clients are receiving fresh DNS information. How do you handle this?

Solution

On Windows clients, open a DOS window and run this command to see the contents of the cache:

```
C:\> ipconfig /displaydns | more
```

This command clears the cache:

```
C:\> ipconfig /flushdns
```

The default TTL is 86,400 seconds, or one day, for positive responses. Answers to negative queries are stored for 300 seconds (5 minutes). You may change these values, or disable caching entirely by editing the Windows Registry. On Windows 2000, open the Registry Editor and change the TTL for positive entries by creating or modifying the DWORD value in:

```
HKEY_LOCAL_MACHINE\SYSTEM\CurrentControlSet\Services\Dnscache\Parameters
DWORD: MaxCacheEntryTtlLimit
Value: 14400
```

14,400 seconds is four hours, which is typical for most ISPs these days. 0 disables all caching. Be sure you enter your values as Decimal Base, not Hexadecimal Base.

Disable negative answers with this key:

```
HKEY_LOCAL_MACHINE\SYSTEM\CurrentControlSet\Services\Dnscache\Parameters
DWORD: NegativeCacheTime
Value: 0
```

On Windows XP and 2003, change the TTL for positive entries with a different DWORD:

```
HKEY_LOCAL_MACHINE\SYSTEM\CurrentControlSet\ Services\Dnscache\Parameters
DWORD: MaxCacheTtl
Value: 14400
```

Turn off negative caching with this one:

```
HKEY_LOCAL_MACHINE\SYSTEM\CurrentControlSet\Services\Dnscache\Parameters
DWORD: MaxNegativeCacheTtl
Value: 0
```

You may disable caching entirely by setting both values to zero. Reboot, as always, to activate the changes.

Discussion

Linux clients do not activate their own DNS caches by default; you have to set these up on purpose. Client-side caching is a nice thing that speeds up lookups. All those caches cause problems only when DNS is changed and the caches get stale.

See Also

- The documentation for your particular flavors of Windows; a quick Google search on "windows dns cache" should get you all the information you need

4.18   Updating the Time at Boot

Problem

You have one of those newfangled routerboards that doesn't have a CMOS battery. BIOS settings are written to nonvolatile RAM, but the time and date are lost with every power-cycle. How do you make it set the time correctly at boot?

Solution

With good ole *ntpdate*. First, edit */etc/default/ntp-servers* so that it points to *pool.ntp.org*:

```
# /sbin/rw
# nano /etc/default/ntp-servers
NTPSERVERS="pool.ntp.org"
```

Then create a startup link so it will run at boot:

```
# ln /etc/init.d/ntpdate /etc/rc2.d/S90ntpdate
```

Now every time you boot up your routerboard, it will set the correct time. You can verify this with the date command:

```
# date
Mon Jan 29 20:52:50 UTC 2007
```

Discussion

If you are familiar with the NTP documentation, you're aware that the fine NTP folks keep trying to get rid of *ntpdate* and replace it with the nptd -g command. However, *ntpdate* still works best for large time corrections.

See Also

- man 1 ntpdate
- Chapter 19, "Keeping Time with NTP," in *Linux Cookbook*, by Carla Schroder (O'Reilly)

## CHAPTER 5

Building a VoIP Server with Asterisk

5.0   Introduction

This chapter introduces Asterisk, the Private Branch eXchange (PBX) implemented entirely in software. Asterisk is the hot new darling of the telephony set; it's both a replacement for existing outmoded and overpriced PBX systems, and it's a doorway to the future. Our current telephone system (at least in the U.S.) is excellent because it's pretty much the same technology invented by Mr. Bell. It has been extensively refined over the years, but hasn't seen much in the way of invention. We won't see videophones, video conferencing, or integration with all manner of software and portable devices on the old-fashioned public switched telephone network (PSTN). That's coming with Voice-over-Internet-Protocol (VoIP), packet-switched networks, and broadband Internet.

Asterisk is a PBX and a powerful IP telephony server. Asterisk supports multiple telephony protocols (including SIP, IAX, and H.323), integrates the PSTN with VoIP, and allows you to mix-and-match services and devices (analog, digital, wired, wireless, IP). You may use it as little more than a glorified answering machine, or as a local PBX that is integrated with your existing telephone service, or as part of a wide-area IP telephone network that spans continents. Anywhere the Internet goes, Asterisk goes.

This chapter covers installing and configuring Asterisk 1.4. We'll set up basic business PBX functions: voicemail, a digital receptionist, Internet call services, integration with analog phone service, user management, conferencing, and customizing hold music and voice prompts. The example configurations in this chapter are as stripped-down and simple as possible. They are fully functional, but needless complexities are left out. Don't let the other geeks pressure you into thinking you have to over-complicate your Asterisk configurations because that is the path to instability and madness. Figuring out dialplan logic is the hard part; once you have that down, you'll be able to easily expand on the recipes in this chapter to accommodate more users and functions.

Asterisk is free in two ways: free of cost and licensed under the GPL. Don't let the word *free* steer you in the wrong direction. VoIP call processing requires a substantial amount of processing power, so don't look to Asterisk as a way to keep old 486s in service. You'll want good-quality hardware and network bandwidth sufficient to handle your workload. How much capacity do you need? There are so many variables involved in calculating this that I'm going to dodge the question entirely, and refer you to the Asterisk support page (*http://www.asterisk.org/support*) and the Voip-info.org Wiki (*http://voip-info.org/wiki/*). These are the mother lodes of Asterisk help and information.

Test-lab Hardware and Software

Asterisk's flexibility is its strength and main drawback—there are so many options that you can easily get lost. You can put together a three-node test lab for practically no money, if you have some old PCs lying around. We'll build one in this chapter consisting of an Asterisk server running on Linux, and two client PCs running software IP phones (*softphones*). You'll need a switch to connect the three PCs, sound cards, and sets of speakers and microphones or headsets. If you get USB headsets you won't need sound cards, speakers, or microphones.

You'll need a broadband Internet connection to place calls over the Internet. VoIP calls consume 30–90 Kbps each way. T1/E1 gives the best call quality. DSL is a decent option, especially if you have a dedicated DSL line just for VoIP. Even better is symmetric DSL instead of the usual ADSL, if you can get it. Cable Internet also works well, if you have a good service provider, and can get adequate upstream bandwidth.

Production Hardware and Software

Asterisk was designed to take advantage of all the cheap power we get in x86 hardware. Asterisk is CPU and memory-intensive, so don't skimp on these. The alternative is much-more-expensive specialized digital sound-processing hardware, so if you find yourself wishing for interface cards that take some of the load off your system's CPU, just remember that they cost more than a PC upgrade.

The types of IP phones you choose can either make your life easy or make it heck because they have a big effect on call quality. Hardware IP phones (*hardphones*) have Ethernet ports and plug directly into your network. Good ones start around $100, and offer all manner of options: speakerphones, headset ports, wireless, and multiple lines. They smooth out echo and jitter, and look and operate like normal office phones.

Headsets combined with softphones (software phones that run on a PC) can save some money because a lot of softphones are free of cost, or less expensive than hardphones. They also save on Ethernet ports and wiring. You'll have the option of wired or wireless headsets, and many different softphones to choose from. You'll want to test them first because there are considerable differences in call quality and usability. A common flaw in many of them is a tiny, cluttered, nonresizable interface. Another factor to watch out for is putting them on underpowered or overworked PCs—it takes a fair number of CPU cycles to process VoIP calls, so the computer must be able to handle call-processing and whatever other jobs the user needs to do.

If you have analog phones you can't bear to part with, you can get individual analog telephone adapters (ATA), or PCI adapters that install in the Asterisk server, like the Digium, Sangoma, or Rhino PCI analog interface cards. You can even get channel banks to handle large numbers of analog phones. There are a wealth of standalone multiport analog adapters with all manner of bells and whistles. These are nice and easy, but watch out for high prices and protocol support. Many of them do not support Inter-Asterisk Exchange (IAX), which is a useful and efficient native Asterisk protocol. Everything should support Session Initiation Protocol (SIP), which has become the most popular VoIP protocol.

Visit the Asterisk and AstLinux user list archives to get information on specific brands and models.

Call Quality

The debate over which type of IP phone to use rages on endlessly, but the reality is there are more differences between brands than between types of phones. In general, hardphones sound and perform the best. Good softphones coupled with decent-quality sound gear perform well. Analog phones require adapters, and have problems with echo. Analog adapter cards should have hardware echo cancellation, and Digium also offers a software High Performance Echo Canceller (HPEC). This is free to Digium customers, and $10 per channel for users of other PCI analog adapters.

Latency is the enemy of VoIP, so you need to ensure that your LAN is squeaky-clean: no hubs, because collision domains kill call quality, and are so last-millennium anyway; no antique cabling, incorrect cabling, flaky NICs, or virus-infected hosts clogging the wires with mass quantities of contagion.

You cannot control what happens when your VoIP bits leave your network. Talk to your ISP to see what it can do to help with your VoIP. It might even offer a service-level agreement with guarantees.

Digium, Asterisk, and the Zapata Telephony Project

Mark Spencer, the inventor of Asterisk, wanted an affordable, flexible PBX for his small business. There was no such thing at the time, so he invented his own. Mr. Spencer sat down and started coding, and implemented PBX functionality in software that runs on Linux on ordinary x86 hardware. But it still couldn't do all that much, because Asterisk had no way to interface with ordinary telephony hardware.

That gap was filled when Jim Dixon of the Zapata Telephony Project invented an interface card to do just that. That first card was called *Tormenta*, or hurricane.

Asterisk and Zapata came together like chocolate and peanut butter and became Digium, Inc. The Tormenta card evolved into the Digium line of T1/E1 cards. Digium also supplies analog adapters for analog telephone lines and analog telephones.

Digium is not the only supplier of interface cards and adapters; a brief Google search will find all sorts of VoIP hardware vendors.

There are recipes in this chapter for recording your own voice prompts. Digium will also sell you professionally recorded custom voice prompts in English, French, or Spanish. English and Spanish voice prompts are recorded by Allison Smith. You can hear her voice in the sound files that come with Asterisk. French and English recordings are made by June Wallack.

Asterisk Implementations

AsteriskNOW (*http://www.asterisknow.org/*) is a software appliance that includes Asterisk, an rPath Linux-based operating system, and excellent web-based administration interfaces for both Asterisk and rPath Linux. It is freely available from Digium.

Asterisk Business and Enterprise Editions (*http://www.digium.com/*) are the commercially-supported versions available from Digium. These are closer to turnkey than the free edition, and Digium's support is good.

Trixbox (*http://www.trixbox.org*) is another popular Asterix bundle. This comes with everything: the CentOS operating system, a graphical management console, MySQL database backend, SugarCRM, HUDLite, and many more nicely integrated goodies. This is a large package—you'll need a couple of gigabytes of drive space just for the installation. The latest release has a modular installer that lets you choose which bits you want to install.

AstLinux (*http://www.astlinux.org/*) is a specialized Linux distribution that contains the operating system and Asterisk in about 40 MB, which makes it a perfect candidate to run on single-board computers like Soekris, PC Engines WRAP boards, and Gumstix Way Small Computers. It also runs fine on small form-factor boxes like Via, and ordinary PC hardware.

FreePBX (*http://www.freepbx.org/*) is a web-based graphical management interface to Asterisk. It used to be called AMP (Asterisk Management Portal), and is included in Trixbox.

The Asterisk Appliance Developer's Kit (*http://www.digium.com/en/products/hardware/aadk.php*) includes application development tools and a specialized hardware appliance for developing customized embedded PBXs. It's a complete package that includes an IP phone, all manner of documentation and training, and even Asterisk memorabilia. This is targeted at resellers, and businesses that have the in-house talent to develop a customized appliance.

Using Asterisk

You can have a test lab up and running in a couple of hours. Asterisk has a rather steep learning curve, so you'll pick it up more quickly if you have both telephony and Linux networking experience. But don't let a lack of experience stop you. Make a little test lab and learn your way around it before trying to build a production system. It's fun, it's endlessly flexible, and having control over your own systems is always good.

While you can compile and run Asterisk on any operating system (or try to), Asterisk works best on Linux. Asterisk is such a fast-moving target that by the time you read this it might run perfectly on all operating systems, so check the current documentation.

AsteriskNOW is an excellent Asterisk implementation that claims it will have you up and running in 30 minutes. See Recipes 5.22 and 5.23 near the end of this chapter for a good introduction to using AsteriskNOW.

See Also

- The History of Zapata Telephony and How It Relates to the Asterisk PBX:
  http://www.asteriskdocs.org/modules/tinycontent/index.php?id=10

5.1   Installing Asterisk from Source Code

Problem

You're not sure what the best way to install Asterisk is—should you install from your distribution's packages, or do a source install?

Solution

Currently, there are packages only for Debian, and they are behind the current stable release. In this chapter, we're going to install Asterisk on CentOS 5.0. CentOS is a Red Hat Enterprise Linux clone. It's very stable, and Asterisk runs well on it.

See Recipe 5.2 for apt-getting your way to Asterisk on Debian.

Hardware requirements are the minimum suggested for a test system. Asterisk needs a lot of horsepower. Your Asterisk server must be a dedicated server—don't try to run other services on it.

Hardware requirements:

- A PC with at least a 500 MHz CPU
- 256 MB RAM
- CD drive
- 10 GB hard drive
- Sound card and speakers, or a USB headset
- An Internet connection for downloading additional sound files during the installation (optional)

Software requirements:

The standard Linux build environment, which includes *gcc*, *automake*, *glibc-devel*, *glibc-headers*, *glibc-kernheaders*, *binutils*, *doxygen*, and *kernel-devel*. Grab all of them at once by installing the Development Tools package group:

```
# yum groupinstall "Development Tools"
```

Then, install these packages to satisfy Asterisk dependencies:

```
# yum install ncurses ncurses-devel openssl openssl-devel zlib zlib-devel newt newt-
devel
```

Now, download the current releases of the three main source tarballs from Asterisk.org (*http://www.asterisk.org/downloads*) into the */usr/src* directory. This example uses the 1.4.4 release:

```
[root@asterisk1 src]# wget http://ftp.digium.com/pub/asterisk/releases/asterisk-1.4.
4.tar.gz \
http://ftp.digium.com/pub/zaptel/releases/zaptel-1.4.3.tar.gz \
http://ftp.digium.com/pub/libpri/releases/libpri-1.4.0.tar.gz
```

Unpack them:

```
[root@asterisk1 src]# tar zxvf asterisk-1.4.4.tar.gz
[root@asterisk1 src]# tar zxvf zaptel-1.4.3.tar.gz
[root@asterisk1 src]# tar zxvf libpri-1.4.0.tar.gz
```

As always, look in each source directory for READMEs, installation notes, and other important information, and review them before starting installation.

The three Asterisk packages must be installed in order. First, enter the Zaptel directory, and run these commands:

```
# cd zaptel-1.4.3
# make clean
# ./configure
# make
# make install
```

Then, change to the *libpri* directory and install it:

```
# cd ../libpri-1.4.0
# make clean
```

```
# make
# install
```

Now comes the big fun—installing Asterisk:

```
# cd ../asterisk-1.4.4
# make clean
# ./configure
# make menuselect
```

make menuselect is a good place to spend a bit of time reviewing your options. This is where you customize Asterisk, unlike previous versions that came in monolithic blobs:

```
************************************
     Asterisk Module Selection
************************************
     Press 'h' for help.
---> 1.  Applications
     2.  Call Detail Recording
     3.  Channel Drivers
     4.  Codec Translators
     5.  Format Interpreters
     6.  Dialplan Functions
     7.  PBX Modules
     8.  Resource Modules
     9.  Voicemail Build Options
     10. Compiler Flags
     11. Module Embedding
     12. Core Sound Packages
     13. Music On Hold File Packages
     14. Extras Sound Packages
```

Navigate with these commands:

```
scroll        => up/down arrows
(de)select    => Enter
select all    => F8
deselect all  => F7
back          => left arrow
quit          => q
save and quit => x
```

In the Module Selection menu, XXX means dependencies have not been met. *menuselect* tells you what you need to satisfy missing dependencies, as this example shows:

```
************************************
     Asterisk Module Selection
************************************
     Press 'h' for help.
     [*] 1.  codec_adpcm
     [*] 2.  codec_alaw
     [*] 3.  codec_a_mu
     [*] 4.  codec_g726
     [*] 5.  codec_gsm
```

```
[*] 6.  codec_ilbc
[*] 7.  codec_lpc10
XXX 8.  codec_speex
[*] 9.  codec_ulaw
[*] 10. codec_zap

Speex Coder/Decoder
Depends on: speex
```

In this example, I need to install the *speex-devel* package to satisfy the dependency. (Speex is great little patent-free compression format designed especially for voice communications.) These must be installed before Asterisk. To save time, go through all the *menuselect* options and note what packages, if any, you need to install. You want the *-devel* packages, which in this example is *speex-devel*. Install them all at once, then rerun make clean, ./configure, and make menuselect.

menuselect is a bit overwhelming, so if you don't understand all the options, accept the defaults. You can always redo it later.

Then run these commands:

```
# make
# make install
# make config
# make progdocs
```

You're all finished, and ready to start learning how to run your Asterisk server.

Discussion

If you are used to Asterisk 1.2, please note that the installation procedure is different. Now there are *./configure* options for the Zaptel drivers and Asterisk, which you can view with ./configure --help.

Soundfiles are installed differently than in 1.2. The Asterisk 1.4 tarball package includes English prompts in GSM format and the FreePlay MOH (Music-on-Hold) files in WAVE format. You may select more from *menuselect*. You might elect to install only the defaults, then add others later because some of the tarballs are huge. For example, *asterisk-extra-sounds-en-wav-1.4.1.tar.gz* is 144 MB.

It might seem unnecessary to run make clean on a new installation, but there are often the odd object files and other random leftover bits floating around. make clean ensures that you start with a clean slate.

Asterisk helpfully makes it clear when an installation command has succeeded, and tells you what to do next:

```
+--------- Asterisk Build Complete ---------+
+ Asterisk has successfully been built, and +
+ can be installed by running:              +
+                                           +
+               make install                +
+-------------------------------------------+
```

It is important to read the READMEs and other informational files in the source trees.

Zaptel drivers control the Digium interface cards, so you might think you don't need to bother with the drivers if you're not using Digium hardware. But you still need a timing device for functions like music on hold and conferencing. The *ztdummy* module provides this. In 2.6 kernels, it interacts directly with the system's hardware clock. In 2.4 kernels, it took its timing from the *usb-uhci* kernel module. Documents that refer to the *usb-uhci* module are outdated. You should be running Asterisk on a Linux distribution with a 2.6 kernel in any case. See the *README* in the Zaptel source directory to see which modules go with which hardware.

To see a list of the package groups on CentOS, use Yum:

```
$ yum grouplist
```

This command displays a list of packages in a group:

```
$ yum groupinfo "Development Tools"
```

See Also

- Asterisk Documentation Project: *http://www.asteriskdocs.org/modules/news/*
- Asterisk Support: *http://www.asterisk.org/support*
- Chapter 2, "Installing and Managing Software on RPM-Based Systems," in *Linux Cookbook*, by Carla Schroder (O'Reilly)

5.2   Installing Asterisk on Debian

Problem

You want to run your Asterisk server on Debian. Can you use *apt-get*? What are the package names?

Solution

Asterisk installs nicely on Debian with *apt-get*, with one exception: you still need to compile the Zaptel modules manually. And even that is easy, thanks to the *module-assistant* utility. First, install Asterisk with these commands:

```
# apt-get install asterisk asterisk-sounds-main asterisk-sounds-extra asterisk-config
asterisk-doc zaptel
```

Then, you will have to compile the Zaptel drivers from sources. The easy way is to use *module-assistant*. This is a slick little program that pulls in everything you need to compile and build kernel modules. Run these commands to install *module-assistant*, and then build and install the Zaptel drivers:

```
# apt-get install module-assistant
# module-assistant prepare
# module-assistant auto-install zaptel
```

This takes a short time if you already have a build environment on your PC; longer if *module-assistant* needs to download a lot of packages. When it's finished, run this command:

```
# update-modules
```

The last step is to configure Asterisk to start at boot, with the *update-rc.d* command:

```
# update-rc.d asterisk start 40 2 3 4 5 . stop 60 0 1 6 .
```

And that's it. Now you can start learning your way around your Asterisk server.

Discussion

What are these Zaptel thingies for, anyway? Zaptel drivers control the Digium interface cards, so you might think you don't need to bother with the drivers if you're not using Digium hardware. But, you still need a timing device for functions like music on hold and conferencing.

The *ztdummy* module provides this. In 2.6 kernels, it interacts directly with the system's hardware clock. In 2.4 kernels, it took its timing from the *usb-uhci* kernel module. Documents that refer to the *usb-uhci* module are outdated.

Debian packages are usually a bit behind the Asterisk releases, especially in Stable. To get newer Asterisk releases, you'll want Testing or Unstable.

Or, you can build Asterisk from the official Asterisk tarballs on Debian just like any other distribution.

See Also

- Asterisk Documentation Project: *http://www.asteriskdocs.org/modules/news/*
- Asterisk Support: *http://www.asterisk.org/support*
- man 8 module-assistant
- Chapter 2, "Installing and Managing Software on Debian-Based Systems," in *Linux Cookbook*, by Carla Schroder (O'Reilly)
- Chapter 7, "Starting and Stopping Linux," in *Linux Cookbook*

5.3   Starting and Stopping Asterisk

Problem

What is the best way to stop and start Asterisk? Does it need to be restarted when you change configuration files, or can you reload changes without disrupting service?

Solution

There are several ways to stop and start Asterisk, depending on what you want to do. You'll have two different command interfaces to use: the Linux command line, and the Asterisk command console. You should use the Asterisk console to control Asterisk.

After installing Asterisk, first reboot the system, then check to see if it is running with *ps*:

```
$ ps ax | grep asterisk
```

It should be, if you ran the `make config` command during installation, because this creates the files necessary to start up automatically at boot.

Then, all you do is attach to the running Asterisk server and open the console with this command:

```
[root@asterisk1 ~]# asterisk -rvvv
Asterisk 1.4.4, Copyright (C) 1999 - 2007 Digium, Inc. and others.
Created by Mark Spencer <markster@digium.com>
Asterisk comes with ABSOLUTELY NO WARRANTY; type 'show warranty' for details.
This is free software, with components licensed under the GNU General Public
License version 2 and other licenses; you are welcome to redistribute it under
certain conditions. Type 'show license' for details.
========================================================================
  == Parsing '/etc/asterisk/asterisk.conf': Found
  == Parsing '/etc/asterisk/extconfig.conf': Found
Connected to Asterisk 1.4.4 currently running on asterisk1 (pid = 31461)
Verbosity was 0 and is now 3

You can exit from the Asterisk console and return to the Linux Bash shell with the
quit or exit commands.

Type help to see a list of Asterisk commands. The list is probably too long for your
screen, so page up and down by holding down the Shift key and pressing Page Up/Page
Down.

Type help [commandname] to get information on specific commands:

asterisk1*CLI> help stop gracefully
Usage: stop gracefully
        Causes Asterisk to not accept new calls, and exit when all
        active calls have terminated normally.
```

Asterisk installs with the usual startup files, and is controlled from the Linux command line with these commands:

```
# /etc/init.d/asterisk start
# /etc/init.d/asterisk restart
# /etc/init.d/asterisk stop
# /etc/init.d/asterisk status
```

These are all right to use in testing, but they disrupt service so they're not appropriate for a production system. Use the Asterisk console commands to reload changes in the following configuration files without interrupting active calls:

sip.conf, sip_notify.conf
> `reload chan_sip.so`

iax.conf, iaxprov.conf
> `reload chan_iax2.so`

extensions.conf
> `dialplan reload`

dnsmgr.conf
> `dnsmgr reload`

extensions.ael
> `ael reload`

Reload all configuration files
> `reload`

Changes in *zaptel.conf* are reloaded with this command:

> `!/sbin/ztcfg`

The exclamation point is used to execute external Linux commands from the Asterisk console. You can also open a Linux shell inside the Asterisk console:

> **`*CLI>` `!`**
> `[root@asterisk1 ~]#`

Type exit to return to Asterisk.

There are several ways to shutdown Asterisk:

`restart gracefully`
> Stop accepting new calls and cold-restart when all active calls have ended.

`restart now`
> Restart Asterisk immediately, callers be danged.

`restart when convenient`
> Restart Asterisk when there is no activity.

`stop gracefully`
> Stop accepting new calls and cold-restart when all active calls have ended.

`stop now`
> Shut down Asterisk immediately.

`stop when convenient`
> Stop Asterisk when there is no activity.

`abort halt`
> Change your mind and cancel a shutdown.

Discussion

Making and loading configuration changes on a running server with a minimum of disruption is one of Asterisk's nicer features, as cutting off callers in mid-stream won't win you any friends. However, on a busy system, you might find yourself waiting a long time for a graceful shutdown, so stop now is a useful option.

If you don't have startup files for Asterisk, or don't want it to start at boot, use this command to start up the Asterisk server:

```
# asterisk -cvvv
```

See Also

- Asterisk Documentation Project: *http://www.asteriskdocs.org/modules/news/*
- Asterisk Support: *http://www.asterisk.org/support*

5.4   Testing the Asterisk Server

Problem

You're ready to start using your Asterisk server and learning your way around it. Where is a good starting point?

Solution

Start at the Asterisk console on the server (previous recipe). Don't change any configuration files yet. If you have a headset or microphone and speakers, you can test all functions. With a USB headset, you won't even need a sound card.

First, listen to the introductory message:

```
asterisk1*CLI> dial 1000
```

This will walk you through the basic calling features: calling a remote server at Digium, performing an echo test, and recording and retrieving voicemail. Use the dial, console answer, and console hangup commands to simulate using a telephone.

Typing help in the Asterisk console displays all the Asterisk commands.

Discussion

Time spent practicing on the Asterisk console is time well-spent because you can run an Asterisk server completely from the console and never touch a configuration file. This is not practical, but testing new configurations on the command line might save a bit of time and find errors before committing them to files.

See Also

- Asterisk Documentation Project: *http://www.asteriskdocs.org/modules/news/*
- Asterisk Support: *http://www.asterisk.org/support*

5.5   Adding Phone Extensions to Asterisk and Making Calls

Problem

Playing around on the Asterisk server is fun, but you're ready to set up some user accounts and make real phone calls. How do you set this up?

Solution

First, we'll set up some local user accounts including voicemail, and test them on the server. (In Recipe 5.6, we'll set up some softphones for some real calling.) You'll be editing these files on the Asterisk server:

- */etc/asterisk/sip.conf*
- */etc/asterisk/extensions.conf*
- */etc/asterisk/voicemail.conf*

The default files are huge and full of helpful comments, but rather a chore to edit, so let's move them out of the way:

```
# mv sip.conf sip.conf.old
# mv extensions.conf extensions.conf.old
# mv voicemail.conf voicemail.conf.old
```

We'll create three users: Ellen Ripley, Sarah Connor, and Dutch Schaeffer. Create a new *sip.conf* with these entries. Note that semicolons are used to comment out lines, not hash marks:

```
;;/etc/asterisk/sip.conf;;
[general]
context=default
port=5060
bindaddr=0.0.0.0
disallow=all
allow=gsm
allow=ulaw
allow=alaw

[ellenr]
;Ellen Ripley
type=friend
username=ellenr
```

```
secret=4545
host=dynamic
context=local-users

[sarahc]
;Sarah Connor
type=friend
username=sarahc
secret=5656
host=dynamic
context=local-users

[dutchs]
;Dutch Schaeffer
type=friend
username=dutchs
secret=6767
host=dynamic
context=local-users
```

Then, create a new *extensions.conf* with these entries:

```
;;/etc/asterisk/extensions.conf;;
[general]
autofallthrough=yes
clearglobalvars=yes

[globals]
CONSOLE=Console/dsp

[default]
;no entries yet

[local-users]
exten => 250,1,Dial(SIP/ellenr,10)
exten => 250,2,VoiceMail(250@local-vm-users,u)

exten => 251,1,Dial(SIP/sarahc,10)
exten => 251,2,VoiceMail(251@local-vm-users,u)

exten => 252,1,Dial(SIP/dutchs,10)
exten => 252,2,VoiceMail(252@local-vm-users,u)

;Internal users can call each other directly with their 3-digit extensions:
exten => _2XX,1,Dial(SIP/${EXTEN},30)
exten => _2XX,n,Voicemail(${EXTEN})
exten => _2XX,n,Hangup

;retrieve messages by dialing ext. 550
exten => 550,1,VoiceMailMain(@local-vm-users)
```

Finally, set up voicemail boxes in *voicemail.conf*:

```
;;/etc/asterisk/voicemail.conf;;
[general]
```

```
format=wav49
skipms=3000
maxsilence=10
silencethreshold=128
maxlogins=3

[local-vm-users]
;mailbox number, password, username
250 => 1234,Ellen Ripley
251 => 3456,Sarah Connor
252 => 4567,Dutch Schaeffer
```

Load the new configurations, then make some calls:

```
asterisk1*CLI> reload
asterisk1*CLI> dial 250@local-vm-users
asterisk1*CLI> console hangup
```

You'll see a lot of console output between these commands, and hear voice prompts that tell you what to do. Leave some voicemail messages, then retrieve them like this example for Ellen, who is at extension 250. You will be prompted for the mailbox number and password:

```
asterisk1*CLI> dial 550
asterisk1*CLI> dial 250
asterisk1*CLI> dial 1234
asterisk1*CLI> console hangup
```

Follow the prompts to listen to the messages. Remember, you have to use the dial command every time you need to enter some numbers. When everything works, you're ready to install and use some softphones.

Discussion

Type help at the Asterisk CLI to see the current command set. The *READMEs*, *changes*, and *UPGRADE.txt* files in the source tarballs are full of useful information, and will tell you what has changed between releases.

A verbosity of 3 (asterisk -rvvv) is just right for monitoring call activities on the server. If there are any errors, you can see them live. Console output and */var/log/ asterisk/messages* are the same.

sip.conf

This file defines all the SIP channels you'll be using. This is where you set up internal users and external trunks. It also contains options for selecting hold music, NAT firewall tweaks, codecs, jitter buffering, and proxies.

The [general] section includes global constants.

port=5060 is the standard SIP port. Don't change this.

`bindaddr=0.0.0.0` means listen on all interfaces. You may change this if your Asterisk server has more than one network interface.

Codecs (coder/decoders) convert analog signals to digital formats. In *sip.conf* and *iax.conf,* you must first deny all codecs with `disallow=all`, then specify the ones you wish to allow in order of preference. Which ones do you allow? This depends on what people calling your network use, what your service provider requires (if you have one), and your own requirements for your network. Any incoming call that uses a codec your server does not support will be transcoded into a format that your server does support. This incurs a CPU hit, and might cause some voice-quality problems. It's most efficient to use the same codec from endpoint to endpoint, though that may not always be possible.

This list shows the most commonly used Asterisk-supported voice codecs and the correct configuration file syntax:

```
Codec name = configuration file entry
G.711u ulaw = ulaw
G.711a alaw = alaw
G.726 = g726
G.729 = g729
GSM = gsm
iLBC = ilbc
LPC10 = lpc10
Speex = speex
```

VoIP codecs are compromises between bandwidth and CPU usage. Compressed codecs require less bandwidth, but at a cost of more CPU cycles. Less compression = less CPU and more bandwidth:

G.711u/a
> G.711 ulaw is used in the U.S. and Japan, while G.711 alaw is used the rest of the world. It is a high-quality companded codec; this is the native language of the modern digital telephone network, and is almost universally supported in VoIP networks and devices. A T1 trunk carries 24 digital PCM (Pulse Code Modulation) channels, and the European E1 standard carries 30 channels. It requires less CPU power, but consumes more bandwidth. It runs at a fixed bitrate of 64 Kbps per call each way, plus around 20 Kbps for packet headers. G.711 has an open source license, and delivers the best voice quality and least latency.

G.726
> G.726 runs at several different bitrates: 16, 24, or 32, and don't forget an additional 20 Kbps or so for headers. 32 Kbps is the most common, and the only one supported by Asterisk. It's easy on CPU usage, has good voice quality, and has an open source license. G.726 is becoming more popular and is supported on most VoIP devices.

G.729

> A high-quality compressed proprietary codec that is easy on bandwidth, with a bitrate of 8 Kbps. (Add about 20 Kbps for headers.) The price for this is more CPU cycles. For example, AstLinux on a Soekris 48xx board can handle about eight concurrent G.711 calls, but only two G.729 calls. Plus, there are patent encumbrances—using G.729 on Asterisk requires a licensing fee of $10 per channel, which you can purchase from Digium.

GSM

> GSM stands for Global System for Mobile communications, which is a cellular phone system standard. It includes a voice codec, and that is the bit that Asterisk uses. It is proprietary, but royalty-free, so anyone can use it. It has a bitrate of 13 Kbps, and uses about 30 Kbps total. GSM delivers acceptable voice quality. (GSM is also the file format of the free voice prompts included with Asterisk.) There are three flavors of the GSM codec. The royalty-free edition is also known as GSM Full-Rate. There are two newer versions that are patent-encumbered: Enhanced Full Rate (EFR) and Half Rate (HR).

iLBC

> iLBC is designed for low-bandwidth high-packet loss networks. It has better voice quality than G.729 for about the same computational price, and it uses a total of about 20–30 Kbps per call each way. Its special strength is graceful degradation over poor-quality networks, so even with packet losses as high as 10 percent, it still sounds good. It is free of cost, and comes with a liberal license that allows modifications.

LPC-10

> This delivers low but clear voice quality, or, as the sample *iax.conf* files says "disallow=lpc10; Icky sound quality...Mr. Roboto." Developed by the U.S. Department of Defense, its main virtue is very low bandwidth and CPU requirements; it uses as little as 2.5 Kbps per call, and you can stuff up to three times as many calls over the wires as you can with GSM. So, don't forget that Asterisk supports it—you just may find yourself in a situation where it will be useful. (OK, so most desert islands don't have Internet. But you never know.)

Speex

> Speex is a high-quality, BSD-style licensed, dynamically variable bitrate codec that was developed as an alternative to restrictive patent-encumbered codecs. It is very flexible, and can be manually fine-tuned in */etc/asterisk/codecs.conf*. Its one drawback is it's the most computationally expensive of the codecs. It has an active developer and user community, and is finding widespread acceptance, so it's bound to continue to improve.

The default *sip.conf* uses phone names instead of people names for the human user extensions. I prefer to name them for the users. There are three types of users: Peers, Users, and Friends. Peers and Users have different sets of privileges, and Friends get all privileges. See the default *extensions.conf* for details.

"Username" and "secret" are the login and password that users will use in their soft-phone configurations to register the phone with the server.

Using host=dynamic tells the server that the phone needs to be registered. This happens every time you start or restart your phone. Then, a timeout is negotiated each time a device registers, usually 3,600 seconds (60 minutes). The device must reregister, or Asterisk removes the registry entry.

You need to name a default context for each user; this tells Asterisk where to start in the dialplan to process calls for each user. This is a nice mechanism for providing different sets of privileges for different groups of users.

Dialplans

extensions.conf is the heart of your Asterisk server because it contains your dialplan. A dialplan has four elements—extensions, contexts, priorities, and applications:

Extensions
> The word *extensions* is a bit unfortunate because it sounds like plain old numbered telephone extensions. But Asterisk extensions are sturdy little workhorses that do all kinds of things. Extension syntax looks like this:
> ```
> exten => name,priority,application( )
> ```
> Names can be words or numbers. Usually, multiple extensions are required to handle a single call; these are called *contexts*.

Contexts
> Named groups of extensions are called *contexts*. Each context is a separate unit, and does not interact with other contexts unless you configure it to do so, with the include directive.

Priorities
> You must always specify a number one priority; this is the first command Asterisk follows when processing a call.

Applications
> Asterisk comes with a large assortment of applications; these are built-in Asterisk commands. You can see a list of applications by running the core list applications command on the Asterisk console.

The *extensions.conf* file has these sections:
```
[general]
[globals]
[contexts]
```

[general] and [globals] are special reserved words, so don't change them. [contexts] are named whatever you want.

The [general] context contains system-wide variables. In this recipe, autofallthrough=yes terminates calls with BUSY, CONGESTION, or HANGUP in case the configuration is not clear on what the next step is supposed to be.

clearglobalvars=yes means that variables will be cleared and reparsed on an extensions reload or Asterisk reload. Otherwise, global variables will persist through reloads, even if they are deleted from *extensions.conf*.

Global constants are set in the [globals] section, such as dialplan and environment values. CONSOLE=Console/dsp sets the default sound device.

Now, we get into the good stuff: user-defined contexts. Contexts define call routing and what users can do. The [local-users] context in this recipe defines the extension numbers for our users, and does their call routing. These examples are as simple as they can be—dial the extension numbers, and if no one answers, you are sent to the appropriate voicemail context. The u voicemail option means "play the unavailable message when no one answers."

The underscores in extensions mean wildcards ahead. In the example that allows users to call each other by their three-digit extensions, the first number dialed must be 2, then the next two numbers dialed are matched to existing extensions. EXTEN is a channel variable that passes in the numbers you dial.

Sequence in contexts is very important—the steps must be numbered or listed in order (you can use "n" for "next" to do so). Using numbered priorities lets you jump around to different priorities, as you'll see later in this chapter.

Extension 550 is configured in the recipe to be the number users dial to retrieve voicemail. You may use any number you want. The recipe uses the VoiceMailMain application, which is Asterisk's built-in voicemail retrieval application, and points to the appropriate voicemail context. When you have more than one voicemail context, you need to specify the correct one, like in the recipe with @local-vm-users:

voicemail.conf

The [general] section defines global constants.

format

The options for this are wav49, gsm, and wav. Voicemails will be recorded in as many formats as you name here. Asterisk will choose the optimum format for playback. If you want to attach voicemail messages to email, use wav49. wav49 is identical to gsm; the difference is it has Microsoft Windows-friendly headers, which makes the file readable to virtually all client software. It creates files about one-tenth the size of WAVE files.

WAVE files are huge because they are uncompressed, but they deliver the best sound quality.

See Also

- Asterisk config *sip.conf*:

    http://www.voip-info.org/wiki-Asterisk+config+sip.conf

- Asterisk config *extensions.conf*:

    http://www.voip-info.org/wiki/view/Asterisk+config+extensions.conf

- Asterisk config *voicemail.conf*:

    http://www.voip-info.org/wiki-Asterisk+config+voicemail.conf

- Asterisk cmd VoiceMailMain:

    http://www.voip-info.org/wiki/index.php?page=Asterisk+cmd+VoiceMailMain

- Asterisk cmd Dial:

    http://www.voip-info.org/wiki/index.php?page=Asterisk+cmd+Dial

- The default *extensions.conf, sip.conf*, and *voicemail.conf*

5.6   Setting Up Softphones

Problem

You're ready to connect some software telephones and do some real IP telephony in your test lab, using Windows and Linux PCs. Where do you find some good softphones, and how do you set them up?

Solution

There are many softphones you can try. This recipe uses the Twinkle softphone for Linux, and the X-Lite softphone for Windows. Both are free of cost. Twinkle is open source, X-Lite is not. Twinkle runs on Linux only, while X-Lite runs on Windows, Linux, and Mac OS X.

Twinkle has a good feature set, a nice easy-on-the-eyes interface, is easy to use, and has good documentation. X-Lite is a bit squinty to read and rather convoluted to configure. But it is very configurable, sound quality is good, and it has volume controls right on the main interface.

You will need the user's login name and password from */etc/asterisk/sip.conf,* and the IP address of the Asterisk server, as Figure 5-1 for Twinkle shows.

You'll find this screen in Edit → User Profile. When you change settings in Twinkle, hit Registration → Register to activate the new settings.

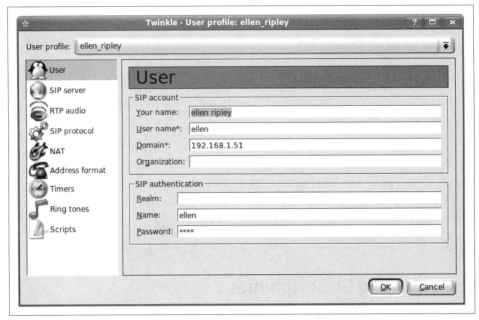

Figure 5-1. Twinkle configuration

In X-Lite, go to the Main Menu → System Settings → SIP Proxy → Default, like Figure 5-2.

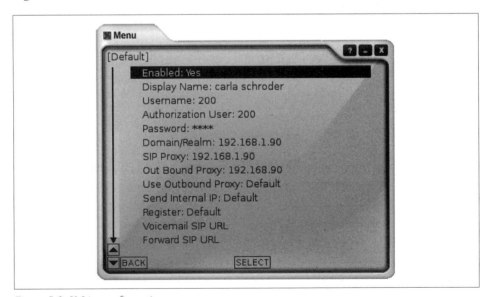

Figure 5-2. X-Lite configuration

Be sure to set Enabled:Yes.

Close X-Lite, then reopen it to activate the changes.

Now, you can try out all the tests you did in the last recipe on the Asterisk console, plus have the two extensions call each other. You can even call the outside world. To do this, copy the [demo] context in the sample */etc/asterisk/extensions.conf* into your working *extensions.conf*. Then, add it to the [local-users] context like this:

```
[local-users]
include => demo
```

Reload the changes in the Asterisk console:

asterisk1*CLI> dialplan reload

Dial 1000 on your softphone to play the Asterisk demonstration. This will walk you through a number of different tasks: an echo test, calling Digium's demonstration server, and testing voicemail. The voicemail test won't work without the default *voicemail.conf*, but because you already tested this in Recipe 5.4 and successfully set up your own *voicemail.conf*, it should be good to go.

Discussion

You'll probably want to test some different softphones, as they vary a lot in usability and sound quality. You'll especially want decent sound gear. Good headsets like Plantronics sound warm and natural, block background noise, and have mute buttons and volume controls. USB headsets don't need sound cards, but contain their own sound-processing circuitry.

Watch out for branded softphones that are customized for a vendor (like Vonage, for example), and can't be used as you like without some serious hacking.

On Linux systems, it's important to use only the Advanced Linux Sound Architecture (ALSA) soundsystem. Don't use aRtsd (the KDE sound server) or the Enlightened Sound Daemon (ESD), which comes with the Gnome desktop. Disable them because they create latency, and latency is the enemy of VoIP sound quality. Additionally, don't use Open Sound System (OSS) because it is obsolete. ALSA provides an OSS emulator for applications and devices that think they need OSS, like the Asterisk console.

See Also

- The documentation for your softphones
- man 1 alsactl
- man 1 alsamixer
- ALSA project: *http://www.alsa-project.org/*

5.7   Getting Real VoIP with Free World Dialup

Problem

You want to get your Asterisk server up and running and connected to the outside world as quickly as you can. So, you want to start off with some basic VoIP services and start making calls over the Internet.

Solution

Connect your Asterisk server to Free World Dialup (FWD). With Free World Dialup, you can make free calls to other FWD users, and to the users on the networks that FWD peers with. (A notable exception is the party pooper Vonage, which does not wish to associate with other VoIP networks.)

First, go to Free World Dialup (*http://www.freeworlddialup.com/*) and sign up for an account. When you receive your welcome email, log in and change your password.

Then, go to the Extra Features link and enable IAX because you'll be setting up an IAX trunk for FWD.

Now, fire up your trusty text editor and configure */etc/asterisk/iax.conf* and *etc/asterisk/extensions.conf*. We'll use */etc/asterisk/sip.conf* and */etc/asterisk/voicemail.conf* from Recipe 5.5.

In these examples, the FWD login is asteriskuser, password 67890, FWD phone number 123456. Incoming FWD calls are routed to Ellen Ripley at extension 250.

```
;;iax.conf;;
[general]
context=default
port=4569
bindaddr=0.0.0.0
disallow=all
allow=gsm
allow=ulaw
allow=alaw
register => 123456:67890@iax2.fwdnet.net

[fwd-trunk]
 type=user
 context=fwd-iax-trunk
 auth=rsa
 inkeys=freeworlddialup

;;extensions.conf;;

[general]
autofallthrough=yes
clearglobalvars=yes
```

```
[globals]
CONSOLE=Console/dsp

;free world dialup settings
FWDNUMBER=123456
FWDCIDNAME=asteriskuser
FWDPASSWORD=67890
FWDRINGS=SIP/ellenr

[default]

include => fwd-iax-trunk

[local-users]
include => default
include => outbound

exten => 250,1,Dial(SIP/ellenr,10)
exten => 250,2,VoiceMail(250@local-vm-users,u)

exten => 251,1,Dial(SIP/sarahc,10)
exten => 251,2,VoiceMail(251@local-vm-users,u)

exten => 252,1,Dial(SIP/dutchs,10)
exten => 252,2,VoiceMail(252@local-vm-users,u)

;Internal users can call each other directly with their 3-digit extensions:
exten => _2XX,1,Dial(SIP/${EXTEN},30)
exten => _2XX,n,Voicemail(${EXTEN})
exten => _2XX,n,Hangup

;retrieve messages by dialing ext. 550
exten => 550,1,VoiceMailMain(@local-vm-users)

[fwd-iax-trunk]
;incoming Free World Dialup
exten => ${FWDNUMBER},1,Dial,${FWDRINGS}

[outbound]
;outgoing FWD
exten => _393.,1,SetCallerId,${FWDCIDNAME}
exten => _393.,2,Dial(IAX2/${FWDNUMBER}:${FWDPASSWORD}@iax2.fwdnet.net/${EXTEN:3},60)
exten => _393.,3,Congestion
```

Load the new dialplan:

```
asterisk1*CLI> dialplan reload
```

Configure your firewall to allow port UDP 4569 traffic. Then, dial the FWD echo test at 393613. You'll be able to talk to yourself. Next, go to your your FWD account profile (*my.FWD*) and click the Callme button. The FWD server will call you and invite you to join a nonexistent conference. Now you know your setup is correct and working.

Discussion

This gives you an easy way to practice setting up an IAX trunk, and to make and receive pure VoIP calls. Friends and associates can call your FWD number with a SIP or IAX phone and avoid toll charges.

Because Ellen doesn't want to play receptionist forever, Recipe 5.9 tells how to set up a digital receptionist to route incoming calls.

Asterisk 1.4 comes with an encryption key for Free World Dialup in */var/lib/asterisk/ keys/freeworlddialup.pub*. If you have any problems with the key, download a fresh one from FWD.

This recipe shows how to use user-defined variables in Asterisk. These go in the [globals] section of *extensions.conf*.

See Also

- The Discussion in Recipe 5.5 for explanations of configuration options
- Recipe 5.9
- Recipe 5.21

5.8   Connecting Your Asterisk PBX to Analog Phone Lines

Problem

You're running a small shop with fewer than 10 analog phone lines. You're not quite ready to give up your nice reliable analog phone service, but you do want to set up an Asterisk server for your local PBX, and to integrate some VoIP services. Your first job is connecting Asterisk to your analog lines—how do you do this?

Solution

First, follow the previous recipes to install and test Asterisk's basic functions. In this recipe, we'll route incoming and outgoing calls through Asterisk. Incoming calls will be routed to our existing extension 250, which is probably not how you want to set up your system permanently, but it's fine for testing. Later in this chapter, we'll set up a proper digital receptionist.

Let's assume you have three analog phone lines. You'll need an Asterisk server, and the Digium TDM400P analog interface PCI card with three FXO ports. You'll also need to load the appropriate Zaptel driver, which for this card is the *wctdm* kernel module.

Install the TDM400P in your Asterisk server. Then, you'll edit */etc/zaptel.conf* and */etc/asterisk/zapata.conf*. First, make a backup copy of the original */etc/zaptel.conf*:

```
# mv zaptel.conf zaptel.conf-old
```

Then, make a new *zaptel.conf* file with these lines in it. Use your own country code—you'll find a complete list in the *zonedata.c* file in the Zaptel source tree:

```
;zaptel.conf
loadzone = us
defaultzone=us
fxsks=1,2,3
```

Now, load the *wctdm* module and verify that it loaded:

```
# modprobe wctdm
# lsmod
Module      Size   Used by
wctdm       34880  0
```

To ensure that the Zaptel module loads automatically at boot, go back to the Zaptel source directory and install the configuration and startup files:

```
# cd /usr/src/zaptel-1.4.3
# make config
```

The next file to edit is */etc/asterisk/zapata.conf*. Back up the original:

```
# mv zapata.conf zapata.conf.old
```

Then, enter these lines in a new empty *zapata.conf*:

```
## zapata.conf
[channels]
context=pstn-test-in
signalling=fxs_ks
language=en
usecallerid=yes
echocancel=yes
transfer=yes
immediate=no
group=1
channel => 1-3
```

Now, add the line TRUNK=Zap/g1 to the [globals] section of */etc/asterisk/extensions.conf*.

Then, create a new [pstn-test-in] context in */etc/asterisk/extensions.conf*. This example routes all incoming calls to the existing extension 250:

```
[pstn-test-in]
;incoming calls go to ext. 250
exten => s,1,Dial(SIP/250,30)
exten => s,n,Voicemail(250)
exten => s,n,Hangup
```

Now, create an [outbound] context so your local users can dial out:

```
[outbound]
ignorepat => 9
```

```
exten => _9NXXXXXX,1,Dial(TRUNK/${EXTEN:1})
exten => _91NXXNXXXXXX,1,Dial(TRUNK/${EXTEN:1})
exten => 911,1,Dial(TRUNK/911)
exten => 9911,1,Dial(TRUNK/911)
```

Add the [pstn-test-in] context to the [default] context:

```
include => pstn-test-in
```

Add the [outbound] context to the [local-users] context.

```
include => outbound
```

Load the new configurations:

asterisk1*CLI> dialplan reload

Now, give it a test drive. You should be able to make calls in the usual way: dial 9 for an outside line, then dial your normal 7-digit local numbers or 10-digit long-distance numbers. This is normal for the U.S., at any rate; you can adapt this as you need for different calling areas.

Discussion

ignorepat (ignore pattern) means keep playing a dial tone after dialing whatever number or numbers you specify.

In *zapata.conf*, we lumped all three channels into a single hunt group, group 1. This means that callers will always be routed to the first available line.

All the Zaptel modules are loaded when you use the default configuration files. This doesn't hurt anything, but you can configure your system to load only the module you need. On CentOS (and Fedora and Red Hat), comment out all the unnecessary modules in */etc/sysconfig/zaptel* (on Debian, it's */etc/default/zaptel*).

A fundamental security measure is to never include an outbound context in any inbound context because you don't want to provide toll calling services to the world.

If you're trying to make sense of this FXS/FXO stuff, you're noticing that the TDM400P has three FXO modules, but the configurations specify FXS signaling. Think of it this way: it accepts and translates FXO signaling on incoming calls, but has to transmit FXS signaling.

Office users are usually accustomed to dialing 9 for an outside line. With Asterisk, it's not necessary, so you don't have to set it up this way. In the example, 911 is programmed to work both ways, so users don't have to remember which is which. This line shows how to configure dialing out without pressing 9 first:

```
exten => _NXXXXXX,1,Dial(TRUNK/${EXTEN})
```

911 service can be a problem with VoIP. If your Asterisk server is down, you won't be able to call 911. Some fallbacks to consider are keeping an analog line or two independently of your Asterisk server, or having your server in a location where you can quickly unplug an analog line from the server and connect it to a telephone.

Because faxing over VoIP is still a big pain, keeping an ordinary analog fax machine with an attached telephone would solve two problems.

See Also

- The sample *extensions.conf*, *sip.conf*, and *voicemail.conf*
- Asterisk Variables:

    http://www.voip-info.org/wiki/index.php?page=Asterisk+Variables
- Asterisk config *zapata.conf*:

    http://www.voip-info.org/wiki-Asterisk+config+zapata.conf
- Asterisk config *zaptel.conf*:

    http://www.voip-info.org/wiki/index.php?page=Asterisk+config+zaptel.conf
- Asterisk config *extensions.conf*:

    http://www.voip-info.org/wiki/view/Asterisk+config+extensions.conf

5.9   Creating a Digital Receptionist

Problem

So far, our incoming calls are routed to extension 250, Ellen Ripley. Ellen has been gracious at playing receptionist, but she has her own work to do. How do you configure Asterisk to take over as a reliable, always courteous digital receptionist?

Solution

Instead of routing all incoming calls to Ellen, program your dialplan to route calls according to an interactive menu, and then record suitable greetings and instructions. (See the next recipe to learn how to use Asterisk to record custom prompts.)

Fire up your trusty text editor and open */etc/asterisk/extensions.conf*. Change the [pstn-test-in] context to look like this:

```
[pstn-test-in]
;interactive menu for incoming calls
exten => s,1,Answer( )
exten => s,2,Set(TIMEOUT(digit)=5)
exten => s,3,Set(TIMEOUT(response)=15)
exten => s,4 Background(local/main-greeting)

;user extensions
exten => 1,1,Goto(local-users,250,1)
exten => 2,1,Goto(local-users,251,1)
exten => 3,1,Goto(local-users,252,1)

;send the caller back to the beginning
;if they enter an invalid option
```

```
exten => i,1,Playback(local/invalid-option)
exten => i,2,Goto(s,2)

;hangup if the timeouts are exceeded
exten => t,1,Hangup
```

Now, record the greetings that will be played for callers. The first one is *main-greeting*, which says something like "Thank you for calling Excellence Itself, Limited. Please press 1 to speak to Ellen Ripley. Press 2 for Sarah Connor, or press 3 for Dutch Schaeffer."

invalid-option responds to incorrect key presses with "I'm sorry, that is not a valid option. Please listen to the available options and try again."

Reload the new dialplan:

```
asterisk1*CLI> dialplan reload
```

Call your server from an outside line and take your new digital receptionist for a test drive.

Discussion

There's a whole lot going on here in a few lines:

```
Set(TIMEOUT(digit)=5)
Set(TIMEOUT(response)=15)
```

Asterisk will hang up if the user takes too long to enter key presses, or too long to respond at all. The defaults are 5 seconds and 10 seconds.

The Background command plays a soundfile, then stops playing the soundfile when it is interrupted by a key press from the caller and goes to the next step in the dialplan.

The t, or *timeout* extension is a special extension that tells Asterisk what to do when timeouts are exceeded.

The i, or *invalid* extension handles incorrect input from callers.

When a caller is routed to a valid user's extension, that's the end of the road. Then, someone either picks up the call, or it goes to voicemail.

See Also

- Asterisk config extensions.conf:

    http://www.voip-info.org/wiki/view/Asterisk+config+extensions.conf

- The sample *extensions.conf, sip.conf, voicemail.conf*

5.10 Recording Custom Prompts

Problem

You've done a bit of research on how to create your own custom prompts for Asterisk, and you know that Digium will sell you nice, professionally recorded custom prompts for a reasonable fee. You know that you can go nuts with recording gear and do it yourself. Both sound like nice options, but for now, you just want quick and cheap.

Solution

You can have quick and cheap. You'll need sound support on your Asterisk server. This can be a sound card plus a microphone and speakers, or a sound card and headset, or a USB headset. (A USB headset replaces a sound card, microphone, and speakers.) Or, call into your server from a client's phone. Then you'll create a context in Asterisk just for recording custom prompts.

First, create two new directories:

```
# mkdir /var/lib/asterisk/sounds/local
# mkdir /var/lib/asterisk/sounds/tmp
```

Then, create this context for recording your custom prompts in /etc/asterisk/extensions.conf:

```
[record-prompts]
;record new voice files
exten => s,1,Wait(2)
exten => s,2,Record(tmp/newrecord:gsm)
exten => s,3,Wait(2)
exten => s,4,Playback(tmp/newrecord)
exten => s,5,wait(2)
exten => s,6,Hangup

;record new messages
exten => 350,1,Goto(record-prompts,s,1)
```

Reload the dialplan:

```
asterisk1*CLI> dialplan reload
```

Now, dial 350. You will hear only a beep—start talking after the beep, then hit the pound key when you're finished. It will replay your new message, then hang up. The first file you're going to record should be an instructional file that says something like, "Wait for the beep to begin recording a new message, then press pound when you are finished."

Next, move the file from the *tmp/* folder to *local/*, and rename it to whatever you want. In this example, it is called *r-make-new-recording*:

```
# mv /var/lib/asterisk/sounds/tmp/newrecord.gsm \
/var/lib/asterisk/sounds/local/r-make-new-recording.gsm
```

Now, record a second message that says, "If you are satisfied with your new recording, press 1. If you wish to record it again, press 2," and rename it *r-keep-or-record.gsm*.

Record a third message that says, "Thank you, your new recording has been saved. Press 2 to record another message, or 3 to exit." Call this one *r-thank-you-message-saved.gsm*.

Then, revise your dialplan to use the new soundfiles:

```
[record-prompts]
;record new voice files
exten => s,1,Wait(1)
exten => s,2,Playback(local/r-make-new-recording)
exten => s,3,Wait(1)
exten => s,4,Record(tmp/znewrecord:gsm)
exten => s,5,Wait(1)
exten => s,6,Playback(tmp/znewrecord)
exten => s,7,Wait(1)
exten => s,8,Background(local/r-keep-or-record)

;copy file to local/ directory and give unique filename
exten => 1,1,System(/bin/mv /var/lib/asterisk/sounds/tmp/znewrecord.gsm /var/lib/
asterisk/sounds/local/${UNIQUEID}.gsm)
exten => 1,2,Background(local/r-thank-you-message-saved)

exten => 2,1,Goto(record-prompts,s,2)

exten => 3,1,Playback(goodbye)
exten => 3,2,Hangup
```

Add this to the [local-users] context:

```
;record new messages
exten => 350,1,Goto(record-prompts,s,1)
```

Reload the dialplan:

asterisk1*CLI> dialplan reload

Now, give it a try by dialing extension 350. This lets you listen to and rerecord your new soundfile until you are satisfied with it, and to record several new soundfiles in a single session without redialing.

Discussion

If you record soundfiles at the Asterisk console instead of from an IP phone on a client PC, you need to specify the context like this:

asterisk1*CLI> dial 350@record-prompts

Let's take a quick walk through the new [record-prompts] context. The s (start) extension is a special extension that kicks in when a specific destination is not named. I think of it as Asterisk answering the call personally, instead of handing it off to a user.

The soundfile names can be anything you want. I prefix them with r- to indicate that they are used for recording. *znewrecord.gsm* puts the temporary sound file last alphabetically in case I get confused and want to find it in a hurry. Asterisk has hundreds of soundfiles, so it's helpful to have a naming convention that keeps them somewhat sorted.

The Goto application jumps to different parts of the dialplan, and to different contexts. If you're an ace programmer, you probably don't think much of Goto, but for Asterisk, it's a simple way to reuse contexts. Without it, dialplans would be unmanageable.

Goto syntax takes a number of options:

```
exten => 100,1,Goto(context,extension,priority)
```

At a minimum, you need a priority. The default is to go to the extension and priority in the current context. I like to make it explicit and spell out everything.

The Playback application plays a soundfile. The default Asterisk soundfile directory is */var/lib/asterisk/sounds/*. So, Asterisk assumes that *tmp/* and *local/* are subdirectories of */var/lib/asterisk/sounds/*.

The Background application plays soundfiles that can be interrupted by keypresses, so this is where you use the "press 1, press 2" instruction soundfiles.

Playback and Background don't need the soundfile extension specified because Asterisk will automatically select the most efficient file available.

Using the colon with the Record command, as in znewrecord:gsm, means record a new sound file named *znewrecord* in the GSM format. You may also use the formats g723, g729, gsm, h263, ulaw, alaw, vox, wav, or WAV. WAV is wav49, which is a GSM-compressed WAVE format. wav49 and GSM files are about one-tenth the size of WAVE files. For recording voice prompts, gsm or wav49 work fine, and save a lot of disk space. GSM is the format for the free prompts that come with Asterisk.

This recipe should help make clear why the different parts of a dialplan are called contexts. The numbers that you dial operate according to context. The familiar "press 1, press 2" dance works because pressing 1 and 2 work differently in different contexts, so you can use the same numbers over and over for different jobs.

The Wait values are in seconds, and can be adjusted to suit. You can leave them out if you like; they give you a chance to take a breath and get ready to talk.

When you hit 1 to tell Asterisk you are satisfied with your recording, it will be copied to */var/lib/asterisk/sounds/local/* and given a unique filename based on the UNIQUEID variable. You'll want to rename the files something descriptive.

See Also

- Asterisk commands:

  http://www.voip-info.org/wiki-Asterisk+-+documentation+of+application+commands

- Asterisk variables:

  http://www.voip-info.org/wiki-Asterisk+variables

5.11   Maintaining a Message of the Day

Problem

You have certain greetings that need to be changed a lot, like the welcome greeting that callers first hear, a greeting that tells your schedule, an inspirational message of the day for staffers—whatever it is, they need to be changed often, so you want an easy way to change them, and you want to restrict who can change them.

Solution

Create a context for listening to and recording each message, then password-protect it.

Start by creating a directory to store your custom prompts in, like */var/lib/asterisk/sounds/local/*. Then, record some instructional prompts using the context created in the previous recipe. Suppose your message tells callers your hours and holiday schedule, and you have named it *store-schedule.gsm*. You'll need instructions like these:

r-schedule-welcome.gsm
> "Welcome to the store schedule management menu. Please enter your password."

r-listen-or-record.gsm
> "To listen to the current store schedule, press 1. To go directly to the recording menu press 2."

r-record-at-tone.gsm
> "To record a new store schedule message, begin speaking after the beep. When you're finished, press the pound key."

r-accept-or-do-over.gsm
> "To rerecord your message, press 2. If you are finished, press 3."

r-thankyou-newschedule.gsm
> "Thank you for updating the store schedule, and have a pleasant day."

r-invalid-option.gsm
> "I'm sorry, that is not a valid option, so I'm sending you back to the beginning."

r-thankyou-new-schedule.gsm
> "Thank you for updating the store schedule. Good-bye."

This is a complete example [record-schedule] context:

```
[record-schedule]
;log in and review existing message
exten => s,1,Wait(1)
exten => s,2,Playback(local/r-schedule-welcome)
exten => s,3,Set(TIMEOUT(digit)=5)
exten => s,4,Set(TIMEOUT(response)=15)
exten => s,5,Authenticate(2345)
exten => s,6,Background(local/r-listen-or-record)
exten => s,7,Background(local/r-accept-or-do-over)

exten => 1,1,Wait(1)
exten => 1,2,Playback(local/store-schedule)
exten => 1,3,Goto(s,6)

;record store-schedule
exten => 2,1,Wait(1)
exten => 2,2,Playback(local/r-record-at-tone)
exten => 2,3,Wait(1)
exten => 2,4,Record(local/store-schedule:gsm)
exten => 2,5,Wait(1)
exten => 2,6,Playback(local/store-schedule)
exten => 2,7,Wait(1)
exten => 2,8,Goto(s,7)

;accept the new message
exten => 3,1,Playback(local/r-thankyou-new-schedule)
exten => 3,2,Hangup

;hangup if the timeouts are exceeded
exten => t,1,Hangup

;send the caller back to the beginning
;if they enter an invalid option
exten => i,1,Playback(local/r-invalid-option)
exten => i,2,Goto(s,2)
```

Put it in your [local-users] context:

```
;record new store schedule
exten => 351,1,Goto(record-schedule,s,1)
```

Now, any of your local-users who have the password can update the store schedule.

Discussion

Contexts can be password-protected with the Authenticate command.

Remember to run the dialplan reload command from the Asterisk CLI every time you make a change to *extensions.conf*.

See Also

- Asterisk commands:

    http://www.voip-info.org/wiki-Asterisk+-+documentation+of+application+commands

5.12   Transferring Calls

Problem

You want your users to be able to transfer calls.

Solution

Just add the t option to their extensions in *extensions.conf*, like this:

```
exten => 252,1,Dial(SIP/dutchs,10,t)
```

To transfer a call, press the pound key on your telephone, then enter the extension number. Asterisk will say "transfer" after you press the pound key, then play a dial tone until you dial the extension number.

Discussion

Giving your users mighty transfer powers is a nice thing, especially when they're helping a customer. Forcing a caller who has gotten lost to call back and navigate your digital receptionist a second time isn't a very nice thing to do.

See Also

- Asterisk cmd Dial:

    http://www.voip-info.org/wiki/index.php?page=Asterisk+cmd+Dial

5.13   Routing Calls to Groups of Phones

Problem

You want callers to be directed to departments, instead of individuals, where they will be answered by whoever picks up first. Or, you have more than one phone, like a desk phone and cell phone, and you want your incoming calls to ring all of them.

Solution

Create *ring groups*. This is a simple configuration that assigns a group of extensions to a single extension, like this:

```
[tech-support]
exten => 380,1,Dial(SIP/604&SIP/605&SIP/606,40,t)
exten => 380,2,VoiceMail(220@local-vm-users)
```

The caller dials extension 380. The listed extensions all ring at the same time. If no one answers it within 40 seconds, it goes to voicemail. Extensions 604, 605, and 606 must already exist, and a voicemail box configured. Transferring is enabled with the lowercase t.

This example is for ringing a desk phone and a cell phone sequentially:

```
[find-carla]
exten => 100,1,Dial(SIP/350,20,t)
exten => 100,2,Dial(Zap/1/1231234567,20,t)
exten => 100,3,VoiceMail(350@local-vm-users)
```

If there is no answer at the first number, Asterisk tries the second number. If Carla is slacking and doesn't answer that one either, it goes to voicemail.

Both phones can be configured to ring at the same time:

```
exten => 100,1,Dial(SIP/350&Zap/1/1231234567,20)
exten => 100,2,VoiceMail(350@local-vm-users)
```

Discussion

This recipe demonstrates that extension numbers and voicemail boxes don't need to be the same.

The Dial command will dial anything that you can dial manually—whatever your Asterisk server supports, Dial can dial it. Well, technically it's not dialing. Funny how old terminology hangs on, isn't it?

See Also

- Asterisk cmd Dial:

    http://www.voip-info.org/wiki/index.php?page=Asterisk+cmd+Dial

5.14 Parking Calls

Problem

You're a mobile kind of worker. Sometimes you get a question that you have to go to a different room to answer, which means your caller is sitting on hold for a long time. Wouldn't it be nice if you could transfer the call and pick it up at your new location?

Solution

Yes, it would, and you can. Asterisk has 20 reserved *parking* slots, 701–720. Activate parking by adding the parkedcalls context to your desired internal context, such as the [local-users] context used in this chapter:

```
[local-users]
include => parkedcalls
```

Make sure you have mighty transfer powers with the t option:

```
exten => 252,1,Dial(SIP/dutchs,10,t)
```

Enabling parked calls requires a server restart:

asterisk1*CLI> restart gracefully

Test it by calling your extension. An easy way to do this is to have a second soft-phone on your test PC configured with a different user account. Cell phones are also great for testing Asterisk.

Transfer the call to extension 700, and Asterisk will automatically park it in the first empty slot. It will tell you the number of the parked extension—to resume the call, pick up another extension, and dial the parked extension number.

If it times out, it will ring the extension originally called, where it will be treated like any call, and go to voicemail if it's not answered.

The lowercase t option allows only the person receiving the call to transfer it. This means you can park a call only once. If you add an uppercase T, like this:

```
exten => 252,1,Dial(SIP/dutchs,10,tT)
```

then you can make transfers whether you're on the receiving or the calling end. So, when you un-park a call, you can park and transfer it yet again.

Discussion

Call parking is configured in */etc/asterisk/features.conf*. While there are a number of configurable options, the only one that really matters to most folks is the parkingtime option, which sets the timeout value.

The default is 45 seconds, which means if you don't pick up within 45 seconds, the call will ring back to your original extension.

See Also

- The sample */etc/asterisk/features.conf*

5.15   Customizing Hold Music

Problem

You want to add your own custom tunes to the hold music that comes with Asterisk, or replace it entirely.

Solution

Easy as falling asleep. Just plunk your own WAVE- or GSM-formatted soundfiles into the */var/lib/asterisk/moh* directory. Then, configure */etc/asterisk/musiconhold* like this:

```
[default]
mode=files
directory=/var/lib/asterisk/moh
random=yes
```

Next, set up a test context for testing your hold music:

```
exten => 1000,1,Answer
exten => 1000,n,SetMusicOnHold(default)
exten => 1000,n,WaitMusicOnHold(30)
exten => 1000,n,Hangup
```

Changes to hold music require a server restart:

```
asterisk1*CLI> restart gracefully
```

Then, dial 1000 to hear your music. It will play for 30 seconds, then hang up.

Discussion

Hold music is enabled globally by default, so you don't need to explicitly turn it on.

See Also

*   Asterisk cmd Musiconhold:

    http://www.voip-info.org/wiki/index.php?page=Asterisk+cmd+Musiconhold

5.16   Playing MP3 Sound Files on Asterisk

Problem

You want to use music on hold in MP3 format, rather than WAVE or GSM. But, they don't work—how do you make them go?

Solution

Download the *asterisk-addons* package to get Asterisk's *format_mp3* player. Follow the instructions in the */usr/src/asterisk-addons-1.4.[version]/format_mp3/README* to install *format_mp3*.

Now, your MP3 files will play just fine.

MP3 files eat more CPU cycles than WAVE or GSM, so don't use them on marginal systems. MP3 files can easily be converted to WAVE format with *lame*:

```
$ lame --decode musicfile.mp3 musicfile.wav
```

Do this to batch-convert all the MP3 files in the current directory:

```
$ for i in *.mp3; do lame --decode $i `basename $i .mp3`.wav; done
```

See Also

- man lame

5.17   Delivering Voicemail Broadcasts

Problem

You want to broadcast inspirational messages to your entire staff with a single call. Or, you might have important information to deliver. At any rate, you want the ability to set up voicemail groups to receive voicemail broadcasts.

Solution

With Asterisk, it's easy. First, create a mailbox group in */etc/asterisk/voicemail.conf*:

```
;broadcast mailbox
375 => 1234,StaffGroup
```

Then, create an extension in */etc/asterisk/extensions.conf* that contains all the mailboxes that belong to the group:

```
;broadcast voicemail extension
exten => 300,1,VoiceMail(375@local-vm-users&250@local-vm-users&251@local-vm-
users&252@local-vm-users)
```

Now, all you do is call extension 375, record your stirring communiqué, and it will copied to all the mailboxes in the group.

A useful option is to delete the master voicemail after it has been sent to the group, like this:

```
375 => 1234,StaffGroup,,,delete=1
```

Discussion

Voicemail contexts have four fields:

```
extension_number => voicemail_password,user_name,user_email_address,user_pager_email_
address,user_options
```

The minimum needed to set up a voicemail box is *extension_number => voicemail_password,user_name*. Any field that you skip needs a comma placeholder, as in this example that sends the user a copy of the voicemail attached to email:

```
103 => 1234,John Gilpin,john@gilpinsride.com,,attach=yes
```

If you use more than one user option, separate them with a pipe symbol:

```
103 => 1234,John Gilpin,john@gilpinsride.com,,attach=yes|delete=1
```

If your users want voicemails emailed to them, you'll want to use the compressed wav49 soundfile format. It's one-tenth the size of uncompressed WAVE files.

See Also

- Asterisk config *voicemail.conf*:

    http://www.voip-info.org/wiki/index.php?page=Asterisk+config+voicemail.conf

- The sample *voicemail.conf*

5.18   Conferencing with Asterisk

Problem

One of the reasons you're using Asterisk is to get inexpensive, easy conferencing. The commercial conferencing services cost a lot, and trying to do it yourself with traditional PBX systems is usually difficult. So, how do you set up conferencing with Asterisk?

Solution

There are two types of conferences: local conferences inside your LAN, and conferences with people outside your organization.

Using conferencing (or *meetme*, as it's often called), inside the LAN is as easy as falling asleep. This is a sample */etc/asterisk/meetme.conf* configuration that sets up three conference rooms:

```
;;/etc/asterisk/meetme.conf
[general]

[conferences]
; Usage is conf => [conference number][,pincode]
; Pincodes are optional
```

```
conf => 8000,1234
conf => 8001,4567
conf => 8002,7890
```

Create extensions for the conference rooms in the [local-users] context in */etc/asterisk/extensions.conf*:

```
;conference rooms 8000, 8001, 8002
exten => 8000,1,Meetme(${EXTEN})
exten => 8001,1,Meetme(${EXTEN})
exten => 8002,1,Meetme(${EXTEN},,7890)
```

Do the usual:

asterisk1*CLI> dialplan reload

And give your new conference rooms a test-drive. You'll be greeted by the voice of Allison Smith, who will ask you for the pincode and tell you how many people are present in the conference. The example for room 8002 enters the pincode for you.

What if you want people outside of your LAN to join the conference? As long as they have the conference number and pincode, and your incoming context includes the conference room extension, all they do is call your office the normal way, then enter the extension and passcode.

Discussion

The extension that you set up to dial the conference room doesn't have to be the same as the conference room number because the room number is an option for the MeetMe application, like this:

```
exten => 100,1,Meetme(8000)
```

Another way to set up conference rooms is to create a single extension for all conference rooms, like this:

```
exten => 8000,1,Meetme( )
```

You can use this single extension for all conference rooms because users will be prompted for both the room number and the pincode. You can limit access further with contexts. For example, you could have two separate user contexts, and each group gets its own conference room:

```
[developers]
exten => 8001,1,Meetme(${EXTEN})

[accounting]
exten => 8002,1,Meetme(${EXTEN})
```

See Also

- The sample *meetme.conf*
- Asterisk cmd MeetMe:

  http://www.voip-info.org/wiki/index.php?page=Asterisk+cmd+MeetMe

5.19 Monitoring Conferences

Problem

You want to keep an eye on conferences, and have mighty administrator powers to mute or even kick users out of the conference.

Solution

Use the *meetme* command on the Asterisk CLI. You can see all the options with the *help* command:

```
asterisk1*CLI> help meetme
Usage: meetme (un)lock|(un)mute|kick|list [concise] <confno> <usernumber>
       Executes a command for the conference or on a conferee
```

This command shows all running conferences:

```
asterisk1*CLI> meetme
Conf Num       Parties      Marked      Activity  Creation
8001           0002         N/A         00:01:10  Static
* Total number of MeetMe users: 2
```

This command lists the users in a conference:

```
asterisk1*CLI> meetme list 8001
User #: 01          250 Ellen Ripley         Channel: SIP/ellen-08d6dc20
(unmonitored)  00:01:58
User #: 02          dutch dutch schaeffer     Channel: SIP/dutch-08d86350
(unmonitored)  00:01:46
2 users in that conference.
```

meetme lock prevents any new users from joining.

To *kick* or *mute* a user, use the conference and user numbers:

```
asterisk1*CLI> meetme kick 8001 02
```

Discussion

Hopefully, your users won't need this sort of babysitting, and you'll only need it to correct technical problems, like a channel not hanging up when the user leaves the conference.

See Also

- The sample *meetme.conf*
- Asterisk cmd MeetMe:

    http://www.voip-info.org/wiki/index.php?page=Asterisk+cmd+MeetMe

5.20 Getting SIP Traffic Through iptables NAT Firewalls

Problem

You're having fits with SIP traffic because it's difficult to get it past NAT firewalls. You could put your Asterisk server in your DMZ, if you have a spare routable public IP address. Or, you could use some kind of a SIP proxy, but those come with a different kind of pain. Can't you just schlep those SIP packets through your NAT-ed *iptables* firewall with connection tracking?

Solution

Yes, you can, thanks to the shiny new *iptables* SIP connection-tracking module. It comes with the 2.6.18 Linux kernel, or, you can use Netfilter's Patch-O-Matic to apply it to older kernels. If you have a 2.6.18 kernel or newer, look in */boot/config-[kernel version]* to see if SIP connection tracking is already enabled. Look for:

```
CONFIG_IP_NF_NAT_SIP=y
CONFIG_IP_NF_SIP=y
```

If you see those magic words, then all you need are a few *iptables* rules in your *iptables* script, and to load the kernel modules. This example is for a standalone NAT firewall and router that forwards your SIP traffic to a separate Asterisk server with a private IP address of 192.168.1.25, and follows the conventions in Chapter 3:

```
$ipt -t nat -A PREROUTING -p tcp -i $WAN_IFACE --dport 5060 -j DNAT --to-destination
192.168.2.25:5060
$ipt -A FORWARD -p tcp -i $WAN_IFACE -o $DMZ_IFACE -d 192.168.2.25 --dport 5060 -j
ACCEPT
```

These rules are for an Asterisk server with a public IP address that is directly exposed to the Internet:

```
$ipt -A INPUT -p udp --dport 5060 -j ACCEPT
$ipt -A FORWARD -o eth0 -p udp --dport 5060 -j ACCEPT
```

Put this in your *iptables* script to load the modules:

```
modprobe ip_conntrack_sip
modprobe ip_nat_sip
```

Reload your *iptables* rules, and you're in business.

Discussion

If you don't have kernel support already, you can patch kernels back to version 2.6.11. You need complete kernel sources (not just headers), a 2.6.11 kernel or newer, and *iptables* sources. I'm going to skip how to set up a kernel build environment; please visit the See Also section for kernel building references.

Once you have a kernel build environment ready to go, fetch the current stable *iptables* source tarball from Netfilter.org (*http://netfilter.org/projects/iptables/downloads.html*). Verify the *md5sum*, and unpack the tarball into whatever directory you want.

Then, download the latest Patch-O-Matic (*ftp://ftp.netfilter.org/pub/patch-o-matic-ng/snapshot/ snapshot*). Verify the *md5sum*. Unpack the tarball into a directory of your choice, and change to its top-level directory. Apply the *sip-conntrack-nat* patch to the kernel sources with this command. You'll need to tell it the filepaths to your kernel and *iptables* sources:

```
$ ./runme sip-conntrack-nat
/home/carla/lib/iptables/
Hey! KERNEL_DIR is not set.
Where is your kernel source directory? [/usr/src/linux]
Hey! IPTABLES_DIR is not set.
Where is your iptables source code directory? [/usr/src/iptables]
Welcome to Patch-o-matic ($Revision$)!
```

You'll get some informational output, and then:

```
The SIP conntrack/NAT modules support the connection tracking/NATing of
the data streams requested on the dynamic RTP/RTCP ports, as well as mangling
of SIP requests/responses.


-----------------------------------------------------------------
Do you want to apply this patch [N/y/t/f/a/r/b/w/q/?]
```

Type y, and the patch is applied.

Now, you must compile a new kernel. When you configure your kernel, be sure to select the SIP support option in Networking → Networking support → Networking options → Network packet filtering → IP: Netfilter Configuration.

Install the new kernel, make and reload your *iptables* rules, and you're in business.

You may install *iptables* sources with Yum on CentOS:

```
# yum install iptables-devel
```

On Debian, run:

```
# apt-get install iptables-dev
```

See Also

- Every Linux distribution has its own kernel-building tools—Debian users can follow Chapter 7 of the Debian Reference Manual (*http://www.debian.org/doc/manuals/reference/ch-kernel.en.html*); CentOS (and Red Hat and Fedora) users can refer to the instructions in their release notes
- Chapter 10, "Patching, Customizing, and Upgrading Kernels," in *Linux Cookbook*, by Carla Schroder (O'Reilly)
- Appendix C

5.21 Getting IAX Traffic Through iptables NAT Firewalls

Problem

You need to know what rules to use to let IAX traffic through *iptables* firewalls.

Solution

Use these rules for an Asterisk server that sits behind a standalone *iptables* firewall and router:

```
$ipt -t nat -A PREROUTING -p tcp -i $WAN_IFACE --dport 4569 -j \
DNAT --to-destination 192.168.2.25:4569
$ipt -A FORWARD -p tcp -i $WAN_IFACE -o $DMZ_IFACE -d 192.168.2.25 \
  --dport 4569 -j ACCEPT
```

These rules are for an Asterisk server with a public IP address that is directly exposed to the Internet, and is running *iptables*:

```
$ipt -A INPUT -p udp --dport 4569 -j ACCEPT
$ipt -A FORWARD -o eth0 -p udp --dport 4569 -j ACCEPT
```

Reload your rules, and you're in business.

These examples follow the conventions in Chapter 3.

Discussion

IAX is a native Asterisk protocol that is efficient, firewall friendly, and able to carry a number of SIP calls over a single IAX trunk.

See Also

- Chapter 3

5.22 Using AsteriskNOW, "Asterisk in 30 Minutes"

Problem

You're not afraid of the command line or of editing text files, but it seems like a lot of work to administer an Asterisk server this way, with a lot of complexity and room for errors. Isn't there a good, clean, graphical administration interface for Asterisk? One that doesn't install with a lot of lard, and lets you make changes from the GUI and the text configuration files without conflicts?

Solution

There is indeed, and it is a product of Digium itself. AsteriskNOW is a software appliance that includes the operating system, Asterisk, and good web-based graphical interfaces for the Asterisk server and the operating system.

Visit AsteriskNOW.org (*http://www.asterisknow.org/*) to download the installation image. You'll have a choice of several different images, including x86-32 and x86-64, a Xen guest image, a VMWare guest image, and a liveCD image.

The installer will look for a DHCP server. Log on to the server to find its IP address with the username *admin*, password *password*. It should tell you the IP address right on the console. If it doesn't, because gosh knows Asterisk is evolving faster than science fiction critters, use the *ifconfig* command.

Alt-F9 takes you to the familiar Asterisk CLI, and Alt-F1 takes you back to the console menu.

Then, log in to the web administration interface from a neighboring PC. Fire up a Firefox web browser, and go to *https://[ip address]*. You'll get a bunch of scary warnings about the server certificate. Accept the certificate, and continue. Log in with *admin*, *password*. This is not the same *admin* user as on the server console, but the web GUI *admin* user. You'll be required to change the password, then relog in and run a setup wizard before you can do anything else. You can quickly skip through the setup wizard if you want to get right into exploring the interface.

On the top right of the AsteriskNOW web GUI, click System Configuration to get into the rPath Linux control panel. This has yet a third separate *admin* user.

An SSH server runs by default, so you can log in remotely this way:

```
$ ssh admin@[ip address]
```

AsteriskNOW does not come with a root password. You can use *sudo* for most chores, but you should still have a root password on the server. On the Asterisk-NOW console, create one this way:

```
[admin@localhost ~]$ sudo passwd root
```

Discussion

Using *sudo* in the way AsteriskNOW has it setup is convenient. You only have to remember one password, and all sudo commands are logged. But, you still need a real root password. Not all commands work with *sudo* because some commands and scripts don't know how to handle *sudo* asking for a password. And, perhaps more importantly, the Ext3 filesystem reserves 5 percent of the filesystem exclusively for the *root* user. This makes it possible for *root* to recover a system when user processes have have gone berserk and completely filled up the filesystem.

AsteriskNOW comes with one-click purchase and provisioning of Polycom IP phones, one-click setup with VoicePulse, and you can upgrade from the free AsteriskNOW to the supported Asterisk Business Edition. Watch for more integration with hardware and service vendors with new AsteriskNOW releases and upgrades.

See Also

- Here be Wikis, forums, and all manner of usefulness:

    AsteriskNOW support: *http://www.asterisknow.org/support*

5.23 Installing and Removing Packages on AsteriskNOW

Problem

Even though AsteriskNOW runs on Linux, it's not the Linux you know. It looks somewhat like Red Hat, but there are no RPM or Yum commands for installing and removing packages. It uses the familiar Bash shell, and */bin* and */sbin* contain all the familiar Linux commands. So, how do you manage the software?

Solution

AsteriskNOW uses rPath Linux, which is a specialized Linux distribution designed for building software appliances like AsteriskNOW. It's designed to be easily customizable and efficient, containing only the packages needed to run your appliance. It uses the Conary build system, which includes custom package repositories and commands.

These commands show short and extended help lists:

```
[admin@localhost ~]$ conary
[admin@localhost ~]$ conary help
```

You can see a list of all packages installed on your system:

```
[admin@localhost ~]$ conary query | less
```

grep helps you find a specific installed program:

```
[admin@localhost ~]$ conary query | grep speex
speex=1.1.10-2-0.1
```

Get information on an installed package:

```
admin@localhost ~]$ conary q speex --info
```

Conary calls dependencies and related packages *troves*. View installed *troves* with this command:

```
admin@localhost ~]$ conary q speex --troves
```

This command shows all *troves*, including those that are not installed:

```
[admin@localhost ~]$ conary q speex --all-troves
```

This command displays dependencies:

```
[admin@localhost ~]$ conary q speex --deps
```

You can see what is available to install:

```
[admin@localhost ~]$ conary rq | less
```

This command installs a new package or updates an installed package:

```
[admin@localhost ~]# conary update [packagename]
```

This command removes a package:

```
[admin@localhost ~]# conary erase [packagename]
```

This command updates the whole system:

```
[admin@localhost ~]# conary updateall
```

Discussion

The rPath web control panel controls network configuration, backups, system updates, *admin* password, and the time and date. You'll need the CLI commands for everything else.

See Also

- You'll find a complete administration manual at Conary system administration:

  http://wiki.rpath.com/wiki/index.php/Conary:User

5.24 Connecting Road Warriors and Remote Users

Problem

You want your traveling staff to be able to log in to your Asterisk server from wherever they may roam, or you have far-flung friends and family that you wish to share your server with so you can keep in touch and avoid toll charges.

Solution

They will need SIP or IAX accounts on your server, broadband Internet, and your server must be Internet-accessible. Then they will need either a soft IP phone, an analog telephone adapter like Digium's IAXy (pronounced *eek-see*) or the Linksys Sipura SPA-1001, or a hard IP phone. The IAXy and SPA-1001 are finicky to configure, but easy for your users.

Using softphones means your users will need their own computers with sound gear and access to broadband Internet. And, if they are behind firewalls, they'll need those configured to allow their VoIP traffic. Follow Recipe 5.6. Make sure your server has a proper, publicly routable IP address.

The IAXy and the SPA-1001 are very small, so users can easily travel with them. They'll need analog phones and broadband Internet to use these. The IAXy uses the IAX protocol, and costs around $100. The SPA-1001 is a SIP device, and is about $70. Both come with good configuration instructions. Your Asterisk server supports IAX and SIP, so either device works fine.

Good-quality hard phones start around $100. These are usually big, multiline desk phones, and not very portable for road warriors. But, they might be nice for Mom and Dad. They'll be easy to use, and have good sound quality. Not many hardphones support IAX, so you'll probably have to set up a SIP account for Mom and Dad.

Discussion

You'll want to configure these remote accounts carefully, so that you are not exposing internal or outbound calling services to the world. If you have PSTN termination on your server, your remote users will have your local calling area for free, and any other services you give them access to. The recipes in this chapter show you how to separate services and privileges.

See Also

- Search VoIP-info.org (*http://voip-info.org/wiki/*) and the Asterisk mailing lists (*http://www.voip-info.org/wiki-Asterisk+Mailing+Lists*) for information and user reviews on specific products
- These are some sites to get you started on shopping:

  VoIP Supply: *http://www.voipsupply.com*
  Telephonyware.com: *http://www.telephonyware.com/*

## CHAPTER 6

Routing with Linux

6.0 Introduction

Linux on ordinary commodity hardware can handle small to medium routing needs just fine. The low- to mid-range commercial routers use hardware comparable to ordinary PC hardware. The main difference is form factor and firmware. Routers that use a real-time operating system, like the Cisco IOS, perform a bit better under heavy loads than Linux-based routers. Big companies with large, complex routing tables and ISPs need the heavy-duty gear. The rest of us can get by on the cheap just fine. You don't want poor-quality hardware; that's always a bad idea. You just don't need to spend the moon for simple routing like this chapter covers.

The highest-end routers use specialized hardware that is designed to move the maximum number of packets per second. They come with multiple fat data buses, multiple CPUs, and Ternary Content Addressable Memory (TCAM) memory. TCAM is several times faster than the fastest system RAM, and many times more expensive. TCAM is not used in lower-cost devices, and no software can shovel packets as fast as TCAM.

But, for the majority of admins, this is not an issue because you have an ISP to do the heavy lifting. Your routing tables are small because you're managing only a few networks that are directly under your care.

In this chapter, we're going to perform feats of static routing using the *route* and *ip* commands, and dynamic routing using two interior routing protocols, Routing Information Protocol (RIP) and Open Shortest Path First (OSPF).

How do you know which one to use? RIP is the simplest to implement. Every 30 seconds it multicasts its entire routing table to your whole network, and all RIP routers update their routing tables accordingly. RIP is known as a *distance-vector routing algorithm* because it measures the distance of a route by the number of hops, and it calls the path to the next hop a *vector*. RIP is limited to 15 hops; if any destination is farther than that, RIP thinks it is unreachable.

RIP works fine for managing stable, less-complex networks.

OSPF is a *link-state* algorithm, which means a router multicasts its information when changes have occurred, and routine updates every 30 minutes. Each OSPF router contains the entire topology for the network, and is able to calculate on its own the best path through the network.

As your network grows, it becomes apparent that updates are the bottlenecks. When you're riding herd on 50 or 100 or more routers, they're going to spend a lot of time and bandwidth talking to each other. OSPF solves this problem by allowing you to divide your network into *areas*. These must all be connected to a common backbone, and then the routers inside each area only need to contain the topology for that area, and the border routers communicate between each area.

Exterior Protocols

You've probably heard of exterior routing protocols like Border Gateway Protocol (BGP) and Exterior Gateway Protocol (EGP). Quagga supports BGP. We're not going to get into these in this chapter because if you need BGP, you'll have a service provider to make sure you're set up correctly. When do you need BGP? When you're a service provider yourself, or when you have two or more transit providers, and you want them configured for failover and redundancy. For example, ISPs boast of things like "four Tier-One Internet connectivity providers…multiple connections, managed with Border Gateway Protocol to optimize routing across connections, ensures low-latency delivery to users worldwide."

If you're in a situation where you need high-availability and no excuses, you might first consider using a hosting service instead of self-hosting. Then someone else has all the headaches of security, maintaining equipment, providing bandwidth, and load-balancing.

There are all kinds of excellent specialized router Linux distributions. See the Introduction to Chapter 3 for a partial list.

Linux Routing and Networking Commands

You'll need to know several similar methods for doing the same things. The *net-tools* package is the old standby for viewing, creating and deleting routes, viewing information on interfaces, assigning addresses to interfaces, bringing interfaces up and down, and viewing or setting hostnames. The *netstat* command is a utility you'll use a lot for displaying routes, interface statistics, and showing listening sockets and active network connections. These are the commands that come with *net-tools*:

- *ifconfig*
- *nameif*

- *plipconfig*
- *rarp*
- *route*
- *slattach*
- *ipmaddr*
- *iptunnel*
- *mii-tool*
- *netstat*
- *hostname*

Debian puts *hostname* in a separate package. *dnsdomainname*, *domainname*, *nisdomainname*, and *ypdomainname* are all part of *hostname*.

In fact, the different Linux distributions all mess with *net-tools* in various ways, so yours may include some different commands.

iproute2 is supposed to replace *net-tools*, but it hasn't, and probably never will. *iproute2* is for policy routing and traffic shaping, plus it has some nice everyday features not found in *net-tools*, and it has the functionality of *net-tools*. It includes these commands:

- *rtmon*
- *ip*
- *netbug*
- *rtacct*
- *ss*
- *lnstat*
- *nstat*
- *cbq*
- *tc*
- *arpd*

ip and *tc* are the most commonly used *iproute2* commands. *ip* does the same jobs as *route*, *ifconfig*, *iptunnel*, and *arp*. Just like *net-tools*, *iproute2* varies between distributions. *tc* is for traffic-shaping.

It would be lovely to have to know only one of these, but you're going to encounter both, so you might as well get familiar with all of them.

6.1   Calculating Subnets with ipcalc

Problem

You often see documentation with instructions like "you must use different subnets for this to work," or "be sure your hosts are all on the same network." But, you're a bit hazy on what this means, and how to make the address calculations—is there a tool to help you?

Solution

There is indeed: *ipcalc*. This is a standard program available for any Linux. This command shows you everything you need to know for a single network:

```
$ ipcalc 192.168.10.0/24
Address:   192.168.10.0          11000000.10101000.00001010. 00000000
Netmask:   255.255.255.0 = 24    11111111.11111111.11111111. 00000000
Wildcard:  0.0.0.255             00000000.00000000.00000000. 11111111
=>
Network:   192.168.10.0/24       11000000.10101000.00001010. 00000000
HostMin:   192.168.10.1          11000000.10101000.00001010. 00000001
HostMax:   192.168.10.254        11000000.10101000.00001010. 11111110
Broadcast: 192.168.10.255        11000000.10101000.00001010. 11111111
Hosts/Net: 254                   Class C, Private Internet
```

So, here you see the old-fashioned dotted-quad notation, the newfangled CIDR notation, the available host address range, the number of hosts you can have on this network, and the binary addresses. *ipcalc* shows the network portion of the address, which is 192.168.10, and the host portion, which is 1–254. And it's a nice visual aid for understanding netmasks.

 On Fedora, *ipcalc* is very different, and not nearly as helpful as the real *ipcalc*. You can install the real *ipcalc* from source, which you can download from *http://freshmeat.net/projects/ipcalc/*, or try *whatmask*. *whatmask* is similar to *ipcalc*, and it is in the Fedora repositories, so you can install it with yum install whatmask.

You need to specify the netmask if it's not /24 (or 255.255.255.0). The more common CIDR netmasks are:

/8
/16
/24

Or, their dotted-quad equivalents:

255.0.0.0
255.255.0.0
255.255.255.0

Use netmasks to differentiate the network part of the address and the host address part. These are the private IPv4 private address ranges:

10.0.0.0–10.255.255.255
172.16.0.0–172.31.255.255
192.168.0.0–192.168.255.255

The first one, 10.0.0.0–10.255.255.255, gives you the most possible addresses. If you use the first quad for the network address, and the last three for host addresses, you'll have 16,777,214 addresses to play with, all in one giant network, which you can see for yourself:

```
$ ipcalc 10.0.0.0/8
Address:   10.0.0.0           00001010. 00000000.00000000.00000000
Netmask:   255.0.0.0 = 8      11111111. 00000000.00000000.00000000
Wildcard:  0.255.255.255      00000000. 11111111.11111111.11111111
=>
Network:   10.0.0.0/8         00001010. 00000000.00000000.00000000
HostMin:   10.0.0.1           00001010. 00000000.00000000.00000001
HostMax:   10.255.255.254     00001010. 11111111.11111111.11111110
Broadcast: 10.255.255.255     00001010. 11111111.11111111.11111111
Hosts/Net: 16777214           Class A, Private Internet
```

A 16,777,214-host network all in one subnet probably isn't what you want, so you can whittle it down into smaller subnets. This example show three subnets that use the first two quads (in bold) for the network portion of the address:

$ ipcalc **10.1**.0.0/16
$ ipcalc **10.2**.0.0/16
$ ipcalc **10.3**.0.0/16

You could number these all the way up to 10.255.0.0/16. You can make even smaller subnets with a bigger netmask:

$ ipcalc **10.1.1**.0/24
$ ipcalc **10.1.2**.0/24
$ ipcalc **10.1.3**.0/24

All the way up to **10.255.255**.0/16.

The host address portions number from 1–254. Remember, the broadcast address is always the highest in the subnet.

ipcalc has one more excellent trick: calculating multiple subnets with one command. Suppose you want to divide a 10.150.0.0 network into three subnets for 100 total hosts. Just tell *ipcalc* your netmask, and how many hosts you want in each segment:

```
$ ipcalc 10.150.0.0/16 --s 25 25 50
```

ipcalc then spells it all out for you, and even shows your unused address ranges.

Discussion

ipcalc has a few simple options, which you can see by running:

```
$ ipcalc --help
```

Classless Inter-Domain Routing (CIDR) notation is compact, and lets you slice and dice your networks finely, all the way down to a single host, which is /32. It is supposed to replace the old dotted-quad netmask notation, but you'll find you need to know both because there are applications that still don't support CIDR.

See Also

- man 1 ipcalc
- RFC 1597—Address Allocation for Private Internets

6.2 Setting a Default Gateway

Problem

You're a bit confused on the concepts of gateways and default gateways. When do you need them? What are they for? How do you configure them?

Solution

Gateways forward traffic between different networks, like different subnets, or your local network and the Internet. Another way to think of them is *next hop routers*. The default gateway contains the default route out of your network. Any host that is allowed access outside of the local network needs a default gateway.

Suppose your network is set up like this:

- Your LAN is on 10.10.0.0/24
- You have a single shared Internet connection with a static WAN address of 208. 201.239.36
- Your ISP has assigned you a default gateway of 208.201.239.1

You'll need to configure two gateways: from your individual LAN hosts to your router, and then from your router to your ISP. Figure 6-1 illustrates this network configuration.

There are several different ways of configuring gateways on your LAN hosts. One way is with *route*:

```
# route add default gw 10.10.0.25
```

Another way is with *iproute2*:

```
# ip route add default via 10.10.0.25
```

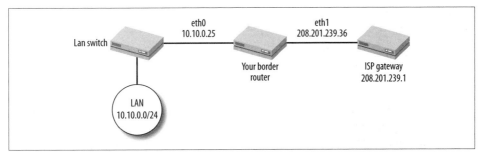

Figure 6-1. LAN, router, and ISP gateway

If your PC has more than one network interface, you can specify a single one:

```
# route add default gw 10.10.0.25 eth2
# ip route add default via 10.10.0.25 dev eth2
```

But, these will not survive a reboot. Debian users have */etc/network/interfaces* for permanent network configurations. For hosts with static IP addresses, add a gateway line to your interface stanzas:

```
gateway 10.10.0.25
```

Fedora users have individual configuration files for each interface in */etc/sysconfig/ network-scripts*, like *ifcfg-eth0*:

```
gateway 10.10.0.25
```

Your router then needs a gateway 208.201.239.1 statement in the configuration for its WAN interface to get Internet access.

Use these commands to remove gateways:

```
# route del default
# route del default gw 10.10.0.25
# ip route del default
# ip route del default via 10.10.0.25
```

ip will not let you set more than one default gateway, which *route* will let you do. There can be only one.

Discussion

Gateways cannot have addresses outside of their own networks. The example used in this recipe demonstrates this—the WAN interface, 208.201.239.36, is on the same network as the ISP, 208.201.239.1. The LAN gateway interface is on the LAN network.

How do you decide which route to make your default gateway? By the number of routes it serves. Your Internet gateway leads you to hundreds of thousands of routes, while you're going to have just a few local routes.

Using *route* or *ip* is great for testing because you can set up and tear down routes as fast as you can type.

Computers do not need routes or default gateways to access other hosts in their own subnet. You can test this easily by deleting your default gateway and running some *ping* tests.

Any hosts that need access outside their own subnet must have default gateways. A computer may have many routes, but it can have only one default gateway. This keeps your routing tables manageable because then you don't need routes for every possible destination.

TCP/IP routing can be thought of as a series of hops. You'll see the term *next hop* a lot. All it means is any router only needs to know the next router to forward packets to. It doesn't have to know how to get all the way to the final destination.

The word *gateway* encompasses a number of meanings. It's the entrance to a network, and it's a translator between different protocols or codecs. In the olden days, you would have needed a gateway between incompatible networking protocols like Token Ring, IPX/SPX, and Ethernet. TCP/IP and Ethernet are pretty much it these days, and most computers support multiple protocols. Voice over IP often requires transcoding of various VoIP protocols, so we have specialized *media gateways* to do this.

See Also

- Chapter 4 to learn how to configure DHCP and DNS using *dnsmasq*
- man 8 ip
- man 8 route

6.3   Setting Up a Simple Local Router

Problem

You have a single shared Internet connection, and your LAN is divided into a number of subnets. You want your subnets to be able to communicate with each other. What do you have to do to make this magic occur?

Solution

Not much. All it takes is a single router, and all of your subnets connected to it. Suppose you have these three subnets:

- 10.25.0.0/16
- 172.32.0.0/16
- 192.168.254.0/24

You router needs to have three network interfaces with one address on each network segment:

- eth0 = 10.25.0.10
- eth1 = 172.32.12.100
- eth2 = 192.168.254.31

Each subnet has its own switch, which is connected to your router, like Figure 6-2.

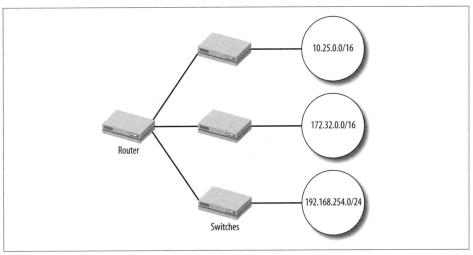

Figure 6-2. Local subnets connected to a single router

Then, turn on IP forwarding on your router. You can do this from the command line:

```
# echo 1 > /proc/sys/net/ipv4/ip_forward
```

This does not survive a reboot, so you can set it permanently in */etc/sysctl.conf*, and then start it immediately:

```
##/etc/sysctl.conf
net.ipv4.ip_forward = 1
```

```
# sysctl -p
```

Next, assign these three addresses as the default gateways for the hosts on each network. All computers in the 10.25.0.0/16 will use 10.25.0.10 as their default gateway, and I think you can extrapolate what the other two networks will use for their default gateways.

Once this is done, your three networks will be able to pass TCP/IP traffic back and forth with ease.

Discussion

You don't have to use addressing from completely different private address ranges like the ones used in this recipe. I used those to make it easier to see the different networks. You can use any nonconflicting addressing scheme, such as in these examples:

```
10.25.0.0/16
10.26.0.0/16
10.27.0.0/16
```

or:

```
172.16.1.0/24
172.16.2.0/24
172.16.3.0/24
```

You must not have duplicate addresses anywhere. Don't be shy about using *ipcalc*—it's a lifesaver.

When you turn on IP forwarding on the router, it automatically forwards packets between between all of its interfaces. This works fine for two types of networks:

- Networks using private addressing
- Networks using public routable addresses

It does not work when you want to share an Internet connection with networks using private addressing because the private address ranges are not routable over the Internet. You need Network Address Translation (NAT) to make this work. Suppose your multihomed router is attached to two local networks using private addresses, and has one public routable IP address on an Internet-connected interface. Your private networks will see each other just fine, but they won't have Internet access until you configure NAT.

Strictly speaking, the private address ranges are routable, as you can see on your local networks, but most ISPs filter out any that find their way on to the Internet and won't forward them. Because, obviously, we can't have random hordes of duplicate private addresses gumming up the Internet.

See Recipe 6.4 to learn a simple way to use NAT to share an Internet connection.

See Also

- man 8 sysctl
- Recipes 3.2 and 3.3 to learn how to configure network interfaces

6.4 Configuring Simplest Internet Connection Sharing

Problem

You want to enable Internet connection sharing on your Linux router. You have one or more networks behind your router using private address ranges. You don't want to set up a firewall because you're taking care of that elsewhere, or you just want to do some testing, so you want plain old simple Internet connection sharing.

Solution

Use this *iptables* script, which follows the conventions used in Chapter 3:

```
#!/bin/sh
##/usr/local/bin/nat_share
#minimal iptables script for
#sharing an Internet connection

#define variables
ipt="/sbin/iptables"
mod="/sbin/modprobe"
WAN_IFACE="eth1"

#load kernel modules
$mod ip_tables
$mod iptable_filter
$mod iptable_nat
$mod ip_conntrack
$mod iptable_mangle
$mod ipt_MASQUERADE
$mod ip_nat_ftp
$mod ip_nat_irc
$mod ip_conntrack_ftp
$mod ip_conntrack_irc

#Flush all active rules and delete all custom chains
$ipt -F
$ipt -t nat -F
$ipt -t mangle -F
$ipt -X
$ipt -t nat -X
$ipt -t mangle -X

#Set default policies
$ipt -P INPUT ACCEPT
$ipt -P FORWARD ACCEPT
$ipt -P OUTPUT ACCEPT
$ipt -t nat -P OUTPUT ACCEPT
```

```
$ipt -t nat -P PREROUTING ACCEPT
$ipt -t nat -P POSTROUTING ACCEPT
$ipt -t mangle -P PREROUTING ACCEPT
$ipt -t mangle -P POSTROUTING ACCEPT

#always have an entry for interface lo
$ipt -A INPUT -i lo -j ACCEPT
$ipt -A OUTPUT -i lo -j ACCEPT

#rewrite source addresses to WAN address
$ipt -t nat -A POSTROUTING -o $WAN_IFACE -j SNAT --to-source 22.33.44.55
```

Of course, you must substitute your own interface name and WAN address. If you don't have a static WAN address, but get it from DHCP, use this line instead:

```
#Enable IP masquerading
$ipt -t nat -A POSTROUTING -o $WAN_IFACE -j MASQUERADE
```

This script offers zero protection—it does no packet filtering at all, but only handles the job of rewriting your private addresses to your WAN address and back again.

Discussion

You're probably looking at this script and wondering "what is so simple about this giant script?" But it really is. All those kernel modules are required. You could get rid of that part of the script by building them into a custom kernel instead of using loadable modules. You could leave out the next section, the part that flushes existing rules and chains, by using a separate script to do this, such as *fw_flush* from Chapter 3. It's important to give *iptables* a clean start so you're not getting interefence from leftover rules or chains. Finally, you have to have the correct policies, or you might get unexpected results. The last line makes it possible to share your Internet connection.

This is a completely insecure setup. Why would you want to use this? It's good for testing, and for when you want to place your firewall somewhere else. For example, you might want to use a separate firewall for each network segment, or one firewall for a DMZ, and another one for your private networks.

There is a lot of overlap between routers and *iptables*, so don't make yourself crazy trying to over-complicate your routers. For example, *ip* also has options for configuring NAT. It's a bit of a pain, and full of perilous pitfalls. *iptables* gives you much finer control and fewer traps. As a general rule, leave routing to your routers, and packet-filtering and mangling to *iptables*.

See Also

- Chapter 3 to learn more about *iptables*
- To learn about NAT and *iproute2*, see Martin Brown's excellent "Guide to IP Layer Network Administration with Linux": *http://linux-ip.net/html/index.html*

6.5   Configuring Static Routing Across Subnets

Problem

You have several private subnets to traverse, and they are not all connected to the same physical router, so how do you give them access to each other?

Solution

There is an easy way and a hard way. The hard way is to create static routes from router to router. Suppose you have three subnets and three routers, like Figure 6-3 shows.

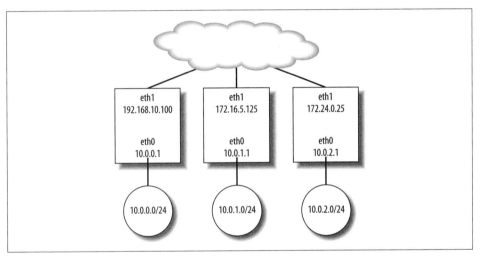

Figure 6-3. Three subnets and three routers

Each router will need two routes. For example, you would set the routes on Router C like this:

```
# route add -net 192.168.10.0/24 gw 172.24.0.25 eth1
# route add -net 172.16.5.0/24 gw 172.24.0.25 eth1
```

Then, Router B:

```
# route add -net 192.168.10.0/24 gw 172.16.5.125 eth1
# route add -net 172.24.0.0/24 gw 172.16.5.125 eth1
```

And, Router A:

```
# route add -net 172.16.5.0/24 gw 192.168.10.100 eth1
# route add -net 172.24.0.0/24 gw 192.168.10.100 eth1
```

Now, hosts on all three subnets can communicate with each other. Deleting routes is done like this:

```
# route del -net 192.168.10.0/24
```

This is a fair bit of work; you have to know netmasks, and be very careful not to make typos. The easy way is to put all three routers on the same network, like in Figure 6-4.

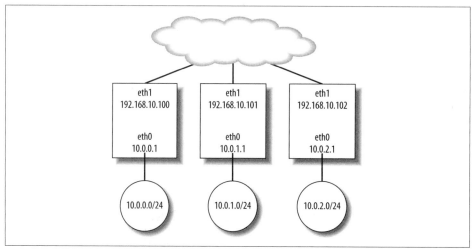

Figure 6-4. Three routers on the same network

Now, you don't need to set routes at all.

Discussion

You may also use *ip* to set and remove routes:

```
# ip route add 172.16.5.0/24 via 192.168.10.100
# ip route del 172.16.5.0/24
```

It doesn't take long for the charm of setting static routes to wear off. The other easy way is to use dynamic routing, which we'll get to starting with Recipe 6.7.

See Also

• man 8 route

6.6   Making Static Routes Persistent

Problem

You don't want to have to retype all those *route* commands every time there's a power blip, or when you make hardware changes. Aren't there some nice configuration files for permanently enshrining your static routes?

Solution

Of course there are. On Debian, add them to */etc/network/interfaces* in the stanza for their corresponding interface:

```
auto eth1
iface eth1 inet static
address  192.168.10.100
netmask 255.255.255.0
gateway 22.33.44.55
broadcast 192.168.10.255

up route add -net 172.16.5.0/24 gw 192.168.10.100 eth1
up route add -net 172.24.0.0/24 gw 192.168.10.100 eth1
down route del -net 172.24.0.0/24
down route del -net 172.16.5.0/24
```

On Fedora, create a */etc/sysconfig/network-scripts/route-* file, like this:

```
##/etc/sysconfig/network-scripts/route-eth1
192.168.10.0/24 via 172.24.0.25
172.16.5.0/24 via 172.24.0.25
```

This uses *ip* command-type syntax. It is important to use the correct filename, with your correct device name, or it won't work. Take the device name from its own configuration file, like */etc/sysconfig/network-scripts/ifcfg-eth1*.

Discussion

On Fedora, don't use */etc/network/static-routes*. That was deprecated several releases ago, and no longer works.

Your routers will need a default gateway if there is another route out of your network, like an Internet connection. If there is no Internet or link to another separate network, they won't need default gateways.

See Also

- man 5 interfaces (Debian)
- man 8 ifup (Debian)
- man 8 ip

6.7 Using RIP Dynamic Routing on Debian

Problem

Your networks aren't all that complex, but you don't want to hassle with manually configuring routes. Isn't this the kind of work that computers should be doing, the repetitive boring stuff? Your routers are Debian-based.

Solution

Indeed, this is the sort of drudgery that computers excel at handling. There are two categories of dynamic routing protocols: interior and exterior. In this recipe, we shall look at Routing Information Protocol, the simplest interior routing protocol. RIP is included in the Quagga suite of routing protocols.

Installation is boringly easy:

```
# aptitude install quagga
```

Now, you must edit some configuration files. Start with */etc/quagga/daemons*, and enable *zebra* and *ripd*:

```
##/etc/quagga/daemons
zebra=yes
bgpd=no
ospfd=no
ospf6d=no
ripd=yes
ripngd=no
isisd=no
```

Next, create */etc/quagga/zebra.conf*:

```
!/etc/quagga/zebra.conf
hostname router1
password bigsecret
enable password bigsecret
service advanced-vty
log file /var/log/quagga/zebra.log
!
!administrative access controls- local machine only
!
access-list localhost permit 127.0.0.1/32
access-list localhost deny any
!
line vty
  access-class localhost
```

Now, create */etc/quagga/ripd.conf*:

```
!/etc/quagga/ripd.conf
hostname router1
password moresecret
enable password moresecret
router rip
network eth1
redistribute static
redistribute connected
service advanced-vty
log file /var/log/quagga/ripd.log
!
!administrative access controls- local machine only
!
```

```
access-list localhost permit 127.0.0.1/32
access-list localhost deny any
!
line vty
  access-class localhost
```

And now, set correct ownership and file permissions:

```
# chown quagga:quagga ripd.conf zebra.conf
# chown :quaggavty vtysh.conf
```

Add these lines to */etc/services*:

```
zebrasrv      2600/tcp          # zebra service
zebra         2601/tcp          # zebra vty
ripd          2602/tcp          # RIPd vty
```

Finally, add this line to */etc/environment*:

```
VTYSH_PAGER=more
```

Now, fire it up:

```
# /etc/init.d/quagga start
```

Do this on all of your routers, and you're finished.

Give it a couple of minutes, then fire up your favorite command to view your routing table:

```
$ /sbin/route
$ ip route show
$ netstat -rn
```

Discussion

Quagga's configuration files use exclamation marks for comments.

All of the Quagga daemons are controlled from a single startup file:

```
# /etc/init.d/quagga {start|stop|restart|force-reload| [daemon]}
```

You could do no more than this recipe and be content. Each Quagga daemon broadcasts its routing table every 30 seconds via multicast to your other RIP-enabled routers, and so you don't have to hassle with creating static routes all over the place.

Debian, by default, limits *vty* access to the local machine in */etc/quagga/debian/conf*, and Fedora uses */etc/sysconfig/quagga*. See Recipe 6.10 to learn how to enable remote logins.

Some definitions for *ripd.conf*:

hostname
:   This is arbitrary, and has nothing to do with the router's Linux hostname. It controls the hostname you see displayed on the *vtysh* or *telnet* command line.

`router rip`
> Specify the `rip` routing protocol here. The default is to send v2 and receive 1 and 2. Other protocol options are `ripng`, `ospf`, `ospf6`, and `bgp`, which of course you would use in their respective configuration files.

`network eth1`
> Which interface or interfaces *ripd* should listen on. Name additional interfaces on separate lines.

`redistribute static`
> Share any static routes; these are listed in *zebra.conf*.

`redistribute connected`
> Share directly connected routes. For example, your router is connected to the 10.0.0.1/24 network, so it will tell your other routers how to get to it.

`service advanced-vty`
> Enables advanced *vty* functions such as command history and tab-completion.

`access-list`
> The two `access-list` lines define a new class, `localhost`. The class name can be anything you want; it doesn't have to be `localhost`. After defining the class, the
>
> ```
> line vty
>   access-class localhost
> ```
>
> lines mean "only allow *vty* logins on the local machine. No remote logins allowed."

The default logging level is `debugging`, which creates the most output. You may specify any of the following loglevels: `emergencies`, `alerts`, `critical`, `errors`, `warnings`, `notifications`, `information`, or `debugging`, like this:

```
log file /var/log/quagga/ripd.log warnings
```

If you don't have a logfile, a crash will generate a */var/tmp/quagga.[daemon name]. crashlog* file. This must be deleted to allow new crashlog files to be generated.

RIP has two versions. RIPv1 is pretty limited, and should be avoided if possible. It does not support classless network notation, and is slow to respond to changing conditions such as a down router. RIPv2 understands classless notation, doesn't get stuck in low gear, and uses triggered updates for quick responses to changes. It is compatible with RIPv1, in case you're stuck with some really old gear. The default is to send v2 and to receive 1 and 2. The `version 2` option tells it to send and receive v2 only.

RIP is limited to 15 hops, so it's no good for large complex networks.

Quagga includes five routing daemons: *ripd*, *ripngd*, *ospfd*, *ospf6d*, and *bgpd*, and one manager daemon, *zebra*. *zebra* must always be started first. Each daemon has its own port that it listens on:

```
zebrasrv    2600/tcp
zebra       2601/tcp
ripd        2602/tcp
ripngd      2603/tcp
ospfd       2604/tcp
bgpd        2605/tcp
ospf6d      2606/tcp
ospfapi     2607/tcp
isisd       2608/tcp
```

See Also

- Quagga documentation: *http://www.quagga.net/docs/docs-info.php*
- */usr/share/doc/quagga/README.Debian*
- man 8 ripd
- man 8 zebra
- Recipe 6.9
- Recipe 6.10

6.8   Using RIP Dynamic Routing on Fedora

Problem

Your networks aren't all that complex, but you don't want to hassle with manually configuring routes. Isn't this the kind of work that computers should be doing, the repetitive boring stuff? Your routers are Fedora-based.

Solution

RIP is configured in exactly the same way on Fedora as it is in Debian (see Recipe 6.7). The one difference is the daemons are started differently. Fedora has a separate control file for each daemon.

Configure *zebra.conf, ripd.conf*, and *vtysh.conf* just like in the previous recipe, and give them the same permissions and ownership.

Next, turn on the startup files for *zebra* and *ripd*:

```
# chkconfig --add zebra
# chkconfig --add ripd
```

Then, you may use the standard Fedora control commands:

```
# /etc/init.d/zebra {start|stop|restart|reload|condrestart|status}
```

Discussion

When you see a line like:

```
# chkconfig: - 16 84
```

in a startup file on Fedora, that means you can run the *chkconfig* command without having to manually specify the runlevels and priorities.

See Also

- Quagga documentation: *http://www.quagga.net/docs/docs-info.php*
- */usr/share/doc/quagga-**
- man 8 ripd
- man 8 zebra

6.9   Using Quagga's Command Line

Problem

You like to run commands from a command shell, and not always have to edit configuration files. How do you do this with Quagga?

Solution

Quagga comes with its own command shell, the Virtual TeletYpe shell *vtysh*. With *vtysh*, you can interact with all Quagga daemons on the local machine. You may also communicate directly with each routing daemon with *telnet*.

First, you need to edit or create */etc/quagga/vtysh.conf*:

```
!/etc/quagga/vtysh.conf
hostname router1
username root nopassword
```

On Debian, add this line to */etc/environment*:

```
VTYSH_PAGER=more
```

Now, open up a new terminal, and fire it up as the *root* user:

```
root@xena:~# vtysh

Hello, this is Quagga (version 0.99.4).
Copyright 1996-2005 Kunihiro Ishiguro, et al.

router1#
```

vtysh has two modes: normal and enable. In normal mode, you can view system status; in enable mode, you can edit configurations and run commands. *vtysh* opens in normal mode. These two commands show both sets of available commands:

```
router1# ?
router1# list
```

You can view all current configurations with one command:

```
router1# write terminal
```

To run any routing commands, or to change configurations, change to *configure* mode:

```
router1# configure terminal
router1(config)#
```

The same commands display all the available commands:

```
router1(config)# ?
router1(config)# list
```

exit closes each session in turn. *vtysh* will run even when no Quagga daemons are running.

A second option is to use *telnet. telnet* can talk to only one daemon at a time, like this example for *ripd*:

```
carla@xena:~$ telnet localhost 2602
Trying 127.0.0.1...
Connected to localhost.
Escape character is '^]'.

Hello, this is Quagga (version 0.99.4).
Copyright 1996-2005 Kunihiro Ishiguro, et al.

User Access Verification

Password:
router1>
```

Any user who knows the daemon's password can log in from *telnet*.

Just like *vtysh*, this opens a session in normal mode. Use the enable command to switch to enable mode, then configure terminal to run configuration commands:

```
router1> enable
router1# configure terminal
router1(config)#
```

exit, end, or quit get you out of there; ? and list show commands.

Discussion

The username root nopassword line is necessary for *vtysh* to even start. The user named here does not need a password to open a *vtysh* session. You may substitute any user you like. Make sure this file is readable and writable only by the user named in the file, and keep in mind there is no way to set a password.

If you get a blank screen with (END) in the bottom-left corner, add VTYSH_PAGER=more to your environment variables, either in your own *.profile*, or globally in */etc/environment*.

The hostname can be anything you want, so you could give each routing daemon a different hostname to help you keep track.

See Also

- Quagga documentation: *http://www.quagga.net/docs/docs-info.php*
- */usr/share/doc/quagga*
- man 8 ripd
- man 8 zebra

6.10   Logging In to Quagga Daemons Remotely

Problem

You understand that Quagga allows *telnet* logins, and that *telnet* is completely inse-cure because it sends all traffic in cleartext. But you feel pretty safe on your own network, so you want to be able to log in and run your routers remotely. Not over the Internet, which would be suicidal, but just on your own LAN.

Solution

You'll need to configure your daemons to listen on all interfaces, and then configure access controls in each daemon's configuration file.

On Debian, edit */etc/quagga/debian.conf* to allow your daemons to listen to all interfaces:

```
vtysh_enable=yes
zebra_options=" --daemon"
ripd_options=" --daemon"
```

Do the same thing in Fedora, in */etc/sysconfig/quagga*.

Then, add these lines to the daemon's configuration files, like this example for *zebra. conf*:

```
access-list localhost permit 127.0.0.1/32
access-list localhost deny any
access-list lan1 permit 192.168.1.0/24
access-list lan1 deny any
access-list lan2 permit 192.168.2.0/24
access-list lan2 deny any
!
line vty
  access-class localhost
  access-class lan1
  access-class lan2
```

That allows logins from localhost and two local subnets, and no one else. Each one is given a separate class; this lets you disable access by commenting out an access-class line.

Then, on Debian, restart Quagga:

```
# /etc/init.d/quagga restart
```

On Fedora, restart each daemon individually:

```
# /etc/init.d/zebra restart
# /etc/init.d/ripd restart
```

Now, you should be able to telnet in from your LAN neighbors by specifying the IP address or hostname and port number:

```
terry@uberpc:~$ telnet xena 2601
```

Discussion

The access-list names, which in this example are localhost, lan1, and lan2, are whatever you want them to be.

The example in this recipe is fairly complex, and controls access per subnet. You could simplify it by lumping everything into a single access list:

```
access-list allowed permit 127.0.0.1/32
access-list allowed permit 192.168.1.0/24
access-list allowed permit 192.168.2.0/24
access-list allowed deny any
!
line vty
 access-class allowed
```

See Also

- Quagga documentation: *http://www.quagga.net/docs/docs-info.php*
- */usr/share/doc/quagga*
- man 8 ripd
- man 8 zebra

6.11 Running Quagga Daemons from the Command Line

Problem

Do you have to edit configuration files? Can't you write them from the Quagga command line, or do commands on the fly?

Solution

Yes, you may do all of those things from both *vtysh* and *telnet*. The commands are exactly the same on the command line as they are in configuration files, so you can write all of your configurations from the command line if you wish. Here is a simple example for *zebra.conf*:

```
carla@xena:~$ telnet localhost 2601
router1> enable
router1> write terminal
router1# configure terminal
router1(config)# hostname zebra2
zebra2(config)# password zebra
zebra2(config)# enable password zebra
zebra2(config)# log file /var/log/quagga/zebra.log
zebra2(config)# write file
Configuration saved to /etc/quagga/zebra.conf
zebra2(config)# write terminal
```

This does not completely overwrite your existing configuration file. It changes existing options and adds new ones, but does not delete any. write terminal shows your current configuration, so if you wish to delete existing options, you can first see what they are, then remove them with the appropriate no command:

```
zebra2(config)# write terminal

Current configuration:
!
hostname zebra2
password zebra
enable password zebra
log file /var/log/quagga/zebra.log
!
interface eth0
 ipv6 nd suppress-ra
!
interface eth1
 ipv6 nd suppress-ra
!
interface lo
!
interface sit0
 ipv6 nd suppress-ra
!
access-list localhost permit 127.0.0.1/32
access-list localhost permit 192.168.1.0/24
access-list localhost permit 192.168.2.0/24
access-list localhost deny any
!
!
line vty
 access-class localhost
```

```
    !
    end

zebra2(config)# no access-list localhost
zebra2(config)# no log file /var/log/quagga/zebra.log
zebra2(config)# write file
Configuration saved to /etc/quagga/zebra.conf
```

Rerun write terminal to view your changes.

You can't do just any old thing with the no command; run the list command to see what no commands are available.

Discussion

A nice bonus of writing configuration files this way is the file permissions are handled automatically for you.

When you configure *zebra.conf* from the command line, it automatically adds ipv6 nd suppress-ra lines for every interface on your system. This means "don't advertise IPv6 routes." If you don't want these, you'll have to delete them directly from *zebra. conf*. If you're not using IPv6, it does no harm to leave them in place.

See Also

- Quagga documentation: *http://www.quagga.net/docs/docs-info.php*
- */usr/share/doc/quagga*

6.12   Monitoring RIPD

Problem

How do you see what RIPD is doing in real time?

Solution

Open a telnet session, and run the built-in RIPD-watching commands:

```
$ telnet localhost 2602
ripd1> show ip rip
ripd1> show ip rip status
ripd1> show work-queues
```

There are a number of helpful debugging commands as well:

```
ripd1> enable
ripd1# debug rip zebra
ripd1# debug rip events
```

Discussion

The first three commands show routes and all manner of statistics, and the communications between routers. The debug commands show probably more details than you'll ever need to know, but when you're tracking down a problem, they usually pinpoint it quickly.

See Also

- Quagga documentation: *http://www.quagga.net/docs/docs-info.php*
- */usr/share/doc/quagga*

6.13   Blackholing Routes with Zebra

Problem

You are getting hit hard by a spammer or other pest, and you would like to drop all traffic from them at your router, instead of hassling with content or packet filters.

Solution

You can set null routes in *zebra.conf* with *ip*:

```
ip route 22.33.44.55/24 null0
```

You may also do this in a telnet session:

```
$ telnet localhost 2601
router1> enable
router1# configure terminal
router1(config)# ip route 22.33.44.55/24 null0
```

Another way to do the same thing is with this command:

```
router1(config)# ip route 22.33.44.55/24 blackhole
```

A variation on this is to use the reject option instead, which sends a "Network is unreachable" error:

```
router1(config)# ip route 22.33.44.55/24 reject
```

Change your mind with a no command:

```
router1(config)# no ip route 22.33.44.55/24 reject
```

Discussion

This blocks everything in the netblock that you specify, so you run the risk of blocking wanted traffic as well as unwanted if you cast your net too widely. Use *ipcalc* to tell you exactly which addresses you are blocking. CIDR notation lets you whittle it finely; for example, 22.33.44.55/32 is a single host address. 22.33.44.55/31 is two hosts, and

22.33.44.55/29 is six hosts. (Yes, *ipcalc* even calculates fake addresses.) 22.33.44.55/24 means you're blocking 254 addresses, and /8 is 16,777,214 addresses.

The incoming packets are not blocked; instead, nothing is sent back to the sender to tell them "neener neener, you're being dev-nulled." Or, to put it in more technical terms, the blackhole option allows in SYN packets, but prevents SYN/ACK packets from being sent in return. So, the sender is ringing the doorbell, but you're pretending you're not home. The connection eventually times out. Using reject closes the connection immediately.

I prefer using *iptables* to do this because *iptables* prevents the unwanted bits from entering your network at all. Additionally, *iptables* lets you fine-tune packet filtering in ways that routing can't. But, blackholing routes is still a useful tool in your network admin arsenal.

See Also

- Quagga documentation: *http://www.quagga.net/docs/docs-info.php*
- man 8 zebra
- */usr/share/doc/quagga*
- Chapter 3

6.14 Using OSPF for Simple Dynamic Routing

Problem

Your network is growing in size and complexity, and you don't feel that *ripd* is doing the job for you anymore. You're riding herd on a growing number of routers, and performance is suffering. Now what?

Solution

This sounds like a job for *ospfd*. *ospfd* is more complex to administer, but it will continue to grow as your site grows, and not fail you.

This is a simple */etc/quagga/ospfd.conf* configuration that does about the same job as *ripd*:

```
!/etc/quagga/ospfd.conf
hostname ospfd1
password bigsecretword
enable password bigsecretword
log file /var/log/quagga/ospfd.log
!
router ospf
  ospf router-id 33.44.55.66
  network 0.0.0.0/0 area 0
```

```
   redistribute connected
   redistribute static
  !
  !administrative access controls- local machine only
  !
  access-list localhost permit 127.0.0.1/32
  access-list localhost deny any
  !
  line vty
    access-class localhost
```

This forwards all routes, with no filtering or restrictions. It's good for testing, but for production systems, you should add authentication and name specific routes:

```
!/etc/quagga/ospfd.conf
hostname ospfd1
password bigsecretword
enable password bigsecretword
log file /var/log/quagga/ospfd.log
!
interface eth0
 ip ospf authentication message-digest
 ip ospf message-digest-key 1 md5 bigsecretword
!
router ospf
 ospf router-id 33.44.55.66
 network 192.168.10.0/0 area 0
 redistribute connected
 redistribute static
 area 0.0.0.0 authentication message-digest
!
!administrative access controls- local machine only
!
access-list localhost permit 127.0.0.1/32
access-list localhost deny any
!
line vty
  access-class localhost
```

ospfd is more efficient than *ripd*, so this could serve your needs for a long time without needing more complex configurations.

On Debian systems, remember to change */etc/quagga/daemons* to read ospfd=yes. Then, restart Quagga:

 # /etc/init.d/quagga restart

On Fedora, just start *ospfd*:

 # /etc/init.d/ospfd start

And remember, *zebra* is the manager daemon, so it must always start first.

Discussion

Give your routers a couple of minutes, then use your favorite routing command to see your new routing table:

```
$ /sbin/route
$ ip route show
$ netstat -rn
```

Here are some definitions:

ospf router-id
> Use this to create an arbitrary, unique 32-bit ID number for each router. An IP address works fine.

passive interface
> Do not use *ospfd* on this interface. Use this for interfaces that are not on a network with your other routers, and on interfaces that lead outside of your network.

See Also

- Quagga documentation: *http://www.quagga.net/docs/docs-info.php*
- man 8 zebra
- */usr/share/doc/quagga*

6.15   Adding a Bit of Security to RIP and OSPF

Problem

All this stuff is going in cleartext between your routers—can't you at least add a password or something, so that the routers must authenticate to each other, and not allow any old host claiming to be a router to mess up your routing tables?

Solution

You can set MD5-hashed passwords on your routers. Add these lines to enable encrypted passwords for *ripd* in */etc/quagga/ripd.conf*:

```
key chain localnet
  key 1
  key-string bigsecretword

interface eth1
  ip rip authentication mode md5
  ip rip authentication key-chain localnet
```

Replace *bigsecretword* with your own password, *localnet* with whatever name you want, and make sure you're specifying the correct network interface.

ospfd uses a slightly different syntax. Add these lines to */etc/quagga/ospfd.conf*:

```
interface eth0
  ip ospf authentication message-digest
  ip ospf message-digest-key 1 md5 bigsecretword

router ospf
  network 172.16.5.0/24 area 0.0.0.1
  area 0.0.0.1 authentication message-digest
```

Use your own password, interface name, and network address. You can create multiple keys for multiple interfaces, numbering them sequentially.

Discussion

Remember to restart your routing daemons after making configuration changes.

RIPv1 does not support any form of authentication. There are two ways to deal with this. One way is to allow only RIPv2 on your network by adding this line to *ripd.conf*:

```
version 2
```

If you must allow RIPv1 support, *ripd* handles this by allowing RIPv1 and other unauthenticated devices to receive routing information, but not to make any changes to the routing tables.

See Also

- Quagga documentation: *http://www.quagga.net/docs/docs-info.php*
- man 8 ospfd
- man 8 ripd
- */usr/share/doc/quagga*

6.16 Monitoring OSPFD

Problem

How do you monitor *ospfd* in real time to see system status and activity, or debug problems?

Solution

Use *ospfd*'s built-in monitoring and debugging commands:

```
$ telnet localhost 2604
ospfd1> show ip ospf
ospfd1> show ip ospf interface
ospfd1> show ip ospf database
ospfd1> show ip ospf database self-originate
```

```
ospfd1> show ip ospf route
ospfd1> enable
ospfd1# debug ospf zebra
ospfd1# debug ospf lsa
ospfd1# debug ospf ism
```

show ip ospf interface displays information on all network interfaces. You may specify one like this:

```
ospfd1> show ip ospf interface eth2
```

Discussion

In addition to these, don't forget your old reliable Linux standbys such as *netstat*, *route*, *traceroute*, *ping*, and *ip*. See Chapter 19 for more information on finding and fixing problems.

See Also

- Quagga documentation: *http://www.quagga.net/docs/docs-info.php*
- man 8 ospfd

CHAPTER 7

Secure Remote Administration with SSH

7.0   Introduction

In this chapter and the next, we'll look at some of the ways Linux offers to administer a server and access your workstation remotely. Linux gives users great flexibility and functionality. You may have command-line only or a full graphical desktop, just as though you were physically present at the remote machine.

OpenSSH is the tool of choice for remote command-line administration. It's secure, and easy to set up and use. It's also good for running a remote graphical desktop because you can tunnel X Windows securely over SSH. This works well over fast local links. However, it's less satisfactory over a dial-up or Internet connection because you'll experience significant lag.

Rdesktop is a simple Linux client for connecting to Windows Terminal Servers, and to the Windows XP Professional Remote Desktop. This is useful for some system administration tasks, and for accessing Windows applications from Linux.

For dial-up users who want a remote graphical desktop over dial-up, FreeNX is just the ticket. It is designed to deliver good performance over slow links. Currently, you can use it to access a Linux PC from Linux, Windows, Mac OS X, and Solaris.

VNC is the reigning champion of cross-platform remote graphical desktops. With VNC, you can do all sorts of neat things: run several PCs from a single keyboard, mouse, and monitor, mix and match operating systems, and do remote technical support.

In this chapter, we'll look at how to use OpenSSH. The next chapter is devoted to Rdesktop, FreeNX, and VNC.

OpenSSH

OpenSSH is the Free Software implementation of the SSH protocol, licensed under a modified BSD license that pretty much lets you do whatever you want with it, including modifying and redistributing it, as long as you include the copyright notices.

OpenSSH is used to foil eavesdropping and spoofing on network traffic by encrypting all traffic during a session, both logins and data transfer. It performs three tasks: authentication, encryption, and guaranteeing the integrity of the data transfer. If something happens to alter your packets, SSH will tell you.

There are two incompatible SSH protocols: SSH-1 and SSH-2. OpenSSH supports both of them, but I do not recommend using SSH-1 at all. If you have to log in to remote systems under someone else's control that are still using SSH-1, consider exercising some tough love and telling them you are not willing to risk your security any more, and they must upgrade. SSH-1 was great in its day, but that was then. It has a number of flaws that are fixed by upgrading to SSH-2. See "CA-2001-35" (*http://www.cert.org/advisories/CA-2001-35.html*) for more information, and don't forget to review the list of references at the end of the article.

SSH Tunneling

You may use SSH port forwarding, also called *tunneling*, to securely encapsulate non-secure protocols like wireless and VNC, which you'll see in various recipes in this book.

OpenSSH supports a number of strong encryption algorithms: 3DES, Blowfish, AES, and *arcfour*. These are unencumbered by patents; in fact, the OpenSSH team has gone to great lengths to ensure that no patented or otherwise encumbered code is inside OpenSSH.

OpenSSH Components

OpenSSH is a suite of remote transfer utilities:

sshd
> The OpenSSH server daemon.

ssh
> Stands for secure shell, though it doesn't really include a shell, but provides a secure channel to the command shell on the remote system.

scp
> Secure copy; this provides encrypted file transfer.

sftp
>   Secure file transfer protocol.

ssh-copy-id
>   Nice little program for installing your personal identity key to a remote machine's *authorized_keys* file.

ssh-keyscan
>   Finds and collects public host keys on a network, saving you the trouble of hunting them down manually.

ssh-keygen
>   Generates and manages RSA and DSA authentication keys.

ssh-add
>   Add RSA or DSA identities to the authentication agent, *ssh-agent*.

ssh-agent
>   Remembers your passphrases over multiple SSH logins for automatic authentication. *ssh-agent* binds to a single login session, so logging out, opening another terminal, or rebooting means starting over. A better utility for this is *keychain*, which remembers your passphrases for as long you don't reboot.

Using OpenSSH

OpenSSH is very flexible, and supports different types of authentication:

Host-key Authentication
>   This uses your Linux login and password to authenticate, and your SSH keys encrypt the session. This is the simplest, as all you need are host keys. An SSH host key assures you that the machine you are logging in to is who it claims to be.

Public-key Authentication
>   Instead of using your system login, authenticate with an SSH identity key. Identity keys authenticate individual users, unlike host keys, which authenticate servers. It's a bit more work to set up because you need to create and distribute identity keys in addition to host keys. This is a slick way to log in to multiple hosts with the same login, plus it protects your system login because the identity key has its own passphrase. Simply distribute copies of your public key to every host that you want to access, and always protect your private key—never share it.

Passphrase-less Authentication
>   This works like public-key authentication, except that the key pair is created without a passphrase. This is useful for automated services, like scripts and *cron* jobs. Because anyone who succeeds in thieving the private key can then easily gain access, you need to be very protective of the private key.

Using a passphrase-less key carries a bit more risk, because then anyone who obtains your private key can masquerade as you. One way to use passphrases with automated processes is to use *ssh-agent* or the *keychain* utility. These remember your passphrases and authenticate automatically. Their one weakness is they do not survive a reboot, so every time you reboot you have to reenter all of your passphrases. See Chapter 17 of *Linux Cookbook* (O'Reilly) for recipes on how to use these excellent utilities.

Key types

There are two different uses for authentication keys: *host keys*, which authenticate computers, and *identity keys*, which authenticate users. The keys themselves are the same type of key, either RSA or DSA. Each key has two parts: the private and the public. The server keeps the private key, and the client uses the public key. Transmissions are encrypted with the public key, and decrypted with the private key. This is a brilliantly simple and easy-to-use scheme—you can safely distribute your public keys as much as you want.

Server and *client* are defined by the direction of the transaction—the server must have the SSH daemon running and listening for connection attempts. The client is anyone logging in to this machine.

7.1   Starting and Stopping OpenSSH

Problem

You installed OpenSSH, and you configured it to start or not start at boot, according to your preference. Now, you want to know how to start and stop it manually, and how to get it to reread its configure file without restarting.

Solution

The answer, as usual, lies in */etc/init.d*.

On Fedora, use these commands:

```
# /etc/init.d/sshd {start|stop|restart|condrestart|reload|status}
```

On Debian systems, use these:

```
# /etc/init.d/ssh {start|stop|reload|force-reload|restart}
```

If you elected to not have the SSH daemon run automatically after installing OpenSSH on Debian, you will need to rename or delete */etc/ssh/sshd_not_to_be_run* before it will start up. Or, you can run `dpkg-reconfigure ssh`.

The OpenSSH configuration file, *sshd.conf*, must be present, or OpenSSH will not start.

Discussion

Port 22, the default SSH port, is a popular target for attack. The Internet is infested with automated attack kits that pummel away at random hosts. Check your firewall logs—you'll see all kinds of garbage trying to brute-force port 22. So, some admins prefer to start up the SSH daemon only when they know they'll need it. Some run it on a nonstandard port, which is configurable in */etc/ssh/ssh_config*, for example:

```
Port 2022
```

Check */etc/services* to make sure you don't use an already-used port, and make an entry for any nonstandard ports you are using. Using a nonstandard port does not fool determined portscanners, but it will alleviate the pummeling a lot and lighten the load on your logfiles. A nice tool for heading off these attacks is the DenyHosts utility; see Recipe 7.15.

Red Hat's condrestart, or conditional restart, restarts a service only if it is already running. If it isn't, it fails silently.

The reload command tells the service to reread its configuration file, instead of completely shutting down and starting up again. This is a nice, nondisruptive way to activate changes.

If you like commands such as condrestart that are not included with your distribution, you may copy them from systems that use them and tweak them for your system. Init scripts are just shell scripts, so they are easy to customize.

See Also

- Chapter 7, "Starting and Stopping Linux," in *Linux Cookbook*, by Carla Schroder (O'Reilly)
- Recipe 7.15

7.2 Creating Strong Passphrases

Problem

You know that you will need to create a strong passphrase every time you create an SSH key, and you want to define a policy that spells out what a strong passphrase is. So, what makes a strong passphrase?

Solution

Use these guidelines for creating your own policy:

- An SSH passphrase must be at least eight characters long.
- It must not be a word in any language. The easy way to handle this is to use a combination of letters, numbers, and mixed cases.

- Reversing words does not work—automated dictionary attacks know about this.
- A short sentence works well for most folks, like "pnt btt3r l*vz m1 gUmz" (peanut butter loves my gums).
- Write it down and keep it in a safe place.

Discussion

Whoever convinced hordes of how-to authors to teach "Don't write down passwords" should be sent to bed without dessert. It doesn't work. If you don't want to believe me, how about a security expert like Bruce Schneier? From his essay "Write Down Your Password" (*http://www.schneier.com/blog/archives/2005/06/write_down_your.html*):

> I recommend that people write their passwords down on a small piece of paper, and keep it with their other valuable small pieces of paper: in their wallet.

Easily remembered passwords are also easily guessed. Don't underestimate the power and sophistication of automated password-guessers. Difficult-to-remember passwords are also difficult to crack. Rarely used passwords are going to evaporate from all but the stickiest of memories.

I use a handwritten file kept in a locked filing cabinet, in a cunningly labeled folder that does not say "Secret Passwords In Here," plus my personal sysadmin notebook that goes with me everywhere. If any thief actually searches hundreds of files and can decode my personal shorthand that tells what each login is for, well, I guess she deserves to succeed at breaking into my stuff!

7.3   Setting Up Host Keys for Simplest Authentication

Problem

You want to know how to set up OpenSSH to log in to a remote host, using the simplest method that it supports.

Solution

Using host-key authentication is the simplest way to set up remote SSH access. You need:

- OpenSSH installed on the machine you want to log into remotely
- The SSH daemon to be running on the remote server, and port 22 not blocked
- SSH client software on the remote client
- A Linux login account on the remote server
- To distribute the public host key to the clients

Your OpenSSH installer should have already created the host keys. If it didn't, see the next recipe.

First, protect your private host key from accidental overwrites:

```
# chmod 400 /etc/ssh/ssh_host_rsa_key
```

Next, the public host key must be distributed to the clients. One way is to log in from the client, and let OpenSSH transfer the key:

```
foober@gouda:~$ ssh reggiano
The authenticity of host 'reggiano (192.168.1.10)' can't be established.
RSA key fingerprint is 26:f6:5b:24:49:e6:71:6f:12:76:1c:2b:a5:ee:fe:fe
Are you sure you want to continue connecting (yes/no)?
Warning: Permanently added 'reggiano 192.168.1.10' (RSA) to the list of known hosts.
foober@reggiano's password:
Linux reggiano 2.6.15 #1 Sun June 10 11:03:21 PDT 2007 i686 GNU/Linux
Debian GNU/Linux
Last login: S Sun June 10 03:11:49 PDT 2007 from :0.0
foober@reggiano:~$
```

Now, Foober can work on Reggiano just as if he were physically sitting at the machine, and all traffic—including the initial login—is encrypted.

The host key exchange happens only once, the first time you log in. You should never be asked again unless the key is replaced with a new one, or you change your personal ~/.ssh/known_hosts file.

Discussion

The public host key is stored in the ~/.ssh/known_hosts file on the client PC. This file can contain any number of host keys.

It is a bad idea to log in as *root* over SSH; it is better to log in as an ordinary user, then *su* or *sudo* as you need after login. You can log in as any user that has an account on the remote machine with the -1 (login) switch:

```
foober@gouda:~$ ssh -1 deann reggiano
```

Or, like this:

```
foober@gouda:~$ ssh deann@reggiano
```

Don't get too worked up over client and server—the server is whatever machine you are logging in to, and the client is wherever you are logging in from. The SSH daemon does not need to be running on the client.

There is a small risk that the host key transmission could be intercepted and a forged key substituted, which would allow an attacker access to your systems. You should verify the IP address and public key fingerprint before typing "yes." Primitive methods of verification, like writing down the fingerprint on a piece of paper, or verifying it via telephone, are effective and immune to computer network exploits.

For the extremely cautious, manually copying keys is also an option; see Recipe 7.4.

See Also

- Chapter 17, "Remote Access," in *Linux Cookbook* by Carla Schroder (O'Reilly)
- man 1 ssh
- man 1 ssh-keygen
- man 8 sshd

7.4   Generating and Copying SSH Keys

Problem

Your OpenSSH installation did not automatically create host keys, or you want to generate new replacement host keys. Additionally, you don't trust the usual automatic transfer of the host's public key, so you want to manually copy host keys to the clients.

Solution

Should you create RSA or DSA keys? Short answer: it doesn't matter. Both are cryptographically strong.

The main difference to the end user is RSA keys can be up to 2,048 bits in length, while DSA is limited to 1,024 bits, so theoretically, RSA keys are more future-proof. The default for either type of key is 1,024 bits.

This example generates a new key pair, using the default host key name from */etc/ssh/sshd_config*. Never create a passphrase on host keys—just hit the return key when it asks for one:

```
# cd /etc/ssh/
# ssh-keygen -t dsa  -f ssh_host_dsa_key
Generating public/private dsa key pair.
Enter passphrase (empty for no passphrase):
Enter same passphrase again:
Your identification has been saved in /etc/ssh/ssh_host_dsa_key.
Your public key has been saved in /etc/ssh/ssh_host_dsa_key.pub.
The key fingerprint is:
26:f6:5b:24:49:e6:71:6f:12:76:1c:2b:a5:ee:fe:fe root@windbag
```

You may wish to be extra cautious and copy the public key manually via floppy disk, USB key, or *scp* over an existing OpenSSH connection to avoid any possible hijacking in transit. You need to modify the key if you're going to copy it manually. Here is the original public host key:

```
ssh-dss
AAAAB3NzaC1kc3MAAACBALeIrq77k2oKUAh8u3RYG1pOiZKAxLQZQzxJ8422d+uPRwvVAARFnriNajoJaB9L7
qu5DOPCSNCOuBMOIkkyHujfXJejQQnMucgkDm8AhMfO8TPyLZ6pG459M+bfwbsBybyWav7eGvgkkTfZYDEd7H
mQK6+Vkd9SYqWd+Q9HkGCRAAAAFQCrhZsuvIuZq5ERrnf5usmMPXlQkQAAAIAUqi61+T7Aa2UjE4Ohn08rSVf
FcuHE6BCmmOFMOoJQbD9xFTztZbDtZcnaOdb5l+6AYxtVInHjiYPj76/hYST5o286/28McWBF8+j8Nn/
tHVUcWSjOE8EJG8Xh2GRxab6AOjgo/
GAQli1qMxlJfCbOlcljVN8VDDF4XtPzqBPHtQAAAIBn7IOv9oM9dUiDZUNXa8s6UV46N4rqcD+HtgkltxDm+t
RiI68kZsU5weTLnLRdZfv/o2P3S9TF3ncrSOYhgIFdGupI//
28gH+Y4sYvrUSoRYJLiDELGm1+2pIO6wXjPpUH2Iajr9TZ9eKWDIE+t2sz6lVqET95SynXq1UbeTsDjQ==
root@windbag
```

Delete the hostname at the end of the file, and prefix the key with the fully qualified domain name and IP address. Make sure there are no spaces between the FQDN and address, and there is one space after the IP address:

```
windbag.carla.com,192.168.1.10 ssh-dss
AAAAB3NzaC1kc3MAAACBALeIrq77k2oKUAh8u3RYG1pOiZKAxLQZQzxJ8422d+uPRwvVAARFnriNajoJaB9L7
qu5DOPCSNCOuBMOIkkyHujfXJejQQnMucgkDm8AhMfO8TPyLZ6pG459M+bfwbsBybyWav7eGvgkkTfZYDEd7H
mQK6+Vkd9SYqWd+Q9HkGCRAAAAFQCrhZsuvIuZq5ERrnf5usmMPXlQkQAAAIAUqi61+T7Aa2UjE4Ohn08rSVf
FcuHE6BCmmOFMOoJQbD9xFTztZbDtZcnaOdb5l+6AYxtVInHjiYPj76/hYST5o286/28McWBF8+j8Nn/
tHVUcWSjOE8EJG8Xh2GRxab6AOjgo/
GAQli1qMxlJfCbOlcljVN8VDDF4XtPzqBPHtQAAAIBn7IOv9oM9dUiDZUNXa8s6UV46N4rqcD+HtgkltxDm+t
RiI68kZsU5weTLnLRdZfv/o2P3S9TF3ncrSOYhgIFdGupI//
28gH+Y4sYvrUSoRYJLiDELGm1+2pIO6wXjPpUH2Iajr9TZ9eKWDIE+t2sz6lVqET95SynXq1UbeTsDjQ==
```

Starting with AAAAB, the file must be one long unbroken line, so be sure to do this in a proper text editor that does not insert line breaks.

You may also use the hostname, or just the IP address all by itself.

If you manually copy additional host keys into the *known_hosts* file, make sure there are no empty lines between them.

Discussion

How much of a risk is there in an automatic host key transfer? The risk is small; it's difficult to launch a successful man-in-the-middle attack, but not impossible. Verifying the host IP address and public key fingerprint before accepting the host key are simple and effective precautions.

It really depends on how determined an attacker is to penetrate your network. The attacker would first have to intercept your transmission in a way that does not draw attention, then possibly spoof the IP address (which is easy) and public-key fingerprint of your trusted server, which is not so easy to do. Because most users do not bother to verify these, most times it's not even necessary. Then, when you type "yes" to accept the key, you get the attacker's host key. To avoid detection, the attacker passes on all traffic between you and the trusted server while capturing and reading everything that passes between you and the trusted server.

How hard is it to hijack Ethernet traffic? On the LAN, it's easy—check out the *arpspoof* utility, which is part of the Dsniff suite of network auditing and penetration-testing tools. How trustworthy are your LAN users? Over the Internet, the attacker would have to compromise your DNS, which is possible, but not easy, assuming your DNS is competently managed. Or, be in a position of trust and a place to wreak mischief, such as an employee at your ISP.

In short, it's a small risk, and the decision is yours.

See Also

- man 1 ssh-keygen

7.5   Using Public-Key Authentication to Protect System Passwords

Problem

You are a bit nervous about using system account logins over untrusted networks, even though they are encrypted with SSH. Or, you have a number of remote servers to manage, and you would like to use the same login on all of them, but not with system accounts. In fact, you would like your remote logins to be decoupled from system logins, plus you would like to have fewer logins and passwords to keep track of.

Solution

Give yourself a single login for multiple hosts by using public-key authentication, which is completely separate from local system accounts. Follow these steps:

Install OpenSSH on all participating machines, and set up host keys on all participating machines. (Host keys always come first.)

Then, generate a new identity key pair as an ordinary unprivileged user, and store it in your *~/.ssh* directory on your local workstation. Be sure to create a passphrase:

```
$ ssh-keygen -t rsa
Generating public/private rsa key pair.
Enter file in which to save the key (/home/carla/.ssh/id_rsa):
Enter passphrase (empty for no passphrase):
Enter same passphrase again:
Your identification has been saved in /home/carla/.ssh/id_rsa.
Your public key has been saved in /home/carla/.ssh/id_rsa.pub.
The key fingerprint is:
38:ec:04:7d:e9:8f:11:6c:4e:1c:d7:8a:91:84:ac:91 carla@windbag
```

Protect your private identity key from accidental overwrites:

```
$ chmod 400 id_rsa
```

Now, copy your new public key (*id_rsa.pub*) to all of the remote user accounts you'll be using, into their *~/.ssh/authorized_keys2* files. If this file does not exist, create it. Using the *ssh-copy-id* utility is the secure, easy way:

```
$ ssh-copy-id -i id_rsa.pub danamania@muis.net
```

Discussion

ssh-copy-id copies identity keys in the correct format, makes sure that file permissions and ownership are correct, and ensures you do not copy a private key by mistake.

The *authorized_keys2* file may be named something else, like *authorized_keys*, or *freds_keys*, or anything you want; just make sure it agrees with the AuthorizedKeysFile line in */etc/ssh/sshd.conf*.

Always put a passphrase on human-user authentication keys—it's cheap insurance. If someone manages to steal your private key, it won't do them any good without the passphrase.

Using public-key authentication combined with *sudo* is a good way to delegate admin chores to your underlings, while limiting what they can do.

Ordinary users may run SSH, which wise network admins know and have policies to control because all manner of forbidden services can be tunneled over SSH, thereby foiling your well-crafted firewalls and network monitors.

See Also

- man 1 ssh-copy-id
- man 1 ssh
- man 1 ssh-keygen
- man 8 sshd
- Recipe 8.21, "Granting Limited Rootly Powers with sudo," in *Linux Cookbook*, by Carla Schroder (O'Reilly)

7.6   Managing Multiple Identity Keys

Problem

You want to use different identity keys for different servers. How do you create keys with different names?

Solution

Use the -f flag of the ssh-keygen command to give keys unique names:

```
[carla@windbag:~/.ssh]$ ssh-keygen -t rsa -f  id_mailserver
```

Then, use the -i flag to select the key you want to use when you log in to the remote host:

```
$ ssh -i id_mailserver  bart@192.168.1.11
Enter passphrase for key 'id_mailserver':
```

Discussion

You don't have to name your keys "id_" whatever, you can call them anything you want.

See Also

- man 1 ssh-copy-id
- man 1 ssh
- man 1 ssh-keygen
- man 8 sshd

7.7   Hardening OpenSSH

Problem

You are concerned about security threats, both from the inside and the outside. You are concerned about brute-force attacks on the *root* account, and you want to restrict users to prevent mischief, whether accidental or deliberate. What can do you to make sure OpenSSH is as hardened as it can be?

Solution

OpenSSH is pretty tight out of the box. There are some refinements you can make; take a look at the following steps and tweak to suit your needs. First, fine-tune */etc/ sshd_config* with these restrictive directives:

```
ListenAddress 12.34.56.78
PermitRootLogin no
Protocol 2
AllowUsers  carla foober@bumble.com  lori meflin
AllowGroups  admins
```

You may want the SSH daemon to listen on a different port:

```
Port 2222
```

Or, you can configure OpenSSH to disallow password logins, and require all users to have identity keys with this line in */etc/sshd_config*:

```
PasswordAuthentication no
```

Finally, configure *iptables* to filter traffic, blocking all but authorized bits (see Chapter 3).

Discussion

Specifying the interfaces that the SSH daemon is to listen to and denying root logins, are basic, obvious precautions.

`Protocol 2` means your server will only allow SSH-2 logins, and will reject SSH-1. SSH-1 is old enough, and has enough weaknesses, that it really isn't worth the risk of using it. SSH-2 has been around for several years, so there is no reason to continue using the SSH-1 protocol.

`AllowUsers` denies logins to all but the listed users. You may use just the login names, or restrict them even further by allowing them to log in only from certain hosts, like *foober@bumble.com*.

`AllowGroups` is a quick way to define allowed users by groups. Any groups not named are denied access. These are normal local Linux groups in */etc/group*.

If you prefer, you may use `DenyHosts` and `DenyGroups`. These work the opposite of the Allow directives—anyone not listed is allowed to log in. Do not mix Allow and Deny directives; only use one or the other.

Changing to a nonstandard port will foil some of the SSH attacks that only look for port 22. However, determined portscanners will find out which port your SSH daemon is listening to, so don't count on it as a meaningful security measure—it's just a way to keep your logfiles from filling up too quickly.

See Also

- `man 1 passwd`
- `man 5 sshd_config`
- Recipe 17.13, "Setting File Permissions on ssh Files," in *Linux Cookbook*, by Carla Schroder (O'Reilly)

7.8   Changing a Passphrase

Problem

You want to change the passphrase on one of your private keys.

Solution

Use the -p switch with the ssh-keygen command:

```
$ ssh-keygen -p -f ~/.ssh/id_dsa
Enter old passphrase:
Key has comment '/home/pinball/.ssh/id_dsa'
Enter new passphrase (empty for no passphrase):
Enter same passphrase again:
Your identification has been saved with the new passphrase.
```

Discussion

Passphrases are not recoverable. If you lose a passphrase, your only option is to create a new key with a new passphrase.

See Also

- man 1 ssh-keygen

7.9   Retrieving a Key Fingerprint

Problem

You are sending a public host key or identity key to another user, and you want the user to be able to verify that the key is genuine by confirming the key fingerprint. You didn't write down the fingerprint when the key was created—how do you find out what it is?

Solution

Use the ssh-keygen command:

```
[carla@windbag:~/.ssh]$ ssh-keygen -l
Enter file in which the key is (/home/carla/.ssh/id_rsa): id_mailserver
1024 ce:5e:38:ba:fb:ec:e7:80:83:3e:11:1a:6f:b1:97:8b id_mailserver.pub
```

Discussion

This is where old-fashioned methods of communication, like telephone and sneaker-net, come in handy. Don't use email, unless you already have encrypted email set up with its own separate encryption and authentication because anyone savvy enough to perpetrate a man-in-the-middle attack will be more than smart enough to crack your email. Especially because the vast majority of email is still sent in the clear, so it's trivial to sniff it.

See Also

- man 1 ssh-keygen

7.10 Checking Configuration Syntax

Problem

Is there a syntax-checker for *sshd_config*?

Solution

But of course. After making your changes, run this command:

```
# sshd -t
```

If there are no syntax errors, it exits silently. If it find mistakes, it tells you:

```
# sshd -t
/etc/ssh/sshd_config: line 9: Bad configuration option: Porotocol
/etc/ssh/sshd_config: terminating, 1 bad configuration options
```

You can do this while the SSH daemon is running, so you can correct your mistakes before issuing a reload or restart command.

Discussion

The -t stands for "test." It does not affect the SSH daemon, it only checks */etc/sshd_config* for syntax errors, so you can use it anytime.

See Also

- man 5 sshd_config
- man 8 sshd

7.11 Using OpenSSH Client Configuration Files for Easier Logins

Problem

You or your users have a collection of different keys for authenticating on different servers and accounts, and different *ssh* command options for each one. Typing all those long command strings is a bit tedious and error-prone. How do you make it easier and better?

Solution

Put individual configuration files for each server in *~/.ssh/*, and select the one you want with the -F flag. This example uses the configuration file *mailserver* to set the connection options for the server *jarlsberg*.

```
[carla@windbag:~/.ssh]$ ssh -F mailserver jarlsberg
```

If you are logging in over the Internet, you'll need the fully qualified domain name of the server:

```
[carla@windbag:~/.ssh]$ ssh -F mailserver jarlsberg.carla.net
```

IP addresses work, too.

Discussion

Using custom configuration files lets you manage a lot of different logins sanely. For example, *~/.ssh/mailserver* contains these options:

```
IdentityFile ~/.ssh/id_mailserver
Port 2222
User mail_admin
```

It's easier and less error-prone to type ssh -F mailserver jarlsberg than ssh -i id_mailserver -p 2222 -l mail_admin jarlsberg.

Don't forget to configure your firewall for your alternate SSH ports, and check */etc/services* to find unused ports.

You may open up as many alternate ports as you want on a single OpenSSH server. Use *netstat* to keep an eye on activities:

```
# netstat -a --tcp -p | grep ssh
tcp6      0      0 *:2222    *:*    LISTEN      7329/sshd
tcp6      0      0 *:ssh     *:*    LISTEN      7329/sshd
tcp6      0      0 ::ffff:192.168.1.1:2222 windbag.localdoma:35474 ESTABLISHED7334/
sshd: carla
tcp6      0      0 ::ffff:192.168.1.11:ssh windbag.localdoma:56374 ESTABLISHED7352/
sshd: carla
```

Remember, */etc/sshd_config* controls the SSH daemon. */etc/ssh_config* contains the global SSH client settings.

You may have any number of different SSH client configuration files in your *~/.ssh/* directory.

The SSH daemon follows this precedence:

* Command-line options
* User's configuration file (*$HOME/.ssh/config*)
* System-wide configuration file (*/etc/ssh/ssh_config*)

User's configuration files will not override global security settings, which is fortunate for your sanity and your security policies.

See Also

* man 1 ssh
* man 5 ssh_config

7.12 Tunneling X Windows Securely over SSH

Problem

OK, all of this command-line stuff is slick and easy, but you still want a nice graphical environment. Maybe you use graphical utilities to manage your headless servers. Maybe you want to access a remote workstation and have access to all of its applications. You know that X Windows has built-in networking abilities, but it sends all traffic in cleartext, which of course is unacceptably insecure, plus it's a pain to set up. What else can you do?

Solution

Tunneling X over SSH is simple, and requires no additional software.

First, make sure this line is in */etc/ssh/sshd_config* on the remote machine:

```
X11Forwarding  yes
```

Then, connect to the server using the -X flag:

```
[carla@windbag:~/.ssh]$ ssh -X stilton
Enter passphrase for key '/home/carla/.ssh/id_rsa':
Linux stilton 2.6.15-26-k7 #1 SMP PREEMPT Sun Jun 3 03:40:32 UTC 2007 i686 GNU/Linux
Last login: Sat June  2 14:55:10 2007
carla@stilton:~$
```

Now, you can run any of the X applications installed on the remote PC by starting them from the command line:

```
carla@stilton:~$ ppracer
```

SSH sets up an X proxy on the SSH server, which you can see with this command:

```
carla@stilton:~$ echo $DISPLAY
localhost:10.0
```

Discussion

The X server runs with the offset specified in */etc/sshd.conf*:

```
X11DisplayOffset 10
```

This needs to be configured to avoid colliding with existing X sessions. Your regular local X session is: 0.0.

The remote system only needs to be powered on. You don't need any local users to be logged in, and you don't even need X to be running. X needs to be running only on the client PC.

Starting with version 3.8, OpenSSH introduced the -Y option for remote X sessions. Using the -Y option treats the remote X client as trusted. The old-fashioned way to do this was to configure *ssh_config* with ForwardX11Trusted yes. (The ForwardX11Trusted default is no.) Using the -Y flag lets you keep the default as no, and to enable trusted X forwarding as you need. Theoretically, you could find that some functions don't work on an untrusted client, but I have yet to see any.

The risk of running a remote X session as trusted matters only if the remote machine has been compromised and an attacker knows how to sniff your input operations (e.g., keystrokes, mouse movements, and copy-and-paste). Also, anyone sitting at the remote machine can do the same thing. Old-timers from the pre-SSH days like to reminisce about their fun days of messing with other user's X sessions and causing mischief.

It is possible to tunnel an entire X session over SSH, and run your favorite desktop or windows manager, like Gnome, KDE, IceWM, and so forth. However, I don't recommend it because there are easier and better ways to do this, as you will see in the next chapter.

Don't use compression over fast networks because it will slow down data transfer.

See Also

- man 1 ssh
- man 5 ssh_config

7.13 Executing Commands Without Opening a Remote Shell

Problem

You have a single command to run on the remote machine, and you think it would be nice to be able to just run it without logging in and opening a remote shell, running the command, and then logging out. After all, is it not true that laziness is a virtue for network admins?

Solution

And, you shall have what you want because OpenSSH can do this. This example shows how to restart Postfix:

```
$ ssh mailadmin@limberger.alrac.net  sudo /etc/init.d/postfix restart
```

This shows how to open a quick game of Kpoker, which requires X Windows:

```
$ ssh -X 192.168.1.10 /usr/games/kpoker
```

You'll be asked for a password, but you'll still save one whole step.

Discussion

You have to use *sudo* when you need root privileges with this command, not *su*, because you can't use *su* without first opening a remote shell. This is also a handy way to script remote commands.

And yes, laziness is a virtue, if it leads to increased efficiency and streamlined methods of getting jobs done.

See Also

- man 1 ssh

7.14   Using Comments to Label Keys

Problem

You have a lot of SSH keys, and you would like a simple way to identify the public keys after they are transferred to your *known_hosts* and *authorized_keys2* files.

Solution

Use the comment option when you create a key to give it a descriptive label:

```
$ ssh-keygen -t rsa -C "mailserver on jarlsberg"
```

The key looks like this:

```
ssh-rsa
AAAAB3NzaC1yc2EAAAABIwAAAIEAoK8bYXg195hp+y1oeMWdwlBKdGkSG8UqrwKpwNU9Sbo+uGPpNxU3iAjRa
LYTniwnoSOj+Nwj+POU5s9KKBf5hx+EJT/
8wl7OKyoyslPghsQAUdODoEwCzNFdIME8nmOvxzlAxS+SO45RxdXBO8j8WMdC92PcMOxIB1wPCIntjiO=
mailserver on jarlsberg
```

This is helpful when you have a lot of keys in *known_hosts* and *authorized_keys2* because even though you can give the keys unique names, the keynames are not stored in these files.

Discussion

OpenSSH ignores the comment field; it's a convenience for human users.

See Also

- man 1 ssh-keygen

7.15 Using DenyHosts to Foil SSH Attacks

Problem

The Internet is full of twits who have nothing better to do than to release automated SSH attacks on the world. You have taken all the sensible security precautions, and feel like your security measures are adequate, but your logfiles are overflowing with this junk. Isn't there some way to head these morons off at the pass?

Solution

Indeed, yes. The excellent DenyHosts utility will take care of you. DenyHosts parses your *auth* log, and writes entries to */etc/hosts.deny* to block future intrusion attempts.

DenyHosts is a Python script, so you need Python 2.3 or newer. Find your Python version this way:

```
$ python -V
Python 2.4.2
```

DenyHosts can be installed with Aptitude or Yum. To install from sources, simply unpack the tarball in the directory where you want to store DenyHosts. This comes with *denyhosts.cfg.dist*, which is a model configuration file. Edit it, then save it as */etc/denyhosts.conf*. (See Recipe 7.16 to learn how to configure a startup script.)

Next, create a whitelist in */etc/hosts.allow*; in other words, add all the important hosts that you never want blocked.

This sample configuration is moderately stern. Make sure the filepaths are correct for your system:

```
WORK_DIR = /var/denyhosts/data
SECURE_LOG = /var/log/auth.log
HOSTS_DENY = /etc/hosts.deny
BLOCK_SERVICE = sshd
DENY_THRESHOLD_INVALID = 3
DENY_THRESHOLD_VALID = 5
DENY_THRESHOLD_ROOT = 1
LOCK_FILE = /tmp/denyhosts.lock
HOSTNAME_LOOKUP=NO
SUSPICIOUS_LOGIN_REPORT_ALLOWED_HOSTS=YES
AGE_RESET_VALID=1d
AGE_RESET_ROOT=25d
AGE_RESET_INVALID=
DAEMON_PURGE = 1h
DAEMON_SLEEP = 30s
DAEMON_LOG_TIME_FORMAT = %b %d %H:%M:%S
ADMIN_EMAIL = carla@kielbasa.net
```

The default configuration file tells you the required options, optional settings, and other useful information.

Discussion

DenyHosts can be run manually, as a *cron* job, or as a daemon. I prefer daemon mode—set it and forget it. To run it manually for testing, simply run the DenyHosts script:

```
# python denyhosts.py
```

Read the *denyhosts.py* script to see the available command options.

This is what the options mean:

BLOCK_SERVICE = sshd

> You may use DenyHosts to protect SSH, or all services with BLOCK_SERVICE = ALL.

DENY_THRESHOLD_INVALID = 2

> Login attempts on nonexistent accounts get two chances before they are blocked. Because the accounts do not exist, blocking them won't hurt anything.

DENY_THRESHOLD_VALID = 5

> Login attempts on legitimate accounts get five chances. Adjust as needed for fat-fingered users.

DENY_THRESHOLD_ROOT = 1

> Root logins get one chance. You should log in as an unprivileged user anyway, then *su* or *sudo* if you need *root*ly powers.

HOSTNAME_LOOKUP = Yes

> DenyHosts will look up hostnames of blocked IP addresses. This can be disabled if it slows things down too much with HOSTNAME_LOOKUP = NO.

SUSPICIOUS_LOGIN_REPORT_ALLOWED_HOSTS

> Set this to YES, then monitor your DenyHosts reports to see if this is useful. It tattles about suspicious behavior perpetrated by hosts in */etc/hosts.allow*, which may or may not be useful.

AGE_RESET_VALID=1d

> Allowed users are unblocked after one day, if they went all fat-fingered and got locked out.

AGE_RESET_INVALID=

> Invalid blocked users are never unblocked.

DAEMON_PURGE = 3d

> Delete all blocked addresses after three days. Your */etc/hosts.deny* file can grow very large, so old entries should be purged periodically.

```
DAEMON_SLEEP = 5m
```
How often should the DenyHosts daemon run? It's a low-stress script, so running it a lot shouldn't affect system performance. Adjust this to suit your situation—if you are getting hammered, you can step up the frequency.

Time values look like this:

s: seconds
m: minutes
h: hours
d: days
w: weeks
y: years

See Also

- The DenyHosts FAQ: *http://denyhosts.sourceforge.net/faq.html*

7.16 Creating a DenyHosts Startup File

Problem

You installed DenyHosts from the source tarball, so you need to know how to set up an *init* script to start it automatically at boot, and for starting and stopping it manually.

Solution

daemon-control-dist is the model startup file; you'll need to edit it for your particular Linux distribution. Only the first section needs to be edited:

```
##########################################
# Edit these to suit your configuration #
##########################################

DENYHOSTS_BIN   = "/usr/bin/denyhosts.py"
DENYHOSTS_LOCK  = "/var/lock/subsys/denyhosts"
DENYHOSTS_CFG   = "/etc/denyhosts.cfg"
```

Make sure the filepaths and filenames are correct for your system. Then give the file a name you can type reasonably, like */etc/init.d/denyhosts*.

Configuring DenyHosts to start at boot is done in the usual manner, using *chkconfig* on Red Hat and Fedora, and *update-rc.d* on Debian:

```
# chkconfig denyhosts --add
# chkconfig denyhosts on

# update-rc.d start 85 2 3 4 5 . stop 30 0 1 6 .
```

Manually stopping and starting DenyHosts is done in the usual manner:

```
# /etc/init.d/denyhosts {start|stop|restart|status|debug}
```

Fedora users also have this option:

```
#  /etc/init.d/denyhosts condrestart
```

This restarts DenyHosts only if it already running; otherwise, it fails silently.

Discussion

When you create a new *init* script on Fedora, you must first add it to the control of *chkconfig* with the `chkconfig --add` command. Then, you can use the `chkconfig foo on/off` command to start or stop it at boot.

See Also

- The DenyHosts FAQ: *http://denyhosts.sourceforge.net/faq.html*
- Chapter 7, "Starting and Stopping Linux," in *Linux Cookbook*, by Carla Schroder (O'Reilly)

7.17   Mounting Entire Remote Filesystems with sshfs

Problem

OpenSSH is pretty fast and efficient, and even tunneling X Windows over OpenSSH isn't too laggy. But sometimes, you want a faster way to edit a number of remote files—something more convenient than *scp*, and kinder to bandwidth than running a graphical file manager over SSH.

Solution

sshfs is just the tool for you. *sshfs* lets you mount an entire remote filesystem and then access it just like a local filesystem.

Install *sshfs*, which should also install *fuse*. You need a local directory for your mountpoint:

```
carla@xena:~$ mkdir /sshfs
```

Then, make sure the *fuse* kernel module is loaded:

```
$ lsmod|grep fuse
fuse                    46612  1
```

If it isn't, run `modprobe fuse`.

Next, add yourself to the *fuse* group.

Then, log in to the remote PC and go to work:

```
carla@xena:~$ sshfs uberpc: sshfs/
carla@uberpc's password:
carla@xena:~$
```

Now, the remote filesystem should be mounted in *~/sshfs* and just as accessible as your local filesystems.

When you're finished, unmount the remote filesystem:

```
$ fusermount -u sshfs/
```

Discussion

Users who are new to *sshfs* always ask these questions: why not just run X over SSH, or why not just use NFS?

It's faster than running X over SSH, it's a heck of a lot easier to set up than NFS, and a zillion times more secure than NFS, is why.

See Also

- man 1 sshfs

## CHAPTER 8

Using Cross-Platform Remote Graphical Desktops

8.0 Introduction

Tunneling X over SSH (covered in the previous chapter) is one good way to run a remote graphical desktop. Like everything else, the Linux world has several good variations on the same theme. In this chapter, we'll look at some more programs for running remote graphical desktops in different ways, such as cross-platform networking and remote helpdesk work. It's a lot easier to take control of a user's computer remotely and fix problems than to talk a poor user through a diagnosis and repair over the telephone. (I'm still puzzled at how anyone ever thought that was a good idea.)

The Linux world offers several ways to get a remote graphical desktop with decent performance, and across different platforms, especially Linux and Windows. In this chapter, we'll look at three different applications: *rdesktop*, FreeNX, and VNC.

rdesktop

rdesktop is a Linux client that uses the Remote Desktop Protocol (RDP) to connect to Windows Terminal Services on Windows NT/2000/2003 servers, and Remote Desktop Connection on Windows XP Pro. *rdesktop* can attach to an existing session or start a new one.

FreeNX

FreeNX runs graphical desktops over low-speed, high-latency connections (e.g., dial-up) at satisfying speeds. So far, it is for logging in to Linux boxes only, from Linux, Windows, Solaris, and Mac OS X clients. It has built-in encryption, and lets you configure any desktop or window manager to use for the remote session. It supports new independent X sessions only, so you cannot attach to an existing X session.

FreeNX has some rough edges. It requires the free-of-cost Linux client from NoMachine, which depends on some very old libraries. (The commercial NXServer uses the same client.) The client version and server version must match, which becomes a problem when NoMachine distributes only the latest clients, and you can't get updated FreeNX server packages. Once you get it up and running, the basic functions work fine, but selecting the desktop you want doesn't always work, and there are problems with file and printer sharing.

NoMachine also distributes a freebie NX server for Linux users, if you can't get the open source FreeNX working the way you want. Like the client, it also depends on some very old libraries that you will likely have to hunt down and install. When it works, it's fast, and the built-in encryption is nice.

In my opinion, VNC and its many derivatives are preferable. It's open source, very flexible, and it's well-maintained and reliable. Need encryption? Tunnel it over SSH.

VNC

Virtual Network Computing (VNC) is the grandmother of cross-platform remote desktops, and the most flexible. It comes in many variations, and supports most operating systems: Mac OS X, Linux, various Unixes, and Windows, so you can remotely log in to anything from anything. On Linux, you may create new independent login sessions, or attach to an existing X session with *x11vnc*. A unique VNC feature is controlling any two computers with a single keyboard and mouse.

VNC has been around long enough to spawn a host of knockoffs and forks. If reliability is what you're after, stick with the established, stable versions:

- TightVNC (*http://www.tightvnc.com/*) is a fast fork of RealVNC. Runs well over slow connections, especially with the new DFMirage video driver for Windows.
- RealVNC (*http://www.realvnc.com/*) offers good free and commercial versions.
- UltraVNC (*http://ultravnc.sourceforge.net/*) is good for Windows-to-Windows remote administration. It has a number of Windows-specific tweaks, such as a mirror video driver similar to DFMirage, encryption, user monitoring, and the ability to log in as any user.
- MSRC4 DSM plug-in (*http://home.comcast.net/~msrc4plugin/*) is an open source encryption plug-in for UltraVNC.
- OS X VNC (*http://www.redstonesoftware.com/VNC.html*) is a VNC server for Mac OS X.
- Chicken of the VNC (*http://sourceforge.net/projects/cotvnc/*) is a VNC viewer for Mac OS X. And a really bad pun.
- Win2VNC (*http://fredrik.hubbe.net/win2vnc.html*) is a Windows VNC server for sharing a mouse and keyboard with a second PC.

- *x2vnc* (*http://fredrik.hubbe.net/x2vnc.html*) is a Linux server for sharing a mouse and keyboard with a second PC.

- *x11vnc* (*http://www.karlrunge.com/x11vnc/*) lets you attach to an existing X session, instead of starting a new one. This is great for roaming users who like to wander from PC to PC, and for remote helpdesk work.

There are a large number of VNC forks for other platforms. Here is a partial list:

- VNC server for MorphOS: *http://binaryriot.com/dreamolers/vncserver/*
- MorphVNC, VNC client for MorphOS: *http://bigfoot.morphos-team.net/files/*
- TwinVNC, a VNC client for MorphOS and AmigaOS: *http://twinvnc.free.fr/*
- J2ME VNC client for Java™-enabled cell phones: *http://j2mevnc.sourceforge.net/*
- PocketPC VNCViewer VNC client: *http://www.cs.utah.edu/~midgley/wince/vnc.html*
- PocketPC VNCServer and WindowsCE.NET server: *http://www.pocketvnc.com/pocketVNC.aspx*
- PalmVNC Palm OS client: *http://palmvnc2.free.fr/*

Built-in Remote Desktop Sharing in KDE and Gnome

Both KDE and Gnome come with remote desktop sharing built-in. On KDE, it's called KDE Remote Desktop Connection; you can start it from the command line with the krdc command. KRDC supports both VNC and RDP (Remote Desktop Protocol), the Windows remote desktop sharing protocol.

Gnome's Remote Desktop Sharing is based on Vino, a VNC server for Gnome. It does not support RDP, just VNC. Both implementations are nicely done and easy to use.

8.1   Connecting Linux to Windows via rdesktop

Problem

You want to log into a Windows NT/2000/2003 server or Windows XP Pro workstation from your Linux workstation. You want to see your own Windows desktop, use your applications, or manage services. You don't want to install additional software on the Windows box to enable remote access, you just want your Linux box to be a Windows Terminal Services client.

Solution

Use *rdesktop*, the open source Remote Desktop Protocol client. Remote Desktop Protocol is the protocol behind Windows Terminal Services. *rdesktop* is a standard package that should come with your Linux distribution.

Follow these steps to get *rdesktop* up and running:

- Install *rdesktop* on Linux.
- Set up Terminal Services on your NT/2000/2003 server, or on XP Professional, set up Remote Desktop Sharing.
- Make sure the accounts that you want to log in to require login passwords.
- Your Windows machine must be booted up, but users do not need to be logged in.
- Log in from Linux, and go to work.

This example shows how to log in to Windows using the IP address and specifying a window size:

```
$ rdesktop -g 1024x768 192.168.1.22
```

You'll see your familiar Windows login box.

rdesktop supports full-screen mode. Hit Ctrl-Alt-Enter to toggle between full-screen and windowed mode. Figure 8-1 shows fine art being created over *rdesktop*.

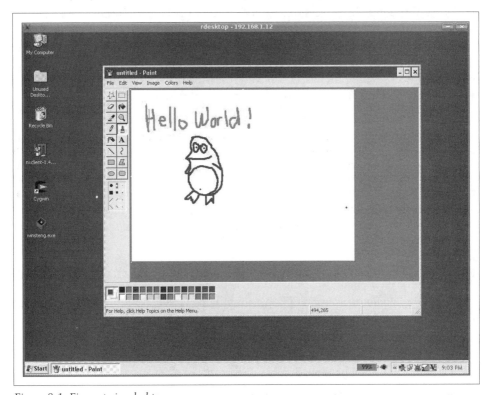

Figure 8-1. Fine art via rdesktop

And that's all there is to it. When you're finished, select Start → Logoff or Start → Disconnect to end your session. Logoff closes all applications; Disconnect leaves them running, so you can pick up where you left off the next time you connect.

Discussion

If you are already logged in to Windows, *rdesktop* will attach to your existing session and lock out local access.

You may log in from all manner of different locations, and pick up where you left off if you remember to Logoff rather than Disconnect. Keep in mind that leaving applications running uses more server resources.

If your Windows Terminal Server is configured to use a different port than 3389, specify a different port at login like this:

```
$ rdesktop -g 1024x768 192.168.1.22:3000
```

And of course, make sure that the port is not blocked by a firewall.

There are some limitations to using Windows Terminal Services and *rdesktop*. It only works on Windows XP Professional, and Windows NT/2000/2003 servers. Terminal Server usually needs to be installed separately on Windows NT and 2000 servers. It is built-in to Windows 2003 and Windows XP Professional. On Windows servers, multiple clients may access the server simultaneously, provided the requisite number and type of licenses are purchased. On XP Professional, only one user may log in at a time, and the desktop is locked to prevent accidental mischief.

System administration is somewhat limited. Installing applications can run into permissions problems because Windows sees the remote administrator user as a different user than the local administrator, and remote configuration could mean you'll end up with two sets of configuration files and Registry entries.

TightVNC is good for running any version of Windows from Linux, and UltraVNC is a good choice for Windows-to-Windows remote administration that works on any version of Windows. Neither one cares about client access or terminal server licenses.

See Also

- man 1 rdesktop
- *Learning Windows Server 2003* by Jonathan Hassell (O'Reilly), and *Securing Windows NT/2000 Servers for the Internet* by Stefan Norberg (O'Reilly) have good chapters on Windows Terminal Services
- Microsoft Knowledge Base article 247930: "Cannot Install Some Programs in a Terminal Services Client Session"
- Search for "Troubleshooting Terminal Server Licensing Problems" on *http://www.microsoft.com*
- NoMachine: *http://nomachine.com/*

8.2   Generating and Managing FreeNX SSH Keys

Problem

You went to FreeNX (*http://freenx.berlios.de/download.php*) to get the FreeNX server and installed it. It came with a set of default SSH keys. Because everyone in the world gets those, how do you make new ones?

Solution

Use */usr/bin/nxkeygen* to generate a new key pair. Then, do not forget to copy the new */var/lib/nxserver/home/.ssh/client.id_dsa.key* to your client PCs, or they will not be able to log in. On Windows, they go in the *\Program Files\NX Client for Windows\ Share* directory. On Linux, Mac OS X, and Solaris they go into */usr/NX/share/*.

Discussion

Mismatched server and client keys are the most common cause of login failures.

See Also

*   NX Server System Administrator's Guide:

    http://www.nomachine.com/documentation/admin-guide.php

8.3   Using FreeNX to Run Linux from Windows

Problem

You want the ability to remotely access a Linux box from your Windows PC. You have some Linux applications you want to use that are not available on Windows, or there are times when all you have is a Windows box to do your remote Linux administration from.

Additionally, you want a full graphical session to run satisfactorily over a slow link, even dial-up, and you want to be able to use the Linux desktop or window manager of your choice.

Solution

You don't want much! Fortunately, FreeNX was designed just to fulfill these needs. Follow these steps to get up and running.

Set up the server

Install the FreeNX server on the Linux box you want to log in to remotely.

Next, add authorized users to the FreeNX server. You must create the login name and password separately. The FreeNX users must already have Linux accounts on the server:

```
# nxserver --adduser pinball
NX> 100 NXSERVER - Version 1.5.0-50 OS (GPL)
NX> 1000 NXNODE - Version 1.5.0-50 OS (GPL)
NX> 716 Public key added to: /home/pinball/.ssh/authorized_keys2
NX> 1001 Bye.
NX> 999 Bye
# nxserver --passwd pinball
NX> 100 NXSERVER - Version 1.5.0-50 OS (GPL)
New password:
Password changed.
NX> 999 Bye
```

Strangely enough, you only get one chance to enter the password, so be careful.

Then, make sure the OpenSSH daemon is running on the FreeNX server, and port 22 is not blocked by your firewall.

Get the client

Go to NoMachine.com (*http://www.nomachine.com/*) to download a free client for your Windows box. Make sure it has the same major and minor version numbers as the FreeNX server. You can find the FreeNX server version number with this command:

```
# nxserver --version
NX> 100 NXSERVER - Version 1.5.0-50 OS (GPL)
```

So, your client needs to be version 1.5.x. If you cannot find a matching client, please see the Discussion.

Once you have a matching client, you can set up your login from Windows.

Set up the connection

Click on NX Client For Windows to open the Connection Wizard, as Figure 8-2 shows.

Enter a name for this configuration on the Session line; for example, let's call our new session *windbag1*.

Enter the hostname or IP address of the server on the Host line.

Select your type of connection, and click Next.

On the Desktop window, select Unix. Then, select the Linux desktop you want to see on your remote session, and the size of the window, as in Figure 8-3.

Check the Enable SSL box to encrypt all traffic, then click Next.

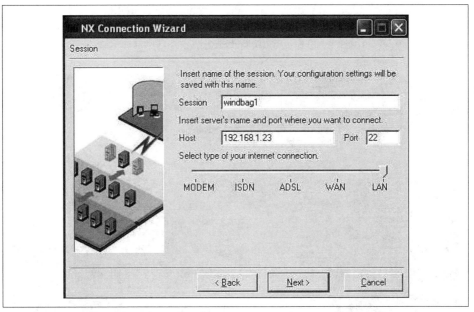

Figure 8-2. NoMachine client setup wizard

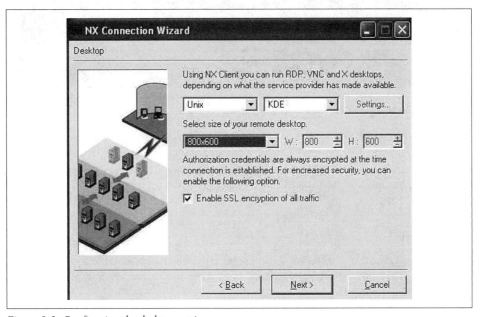

Figure 8-3. Configuring the desktop settings

Check "Create shortcut on desktop" and Nxclient will make a shortcut called *windbag1*. Make sure your login name has the correct case, type in your password, click to log in, and there you are. Figure 8-4 shows an active session.

Figure 8-4. See the pretty Linux desktop on Windows

To close your FreeNX session, log out from your remote desktop in the usual manner. You may also click the Close button on the Nxclient window. This brings up a dialog that asks you if you want to Suspend or Terminate. Suspend does not close running applications, so you can log in later and pick up where you left off; Terminate closes all applications.

Discussion

If you try to connect to the server and get the error message: "Unable to create the X authorization cookie," it means Nxclient is looking in the incorrect location for the *xauth* program. Fix this by creating a symlink:

```
# cd /usr/X11R6/bin
# ln -sf /usr/bin/xauth
```

When NoMachine released its 2.0 versions, it left FreeNX behind. FreeNX 1.5 doesn't work with NoMachine 2.0 clients without a bit of tweaking, and even then, it may not work reliably. At the time this was written, you could download older NoMachine clients from Industrial-Statistics.com: *http://www.industrial-statistics. com/info/nxclients?IndStats=47ebcaa422e76eba8af14a1b6f31d971*.

Another option is to modify FreeNX 1.5 to work with the NoMachine 2.0 client. See FreeNX FAQ/Problem Solving: *http://openfacts.berlios.de/index-en.phtml?title=FreeNX_ FAQ/Problem_Solving*.

Nxclient, by default, enters the name of the current Windows user on the Nxclient login screen, with the first letter capitalized. Linux logins are case-sensitive, so beware. You may log in as any FreeNX user; it doesn't matter which Windows login is active.

You may save your password in the Nxclient login; this is convenient, but an obvious security risk.

Enabling SSL encrypts all traffic, and is good to use all the time.

You'll probably want to increase the font size used in the logfiles; the default is nearly unreadable. Do this on the Environment tab; open "NX Client For Windows," then click the Configure button to get to all the configuration tabs.

You may use any desktop environment or window manager, as long as it is installed on the FreeNX server. However, when this was written, selecting anything other than KDE or Gnome didn't work correctly.

When a new user is added to the FreeNX server, the user key is copied from */etc/ nxserver/users.id_dsa.pub* to */home/user/.ssh/authorized_keys2*.

FreeNX user's passwords are hashed and stored in */etc/nxserver/passwords*.

See Also

- NoMachine's download page:

    http://www.nomachine.com/download.php

- nomachine.com's Support Center:

    http://www.nomachine.com/support.php

- NX Server System Administrator's Guide:

    http://www.nomachine.com/documentation/admin-guide.php

8.4   Using FreeNX to Run Linux from Solaris, Mac OS X, or Linux

Problem

You don't want to remotely access your nice Linux box from Windows—you have a Solaris, Mac OS X, or Linux PC that you want to use. How do you set them up as FreeNX clients?

Solution

Just the same as on Windows, as in the previous recipe. After setting up the FreeNX server, download and install the appropriate client from NoMachine's download page (*http://www.nomachine.com/download.php*).

Start the NX Connection Wizard with the /usr/NX/bin/nxclient --wizard command.

Configure it in exactly the same way as for Windows; the client interface looks the same on all platforms.

There is one important difference: when you copy the client key, it goes into */usr/NX/share/keys/*. Otherwise, it's all the same.

Debian users, if you get an error message saying that you need *libstdc++2.10-glibc2.2* and *libpng.so* when you try to install *nxclient*, it means you need to track down these old libraries and install them. They should be in the Debian Woody repositories.

Fedora users need the *compat-libstdc++-296* package.

Discussion

When NoMachine released its 2.0 versions, it left FreeNX behind. FreeNX 1.5 doesn't work with NoMachine 2.0 clients without a bit of tweaking, and even then it may not work reliably. At the time this was written, you could download older NoMachine clients from Industrial-Statistics.com (*http://www.industrial-statistics.com/info/nxclients?IndStats=47ebcaa422e76eba8af14a1b6f31d971*).

Another option is to modify FreeNX 1.5 to work with the NoMachine 2.0 client. See FreeNX FAQ/Problem Solving (*http://openfacts.berlios.de/index-en.phtml?title=FreeNX_FAQ/Problem_Solving*).

You may be asking why use FreeNX on Unix platforms, when tunneling X over OpenSSH is standard and easy? Because FreeNX offers significantly faster performance, especially over slow links. Kurt Pfeifle, one of the primary FreeNX developers, says that "a full-screen KDE 3.2 session start-up sequence transfers 4.1 MB of data over the wire, if it is run over a plain vanilla remote X connection...if run over NX, the second startup data transfer volume drops down to 35 KB, due to the combined compression, cache and minute differential effects of NX," (*Linux Journal* online, "The Arrival of NX, Part 4" at *http://www.linuxjournal.com/node/8489/*).

So, this means that users on a dial-up link of at least 40 Kbps will experience little perceptible lag. Using a lightweight window manager like IceWM or Xfce will see even better performance—if you can get them to work.

See Also

- NoMachine's download page:

  http://www.nomachine.com/download.php
- NoMachine's Support Center:

  http://www.nomachine.com/support.php
- NX Server System Administrator's Guide:

  http://www.nomachine.com/documentation/admin-guide.php

8.5 Managing FreeNX Users

Problem

You want to know how to list, add, and delete FreeNX users.

Solution

Use these commands, as *root*, to list, add, or delete users. We'll use our favorite user *pinball* to demonstrate in these examples:

```
# /usr/bin/nxserver --listuser
# /usr/bin/nxserver --adduser pinball
# /usr/bin/nxserver --deluser pinball
```

You can change users' passwords, and users can change their own passwords with the --passwd option:

```
# /usr/bin/nxserver --passwd pinball
```

Discussion

Remember, FreeNX users must first be Linux users—they must have accounts to log in to.

See Also

- Run /usr/bin/nxserver --help as *root* to see all server commands
- NoMachine's Support Center:

  http://www.nomachine.com/support.php
- NX Server System Administrator's Guide:

  http://www.nomachine.com/documentation/admin-guide.php

8.6   Watching Nxclient Users from the FreeNX Server

Problem

You want a central management console to keep an eye on who is logged in to your FreeNX server. You want to be able to terminate sessions, view user histories, and send vitally important messages to users.

Solution

Use */usr/bin/nxserver*. You can see who is currently logged in:

```
# nxserver --list
NX> 100 NXSERVER - Version 1.5.0-50 OS (GPL)
NX> 127 Sessions list:

Display Username        Remote IP        Session ID
------- --------------- ---------------- --------------------------------
1003    carla   192.168.1.17    1D0FB6F2759E350067E911D245E9
1001    pinball 192.168.1.19    64A6BBAE7E9BDD8BC79EE5FCAB
NX> 999 Bye
```

View user history:

```
# nxserver --history pinball
NX> 100 NXSERVER - Version 1.5.0-50 OS (GPL)
NX> 127 Session list:

Display Username        Remote IP       Session ID                        Date
Status
------- --------------- --------------- -------------------------------- ------------
------- -----------
1000    pinball 192.168.1.17    B5870BA4DF456E9126B0561402       2006-12-14 04:25:06
Finished
1001    pinball 192.168.1.17    64A6BBAE7E9BDB1C79EE5FCAB        2006-12-18 09:56:12
Running
NX> 999 Bye
```

pinball is being a pain, so you want to kick her off the server. You may terminate a single session, using the session ID:

```
# nxserver --terminate 64A6BBAE7E9BDB1C79EE5FCAB
```

Or, you can knock all of *pinball*'s sessions offline with her username:

```
# nxserver --terminate pinball
```

You may send messages to single users, or to all users:

```
# nxserver --send pinball "Save your work, I'm disconnecting you in five seconds"
# nxserver --broadcast "Save your work, I'm disconnecting you in five seconds and
then we're going out for treats"
```

This is a useful command for cleaning up stray sessions leftover after a power outage:

```
# nxserver --cleanup
```

Discussion

This is also useful if you have problems with your own remote FreeNX sessions. For example, if you have logged in from a number of different locations, you can SSH in to the FreeNX server and run the nxserver commands to see how many active sessions you have, and shut them down.

See Also

- Run /usr/bin/nxserver --help as *root* to see all server commands
- NoMachine's Support Center:

    http://www.nomachine.com/support.php
- NX Server System Administrator's Guide:

    http://www.nomachine.com/documentation/admin-guide.php

8.7 Starting and Stopping the FreeNX Server

Problem

You don't see an *nx* or FreeNX daemon running anywhere, yet it works—how do you stop and start it, and how do you check the status?

Solution

With these three commands:

```
# /usr/bin/nxserver --start
# /usr/bin/nxserver --stop
# /usr/bin/nxserver --status
```

FreeNX uses services provided by *ssh*, so you won't see any sort of FreeNX daemon running. However, stopping FreeNX won't affect *ssh* or other login services at all.

Discussion

Here is what your command output should look like:

```
# nxserver --status
NX> 100 NXSERVER - Version 1.5.0-50 OS (GPL)
NX> 110 NX Server is running
NX> 999 Bye
# nxserver --stop
NX> 100 NXSERVER - Version 1.5.0-50 OS (GPL)
NX> 123 Service stopped
NX> 999 Bye
# nxserver --status
NX> 100 NXSERVER - Version 1.5.0-50 OS (GPL)
NX> 110 NX Server is stopped
NX> 999 Bye
```

```
# nxserver --start
NX> 100 NXSERVER - Version 1.5.0-50 OS (GPL)
NX> 122 Service started
NX> 999 Bye
```

FreeNX is pretty low-maintenance, and usually doesn't need configuration tweaks. The main configuration file is */etc/nxserver/node.conf*. */usr/bin/nxserver* is just a big old shell script, if you have a desire to hack at it.

See Also

- Run /usr/bin/nxserver --help as *root* to see all server commands
- NoMachine's Support Center:

    http://www.nomachine.com/support.php
- NX Server System Administrator's Guide:

    http://www.nomachine.com/documentation/admin-guide.php

8.8   Configuring a Custom Desktop

Problem

The Connection Wizard only gives you four choices for your remote desktop: KDE, Gnome, CDE, and Custom. You don't want KDE, Gnome, or CDE, you want something else like IceWM or Xfce, so Custom is the obvious choice. How do you configure a custom desktop?

Solution

First, make sure the desktop you want to use is installed on your FreeNX server. Then, fire up the Connection Wizard on the client.

On the Desktop tab of the Connection Wizard, click Custom, then Settings.

On the Settings window, click "Run the following command," and type in the command to start up your chosen desktop.

Check "New virtual desktop."

Finish the rest of the setup, and you're done. See Figure 8-5 for an example.

Discussion

You may or may not be able to get a custom desktop to work; currently, there are some problems with these.

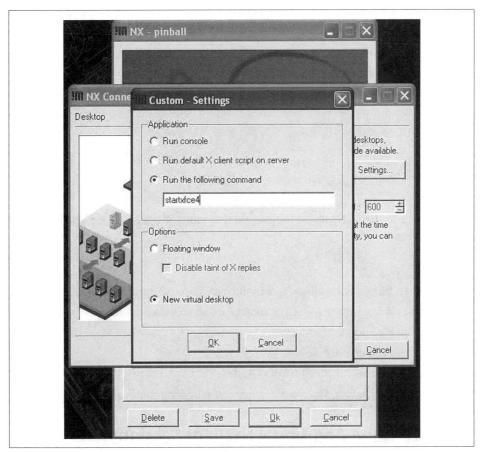

Figure 8-5. Configuring a custom desktop

Make sure your server and client versions match, or your remote desktops might get garbled, or even be unusable. They must have the same major and minor version numbers, so the server version 1.5.0-50 must be paired with a client version starting with 1.5.

Gnome and KDE run well even over slow links. To get even better performance, try lightweight window managers like IceWM or Xfce. These are fully featured, but a lot less resource-hungry. However, FreeNX is so efficient, you probably won't notice a lot of difference.

Be sure to check the documentation for your window manager or desktop to find the correct start command. Some need only to execute the binary, some have a startup script. Table 8-1 lists some examples.

Table 8-1. Startup commands for popular window managers

Window manager	Startup command
Afterstep	afterstep
Enlightenment	enlightenment
FVWM	fvwm2
Gnome	gnome-session
IceWM	icewm
KDE	startkde
TWM	twm
Xfce	startxfce4

You won't need the full path as long as these commands are in your $PATH on your FreeNX server.

See Also

- XWinman (*http://xwinman.org/*) for information on all kinds of window managers
- Run /usr/bin/nxserver --help as *root* to see all server commands
- NoMachine's Support Center:

    http://www.nomachine.com/support.php
- NX Server System Administrator's Guide:

    http://www.nomachine.com/documentation/admin-guide.php

8.9   Creating Additional Nxclient Sessions

Problem

You have several remote Linux machines that you want to log in to. How do you set up additional Nxclient sessions?

Solution

Run the NX Connection Wizard every time you want to create a new session. On Windows, run Start → NX Client For Windows → NX Connection Wizard.

On Linux, Solaris, and Mac OS X, run /usr/NX/bin/nxclient --wizard.

You can create a new desktop shortcut for each one, and it will also populate the drop-down menu in the Nxclient login screen with the name of each new session.

Discussion

Nxclient comes with all the fixings to create menu and desktop icons, even on Linux. Whether they will actually be installed depends on your chosen Linux distribution.

See Also

- Run /usr/bin/nxserver --help as root to see all server commands
- NoMachine's Support Center:

    http://www.nomachine.com/support.php
- NX Server System Administrator's Guide:

    http://www.nomachine.com/documentation/admin-guide.php
- Monitoring Nxclient Sessions With NX Session Administrator

Problem

You want to monitor and control your Nxclient sessions—start new ones, stop existing ones, view logs, collect statistics, and monitor performance. How do you do this?

Solution

Use the NX Session Administrator, which comes with Nxclient. On Windows clients, look for the NX Session Administrator shortcut.

On Linux, Mac OS X, and Solaris, run /usr/NX/bin/nxclient --admin.

Using it is self-explanatory; just check out the different menus. The Session menu is interesting—here, you can see all the logs, statistics, and see for yourself how bandwidth-efficient FreeNX really is.

Discussion

KDE and Gnome are both working toward integrating FreeNX and Nxclient, so keep your eyes peeled for KDE and Gnome-specific utilities.

See Also

- Run /usr/bin/nxserver --help as *root* to see all server commands
- NoMachine's Support Center:

    http://www.nomachine.com/support.php
- NX Server System Administrator's Guide:

    http://www.nomachine.com/documentation/admin-guide.php

8.10 Enabling File and Printer Sharing, and Multimedia in Nxclient

Problem

You have Samba set up already for file and printer sharing, and CUPS is your printing subsystem. You want to share files and printers through FreeNX, instead of running a separate Samba client, or messing with CUPS. And, you noticed that sound effects don't play on your Nxclient, but they do play on the host PC. How do you get the sound effects to work remotely?

Solution

On Microsoft Windows, open NXclient For Windows; on Linux, Mac OS X, and Solaris, run */usr/NX/bin/nxclient*.

Click the Configure button, and go to the Services tab. Here are all the checkboxes to enable multimedia, shared printing, and file sharing.

Discussion

You must have Samba and CUPS already configured and working. Nxclient automatically finds all available shares—all you do is select the ones you want from a drop-down list.

See Also

- Chapters 14, 15, and 23 in *Linux Cookbook*, by Carla Schroder (O'Reilly) to learn how to set up CUPS and Samba
- Run /usr/NX/bin/nxclient --help to see all available commands

8.11 Preventing Password-Saving in Nxclient

Problem

You want to tighten up the client-side a bit by not allowing users to be able to save passwords in the Nxclient login screen.

Solution

Create an empty file on the client named */usr/NX/share/nopasswd*:

```
# touch /usr/NX/share/nopasswd
```

On Windows clients, create *\Program Files\NX Client for Windows\Share\nopasswd*.

This disables saving the login and password.

Discussion

If you have chronically roaming users, or users sharing Windows PCs, or generic public terminals, it is wise to disable login and password saving.

Obviously, you must make sure that the *nopasswd* file is read-only by the user. On Linux, this is easy:

```
# chown root:root nopasswd
# chmod 644 nopasswd
```

On Windows, it isn't so easy. Windows NT, 2000, 2003, and XP Pro running the NTFS filesystem let you tweak individual file permissions; just right-click on the file icon, and go to the Security tab to set ownership and access permissions.

However, any Windows running the FAT32 filesystem does not have ACLs. Windows XP Home does not include an ACL-capable filesystem, nor does Windows XP Pro in Simple File Sharing mode.

Simple File Sharing is on in XP Pro by default; to turn it off, open My Computer → Tools → Folder Options → View → Advanced Settings, and uncheck "Use simple file sharing (Recommended)."

You should do this as Administrator because Simple File Sharing is enabled/disabled per user. So, make sure the boss has control, however feeble. You can also make *nopasswd* a hidden file, for a wee bit of extra obscurity.

See Also

- Run /usr/bin/nxserver --help as *root* to see all server commands
- NoMachine's Support Center:

    http://www.nomachine.com/support.php
- NX Server System Administrator's Guide:

    http://www.nomachine.com/documentation/admin-guide.php

8.12 Troubleshooting FreeNX

Problem

You cannot connect—help!

Solution

Check the server logfile first, */var/log/nxserver.log*. If the logfile is not detailed enough, go into */etc/nxserver/node.conf,* and bump up the logging level. Available levels are 0–7. Level 6 is usually sufficient:

```
NX_LOG_LEVEL=6
```

Nxclient has its own log viewer in the NX Session Administrator, at Session → View session log.

The logfiles don't always tell you what you need to know. Here are a number of common problems that are easy to remedy:

- Make sure TCP port 3389 is not blocked on the clients.
- Make sure TCP port 22 is not blocked on the server.
- Make sure you are using the correct hostname or IP address of your FreeNX server.
- Make sure that you have distributed the correct client keys—probably the most common error is creating a new key pair when installing the server, and forgetting to distribute the client key.
- Check filepaths in */etc/nxserver/node.conf* and in the NX Clients.

See Also

- NoMachine's Support Center:

    http://www.nomachine.com/support.php

- NX Server System Administrator's Guide:

    http://www.nomachine.com/documentation/admin-guide.php

8.13   Using VNC to Control Windows from Linux

Problem

You want to control your Windows workstation or server remotely from your Linux box. Or, you want to be able to remotely control user's Windows PCs for helpdesk chores or remote administration.

Solution

Virtual Network Computing (VNC) is just what you need. There are several variants of VNC; in these recipes, we'll use TightVNC. VNC has two parts: the server and the client (which is called the *viewer*).

Install the TightVNC server and the DFMirage driver on Windows (see TightVNC, *http://www.tightvnc.com/*).

Install any VNC viewer on Linux. Chances are, one is already installed by default. The TightVNC viewer includes a Java viewer, so any Java-enabled web browser can be a VNC viewer.

The Windows installer will take you through a number of steps. The main question is, do you want TightVNC to run as a service or in application mode? You can change this at any time with the "Install VNC Service" or "Remove VNC Service" commands. Use application mode for occasional use, and run it as a service for frequent use.

These configuration options are important:

- On the Server tab, be sure to enable Accept Socket Connections.
- Make sure there are passwords for Primary Password and View-Only Password. Passwords may not be more than eight characters.
- On the Administration tab, check Disable Empty Passwords.
- To enable using a web browser as a client, check Enable built-in HTTP server.
- Enable logging; it's not necessary to turn on debugging unless you're having problems.

Now, you can connect from any VNC viewer on any operating system by entering the IP address or hostname of the Windows box. Figure 8-6 shows the Xvnc4viewer login screen.

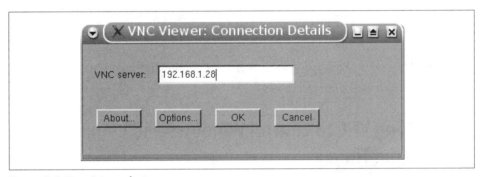

Figure 8-6. Xvnc4viewer login screen

You may use any VNC-capable viewer, like the KDE Remote Desktop Connection, the Gnome remote desktop, *jtightvncviewer*, *vncviewer*, or *xvnc4viewer*.

To close out your remote session, just close the window.

To open a VNC session in a web browser, type *http://[hostname-or-IP-address]:5800* in the address bar.

Please note that all transmissions are sent in the clear, and authentication is weakly protected, so you do not want to use this over untrusted networks.

Discussion

On Debian, the TightVNC Java viewer is a separate package, *tightvnc-java*.

You can encrypt a VNC session by tunneling VNC over SSH (see Recipe 8.21). This works on any platforms that support SSH and VNC.

Unlike *rdesktop*, VNC works for any version of Windows.

Because the TightVNC server has its own password, you can log in to any active Windows session; it doesn't matter which Windows user is logged in.

In application mode, you need a Windows user already logged in on the Windows PC to enable remote logins. When it's running as a service, you don't.

Only Windows users with administrative privileges can make any changes to the TightVNC server configuration when it runs as a service. This prevents remote users from shutting down the VNC server or changing its settings.

When the TightVNC server runs in application mode, then any Windows user can run it as they please, and remote users can change VNC settings, and even shut it down. This is a nice convenience for users, and also a potential security hole.

See Also

- RealVNC:

    http://www.realvnc.com/
- TightVNC:

    http://www.tightvnc.com/
- UltraVNC for Windows-to-Windows remote administration:

    http://ultravnc.sourceforge.net/

8.14 Using VNC to Control Windows and Linux at the Same Time

Problem

You need to use a Windows PC and a Linux PC a lot. Sure, you get some exercise hopping back and forth from chair to chair, or scooting your chair about, but it would be nice to control both from a single keyboard and mouse, and you would rather not spend money on a hardware switch.

Solution

As usual, the Linux world provides an abundance of useful goodies. In addition to a Windows VNC server (see the previous recipe), you'll need the *x2vnc* program.

Of course, Linux must be in charge, and will control both computers. First, install *x2vnc* on Linux.

Make sure the Windows VNC server is running and accepting connections.

Then, fire up *x2vnc*:

```
$ x2vnc 192.168.1.28:0 -west
x2vnc: VNC server supports protocol version 3.7 (viewer 3.3)
Password:
x2vnc: VNC authentication succeeded
x2vnc: Desktop name "powerpc-w2k"
x2vnc: Connected to VNC server, using protocol version 3.3
x2vnc: VNC server default format:
```

And there you are. -west means left, so you can move your cursor to the left off the edge of your Linux screen, and it will reappear on your Windows screen. Now, you control both computers with the same keyboard and mouse.

Discussion

You'll notice that this is quite a bit peppier than a regular VNC session because you are running native sessions on each computer, rather than creating virtual graphics servers.

This can only be used to control Windows from Linux. If you want to run your primary session from a Windows PC, use Win2VNC on Windows, and the VNC server of your choice on Linux.

Running two Linux PCs requires *x11vnc* for the VNC server.

x2vnc works by creating a one-pixel-wide trigger window at the edge of the screen, which causes *x2vnc* to take control and send mouse movements and keystrokes to the Windows PC.

Here are some useful options:

-resurface
    This keeps the trigger window on top, so it can't be covered by another window.

-edgewidth 3
    If you have problems with the trigger window, you can try making it wider. Setting it to 0 disables it entirely, if you would rather use the hotkey to switch back and forth.

-debug
    If you are having problems, crank up the verbosity.

-hotkey
    A common error message is "Warning: Failed to bind x2vnc hotkey, hotkey disabled." Use the -hotkey option to specify which hotkey you want, like this:

    ```
    $ x2vnc -hotkey F12 192.168.1.28:0 -west
    ```

    Hitting F12 switches the cursor back and forth between your two screens. The default is Ctrl-F12; you may use any combination of meta keys that you like.

See Also

- man 1 x2vnc

8.15   Using VNC for Remote Linux-to-Linux Administration

Problem

You want to use VNC to control other Linux PCs from your Linux box.

Solution

Install the VNC server and viewers of your choice on both Linux PCs. In this recipe, we'll use TightVNC. Fire up the VNC server on the first PC. This example shows a first-time startup that creates the server's configuration files and password:

```
carla@windbag:~$ tightvncserver
You will require a password to access your desktops.
Password:
Verify:
New 'X' desktop is windbag:1
Creating default startup script /home/carla/.vnc/xstartup
Starting applications specified in /home/carla/.vnc/xstartup
Log file is /home/carla/.vnc/windbag:1.log
```

Then, it exits. Start it up again:

```
carla@windbag:~$ tightvncserver
New 'X' desktop is windbag:2
Starting applications specified in /home/carla/.vnc/xstartup
Log file is /home/carla/.vnc/windbag:2.log
```

Notice that it helpfully tells you everything you need to know: the connection parameters, configuration file, and logfile locations.

Now, run over to Linux PC number two, open a VNC viewer, and connect with the hostname:

```
windbag:2
```

Or, use the IP address:

```
192.168.1.28:2
```

It will ask for a password, and there you are.

You can shutdown *tightvncserver* sessions on the server like this, specifiying the session number:

```
$ tightvncserver -kill :2
Killing Xtightvnc process ID 24306
```

Note that you must append a session number because Linux supports running multiple VNC servers at the same time.

Discussion

If you configured the server to use a different port number than the default 5800 (for HTTP) or 5900 (VNC viewer), you'll need to specify the port number in the client, like this for port 6000:

```
windbag:6002
```

VNC adds the session number to the port number, so session 3 is 6003, and so forth.

You'll notice this is quite a bit faster than using VNC to run Windows from Linux. This is because VNC only needs to handle X Windows, which was designed from the start to support networking. So, all VNC needs to do is transmit keyboard and mouse input over TCP/IP, rather than replicating the entire screen like it does with Windows, which uses an entirely different graphical subsystem. In effect, VNC must repeatedly screen scrape and transmit a copy of the Windows display.

You may run as many VNC servers on a single Linux PC as you like. Just open new instances of the VNC server, and it will automatically assign a new display:

```
$ tightvncserver
New 'X' desktop is windbag:3
Starting applications specified in /home/carla/.vnc/xstartup
Log file is /home/carla/.vnc/windbag:3.log
```

You can go nuts and connect back and forth as much as you like, or daisy-chain several VNC sessions by connecting to other PCs from inside the remote sessions.

Run ps ax | grep vnc to see how many servers you have running locally:

```
18737 pts/1   S      0:00 Xtightvnc :1 -desktop X -httpd /usr/share/tightvnc-java -
auth /home/carla/.Xauthority -geometry 1024x768 -depth 24 -rfbwait 120000 -rfbauth /
home/carla/.vnc/passwd -rfbport 5901 -fp /usr/share/X11/fonts/misc,/usr/share/X11/
fonts/cyrillic,/usr/share/X11/fonts/100dpi/:unscaled,/usr/share/X11/fonts/75dpi/:
unscaled,/usr/share/X11/fonts/Type1,/usr/share/X11/fonts/CID,/usr/share/X11/fonts/
100dpi,/usr/share/X11/fonts/75dpi,/var/lib/defoma/x-ttcidfont-conf.d/dirs/TrueType,/
var/lib/defoma/x-ttcidfont-conf.d/dirs/CID -co /usr/X11R6/lib/X11/rgb

19479 pts/5   S      0:00 Xtightvnc :2 -desktop X -httpd /usr/share/tightvnc-java -
auth /home/carla/.Xauthority -geometry 1024x768 -depth 24 -rfbwait 120000 -rfbauth /
home/carla/.vnc/passwd -rfbport 5902 -fp /usr/share/X11/fonts/misc,/usr/share/X11/
fonts/cyrillic,/usr/share/X11/fonts/100dpi/:unscaled,/usr/share/X11/fonts/75dpi/:
unscaled,/usr/share/X11/fonts/Type1,/usr/share/X11/fonts/CID,/usr/share/X11/fonts/
100dpi,/usr/share/X11/fonts/75dpi,/var/lib/defoma/x-ttcidfont-conf.d/dirs/TrueType,/
var/lib/defoma/x-ttcidfont-conf.d/dirs/CID -co /usr/X11R6/lib/X11/rgb
```

Run killall Xtightvnc to stop all of them.

Don't run Xtightvnc directly, because *tightvncserver* is a wrapper script that performs sanity checks and emits useful error messages.

See Also

- RealVNC:

    http://www.realvnc.com/

- TightVNC:

    http://www.tightvnc.com/

- UltraVNC for Windows-to-Windows remote administration:

    http://ultravnc.sourceforge.net/

8.16   Displaying the Same Windows Desktop to Multiple Remote Users

Problem

You want to run a remote demo to several of your users, or conduct a class, or otherwise set it up so that several people can share the same remote Windows desktop.

Solution

TightVNC supports multiple concurrent users. Anyone with a VNC viewer can connect: Linux, Mac, or other Windows users.

First, configure the TightVNC server on Windows to accept multiple connections. Double-click the systray VNC icon, or open Start → TightVNC → Show User Settings. Go to the Administration tab, and check "Automatic shared sessions."

Now, your users can log in to Windows in the usual manner by entering the hostname or IP of the Windows PC in their VNC clients. In VNC viewers, the port number is 5900. In the KDE Remote Desktop Connection (KRDC) viewer, it looks like Figures 8-7 and 8-8.

Now, imagine what happens when all of your users are connected—do you want them to have control of the mouse and keyboard, or do you wish to lock them out? Do you want to allow remote control only when the local Windows user is idle? Configure these options on the Server tab under Input handling.

Discussion

TightVNC does not have any sort of user-monitoring tools—the only way it shows client connections is that the systray icon changes color. There are a couple of useful client-management options when you right-click the systray icon. You can block new users from connecting, or kick off the entire lot of connected clients.

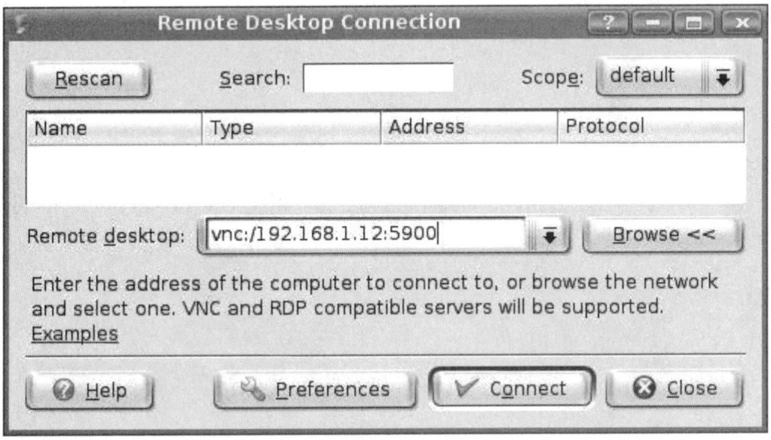

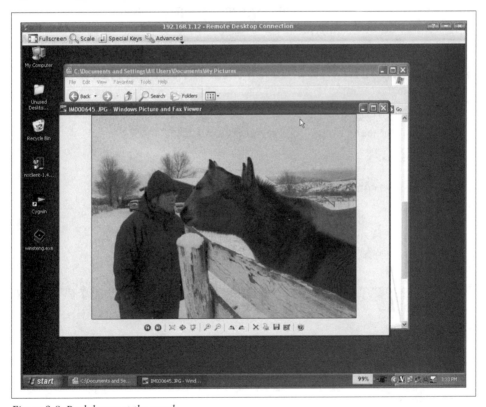

Figure 8-7. Login screen

Figure 8-8. Back home at the ranch

You may also view the session in a Java-enabled web browser. Enter the connection parameters in standard URL form, plus the port number:

```
http://powerpc:5800
```

Or, use the IP address:

```
http://192.168.1.28:5800
```

On Debian, you need the *tightvnc-java* package installed on the server. The TightVNC server RPMs and source tarballs include the Java component.

See Also

- RealVNC:

    http://www.realvnc.com/

- TightVNC:

    http://www.tightvnc.com/

- UltraVNC for Windows-to-Windows remote administration:

    http://ultravnc.sourceforge.net/

8.17   Changing the Linux VNC Server Password

Problem

How do you change the Linux VNC server password?

Solution

Use the vncpasswd command:

```
$ vncpasswd
Password:
Verify:
```

Discussion

Remember to inform users when you change the password. You may do without passwords entirely, if you really really want to.

See Also

- man 1 vncpasswd
- RealVNC: *http://www.realvnc.com/*
- TightVNC: *http://www.tightvnc.com/*
- UltraVNC for Windows-to-Windows remote administration:

    http://ultravnc.sourceforge.net/

8.18   Customizing the Remote VNC Desktop

Problem

The default VNC remote desktop on Linux is little better than a plain vanilla SSH session—all you get is some barebones window manager like TWM or Metacity, and an Xterm. How do you get the window manager or desktop of your choice?

Solution

Edit your *~/.vnc/xstartup* file on the server. This is the default:

```
#!/bin/sh
xrdb $HOME/.Xresources
xsetroot -solid grey
x-terminal-emulator -geometry 80x24+10+10 -ls -title "$VNCDESKTOP Desktop" &
x-window-manager &
```

If there is no *~/.Xresources* file, comment that line out.

Simply replace -window-manager with the startup command for the window manager of your choice, like this:

```
icewm &
```

Whenever you make changes in this file, you need to stop and restart the server:

```
$ tightvncserver -kill :1
$ tightvncserver
```

Then, log in again from your remote PC.

Table 8-2 lists some startup commands for various window managers, which must be installed on the server if you want to use them.

Table 8-2. Startup commands for popular window managers

Window manager	Startup command
Afterstep	afterstep
Enlightenment	enlightenment
FVWM	fvwm2
Gnome	gnome-session
IceWM	icewm
KDE	startkde
TWM	twm
Xfce	startxfce4

Discussion

Check the logfiles in *~/.vnx* first if you have problems making this work.

You'll find all sorts of misinformation on the Internet about how to do this. The VNC documentation isn't exactly helpful, either. Which is too bad, because customizing your remote environment is easy. All you do is edit the *~/.vnc/xstartup* file, as this example shows:

```
#!/bin/sh
xsetroot -gray
kwrite &
konqueror &
icewm &
```

xsetroot sets the background color of your window manager.

List any applications you want to start automatically, one per line, and be sure to end each line with the & operator. If you don't, your apps will be locked in place and nothing will work. The & operator tells Bash to continue parsing each line; otherwise, it stops and waits for the first command to complete before proceeding.

See Also

- man 1 vncserver

8.19   Setting the Remote VNC Desktop Size

Problem

Your custom VNC desktop works fine, except it's too big. How do you change this?

Solution

The default remote desktop size is 1024×768. You can change this on the command line when you start the server:

```
$ tightvncserver -geometry 800x600
```

Be sure to use standard values only, or applications will look all wrong, or not work at all. The standard values are:

```
1600×1200
1280×1024
1024×768
800×600
640×480
```

You can set the desktop size in a configuration file, either system-wide in */etc/vnc.conf* or per-user in *~/.vncrc*. User settings override global settings, and the command line overrides all. For example, to set the default desktop size to 800×600, use this line:

```
geometry = "800x600";
```

The default */etc/vnc.conf* contains a lot of sample options and shows the correct syntax.

Discussion

There are so many ways to do this on Linux and on Windows from Cygwin that it gets a bit mind-boggling. For example, you could log in to your VNC server via SSH and start up the VNC server with customized options. Or, edit its configuration files and restart it. You can get a pretty good hall-of-mirrors effect going.

See Also

- man 1 vncserver
- man 5 vnc.conf

8.20   Connecting VNC to an Existing X Session

Problem

You want to be able to connect to your Linux workstation remotely, and you want to attach to your existing X session instead of starting a new independent one. You want to be able to roam about and log in from other locations, picking up where you left off. Or, you want to use this as a helpdesk tool so you can take control of user's Linux PCs remotely and fix problems yourself, instead of spending way too much time trying to talk users through a diagnosis and repair over the telephone.

Solution

Easy as pie with *x11vnc*. You need *x11vnc* on the remote server, and a VNC viewer on your local Linux workstation. After installing *x11vnc*, create a login password. In this example, it is stored in */home/carla/x11vnc/passwd*. Make sure it is readable only by the user:

```
carla@windbag:~/x11vnc$ x11vnc -storepasswd 'password' passwd
stored passwd in file passwd
carla@windbag:~/x11vnc$ chmod 0600 passwd
```

Now, create a *~/.x11vncrc* file. This is the user-specific configuration file that *x11vnc* will automatically look for. Put a line in this file pointing to your password file:

```
rfbauth   /home/carla/x11vnc/passwd
```

Then, start up *x11vnc*:

```
$ x11vnc
07/01/2007 21:25:12 passing arg to libvncserver: -rfbauth
07/01/2007 21:25:12 passing arg to libvncserver: /home/carla/x11vnc/passwd
[...]
Using X display :0
Read initial data from X display into framebuffer.

07/01/2007 18:51:01 Using X display with 16bpp depth=16 true color
07/01/2007 18:51:01 Autoprobing TCP port
07/01/2007 18:51:01 Autoprobing selected port 5900
07/01/2007 18:51:01 screen setup finished.
07/01/2007 18:51:01 The VNC desktop is stinkpad:0
PORT=5900
```

Next, start the VNC viewer on the other PC, like this:

```
$ vncviewer stinkpad:0
```

Enter the password on the login screen, and you are logged in.

x11vnc automatically exits after a single log in, so you won't be able to log in again without restarting it. To leave it running continuously, use the -forever and -bg options:

```
$ x11vnc -forever -bg
```

-bg sends it into the background.

Discussion

A common desire is to make *x11vnc* to run as a service, surviving reboots. It is difficult, and in my opinion dangerous, as its authentication is weakly protected, data are sent in the clear, and it requires configuring X Windows, which is just as insecure. I recommend starting it up only when you want to use it. A safer method is to log in to remote PCs with OpenSSH first, then start up *x11vnc*. Even better is to tunnel *x11vnc* over SSH, which the next recipe tells you how to do.

See Also

- *x11vnc* has dozens of options; to see all of them, run:
    ```
    $ x11vnc -opts
    ```
- This command gives long descriptions for each one:
    ```
    $ x11vnc -help
    ```
- *x11vnc* home page: *http://www.karlrunge.com/x11vnc*

8.21   Securely Tunneling x11vnc over SSH

Problem

x11vnc is great for remote helpdesk and roaming users, but you're not comfortable with sending everything in cleartext. You want to tunnel *x11vnc* over SSH for secure encryption, so how is this done?

Solution

This example shows you how to tunnel *x11vnc* over SSH, establishing the tunnel and starting *x11vnc* with one command. No remote user intervention is needed at all, providing that *sshd* is running on their PC. Windbag is the local PC, and Stinkpad is the remote machine:

```
carla@windbag:~$ ssh -L 5900:windbag:5900 stinkpad 'x11vnc -localhost -display :0'
```

Then, open a second command shell on the local machine, and connect with this command:

```
carla@windbag:~$ vncviewer localhost:0
```

Just like VNC, you may run as many *x11vnc* sessions as you want. They are numbered sequentially.

If you don't want to keep your password in a configuration file, and would rather enter it on the command line, use the -passwd flag:

```
$ x11vnc -passwd [password] -bg
```

x11vnc is a stateless connection, so you can log in, log out, wander around, and log in again, picking up where you left off.

x11vnc has many dozens of options; to see a list of them, run:

```
$ x11vnc -opts
```

This command gives long descriptions for each one:

```
$ x11vnc -help
```

Discussion

This should work for any version of VNC.

See Also

- *x11vnc* home page: *http://www.karlrunge.com/x11vnc*

8.22 Tunneling TightVNC Between Linux and Windows

Problem

You're not comfortable with VNC's lack of data encryption and its weak authentication, so you want to know how to add strong security, especially for traffic over untrusted networks. And, you want something that works cross-platform (for example, when you administer Windows PCs from your Linux workstation).

Solution

Tunnel VNC over SSH.

We'll assume the following for this recipe:

- You have a Windows 2000 machine or greater capable of running Cygwin and TightVNC.
- You have a Linux machine with the *vncviewer* program installed on it.
- The Windows PC is named "cygwin" and the Linux PC is named "linux."

To install Cygwin and OpenSSH on Windows, go to Cygwin.com (*http://cygwin. com*), and hit "Install Cygwin Now." This downloads a tiny *setup.exe* file; double-click this file to bring up the Cygwin installation menu.

The default installation will work fine, except you need to add OpenSSH. You'll find this in the Net submenu. Throw in *ping* for good measure; it will save you the hassle of opening a DOS window when you need to use *ping* while you're running Cygwin.

After installation, open a Cygwin *bash* shell (there should be a menu command "Cygwin Bash Shell"), then run:

```
$ ssh-host-config
```

This generates new SSH keys and configuration files. Say "yes" to:

- Privilege separation
- Create a local user "sshd"
- Install sshd as a service

Then, add the CYGWIN=ntsec tty environment variables.

Next, start up the *ssh* daemon:

```
$ net start sshd
The CYGWIN sshd service is starting.
The CYGWIN sshd service was started successfully.
```

Download TightVNC from tightvnc.com (*http://www.tightvnc.com/download.html*), and install it onto your Win32 machine and reboot. You can access the Current User Properties by double-clicking on the VNC icon in the system tray. Do this to set a password, and then click the Advanced button. In the next menu, check "Allow Loopback Connections."

Test that you can get to the VNC server with the password you specified in the previous step from the Linux machine by running the `vncviewer cygwin` command from the Linux machine, or `vncviewer [windows-IP-address]`.

Next, let's generate a passwordless DSA key on the Linux PC. Accept the defaults for all questions by hitting Enter for each one:

```
carla@linux:~ $ ssh-keygen -t dsa
Generating public/private dsa key pair.
Enter file in which to save the key (/home/carla/.ssh/id_dsa):
Enter passphrase (empty for no passphrase):
Enter same passphrase again:
Your identification has been saved in /home/carla/.ssh/id_dsa.
Your public key has been saved in /home/carla/.ssh/id_dsa.pub.
The key fingerprint is:
2b:cb:9a:df:f8:34:2d:2f:0c:29:76:5c:c6:52:43:92
```

Then, on the Windows machine, back at the Cygwin command line, copy the key from the Linux box:

```
$ scp carla@linux:.ssh/id_dsa.pub .$ cat id_dsa.pub >> .ssh/authorized_keys
```

Finally, test that the key allows you to log in to Windows without a password:

```
carla@linux:~$ ssh user@cygwin
Last login: Sun Sep 24 15:42:48 2006 from 192.168.1.15
```

So, you can create the SSH tunnel from the Linux host to the Windows host with the following command:

```
carla@linux:~$ ssh -L 5900:localhost:5900 user@cygwin
Last login: Sun Jun 3 20:59:54 2007 from 192.168.1.15
Carla@cygwin ~
$
```

Now that you are logged in, open a second terminal on your Linux machine, and fire up VNC:

```
carla@linux:~$ vncviewer localhost
```

You should be prompted for a password to the VNC server, make the connection, and just like in a bad movie, yell, "I'm in!"

Future logins will be easy—just create the tunnel, then run VNC.

Discussion

It's easy to test that your VNC session is running over the SSH tunnel. Just log out from the SSH session, and VNC will go away.

SSH tunneling works with any operating system that runs SSH; it works great for Linux-on-Linux sessions, and is a must for connecting over the Internet. SSH is efficient, so you shouldn't see a performance hit.

You don't need to do anything different to VNC, just configure and use it as you normally would. Once the tunnel is established, use all the ordinary VNC commands.

Let's take a look at the command that created the tunnel:

```
ssh -L 5900:windbag:5900 user@cygwin
```

The -L switch tells SSH to forward everything sent to the specified local port onward to the remote port and address. So, any traffic sent to TCP 5900 will be forwarded, not just VNC. (The VNC port is specified in the VNC server configuration.) You may, of course, use IP addresses instead of hostnames.

If you're tunneling over the Internet, be sure to use fully qualified domain names:

```
$ ssh -L 5900:homepc.pinball.net:5900 cygwin.work.com
```

The second command:

```
vncviewer windbag
```

must be directed to the local machine instead of the remote machine because the entrance to the tunnel is on the local PC.

The CYGWIN=ntsec environment variable creates more Unix-like file permissions on Windows NTFS filesystems.

The CYGWIN=tty environment variable enables Bash job control.

Cygwin environment variables are in *C:\cygwin.bat*, which you may edit to suit.

See Also

- Chapter 7
- Chapter 2, "Setting Up Cygwin," in *Cygwin's User Guide*:
    http://www.cygwin.com/cygwin-ug-net/cygwin-ug-net.html

## CHAPTER 9

Building Secure Cross-Platform Virtual Private Networks with OpenVPN

9.0 Introduction

Granting safe, controlled access to your company network for road warriors, telecommuters, and branch offices isn't difficult when you use OpenVPN. OpenVPN is a great Secure Sockets Layer-based Virtual Private Network (SSL VPN) program that is free of cost, open source, easy to administer, and secure. OpenVPN is designed to be as universal as possible, so it runs on Linux, Solaris, Windows, Mac OS X, and several other platforms. It runs as a client or server from the same installation, so client setup is a breeze. There are no hassles with vendor compatibility or finding a decent client, as there are with other VPN products.

In this chapter, we're using OpenVPN 2.0.7. (Use the command `openvpn --version` to see what yours is.) Don't use anything older; it's free, and it's easy to install and upgrade, so there's no point in using old mold. If you're not experienced with OpenVPN, try out the recipes in order, or at least run the first two recipes before you try anything else. These will help you understand how OpenVPN works.

The subject of VPNs is muddled by misleading marketing and incorrect information about SSL VPN products, IPSec VPNs, what they can do, and what they actually do, so first let's discuss some basics.

To start out, let's define a VPN—it is an encrypted network-to-network virtual tunnel that connects trusted endpoints. Both the VPN server and client must authenticate to each other. It is a secure extension of your network that makes all the same services available to remote workers, such as telecommuters and road warriors, that local users have. Think of it as a secure Ethernet cable that extends your network through hostile territory. A VPN connects two networks, like branch offices, or lone remote users to the office.

SSL VPNs rely on SSL/TLS for security. Secure Sockets Layer (SSL) is the predecessor to Transport Layer Security (TLS). The terms are used interchangeably; the two are very similar. These are cryptographic protocols used to protect transmissions over untrusted networks. They aim to prevent eavesdropping, tampering, message forgery, and to provide authentication.

An alarming number of commercial SSL VPN products treat your network like a shopping web site: in other words, all clients are trusted. This works fine for online shopping, but can be disastrous for remote LAN access. These are not real VPNs, but application portals. What makes a VPN strong is trusted endpoints. You don't want your users logging in from arbitrary machines, and especially not from coffee shops or other public terminals. Sure, it's convenient not to have to install and configure client software and copy encryption keys. But, that is shortsighted—the last thing you need is users logging in from random PCs infected with keyloggers and spyware, and then being given a warm welcome into your LAN. Prevention is more convenient than cleaning up after a successful intrusion. Any SSL VPN product that promises "Easy clientless configuration!" should be viewed with a large dose of skepticism. A real VPN is not an SSL-enabled web browser with pretty icons. A real VPN doesn't need a web browser. Don't trust your security to prettified web browsers.

What About IPSec?

To further complicate the issue, some IPSec proponents claim that IPSec is superior and that SSL VPNs are not worthy. IPSec, especially in IPv4 networks, has a number of problems. It is complex and difficult to administer, which are not good traits for security products. It is tightly coupled to the kernel, which means a failure can bring down your whole system, or a flaw opens a root door to an intruder. If you really want to use an IPSec VPN, try OpenBSD. It comes with a great IPSec implementation that is easy to get up and running. Its one weakness is on the client side—you're on your own for hunting down IPSec clients.

As IPv6 is implemented, IPSec may become easier because it is integrated into IPv6, rather than bolted-on as it is for IPv4.

OpenVPN

OpenVPN is, I think, the best VPN product available. OpenVPN creates a true VPN, an encrypted extension of your network that requires a mutual trust to be established between the server and the client. The first step to setting this up is creating your own Public Key Infrastructure (PKI), which means using OpenSSL to create your own Certificate Authority (CA), and server and client keys and certificates. Having your own CA simplifies certificate management considerably. The server doesn't need to know anything about the individual client certificates because the CA authenticates them. If a client is compromised, its certificate can be revoked from the server. OpenVPN comes with a batch of scripts that make managing your PKI easy.

OpenVPN's encryption process is complex. First, the SSL/TLS handshake authenticates both ends, then four different new keys are generated: Hashed Message Authentication Code (HMAC) send and receive keys, an encrypt/decrypt send key, and an encrypt/decrypt receive key. This is all delightfully complex, and happens in an eyeblink; the result is that any attacker is going to have a very hard time getting anywhere. To learn about this in detail, read Charlie Hosner's excellent paper, "Open-VPN and the SSL Revolution" (*http://www.sans.org/reading_room/whitepapers/vpns/1459.php?portal=c7da694586dcdad815fd41098461e495*).

Client configuration is the easiest of any VPN. OpenVPN runs as either client or server on Linux, Solaris, OpenBSD, Mac OS X, FreeBSD, NetBSD, and Windows 2000 and up, so you don't have to hunt for client software, or suffer the pain of testing poor-quality client software. Configuration files are pretty much the same on all platforms. Just remember that slashes lean in the wrong direction on Windows.

OpenVPN runs as a user-space daemon. It uses TAP/TUN drivers to manage network access. TAP/TUN drivers are standard on most operating systems; these provide a way for user-space applications to access network interfaces without needing *root* privileges. The TAP driver provides low-level kernel support for IP tunneling, and the TUN driver provides low-level kernel support for Ethernet tunneling. You'll see this on Linux and Unix systems as character devices named */dev/tapX* and */dev/tunX*. In *ifconfig*, they will appear as *tunX* and *tapX*. Use the TUN driver when your VPN tunnel is routed, and the TAP driver when it's bridged. You'll configure this in *openvpn.conf*.

In an ideal world, your remote users only log in from PCs that have been carefully screened by your ace security staff, and your users are wise and careful, and don't let other people use their computers. In the real world, it's messier, of course. But using OpenVPN is a strong security measure that prevents many ills.

OpenVPN is a standard package on most Linux-based firewall distributions, such as Shorewall, IPCop, Pyramid, Open WRT, Bering uClibc, and DD-WRT. On others, it's just a `yum install openvpn` or `apt-get install openvpn` away, and of course, you may build it from sources if you prefer.

9.1   Setting Up a Safe OpenVPN Test Lab

Problem

You don't want to be messing around with trying to test OpenVPN over the Internet; you want a safe, controlled environment for testing before you deploy it.

Solution

Not a problem. Just build a little test lab with three computers. One acts as the remote PC, the second one is the OpenVPN server and router, and the third one represents your LAN. The PC acting as the OpenVPN server and router needs two Ethernet interfaces. With this setup, you can test OpenVPN configurations and firewall rules safely, and in a realistic manner. These should be in physical proximity to each other because when you start messing with networking, you're going to lose connectivity. You should use Ethernet cables and a switch; don't try this with wireless unless you enjoy introducing more problems.

Before you do anything else, install OpenVPN on the remote PC and the machine that is going to be your OpenVPN server. In this recipe, all three computers are running Linux. (We'll get to other clients later in the chapter.) OpenVPN is included in most Linux distributions, so it's just a yum install openvpn or aptitude install openvpn away.

Setting up routes can get a bit confusing, especially if you still rely on cheat sheets for calculating subnets (like I do), and have to draw network diagrams even for simple setups (which I must also do), so take it slowly and follow these steps exactly. You can always change addresses and routes later. Your test network should look like Figure 9-1.

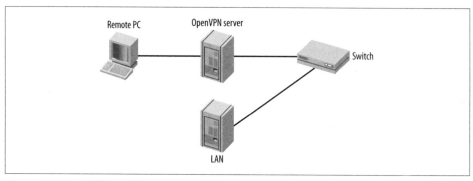

Figure 9-1. OpenVPN test lab

Connect the remote PC to the server directly with a crossover cable. In this recipe, I'll use Xena as the name of the OpenVPN server, Stinkpad as the remote client, and Uberpc represents the rest of the LAN.

Xena and Stinkpad need to be on different subnets, so our network addressing looks like this:

Stinkpad
> eth0
>
> address 192.168.2.100
>
> netmask 255.255.255.0
>
> broadcast 192.168.2.255

Xena
> eth0- LAN interface
>
> address 192.168.1.10
>
> netmask 255.255.255.0
>
> broadcast 192.168.1.255

eth1- "Internet" interface

address 192.168.3.10

netmask 255.255.255.0

broadcast 192.168.3.255

Uberpc

eth0

address 192.168.1.76

netmask 255.255.255.0

broadcast 192.168.1.255

default gateway 192.168.1.10

It doesn't matter what network configurations your PCs already have because we'll set them temporarily for testing, so you don't need to touch any configuration files. Set their IP addresses with these commands:

```
root@stinkpad:~# ifconfig eth0 192.168.2.100 netmask 255.255.255.0 up
root@xena:~# ifconfig eth0 192.168.1.10 netmask 255.255.255.0 up
root@xena:~# ifconfig eth1 192.168.3.11 netmask 255.255.255.0 up
root@uberpc:~# ifconfig eth1 192.168.1.76 netmask 255.255.255.0 up
```

Now, create some static routes, and turn on forwarding on Xena, so that the bits may flow freely:

```
root@stinkpad:~# route del default
root@stinkpad:~# route add -net 192.168.3.0/24  gw 192.168.2.100  eth0
root@xena:~# route del default
root@xena:~# route add -net 192.168.2.0/24  gw 192.168.3.10  eth1
root@xena:~# echo 1 > /proc/sys/net/ipv4/ip_forward
root@uberpc:~# route del default
root@uberpc:~# route add default gw 192.168.1.10 eth0
```

View your routes with the *route* command. If you make a mistake, routes are deleted this way, using your own network address, of course:

```
# route del -net 192.168.3.0/24
```

Stinkpad and Uberpc should now be able to *ping* each other. Once *ping* is working, you can go to the next recipe to start testing OpenVPN.

Discussion

If you get hopelessly messed up, simply reboot and start over.

This is designed to mimic the Internet. A real Internet connection would have routers between Stinkpad and Xena, so to emulate this, Stinkpad must be its own router and gateway. Stinkpad only needs to be routed to Xena; routing into the LAN behind Xena will be handled by the OpenVPN server, which we'll get to later in this chapter.

You may add more computers if you wish—just remember to put them on the same LAN as Stinkpad (192.168.1.0/24), and make Stinkpad's LAN IP address their default gateway.

If you set two default gateways on a computer, you can select which one to delete, like this:

```
# route del default gw 192.168.1.25
```

There can be only one default gateway. It's not necessary to have default gateways during testing, but you should on production machines.

It is possible to have a large number of routes, and to have your usual Internet connectivity if you configure everything correctly. Feel free to be as much of a routing guru as you like; I prefer to keep it as simple as possible for easier debugging. That is why the default routes are deleted, so they aren't hanging around to confuse you. If you have other routes that do not pertain to testing OpenVPN, get rid of them, too.

Stinkpad (the remote PC), must connect directly to the router, Xena, because different broadcast domains need routing between them. (Or bridging, which we'll get to later.)

See Also

- man 8 route
- man 8 ifconfig

9.2   Starting and Testing OpenVPN

Problem

You followed the previous recipe and your little test lab works, and you're ready to start running OpenVPN. Now what?

Solution

First, check both OpenVPN machines to see if OpenVPN is already running:

```
$ ps ax | grep vpn
```

If it is, stop it:

```
# killall openvpn
```

Then, open a quick, insecure tunnel between the remote PC and your OpenVPN server with these commands:

```
root@xena:~# openvpn --remote 192.168.2.100  --dev tun0 \
--ifconfig 10.0.0.1  10.0.0.2
root@stinkpad:~# openvpn --remote 192.168.3.10  \
--dev tun0 --ifconfig 10.0.0.2  10.0.0.1
```

This message shows success, and should be seen on both sides of the connection:

```
Wed Feb 14 12:53:45 2007 Initialization Sequence Completed
```

Now, open some new terminals, and try *pinging* your new virtual IP addresses:

```
carla@xena:~$ ping 10.0.0.2
PING 10.0.0.2 (10.0.0.2) 56(84) bytes of data.
64 bytes from 10.0.0.2: icmp_seq=1 ttl=64 time=0.421 ms
64 bytes from 10.0.0.2: icmp_seq=2 ttl=64 time=0.314 ms
carla@stinkpad:~$ ping 10.0.0.1
PING 10.0.0.1 (10.0.0.1) 56(84) bytes of data.
64 bytes from 10.0.0.1: icmp_seq=1 ttl=64 time=0.360 ms
64 bytes from 10.0.0.1: icmp_seq=2 ttl=64 time=0.317 ms
```

You may also specify which interface for *ping* to use:

```
carla@xena:~$ ping -I tun0 10.0.0.2
carla@stinkpad:~$ ping -I tun0  10.0.0.1
```

Go ahead and give your tunnels a test drive by opening SSH sessions everywhere:

```
carla@xena:~$ ssh  10.0.0.2
carla@stinkpad:~$ ssh 10.0.0.1
```

Exit your SSH sessions, and hit Ctrl-C to shut down OpenVPN and close the tunnels.

Discussion

What you did here was create an unencrypted tunnel between a remote PC, Stinkpad, and Xena, which is functioning like a border router. Stinkpad and Xena can exchange TCP and UDP traffic, but the LAN behind Xena is not yet accessible to Stinkpad. Because these are routed connections, broadcast traffic like Samba will not cross the router.

If you see UDPv4 [ECONNREFUSED]: Connection refused (code=111), it means only one tunnel endpoint has been created, so you still need to create the other end.

The message TCP/UDP Socket bind failed on local address [ip-address]:1194: Address already in use means OpenVPN is already running.

The --ifconfig option first sets the local tunnel endpoint address, then the remote tunnel endpoint. These can be pretty much anything you want, as long as they are different from your other subnets. (Subnets and broadcast domains are the same things.) You don't have to use completely different address classes; for example, you could stick to using IPv4 class C addresses for everything, which is 192.168.0.0–192.168.255.255.

Use *ifconfig* to see the new *tun0* interface:

```
$ /sbin/ifconfig -i tun0
tun0      Link encap:UNSPEC  HWaddr 00-00-00-00-00-00-00-00-00-00-00-00-00-00-00-00
          inet addr:10.0.0.2  P-t-P:10.0.0.1  Mask:255.255.255.255
          UP POINTOPOINT RUNNING NOARP MULTICAST  MTU:1500  Metric:1
          RX packets:0 errors:0 dropped:0 overruns:0 frame:0
```

```
              TX packets:0 errors:0 dropped:0 overruns:0 carrier:0
              collisions:0 txqueuelen:100
              RX bytes:0 (0.0 b)   TX bytes:0 (0.0 b)
```

Use *route* to see your new routes:

```
carla@xena:~$ /sbin/route
Kernel IP routing table
Destination     Gateway         Genmask         Flags Metric Ref    Use Iface
10.0.0.2        *               255.255.255.255 UH    0      0        0 tun0
192.168.3.0     *               255.255.255.0   U     0      0        0 eth1
192.168.2.0     192.168.3.10    255.255.255.0   UG    0      0        0 eth1
192.168.1.0     *               255.255.255.0   U     0      0        0 eth0
carla@stinkpad:~$ /sbin/route
Kernel IP routing table
Destination     Gateway         Genmask         Flags Metric Ref    Use Iface
10.0.0.1        *               255.255.255.255 UH    0      0        0 tun0
192.168.3.0     192.168.2.100   255.255.255.0   UG    0      0        0 eth0
192.168.2.0     *               255.255.255.0   U     0      0        0 eth0
default         192.168.2.100   0.0.0.0         UG    0      0        0 eth0
```

See Also

- man 8 route
- man 8 ifconfig
- man 8 openvpn
- OpenVPN How-to: *http://openvpn.net/howto.html*

9.3   Testing Encryption with Static Keys

Problem

Now you want to test using encryption keys with OpenVPN, and you want the simplest method for testing possible.

Solution

Use shared static keys. This is less secure than creating a proper Public Key Infrastructure (PKI), but is easy to set up for testing. Follow these steps:

1. Follow the previous recipes.
2. Generate a special static encryption key, and copy the static key to the server and client.
3. Create simple configuration files on both of your test PCs.
4. Fire up OpenVPN from the command line to test it.

In this recipe, the OpenVPN server is again Xena at IP address 192.168.3.10, and the client is Stinkpad at 192.168.2.100. First, create the shared static key on the Open-VPN server with this command:

```
root@xena:~# openvpn --genkey --secret static.key
```

Then, copy it to the client PC:

```
root@xena:~# scp static.key 192.168.2.100:/etc/openvpn/keys/
```

Now, create the server configuration file. I call it */etc/openvpn/server1.conf*; you can call it anything you like. Use IP addresses that are on a different subnet than your server. Xena is at 192.168.3.10, so let's make Xena's tunnel endpoint address 10.0.0.1:

```
## openvpn server1.conf
dev tun
ifconfig 10.0.0.1 10.0.0.2
secret /etc/openvpn/keys/static.key
local 192.168.3.10
```

Then, create the client configuration file on Stinkpad. Stinkpad's tunnel endpoint address is 10.0.0.2:

```
## openvpn client1.conf
remote 192.168.3.10
dev tun
ifconfig 10.0.0.2 10.0.0.1
secret /etc/openvpn/keys/static.key
```

Make sure that OpenVPN is not already running on the client or server, then start it up on both with these commands:

```
root@xena:~# openvpn /etc/openvpn/server1.conf
root@stinkpad:~# openvpn /etc/openvpn/client1.conf
```

Just like in the previous recipe, you'll see Initialization Sequence Completed when the tunnel is completed, and both machines can *ping* each other:

```
carla@xena:~$ ping 10.0.0.2
terry@stinkpad:~$ ping 10.0.0.1
```

Hit Ctrl-C on both tunnel endpoints to shut it down.

Discussion

Watch your messages when you establish the tunnels. When you set up the unencrypted tunnel, the warning:

```
******* WARNING *******: all encryption and authentication features disabled -- all
data will be tunnelled as cleartext
```

was displayed. That should be gone now.

This isn't quite good enough for production machines; see the next recipe to learn a better setup for the real world.

The problem with using static keys is that you lose perfect forward secrecy because your static key never changes. If an attacker found a way to sniff and capture your network traffic, and then captured and cracked your encryption key, the attacker could then decrypt everything, past and future. OpenVPN supports using PKI, which is more complex to set up, but ensures perfect forward secrecy. OpenVPN's PKI uses a complex process that generates four different encryption keys, including separate encrypt/decrypt send and encrypt/decrypt receive keys, which are changed every hour. So, at best, a successful attacker can decrypt one hour's worth of traffic at a time, and then has to start over. See Charlie Hosner's excellent paper, "OpenVPN and the SSL Revolution" (*http://www.sans.org/reading_room/whitepapers/vpns/1459. php?portal=c7da694586dcdad815fd41098461e495*), for more details on how this works.

See Also

- man 8 openvpn
- OpenVPN How-to: *http://openvpn.net/howto.html*

9.4 Connecting a Remote Linux Client Using Static Keys

Problem

You followed the previous recipes and everything works. Now, what do you do for a production VPN server? You want to set it up so that you can connect to your work network from your home Linux PC. Your work Internet account has a static, routable IP address. Your home PC has no overlapping addresses with your work network or your OpenVPN addressing. Your OpenVPN server is on your border router.

Solution

Again, keep in mind that using a static key is less secure than using a proper Public Key Infrastructure (PKI).

Follow the previous recipe to generate and distribute the shared static key. Then, you'll need more options in your configuration files, and to configure your firewall to allow the VPN traffic.

Your setup should look something like Figure 9-2.

Next, copy these client and server configurations, using your own IP addresses and domain names. The local IP address must be your WAN address. These files have different names than in the previous recipe, which speeds up testing as you will see:

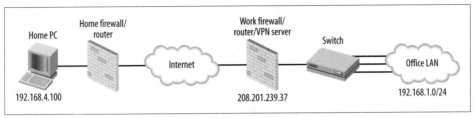

Figure 9-2. Remote user logging in over VPN from home

```
## openvpn server2.conf
dev tun
proto udp
ifconfig 10.0.0.1 10.0.0.2
local 208.201.239.37
secret /etc/openvpn/keys/static.key
keepalive 10 60
comp-lzo
daemon
```

Next, the client configuration file:

```
## openvpn client2.conf
remote router.alrac.net
dev tun
ifconfig 10.0.0.2 10.0.0.1
route 192.168.1.0 255.255.255.0
secret /etc/openvpn/keys/static.key
keepalive 10 60
comp-lzo
```

Then, you'll need to allow the VPN traffic through your work firewall through UDP port 1194. If you're using a nice stout *iptables* firewall, use these rules:

```
iptables -A INPUT -p udp --dport 1194 -j ACCEPT
iptables -A INPUT -i tun+ -j ACCEPT
iptables -A FORWARD -i tun+ -j ACCEPT
```

Now, start OpenVPN manually and test it, just like we did in previous recipes:

```
root@xena:~# openvpn /etc/openvpn/server2.conf
root@stinkpad:~# openvpn /etc/openvpn/client2.conf
```

Discussion

This is a nice simple setup when you control your work and home networks. Don't do this for others—just for yourself.

What if your work site does not have a static IP address, but a dynamically assigned address? Use the free dynamic DNS (DDNS) service at DynDns.com (*http://www. dyndns.com/*) to give it a persistent address.

The route option in *client2.conf* lets your remote client access the whole LAN.

`keepalive 10 60` keeps the connection alive by sending a *ping* every 10 seconds. If there is no response after 60 seconds, OpenVPN assumes the connection is broken.

`comp-lzo` compresses your traffic. This option must be present in server and client configuration files.

`daemon` runs OpenVPN in listening mode. As soon as you run the `openvpn /etc/openvpn/server2.conf` command, it drops into the background and returns you to the command prompt.

The plus mark in the *iptables* rules is a wildcard, so tun+ means "all tun devices."

Using a proper PKI is only a little more work than using static keys, and many times more secure. See the next recipe to learn how to do this.

See Also

- man 8 openvpn
- OpenVPN How-to: *http://openvpn.net/howto.html*
- Chapter 3

9.5   Creating Your Own PKI for OpenVPN

Problem

You want to run OpenVPN as securely as possible, so you're ready to set up a proper Public Key Infrastructure.

Solution

This isn't hard at all, and is many times more secure than using static keys. Follow these steps:

1. Create your own Certificate Authority (CA) certificate.
2. Create an OpenVPN server certificate.
3. Generate client certificates.

OpenVPN comes with a batch of scripts that make this easy. First, find the *easy-rsa/2.0* directory, and copy it to */etc/openvpn*:

```
# cp /usr/share/doc/openvpn/examples/easy-rsa/2.0 /etc/openvpn/easy-rsa/2.0
```

Change to the 2.0 directory:

```
# cd /etc/openvpn/easy-rsa/2.0
```

Open the *vars* file, and assign your own values to these lines. Don't leave any blank. Use NA if you don't want to assign your own value:

```
export KEY_SIZE=2048
export KEY_COUNTRY=US
export KEY_PROVINCE=NA
export KEY_CITY=Linuxville
export KEY_ORG="Alrac.net-test"
export KEY_EMAIL="carla@alrac.net"
```

Then, run these commands just as they are shown, and follow their prompts. After the leading dot in . ./vars there is a space.

```
# . ./vars
# ./clean-all
# ./build-ca
```

When it asks you for a Common Name, use something descriptive, like *vpn-ca*. Then, run this command to create the server certificate, naming it with your own server name:

```
# ./build-key-server xena
```

Use the fully qualified domain name, like *xena.alrac.net*, for the Common Name. Answer yes to "Sign the certificate? [y/n]" and "1 out of 1 certificate requests certified, commit? [y/n]."

Next, create unique keys for all of your clients. This example generates a passphrase-less key pair for the laptop named Stinkpad:

```
# ./build-key stinkpad
```

Or, you may wish to password-protect the client key. Use this command instead:

```
# ./build-key-pass stinkpad
```

The user will be asked for the password every time they initiate a connection. Use the hostname for the Common Name. Now, generate the Diffie-Hellman parameters:

```
# ./build-dh
```

Finally, create a TLS-AUTH key. The server and all clients need a copy of this key:

```
# cd keys/
# openvpn --genkey --secret ta.key
```

You should now have something like this in your keys directory:

```
01.pem
02.pem
ca.crt
ca.key
dh2048.pem
index.txt
index.txt.attr
index.txt.attr.old
index.txt.old
serial
serial.old
```

```
stinkpad.crt
stinkpad.csr
stinkpad.key
ta.key
xena.crt
xena.csr
xena.key
```

For your own sanity, keep your certificate-creation directory separate. It can even be on a separate PC. Create a new keys directory, and move your new server keys and certificates into it. These commands are all run from */etc/openvpn/easy-rsa/2.0*:

```
# mkdir -m 0700 /etc/openvpn/keys
# cp ca.crt ../../keys
# mv dh2048.pem ta.key xena.crt xena.key ../../keys
```

stinkpad.key, stinkpad.crt, and copies of *ta.key* and *ca.crt* must be moved to the appropriate directory on Stinkpad. You must create a unique key pair for each additional client.

See the next recipe to learn how to configure your server and clients to use your nice new PKI.

Discussion

You can read your X509 certificates with this command:

```
$ openssl x509 -in [certificate name] -text
```

Anything ending in *.key* is a private key, which must be carefully protected and never shared. *.crt* is a public certificate, and can be shared. *ca.key* is your private root certificate authority key.

The most paranoid way is to do all this on a PC that is never connected to any network, and use USB flash devices or directly connected crossover cables to transfer them to their appropriate hosts. Secure copy over your LAN works, too, assuming you have SSH set up on your systems:

```
# scp stinkpad.crt stinkpad:/etc/openvpn/keys/
```

Generating a certificate/key pair for every client is a bit of work, but that's the magic bit that makes your OpenVPN tunnel secure. If you've ever created key pairs from scratch using OpenSSL instead of OpenVPN's excellent scripts, you will appreciate how much the OpenVPN developers have streamlined the process.

Consider requiring password-protected client certificates on all laptops. Any client PCs outside of the office are at risk for theft and misuse, especially laptops.

Use the Common Name to create a unique name for each key pair. I like to use the convention of *vpnserver* and *vpnclient* because they are different types of keys, which you can see by reading the *build-key* scripts. Using the hostname as the key name is a quick way to see what belongs where. It's easy to get confused when you're rolling out a batch of these; smart naming will keep you on track.

The Diffie-Hellman parameter is the encryption mechanism that allows two hosts to create and share a secret key. Once the OpenVPN client and server authenticate to each other, additional send and receive keys are generated to encrypt the session.

See Also

- See Charlie Hosner's excellent paper, "OpenVPN and the SSL Revolution," for more details on how this works: *http://www.sans.org/reading_room/whitepapers/vpns/1459.php?portal=c7da694586dcdad815fd41098461e495*

- man 8 openvpn

- OpenVPN How-to: *http://openvpn.net/howto.html*

9.6 Configuring the OpenVPN Server for Multiple Clients

Problem

You have your PKI (Public Key Infrastructure) all set up, and clients keys copied to your clients. Now, how do you configure your server and clients?

Solution

Follow these examples:

```
## server3.conf
local 192.168.3.10
port 1194
proto udp
dev tun
daemon
server 10.0.0.0 255.255.255.0
push "route 192.168.1.0 255.255.255.0"
push "dhcp-option DNS 192.168.1.50"
max-clients 25

ca     /etc/openvpn/keys/ca.crt
cert   /etc/openvpn/keys/xena.crt
key    /etc/openvpn/keys/xena.key
dh     /etc/openvpn/keys/dh1024.pem
tls-auth /etc/openvpn/keys/ta.key 0

cipher BF-CBC
comp-lzo
keepalive 10 120
log-append  /var/log/openvpn.log
status /var/log/openvpn-status.log
ifconfig-pool-persist  /etc/openvpn/ipp.txt
```

```
mute 20
verb 4

## client3.conf
client
pull
dev tun
proto udp
remote 192.168.3.10 1194

ca    /etc/openvpn/keys/ca.crt
cert  /etc/openvpn/keys/xena.crt
key   /etc/openvpn/keys/xena.key
tls-auth /etc/openvpn/keys/ta.key 1

cipher BF-CBC
comp-lzo
verb 4
mute 20
ns-cert-type server
```

Fire up OpenVPN in the usual way:

```
root@xena:~# openvpn /etc/openvpn/server3.conf
root@stinkpad:~# openvpn /etc/openvpn/client3.conf
```

Copy the client configuration file to as many Linux clients as you want and try connecting. Your OpenVPN server should welcome all of them.

Discussion

You now have an excellent, strong, genuine Virtual Private Network up and running. Now, your remote clients can access your network almost as if they were physically present. There are a few limitations: remote clients cannot see each other, and broadcast traffic, with Samba being the most famous example, cannot cross a router.

I like to keep different versions of configuration files, like *server2.conf* and *server3.conf*, for quick and easy testing different setups. You are welcome to call them anything you want.

Let's take a quick cruise over the configuration options. The manpage is thorough, so we'll hit the high points.

The server line tells OpenVPN to run in server mode, and to automatically configure routing and client addressing. The syntax is *server network netmask*. The server assigns itself the .1 address for its end of the tunnel, automatically reserves a pool of client addresses, and pushes out the correct VPN route to clients. You can see this when you run the route command on the clients.

The push "route" option sends the correct route so that VPN clients can access the LAN behind the OpenVPN server.

push "dhcp-option DNS" tells your remote clients where your DNS server is, which is a very nice thing for them to know.

The ns-cert-type server option in client files prevents clients from connecting to a server that does not have the nsCertType=server designation in its certificate. The *build-key-server* script does this for you. It's an extra bit of prevention that helps prevent man-in-the-middle attacks.

To add another layer of verification, use the tls-remote option in client configuration files. This takes the Common Name from the server certificate, like this:

```
tls-remote xena.alrac.net
```

If the client doesn't see the correct Common Name, it won't connect.

See Also

- man 8 openvpn
- OpenVPN How-to: *http://openvpn.net/howto.html*

9.7 Configuring OpenVPN to Start at Boot

Problem

You don't want to start your OpenVPN server manually, but want it to start at boot, like any other service.

Solution

First, edit edit */etc/init.d/openvpn*, and make sure this line points to your configuration directory:

```
CONFIG_DIR=/etc/openvpn
```

Then, make sure that you have only one configuration file in there. The startup file looks for files ending in *.conf*, and tries to start all of them. The newest versions of OpenVPN handle multiple tunnels, but for now, we'll run just one.

Debian creates startup files automatically, so Debian users can go to the next recipe.

On Fedora, run chkconfig --add openvpn to create the startup files.

On Debian and Fedora systems, OpenVPN can be controlled with the usual /etc/init.d/openvpn start|stop|restart commands.

You probably don't want to set up most clients this way. For your intrepid Linux road warriors, create either a command-line alias or a nice deskstop icon to launch their OpenVPN tunnel. Create a command alias this way:

```
$ alias opensesame='openvpn /etc/openvpn/client3.conf'
```

Now, typing opensesame opens a VPN session. To see your aliases, use alias -p. Run unalias *alias name* to delete individual aliases.

Creating desktop icons depends on which desktop environment or window manager they use. In KDE, right-click the K Menu icon, and open the menu editor. Paste in the whole command; don't use aliases. In Gnome, use the nice new Alacarte menu editor.

Discussion

Obviously, this presents some security concerns because anyone with access to the remote computer has access to your network. Laptops get stolen all the time; home computers are savaged by family members. There are a number of possible methods that aim to prevent the wrong people from logging in to your network. Using the *build-key-pass* script to create passphrase-protected keys adds a useful extra layer of security. You might consider requiring that all laptops use some form of disk encryption.

OpenVPN gives you one powerful tool for protection from mishaps—using PKI gives you the power to revoke certificates, which prevents the user from logging in at all. See the next recipe to learn how to do this.

See Also

- man 8 openvpn
- OpenVPN How-to: *http://openvpn.net/howto.html*
- man 1 bash

9.8   Revoking Certificates

Problem

Your OpenVPN setup is working perfectly, and everyone is happy. You've just gotten the news that an employee has left the company, or perhaps one of your road warriors has lost a laptop. At any rate, you need to terminate a user's access. How is this done?

Solution

Change to the */etc/openvpn/easy-rsa/* directory on the server, and run these two commands, using the name of the client certificate you need to revoke:

```
# . ./vars
# ./revoke-full stinkpad
Using configuration from /etc/openvpn/easy-rsa/openssl.cnf
DEBUG[load_index]: unique_subject = "yes"
Revoking Certificate 01.
```

```
Data Base Updated
Using configuration from /etc/openvpn/easy-rsa/openssl.cnf
DEBUG[load_index]: unique_subject = "yes"
stinkpad.crt: /C=US/ST=NA/O=Alrac.net-test/CN=openvpnclient-stinkpad/
emailAddress=carla@alrac.net
error 23 at 0 depth lookup:certificate revoked
```

error 23 means your revocation was successful. You'll see a new file, */etc/openvpn/easy-rsa/keys/crl.pem*, that contains your control revocation list.

Now, you need to add this line to your server configuration file:

```
crl-verify /etc/openvpn/easy-rsa/crl.pem
```

Restart the OpenVPN server:

 # /etc/init.d/openvpn restart

You're done, and the user is locked out. For future revocations, you don't need to restart the server. If the user is connected, OpenVPN will kick them off in an hour anyway when it negotiates new send and receive keys.

Or, you can send a SIGHUP, and kick them off immediately:

 # /etc/init.d/openvpn reload

This flushes all clients, but they shouldn't notice any disruption. Except the one you kicked off.

Discussion

When a user forgets their passphrase, you can revoke their certificate, then create a new one using the same common name.

Make sure that *crl.pem* is world-readable.

You should also add these lines to your server configuration:

```
ping-timer-rem
persist-tun
```

ping-timer-rem doesn't start clocking *ping* timeouts until clients actually connect.

persist-tun keeps the tunnel open even when SIGHUPs or *ping* restarts occur.

See Also

- man 8 openvpn
- OpenVPN How-to: *http://openvpn.net/howto.html*
- man 7 signal

9.9 Setting Up the OpenVPN Server in Bridge Mode

Problem

You want to run your OpenVPN server in bridged mode because you aren't supporting a lot of users. You're trading the slower performance of an Ethernet bridge for its ease of administration. You've made sure your VPN clients do not have conflicting addresses with your LAN.

Solution

First, make sure you have the *bridge-utils* package installed. Then, fetch the example *bridge-start* script. If your distribution does not include it, you'll find it in the OpenVPN source tarball, or online at OpenVPN.net (*http://openvpn.net/bridge.html#linuxscript*). Edit the first section to include your own bridge address, tap address, and your own IP address:

```
# Define Bridge Interface
br="br0"

# Define list of TAP interfaces to be bridged,
# for example tap="tap0 tap1 tap2".
tap="tap0"

# Define physical ethernet interface to be bridged
# with TAP interface(s) above.
eth="eth0"
eth_ip="192.168.1.10"
eth_netmask="255.255.255.0"
eth_broadcast="192.168.1.255"
```

Next, copy it to */usr/sbin/openvpn*, along with *bridge-stop*, which needs no changes.

Now, change two lines in your server configuration, which we'll call */etc/openvpn/server-bridge.conf*. Change dev tun to dev tap0, then comment out your server and push lines, and replace them with this:

```
server-bridge 192.168.1.10 255.255.255.0 192.168.1.128 192.168.1.254
```

This configures server-bridge with your own gateway, netmask, client IP-range-start, and client IP-range-end.

VPN clients also need dev tun changed to dev tap0.

To test it manually, run these commands:

```
# bridge-start
# openvpn /etc/openvpn/server-bridge.conf
```

Test your connectivity. You should see Samba shares and everything. When you're finished testing, hit Ctrl-C to stop OpenVPN, then run the *bridge-stop* script to tear down the bridge.

To make everything start and stop automatically, add these lines to *server-bridge.conf*:

```
up /usr/sbin/openvpn/bridge-start
down /usr/sbin/openvpn/bridge-stop
```

Discussion

If you have an *iptables* firewall, use these rules to move VPN traffic across the bridge:

```
$ipt -A INPUT -i tap0 -j ACCEPT
$ipt -A INPUT -i br0 -j ACCEPT
$ipt -A FORWARD -i br0 -j ACCEPT
```

Ethernet bridging is simpler than routing in some ways, but you pay a performance penalty because you have broadcast traffic crossing your bridge from both sides. It works fine for smaller networks, and saves a bit of routing hassles.

See Also

- man 8 openvpn
- OpenVPN How-to: *http://openvpn.net/howto.html*

9.10   Running OpenVPN As a Nonprivileged User

Problem

On many Linux distributions, you already have the *nobody* user and group. All you need to do to configure OpenVPN to run as the nonprivileged user *nobody* user is add user nobody and group nobody to the server configuration file. Or, your Linux distribution may have created a unique OpenVPN user and group. But Debian doesn't have a *nobody* user or group, nor does it create unique users. What do you do?

Solution

No problem whatsoever. Just create an *openvpn* user and group, and use them:

```
# groupadd openvpn
# useradd -d /dev/null -g test -s /bin/false openvpn
```

Then, add these lines to your OpenVPN configuration files:

```
user openvpn
group openvpn
persist-key
```

Do this for both servers and clients.

Discussion

The *nobody* user tends to get a bit overburdened, so you should create a unique user for OpenVPN and not use *nobody*.

persist-key keeps the connection up even after OpenVPN has dropped to the unprivileged *openvpn* user, which cannot read private keys or other *root*-only files.

See Also

- man 8 openvpn
- OpenVPN How-to: *http://openvpn.net/howto.html*
- man 8 useradd

9.11   Connecting Windows Clients

Problem

You want to equip your remote Windows users with OpenVPN. How do you set up Windows as an OpenVPN client?

Solution

First of all, you need Windows 2000, 2003, or XP. Older versions of Windows won't work.

It's not all that different from running it on Linux. Download and install the Windows version of OpenVPN. You need Administrator rights to do this. Then, create the *\Program Files\OpenVPN\keys* directory, and copy over the client key to it.

Next, go to *\Program Files\OpenVPN\sample-config\client.ovpn* and edit it just like the Linux clients in Recipes 9.4 and 9.5. Save it as *\Program Files\OpenVPN\config\client.ovpn*. Then, right-click on the file icon, and click "Start OpenVPN on this config file." You can then drag it to the desktop, or copy it to your user's Desktop directories for their convenience.

Discussion

Windows doesn't have the user or group *nobody*, so ignore those options in *client.ovpn*. You can control OpenVPN like any other service on the Services control panel, though you probably want users starting OpenVPN when they need it, and not leaving it running all the time.

See Also

- man 8 openvpn
- OpenVPN How-to: *http://openvpn.net/howto.html*

## CHAPTER 10

Building a Linux PPTP VPN Server

10.0 Introduction

Point-to-Point Tunneling Protocol (PPTP) is often used on Windows networks to create Virtual Private Networks (VPNs). Setting up a Windows PPTP server means shoveling out money for Windows server licenses. If you already have a Windows server, then you have a built-in VPN via its Routing and Remote Access Server (RRAS), so you might as well use that. But if you don't, you can set up a nice PPTP-based VPN server for no more than the cost of the hardware using Linux and the Poptop *pptpd* server. It will need at least two network interfaces, as it will be acting as a router and forwarding traffic.

Where does your VPN server belong in your network? A common practice is to put a VPN gateway on border routers. If you have a nice Linux-based border router, then this is easy-peasy. For other circumstances, you might want a standalone VPN gateway, which would sit behind a border router like Figure 10-1 shows.

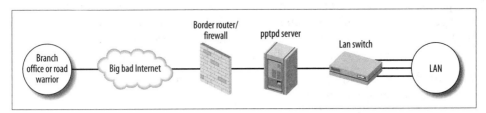

Figure 10-1. Standalone VPN server

PPTP was created in the days of dial-up networking, so you'll still see a lot of references to dial-up in documentation and on your Windows clients. You may use it over any type of network: dial-up, Ethernet, ISDN, Internet, whatever.

A PPTP-based VPN is a weak VPN. It is Point-to-Point Protocol (PPP) over a Generic Routing Encapsulation (GRE) tunnel, neither of which was designed with security in mind. PPTP adds single-factor authentication, requiring only a login and password from the client. Microsoft's implementation relies on Microsoft Challenge Handshake Authentication (MS-CHAP V2) for authentication, and Microsoft Point-to-Point Encryption (MPPE) for encryption. MPPE uses the RC4 algorithm to generate a 128-bit encryption and decryption key, which is derived from the cleartext authentication password of the user. The same key is used at both ends of the tunnel. The tunnel itself is trusted from the start, and needs no authentication. An attacker needs only to capture a chunk of the datastream, and then brute-force the password offline at leisure. Once the password is cracked, the attacker owns the works.

Contrast this with how OpenVPN (see Chapter 9) uses a proper Public Key Infrastructure (PKI) and several levels of encryption. So, why use a PPTP-based VPN, when OpenVPN is free of cost, cross-platform, and far stronger? Because you may not have a choice; because PPTP is quick and easy; because all versions of Windows already have clients (sort of); or because you may be stuck with legacy networking gear that does not support Windows' IPSec implementation, and PPTP is your only common VPN option.

You can easily set up a good test lab with three PCs; just follow Recipe 9.1.

Windows Client Necessary Updates

Windows 9x and ME need the MSDun 1.4 update. Windows 2000 requires installing the Windows 2000 High Encryption Pack. This enables 128-bit encryption. These are free downloads from *http://microsoft.com*.

PPTP Security

Your best defense is to enforce a very strong password policy. The maximum is 20 characters, so why not use them all? Don't use words or names, but random characters like 9/'wx1$)E6^bB-L3%=sP. Your users are probably going to tick the "remember this password" button in their clients anyway, so they don't have to be memorable. Change them periodically. Remember how OpenVPN limits the damage from successful intrusions by changing the encryption/decryption keys hourly? Your PPTP keys are only going to be changed when you change the passwords.

If you need help generating passwords, there are all kinds of password generator programs and web sites to help you.

IPSec VPN

Windows also supports L2TP/IPsec-based VPNs. L2TP/IPsec-based VPNs require a PKI, so they are more work to set up, but significantly stronger.

L2TP means Layer 2 Tunneling Protocol. L2TP is a blend of the best features of Microsoft's original PPP and Cisco's Layer 2 Forwarding (L2F).

IPSec is Internet Protocol Security. It is a suite of protocols for encrypting and authenticating network traffic. Microsoft, for reasons that must seem good to them, combine L2TP and IPSec almost inseparably, which considerably complicates client support on non-Windows platforms, and hurts compatibility with other VPN gear. IPSec alone works fine, and is widely supported.

Server and client support for the three protocols varies in the extended Windows family:

PPTP-based RAS (Remote Access Server)
 NT4 Server

PPTP and L2TP/IPsec RRAS (Routing and Remote Access Server)
 Windows 2000 server and 2003 Server

PPTP and L2TP/IPsec single-connection RAS
 Windows 2000 Professional, XP Professional, and Vista

PPTP and L2TP/IPsec client
 Windows 98, ME, NT4, 2000, 2003, XP, and Vista

The single-connection RAS is used to open up a remote VPN to your PC. It is configured in the Incoming Connections part of the Network Connections folder.

Windows 95 only supports a PPTP client. Windows 98 and ME did not ship with PPTP clients, but should have received them through routine updates, along with L2TP/IPsec client support. They'll want the MSdun1.4 update.

Router-to-router L2TP/IPSec connections are possible only with:

- A Windows server running RRAS.
- A third-party VPN router that supports L2TP/IPSec.

Windows NT4 Server does not support L2TP/IPSec.

As a rather amusing side note, Microsoft is developing SSTP, or Secure Socket Tunneling Protocol, which is based on HTTP over SSL, just like the many SSL-based "VPNs" by Cisco, Juniper, Nortel, and so forth. It is scheduled to be included in Longhorn server. Please refer to Charlie Hosner's excellent paper "OpenVPN and the VPN Revolution" (*http://www.sans.org/reading_room/whitepapers/vpns/*) for a discussion of what is a real VPN and what isn't.

Linux Requirements

The easy way is to use a Linux distribution with a kernel newer than 2.6.15-rc1, and to make sure you have the exactly correct *ppp* version. With Poptop *pptpd* versions 1.3.0 to 1.3.4, this is *ppp* 2.4.3. At the time this was written, most newer Linux distribution releases were shipping with *ppp* 2.4.4. Debian users can rest easy—it works fine without any hassles. Fedora users should download the matching *ppp* RPM along with the *pptpd* RPM from the Poptop download site. Ubuntu users may have some difficulties, which are addressed in Recipe 10.10.

Older kernels need to be patched to get MPPE support; visit Poptop (*http://www. poptop.org/*) for more information.

Is PPTP Really Easier?

In my opinion, this is debatable. The main argument for PPTP over stronger VPNs is that it's easier because you don't have to install client software, which is only partly true—Windows 2000 requires an update to support 128-bit encryption, and older Windows versions require updates to get PPTPD clients and 128-bit support. If you have kept your systems upgraded, you're in good shape. If you have to install client software, consider using OpenVPN instead. For the same amount of work, you get a much stronger system.

See Also

- PPTP Security: *http://pptpclient.sourceforge.net/protocol-security.phtml*

10.1   Installing Poptop on Debian Linux

Problem

You have a gaggle of Windows clients on your LAN, and no available Windows servers or nice VPN gateways, so you want to set up a Debian Linux-based VPN server running Poptop to allow remote access to your LAN.

Solution

On Debian, it's as easy as falling over. First, verify that you have *ppp-2.4.3* or newer, and a kernel newer than 2.6.15-rc1:

```
$ apt-show-versions ppp
ppp/etch uptodate 2.4.4

$ uname -r
2.6.17-10
```

Then, confirm that your kernel has the necessary Microsoft Point-to-Point Encryption (MPPE) support:

```
# modprobe ppp-compress-18 && echo success
success
```

Now, go ahead and install *pptpd* in the usual manner:

```
# aptitude install pptpd
```

The *pptp* daemon will automatically start at boot, and is controlled in the usual manner with /etc/init.d/pptpd [start|stop|restart]. One gotcha to look out for is restart will not close any existing sessions, so to completely restart it you must stop, then start it.

Now, you're ready to configure your server.

Discussion

If loading the *ppp-compress-18* module fails, you'll see this message:

```
FATAL: Module ppp-compress-18 not found
```

This is very unlikely, however, as long as you have the correct kernel version or have an older kernel that is patched.

See Also

- man 8 aptitude
- man 8 modprobe

10.2   Patching the Debian Kernel for MPPE Support

Problem

Oops, you have an older (pre-2.6.15-rc1) kernel on your Debian system, so you need to build the MPPE kernel module. How do you do this?

Solution

Follow these steps. First, download the necessary tools, kernel sources, and MPPE patch:

```
# apt-get install gcc bin86 libc6-dev bzip2 kernel-package kernel-patch-mppe
```

Find your kernel version:

```
# uname -r
2.6.8
```

Then, download, unpack, and prepare the kernel source package:

```
# apt-get install kernel-source-2.6.8
# cd /usr/src
# tar xfj kernel-source-2.6.8.tar.bz2
# cd kernel-source-2.6.8
# make-kpkg clean
```

Copy over your existing kernel configuration file to use for building your new kernel:

```
# cp /boot/config-2.6.8 ./.config-2.6.8
```

Finally, build your new kernel package:

```
# cd /usr/src/kernel-source-2.6.8
 # make-kpkg \
   --added-patches mppe \
   --append-to-version -mppe \
   --config oldconfig \
```

```
--initrd \
kernel_image
```

When you're configuring the new kernel, be sure to enable `CONFIG_PPP_MPPE` as a module:

```
PPP MPPE compression (encryption) (PPP_MPPE) [N/m/?] (NEW) m
```

When that's all finished, and the kernel is compiling, you might as well go take a walk because it will take a few minutes. Maybe a lot of minutes, depending on what type of machine it's compiling on. When it's all finished, install the new kernel:

```
# dpkg --install /usr/src/kernel-image-2.6.8-mppe_10.00.Custom_all.deb
```

Reboot to load the new kernel, then test for MPPE support:

```
# modprobe ppp-compress-18 && echo success
success
```

Hurrah! All finished, and now you can configure your Poptop server.

Discussion

A build environment needs a bit of elbow room; give yourself a couple of gigabytes. You can set up a PC as a build machine, then copy your new kernel image to its final destination. You'll want to be careful to tailor it for the hardware it's going to run on.

Debian offers up a limited number of official kernel versions:

- kernel-source-2.4.27
- kernel-source-2.6.8
- linux-source-2.6.18
- linux-source-2.6.20

You can find more kernel versions at the Debian snapshot site (*http://snapshot.debian.net/*), but as the site warns you, there could be problems with the packages archived here.

When Debian Etch was released, Debian moved to a new kernel-package naming convention. The old convention for source packages was *kernel-source-[version]*, and binary packages were named *kernel-image-[version]*. In anticipation of some-day supporting other kernels, such as the Hurd, the new naming conventions are *linux-source-[version]* and *linux-image-[version]*.

See Also

- Debian MPPE HOWTO patch your own kernel:

  http://pptpclient.sourceforge.net/howto-debian-build.phtml

10.3   Installing Poptop on Fedora Linux

Problem

You have a gaggle of Windows clients on your LAN, and no available Windows servers or nice VPN routers, so you want to set up a Fedora Linux-based VPN server running Poptop to allow remote access to your LAN.

Solution

The easy way is to use Fedora 5 or newer. Then, you'll have kernels with MPPE support already, so you can get down to the business of installing and running your Poptop server.

Make sure you have MPPE support:

```
# modprobe ppp-compress-18 && echo success
success
```

Check your *ppp* version:

```
$ rpm -q ppp
ppp-2.4.4-1.fc6
```

Oops. This won't work, and must be replaced with a 2.4.3 version. Remove it:

```
# yum remove ppp
```

Then, download and install the matching RPMs from Poptop's download site on Sourceforge.net (*http://sourceforge.net/project/showfiles.php?group_id=44827*). The current releases are *ppp-2.4.3-5* and *pptpd-1.3.4*.

Then, configure *pptpd* to start at boot in the usual way with *chkconfig*:

```
# chkconfig pptpd on
```

Note that the *pptpd* daemon is controlled with the usual /etc/init.d/pptpd [start|stop|restart|status|condrestart] commands. A small gotcha is only stop will completely shut it down and close all sessions, so you must stop and start it for a complete restart.

Now, you're ready to move on to configuration.

Discussion

You must have the correct *ppp* version, or your *pptp* server will not work. At the time this was written, the documentation was a bit unclear on this, and different Linux distributions did not package *pptp* with a dependency on the correct version of *ppp*. For more information, see Recipe 10.10.

See Also

- Poptop, The PPTP Server for Linux: *http://www.poptop.org/*

10.4 Patching the Fedora Kernel for MPPE Support

Problem

Oops, you have an older (pre-2.6.15-rc1) kernel on your Fedora, Red Hat, CentOS, or Red Hat-like system. You don't want to upgrade, so you need to build the MPPE kernel module. How do you do this?

Solution

The fine Poptop maintainers use Dynamic Kernel Module Support (DKMS) to generate the MPPE kernel module, which is much easier than the traditional way. First, test for MPPE support:

```
# modprobe ppp-compress-18 && echo ok
FATAL: Module ppp-compress-18 not found.
```

Then, you need to build a new kernel module. Follow these steps. First, find your kernel version:

```
# uname -r
2.6.11-1.1369.fc6
```

Then, download the matching *kernel-devel* package. First, list the available versions:

```
# yum search kernel-devel
[...]
kernel-devel.i586    2.6.11-1.1369.fc6    core
Matched from:
kernel-devel
[...]
```

If there is more than one, install the one that matches your kernel:

```
# yum install kernel-devel-2.6.11-1.1369_fc4.i586
```

If there is only one, save yourself some typing:

```
# yum install kernel-devel
```

Now, install the DKMS package, which is a great tool that simplifies building new kernel modules:

```
# yum install dkms
```

Finally, download and install the MPPE module builder RPM (currently *dkms-2.0.10-1* from Poptops's Sourceforge download site (*http://sourceforge.net/project/showfiles. php?group_id=44827*). Reboot, then try loading the MPPE module:

```
# modprobe ppp-compress-18 && echo success
success
```

Very good! Now you can move on to installing and running your *pptpd* server.

Discussion

Another way to install the *kernel-devel* package is to hunt down and download the RPM, then use Yum to install it this way:

```
# yum localinstall kernel-devel-2.6.11-1.1369_FC4.i686.rpm
```

This is an option if you can't find a *kernel-devel* package with Yum to match your installed kernel. They must match, or your new kernel module might not work.

See Also

- man 8 yum
- man 8 modprobe

10.5   Setting Up a Standalone PPTP VPN Server

Problem

You have a small gaggle of Windows clients on your LAN, and no Windows servers, so you want to set up a Linux VPN server running Poptop to allow remote access to your LAN. You've already installed Poptop on your favorite Linux distribution on a machine with at least two network interfaces. Networking is configured and ready to go.

Solution

Your Windows clients should have all received their necessary updates. (See the chapter Introduction to learn more about these.)

Now, you will edit three files:

> */etc/pptpd.conf*
> */etc/ppp/pptpd-options* (Debian)
> */etc/ppp/options.pptpd* (Fedora)
> */etc/ppp/chap-secrets*

Here are complete examples of all three:

```
##/etc/pptpd.conf
option /etc/ppp/pptpd-options
logwtmp
localip 192.168.0.10
remoteip 192.168.0.100-254
```

```
##/etc/ppp/pptpd-options/- /etc/ppp/options.pptpd
name pptpd
refuse-pap
refuse-chap
refuse-mschap
require-mschap-v2
require-mppe-128
proxyarp
nodefaultroute
debug
dump
lock
nobsdcomp
novj
novjccomp
nologfd


##/etc/ppp/chap-secret
# a single client for testing
# client    server    secret    IP addresses
foober    pptpd    password    *
```

Copy these exactly, with these exceptions:

/etc/pptpd.conf

Use your own addressing for localip and remoteip. These values are arbitrary. They must be on different networks from your LAN.

/etc/ppp/chap-secrets

This file holds your usernames and passwords. The server name comes from the name line in */etc/ppp/pptpd-options*.

Now, start up your *pptpd* server:

```
# /etc/init.d/pptpd stop
# /etc/init.d/pptpd start
```

Confirm that it's running with *netstat* or *ps*:

```
# netstat -untap | grep pptpd
tcp    0    0 0.0.0.0:1723    0.0.0.0:*    LISTEN    4167/pptpd
$ ps ax | grep pptpd
 4167 ?    Ss    0:00 /usr/sbin/pptpd
```

Add this line to */etc/sysctl.conf* to turn on IP forwarding:

```
net.ipv4.ip_forward = 1
```

Then, run this command to load the new setting:

```
# sysctl -p
```

Make sure that ports TCP 47 and TCP 1723 are not blocked, and you're ready to connect clients.

Discussion

You'll need to configure these items in your Windows clients to be able to connect to your *pptpd* server:

- `client`, `server`, and `password` from */etc/ppp/chap-secret*
- The "real" IP address of the *pptpd* server (not the `localip`)
- The correct type of encryption: MS-Chapv2, 128-bit only

Restarting *pptp* does not shut it down and close any existing tunnels, so when you want a complete restart, you must stop it, then start it. Here are some configuration options explained:

`logwtmp`

This tracks client connections so you can use the `who` and `last` commands to see who is currently logged in, and a history of client logins.

`localip`

You may use either a single IP address or a range of addresses. This assigns an address to the server end of the tunnel. You may use a single address or a range of addresses. If you define a range of addresses, each client will be assigned a different server IP address. There's no advantage to either method; use what suits you. The `localip` is arbitrary and has no relationship to the server's real IP address.

`remoteip`

Client addresses are assigned from the range that you define here.

`name`

An arbitrary name for your PPTPD server; just like `localip`, it has no relationship to the server's real hostname.

`refuse-pap`, `refuse-chap`, `refuse-mschap`, `require-mschap-v2`, `require-mppe-128`

Allow only the strongest encryption.

`proxyarp`

Add the *pptpd* tunnel endpoints to the local ARP table, so that they all appear to be on the local network.

`nodefaultroute`

Don't replace the local system's default route.

`debug`, `dump`

Turn these on during testing and whenever you have problems. debug goes into */var/log/debug*, dump goes into */var/log/messages*.

`novj`, `novjccomp`

Disable Van Jacobson compression; this may or may not help with Windows 2000 client connection problems. It doesn't seem to hurt anything to enable these. This mailing list thread hosted on The Aims Group site (*http://marc. theaimsgroup.com/?t=111343175400006&r=1&w=2*) tells more about it.

See Also

- Poptop, The PPTP Server for Linux: *http://www.poptop.org/*
- man 5 pptpd.conf
- man 8 pptpd

10.6 Adding Your Poptop Server to Active Directory

Problem

You have an Active Directory domain under your care, and you want your Linux *pptp* server to be an Active Directory member, so you want to manage it just like any other AD object. Your DNS house is in order, and you already have a Kerberos Key Distribution Center (KDC).

Solution

Use Samba, Winbind, and Kerberos on your Linux Poptop server to become a full Active Domain member. See Recipe 11.6 to learn how to do this.

Then, configure your Poptop server according to the previous recipes, and add these lines to */etc/ppp/options.pptpd*:

```
##/etc/ppp/options.pptpd
[...]
#if you are using MS-DNS, enter the server IP address
ms-dns 1.2.3.5
#if you use a WINS server, enter the IP address
ms-wins 1.2.3.4
plugin winbind.so
ntlm_auth-helper "/usr/bin/ntlm_auth --helper-protocol=ntlm-server-1"
```

Start it up, and make sure it's running with *netstat* or *ps*:

```
# /etc/init.d/pptpd stop
# /etc/init.d/pptpd start
# netstat -untap | grep pptpd
tcp    0    0 0.0.0.0:1723    0.0.0.0:*    LISTEN    4167/pptpd
$ ps ax | grep pptpd
 4167 ?    Ss    0:00 /usr/sbin/pptpd
```

Now, connect some Windows clients, and life should be good. Windows 2000 clients and up can use Active Directory authentication, and don't need entries in */etc/ppp/chap-secrets*.

Discussion

Put your plug-ins at the end of the */etc/ppp/options.pptpd* file; this helps to avoid any possible conflicts.

/usr/bin/ntlm_auth is part of Winbind.

See Also

- Poptop, the PPTP Server for Linux: *http://www.poptop.org/*
- PPTP Client: *http://pptpclient.sourceforge.net/*

10.7 Connecting Linux Clients to a PPTP Server

Problem

You want to connect your Linux PC to a Windows or Linux PPTP server.

Solution

No problem, just install the *pptp* client, and away you go. On Debian:

```
# aptitude install pptp-linux
```

On Fedora:

```
# yum install pptp
```

Your */etc/ppp/options.pptp* file should have these options:

```
##/etc/ppp/options.pptp
lock
noauth
refuse-eap
refuse-chap
refuse-mschap
nobsdcomp
nodeflate
require-mppe-128
```

Then, enter your password and login in */etc/ppp/chap-secrets*:

```
##/etc/ppp/chap-secrets
# client    server    secret     IP addresses
foober   server1    tuffpassword  *
```

If you are authenticating to a Windows RAS server, you'll need the domain name:

```
alrac.net\\foober server1 tuffpassword  *
```

Next, create a */etc/ppp/peers/$TUNNEL* file. In this example, the tunnel name is server1:

```
##/etc/ppp/peers/server1
pty "pptp rasserver --nolaunchpppd"
name alrac.net\\foober
remotename server1
require-mppe-128
file /etc/ppp/options.pptp
ipparam server1
```

Using the venerable old *pon/poff* commands starts and stops the tunnel manually:

```
$ pon server1
$ poff server1
```

The *pon* command with these options makes it run in the background:

```
$ pon provider updetach && pon server1 updetach
```

You can alias this to save a bit of typing:

```
$ alias vpn1on='pon provider updetach && pon server1 updetach'
$ alias vpn1off='poff server1'
```

Now, typing vpn1 will get you connected, and vpn1off closes the connection.

Discussion

All Linux window managers and desktops have ways to attach a custom command to a menu icon so you can start and stop your VPN connection with a mouse click.

You can also download a nice graphical client, *pptpconfig*, from PPTP Client (*http://pptpclient.sourceforge.net*). Another good one is KVpnc (*http://home.gna.org/kvpnc/en/*), a KDE client for all VPNs.

See Also

- PPTP Client: *http://pptpclient.sourceforge.net*
- KVpnc: *http://home.gna.org/kvpnc/en/*

10.8   Getting PPTP Through an iptables Firewall

Problem

How do you configure your *iptables* firewall to pass your Poptop VPN traffic?

Solution

It depends if the Poptop *pptp* server is running on your border firewall, or on a separate server behind it. If it's on the firewall, use these rules, which follow the conventions used in Chapter 3:

```
$ipt -A INPUT -p tcp –dport 1723 -j ACCEPT
$ipt -A INPUT -p 47 -j ACCEPT
```

If you have a restrictive OUTPUT policy, add these rules to allow outgoing packets:

```
$ipt -A OUTPUT -p tcp –sport 1723 -j ACCEPT
$ipt -A OUTPUT -p 47 -j ACCEPT
```

Use these rules on a NAT *iptables* firewall to forward traffic to a separate *pptp* server, substituting your own interface names and network addresses. In this example, 172.16.1.10 is the address of the *pptp* server, and 2.3.4.5 is the WAN address:

```
$ipt -t nat -A PREROUTING -i $WAN_IFACE -p tcp -d 2.3.4.5 --dport 1723 -j DNAT \
   --to-destination 172.16.1.10
$ipt -t nat -A PREROUTING -i $WAN_IFACE -p gre -d 2.3.4.5 -j DNAT \
   --to-destination 172.16.1.10
```

```
$ipt -A FORWARD -i $WAN_IFACE -o $LAN_IFACE -p tcp --dport 1723 -d 172.16.1.10 -m \
  state --state NEW,ESTABLISHED,RELATED -j ACCEPT
$ipt -A FORWARD -i $WAN_IFACE -o $LAN_IFACE -p gre -d 172.16.1.10 -m state \
  --state NEW,ESTABLISHED,RELATED -j ACCEPT
```

If you have a restrictive FORWARD policy, these rules will let your VPN packets out:

```
$ipt -A FORWARD -i $LAN_IFACE -o $WAN_IFACE -p tcp -s 172.16.1.10 --sport 1723 \
  -m state --state ESTABLISHED,RELATED -j ACCEPT
$ipt -A FORWARD -i $LAN_IFACE -o $WAN_IFACE -p gre -s 172.16.1.10 -m state \
  --state ESTABLISHED,RELATED -j ACCEPT
```

Discussion

Refer to your */etc/protocols* file for a short list of IP protocols. The Nmap package comes with a much longer list. *gre* and *47* are the same thing; all protocols also have a number designation.

See Also

- Chapter 3

10.9   Monitoring Your PPTP Server

Problem

How do you keep track of who is logged in to your Poptop server?

Solution

This is easy: use the *who* and the *last* commands. *who* shows you who is currently logged in, and *last* shows a history of logins:

```
$ who
[...]
carla    :0          2007-05-03 08:02
foober   ppp0        2007-05-03 10:09 (1.2.3.4)
arlene   ppp0        2007-05-03 10:17 (2.3.4.5)
$ last
foober   ppp0        1.2.3.4     Thu May  3 10:09   still logged in
arlene   ppp0        2.3.4.5     Thu May  3 10:17   still logged in
carla    :0                      Thu May  3 08:02   still logged in
reboot   system boot 2.6.17-10-generi Thu May  3 08:02 - 10:10  (02:08)
wtmp begins Tue May  1 22:31:38 2007
```

Discussion

Don't forget *grep* for weeding out the extraneous entries:

```
$ last |grep ppp
foober   ppp0        1.2.3.4     Thu May  3 10:09   still logged in
arlene   ppp0        2.3.4.5     Thu May  3 10:17   still logged in
```

See Also

- man 1 who
- man 1 last

10.10 Troubleshooting PPTP

Problem

You're having trouble establishing a connection from a Windows client to your Linux Poptop server. What do you do?

Solution

First, make sure your *pptp* server is running with the *netstat* command:

```
# netstat -untap | grep pptp
tcp 0 0    0.0.0.0:1723  0.0.0.0:*   LISTEN     12893/pptpd
```

Then, use the good old *ping* command to test connectivity. When that's established, your Windows client error messages can be helpful. Figure 10-2 shows what it looks like on Windows XP when the server is unreachable.

You can take the number of the error message and look it up online, because Windows uses the standard Remote Access Server (RAS) error codes.

Next, make sure your firewall isn't blocking your VPN. The easy but scary way is to turn it off. Another way to do this for an *iptables* firewall is to run the *fw_status* script (see Chapter 3), and look for lines like these:

```
Chain PREROUTING (policy ACCEPT 74530 packets, 7108K bytes)
num   pkts bytes target     prot opt in     out     source        destination
1   0   0 DNAT   tcp  -- eth1 any  anywhere   foo.net tcp dpt:1723 to:192.168.1.10
2   0   0 DNAT   gre  -- eth1 any  anywhere   foo.net to:192.168.1.10
7   0   0 ACCEPT tcp  -- eth1 eth0 anywhere   xena.alrac.net  tcp dpt:1723 state
NEW,RELATED,ESTABLISHED
8   0   0 ACCEPT gre  -- eth1 eth0 anywhere   xena.alrac.net  state
NEW,RELATED,ESTABLISHED
```

You can check your destination address, state matches, interfaces name, and protocol matches.

Enabling the `dump` and `debug` options in */etc/pptpd.conf* generates bales of helpful output in */var/log/debug* and */var/log/messages*.

This particular error plagues Ubuntu Edgy Eft users, and possibly users of some other Debian-derived distributions as well.

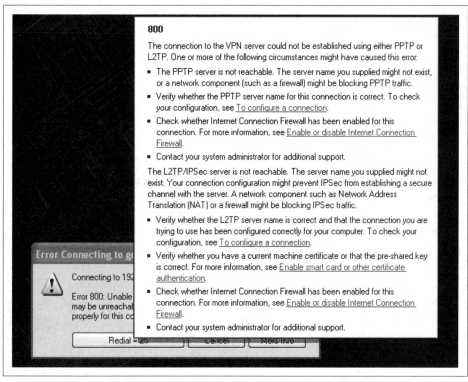

Figure 10-2. Windows XP cannot find the PPTP server

```
April 17 08:19:31 router3 pptpd[6762]: CTRL: Starting call (launching pppd, opening
GRE)
April 17 08:19:31 router3 pppd[6763]: Plugin /usr/lib/pptpd/pptpd-logwtmp.so is for
pppd version 2.4.3, this is 2.4.4
April 17 08:19:31 router3 pptpd[46762]: GRE: read(fd=6,buffer=6808440,len=8196) from
PTY failed: status = -1 error = Input/output error, usually caused by unexpected
termination of pppd, check option syntax and pppd logs
```

Your clients won't be able to establish a connection, and typically will get various unhelpful error messages. The problem is a version mismatch between *ppp* and *logwtmp*. A quick fix is to comment it out in */etc/pptpd.conf*:

```
#logwtmp
```

But then, you won't be able to monitor your *pptp* server with the *who* and *last* commands. To fix it, you need to download the source code for *pptpd*, edit a header file, then compile and install the new binary. It's really not hard, just change to the *root* user, and follow these steps:

```
# cd
# apt-get install libwrap0-dev debhelper
# apt-get source pptpd
# cd pptpd-1.3.0/plugins
```

Open the *patchlevel.h* file with your favorite editor and change this line:

```
#define VERSION    "2.4.3"
```

to:

```
#define VERSION    "2.4.4"
```

Save the file and exit. Then, run these commands:

```
# cd ../..
# apt-get -b source pptpd
# dpkg -i pptpd_1.3.0-1ubuntu1_i386.deb
# dpkg -i bcrelay_1.3.0-1ubuntu1_i386.deb
```

And that's all there is to it. Double-check your configurations, which should not have been touched, and everything should work.

Discussion

Hopefully, this version mismatch will not exist by the time you read this.

Here are some other things to look for:

- Windows host firewalls.
- Passwords over 20 characters in length.
- Wrong server name or address.
- Wrong password.
- Windows clients without 128-bit encryption support. Remember, 9x clients require the MSDun 1.4 updates; Windows 2000 requires the High Encryption Pack.

See Also

- The mailing lists at Poptop: *http://www.poptop.org/*

## CHAPTER 11

Single Sign-on with Samba for Mixed Linux/Windows LANs

11.0 Introduction

As delightful as it would be to have a job where you have to deal only with nice reliable Linux boxes, the reality is that mixed networks are more usual. The real world demands that we know how to integrate multiple platforms, primarily Windows, Linux, and Unix, with occasional dashes of Mac OS X and Classic Mac. This chapter tells you how to integrate Linux and Windows, as those are the dominant platforms. Unix and Mac OS X are similar enough to Linux that you can figure them out pretty easily. If you need help with other platforms, or with running a Windows domain, please see Appendix A for good reference materials.

We'll approach the problem of integrating Windows and Linux from two angles: you have a Windows Active Directory domain that you want to add some Linux hosts to, or you have a Linux network that you want to add some Windows hosts to. There are several possible roles for Samba:

- Login server/domain controller
- Fileserver
- Printer server
- Domain client for both workstations and servers

Linux machines can tuck in nicely just about anywhere, and thanks to Samba and Winbind, they can even become fully fledged Active Directory objects. Samba is the key to making all of this work; you'll need it on all participating Linux hosts.

Replacing an NT4 Domain Controller

If you're running a Windows NT4 domain controller and thinking of upgrading, consider replacing it with Samba. Samba works great as a drop-in replacement for an NT domain controller. A Linux server running Samba handles a bigger load, and is more stable and secure. It does not replace a Windows 2000/2003 server running Active Directory, because Active Directory comes with user and resource management tools that Samba does not provide. But, as a straight-across NT4-type domain controller, Samba excels. It has these advantages:

- Easily integrates Linux hosts into your LAN
- Saves you from expensive, Byzantine licensing schemes and fear of the license police
- Greater stability, reliability, and performance
- Multiple choices of database backends
- Community and commercial support
- Secure remote administration via SSH
- Reliable, efficient synchronization of backup Samba servers via *rsync*

If you start out with Samba as your domain controller, and then decide you want to upgrade to Active Directory, no problem. Samba 3 fits right into Active Directory with a few configuration tweaks, unlike NT4, which requires a complete reinstallation to change its role from a domain controller to a domain member.

Samba makes a great file and print server for mixed Windows/Linux LANs, so once you learn any part of Samba, you can continue to build on your knowledge.

With Linux, there are no artificial distinctions between server and workstation versions. Any Linux can be customized to serve whatever role you wish; you won't find yourself wrestling with crippled editions designed solely to extract more money from you.

Hardware Requirements

Calculating how much horsepower and storage you need is an imprecise endeavor, but we can cobble up some useful guidelines. For 50 users or fewer, any old Pentium II or better with at least 128 MB of RAM and enough disk space will do the job just fine. If you're running X Windows, make it 256 MB of RAM. Of course, much depends on how hard your users pummel the server, how many users you have, how much file storage is on the server, and how many programs you have running on the server.

As your userbase grows, you can calculate memory requirements, as this simple illustration for 100 users shows:

```
Application  Memory per User    User
    Name         (MBytes)       Total

Samba (nmbd)      16.0           16
Samba (winbind)   16.0           16
Samba (smbd)       4.0          400
Basic OS          128           128
total             167.5         560
```

Samba spawns a process for every user. As your userbase grows, having adequate memory and a fast disk subsystem improve performance more than having a fast CPU.

In addition to shared files, users have private home directories on the server. You can set quotas on users in the ordinary manner to keep storage under control, using the quota command (see Recipe 8.22, "Using Disk Quotas," in *Linux Cookbook* [O'Reilly]).

Sanity Quest

Searching for sanity in Windows networking is a bit of a quest. Windows XP Home cannot join any domain—neither a Windows domain, nor a Samba domain. Windows NT 3.x, Windows 95 pre-OSR2, and Windows NT 4 pre-Service Pack 3 do not support encrypted passwords, which Samba uses by default, so you cannot join these to a normal Samba domain. You can download a patch to enable encrypted passwords in Windows 95, *Vrdrupd.exe*. Search the Microsoft Knowledge Base for kb 165403 to find the download and instructions. Windows 9x/ME introduce a number of potential security holes because they do not support the more secure NTFS filesystem. The best choices for domain clients are Windows NT, 2000, 2003, and XP Pro, running on the NTFS filesystem. Vista also works with Samba; there are some authentication issues we'll cover in the Vista recipe.

11.1   Verifying That All the Pieces Are in Place

Problem

You are ready to integrate some Linux and Windows hosts. You want a single central authentication mechanism for all users. You have chosen Samba because you're not ready to start migrating to an LDAP backend, or because it is fairly simple to implement, and you're already familiar with it. You want to know what software you need to install.

Solution

You will need some or all of these programs installed. Each recipe in this chapter tells you which ones you'll need:

- Samba 3.0.20 or newer
- MIT Kerberos 1.4 or newer
- OpenLDAP
- Winbind 3.0.20 or newer (part of Samba, but may be packaged separately)

Then, you need support for these compiled into Samba:

- Kerberos
- LDAP
- Winbind
- Active Directory

Debian and Fedora keep their binary packages fairly up-to-date and built with the options you need, so you'll be fine using Aptitude or Yum to install Samba.

Discussion

Debian tends to split programs into a lot of little packages, so finding all the pieces you want can be a bit of a chore. For Samba, you'll need these: *samba*, *samba-common*, *samba-doc*, *smbclient*, and *winbind*.

Fedora users need *samba*, *samba-client*, and *samba-common*.

Find the installed Samba version information with these commands:

```
$ /usr/sbin/smbd --version
Version 3.0.23-Debian
$ /usr/sbin/winbindd --version
Version 3.0.23-Debian
```

On Debian, check your Kerberos version with *dpkg*:

```
$ dpkg -l | grep krb5
ii  libkrb53  1.4.4-etch        MIT Kerberos runtime libraries
```

On Fedora, use *rpm*:

```
$ rpm -q krb5-workstation
krb5-workstation-1.5-21
```

Samba comes with a great little command that shows all of its compiled options:

```
$ /usr/sbin/smbd -b
```

However, that spits out pages of output, so you should narrow your search with *grep*:

```
$ smbd -b | grep -i ldap
HAVE_LDAP_H
HAVE_LDAP
HAVE_LDAP_DOMAIN2HOSTLIST
...
$ smbd -b | grep -i krb5
HAVE_KRB5_H
HAVE_ADDRTYPE_IN_KRB5_ADDRESS
HAVE_KRB5
...
$ smbd -b | grep -i ads
WITH_ADS
WITH_ADS
```

```
$ smbd -b | grep -i winbind
WITH_WINBIND
WITH_WINBIND
```

You'll see more output than is printed here. This shows you are ready to proceed to the rest of the recipes in this chapter.

A blank line indicates that support for that particular item is not compiled into Samba, which means you'll have to recompile it yourself. See Recipe 11.2 to learn how to do this.

If you are familiar with Heimdal Kerberos, that works just fine. Some admins prefer it, as it is outside of the United States' export controls. The examples in this chapter will use MIT Kerberos.

Fedora users need *krb5-workstation*, containing client utilities, and *krb5-libs* for the server. Debian splits it up into several smaller packages, as you can see from searching the Debian packages list (*http://www.us.debian.org/distrib/packages*), or searching your own local package list:

```
$ apt-cache search krb5
libpam-krb5 - PAM module for MIT Kerberos
krb5-admin-server - MIT Kerberos master server (kadmind)
krb5-clients - Secure replacements for ftp, telnet and rsh using MIT Kerberos
krb5-config - Configuration files for Kerberos Version 5
krb5-doc - Documentation for krb5
krb5-ftpd - Secure FTP server supporting MIT Kerberos
krb5-kdc - MIT Kerberos key server (KDC)
krb5-user - Basic programs to authenticate using MIT Kerberos
libkrb53 - MIT Kerberos runtime libraries
ssh-krb5 - Secure rlogin/rsh/rcp replacement (OpenSSH with Kerberos)
```

For this chapter, you'll need *krb5-config*, *krb5-doc*, *krb5-admin-server*, *krb5-kdc*, and *krb5-user*.

Fedora users need these packages to get OpenLDAP: *openldap*, *openldap-servers*, and *openldap-clients*.

On Debian, you'll need *ldap-utils*, *ldapscripts*, *libldap2*, and *slapd*.

See Also

- man 8 rpm
- man 8 dpkg
- Chapters 2, 3, and 4 in Carla Schroder's *Linux Cookbook* (O'Reilly) go into detail on installing, updating, and removing Linux software

11.2 Compiling Samba from Source Code

Problem

Your Linux distribution did not compile support for all the options you need into Samba (see the previous recipe), so you need to rebuild it from scratch and ensure that it has everything you need built-in. Or, you just prefer source installations.

Solution

Follow these steps.

First, make sure you have the necessary development tools installed on your system. Debian users need:

- build-essential
- autoconf
- autogen
- libkrb5-dev
- krb5-user
- gnugpg

Fedora users need:

- autoconf
- autogen
- krb5-workstation
- krb5-libs
- krb5-devel
- gnugpg

The command yum groupinstall 'Development Tools' installs all of the basic Linux development tools that you need for a source build on Fedora.

Obtain the Samba source code tarball from *samba.org*, the signature file, and the GPG key. Verify the filenames before downloading, making sure you have the latest stable versions:

```
$ wget http://us1.samba.org/samba/ftp/samba-3.0.25a.tar.asc
$ wget http://us1.samba.org/samba/ftp/samba-pubkey.asc
$ wget http://us1.samba.org/samba/ftp/samba-3.0.25a.tar.gz
```

Uncompress the tarball into a directory where you have write permissions, like in your home directory:

```
$ gunzip -d samba-3.0.25a.tar.gz
```

Import the GPG key into your GPG keyring:

```
$ gpg --import samba-pubkey.asc
gpg: key F17F9772: public key "Samba Distribution Verification Key <samba-bugs@samba.
org>" imported
gpg: Total number processed: 1
gpg:              imported: 1
```

Then, verify the uncompressed tarball:

```
$ gpg --verify samba-3.0.25a.tar.asc
gpg: Signature made Wed Oct 12 19:20:25 2005 PDT using DSA key ID F17F9772
gpg: Good signature from "Samba Distribution Verification Key
<samba-bugs@samba.org>"
Primary key fingerprint: 2FD9 BC31 99F3 AEB0 8D30  2233 A037 FC69 F17F 9772
```

Now, you can unpack the tarball:

```
$ tar xvf samba-3.0.25a.tar
```

Next, change to the directory in the Samba source tree that contains the *autogen.sh* script, and run the script:

```
$ cd samba-3.0.25b/source
$ ./autogen.sh
./autogen.sh: running script/mkversion.sh
./script/mkversion.sh: 'include/version.h' created for Samba("3.0.25a")
./autogen.sh: running autoheader
./autogen.sh: running autoconf
```

To see a complete list of build options, run:

```
$ ./configure --help
```

Select these options to support Active Directory, Kerberos, Winbind, and LDAP:

```
$ ./configure --with-ldap --with-ads --with-krb5=/usr --with-winbind
```

Make sure that --with-krb5 points to the directory containing your Kerberos libraries. Additionally, these build options are also useful:

```
--with-automount -with-smbmount --with-pam --with-pam_smbpass \
 --with-ldapsam  --with-syslog  --with-quotas --with-sys-quotas
```

Then su to *root*, build, and install Samba:

```
$ su
# make
# make install
```

The final steps are configuring Samba to start automatically at boot. See Recipe 11.3.

Discussion

There are all manner of build options, as ./configure --help shows. You can control installation directories, fine-tune debugging output, and make platform-specific tweaks. The default installation directory is */usr/local/samba/*, which makes it easy to wipe out a troublesome installation and start over.

The Samba tarball includes files and instructions for building packages for Debian, Red Hat, Solaris, and many others; see the *packaging/* directory in the Samba tarball.

You'll need a build environment for compiling programs from source code. The tools you need are standard on all Linux distributions, though they may not be installed, depending on what sort of installation you choose:

- GNU coreutils
- GNU binutils
- gcc
- gunzip
- bunzip2
- GNU tar
- make

See Also

- Chapter 4, "Installing Programs from Source Code," in *Linux Cookbook* by Carla Schroder (O'Reilly)

11.3   Starting and Stopping Samba

Problem

You want to know how to make Samba start automatically at boot, and you need to know the commands for manually starting, stopping, and restarting Samba.

Solution

Samba has two daemons: *smbd* and *nmbd*. If you installed Samba from packages (RPM or deb), startup scripts will have been created for you in */etc/init.d*. Debian starts it up automatically. On Fedora, you need to run *chkconfig*:

```
# chkconfig --add samba
```

Manually stopping and starting Samba is done on Fedora systems with these commands:

```
# /etc/init.d/smb {stop|start|restart|reload|condrestart}
```

On Debian, use these commands:

```
# /etc/init.d/samba {stop|start|restart|reload|force-reload}
```

Check to see if it is running with this command:

```
$ ps ax | grep mbd
 5781 ?        Ss     0:00 /usr/sbin/nmbd -D
 5783 ?        Ss     0:00 /usr/sbin/smbd -D
```

If you installed Samba from source code, you'll find *init* scripts for various distributions in the packaging directory in the source tarball.

Discussion

condrestart is a conditional restart; it only restarts Samba if it's already running.

reload rereads *smb.conf* rather than restarting the *smbd* and *nmbd* daemons.

Samba rereads *smb.conf* periodically, so it's not strictly necessary to restart or reload with every change.

See Also

- man 8 chkconfig
- man 8 update-rc.d
- Chapter 7, "Starting and Stopping Linux," in *Linux Cookbook*, by Carla Schroder (O'Reilly) for recipes on managing runlevels and controlling services

11.4   Using Samba As a Primary Domain Controller

Problem

You want a central login and authentication server on your network; you have either Windows hosts, or a mixed LAN of Windows and Linux hosts. You may also want this server to provide access to network resources, such as file shares and printers. You do not have a Windows domain controller or existing password server, but a mish-mash of peer networking plus sneakernet, or just shared Internet, so you are starting from scratch.

Solution

There are seven steps to building a Samba domain controller:

1. Install Samba.
2. Configure */etc/samba/smb.conf*.
3. Create a Samba *root* user.
4. Create a group for machine accounts.
5. Join all Windows NT/200x/XP/Vista computers in the domain to the Samba server.
6. Create user accounts on both Linux and Samba.
7. Fire it up and connect clients for testing.

Here is a complete, basic */etc/samba/smb.conf* for your new domain controller. Substitute your own workgroup name (which is the name of the primary domain), NetBIOS name, server string, and network IP:

```
[global]
    workgroup = bluedomain
    netbios name = samba1
    server string = Samba PDC
    domain master = yes
    os level = 64
    preferred master = yes
    domain logons = yes
    add machine script = /usr/sbin/useradd -s /bin/false -d /dev/null -g machines '%u'

    passdb backend = tdbsam
    security = user
    encrypt passwords = yes
    log file = /var/log/samba/log
    log level = 2
    max log size = 50
    hosts allow = 192.168.1.
    wins support = yes

[netlogon]
    comment = Network Logon Service
    path = /var/lib/samba/netlogon/
    browseable = No
    writable = No

[homes]
    comment = Home Directories
    valid users = %S
    browseable = No
    writable = Yes
```

Create */var/lib/samba/netlogon/* if it does not already exist:

```
# mkdir -m 0755 /var/lib/samba/netlogon/
```

Create a *netlogon.bat* script containing these lines to automatically mount shares on user's Windows PCs, and put it in */var/lib/samba/netlogon/*, mode 0644. You may use any drive letter you like, as long it doesn't conflict with user's existing drives:

```
## netlogon.bat
REM NETLOGON.BAT
net use z: \\linux\samba /yes
```

Save and close *smb.conf,* then run *testparm* to check for syntax errors:

```
# testparm
Load smb config files from /etc/samba/smb.conf
Loaded services file OK.
Server role: ROLE_DOMAIN_PDC
Server role: ROLE_DOMAIN_PDC is the line you want to see.
```

Fix syntax errors, if any, then restart Samba. (See Recipe 11.3 to learn how to start and stop Samba.)

Next, create a Samba *root* user account with *smbpasswd*. Do not use the same password as the Linux *root* user:

```
# smbpasswd -a
New SMB password:
Retype new SMB password:
Added user root.
```

Then create a *machines* group:

```
# groupadd -g machines
```

You must now make the first domain logins from the Windows NT/200x/XP/Vista PCs as the Samba *root* user. Don't forget to do this, or your Windows NT/200x/XP/Vista users will not be able to log in to the domain. Log in as soon as possible to synchronize with the server, and to prevent someone else from possibly hijacking the account.

Finally, create Linux accounts on the Samba box for all users in the domain. This example disables Linux logins, so that users can access their home directories on the server only via Samba:

```
#  useradd -m -s /bin/false foober
```

Then, use the Samba *smbpasswd* command to create Samba user accounts:

```
# smbpasswd -a foober
New SMB password:
Retype new SMB password:
Added user foober.
```

Be sure to give *foober* his new password. Yes, it's tedious. (Check the See Also section for tips for easing the process.)

Finally, start or restart Samba.

Discussion

wins support = yes means Samba is the WINS server. You don't have to do anything other than add this line to *smb.conf*, and it will automatically keep a list of all NetBIOS names registered with them, acting as a DNS server for NetBIOS names. Remove it if there is already a WINS server on the network, because having two causes problems.

Users will have two home directories: one on their local PCs, and one on the Samba server. You can limit user's storage space on the Samba server in the usual manner, with the *quota* command. You may do away with home directories on the server entirely, but then you run the risk of some things not working right, like Kerberos if you ever implement it, or joining Samba to an Active Directory domain.

Machine Trust Accounts are user accounts owned by a single computer. The password of a Machine Trust Account acts as the shared secret for secure communication with the Domain Controller. This prevents an unauthorized machine from masquerading the NetBIOS name and gaining access. A Windows 9x/ME host cannot possess a Machine Trust Account, so this opens a potential security hole in your domain (among many other potential security holes, such as the fact that multiple users on a Windows 9x/ME machine can freely access each other's files, and by default it caches passwords).

The *add machine* script directive simplifies creating machine accounts. Creating them manually is done this way, using the host "tinbox" as an example:

```
# useradd -g machines -d /dev/null  -s /bin/false tinbox$
# smbpasswd -a -m tinbox
```

Note that the machine account is created with no login shell and a locked password, so it is impossible to log in to Linux using the machine account. This is an important security measure.

You can easily add file and printer shares as you need, just like for any Samba server.

These are the directives that tell Samba it is a primary domain controller:

```
domain master = yes
os level = 64
preferred master = yes
domain logons = yes
```

The passdb backend = tdbsam directive selects the *tdbsam* database for storing user account information, rather than the default *smbpasswd*. The Samba team recommends using *tdbsam* over *smbpasswd*, which is being phased out. Don't confuse the *smbpasswd* database with the *smbpasswd* command—the *smbpasswd* command is used to manage user accounts with *tdbsam* and other supported databases.

Any users that you add with *smbpasswd* must already have system accounts on the Samba server. If they are not in */etc/passwd*, you will get this error:

```
Failed to initialise SAM_ACCOUNT for user foo.
Failed to modify password entry for user foo
```

Remember, There Can Be Only One—don't put two primary domain controllers (PDCs) on the same domain, or nothing will work right. You may have multiple Samba servers, but only one PDC.

See Also

- man 8 useradd
- man 1 passwd
- man 5 smb.conf is thorough and understandable—keep it close to your Samba server; be sure to review it for the configuration defaults

- Recipes 8.17, 8.18, and 8.19 in *Linux Cookbook*, by Carla Schroder (O'Reilly) explain how to automate adding Linux system users. Be sure to check out the wonderful *mass_useradd* and *mass_passwd* scripts

- Chapter 23, "File and Printer Sharing, and Domain Authentication with Samba," in *Linux Cookbook*

- Chapter 4, "Domain Control," in *The Official Samba-3 HOWTO and Reference Guide (http://www.samba.org/samba/docs/man/Samba-HOWTO-Collection/)*

11.5 Migrating to a Samba Primary Domain Controller from an NT4 PDC

Problem

Microsoft's support for Windows NT4 ended December 31, 2004. You have an NT4 domain controller or controllers, and are wondering what to do next—keep them? Upgrade to Windows 2003 with Active Directory, which is expensive, has a learning curve, and probably means buying new computers as well? Find something else entirely?

Solution

Find something else entirely—a nice Linux system running Samba 3 makes a dandy drop-in NT4 PDC replacement. Your users will never know the difference, except perhaps in better performance.

Follow these steps:

1. Do some housecleaning first—get rid of unused and duplicate accounts on the NT4 PDC.

2. Make a Backup Domain Controller (BDC) account for Samba using NT Server Manager.

3. Configure Samba.

4. Join the Samba BDC to your NT4 domain.

5. Migrate user and machine accounts.

6. Shut down the NT4 domain controller.

7. Promote Samba to a PDC.

This is a simple */etc/samba/smb.conf* designed just for migration from NT4. The workgroup name is the existing domain name—do not change it! The netbios name can be anything you want, and you must use the real IP of your WINS server:

```
[global]
    workgroup = reddomain
    netbios name = samba11
```

```
passdb backend = tdbsam
security = user
domain master = No
domain logons = Yes
os level = 33
add user script = /usr/sbin/useradd -m '%u'
delete user script = /usr/sbin/userdel -r '%u'
add group script = /usr/sbin/groupadd '%g'
delete group script = /usr/sbin/groupdel '%g'
add user to group script = /usr/sbin/usermod -G '%g' '%u'
add machine script = /usr/sbin/useradd -s /bin/false -d /dev/null '%u'
wins server = 192.168.1.30
```

Run *testparm* to check syntax:

```
$ testparm
Load smb config files from /etc/samba/smb.conf
Loaded services file OK.
Server role: ROLE_DOMAIN_BDC
Press enter to see a dump of your service definitions
```

Start or restart Samba, then join it to the domain using the IP address or NetBIOS name of the NT4 PDC, and the NT4 Administrator login, or any NT4 user with administrative rights:

```
# net rpc join -S ntpdc -U Administrator%password
Joined domain REDDOMAIN.
```

Now comes the fun part; this is where you get to *vampire* your accounts from the NT4 box to Samba:

```
# net rpc vampire -S ntpdc -W reddomain -U Administrator%password
Fetching REDDOMAIN database
SAM_DELTA_REDDOMAIN_INFO not handled
Creating unix group: 'Domain Admins'
Creating unix group: 'Domain Users'
Creating unix group: 'Domain Guests'
Creating unix group: 'Web_team'
Creating unix group: 'Sysadmins'
...
Creating account: Administrator
Creating account: Guest
Creating account: NTSERVER$
Creating account: 'carla'
Creating account: 'foober'
...
```

Verify that your user accounts moved over by running *pbdedit* to show a list of migrated accounts:

```
# pdbedit -L
powerpc-w2k$:1010:POWERPC-W2K$
stinkpad$:1012:STINKPAD$
```

```
alrac:1013:
root:0:root
foober5:1007:
...
```

Finally, promote Samba to Primary Domain Controller by reworking */etc/samba/smb. conf* to look just like the example in Recipe 11.4. Restart Samba, and your users should be able to log in without a hitch.

Shut down your old NT4 domain controller and find it another job, perhaps as a nice Samba file or printer server.

Discussion

If you change the domain name you're committed to starting over, and will have to enter all user accounts manually, so don't.

See Also

- man 8 pdbedit
- man 5 smb.conf
- Chapter 8, "Managing Users and Groups," in *Linux Cookbook*, by Carla Schroder (O'Reilly)
- Chapter 23, "File and Printer Sharing, and Domain Authentication with Samba," in *Linux Cookbook*

11.6   Joining Linux to an Active Directory Domain

Problem

You are running a Windows network managed by an Active Directory domain. You know you can stick Linux hosts on the network and make them accessible to Windows hosts, but what you really want is for the Linux boxes to be full members of your Active Directory domain. This allows you to manage them just like any other AD object, have a unified login for all hosts, and manage Linux users from Active Directory. Your DNS house is in order, and you already have a Kerberos Key Distribution Center (KDC).

Solution

You need all Samba, Winbind, and the Kerberos client packages installed, and support for Kerberos, LDAP, Active Directory, and Winbind compiled into Samba. Please see Recipe 11.1 to learn exactly what you need.

Also needed are accounts for the Linux users and computers already present in Active Directory.

These are the steps to follow:

1. Make sure you have a reliable Network Time Protocol (NTP) server available to your LAN, and that all hosts are synchronized.

2. Delete all *.tdb* files to get rid of stale data: */etc/samba/secrets.tdb* (which may not exist) and in */var/lib/samba*. Keep backup copies, though you probably won't need them.

3. Stop the Samba and Winbind daemons.

4. Create a Linux group for machine accounts.

5. Configure */etc/hosts*.

6. Configure */etc/resolv.conf*.

7. Configure Samba.

8. Configure NSS.

9. Configure PAM.

10. Restart all daemons and test.

When the first two steps are accomplished, stop the Samba and Winbind daemons. On Fedora:

```
# /etc/init.d/smb stop
# /etc/init.d/winbind stop
```

On Debian, use these commands:

```
# /etc/init.d/samba stop
# /etc/init.d/winbind stop
```

Then, create a Linux group to hold Machine Trust Accounts:

```
# groupadd machines
```

Next, add important hosts to */etc/hosts* as a fallback:

```
## /etc/hosts
192.168.1.25    samba1.bluedomain.com    samba1
192.168.1.20    windows1.bluedomain.com  windows1
```

Also, make sure that */etc/resolv.conf* contains your DNS server:

```
nameserver 192.168.1.21
```

Now, test connecting to the KDC. It should report no errors:

```
# kinit fredfoober@BLUEDOMAIN.COM
Password for fredfoober@BLUEDOMAIN.COM:
```

Edit */etc/samba/smb.conf* to authenticate against Active Directory, using your own domain name, NetBIOS name, server string, and Kerberos realm. This is a complete example file:

```
[global]
    workgroup = bluedomain
    netbios name = samba1
```

```
    realm = BLUEDOMAIN.COM
    server string = Samba server one
    security = ADS
    encrypt passwords = yes

    idmap uid = 10000-20000
    idmap gid = 10000-20000
    winbind use default domain = yes
    winbind enum users = Yes
    winbind enum groups = Yes
    winbind separator = +

    log file = /var/log/samba/log
    log level = 2
    max log size = 50
    hosts allow = 192.168.1.

[homes]
    comment = Home Directories
    valid users = %S
    read only = No
    browseable = No
```

Now, edit */etc/nsswitch.conf* to include these lines:

```
passwd:        files winbind
group:           files winbind
shadow:            files
```

Start up Samba and Winbind. Join the Linux PC to the Active Directory domain, and set up a machine trust account, using the Administrator account on the AD server, or any administrative user:

```
# net ads join -U Administrator%password
Using short domain name -- BLUEDOMAIN
Joined 'SAMBA1' to realm 'BLUEDOMAIN.COM.'
```

You should now see a new computer account with the NetBIOS name of your Linux machine (*samba1*) in Active Directory, under Users and Computers in the Computers folder.

Finally, you need to configure Pluggable Authentication Modules (PAM) to allow authentication via Winbind. First, make a backup copy:

```
# cp /etc/pam.d/login /etc/pam.d/login-old
```

Edit */etc/pam.d/login* to include the Winbind modules, and the *pam_mkhomedir.so* module:

```
auth        requisite  pam_securetty.so
auth        requisite  pam_nologin.so
auth        required    pam_env.so
auth        sufficient pam_winbind.so
auth        required    pam_unix.so nullok use_first_pass
```

```
account     requisite   pam_time.so
account     sufficient  pam_winbind.so
account     required    pam_unix.so

session     required    pam_unix.so
session     optional    pam_lastlog.so
session     optional    pam_motd.so
session     optional    pam_mail.so standard noenv
session     required    pam_mkhomedir.so skel=/etc/skel umask=0027
```

Your existing */etc/pam.d/login* may look a lot different than this; see the Discussion for more information and more sample configurations.

Now, it's time to test everything. Reboot your Linux box, and try to log in to the domain. If that works, you're all finished.

Discussion

This may seem like a lot of steps, but don't be fooled—it really is complex because by design, Windows hinders interoperability. Fortunately, heroic Linux coders like the Samba team make interoperability and mixed networks possible.

The *pam_mkhomedir.so* directive creates home directories for users on the fly, at their first login.

In a more complex network, you may specify a particular Kerberos realm to join:

```
# kinit fredfoober@BLUEDOMAIN.COM
# net ads join "Computers\TechDept\Workstations" \
  -U Administrator%password
```

Because user accounts are managed on the Active Directory server, and are made available to Linux via Winbind and PAM, you do not need to create duplicate user accounts on the Linux PC. However, you may still have local accounts on the Linux machine; these are invisible to Active Directory, and allow administrative users to freely access the server either locally, or remotely via SSH. And, you must have at least a local *root* account—don't depend on a remote login server for everything, or you could get locked out.

A lot of documentation tells you to edit */etc/krb5.conf* to point to your KDC server. This isn't necessary if Active Directory and your Microsoft DNS server are correctly configured because AD automatically creates SRV records in the DNS zone *kerberos._tcp.REALM.NAME* for each KDC in the realm. Both the MIT and Heimdal Kerberos automatically look for these SRV records so they can find all available KDCs. And */etc/krb5.conf* only lets you specify a single KDC, rather than allowing automatic selection of the first available KDC. If you are not using Microsoft DNS, you'll have to enter these DNS records manually.

If for whatever reason Kerberos cannot find the KDC via DNS, this simple example */etc/krb5.conf* works for most setups, using your own domain names, of course:

```
[libdefaults]
        default_realm = BLUEDOMAIN.COM
[realms]            BLUEDOMAIN.COM = {
        kdc = windows1.bluedomain.com
        }

[domain_realms]
        .carla.com = BLUEDOMAIN.COM
```

Once you have your Samba setup debugged and working, simply replicate it for any Linux host that needs to be an Active Directory member.

See Also

- man 5 smb.conf

11.7 Connecting Windows 95/98/ME to a Samba Domain

Problem

You set up a new Samba primary domain controller (PDC) like in Recipe 11.4, and you did not have a domain controller before, so your clients are not configured to log in to a domain. How do you log in from a Windows 95/98/ME client?

Solution

First, confirm that Windows networking is set up correctly: TPC/IP and Client For Microsoft Networks must be installed, in Start → Settings → Control Panel → Network.

Then, go to Control Panel → Network → Client for Microsoft Networks → Properties. Check "Logon to NT Domain." Enter the domain name.

Check "Logon and restore network connections." Click OK. It may ask you for your Windows CD, and then you must reboot to activate the changes.

After reboot, you can log in to the domain; you'll be presented with a login screen with the domain name.

To boot up Windows without logging in to the domain, hit the Cancel button.

Discussion

Even though you can set up multiple users on Windows 95/98/ME, there is no real separation or security. Everyone may access everyone's files, all the applications are configured globally, and the only user-unique features are the desktop decorations.

See Also

- Recipe 23.4, "Enabling File Sharing on Windows PCs," in *Linux Cookbook*, by Carla Schroder (O'Reilly) for more information on configuring Windows networking
- Chapter 3, "Configuring Windows Clients," in *Using Samba,* Second Edition, by Jay Ts et al. (O'Reilly)

11.8   Connecting Windows NT4 to a Samba Domain

Problem

You have set up a new Samba primary domain controller (PDC) like in Recipe 11.4, and you did not have a domain controller before, so your clients are not configured to log in to a domain. How do you login from a Windows NT4 client?

Solution

First, confirm that Windows networking is set up correctly: TPC/IP and Client For Microsoft Networks must be installed, and the appropriate network settings in place, which you'll find in Start → Settings → Network and Dial-up Connections.

Then, go to Control Panel → Network → Identification → Change. Select the Domain button and enter the domain name, which is the workgroup name in *smb.conf.*

Reboot and log in to the domain.

Discussion

You'll initiate logins with Ctrl-Alt-Del. Note that you can either log in to the domain, or to the local machine without logging in to a domain by clicking the Options button to expose a drop-down menu listing your login choices.

See Also

- Recipe 23.4, "Enabling File Sharing on Windows PCs," in *Linux Cookbook*, by Carla Schroder (O'Reilly) for more information on configuring Windows networking
- Chapter 3, "Configuring Windows Clients," in *Using Samba,* Second Edition, by Jay Ts et al. (O'Reilly)

11.9 Connecting Windows NT/2000 to a Samba Domain

Problem

You have set up a new Samba primary domain controller (PDC) like in Recipe 11.4, and you did not have a domain controller before, so your clients are not configured to log in to a domain. How do you login from a Windows 2000 client?

Solution

First, confirm that Windows networking is set up correctly: TPC/IP and Client For Microsoft Networks must be installed, and the appropriate network settings in place, which you'll find in Start → Settings → Network and Dial-up Connections.

Then, right-click My Computer, click Properties, Network Identification Tab, and click the Network ID button. This will open the Network Identification Wizard, which will take you through all the necessary steps.

Discussion

You'll intitiate logins with Ctrl-Alt-Del. Note that you can either log in to the domain, or to the local machine without logging in to a domain, by clicking the Options button to expose a drop-down menu listing your login choices.

See Also

- Recipe 23.4, "Enabling File Sharing on Windows PCs," in *Linux Cookbook*, by Carla Schroder (O'Reilly) for more information on configuring Windows networking
- Chapter 3, "Configuring Windows Clients," *Using Samba,* Second Edition, by Jay Ts et al. (O'Reilly)

11.10 Connecting Windows XP to a Samba Domain

Problem

You have set up a new Samba primary domain controller (PDC) like in Recipe 11.4, and you did not have a domain controller before, so your clients are not configured to log in to a domain. How do you log in from a Windows XP client?

Solution

First, confirm that Windows networking is set up correctly: TPC/IP and Client For Microsoft Networks must be installed, and the appropriate network settings in place, which you'll find in Start → Control Panel → Network Connections.

Then, right-click My Computer, click Properties, Network Identification Tab, and click the Network ID button. This will open the Network Identification Wizard, which will take you through all the necessary steps.

Discussion

You'll intitiate logins with Ctrl-Alt-Del. Note that you can either log in to the domain, or to the local machine without logging in to a domain, by clicking the Options button to expose a drop-down menu listing your login choices.

See Also

- Recipe 23.4, "Enabling File Sharing on Windows PCs," in *Linux Cookbook*, by Carla Schroder (O'Reilly) for more information on configuring Windows networking
- Chapter 3, "Configuring Windows Clients," in *Using Samba,* Second Edition, by Jay Ts et al. (O'Reilly)

11.11 Connecting Linux Clients to a Samba Domain with Command-Line Programs

Problem

Your shiny new Samba domain controller is in service and ready to rock. Your Windows clients are successfully logging in and finding shares just like they're supposed to. How do your Linux PCs join the party using command-line utilities?

Solution

These command-line tools are for browsing, logging in, and mounting Samba shares:

smbtree
> Browses the network and displays all domains, servers, and shares in a tree structure. It is part of the Samba suite.

smbclient
> Network browser and file manager. *smbclient* displays domains, servers, and shares, and uses FTP-type commands to transfer files. You don't need to mount the shares to get access to the files. Also part of the Samba suite.

smbmount/smbumount

These commands are for mounting and unmounting Samba shares. Part of the *smbfs* package.

Discussion

Linux does not see domains the same way that Windows does, which is no surprise because the domain structure is a Windows convention. Linux sees filesystems that it has either permission to access or no permission to access. Unlike Windows, which can either log in to a domain or log in locally, but not both, Linux users log in first to their local systems in the normal fashion, then log in to domain shares as needed. Domain shares can be configured to auto-mount in */etc/fstab*, just like any other filesystem.

To browse the network and see all the domains, servers, and shares with *smbtree*, run it with the -N (no password) switch. This will not show nonbrowseable shares, such as user's home directories:

```
$ smbtree -N
REDDOMAIN
        \\STINKPAD                      thinkpad r32
        \\SAMBA11                       Samba PDC
                \\SAMBA11\HP6L              HP6L b&w laser printer
                \\SAMBA11\ADMIN$           IPC Service (Samba PDC)
                \\SAMBA11\IPC$             IPC Service (Samba PDC)
                \\SAMBA11\share1          testfiles
```

You may also browse by either hostname, IP address, or NetBIOS name. In this example, *windbag* is the hostname, and *samba11* is the NetBIOS name as specified in *smb.conf*:

```
$ smbtree -N windbag
$ smbtree -N samba11
```

But not the domain name, because the domain name is not a resolvable name.

You may see nonbrowseable shares that are accessible to you by using your username and password:

```
$ smbtree -U foober
Password:
REDDOMAIN
        \\STINKPAD                      thinkpad r32
                \\STINKPAD\C$              Default share
                \\STINKPAD\ADMIN$         Remote Admin
                \\STINKPAD\F$             Default share
                \\STINKPAD\print$         Printer Drivers
                \\STINKPAD\SharedDocs
                \\STINKPAD\IPC$           Remote IPC
        \\SAMBA11                       Samba PDC
                \\SAMBA11\foober          Home Directories
                \\SAMBA11\HP6L            HP6L
                \\SAMBA11\ADMIN$          IPC Service (Samba PDC)
                \\SAMBA11\IPC$            IPC Service (Samba PDC)
                \\SAMBA11\share1          testfiles
```

When you see the share you want, mount the share on your system with *smbmount*, using a directory already created for this purpose, and mind your slashes. In this example, user *foober* mounts his Samba home directory in the local directory *samba*:

```
$ mkdir samba
$ smbmount //samba11/foober samba
$ password:
```

The smbumount command unmounts the share:

```
$ smbumount  samba
```

You may use *smbclient* to access file shares without having to mount the shares. Instead, *smbclient* uses FTP-like commands to transfer files. This command shows you how to browse the network. You must specify the hostname or NetBIOS name; this shows the hostname:

```
$ smbclient -N -L windbag
Anonymous login successful
Domain=[REDDOMAIN] OS=[Unix] Server=[Samba 3.0.10-Debian]

        Sharename       Type      Comment
        ---------       ----      -------
        share1          Disk      testfiles
        IPC$            IPC       IPC Service (Samba PDC)
        ADMIN$          IPC       IPC Service (Samba PDC)
        HP6L            Printer   HP6L
Anonymous login successful
Domain=[REDDOMAIN] OS=[Unix] Server=[Samba 3.0.10-Debian]

        Server            Comment
        ---------         -------
        SAMBA11           Samba PDC

        Workgroup         Master
        ---------         -------
        REDDOMAIN         SAMBA11
```

You can find your home directory by browsing with your login:

```
$ smbclient -L samba11 -U carla
Password:
Domain=[REDDOMAIN] OS=[Unix] Server=[Samba 3.0.10-Debian]

        Sharename       Type      Comment
        ---------       ----      -------
        share1          Disk      testfiles
        IPC$            IPC       IPC Service (Samba PDC)
        ADMIN$          IPC       IPC Service (Samba PDC)
        HP6L            Printer   HP6L
        carla           Disk      Home Directories
...
```

Use this command to connect to your home share:

```
$ smbclient -U carla //samba11/carla
Password:
Domain=[REDDOMAIN] OS=[Unix] Server=[Samba 3.0.10-Debian]
smb: \>
```

When you are at the smb: \> prompt, type ? to show a commands list:

```
smb: \> ?
?               altname     archive     blocksize   cancel
case_sensitive  cd          chmod       chown       del
dir             du          exit        get         hardlink
help            history     lcd         link        lowercase
...
```

See? Same old familiar Linux commands. The following commands list files, then transfer the *foo* directory from the server to the local working directory, and renames it to *foo-copy*:

```
smb: \> ls
smb: \> get foo foo-copy
getting file \foo of size 2131 as foo-copy (1040.5 kb/s) (average 1040.5 kb/s)
smb: \>
```

Uploading files to the Samba share is done with the old familiar put command:

```
smb: \> put foo-copy
putting file foo-copy as \foo-copy (0.0 kb/s) (average 0.0 kb/s)
```

To close your connection to the share:

```
smb: \> quit
```

The *smbmount* and *smbumount* commands call *smbmnt*. If you run into permissions problems, such as "smbmnt must be installed suid root for direct user mounts," make *smbmnt* SUID with *chmod*:

```
# chmod +s /usr/bin/smbmnt
```

If you are nervous about using SUID, set up *sudo* for authorized *smbmnt* users.

See Also

- Chapter 8, "Managing Users and Groups," in *Linux Cookbook*, by Carla Schroder (O'Reilly) to learn how to configure *sudo*
- man 8 smbmount
- man 8 smbumount
- man 1 smbtree
- man 1 smbclient

11.12 Connecting Linux Clients to a Samba Domain with Graphical Programs

Problem

You or your users prefer a nice graphical interface to find and connect to Samba shares. You want to know what is available for Gnome and KDE, and also if there are any standalone programs to use in any X Windows environment.

Solution

Here are the four best graphical utilities for network browsing and connecting to Samba shares:

- The Konqueror file manager, in KDE
- The Nautilus file manager, in Gnome
- Smb4k, a nice add-on for Konqueror
- LinNeighborhood, a standalone program than works in any X Windows environment

Discussion

Each program has its quirks. Let's look at how to use each one:

Konqueror

To browse the network, type *smb:/* in the Location bar.

To browse specific hosts, type *smb://netbios name or hostname*.

You can open and edit documents directly, and save them back to the share.

Nautilus

To browse the network, type *smb:* in the Location bar.

To go directly to a share, type *smb://servername/sharename*, like *smb://samba11/carla*.

Nautilus browses only. It does not mount shares, and it does not permit you to edit files directly. What you have to do is open a file, save it to a local drive, edit it, and then drag-and-drop a copy of the file back to the Samba share.

Smb4k

Smb4k is the easiest one to use, and has the best feature set. When you start it up, it automatically scans the network and lists all shares, and shows a nice graphic of available space on the shares. When you click on a share, it is automatically mounted in your */home/smb4k/* directory. You may configure this, as well as a number of other useful tasks, like automatically logging you in, selecting a specific server for retrieving a browse list, and configuring a list of hosts and shares that use different logins.

LinNeighborhood

LinNeighborhood is a nice, standalone LAN browser that runs in any Linux graphical environment. LinNeighborhood usually requires a bit of configuration. Open Edit → Preferences. Then, under the Scan tab, enter either the hostname or NetBIOS name of your master browser, which in this chapter is "windbag" or "samba11."

Start a new network scan with Options → Browse Entire Network.

On the Miscellaneous tab, you can enter a default username and select your default mount directory. This should be a file that already exists in your home directory, something like */home/carla/samba*.

On the Post Mount tab, configure your default file manager. Be sure to hit Save on every tab, and after you close the Preferences menu, click Edit → Save Preferences.

You can bring up a menu for logging in as different users on different shares simply by clicking on the share you want.

See Also

- Chapter 8, "Managing Users and Groups," in *Linux Cookbook*, by Carla Schroder (O'Reilly)
- Smb4K, A SMB share browser for KDE: *http://smb4k.berlios.de/*
- LinNeighborhood: *http://www.bnro.de/~schmidjo/*
- Konqueror: *http://www.konqueror.org/*
- Nautilus: *http://www.gnome.org/projects/nautilus/*

## CHAPTER 12

Centralized Network Directory with OpenLDAP

12.0 Introduction

I believe that knowing how to administer a Lightweight Directory Access Protocol (LDAP) directory server has become an essential skill for a network administrator. An LDAP directory is your key to network simplicity. It is your universal directory across all platforms and applications, supporting simplified network authentication and a centralized company data store. The LDAP protocol is cross-platform, network-aware, and standards-based. There are a large number of LDAP implementations; in this chapter, we'll use the excellent free-of-cost, free-software OpenLDAP.

LDAP is widely supported by applications; for example, most email clients come with LDAP clients. Additionally, various databases, Content Management Systems (CMS), groupware and messaging servers, authentication servers, customer management applications, and application servers can all speak to an LDAP server.

Some folks like to argue about whether LDAP is a database. Strictly speaking, it is a protocol, not a database. It accesses a special kind of database that is optimized for very fast reads. Use it for relatively static information, such as company directories, user data, customer data, passwords, asset tracking, and security keys. OpenLDAP uses the Sleepycat Berkeley DB.

Why not use an ordinary relational database like PostgreSQL, Oracle, or MySQL? You can if you like, but then you'll lose the advantages of LDAP, which are:

- Very fast reads
- Flexible data types
- Nearly universal application support
- Fine-grained control over access to data
- Distributed storage and replication
- No need for elite database guru admins
- No need for custom APIs

You don't want to use OpenLDAP for for a retail or web site backend, for example, or any application that needs fast, frequent changes. That's where you want an RDBMS.

The structure of the Sleepycat BDB is different from a relational database. Rather than storing information in columns and rows, and having a rigid set of indexes and fields, data are stored in attribute-type/attribute-value pairs. This structure offers great flexibility in designing records. A particular user record, for example, can have new types of data added without having to redesign the entire database. You can store any kind of text or binary data. Because it is simple like a large flat file, adding new entries is easy—just tack them on. OpenLDAP supports a distributed architecture, replication, and encryption.

LDAP Directory Structure

Let's take a run through the basic concepts and structure of an LDAP directory. This is more important than having an encyclopedic knowledge of configuration options, because if you don't have a clear idea of what you need and how everything fits together, LDAP will remain a mysterious mess. But it's not really all that mysterious; once you grasp the basics, you'll be in fine shape. As coaches always say, first master the fundamentals. An LDAP directory can be pictured as a standard upside-down tree structure, with the root portrayed as being the top, and the branches flowing downward. Figure 12-1 is a hierarchical namespace; it is also called the *directory information tree* (DIT).

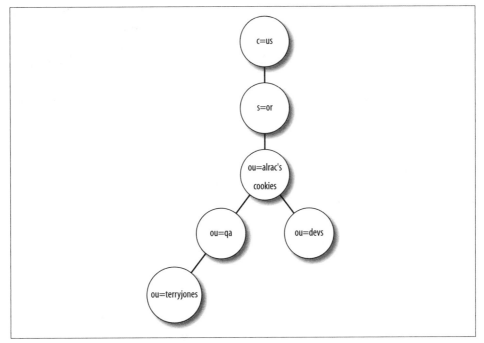

Figure 12-1. An example of an LDAP hierarchy

The root of this example directory is the *country* entry. The next stop is the *state* entry, then the *organizational unit* (OU) entry, which is the company's name. This branches off into different company entries, which are also called *organizational units*. The lefthand branch terminates at a user ID (UID). The Quality Assurance (QA) OU could hold many more users than just the one in the example.

Now comes the important bit: Terry Jones has a *distinguished name* (DN), which consists of Terry's Relative Distinguished Name (RDN), which in this example is the UID, plus tacking on all the ancestor entries: uid=terryjones, ou=qa, ou=alrac's cookies, ou=or, c=us. Any attribute can be the RDN; it must be unique within the level that the entry belongs to. The UID is usually unique because it is a common practice to make it the user's login, but you could use any other attribute. Obviously, a little common sense goes a long way here; for example, there are many duplicate surnames, so using the SN attribute would cause problems. The most common RDN for people is a UID or common name (CN).

The basic unit of your directory is an *entry*. An entry is also called a *record* or *directory object*. Terry Jones' entry contains a number of *attributes*, such as name, phone number, email address, and so forth. You can't just invent attributes out of thin air; these must be already defined in OpenLDAP. An easy way to view them is with the GQ LDAP client (*http://sourceforge.net/projects/gqclient/*). You may also see them in the files in */etc/ldap/schema* (on Fedora, */etc/openldap/schema*) in the *objectClass* definitions.

You may create your own custom objectClass definitions and attribute types. I don't recommend this unless you absolutely need something that's not included. The default *schema* are extensive, and a lot of effort has gone into making them universal; there's no need to reinvent the wheel. On the other hand (there is always another hand, isn't there), this makes OpenLDAP flexible and extensible, and it's easy to share custom schema.

Each attribute is made up of an *attribute type* and an *attribute value*. Attributes can have multiple values. For example, Terry Jones' entry could look like this:

```
uid=terryjones
cn=Terry Jones
gn=Terry
sn=Jones
telephoneNumber=123-456-7890
telephoneNumber=123-456-7891
mail=tjones@alrac.com
```

This shows a couple of duplicate attributes. You may use as many as you like. A common use for duplicate attributes is for people's names, like this:

```
cn=Terry Jones
cn=T. Jones
cn=Terry "codefiend" Jones
cn=Codefiend
```

The result of this is a search on any of these attribute values will succeed, so Terry Jones has nowhere to hide.

The *suffix* or *naming context* is the top of your LDAP hierarchy. In our simple example, the suffix is c=us. A common approach these days is to use your company's domain name, like dc=alrac,dc=net. DC stands for *domain component*.

Schemas, objectClasses, and Attributes

When you create an entry in a DIT, its data are contained in attributes. These belong to objectClasses. Schemas can be thought of as big bags of organized objectClasses. So, when you hear someone talking about OpenLDAP schemas, you know they are referring to the files that define the organization and types of data that go into an OpenLDAP directory. In OpenLDAP, some schema are hardcoded into *slapd* itself.

An objectClass is part of an objectClass hierarchy. It inherits all the properties of its parents. For example, the inetOrgPerson objectClass is one you'll use a lot. If you look inside */etc/ldap/schema/inetorgperson.schema*, you'll find this definition:

```
objectclass    ( 2.16.840.1.113730.3.2.2
    NAME 'inetOrgPerson'
    DESC 'RFC2798: Internet Organizational Person'
    SUP organizationalPerson
    STRUCTURAL
```

This snippet shows that the long objectClass number is an official Object ID (OID) number. All of the LDAP OIDs are globally unique; you can't just make them up. This only matters when you create a custom schema and need some new OIDs. Then, find a registrar to assign some to you, such as Internet Assigned Numbers Authority (IANA).

The SUP (superior) organizationalPerson line tells you that its parent objectClass is organizationalPerson, which is a child of person, which is a top-level objectClass. The objectClass defines the required and optional attributes of all of its children, which you can read in any LDAP browser.

STRUCTURAL means this objectClass can be used to create entries in your DIT. You'll also see AUXILARY objectClasses; these cannot stand alone, but must be used alongside a STRUCTURAL objectClass.

An objectClass is also an attribute.

Don't worry if this doesn't make a lot of sense right now. After you create a simple directory, you'll see how it all fits together.

The "Secret" RootDSE

One more thing you should know about: the rootDSE. This is one of those clever self-referential geek names: DSE stands for DSA Specific Entry, and DSA means Directory System Agent. This is the invisible topmost entry in your LDAP hierarchy; the built-in attributes of your LDAP server. To see these, run these two commands on your LDAP server:

```
$ ldapsearch -x -s base -b "" +
# extended LDIF
#
# LDAPv3
# base <> with scope baseObject
# filter: (objectclass=*)
# requesting: +
#

#
dn:
structuralObjectClass: OpenLDAProotDSE
configContext: cn=config
namingContexts: dc=alrac,dc=net
supportedControl: 2.16.840.1.113730.3.4.18
supportedControl: 2.16.840.1.113730.3.4.2
[...]
supportedFeatures: 1.3.6.1.4.1.4203.1.5.4
supportedFeatures: 1.3.6.1.4.1.4203.1.5.5
supportedLDAPVersion: 3
supportedSASLMechanisms: DIGEST-MD5
supportedSASLMechanisms: CRAM-MD5
supportedSASLMechanisms: NTLM
entryDN:
subschemaSubentry: cn=Subschema

# search result
search: 2
result: 0 Success

# numResponses: 2
# numEntries: 1
```

All those long numbers are official Object Identifiers (OIDs). To learn more about these, visit *http://www.alvestrand.no/objectid/*. This includes a searchable database, so you can see what a particular OID means.

This shows the same output, plus a bale of *subschema*:

```
$ ldapsearch -x -s base -b "cn=subschema" objectclasses
[...]
# Subschema
dn: cn=Subschema
objectClasses: ( 2.5.6.0 NAME 'top' DESC 'top of the superclass chain' ABSTRAC
 T MUST objectClass )
```

```
objectClasses: ( 1.3.6.1.4.1.1466.101.120.111 NAME 'extensibleObject' DESC 'RF
  C2252: extensible object' SUP top AUXILIARY )
objectClasses: ( 2.5.6.1 NAME 'alias' DESC 'RFC2256: an alias' SUP top STRUCTU
  RAL MUST aliasedObjectName )
objectClasses: ( 2.16.840.1.113730.3.2.6 NAME 'referral' DESC 'namedref: named
  subordinate referral' SUP top STRUCTURAL MUST ref )
objectClasses: ( 1.3.6.1.4.1.4203.1.4.1 NAME ( 'OpenLDAProotDSE' 'LDAProotDSE'
  ) DESC 'OpenLDAP Root DSE object' SUP top STRUCTURAL MAY cn )
objectClasses: ( 2.5.17.0 NAME 'subentry' SUP top STRUCTURAL MUST ( cn $ subtr
  eeSpecification ) )
[...]
```

That's all the same information you have in *etc/ldap/schema*. You don't need to do anything with the rootDSE; this is just to show it's there, and what it looks like. The rootDSE is sometimes confused with the *root DN*, but they are not the same thing. The rootDSE is your bare OpenLDAP server; i.e., the *schema* and supported protocols. You'll see *root DN* in a lot of documentation as your suffix name, or the base name of your data hierarchy. I avoid using the term *root DN*; it's too confusing. Oh, and then there is the rootdn. That's your directory superuser; the rootdn and rootpw directives go in *slapd.conf*. Yes, it is a bit confusing. The rootdn is all-powerful; many admins prefer to not have a rootdn at all, but instead create some sort of admin user that is defined inside the directory itself.

Deciding How Deep Your Directory Is

You're trying to plan for the future, and you want to design your DIT so smartly that it will seamlessly expand as your organization grows. It's a noble goal, for sure! So, you're wondering if you should structure it widely and shallowly, or more narrowly and deeply. This is the problem that all LDAP administrators face, and as always, the definitive answer is "it depends." My own preference is toward a shallower directory structure because it's easier to maintain, and because LDAP is optimized for searches along a level, rather than up and down the hierarchy.

Figure 12-2 shows a DIT with three OUs.

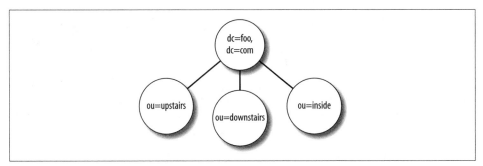

Figure 12-2. The DIT sprouts limbs

This seems all nice and organized, doesn't it? Three separate departments each with their own OU, which feels all satisfying, like a tidy filing cabinet. But think about it—what if Jenn from Upstairs gets moved to Downstairs? You'll have remove her entry from Upstairs and create a new one in Downstairs, which is several steps, no matter how efficient you are.

Now, take a look at Figure 12-3.

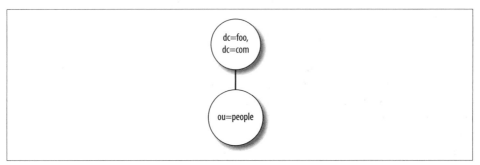

Figure 12-3. The DIT is amputated

All users are lumped into the People OU. How do we know what departments they belong to? By giving them an extra OU attribute, like this:

```
dn: cn=Jenn Dancer,ou=people,dc=foo,dc=com
objectClass: inetOrgPerson
cn: Jenn Dancer
ou=Upstairs
[...]
```

Jenn wants to move Downstairs? Piece of cake. All I do is run *ldapmodify* or a graphical LDAP browser to change ou=Upstairs to ou=Downstairs, and anything else that changes (e.g., phone number and title). This is less than half the work of moving her entry to a new OU, which requires these steps:

- Export the existing entry to an LDIF file with *ldapsearch*.
- Delete the record with *ldapdelete*.
- Edit the LDIF file.
- Add it to the new OU with *ldapadd*.

You might also think in terms of delegating responsibility to junior admins, or figuring out how to protect sensitive data. This might mean storing some data in different subtrees or separate databases, which makes administration a bit more complex, but gives you more control over who has read and write access.

This is never an easy subject, and if you ask five other LDAP admins for their advice, you'll get eight different opinions. *LDAP System Administration,* by Gerald Carter (O'Reilly), is especially helpful with figuring out your directory topology.

12.1 Installing OpenLDAP on Debian

Problem

You're ready to go to work and get your OpenLDAP server up and running. What's the best way to install it on Debian?

Solution

Just fire up Aptitude and install these packages:

```
# aptitude install slapd ldap-utils gq db4.3-doc db4.2-util
```

You will be asked to create an LDAP *admin* password. Debian will then create the LDAP *admin* user, and take your existing domain name as the suffix, or naming context.

Then, run this simple search to make sure the server is running and responding to requests:

```
# ldapsearch -xb '' -s base '(objectclass=*)' namingContexts
[...]
dn:
namingContexts: dc=alrac,dc=net
[...]
```

Run this command to show the *admin* user:

```
$ ldapsearch -xb 'dc=alrac,dc=net'
[...]
# admin, alrac.net
dn: cn=admin,dc=alrac,dc=net
objectClass: simpleSecurityObject
objectClass: organizationalRole
cn: admin
description: LDAP administrator
[...]
```

Very good! This shows success. Now, you are ready to move on to the next steps.

Discussion

Debian creates a bare-bones configuration, creates an *openldap* user, which you can see in */etc/passwd*, creates startup files and starts it at boot, and gives all the files the correct ownership and permissions. It also creates the OpenLDAP *admin* user, which is not a system user like *openldap*, but a user in the OpenLDAP directory.

You've probably seen OpenLDAP How-tos that create a rootdn and rootpw in *slapd.conf*. The rootdn is the database superuser, just like our *admin* user, and rootpw is the rootdn's password. This is necessary for the initial creation of your directory, and you may prefer to configure your database superuser this way. rootdn automatically has unrestricted access to everything, and does not need access controls, which our *admin* user does.

Some admins don't want the rootpw in *slapd.conf* for security reasons. Some admins don't want the superuser in the directory, like our *admin* user, for security reasons. If you do keep it in *slapd.conf*, make triple-sure that file is protected—make it readable only by the owner and group owner, and turn on write access only when you need to make changes.

OpenLDAP depends on the Sleepycat Berkeley DB for its backend database. Aptitude should pull in the version you need. The *db4.2-util* package includes essential commands for managing the BDB.

The *db4.3-doc* package contains the complete Sleepycat BDB manual. It's targeted at programmers, but it contains a lot of helpful information for server administrators, too. (There is no *db4.2-doc* package, but the package version mismatch doesn't matter.)

Get the version of *db4.*-util* that matches your Berkeley DB version. If you don't know which package name to look for, *dpkg* shows you what is installed on your system:

```
$ dpkg -l | grep db4
ii  libdb4.2    4.2.52+dfsg-2 Berkeley v4.2 Database Libraries [runtime]
ii  libdb4.3    4.3.29-8      Berkeley v4.3 Database Libraries [runtime]
ii  libdb4.4    4.4.20-8      Berkeley v4.4 Database Libraries [runtime]
```

You'll probably have multiple versions because a lot of applications use Berkeley DB for their backends. Find the correct version that goes with *slapd* with *apt-cache*:

```
$ apt-cache depends slapd | grep db4
Depends: libdb4.2
```

You can see your suffix, which is the base name of your directory, in */etc/ldap/slapd.conf*:

```
# The base of your directory in database #1
suffix          "dc=alrac,dc=net"
```

This is what the *ldapsearch* options mean:

-x

Bind to the directory with plaintext authentication.

-b

Start the search here.

-s

Define the scope of the search. Your choices are base, one, or sub. base means search the base object, one searches the immediate children of an entry and does not include the entry itself, sub is search the whole subtree and the entry. The default is sub.

You may install from sources if you really really want to. Please visit OpenLDAP.org (*http://www.openldap.org/*) for instructions.

See Also

- man ldapsearch
- OpenLDAP.org: *http://www.openldap.org/*
- *LDAP Directories Explained: An Introduction and Analysis*, by Brian Arkills (Addison-Wesley)

12.2   Installing OpenLDAP on Fedora

Problem

You're ready to go to work and get your OpenLDAP server up and running. What's the best way to install it on Fedora?

Solution

Fire up Yum, and install these packages:

```
# yum install openldap openldap-servers openldap-clients db4-utils gq
```

Discussion

Fedora's OpenLDAP implementation does little hand-holding. You'll have to configure it from scratch, correct some file ownerships, and create a database configuration file, which we'll get to in the next recipe. It does create startup files and an *ldap* system user, and Yum handles dependencies.

You may install from sources if you really really want to. Please visit OpenLDAP.org (*http://www.openldap.org/*) for instructions.

See Also

- OpenLDAP.org: *http://www.openldap.org/*
- *LDAP Directories Explained: An Introduction and Analysis*, by Brian Arkills (Addison-Wesley)

12.3   Configuring and Testing the OpenLDAP Server

Problem

Installing your OpenLDAP server went fine; now what do you do to start and test it?

Solution

Debian users don't need to follow this recipe because the Debian installer does all this, but it might be useful to review it anyway.

Fedora users, copy this example: */etc/openldap/slapd.conf*. Substitute your own domain name (any one will do, even *example.com*) in the brackets, and invent your own rootpw:

```
####################################################################
# Global Directives:

# Schema and objectClass definitions
include         /etc/ldap/schema/core.schema
include         /etc/ldap/schema/cosine.schema
include         /etc/ldap/schema/nis.schema
include         /etc/ldap/schema/inetorgperson.schema

pidfile         /var/run/slapd/slapd.pid
argsfile        /var/run/slapd/slapd.args

# Read slapd.conf(5) for possible values
loglevel        -1

# Where the dynamically loaded modules are stored
modulepath      /usr/lib/ldap
moduleload      back_bdb

# The maximum number of entries that is returned for a search operation
sizelimit 500

# The tool-threads parameter sets the actual amount of cpus that is used
# for indexing.
tool-threads 1

####################################################################
# Specific Backend Directives for bdb:
# Backend specific directives apply to this backend until another
# 'backend' directive occurs
backend         bdb
checkpoint 512 30

####################################################################
# Specific Directives for database #1
database        bdb
suffix "dc=[alrac],dc=[net]"
rootdn "cn=admin,dc=[alrac],dc=[net]"
rootpw [password]

# Where the database file are physically stored for database #1
directory       "/var/lib/ldap"

# Indexing options for database #1
index           objectClass eq
```

```
# Save the time that the entry gets modified, for database #1
lastmod         on

# admin can read/write all passwords
# users can change their own passwords
access to attrs=userPassword,shadowLastChange
        by dn="cn=admin,dc=alrac,dc=net" write
        by anonymous auth
        by self write
        by * none

# many applications need read access to the rootDSE
# especially to read supported SASL mechanisms
# this restricts them to the rootDSE; they cannot read past this level
access to dn.base="" by * read

# admin gets unlimited read/write access to database
# everyone else read-only
access to *
        by dn="cn=admin,dc=alrac,dc=net" write
        by * read
#######################################################################
```

Then, make sure that the files in */var/lib/ldap* are owned by the *ldap* user:

```
# chown -R ldap:ldap /var/lib/ldap
```

If there is no */var/lib/ldap/DB_CONFIG* file, create an empty one:

```
# touch /var/lib/ldap/DB_CONFIG
```

Next, run the slaptest command to check */etc/ldap/slapd.conf*:

```
# slaptest
config file testing succeeded
```

Now, start it up:

```
# /etc/init.d/ldap start
Checking configuration files for slapd: config file testing succeeded
                                                        [  OK  ]
Started slapd:                                          [  OK  ]
```

Finally, run this simple search to make sure the server is running and responding to requests:

```
# ldapsearch -x -b '' -s base '(objectclass=*)' namingContexts
[...]
dn:
namingContexts: dc=alrac,dc=net
[...]
```

Very good! This shows success. Now, you are ready to move on to the next steps.

Discussion

Debian users don't need `rootpw` or `rootdn`; these will go away in the next recipe anyway.

`loglevel -1` means log everything, and this can add up to megabytes dumped into the *syslog* in a hurry. See Recipe 12.12 for more information.

See the Discussion in Recipe 12.1 for an explanation of the *ldapsearch* options.

When you run *slaptest*, you may see warnings. *slapd* should run anyway, but you should always fix whatever is causing the warnings. Some common errors on Fedora are caused by:

- Incorrect file permissions or ownership
- A missing */var/lib/ldap/DB_CONFIG*

Following the steps in this recipe should prevent any errors. For example, if the files in */var/lib/ldap* are not owned by the *ldap* user, you'll get "permission denied" errors. If *DB_CONFIG* is missing, you'll get a warning, but *slapd* will still run.

DB_CONFIG contains options to tune the Berkeley DB backend. See Recipe 12.11 to learn how to configure it.

This is a bare setup just to test the basics; having a `rootpw` password in *slapd.conf* isn't the best thing to do from a security perspective, and we haven't really built a directory yet. But we are getting there.

See Also

- `man ldapsearch`
- OpenLDAP.org: *http://www.openldap.org/*
- *LDAP Directories Explained: An Introduction and Analysis*, by Brian Arkills (Addison-Wesley)

12.4 Creating a New Database on Fedora

Problem

Your Fedora OpenLDAP installation does not yet include an administrative user, nor any users at all. You need to create an *admin* user to manage your directory, and you also need to define your *suffix*.

Solution

There are three steps:

1. Create an LDIF file with the new information.

2. Use the *ldapadd* command to add the new entries to Berkeley DB.

3. Configure read-write permissions in *slapd.conf*.

First, create the LDAP Data Interchange Format (LDIF) file, which in this example is named *first.ldif*. Substitute your own domain name, company name, description, and password. Trim all leading and trailing spaces. A blank line separates entries, comments must go on their own lines, and there must be one space after each colon:

```
##first.ldif
# root dn entry
dn: dc=alrac,dc=net
objectclass: dcObject
objectclass: organization
o: Alrac's Fine Cookies and Beer
dc: alrac

# directory administrator
dn: cn=admin,dc=alrac,dc=net
objectClass: simpleSecurityObject
objectClass: organizationalRole
cn: admin
userPassword: bigsecretword
description: LDAP administrator
```

Second, run this *ldapadd* command. You'll be asked for the rootpw password you entered in *slapd.conf*:

```
# ldapadd -x -D "cn=admin,dc=alrac,dc=net" -W -f first.ldif
Enter LDAP Password:
adding new entry "dc=alrac,dc=net"
adding new entry "cn=admin,dc=alrac,dc=net"
```

Let us admire the new entries:

```
$ ldapsearch -x -b 'dc=alrac,dc=net'
[...]
# alrac.net
dn: dc=alrac,dc=net
objectClass: dcObject
objectClass: organization
o: Alrac's Fine Cookies and Beer
dc: alrac

# admin, alrac.net
dn: cn=admin,dc=alrac,dc=net
objectClass: simpleSecurityObject
objectClass: organizationalRole
cn: admin
userPassword: fji8Hu11hs
description: LDAP administrator
[...]
```

Comment out the `rootpw` and `rootdn` entries in *slapd.conf*. Then, restart OpenLDAP, and view the directory entries again:

```
# /etc/init.d/ldap restart
$ ldapsearch -x -b 'dc=alrac,dc=net'
```

Now, the *admin* user has complete control of the database.

Discussion

Mind the whitespace in your LDIF files. A blank line delimits each entry. A single leading space on a line means it is a continuation of the previous line, commas delimit each name/value pair, and any literal commas must be escaped, like this example shows:

```
dn: uid=twhale,ou=people,ou=factory,ou=bluecollars,
    o=widgets\, inc.,c=au,dc=widgets,dc=com
```

The *admin* user can have any name, such as *db-admin*, or *ldapgoddess*, or whatever you like. You'll see the *Manager* user in a lot of LDAP documentation, which is the same as our *admin* user.

The *first.ldif* file contains two separate entries. The first one defines our *suffix*. That's the *root* of our directory tree. The second entry defines the *admin* user, who is given read/write access to the entire database in *slapd.conf*. All other users are given read access only. They can change their own passwords, and they cannot see anyone else's password.

Each entry requires its own unique DN. Remember, these are made by combining the Relative Distinguished Name (RDN) with all of its ancestors. (See this chapter's Introduction for more information.)

Your LDIF files don't have to use the *.ldif* file extension. It's probably less confusing to keep it, though.

Why replace the `rootdn` and `rootpw` in *slapd.conf*? The `rootdn` is the database superuser, just like our *admin* user, and `rootpw` is the `rootdn`'s password. This is necessary for the initial creation of your directory, and you may prefer to configure your database superuser this way. Some admins don't want a `rootdn` in *slapd.conf* for security reasons. Some admins don't want the superuser in the directory, like our *admin* user, for security reasons. If you do keep it in *slapd.conf*, make triple-sure that file is protected—make it readable only by the owner and group owner, and turn on write access only when you need to make changes.

The *admin* ACLs we created in the previous recipe in *slapd.conf* are not necessary if you choose to keep `rootdn` in *slapd.conf*. `rootdn` does not need explicit access rules.

ObjectClasses and attributes

Fire up a graphical LDAP browser like *gq* to see the available attributes for each objectClass. This is an easy way to see what your choices are. You may also look in the schema files in */etc/ldap/schema/* (*/etc/openldap* on Fedora). inetOrgPerson is one you'll use a lot. */etc/ldap/schema/inetorgperson.schema* defines what attributes are required, and which ones are optional:

```
# inetOrgPerson
# The inetOrgPerson represents people who are associated with an
# organization in some way.  It is a structural class and is derived
# from the organizationalPerson which is defined in X.521 [X521].
objectclass     ( 2.16.840.1.113730.3.2.2
    NAME 'inetOrgPerson'
    DESC 'RFC2798: Internet Organizational Person'
    SUP organizationalPerson
    STRUCTURAL
    MAY (
        audio $ businessCategory $ carLicense $ departmentNumber $
        displayName $ employeeNumber $ employeeType $ givenName $
        homePhone $ homePostalAddress $ initials $ jpegPhoto $
        labeledURI $ mail $ manager $ mobile $ o $ pager $
        photo $ roomNumber $ secretary $ uid $ userCertificate $
        x500uniqueIdentifier $ preferredLanguage $
        userSMIMECertificate $ userPKCS12 )
    )
```

As this shows, all of them are optional. The simpleSecurityObject is less complex; it has only a single required attribute:

```
objectclass ( 0.9.2342.19200300.100.4.19 NAME 'simpleSecurityObject'
    DESC 'RFC1274: simple security object'
    SUP top AUXILIARY
    MUST userPassword )
```

See Also

- man 1 ldapsearch
- OpenLDAP.org: *http://www.openldap.org/*
- *LDAP Directories Explained: An Introduction and Analysis*, by Brian Arkills (Addison-Wesley)
- *LDAP System Administration*, by Gerald Carter (O'Reilly)

12.5   Adding More Users to Your Directory

Problem

You're ready to start stuffing more users into your OpenLDAP directory. How do you do this?

Solution

Make sure your OpenLDAP server is running. Next, create an LDIF file containing your new user entries, then use *ldapadd* to export them into your OpenLDAP directory.

We're going to expand our directory structure a bit, because right now it's just a plain old one-level directory. We want to be organized and not just dump everything into the top level, so we're going to add a people Organizational Unit (OU). Our directory now looks like Figure 12-4.

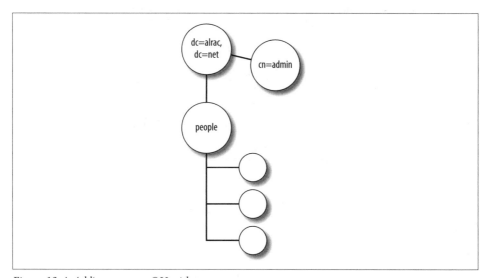

Figure 12-4. Adding one new OU with users

You can see our *admin* user hanging out there all alone. (It's lonely at the top.)

This example *users.ldif* file adds the new OU and two human users. Mind your whitespace! Comments must be on separate lines, there must be one space after each colon, and a blank line separates entries:

```
##/etc/ldap/ldif/users.ldif
dn: ou=people,dc=alrac,dc=net
ou: people
description: All people in organisation
objectClass: organizationalUnit

dn: uid=cschroder,ou=people,dc=alrac,dc=net
objectClass: inetOrgPerson
```

```
cn: Carla Schroder
sn: Schroder
uid: cschroder
userPassword: password
telephoneNumber: 444-222-3333
homePhone: 555-111-2222
mail: carla@bratgrrl.com
mail: carla@gmail.com
description: indescribable

dn: uid=thanson,ou=people,dc=alrac,dc=net
objectClass: inetOrgPerson
cn: Terry Hanson
sn: Hanson
uid: thanson
userPassword: password
telephoneNumber: 222-333-4455
homePhone: 112-334-5678
mail: terry@bratgrrl.com
mail: terry@gmail.com
description: absolutely fabulous
```

Now, add the new entries to the database:

```
# ldapadd -x -D "cn=admin,dc=alrac,dc=net" -W -f users.ldif
Enter LDAP Password:
adding new entry "ou=people,dc=alrac,dc=net"
adding new entry "uid=cschroder,ou=people,dc=alrac,dc=net"
adding new entry "uid=thanson,ou=people,dc=alrac,dc=net"
```

Then, run the usual *ldapsearch* command to verify your entries:

```
$ ldapsearch -x -b 'dc=alrac,dc=net'
```

To add more users, you need to create a new *.ldif* file, or overwrite the old one. You can't just add new entries to your existing file, because when *ldapadd* finds an existing entry, it stops and does not read the rest of the file.

Discussion

ldapadd requires a running server; it won't work if *slapd* is not running. All commands that start with "ldap" operate on a running server. The "slap" commands, like *slapcat* and *slapadd*, require that *slapd* is not running. See the Discussion in the previous recipe to learn the finer points of creating LDIF files.

See Also

- man 1 ldapsearch
- OpenLDAP.org: *http://www.openldap.org/*
- *LDAP Directories Explained: An Introduction and Analysis*, by Brian Arkills (Addison-Wesley)
- *LDAP System Administration*, by Gerald Carter (O'Reilly)

12.6   Correcting Directory Entries

Problem

Users changed, or you made a mistake, so you want to change an existing directory entry. How do you do this?

Solution

One way is using *ldapmodify*. You'll need to create a new LDIF file in a special format. This example adds a title, changes the email address, and adds a photograph:

```
##/etc/ldap/modfile.ldif
dn: uid=thanson,ou=people,dc=alrac,dc=net
changetype:modify
add:title
title:Fire Marshal
-
replace:mail
mail:terry@wolfgrrl.com
-
add: jpegphoto
jpegphoto:< file:///filename.jpg
```

Next, use the LDIF file this way:

```
# ldapmodify -x -D "cn=admin,dc=alrac,dc=net" -W -f modfile.ldif
Enter LDAP Password:
modifying entry "cn=Terry Hanson,ou=people,dc=alrac,dc=net"
```

Then, verify it with *ldapsearch*:

```
$ ldapsearch -xtb 'dc=alrac,dc=net' 'cn=terry hanson'
[...]
# Terry Hanson, people, alrac.net
dn: cn=Terry Hanson,ou=people,dc=alrac,dc=net
objectClass: inetOrgPerson
cn: Terry Hanson
sn: Hanson
uid: thanson
telephoneNumber: 333.444.4545
homePhone: 222-333-5555
description: burning down the house
title: Fire Marshal
mail: terry@wolfgrrl.com
jpegPhoto:< file:///tmp/ldapsearch-jpegPhoto-Sx11P8
[...]
```

Discussion

For changes to a small number of entries, a graphical LDAP browser (see Recipe 12.10) is usually faster and easier. Using LDIFs is usually faster for bulk changes and for ace scripting gurus.

Note the new -t option to ldapsearch. This tells *ldapsearch* to store photos, audio files, or other noncharacter data in temporary files. If you don't use this, you'll get masses of encoding, like this:

```
fdtvWuJG2BwGFzjms1d7eTubLmBp5EFktAAPZfvNUzNVthoyz6sMbkgtSAd6dj3mqudjOCW6QxUAItBmSbQw
638J7W+NQArNTIZ4wNQbkdXh3sATNVnpSns2yveXHeYU5+1o46yelp6puO2LGcYBKimkNyRuq/j+/QUGJBp
3mdwf3q2PTbca2gFkCkkKVRixIltTMw4m3+91vTmZYaGy5Ktbxnq0
```

When you're adding a JPEG photograph, it must be available, or *ldapmodify* will return with the message ldapmodify: invalid format. That is a long way from "I can't find the file," but that's what it means. JPEGs are imported into the database in base-64 MIME encoding. If you're going to include ID photographs of people, make sure they are small in physical and file size, or they're going to look strange in your LDAP clients.

OpenLDAP is finicky about the format and syntax of a changefile. Start with the DN to identify the entry, then the keyword changetype followed by the type of change: add, modify, modrdn, or delete. Deleting an entry requires only two lines:

```
dn: cn=Terry Hanson,ou=people,dc=alrac,dc=net
changetype:delete
```

The syntax for the jpegPhoto and audio attributes is fussy:

```
jpegphoto:< file:///filename.jpg
```

There must be no space between :<, and then one space. file:// has two slashes, then the filename.

When you're modifying an existing entry, your possible keywords are add, replace, or delete. replace is all-or-nothing; for example, if the entry has three email addresses, and your LDIF file contains:

```
replace: mail
mail: thanson@foosite.com
```

It will delete the three old addresses, and then add the one new one.

delete can be all-or-nothing, or selective. If your entry has three homePhone attributes, and you use:

```
delete: homephone
```

then all three will be deleted. To delete a single attribute, do this:

```
delete: homephone
homePhone: 222-333-5555
```

See Also

- OpenLDAP.org: *http://www.openldap.org/*
- *LDAP Directories Explained: An Introduction and Analysis*, by Brian Arkills (Addison-Wesley)
- *LDAP System Administration*, by Gerald Carter (O'Reilly)

12.7 Connecting to a Remote OpenLDAP Server

Problem

You're not always going to be sitting at your physical server, or you want to run it headless, so you need to know how to administer your OpenLDAP server remotely.

Solution

All of the OpenLDAP commands use the same -H option to connect to a remote host, like this example for a local network that uses the server's hostname:

```
# ldapsearch -H ldap://xena -xtb 'dc=alrac,dc=net'
```

Or, you may use the fully qualified domain name:

```
# ldapsearch -H ldap://xena.alrac.net -xtb 'dc=alrac,dc=net'
```

Or, specify the port. You don't need to do this unless you're using an alternate port:

```
# ldapsearch -H ldap://xena.alrac.net:389 -xtb 'dc=alrac,dc=net'
```

Discussion

A lot of documentation still refers to using the lowercase -h, but this has been deprecated, and someday will go away for good.

You don't have to use just the options in the example commands; any OpenLDAP command can be run remotely (e.g., searches, making changes, etc.).

See Also

- man 1 ldapsearch
- man 1 ldapmodify
- OpenLDAP.org: *http://www.openldap.org/*
- *LDAP Directories Explained: An Introduction and Analysis*, by Brian Arkills (Addison-Wesley)
- *LDAP System Administration*, by Gerald Carter (O'Reilly)

12.8 Finding Things in Your OpenLDAP Directory

Problem

Your directory is growing, and you want to know how to fine-tune your searches so you can pluck out just the information you want, and not have to wade through a bunch of irrelevant stuff.

Solution

The ldapsearch command comes with a host of options for searching on every imaginable attribute. This command searches for a specific user by common name (CN):

```
$ ldapsearch -xtb 'dc=alrac,dc=net' 'cn=carla'
```

If you're not quite sure what to look for, you can use wildcards. This example searches for UIDs that end in *schroder*:

```
$ ldapsearch -xtb 'dc=alrac,dc=net' 'uid=*schroder'
```

Maybe you want all the entries with a certain phone prefix:

```
$ ldapsearch -xtb 'ou=people,dc=alrac,dc=net' '(telephoneNumber=333*)'
```

You might want a list of attributes only, without the values:

```
$ ldapsearch -xtb 'dc=alrac,dc=net' 'cn=carla' -A
```

You can start from a different level in your DIT:

```
$ ldapsearch -xtb 'ou=people,dc=alrac,dc=net' 'cn=carla'
```

You can limit the size of your search, like this example that searches for entries with photos, and limits the results to 10 entries:

```
$ ldapsearch -z 10 -xtb 'ou=people,dc=alrac,dc=net' '(jpegPhoto=*)'
```

This command makes a list of objectClasses used in your directory:

```
$ ldapsearch -xb 'dc=alrac,dc=net' '(objectclass=*)' dcObject
```

Or, search for entries with specific objectClasses:

```
$ ldapsearch -xb 'dc=alrac,dc=net' '(objectclass=simpleSecurityObject)'
```

Combine attributes to narrow searches, such as users with a certain phone prefix and mail domain:

```
$ ldapsearch -xtb 'dc=alrac,dc=net' '(&(mail=*domain.com)(telephoneNumber=333*))'
```

Or, list all users at a specific mail domain except the ones with the specified phone prefix (mind your parentheses):

```
$ ldapsearch -xtb 'dc=alrac,dc=net' '(&(mail=*domain.com)(!(telephoneNumber=333*)))'
```

Discussion

If you're thinking, "Forget this, I'm making a beeline to those nice graphical LDAP clients," slow down. Those nice graphical interfaces still require a knowledge of the OpenLDAP commands.

Here are some examples of the syntax for various search expressions:

Match this value

```
(attribute=value)
(objectclass=name)
```

Approximately match this value; this requires an approx index; see Recipe 12.9 for more information

    (attribute~=value)

Match all these values

    (&(exp1)(exp2)(exp3))

Match any of these values; exp1 OR exp2 OR exp3

    (|(exp1)(exp2)(exp3))

Exclude this value

    (!(exp1))

Exclude both of these values

    (&(!(exp1))(!(exp2)))

Exclude either of these values

    (|(!(exp1))(!(exp2)))

There are some other available search types, though I haven't found them to be useful because these depend on the attribute having an *ordering* rule, and most of them don't:

Match results that are greater than

    (attribute>=value)

Match results that are less than

    (attribute<=value)

See Also

- man 1 ldapsearch
- OpenLDAP.org: *http://www.openldap.org/*
- *LDAP Directories Explained: An Introduction and Analysis*, by Brian Arkills (Addison-Wesley)
- *LDAP System Administration*, by Gerald Carter (O'Reilly)

12.9   Indexing Your Database

Problem

You noticed there are some indexing options in *slapd.conf*—what's that all about? Will they make your directory go faster?

Solution

Indeed they will. Indexing attributes that are frequently searched for will speed up performance. Here are some sample indexes for different uses:

```
#always have this one
index  objectClass  eq
```

```
#for common name searches
index cn,sn,uid   pres,eq,sub

#email address searches
index mail   pres,eq
```

These go into *slapd.conf*.

Discussion

If you change the index settings while *slapd* is running, an internal task will automatically run and generate the new indexes. You don't need to explicitly regenerate the indexes. However, if *slapd* is stopped before the indexing task is finished, you'll have to manually generate the new indexes with the slapindex command:

```
# /etc/init.d/slapd stop (Debian)
# /etc/init.d/ldap stop (Fedora)
#  slapindex
```

When it's finished, restart OpenLDAP. If you have a large directory, this process will take a few minutes.

Indexing increases the size of your *id2entry* file. The larger your database and the more indexes you have, the bigger this file will grow. This post from the OpenLDAP-devel list (*http://www.openldap.org/lists/openldap-devel/200510/msg00131.html*) says:

> For my test database with 360 MB input LDIF and 285,000 entries and 15 indexed attributes, using a 512 MB BDB cache…. The resulting id2entry database is about 800 MB; with all indexing the total size is around 2.1 GB.

The syntax for indexing is:

```
index [attributes] [index type]
```

Multiple attributes and index types are comma-delimited. These are the most useful index types:

pres
> Match on the attribute type, rather than the value of the attribute. For example, search for attributes like (objectclass=inetOrgPerson) or (attribute=mail).

eq
> Match the exact *attribute* value, like (cn=fred) returns only exact "fred" matches.

sub
> Indexes for wildcard searches, like (cn=lisa*). There are several variations on sub. For example, subinitial is optimized for (cn=lisa*)-type searches, subfinal is optimized for (cn=*smith)-type searches, and *subany* is optimized for (cn=*isa*).

Creating unnecessary indexes will hurt performance. Unindexed searches will always succeed; your goal is to index the most common searches, and not worry about infrequent search types. Smart indexing will boost performance noticeably. Watch your logfiles to see what your users or applications are looking for; that's your best guide to deciding what to index. See Recipe 12.12 for more information.

See Also

- man 8 slapindex
- OpenLDAP.org: *http://www.openldap.org/*
- *LDAP Directories Explained: An Introduction and Analysis*, by Brian Arkills (Addison-Wesley)
- *LDAP System Administration*, by Gerald Carter (O'Reilly)

12.10 Managing Your Directory with Graphical Interfaces

Problem

You want some nice graphical tools for managing your LDAP directory.

Solution

There are quite a number of graphical LDAP directory viewers and managers in varying degrees of usefulness and polish. You still need to know the OpenLDAP commands, but a good graphical interface can make you more efficient. Here are some nice open source applications:

GQ (http://gq-project.org/)
> This is a fairly simple standalone LDAP client. It is a browser and an editor. You can easily browse schema details, and see your directory structure as Figure 12-5 shows. You may also authenticate to create or edit entries.

Web browsers
> Konqueror and Internet Explorer include simple LDAP viewers. You can see your directory, but not edit it. Enter a URL containing your suffix, like *ldap:// localhost:389/dc=alrac,dc=net*, and you'll see something like Figure 12-6.

LAT, LDAP Administration Tool (http://dev.mmgsecurity.com/projects/lat/)
> A nice, fully featured viewer and editor (see Figure 12-7). It includes tools for Samba and Active Directory integration, a good search tool, LDIF imports and exports, and other essential management features.

Web-based LDAP managers
> phpLDAPadmin (*http://phpldapadmin.sourceforge.net/*) and Gosa (*https://www. gosa-project.org/*) are two popular web-based LDAP managers. They're rather complex, as PHP applications tend to be, because they depend on HTTP servers, PHP, and various modules and libraries. So, they both have learning curves, but the advantages are attractive interfaces, universal clients, and the fact that any PHP coder can extend and customize them.

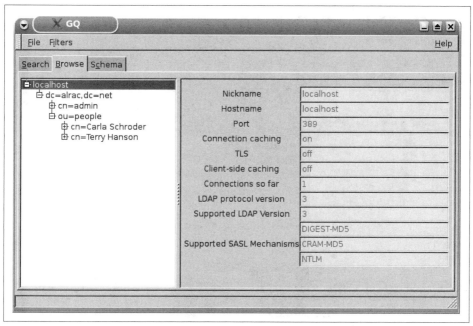

Figure 12-5. GQ's view of our LDAP directory

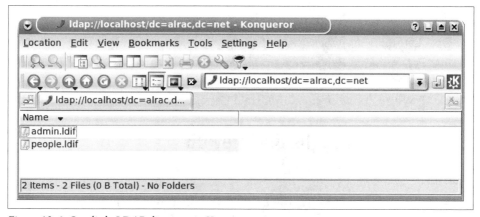

Figure 12-6. Our little LDAP directory in Konqueror

Discussion

Like all good Linux admins, you don't want to run X Windows on your LDAP server, and with any of these applications, you won't need to because they all support secure remote access.

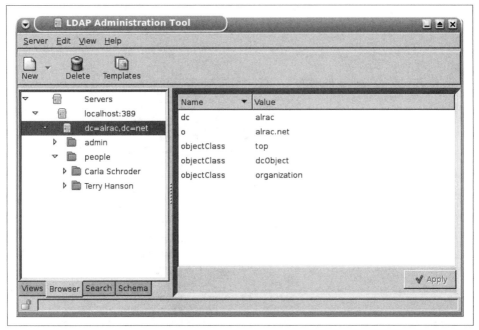

Figure 12-7. LAT's view of the directory

See Also

- OpenLDAP.org: *http://www.openldap.org/*
- *LDAP Directories Explained: An Introduction and Analysis*, by Brian Arkills (Addison-Wesley)
- *LDAP System Administration*, by Gerald Carter (O'Reilly)

12.11 Configuring the Berkeley DB

Problem

You know that you need to use the */var/lib/ldap/DB_CONFIG* file to configure the database backend to your LDAP directory (Berkeley DB) so that it will perform peppily and not get all bogged down. How do you know what options and values to use?

Solution

We'll start off with some reasonable values for starters, and then learn how to make some calculations to fine-tune them.

Be sure to check your *slapd.conf* for duplicate BDB entries and get rid of them. They can go in either file, but it's best to keep them all in *DB_CONFIG*. You don't want duplicates or conflicting entries.

First, make sure there is a cachesize entry in *slapd.conf*:

```
cachesize 5000
```

Then, enter these options and values into */var/lib/ldap/DB_CONFIG*:

```
##/var/lib/ldap/DB_CONFIG
set_cachesize 0 1048576 0
set_lk_max_objects 1500
set_lk_max_locks 1500
set_lk_max_lockers 1500
#
#logging settings
set_lg_regionmax 1048576
set_lg_bsize 32768
set_lg_max 131072
set_lg_dir /var/log/openldap
```

The set_cachesize value is in bytes, and must be a power of 2, so the example is one megabyte. How do you know how much to use? Use the *db4.2_stat* command on Debian, and the *db_stat* command on Fedora to generate statistics from *id2entry.bdb* and *dn2id.bdb*, which are the two main database files:

```
# db4.2_stat -d /var/lib/ldap/id2entry.bdb
53162    Btree magic number.
9        Btree version number.
Flags:   little-endian
2        Minimum keys per-page.
16384    Underlying database page size.
1        Number of levels in the tree.
6        Number of unique keys in the tree.
6        Number of data items in the tree.
0        Number of tree internal pages.
0        Number of bytes free in tree internal pages (0% ff).
1        Number of tree leaf pages.
12374    Number of bytes free in tree leaf pages (24% ff).
0        Number of tree duplicate pages.
0        Number of bytes free in tree duplicate pages (0% ff).
0        Number of tree overflow pages.
0        Number of bytes free in tree overflow pages (0% ff).
0        Number of pages on the free list.

# db4.2_stat -d /var/lib/ldap/dn2id.bdb
53162    Btree magic number.
9        Btree version number.
Flags:   duplicates, little-endian
2        Minimum keys per-page.
4096     Underlying database page size.
1        Number of levels in the tree.
13       Number of unique keys in the tree.
19       Number of data items in the tree.
0        Number of tree internal pages.
0        Number of bytes free in tree internal pages (0% ff).
1        Number of tree leaf pages.
3378     Number of bytes free in tree leaf pages (18% ff).
```

```
0        Number of tree duplicate pages.
0        Number of bytes free in tree duplicate pages (0% ff).
0        Number of tree overflow pages.
0        Number of bytes free in tree overflow pages (0% ff).
0        Number of pages on the free list.
```

You can see that each *id2entry.bdb* page requires 16 KB, and *dn2id.bdb* needs 4 KB per page, and the number of internal pages each one is using. So, you can use this formula to calculate a bare minimum memory requirement:

((50+1) * 4096) + ((12+1) * 16384)) = 421,888 bytes

This does not take into account other library overhead or indexing. As a shortcut, double this figure for decent performance. So, for this example, we could round it up to a whopping 1 MB of RAM.

How do you know what values to assign to set_lk_max_objects 1500, set_lk_max_locks 1500, and set_lk_max_lockers 1500? Use the db4.2_stat -c (db_stat on Fedora) command:

```
# cd /var/lib/ldap
# db4.2_stat -c
100      Last allocated locker ID.
2147M    Current maximum unused locker ID.
9        Number of lock modes.
1500     Maximum number of locks possible.
1500     Maximum number of lockers possible.
1500     Maximum number of lock objects possible.
3        Number of current locks.
11       Maximum number of locks at any one time.
12       Number of current lockers.
19       Maximum number of lockers at any one time.
3        Number of current lock objects.
8        Maximum number of lock objects at any one time.
1170     Total number of locks requested.
1167     Total number of locks released.
0        Total number of lock requests failing because DB_LOCK_NOWAIT was set.
0        Total number of locks not immediately available due to conflicts.
0        Number of deadlocks.
0        Lock timeout value.
0        Number of locks that have timed out.
0        Transaction timeout value.
0        Number of transactions that have timed out.
552KB    The size of the lock region..
0        The number of region locks granted after waiting.
2579     The number of region locks granted without waiting.
```

1500 is a reasonable starting point for a smaller directory; use your db4.2_stat -c output to decide if you need to increase it. When usage hits 85 percent of your allocated values, increase them. Look at your *Number of current values* outputs, timeouts, and failures.

For OpenLDAP versions 2.3 and above, all you need to do after changing *DB_CONFIG* is restart *slapd*:

```
# /etc/init.d/slapd restart (Debian)
# /etc/init.d/ldap restart  (Fedora)
```

However, this doesn't always work, so if *slaptest* returns errors, and is on 2.2 and older, Debian users need to use the database recovery command:

```
# /etc/init.d/slapd stop
# db4.2_recover -h /var/lib/ldap
# /etc/init.d/slapd start
```

Fedora users have slightly different commands:

```
# /etc/init.d/ldap stop
# db_recover -h /var/lib/ldap
# /etc/init.d/ldap start
```

Then, run this command to verify your new cache size. These examples are based on a value of 16777216 in *DB_CONFIG*. As usual, the Debian command is first, Fedora second:

```
# db4.2_stat -h /var/lib/ldap -m | head -n 2
20MB 1KB 604B   Total cache size.
1        Number of caches.
# db_stat -h /var/lib/ldap -m | head -n 2
```

Now, keep an eye on the performance while *slapd* is running. Change to the directory your database is stored in:

```
# cd /var/lib/ldap
# db4.2_stat -m  (Debian)
# db_stat -m  (Fedora)
```

This displays complete cache statistics.

Discussion

cachesize defines the number of entries that the LDAP backend will keep in memory. For best performance, this number is equal to the number of entries in your directory, but it can be smaller. This is not the BDB cache, but OpenLDAP's own internal cache. The default is 1000.

Watch your disk I/O—*iostat* is a good tool for this—and keep an eye on the *Requested pages found in the cache* value, which you get from running db_stat -m in your database directory. You want this to be as close to 100 percent as possible, and the pages forced from the cache should be 0. If it falls under 95 percent, increase your set_cachesize value. You want requests to be answered from the memory cache as much as possible; you don't want a lot of disk thrashing.

set_cachesize has three fields: <gbytes>, <bytes>, and <ncache>. If you want to create a 2 GB cache, it looks like set_cachesize 2 0 0. You may combine both gigabytes and bytes. The maximum is 4 GB. Don't make your cache larger than your total system memory. Any cache size less than 500 MB is automatically increased by 25 percent to account for buffer pool overhead.

ncache tells BDB if it should use one contiguous section of memory, or more than one. 0 or 1 means one segment; a larger number means create that number of segments. Modern Linux kernels support 1–3 GB per user process on 32-bit x86 systems, and don't forget that the kernel needs a good-sized chunk as well. This example splits a 2 GB cache across two segments:

```
set_cachesize 2 0 2
```

On 64-bit systems, theoretically your whole memory space, except the bit reserved for the kernel, can be used by a single process.

Creating a too-big set_cachesize value can hurt overall system performance, but it won't hurt OpenLDAP, so you can set a generous value if you have abundant RAM. If you need to be frugal with your available RAM, check the See Also section for detailed references on making finer calculations.

The set_lk_max_locks, set_lk_max_lockers, and set_lk_max_objects set the maximum number of locks, lockers, and locked objects, respectively. If the values are too small, requests for locks will fail. If the values are too large, the locking subsystem will use more resources than it really needs. It's safer to have too much. Run db4.2_stat -c (db_stat -c in Fedora) in your database directory to keep tabs on this.

The locking subsystem keeps reads and writes in order. Anything that is writing to the BDB gets an exclusive lock on the object it is writing to. Reads are shared.

Configuring logging will also affect performance. This is what the examples mean:

set_lg_regionmax
: The maximum memory cache in bytes for database file name caching. Increase this value as the number of database files increases. Every attribute that you configure for indexing uses one file to store its index, plus *id2entry* and *dn2id* which always exist.

set_lg_bsize
: The size of the memory cache for logging data, in bytes. When the cache is full, it will be flushed to disk.

set_lg_max
: Maximum size of logfile, in bytes. When it reaches the limit, the file is rotated. This should be a minimum of four times set_lg_bsize.

set_lg_dir
: Directory for the logfiles. For best performance, store logfiles on a separate disk, or remote network share.

slapd -V
: Gives the OpenLDAP server version.

See Also

- OpenLDAP Performance Tuning:

    http://www.openldap.org/faq/data/cache/190.html

- Getting Started with Berkeley DB:

    http://www.oracle.com/technology/documentation/berkeley-db/db/gsg/C/index.html

- Chapter 4 of *Getting Started with Berkeley DB XML Transaction Processing* (*http://www.oracle.com/technology/documentation/berkeley-db/xml/gsg_xml_txn/java/blocking_deadlocks.html*); see the section, "Locks, Blocks, and Deadlocks"

12.12 Configuring OpenLDAP Logging

Problem

OpenLDAP's default setup dumps logging into the *syslog*, and you would rather it have its own separate logfile. How do you do this?

Solution

First, we'll create a separate directory and an empty logfile:

```
# mkdir /var/log/openldap
# touch /var/log/openldap/ldap.log
```

Then, add these lines to */etc/syslog.conf*:

```
#Logging for openldap
local4.* /var/log/openldap/ldap.log
```

And set your desired logging level in *slapd.conf,* in the Global section:

```
loglevel        256
```

Now, restart both OpenLDAP and the *syslog* daemon:

```
# /etc/init.d/slapd restart (Debian)
# /etc/init.d/ldap restart   (Fedora)
# /etc/init.d/sysklogd restart (Debian)
# /etc/init.d/syslog restart (Fedora)
```

Run some searches to generate some activity, then check your logfile. It should be full of entries like this:

```
May 22 11:53:32 xena slapd[7686]: conn=5 fd=11 ACCEPT from IP=127.0.0.1:33643 (IP=0.
0.0.0:389)
May 22 11:53:32 xena slapd[7686]: conn=5 op=0 BIND dn="" method=128
May 22 11:53:32 xena slapd[7686]: conn=5 op=0 RESULT tag=97 err=0 text=
May 22 11:53:32 xena slapd[7686]: conn=5 op=1 SRCH base="dc=alrac,dc=net" scope=2
deref=0 filter="(objectClass=*)"
```

Discussion

The available logging levels for OpenLDAP are a bit complicated. `man 5 slapd.conf` lists all of them. The default is `256`, which logs statistics like connections, operations, and results. `-1` logs everything, so beware! A busy OpenLDAP server will generate megabytes of logfiles at this level in no time. Some admins disable logging entirely with the `0` option, and turn it on periodically for analysis or troubleshooting. Some high-priority messages are logged regardless of your logging level, so you should still route them to a separate file.

Logging can bog down performance noticeably, so one tweak you can make is to use the minus prefix in *syslog.conf*:

```
local4.*  -/var/log/openldap/ldap.log
```

This tells the *syslog* daemon to not synchronize the file after every write. The risk is you could lose some data if the system crashes, but it makes a noticeable difference in performance on a heavily loaded server.

Each logging level is not a different verbosity, but a different subsystem. So, you can combine them like this to log different activities:

```
256 + 32 + 8
```

Using a remote logging server takes a lot of the load away from your OpenLDAP server. See Chapter 19 for recipes on setting up a logging server using Syslog-ng.

See Also

- `man 5 slapd.conf`
- OpenLDAP.org: *http://www.openldap.org/*
- *LDAP Directories Explained: An Introduction and Analysis*, by Brian Arkills (Addison-Wesley)
- *LDAP System Administration*, by Gerald Carter (O'Reilly)

12.13 Backing Up and Restoring Your Directory

Problem

Is there a special way to back up and restore your OpenLDAP directory, or can you use standard Linux utilities like *rsync*?

Solution

You can copy your database files just like any other files, so go ahead and include them in your normal system backup. The `directory` option in *slapd.conf* defines the database directory. You should also use the two special OpenLDAP commands for backups and restores: *slapcat* and *slapadd*.

slapcat exports the contents of your database (which is defined in *slapd.conf*) into an LDIF-formatted file. If you have only one database, first stop your server, then run *slapcat*:

```
# /etc/init.d/slapd stop (Debian)
# /etc/init.d/ldap stop (Fedora)
# slapcat -l backupfile.ldif
```

If you have more than one, you should dump them separately. Use the -b option to select them by suffix:

```
# slapcat -b 'dc=alrac,dc=net' -l backupfile.ldif
```

Restoring your data is done with *slapadd*. First, delete or move the existing database files from */var/lib/ldap*, or wherever you are keeping them, then run this command:

```
# slapadd -l backupfile.ldif
```

Just like *slapcat*, use the -b option to select a specific database to restore to:

```
# slapadd -b 'dc=alrac,dc=net' -l backupfile.ldif
```

Start up your OpenLDAP server, and you're back in business.

You may also use *slapadd* to build a brand-new database.

Want to automate your backups? Try this script:

```
#!/bin/sh
##/usr/local/bin/ldap-backup.sh
BACKUPDIR=/root/ldap.backup
ROTATION=30

mkdir -p $BACKUPDIR

/etc/init.d/slapd stop

#append the date to the filename
#and compress the file
FILENAME=$BACKUPDIR/ldap.backup.$(date +%Y%m%d)
/usr/sbin/slapcat | gzip --best >${FILENAME.new.gz}
mv -f ${FILENAME.new.gz} ${FILENAME.gz}

/etc/init.d/slapd start

# Delete old copies after 30 days
OLD=$(find $BACKUPDIR/ -ctime +$ROTATION -and -name 'ldap.backup.*')
[ -n "$OLD" ] && rm -f $OLD
```

Stick it in */etc/crontab*; this runs it every morning at 1 a.m.:

```
# m h dom mon dow user command
00 1 * * * root /usr/local/bin/ldap-backup.sh
```

Discussion

There are a number of potential problems with automating *slapcat*. You have to shut down the directory, and the time it takes is unpredictable. Even the best script doesn't always succeed in restarting daemons. So, consider this script as a starting point for adding your own error checks and refinements.

LDIF files have several advantages over the binary database files. They are in plaintext, version-independent, and platform-independent, so they can be imported into virtually any LDAP directory. Plaintext files are editable, so you can clean them up or copy selected bits, or mangle them with the usual Unix tools like Perl, *grep*, *sed*, and *awk* to pick out selected bits. Whether you make your dumps manually or automatically, you should always keep current *slapcat* dumps of your OpenLDAP directory.

See Also

- man 8 slapcat
- man 8 slapadd
- OpenLDAP.org: *http://www.openldap.org/*
- *LDAP Directories Explained: An Introduction and Analysis*, by Brian Arkills (Addison-Wesley)
- *LDAP System Administration*, by Gerald Carter (O'Reilly)

12.14 Refining Access Controls

Problem

Right now, your directory is read-only for everyone, and read/write for the *admin* user. Is there a way to allocate access controls more finely?

Solution

Of course there is. Let's start with our simple example DIT, the one with the suffix of dc=alrac,dc=net, and its single second-level ou=people:

```
dc=alrac,dc=net
    |
ou=people
```

Let's say we have a number of users in people with the following attributes:

```
objectClass:
cn:
sn:
uid:
title:
```

```
jpegPhoto:
telephoneNumber:
homePhone:
homePostalAddress:
mail:
description:
```

It would be nice to let users control some of their own data, such as passwords, email addresses, and telephone numbers. But, not everything: UIDs, titles, CNs, and such should be protected from mischievous users. So, let's take our access controls from Recipe 12.4 and add to them. The new entries are in bold, and our ACLs are now numbered so we can keep track more easily:

```
#ACL 1
access to attrs=userPassword,shadowLastChange
        by dn="cn=admin,dc=alrac,dc=net" write
        by anonymous auth
        by self write
        by * none

#ACL 2
access to attrs=homePostalAddress,homePhone,telephoneNumber,mail
    by dn="cn=admin,dc=alrac,dc=net" write
    by self write
    by * none

#ACL 3
access to dn.base="" by * read

#ACL 3
access to *
        by dn="cn=admin,dc=alrac,dc=net" write
        by * read
```

Save your changes, run *slaptest*, and restart *slapd*; then fire up an LDAP client, and verify that users can make their own changes:

```
$ ldapmodify -xD "uid=cschroder,ou=people,dc=alrac,dc=net" -W
Enter LDAP Password:
dn: uid=cschroder,ou=people,dc=alrac,dc=net
changetype: modify
replace:mail
mail: newmail@newmail.com

modifying entry "uid=cschroder,ou=people,dc=alrac,dc=net"
```

Hit the return key twice to write your changes, and Ctrl-D to exit.

Now for some trickier stuff. Maybe you want select other persons to have write access to user's entries, such as human resources. We can do this with *groups*. Create a new OU just for them, like Figure 12-8 shows.

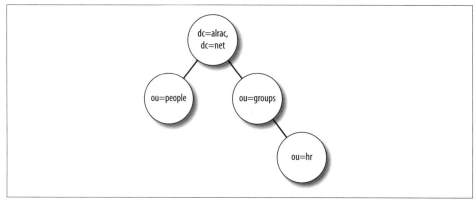

Figure 12-8. The new groups and HR OUs

Create a new LDIF file to add these to your directory:

```
##groups.ldif
dn: ou=groups,dc=alrac,dc=net
objectclass:organizationalUnit
ou: groups
description: special administrative groups

dn: ou=hr,ou=groups,dc=alrac,dc=net
objectclass: groupOfNames
ou: hr
cn: Human Resources
description: Human Resources staff
member: uid=thanson,ou=people,dc=alrac,dc=net
member: uid=ajones,ou=people,dc=alrac,dc=net
```

Add these new entries to the directory:

```
# ldapadd -xD "cn=admin,dc=alrac,dc=net" -W -f groups.ldif
```

Now, add this as ACL #3 to *slapd.conf*:

```
# ACL 3
access to dn.one="ou=people,dc=alrac,dc=net"
    by dn="cn=admin,dc=alrac,dc=net" write
    by group.exact="ou=hr,ou=groups,dc=example,dc=com" write
    by users read
    by * none
```

Let's do one more. This lets human resources people edit all of their own data:

```
# ACL 4
access to *
    by dn="cn=admin,dc=alrac,dc=net" write
    by self write
    by group.exact="ou=hr,ou=groups,dc=alrac,dc=net" write
    by users read
    by * none
```

Discussion

Order is important. As soon as a match is found, it is executed. As a rule of thumb, the most specific rules come first, and more general rules later.

ACLs are real power tools, and they can drive you nuts. Please study man 5 slapd. access; it's not the most riveting reading, but it is the most accurate and detailed.

These are the most common user matches:

*

> Any connected user, including anonymous binds.

self

> The current user, who has successfully authenticated. The *ldapmodify* example in this recipe demonstrates this.

anonymous

> Nonauthenticated user connections.

users

> Authenticated user connections.

These are the access levels:

write

> Can do any kind of search and make changes.

read

> Can search and read complete entries.

search

> Can search and read whatever attributes permission is given for.

compare

> Compare attributes, but not search for them.

auth

> Permission to authenticate; this means anonymous users have to provide a DN and password, or some other credential.

> I hear you knocking, but you can't come in.

See Also

- man 5 slapd.access
- OpenLDAP.org: *http://www.openldap.org/*
- *LDAP Directories Explained: An Introduction and Analysis*, by Brian Arkills (Addison-Wesley)
- *LDAP System Administration*, by Gerald Carter (O'Reilly)

12.15 Changing Passwords

Problem

How do you change your own password?

Solution

Use *ldappasswd* with your own DN:

```
$ ldappasswd -xD "uid=cschroder,ou=people,dc=alrac,dc=net" -WS
New password:
Re-enter new password:
Enter LDAP Password:
Result: Success (0)
```

If you leave off the -S flag, it will create a new password for you:

```
$ ldappasswd -xD "uid=cschroder,ou=people,dc=alrac,dc=net" -W
Enter LDAP Password:
New password: MzJiHq8n
Result: Success (0)
```

ldapwhoami is a great way to test logins:

```
$ ldapwhoami -x -D "uid=cschroder,ou=people,dc=alrac,dc=net" -W
Enter LDAP Password:
dn:uid=cschroder,ou=people,dc=alrac,dc=net
Result: Success (0)
```

Discussion

Naturally, if you prefer a graphical LDAP client, it's usually easier and faster. You should still be familiar with *ldappasswd* and *ldapwhoami* for troubleshooting because using graphical clients still requires a knowledge of OpenLDAP commands.

By default, *ldappasswd* hashes passwords with SSHA. You may choose a different mechanism with the -Y flag: SHA, SMD5, MD5, CRYPT, or CLEARTEXT. You may also set a different default in *slapd.conf*, like this:

```
password-hash  {MD5}
```

See Also

- man 1 ldappasswd
- man 1 slapd.conf
- man 1 ldapwhoami
- OpenLDAP.org: *http://www.openldap.org/*
- *LDAP Directories Explained: An Introduction and Analysis*, by Brian Arkills (Addison-Wesley)
- *LDAP System Administration*, by Gerald Carter (O'Reilly)

## CHAPTER 13

Network Monitoring with Nagios

13.0 Introduction

In this chapter, you'll learn how to install and configure Nagios to monitor network services, host processes, and hardware. Nagios is so flexible it would take a couple of books to detail everything it can do, so we're going to focus on the most common functions to build a good foundation that will let Nagios grow as your network grows.

In this chapter, you will learn how to:

- Monitor services like HTTP, SSH, name services, and mail services
- Monitor system processes and hardware usage
- Receive alerts when there are problems

Why Nagios, when the FOSS world offers a multitude of good network monitors? You could probably choose one with a coin toss and be happy with it. Nagios' strength is its modular design, which permits the greatest flexibility and room for growth. The grunt work is done with plug-ins. You may use or modify the official Nagios plug-ins, try some of the many third-party plug-ins, or write your own. Plug-ins make Nagions future-proof; for example, as more devices become SNMP-aware, you may wish to add or write SNMP plug-ins.

One caveat about plug-ins: Nagios is Free Software, licensed under GPL2. Third-party plug-ins are released under all manner of licenses, so you'll want to be careful and not assume they are also GPL.

Nagios sees your network as hosts or services. Host checks are simple *pings*. Service checks encompass everything, including the usual services such as HTTP, DNS, SSH, as well as processes such as numbers of users, CPU load, disk space, and logfiles. Host checks are done only as required—Nagios knows that as long as its services are running, the host is fine, so host checks are run only when services fail.

We'll install Nagios from source code because the Nagios packages in most Linux distributions are several releases behind. If you prefer a package installation, such as Aptitude or Yum, the recipes will still work; files will be in different places, and you shouldn't have to hassle with creating the Nagios user and group, or tweaking file ownership and permissions.

See Also

- Nagios.org: *http://www.nagios.org/*
- Nagios Exchange (*http://www.nagiosexchange.org/*) is a central plug-in repository and trading post

13.1 Installing Nagios from Sources

Problem

You prefer to build Nagios from source code so that you can control the compile-time options. You also want to get the latest version because the packages in your Linux distribution are several versions behind. What additional libraries do you need?

Solution

You need an HTTP server such as Apache or Lighttpd, the usual Linux build environment, plus libraries to support the statusmap, trends, and histograms. Nagios uses a lot of Common Gateway Interface (CGI) scripts (these are scripts used by web servers to generate pages), so it needs the GD libraries and their dependencies. On Fedora, install these packages:

- The Development Tools package group (`yum install 'Development Tools'`)
- `libgd`
- `libgd-devel`
- `libpng`
- `libpng-devel`
- `libjpeg`
- `libjpeg-devel`
- `zlib`
- `zlib-devel`

On Debian, you need these packages:

- `build-essential`
- `libgd2`

- `libgd2-dev`
- `libpng12-0`
- `libgd2-dev`
- `libjpeg62`
- `libjpeg62-dev`
- `zlib1g`
- `zlib1g-dev`

There are four Nagios tarballs. These are the versions that were current when this was written:

- *nagios-2.9.tar.gz*
- *nagios-plugins-1.4.8.tar.gz*
- *nrpe-2.8.1.tar.gz*
- *nsca-2.7.1.tar.gz*

The first two contain the core Nagios framework and plug-ins. With these, you can perform host and service checks without installing any client software. The second two require you to install and configure Nagios on the client computers. *nrpe* performs additional checks, such as CPU status and other hardware checks. *ncsa* adds all kinds of encryption and security. These might be useful for monitoring important Linux or Unix servers; in this chapter, we're going to focus on configuring only the Nagios server, and setting up the service and host checks that do not require client software.

Installing Nagios from sources is more complex than for most applications, so follow these steps to achieve Nagios nirvana. First, download the two current stable *nagios* and *nagios-plugins* tarballs from Nagios.org (*http://www.nagios.org/download*) into the directory of your choice. Compare the md5sums, which are posted on the download page:

```
$ md5sum nagios-2.9.tar.gz
bb8f0106dc7f282c239f54db1f308445  nagios-2.9.tar.gz
```

Then, unpack them:

```
$ tar zxvf nagios-2.9.tar.gz
$ tar zxvf nagios-plugins-1.4.8.tar.gz
```

Create a *nagios* group and user, and create */usr/local/nagios* as its home directory:

```
# groupadd nagios
# useradd -g nagios -md /usr/local/nagios nagios
```

Now, create an external command group. First find out which user Apache runs as. On Fedora, use this command:

```
$ grep 'User ' /etc/httpd/conf/httpd.conf
User apache
```

On Debian, use this command:

```
$ grep 'User ' /etc/apache2/apache2.conf
User www-data
```

The rest of the steps are the same for both. Create a *nagioscmd* group, and add the Apache user and *nagios* user to it:

```
# groupadd nagioscmd
# usermod -G nagioscmd [your Apache user]
# usermod -G nagioscmd nagios
```

Next, enter the nagios-2.9 directory, and run the *configure* script with the options shown here. Then, install Nagios and the Nagios helpers:

```
$ cd nagios-2.9
$ ./configure --with-cgiurl=/nagios/cgi-bin --with-htmurl=/nagios \
--with-nagios-user=nagios --with-nagios-group=nagios \
--with-command-group=nagioscmd
$ make all
# make install
# make install-init
# make install-commandmode
# make install-config
```

Now, enter the *nagios-plugins-1.4.8* directory and install the plug-ins:

```
# cd ../nagios-plugins-1.4.8
# ./configure
# make
# make install
```

The plug-ins will be installed in */usr/local/nagios/libexec*.

Nagios will not start until you create a basic working configuration. You can now view the Nagios HTML documentation at */usr/local/nagios/share/index.html*, as Figure 13-1 shows. You can read the help docs even though Nagios is not running.

The next recipe tells you how to configure Apache to serve up the Nagios pages.

If you need to start over and recompile Nagios, be sure to run the make devclean command first to clean up leftover object files and get a fresh start.

Discussion

On small networks, you can get away with using your HTTP server to run Nagios and a bunch of other services, but it's better to use a dedicated HTTP plus Nagios installation.

That takes care of installing your basic Nagios framework. The source install puts everything in */usr/local/nagios*. Of course, you may customize the file locations with configure options; run configure --help to see all the available options.

The installation options for Nagios version 2.9 are mostly self-explanatory, except for these two:

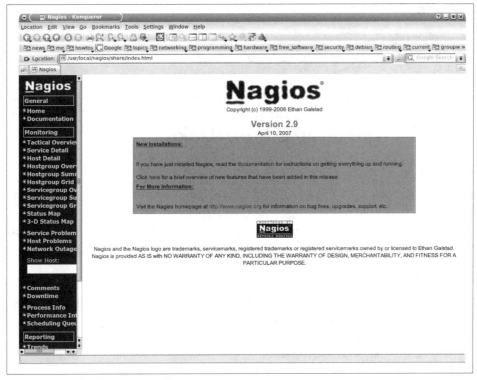

Figure 13-1. A fresh Nagios installation

`--with-cgiurl=`
Defines the web directory where the Nagios CGI scripts will go.

`--with-htmurl=`
Defines the URL for the Nagios web interface.

This is what the Makefile targets do:

make all; make install
Compile and install Nagios.

make install-init
Install the start-up script.

make install-commandmode
Set appropriate file permissions.

make install-config
Install sample configuration files.

Review the *INSTALLING* and *README* files in the Nagios tarball, and the *INSTALL* and *REQUIREMENTS* files in *nagios-plugins* for current options and requirements. Look in */usr/local/nagios/share* for the HTML documentation.

See Also

- Nagios.org: *http://www.nagios.org/*
- Chapter 8, "Managing Users and Groups," in *Linux Cookbook*, by Carla Schroder (O'Reilly)
- Chapter 4, "Installing Programs from Source Code," in *Linux Cookbook*

13.2   Configuring Apache for Nagios

Problem

You can read the Nagios HTML docs in a local web browser or HTML-enabled file browser like Konqueror, but Apache doesn't seem to know they exist. Nagios needs Apache support to be fully functional and to display all the status pages and command pages. How do you make it go?

Solution

You need to use Apache's access controls. First, create an Apache password for the Nagios user:

```
# cd /usr/local/nagios/etc/
# htpasswd -c htpasswd.users nagios
New password:
Re-type new password:
Adding password for user nagios
```

Then, make the password file owned and readable/writable only by the HTTP user:

```
# chown HTTP user htpasswd.users
# chmod 0600 htpasswd.users
```

On Fedora, add this directive to your */etc/httpd/conf/httpd.conf* file:

```
Include /etc/httpd/conf.d
```

Next, create */etc/httpd/conf.d/nagios*. On Debian. create */etc/apache2/conf.d/nagios*. Add these directives to the file, using your own subnet on the line `Allow from 192.168.1.`:

```
## conf.d/nagios
ScriptAlias /nagios/cgi-bin /usr/local/nagios/sbin
<Directory "/usr/local/nagios/sbin">
    Options ExecCGI
    AllowOverride None
    Order allow,deny
    HostnameLookups On
    Allow from localhost
    Allow from 127.0.0.1
    Allow from 192.168.1.
    AuthName "Nagios Access"
    AuthType Basic
```

```
     AuthUserFile /usr/local/nagios/etc/htpasswd.users
     Require valid-user
</Directory>

Alias /nagios /usr/local/nagios/share
<Directory "/usr/local/nagios/share">
    Options None
    AllowOverride None
    Order allow,deny
    HostnameLookups On
    Allow from localhost
    Allow from 127.0.0.1
    Allow from 192.168.1.
    AuthName "Nagios Access"
    AuthType Basic
    AuthUserFile /usr/local/nagios/etc/htpasswd.users
    Require valid-user
</Directory>
```

Restart Apache on Fedora with this command:

 # /etc/init.d/httpd restart

This command restarts it on Debian:

 # /etc/init.d/apache2 restart

Now, enter this URL in a web browser on the Nagios server:

http://localhost/nagios

It should pop up a login window. Log in as *nagios*, using the password you just created, and there you are, just like in Figure 13-1, shown in the previous recipe.

http://127.0.0.1/nagios and the IP address and hostname of the server should all work as well. Try logging in from a neighboring PC using the IP address or hostname of your Nagios server.

You have successfully enabled using and administering Nagios on your LAN only, and blocked it from the outside world.

Discussion

Apache is not required; you may use any HTTP server. You should consider using an HTTP server dedicated only to Nagios, and not running other services. You'll get better performance, and it's easier to manage.

To find the name of your HTTP user, search your main Apache configuration file. Use this command on Fedora:

$ grep 'User ' /etc/httpd/conf/httpd.conf
User apache

On Debian, use this command:

$ grep 'User ' /etc/apache2/apache2.conf
User www-data

You may call the *htpasswd.users* file anything you like. If you wish to add more Nagios admins, use the htpasswd command without the -c option because -c means "create a new file:"

```
# htpasswd /usr/local/nagios/etc/htpasswd.users admin-user2
```

At this point, Nagios is not running. All you can do is read the user manual, and click on the links to see exciting error messages like "Whoops! Error: Could not open CGI config file '*/usr/local/nagios/etc/cgi.cfg*' for reading!" There is no basic configuration framework set up yet, and Nagios will not run without one.

Apache's Basic authentication isn't particularly strong. Passwords are stored encrypted in a plaintext file, and all traffic goes across the wires unencrypted, including the encrypted password. Anyone on your LAN could sniff the encrypted password and try to crack it, or just snoop on the data traffic. You definitely do not want to run unencrypted Nagios sessions over the Internet. An easy way to add encryption is to tunnel your Nagios sessions over SSH; see Recipe 13.14 to learn how. Another option is to add SSL support. Unlike SSH, this doesn't require you to log in to a user account on the Nagios server. See Recipe 13.15 to learn how to do this.

See Also

- "Setting up the web interface" section of your local Nagios documentation:

  http://localhost/nagios

- Nagios.org: *http://www.nagios.org/*

- Chapter 22, "Running an Apache Web Server," in *Linux Cookbook*, by Carla Schroder (O'Reilly)

13.3 Organizing Nagios' Configuration Files Sanely

Problem

You're looking at the sample configuration files in */usr/local/nagios/etc* and studying the documentation, and you realize that you're going to be managing a whole lot of interdependent files. How are you going to keep track of everything?

Solution

A simple hack to keep your sanity is to use a single directory to store all configuration files—with three exceptions, which we'll get to in a moment—and then use the cfg_dir option in *nagios.cfg* instead of the cfg_file option to include them. cfg_dir means "use all the files in this directory," so you can easily control which files Nagios uses by simply adding or removing them. This is easier than keeping track of a herd of individual cfg_file options.

This is what the default *usr/local/nagios/etc* directory looks like after following the previous recipes:

```
$ cd /usr/local/nagios/
$ tree etc
etc
|-- cgi.cfg-sample
|-- commands.cfg-sample
|-- htpasswd.users
|-- localhost.cfg-sample
|-- nagios.cfg-sample
`-- resource.cfg-sample

|-- bigger.cfg-sample
|-- cgi.cfg-sample
|-- commands.cfg-sample
|-- minimal.cfg-sample
|-- misccommands.cfg-sample
|-- nagios.cfg-sample
`-- resource.cfg-sample
```

I like to organize them like this:

```
$ tree --dirsfirst etc
etc
|-- lan_objects
|   |-- commands.cfg
|   |-- contacts.cfg
|   |-- hosts.cfg
|   |-- commands.cfg
|   |-- services.cfg
|   `-- timeperiods.cfg
|-- sample
|   |-- cgi.cfg-sample
|   |-- commands.cfg-sample
|   |-- localhost.cfg-sample
|   |-- nagios.cfg-sample
|   `-- resource.cfg-sample
|-- cgi.cfg
|-- htpasswd.users
|-- nagios.cfg
`-- resource.cfg
```

How do all those files get there? First, move all the sample files into the *sample/* directory. Then, enter the *sample/* directory and copy these files into *etc/* and *lan_objects/*:

```
$ cd etc
# mkdir lan_objects
# mkdir sample
# mv *sample sample
# cd sample
# cp cgi.cfg-sample ../cgi.cfg
# cp resource.cfg-sample ../resource.cfg
# cp commands.cfg-sample ../lan_objects/commands.cfg
```

The rest will be created as we need them in the next few recipes.

See the next recipe to learn how to configure Nagios to use your nice new directory organization, and to get started monitoring the local system.

Discussion

All Nagios configuration files must end in *.cfg*.

You are perfectly welcome to use a graphical file manager to shuffle everything around. It's easier and faster.

cgi.cfg, nagios.cfg, and *resource.cfg* are the primary Nagios configuration files, so they don't go with the others. *htpasswd.users* must be in the same directory as *nagios.cfg*.

The files in the *lan_object/* directory are called *object* files. A Nagios object is a single unit, such as a host, a command, a service, a contact, and the groups they belong to. These objects are inheritable and reusable, which simplifies administration.

See Also

- man 1 tree
- man 1 cp

13.4 Configuring Nagios to Monitor Localhost

Problem

You've successfully installed Nagios, configured Apache, and set up your configuration files in an orderly manner as outlined in the previous recipe. Reading the local Nagios documentation at *http://localhost/nagios* is nice, but you really want to get going on setting up Nagios to keep an untiring eye on your network. What's the next step?

Solution

Nagios is best set up in small steps, so we'll start with monitoring five basic functions on the Nagios server: *ping*, disk usage, local users, total processes, and CPU load. This is a long recipe, but when you're finished, you'll have your basic Nagios framework constructed.

Copy the following five configuration files exactly as shown, except where it says to use your own information, and put them in the directories as outlined in the previous recipe:

- */usr/local/nagios/etc/nagios.cfg*
- */usr/local/nagios/etc/lan_objects/timeperiods.cfg*
- */usr/local/nagios/etc/lan_objects/contacts.cfg*

- */usr/local/nagios/etc/lan_objects/hosts.cfg*
- */usr/local/nagios/etc/lan_objects/services.cfg*

Obviously, retyping all this is the path to madness, so please visit *http://www.oreilly. com/catalog/9780596102487* to download them.

First, create *nagios.cfg*:

```
###############
# nagios.cfg
# main Nagios configuration file
###############
log_file=/usr/local/nagios/var/nagios.log
cfg_dir=/usr/local/nagios/etc/lan_objects
object_cache_file=/usr/local/nagios/var/objects.cache
resource_file=/usr/local/nagios/etc/resource.cfg
status_file=/usr/local/nagios/var/status.dat

nagios_user=nagios
nagios_group=nagios

check_external_commands=1
command_check_interval=-1
command_file=/usr/local/nagios/var/rw/nagios.cmd

comment_file=/usr/local/nagios/var/comments.dat
downtime_file=/usr/local/nagios/var/downtime.dat
lock_file=/usr/local/nagios/var/nagios.lock
temp_file=/usr/local/nagios/var/nagios.tmp
event_broker_options=-1

log_rotation_method=d
log_archive_path=/usr/local/nagios/var/archives
use_syslog=1
log_notifications=1
log_service_retries=1

log_host_retries=1
log_event_handlers=1
log_initial_states=0
log_external_commands=1
log_passive_checks=1

service_inter_check_delay_method=s
max_service_check_spread=30
service_interleave_factor=s
host_inter_check_delay_method=s
max_host_check_spread=30

max_concurrent_checks=0
service_reaper_frequency=10
auto_reschedule_checks=0
auto_rescheduling_interval=30
auto_rescheduling_window=180
```

```
sleep_time=0.25
service_check_timeout=60
host_check_timeout=30
event_handler_timeout=30
notification_timeout=30

ocsp_timeout=5
perfdata_timeout=5
retain_state_information=1
state_retention_file=/usr/local/nagios/var/retention.dat
retention_update_interval=60

use_retained_program_state=1
use_retained_scheduling_info=0
interval_length=60
use_aggressive_host_checking=0
execute_service_checks=1

accept_passive_service_checks=1
execute_host_checks=1
accept_passive_host_checks=1
enable_notifications=1
enable_event_handlers=1

process_performance_data=0
obsess_over_services=0
check_for_orphaned_services=0
check_service_freshness=1
service_freshness_check_interval=60

check_host_freshness=0
host_freshness_check_interval=60
aggregate_status_updates=1
status_update_interval=15
enable_flap_detection=0

low_service_flap_threshold=5.0
high_service_flap_threshold=20.0
low_host_flap_threshold=5.0
high_host_flap_threshold=20.0
date_format=us

p1_file=/usr/local/nagios/bin/p1.pl
illegal_object_name_chars=`~!$%^&*|'"<>?,()=
illegal_macro_output_chars=`~$&|'"<>
use_regexp_matching=0
use_true_regexp_matching=0

admin_email=nagios
admin_pager=pagenagios
daemon_dumps_core=0
```

Now, create *timeperiods.cfg*:

```
# Time periods
# All times are valid for all
# checks and notifications

define timeperiod{
        timeperiod_name 24x7
        alias           24 Hours A Day, 7 Days A Week
        sunday          00:00-24:00
        monday          00:00-24:00
        tuesday         00:00-24:00
        wednesday       00:00-24:00
        thursday        00:00-24:00
        friday          00:00-24:00
        saturday        00:00-24:00
        }
```

Next, create *contacts.cfg*. The contact_name must be a Nagios user with a Nagios login in *htpasswd.users*, and an email account:

```
################
# Contacts- individuals and groups
################
define contact{
        contact_name                    nagios
        alias                           Nagios Admin
        service_notification_period     24x7
        host_notification_period        24x7
        service_notification_options    w,u,c,r
        host_notification_options       d,r
        service_notification_commands   notify-by-email
        host_notification_commands      host-notify-by-email
        email                           nagios@alrac.net
        }

# contact groups
# Nagios only talks to contact groups, not individuals
# members must be Nagios users, alias and contact_group
# are whatever you want

define contactgroup{
        contactgroup_name       admins
        alias                   Nagios Administrators
        members                 nagios
        }
```

Next, create *hosts.cfg*:

```
################
# Hosts file- individual hosts and host groups
################
# Generic host definition template - This is NOT a real host, just a template!

define host{
  name                  generic-host
```

```
        notifications_enabled      1
        event_handler_enabled      1
        flap_detection_enabled     1
        failure_prediction_enabled 1
        process_perf_data          1
        retain_status_information  1
        retain_nonstatus_information 1
; DONT REGISTER THIS DEFINITION - ITS NOT A REAL HOST, JUST A TEMPLATE!
        register  0
                }
# local host definition

define host{
        use                  generic-host
        host_name            localhost
        alias                Nagios Server
        address              127.0.0.1
        check_command        check-host-alive
        max_check_attempts   10
        check_period         24x7
        notification_interval 120
        notification_period  24x7
        notification_options d,r
        contact_groups     admins
                }


##############
# Host groups
##############

# Every host must belong to a host group

define hostgroup{
        hostgroup_name  test
        alias           Test Servers
        members         localhost
                }
```

Finally, create *services.cfg*:

```
################
# Services
################

# Generic service definition template - This is NOT a real service, just a template!

define service{
   name            generic-service
   active_checks_enabled    1
   passive_checks_enabled   1
   parallelize_check        1
   obsess_over_service      1
   check_freshness          0
   notifications_enabled       1
   event_handler_enabled       1
```

```
    flap_detection_enabled      1
    failure_prediction_enabled  1
    process_perf_data           1
    retain_status_information    1
    retain_nonstatus_information 1
; DONT REGISTER THIS DEFINITION - ITS NOT A REAL SERVICE, JUST A TEMPLATE!
 register    0
        }

# Define a service to "ping" the local machine

define service{
        use                     generic-service
        host_name               localhost
        service_description     PING
        is_volatile             0
        check_period            24x7
        max_check_attempts      4
        normal_check_interval   5
        retry_check_interval    1
        contact_groups          admins
        notification_options     w,u,c,r
        notification_interval   960
        notification_period     24x7
        check_command           check_ping!100.0,20%!500.0,60%
        }

# Define a service to check the disk space of the root partition
# on the local machine.  Warning if < 20% free, critical if
# < 10% free space on partition.

define service{
        use                     generic-service
        host_name               localhost
        service_description     Root Partition
        is_volatile             0
        check_period            24x7
        max_check_attempts      4
        normal_check_interval   5
        retry_check_interval    1
        contact_groups          admins
        notification_options     w,u,c,r
        notification_interval   960
        notification_period     24x7
        check_command           check_local_disk!20%!10%!/
        }

# Define a service to check the number of currently logged in
# users on the local machine.  Warning if > 20 users, critical
# if > 50 users.

define service{
        use                     generic-service
        host_name               localhost
        service_description     Current Users
```

```
        is_volatile                  0
        check_period                 24x7
        max_check_attempts           4
        normal_check_interval        5
        retry_check_interval         1
        contact_groups               admins
        notification_options          w,u,c,r
        notification_interval        960
        notification_period          24x7
        check_command                check_local_users!20!50
        }
```

```
# Define a service to check the number of currently running procs
# on the local machine.  Warning if > 250 processes, critical if
# > 400 users.
```

```
define service{
        use                          generic-service
        host_name                    localhost
        service_description          Total Processes
        is_volatile                  0
        check_period                 24x7
        max_check_attempts           4
        normal_check_interval        5
        retry_check_interval         1
        contact_groups               admins
    notification_options        w,u,c,r
        notification_interval         960
        notification_period           24x7
    check_command               check_local_procs!250!400
        }
```

```
# Define a service to check the load on the local machine.
```

```
define service{
        use                          generic-service
        host_name                    localhost
        service_description          Current Load
        is_volatile                  0
        check_period                 24x7
        max_check_attempts           4
        normal_check_interval        5
        retry_check_interval         1
        contact_groups               admins
         notification_options          w,u,c,r
        notification_interval        960
        notification_period          24x7
        check_command                check_local_load!5.0,4.0,3.0!10.0,6.0,4.0
        }
```

OK, we're almost there! Make all the files in *lan_objects/* owned and writable by the *nagios* user:

```
# chown nagios:nagios /usr/local/nagios/etc/lan_objects/*
# chmod 0644 /usr/local/nagios/etc/lan_objects/*
```

Adjust these file ownerships and modes as shown:

```
# chown nagios:nagios /usr/local/nagios/etc/nagios.cfg
# chmod 0644 /usr/local/nagios/etc/nagios.cfg
# chown nagios:nagios /usr/local/nagios/etc/resource.cfg
# chmod 0600 /usr/local/nagios/etc/resource.cfg
# chown nagios:nagios /usr/local/nagios/etc/cgi.cfg
# chmod 0644 /usr/local/nagios/etc/cgi.cfg
```

Now, you can run Nagios' syntax checker. You need to do this as *root*:

```
# /usr/local/nagios/bin/nagios -v /usr/local/nagios/etc/nagios.cfg
```

You should see a lot of output ending in these lines:

```
Total Warnings: 0
Total Errors:   0
Things look okay - No serious problems were detected during the pre-flight check
```

If there are any errors, it will tell you exactly what you need to fix. When you get a clean run, start up the Nagios daemon:

```
# /etc/init.d/nagios start
```

Now, log in to the Nagios web interface at *http://localhost/nagios*, and start clicking on various links in the left navigation bar. The Service Detail page should look like Figure 13-2.

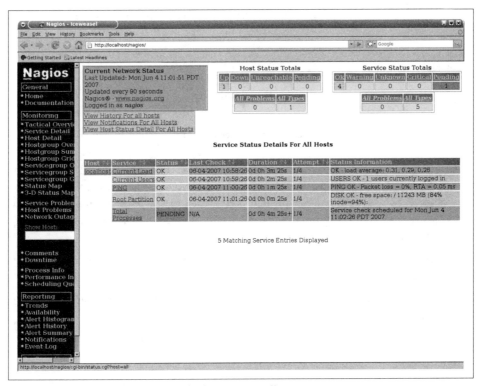

Figure 13-2. Service Detail page on a fresh Nagios installation

This means you have successfully gotten Nagios up and running and monitoring localhost. Congratulations!

Discussion

You may name Nagios configuration files whatever you want, as long they have the *.cfg* extension—this is required.

You won't be able to access all of the Nagios web interface pages yet; you'll get an "It appears as though you do not have permission to view the information you requested…" error on some of them because we haven't set the correct CGI permissions yet. See the next recipe to learn how to do this.

During its initial run, my Nagios system couldn't run the "Total Processes" check. The error message was *check_procs: Unknown argument—(null)*. This means that either one of the options in the command definition (*commands.cfg*) was incorrect, or the service definition (*services.cfg*) was incorrect. I used the default files, so chances are you fine readers might encounter the same error. A quick comparison showed a mismatch between the two:

```
# commands.cfg
# 'check_local_procs' command definition
define command{
        command_name    check_local_procs
        command_line    $USER1$/check_procs -w $ARG1$ -c $ARG2$ -s $ARG3$
        }

# services.cfg
define service{
        use                     generic-service
        host_name               localhost
        service_description     Total Processes
<...>
    check_command           check_local_procs!250!400!
        }
```

Compare the command_line and check_command lines. The check_local_procs command wants three arguments, but the service definition check_local_procs!250!400! only defined two. Because all I want is to keep track of the total number of running processes, the first two arguments are sufficient. Deleting -s $ARG3$ and restarting Nagios fixed it.

When the total number of running processes reaches 250, Nagios sends a warning. 400 is critical.

The exclamation points simply separate the two alert values; they don't mean you need to get excited.

See Also

- Local Nagios documentation: *http://localhost/nagios*
- For definitions of the options in object definition files, which are all the files in *lan_objects/*, start at "Template-Based Object Configuration": *http://localhost/nagios/docs/xodtemplate.html*
- For *nagios.cfg* and *resources.cfg*, see "Main Configuration File Options": *http://localhost/nagios/docs/configmain.html*
- For *cgi.cfg*, see "CGI Configuration File Options" (*http://localhost/nagios/docs/configcgi.html*) and "Authentication And Authorization In The CGIs" (*http://localhost/nagios/docs/cgiauth.html*)
- Nagios.org: *http://www.nagios.org/*

13.5 Configuring CGI Permissions for Full Nagios Web Access

Problem

You have followed all the steps so far, but when you log in to the Nagios web interface, you can't access all of the pages. Instead, you get this error: "It appears as though you do not have permission to view information you requested.... If you believe this is an error, check the HTTP server authentication requirements for accessing this CGI and check the authorization options in your CGI configuration file." How do you fix this?

Solution

Uncomment these lines in */usr/local/nagios/etc/cgi.cfg*, and make sure the correct Nagios user is named, which in this chapter is *nagios*:

```
authorized_for_all_services=nagios
authorized_for_all_hosts=nagios
authorized_for_system_commands=nagios
authorized_for_configuration_information=nagios
authorized_for_all_service_commands=nagios
authorized_for_all_host_commands=nagios
```

Make sure this line is uncommented and set to 1:

```
use_authentication=1
```

This requires all CGI scripts to use authentication. Disabling this opens a great big security hole; for example, any random person on your LAN could write whatever they want to your command file.

Save the changes, and try again. Now, your *nagios* user should have full access to all pages on the Nagios web interface, including the ability to run commands.

Discussion

At the end of the file, you can activate some sound alerts if you really really want to.

It is better to administer Nagios as an unprivileged user, rather than as the system's *root* user. You may add more authorized users in a comma-delimited list. These aren't very fine-grained access controls, but you do get a little bit of flexibility. Each Nagios user must be added to *htpasswd.users*; see the next recipe to learn how to do this.

This a complete sample *cgi.cfg*:

```
# example cgi.cfg that gives complete administrative
# powers to 'nagios' user
main_config_file=/usr/local/nagios/etc/nagios.cfg
physical_html_path=/usr/local/nagios/share
url_html_path=/nagios
show_context_help=0
use_authentication=1

authorized_for_system_information=nagios
authorized_for_configuration_information=nagios
authorized_for_system_commands=nagios
authorized_for_all_services=nagios
authorized_for_all_hosts=nagios

authorized_for_all_service_commands=nagios
authorized_for_all_host_commands=nagios
default_statusmap_layout=5
default_statuswrl_layout=4
ping_syntax=/bin/ping -n -U -c 5 $HOSTADDRESS$
refresh_rate=90
```

See Also

- Local documentation at "Configuring authorization for the CGIs" (*http://localhost/nagios/docs/cgiauth.html*) and "CGI Configuration File Options" (*http://localhost/nagios/docs/configcgi.html*)
- Nagios.org: *http://www.nagios.org*

13.6   Starting Nagios at Boot

Problem

Nagios created a nice start/stop script for itself in */etc/init.d*, but it doesn't start automatically on boot, and you want it to do this.

Solution

You need to set this up yourself. On Fedora, use *chkconfig*:

```
# chkconfig --level 2345 nagios on
# chkconfig --level 016 nagios off
```

Confirm that it worked:

```
# chkconfig --list nagios
nagios 0:off 1:off 2:on 3:on 4: on 5: on 6:off
```

On Debian, use *update-rc.d*:

```
# update-rc.d nagios start 99 2 3 4 5 . stop 01 0 1 6 .
```

Discussion

Both of these commands start Nagios on runlevels 2, 3, 4, and 5, and stop it on runlevels 0, 1, and 6. The Debian start priority is 99, and the stop priority is 01, so it's low priority to start, and high priority to stop. Nagios is not an essential system service, so these priorities are appropriate. Of course, you may adjust them to suit.

See Also

- Chapter 7, "Starting and Stopping Linux," in *Linux Cookbook*, by Carla Schroder (O'Reilly)

13.7   Adding More Nagios Users

Problem

You don't want to be stuck with administering Nagios all by yourself, but you want to add some junior admins to help out.

Solution

Your new admins must have system accounts on the Nagios server, and passwords in *htpasswd.users*:

```
# useradd -m -G nagioscmd admin2
# passwd admin2
# htpasswd /usr/local/nagios/etc/htpasswd.users admin2
```

Then, you need to configure access to whatever Nagios functions you want them to have in *cgi.cfg*, using comma-delimited lists like this example shows:

```
authorized_for_all_services=nagios,admin2
authorized_for_all_hosts=nagios,admin2
```

Restart Nagios to activate the changes:

```
# /etc/init.d/nagios restart
```

Discussion

Do not have any user in the *nagios* group but *nagios*.

These aren't the most fine-grained access controls, but they do let you limit what your underlings can do:

authorized_for_system_information
> View Nagios process information.

authorized_for_configuration_information
> View all configuration information, both hosts and commands.

authorized_for_system_commands
> Shutdown, restart, and put Nagios on standby.

authorized_for_all_services, authorized_for_all_hosts
> View information for all hosts and services. By default, Nagios users can only view hosts or services they are named as contacts for.

authorized_for_all_service_commands, authorized_for_all_host_commands
> Issue service or host commands. By default, Nagios users can only run commands for the hosts or services they are named as contacts for.

See Also

- "CGI Configuration File Options": *http://localhost/nagios/docs/configcgi.html*
- "Authentication And Authorization In The CGIs":

  http://localhost/nagios/docs/cgiauth.html
- Nagios.org: *http://www.nagios.org/*

13.8   Speed Up Nagios with check_icmp

Problem

You've seen on some Nagios forums or mailing lists that you should use the check_icmp plug-in instead of check_ping because it is faster and more efficient. So, you've tried it, but it doesn't work; you get a *check_icmp: Failed to obtain ICMP socket: Operation not permitted* error. This doesn't seem like an improvement—now what?

Solution

The check_icmp plug-in needs *root* permissions to work, so you need to set the SUID bit to allow unprivileged users to run it with *root* privileges.

First, replace all instances of check_ping in your configuration files with check_icmp. Use the *grep* command to find them:

```
# grep -r check_ping  /usr/local/nagios/etc/
```

Then, set the SUID bit on check_icmp, and make it a member of the *nagios* group:

```
# cd /usr/local/nagios/libexec
# chown root:nagios check_icmp
# chmod 4711 check_icmp
```

Now, it will work without complaints.

Discussion

check_ping calls the external */bin/ping*, while check_icmp is an internal Nagios command. Nagios uses ICMP echo request and ICMP echo reply a lot, so this adds up to a nice performance enhancement.

See Also

- The FAQ in the *nagios-plugins* source tree, plus the *README* and *REQUIREMENTS*
- Chapter 8, "Managing Users and Groups," in *Linux Cookbook*, by Carla Schroder (O'Reilly)

13.9   Monitoring SSHD

Problem

You use the SSH daemon on all of your servers for secure remote administration, so you want to set up Nagios to monitor SSH and alert you if it becomes unavailable. You also want to be able to add new servers for monitoring easily.

Solution

Start by setting it up for one server. You'll create a command definition, a host definition, and a service definition by editing *commands.cfg, hosts.cfg,* and *services.cfg.* Then, you'll be able to add new servers simply by creating new host definitions, and adding the server names to the service definition.

The default *commands.cfg* does not contain a command definition for SSH, so add this to *commands.cfg*:

```
# 'check_ssh' command definition
define command{
        command_name    check_ssh
        command_line    $USER1$/check_ssh -H $HOSTADDRESS$
        }
```

Next, add a host definition to *hosts.cfg*, using your own hostname and IP address:

```
# SSH servers
define host{
        use                     generic-host
```

```
host_name              server1
alias                  backup server
address                192.168.1.25
check_command          check-host-alive
max_check_attempts     10
check_period          24x7
notification_interval  120
notification_period   24x7
notification_options   d,r
contact_groups         admins
}
```

Add your new server to an existing group, or create a new group for it, as this example shows:

```
define hostgroup{
        hostgroup_name  misc_servers
        alias           Servers
        members         server1
        }
```

Now, define the SSH service in *services.cfg*:

```
# Define a service to monitor SSH
define service{
        use                     generic-service
        host_name               server1
        service_description     SSH
        is_volatile             0
        check_period            24x7
        max_check_attempts      4
        normal_check_interval   5
        retry_check_interval    1
        contact_groups          admins
         notification_options       w,u,c,r
        notification_interval   960
        notification_period     24x7
        check_command           check_ssh
        }
```

Run the syntax checker, then restart Nagios:

```
# /usr/local/nagios/bin/nagios -v /usr/local/nagios/etc/nagios.cfg
# /etc/init.d/nagios restart
```

Refresh the Nagios web interface, and you'll see the new entry's status listed as PENDING. In a few minutes, Nagios will run the new service check, and it will no longer be PENDING, but displaying status information. If you don't want to wait, go to Service Detail → SSH → Reschedule Next Service Check, and run it immediately.

Discussion

If you are using ports other than port 22, use the -p option to specify the correct port.

You can use this recipe as a copy-and-paste template for most services.

Look in */usr/lib/nagios/libexec* to view your available plug-ins. Run [plugin-name] --help to see the available options.

Host and service definitions have several required fields; see "Template-Based Object Configuration" (*http://localhost/nagios/docs/xodtemplate.html*) in your local Nagios documentation for details.

Command definitions

The *check_ssh* command demonstrates the most basic Nagios command definition. All Nagios command definitions must have a *command_name* and a *command_line*. The *command_name* can be anything you want. The *command_line* must be the name of a plug-in, followed by options.

$USER1$ is a special macro defined in *resource.cfg*; this is a shortcut for the path to the plug-in. You may have up to 32 $USERx$ macros. Nagios automatically expands the macro before it runs the command. $USERx$ macros can also store passwords and usernames. This is a nice shortcut when you're managing groups of complex configuration files.

-H means "hostname or address," and $HOSTADDRESS$ is a built-in macro that takes the IP address from the host definition. You can use hostnames with the $HOSTNAME$ macro, but adding DNS lookups to your monitoring can slow it down, and it adds a point of failure.

Run the plug-in from the command line to see help and options:

```
root@xena:/usr/local/nagios/libexec# ./check_ssh -h
```

Most plug-ins have the -h or --help option.

It is best to keep your command definitions generic with macros, and to use explicit values in the service definitions.

Host definitions

Every host needs its own host definitions. Host definitions tell Nagios where to find your servers, and define basic monitoring and alerting behaviors.

check_command check-host-alive is a special *ping* command. It is used only when other services on the host do not respond. Nagios knows that as long as the services are up, it doesn't need to *ping* the host to see if it is alive.

notification_options d,r means send a notification when the host is down, or has recovered from a down state and is now OK. Here are other options you can use:

u

Send notifications on an unreachable state.

f

Send notifications when the host starts and stops flapping, which is changing state very rapidly.

n

Send no notifications.

Service definitions

These are similar to Host Definitions, with one large difference: they are reusable. Once you create a service definition, you can add more hosts to it, rather than creating a new service definition every time you need to add a new machine. Just add more servers on the host_name line in a comma-delimited list:

```
host_name        stinkpad,uberpc,xena
```

Another option is to create a hostgroup for your servers, then use the hostgroup_name directive instead:

```
hostgroup_name       backup_servers
```

The notification_options are a bit different:

w

Send notifications on a warning state.

u

Send notifications on an unknown state.

c

Send notifications on a critical state.

r

Send notifications on recoveries.

f

Send notifications when the service starts and stops flapping.

See Also

- "Using Macros In Commands" (*http://localhost/nagios/docs/macros.html*) in your local Nagios documentation for a list of built-in macros
- For definitions of the options in object definition files, which are all the files in *lan_objects/*, start at "Template-Based Object Configuration": *http://localhost/nagios/docs/xodtemplate.html*
- For *nagios.cfg* and *resources.cfg*, see "Main Configuration File Options": *http://localhost/nagios/docs/configmain.html*
- "Flapping": *http://localhost/nagios/docs/flapping.html*
- Nagios.org: *http://www.nagios.org/*

13.10 Monitoring a Web Server

Problem

You have a web server you want Nagios to monitor. You want to make sure that the server is alive, and that HTTP and SSH are functioning. If one of the services stops, or the server goes down, you want to receive an alert.

Solution

Create a new host definition for the server, and an HTTP service definition. Then, add the new server to the existing SSH service definition (see previous recipe). Restart Nagios, and you're done.

This is a sample host definition in *hosts.cfg*, using the host *apache1* with an IP address of 192.168.1.26. Use your own hostname and IP address, of course:

```
# HTTP servers
define host{
        use                     generic-host
        host_name               apache1
        alias                   Apache web server
        address                 192.168.1.26
        check_command           check-host-alive
        max_check_attempts      10
        check_period            24x7
        notification_interval   120
        notification_period     24x7
        notification_options    d,r
        contact_groups          admins
        }
```

Add your new server to an existing group, or create a new group for it, as this example shows:

```
define hostgroup{
        hostgroup_name  apache_servers
        alias           Web Servers
        members         apache1
        }
```

Next, define the HTTP service in *services.cfg*:

```
# Define a service to monitor HTTP
define service{
        use                     generic-service
        host_name               apache1
        service_description     HTTP
        is_volatile             0
        check_period            24x7
        max_check_attempts      4
        normal_check_interval   5
        retry_check_interval    1
```

```
        contact_groups          admins
        notification_options        w,u,c,r
        notification_interval   960
        notification_period     24x7
        check_command           check_http
        }
```

Add the new server to the SSH service definition:

```
# Define a service to monitor SSH
define service{
        use                     generic-service
        host_name               server1,apache1
        service_description     SSH
        is_volatile             0
        check_period            24x7
        max_check_attempts      4
        normal_check_interval   5
        retry_check_interval    1
        contact_groups          admins
        notification_options        w,u,c,r
        notification_interval   960
        notification_period     24x7
        check_command           check_ssh
        }
```

Run the syntax checker, then restart Nagios:

```
# /usr/local/nagios/bin/nagios -v /usr/local/nagios/etc/nagios.cfg
# /etc/init.d/nagios restart
```

Refresh the Nagios web interface, and you'll see the new entries listed as PENDING, as Figure 13-3 shows.

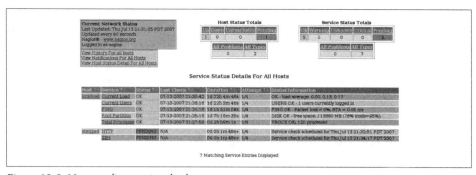

Figure 13-3. New pending service checks

In a few minutes, Nagios will run the new service checks; then, they will no longer be PENDING, and instead display status information.

Discussion

check_http takes a number of options. It checks normal (HTTP) and secure (HTTPS) connections, and reports if SSL certificates are still valid. You can test it on the command line first. This shows your command options:

```
root@xena:/usr/local/nagios/libexec# ./check_http -h
```

Use it this way to give you 30 days' notice on expiring SSL certificates:

```
# ./check_http www.yourdomain.com -C 30
```

The -p option specifies the port number, when you're using a nonstandard port:

```
# ./check_http www.yourdomain.com -p 8080
```

Using the -w and -c options lets you test response time, in seconds:

```
# ./check_http -w 5 -c 10
```

That issues a warning if there is no response after 5 seconds, and it goes critical after 10 seconds.

Use the -ssl option to connect to SSL-enabled servers:

```
# ./check_http --ssl www.yourdomain.com
```

Once you get the initial Nagios framework configured, adding new servers and services is fairly simple. Just copy and paste existing entries and modify them for the new hosts and services.

Using hostgroups is a simple way to control groups of related servers. Use the hostgroup_name option in *services.cfg* instead of host_name, and simply add or remove servers from the hostgroup.

See Also

- "Using Macros In Commands" (*http://localhost/nagios/docs/macros.html*) in your local Nagios documentation for a list of built-in macros
- For definitions of the options in object definition files, which are all the files in *lan_objects/*, start at "Template-Based Object Configuration": *http://localhost/nagios/docs/xodtemplate.html*
- For *nagios.cfg* and *resources.cfg*, see "Main Configuration File Options": *http://localhost/nagios/docs/configmain.html*
- "Flapping": *http://localhost/nagios/docs/flapping.html*
- Nagios.org: *http://www.nagios.org/*

13.11 Monitoring a Mail Server

Problem

You want to know how to use Nagios to monitor your mail server. You want it to keep an eye on SMTP, POP, SSH, and IMAP services.

Solution

Add new host and service definition entries to the *hosts.cfg* and *services.cfg* files. You may also need some new command definitions in *commands.cfg*.

First, make sure these entries exist in *commands.cfg*:

```
# 'check_pop' command definition
define command{
        command_name    check_pop
        command_line    $USER1$/check_pop -H $HOSTADDRESS$
        }

# 'check_smtp' command definition
define command{
        command_name    check_smtp
        command_line    $USER1$/check_smtp -H $HOSTADDRESS$
        }

# 'check_imap' command definition
define command{
        command_name    check_imap
        command_line    $USER1$/check_imap -H $HOSTADDRESS$
        }

# 'check_ssh' command definition
define command{
        command_name    check_ssh
        command_line    $USER1$/check_ssh -H $HOSTADDRESS$
        }
```

Next, create a host definition for the server:

```
# define a Mail server host
define host{
        use                     generic-host
        host_name               postfix1
        alias                   mail server1
        address                 192.168.1.27
        check_command           check-host-alive
        max_check_attempts      10
        check_period            24x7
        notification_interval   120
        notification_period     24x7
        notification_options    d,r
        contact_groups          admins
        }
```

Add your new server to an existing group; or, create a new group for it, as this example shows:

```
define hostgroup{
        hostgroup_name   mail_servers
        alias            Mail Servers
        members          postfix1
        }
```

Next, define the four services (POP, IMAP, SMTP, and SSH) in *services.cfg*. Each service requires a separate definition. The easy way is to copy and paste the following example, replacing only the hostname, service_description, and check_command values:

```
# Define a service to monitor POP/SMTP/IMAP/SSH
define service{
        use                     generic-service
        host_name               postfix1
        service_description     POP
        is_volatile             0
        check_period            24x7
        max_check_attempts      4
        normal_check_interval   5
        retry_check_interval    1
        contact_groups          admins
        notification_options      w,u,c,r
        notification_interval   960
        notification_period     24x7
        check_command           check_pop
        }
```

If any of these services are already defined, all you do is add the hostnames or hostgroups to the existing service definition:

```
host_name               postfix1,postfix2,exim1
```

or:

```
hostgroup_name          mail_servers
```

Run the syntax checker, then restart Nagios:

```
# /usr/local/nagios/bin/nagios -v /usr/local/nagios/etc/nagios.cfg
# /etc/init.d/nagios restart
```

Refresh the Nagios web interface, and you'll see the new entries listed as PENDING. In a few minutes, Nagios will run the new service checks, and they will no longer be PENDING, but will display status information.

Discussion

Reuse and recycle are the keys to Nagios sanity. Remember:

commands.cfg contains your command definitions. Each command definition only needs to be created once.

Each new host needs its own host definition in *hosts.cfg*.

Service definitions are created once per service in *services.cfg*, then simply add additional host_name or hostgroup_name entries.

Using hostgroups is one way to organize related servers; another way is by using servicegroups. Servicegroups let you group related services in the Nagios web interface. See the next recipe to learn how to do this.

See Also

- "Using Macros In Commands" (*http://localhost/nagios/docs/macros.html*) in your local Nagios documentation for a list of built-in macros
- For definitions of the options in object definition files, which are all the files in *lan_objects/*, start at "Template-Based Object Configuration": *http://localhost/nagios/docs/xodtemplate.html*
- For *nagios.cfg* and *resources.cfg*, see "Main Configuration File Options": *http://localhost/nagios/docs/configmain.html*
- "Flapping": *http://localhost/nagios/docs/flapping.html*
- Nagios.org: *http://www.nagios.org/*

13.12 Using Servicegroups to Group Related Services

Problem

Some of your servers are running multiple services, and on the Nagios web interface, you want to see related services grouped together (e.g., SSH, FTP, HTTP, and anything you have running on multiple servers).

Solution

Create servicegroups. You can group together any host or service combinations you like. This example shows an SSH servicegroup:

```
# ssh servicegroup
define servicegroup{
  servicegroup_name     ssh
  alias                 all ssh servers
  members               uberpc,SSH,stinkpad,SSH
}
```

The members must already have service definitions in *services.cfg*. You may group together any combination of host/service pairs.

When you're finished, run the syntax-checker, and restart Nagios:

```
# /usr/local/nagios/bin/nagios -v /usr/local/nagios/etc/nagios.cfg
# /etc/init.d/nagios restart
```

Then, click on the various "Servicegroup" links on the Nagios web interface to see them.

Discussion

The services don't have to all be the same; you can group any services you want. The members definitions are case-sensitive, so make sure they match their host and service definitions.

See Also

- "Template-Based Object Configuration" (*http://localhost/nagios/docs/xodtemplate.html*) in your local Nagios documentation
- Nagios.org: *http://www.nagios.org/*

13.13 Monitoring Name Services

Problem

You want Nagios to monitor your DNS and DHCP servers.

Solution

Add the DNS and DHCP command definitions to *commands.cfg* if they do not already exist, then create new host and service definitions just like we did in Recipes 13.9 through 13.12.

DNS uses an ordinary command definition:

```
# commands.cfg
# 'check_dns' command definition
define command{
        command_name    check_dns
        command_line    $USER1$/check_dns -H $ARG1$
        }
```

Then, define your DNS query parameters in the service definition, specifying a domain or hostname to use for testing the server:

```
check_command    check_dns!host.domain.com
```

DHCP is bit more work to set up because the *check_dhcp* plug-in requires *root* privileges to get full access to the network interface. Give it the SUID bit, owned by *root*, in the *nagios* group:

```
# chown root:nagios check_dhcp
# chmod 4750 check_dhcp
```

To query DHCP functionality on the network, don't specify any options:

```
# 'check_dhcp' command definition
define command{
        command_name    check_dhcp
        command_line    $USER1$/check_dhcp
        }
```

Add the -s option to specify a server to check:

```
$USER1$/check_dns -s $ARG1$
```

Then, specify the server in the service definition:

```
check_command       check_dhcp!12.34.56.78
```

Discussion

check_dns requires that you specify a hostname to check. This can be a local host or a remote host that you can reasonably expect to be up, such as Google, Yahoo, or your ISP. Be nice—don't bombard other people's servers. By default, *check_dns* queries the servers in */etc/resolv.conf*. Use the -s option to specify a specific nameserver, like this example:

```
$USER1$/check_dns -H $ARG1$ -s $ARG2$
```

Then, the service definition specifies the hostname to resolve and the nameserver:

```
check_command       check_dns!host.domain.com!ns1.domain.net
```

You can take this a step further and specify the IP address that the hostname should resolve to:

```
$USER1$/check_dns -H $ARG1$ -s $ARG2$ -a $ARG3$
check_command       check_dns!host.domain.com!ns1.domain.net!12.34.56.78
```

check_dhcp works by sending a standard DHCP-DISCOVER broadcast request via UDP 67. When the server replies with DHCPOFFER, *check_dhcp* says thank you and does not pester the server further.

See Also

- "Using Macros In Commands" (*http://localhost/nagios/docs/macros.html*) in your local Nagios documentation for a list of built-in macros
- For definitions of the options in object definition files, which are all the files in *lan_objects/,* start at "Template-Based Object Configuration": *http://localhost/nagios/docs/xodtemplate.html*
- Nagios.org: *http://www.nagios.org/*

13.14 Setting Up Secure Remote Nagios Administration with OpenSSH

Problem

You're not comfortable with running remote Nagios sessions over HTTP because all transmissions are sent in the clear. You could set up SSL, but that seems like a big hassle because you'll have to create a certificate and configure Apache to use SSL. So, why not just set up a nice, easy, secure OpenSSH tunnel?

Solution

No reason why not. OpenSSH is an amazingly flexible, useful program. Setting a tunnel on your LAN is easy. Our two example hosts are *nagiospc* and *neighborpc*. You need system accounts on both hosts. Run a command like this from *neighborpc* to set up a tunnel to your Nagios server:

```
user@neighborpc:~$ ssh user@nagiospc -L 8080:nagiospc:80
```

Now, fire up a Web browser on *neighborpc*, and go to *http://localhost:8080/nagios*. The entire session will be safely tucked inside an SSH tunnel, and safe from snoopers.

To run a Nagios session over the Internet, see Chapter 7 to learn how to get SSH tunnels past your NAT firewall.

Discussion

When logging in over SSH, don't use the *nagios* user, because by default it has no password and cannot log in. Instead, log in as some other unprivileged user, then authenticate in the usual manner on the Nagios web interface.

The command syntax can be a little confusing, so let's break it into bite-sized chunks. The first part is the same as any remote SSH login: *user@remote_host*.

The -L flag means "create a tunnel."

8080, or whatever port you select, is the outgoing port on your local PC. Be sure to choose an unused, high-numbered (higher than 1024) port.

nagiospc:80 is the remote server and port. So, you'll always need to know which port the service you want to tunnel is using.

See Also

- Chapter 7
- Chapter 17, "Remote Access," in *Linux Cookbook*, by Carla Schroder (O'Reilly)

13.15 Setting Up Secure Remote Nagios Administration with OpenSSL

Problem

Remote Nagios logins over SSH are OK, but you would like it to be even easier. Just fire up a web browser, log in to Nagios, and be done with it. You know you can do this with OpenSSL. How do you set it up?

Solution

On Fedora, it's as easy as falling over. Simply install Apache's SSL module with this command:

```
# yum -y install mod_ssl
```

To restrict all access to HTTPS only, make sure these lines exist in *httpd.conf*:

```
#Listen 80
Listen 443
```

On Debian, it's a few more steps. Run these commands:

```
# apt-get install apache2.2-common
# a2enmod ssl
# cp /etc/apache2/sites-available/default /etc/apache2/sites-available/ssl
# ln -s /etc/apache2/sites-available/ssl /etc/apache2/sites-enabled/ssl
```

Then, create a new self-signed SSL certificate with the apache2-ssl-certificate script, which is part of *apache2-common*:

```
# /usr/sbin/apache2-ssl-certificate -days 365
```

Now, edit */etc/apache2/sites-enabled/ssl*. Replace the first three lines with these lines, using your own server name or IP address:

```
NameVirtualHost *:443
<VirtualHost *:443>
ServerName windbag.alrac.net
SSLEngine On
SSLCertificateFile /etc/apache2/ssl/apache.pem
```

Put these lines in */etc/apache2/ports.conf*:

```
#Listen 80
Listen 443
```

Restart Apache with a force-reload:

```
# /etc/init.d/apache2 force-reload
* Forcing reload of apache 2.0 web server...    [ ok ]
```

Now, fire up a web browser and try *http://localhost/nagios* and *https://localhost/ nagios*. Only the second one should work. The first time you connect, your browser will ask you if you want to accept the certificate. You can view it to make sure it's the right one.

Discussion

Managing SSL with Apache changed a lot between Apache 1.3 and Apache 2. Keep in mind you want *mod_ssl* for Apache 2, not *apache_ssl*.

Debian's apache2-ssl-certificate script is a small wrapper to the standard OpenSSL certificate-creation commands. It defaults to a 30-day expiration, which is probably too short for most circumstances.

See Also

- Apache HTTP Server Documentation: *http://httpd.apache.org/docs/*

CHAPTER 14

Network Monitoring with MRTG

14.0 Introduction

MRTG, the Multi-Router Traffic Graph, was originally designed to collect SNMP traffic counters of routers, log the data, and convert the data to graphs. These graphs are embedded in web pages, and can be read from any web browser. Because MRTG is based on SNMP, you may use it to graph practically any device or service that is SNMP-enabled. This also means you need to pay attention to SNMP, because if SNMP doesn't work, MRTG doesn't work.

MRTG builds daily, weekly, monthly, and yearly graphs, so it's a great tool for seeing trends at a glance. "A picture is worth a thousand words" is especially true when you're riding herd on a network.

MRTG only collects data and creates graphs; it does not send alerts. It stores data in its own logfiles, which helpfully manage themselves. MRTG automatically consolidates its logs, so you don't have to worry about them ballooning out of control. It keeps data for two years.

MRTG also depends on an HTTP server. In this chapter, we'll use Lighttpd because it is a fast, lightweight HTTP server that is well-suited for MRTG. Of course, you may use whatever you like.

There are three versions of SNMP: SNMPv1, SNMPv2, and SNMPv3. SNMPv1 is the most widespread, and probably will be for some time to come. The main objection to v1 is the lack of security; all messages are sent in cleartext. v2 was developed to add security, but it seems that development got a bit out of hand, and we ended up with four versions:

- SNMPv2p
- SNMPv2c
- SNMPv2u
- SNMPv2 "star" or SNMPv2*

Only the first three are documented in RFCs, as a proper standard should be. Though in the case of SNMP, having RFCs may not be all that helpful because there are dozens upon dozens of the things. v2 also includes some new features and functionality that adds complexity, so it's a bit confused. It is backward compatible with v1.

SNMPv3 is supposed to restore order and sanity, and it is a nice implementation that has real security, so over time it may replace v1 and v2. In this chapter, we'll stick with v1 and v2c because they are the most widely deployed and the simplest to use. SNMPv3 encrypts all traffic and requires authentication from all hosts, so it's more work to set up and maintain, and a lot of devices still don't support it. Because MRTG only reads data, we'll create a simple read-only SNMP configuration in this chapter. Nobody will need any write permissions. If you want all the encryption and authentication goodies, *Essential SNMP*, Second Edition, by Douglas Mauro and Kevin Schmidt (O'Reilly) has an excellent chapter on using SNMPv3.

14.1 Installing MRTG

Problem

You're all ready to get MRTG up and running. What's the best way to install it—from sources, or with your nice easy dependency-resolving installers like Aptitude and Yum?

Solution

There isn't much to be gained from a source install, other than control over file locations and build options, so using the easy way is perfectly OK. You need *snmp*, an HTTP server, and MTRG. On Debian, install it this way:

```
# aptitude install snmp snmpd mrtg lighttpd
```

On Fedora, install it with this command:

```
# yum install net-snmp-utils net-snmp mrtg lighttpd
```

And that's all there is to it. See the next recipes to get up and running.

Discussion

Even in this modern era of sophisticated dependency-resolving package managers like Aptitude and Yum, we are still at the mercy of our distribution maintainers for keeping binary packages up-to-date, and built with useful options. So sometimes a source build is the better option, even though it means more difficult updates and patching. Fortunately, MRTG is popular and well-maintained on most Linux distributions.

The Debian and Fedora packages are based on *net-snmp*, which contains an SNMP agent, command-line management tools, and a Management Information Browser (MIB).

MRTG depends on SNMP and requires an HTTP server. I like Lighttpd because it is a nice, lightweight HTTP server that is perfect for chores like this, when you don't need all the bells and whistles of Apache. Of course, you may use any HTTP server you like.

See Also

- Net-SNMP: *http://net-snmp.sourceforge.net/*
- Tobi Oetiker's MRTG: *http://oss.oetiker.ch/mrtg/*
- Lighttpd: *http://www.lighttpd.net/*

14.2 Configuring SNMP on Debian

Problem

You need to make sure SNMP is operating correctly before you configure MRTG. What's a good basic configuration, and how do you test it?

Solution

You need to first make sure that *snmpd* is running. The installer should have automatically started it. Check *snmpd* with this command:

```
$ snmpwalk -v 2c -c public localhost system
SNMPv2-MIB::sysDescr.0 = STRING: Linux xena 2.6.20-16-generic #2 SMP Thu Jun 7 20:19:
32 UTC 2007 i686
SNMPv2-MIB::sysObjectID.0 = OID: NET-SNMP-MIB::netSnmpAgentOIDs.10
DISMAN-EVENT-MIB::sysUpTimeInstance = Timeticks: (359297) 0:59:52.97
SNMPv2-MIB::sysContact.0 = STRING: Root <root@localhost> (configure /etc/snmp/snmpd.
local.conf)
SNMPv2-MIB::sysName.0 = STRING: xena
[...]
```

Now, we'll move the default *snmpd.conf* file out of the way, and replace it with our own bare bones edition:

```
# cd /etc/snmp
# mv snmpd.conf snmpd.conf-old
# chmod 0600 snmpd.conf
# chmod 0666 snmpd.conf-old
```

The last command is optional; it makes the default file available to ordinary users for study and reference. Our new *snmpd.conf* consists of just a few lines. Replace password with your own choice for a password. Don't use public or private, the default *snmp* passwords:

```
###/etc/snmp/snmpd.conf
##        sec.name    source            community
##        ========    ======            =========
com2sec  local       localhost         password
com2sec  lan         192.168.1.0/24    password
```

```
##        Access.group.name   sec.model   sec.name
##        =================   =========   ========
group     ROGroup_1              v1        local
group     ROGroup_1              v1        lan
group     ROGroup_1              v2c       local
group     ROGroup_1              v2c       lan

##   MIB.view.name      incl/excl   MIB.subtree   mask
##   =============      =========   ===========   ====
view all-mibs           included      .1           80

##        MIB
##        group.name   context sec.model sec.level prefix read    write notif
##        ==========   ======= ========= ========= ====== ====    ===== =====
access    ROGroup_1      ""      v1        noauth    exact all-mibs none  none
access    ROGroup_1      ""      v2c       noauth    exact all-mibs none  none
```

Make sure this file is owned and readable only by *root*. Then, restart *snmpd*:

 # /etc/init.d/snmpd restart

Next, try the *snmpwalk* command again:

```
$ snmpwalk -v 2c -c public localhost system
Timeout: No Response from localhost
```

Now, try it with your new password, which in SNMP lingo is called the *community string*:

```
$ snmpwalk -v 2c -c password localhost system
SNMPv2-MIB::sysDescr.0 = STRING: Linux xena 2.6.20-16-generic #2 SMP Thu Jun 7 20:19:
32 UTC 2007 i686
SNMPv2-MIB::sysObjectID.0 = OID: NET-SNMP-MIB::netSnmpAgentOIDs.10
DISMAN-EVENT-MIB::sysUpTimeInstance = Timeticks: (105655) 0:17:36.55
SNMPv2-MIB::sysContact.0 = STRING: root
SNMPv2-MIB::sysName.0 = STRING: xena
[...]
```

OK then! It works.

snmpd is controlled via the usual Debian *init* commands:

 # /etc/init.d/snmpd {start|stop|restart|reload|force-reload}

Discussion

Let's take a look at what we did. There are four keywords that we're using for setting up access controls: com2sec, view, group, and access.

com2sec

   com2sec, or community-to-security, defines a security name (sec.name), which is a combination of the community string and source IP address.

view

Defines which parts of the MIB tree are available to view. This example allows access to the entire tree.

group

This creates named groups and maps them to their security names.

access

This specifies who has access to which bits of the MIB tree. This example lets everyone in the Read-only Group (ROGroup_1) read all MIBs, using SNMP v1 or v2c. ROGroup_1 is an arbitrary name; you may call it anything you want.

There is a simpler way to do the same thing:

```
rocommunity password
```

That single line replaces the entire example file. You're welcome to use this if you prefer; it's simpler and makes debugging easier. Using and understanding the longer file will help you later as you create more complex *snmpd.conf* configurations.

snmpwalk syntax is pretty simple:

```
snmpwalk [options] community hostname [OID]
```

This is what the options mean:

-v

Selects which SNMP protocol to use. Your choices are v1, v2c, and v3 (the default).

-c

Set the community string, which is the same as a password. The default *snmp. conf* creates two default community strings: public and private. Because everyone in the world knows these, we got rid of them.

localhost

Specify which device you're querying.

system

system is a shortcut name for all the OIDs under the 1.3.6.1.2.1.1 hierarchy. snmpwalk -v 1 -c password localhost .1.3.6.1.2.1.1 returns the same results. In the examples, I use system just to reduce the quantity of output. Leave it off, and you'll see lots more.

See Also

- ASN.1 Information: *http://asn1.elibel.tm.fr/en/index.htm*
- Net-SNMP: *http://net-snmp.sourceforge.net*
- man snmpd.conf

14.3   Configuring SNMP on Fedora

Problem

You need to make sure SNMP is operating correctly before you configure MRTG. What's a good basic configuration, and how do you test it?

Solution

Start it manually with this command:

```
# /etc/init.d/snmpd start
```

To have it start automatically at boot, use *chkconfig*:

```
# chkconfig  snmpd on
# chkconfig --list snmpd
snmpd    0:off 1:off 2:on 3:on 4:on 5:on 6:off
```

snmpd is controlled via the usual startup scripts:

```
/etc/init.d/snmpd {start|stop|status|restart|condrestart|reload}
```

Now, you can go back to the previous recipe, and follow the steps there.

Discussion

This is a bare bones SNMP configuration that allows you to get MRTG up and running with a minimum of fuss, and to reduce the number of potential complications. See the Discussion in Recipe 14.2 for information on configuration options.

See Also

- Net-SNMP: *http://net-snmp.sourceforge.net*
- man snmpd.conf

14.4   Configuring Your HTTP Service for MRTG

Problem

You installed Lighttpd to serve up your MRTG pages. What do you have to do to prepare it for MRTG?

Solution

There is hardly anything to this, because MRTG comes with a script to create its own *root* web directory. So, all you need to do is configure the Lighttpd startup files. The Debian installer creates startup files, and starts up the HTTP daemon for you. On Fedora, you need to do this yourself:

```
# /etc/init.d/lighttpd start
```

To have it start automatically at boot, use *chkconfig*, and confirm that it worked:

```
# chkconfig lighttpd on
# chkconfig --list lighttpd
lighttpd    0:off 1:off 2:on 3:on 4:on 5:on 6:off
```

Then, check by opening a web browser to *http://localhost/*. This should display the default HTTP server page, like Figure 14-1 shows.

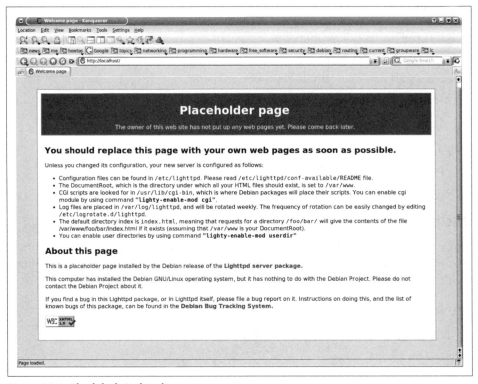

Figure 14-1. The default Lighttpd page

lighttpd is controlled on Fedora via the usual startup script commands:

```
# /etc/init.d/lighttpd {start|stop|status|restart|condrestart|reload}
```

Debian's are little bit different:

```
# /etc/init.d/lighttpd {start|stop|restart|reload|force-reload}
```

Discussion

This works for any HTTP server; just substitute the correct name in the commands.

See Also

- Lighttpd: *http://www.lighttpd.net/*

14.5 Configuring and Starting MRTG on Debian

Problem

OK already, enough with the preliminaries. Your SNMP and HTTP daemons are installed and running, and you want to get going with MRTG and start making nice network graphs like everyone else. What do you do now?

Solution

First, we'll have MRTG monitor all the up network interfaces on our server.

Run this command to create the initial MRTG configuration file. password is whatever SNMP community string you set:

```
# cfgmaker --output=/etc/mrtg.cfg \
--global "workdir: /var/www/mrtg" -ifref=ip \
--global 'options[_]: growright,bits' \
password@localhost
```

Then, start it manually:

```
# mrtg /etc/mrtg.conf
----------------------------------------------------------------------
ERROR: Mrtg will most likely not work properly when the environment
       variable LANG is set to UTF-8. Please run mrtg in an environment
       where this is not the case. Try the following command to start:

       env LANG=C /usr/bin/mrtg /etc/mrtg.cfg
----------------------------------------------------------------------
```

So, do that:

```
# env LANG=C mrtg /etc/mrtg.cfg
```

If your default is already LANG=C, then you won't see that message. If you get "Rateup WARNING" error messages, repeat the command until they go away. This usually takes three tries.

Run this command to create the HTML index file:

```
# indexmaker --output=/var/www/mrtg/index.html /etc/mrtg.cfg
```

Now, point a web browser to localhost (*http://localhost/mrtg/*), and you should see nice graphs tracking all of your up interfaces, like in Figure 14-2.

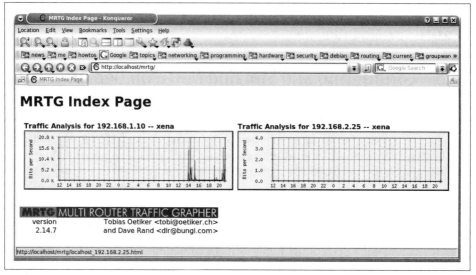

Figure 14-2. MRTG graphs of two active local network interfaces

Click on any graph to view detailed statistics, as shown in Figure 14-3.

This shows that it is working correctly.

Discussion

Let's take a look at what we did in the command:

`--output=/etc/mrtg.cfg`
> This tells the `cfgmaker` command where to create the MRTG configuration file.

`--global "workdir: /var/www/mrtg" -ifref=ip`
> This setting goes in the global section of *mrtg.cfg*, and defines the directory where the HTML files are stored. `-ifref=ip` tells MRTG to track your network interfaces by IP address.

`--global 'options[_]: growright,bits'`
> This means your graphs will expand to the right, and network traffic will be measured in bits.

`password@localhost`
> The community string (password) for *snmpd*.

Debian installs a *crontab* for MRTG in */etc/cron.d/mrtg* that updates the graphs every five minutes, so you don't need to take any additional steps to keep it running.

Running env `LANG=C mrtg /etc/mrtg.cfg` commonly emits error messages like this:

```
Rateup WARNING: /usr/bin/rateup could not read the primary log file for localhost_
192.168.1.10
Rateup WARNING: /usr/bin/rateup The backup log file for localhost_192.168.1.10 was
invalid as well
```

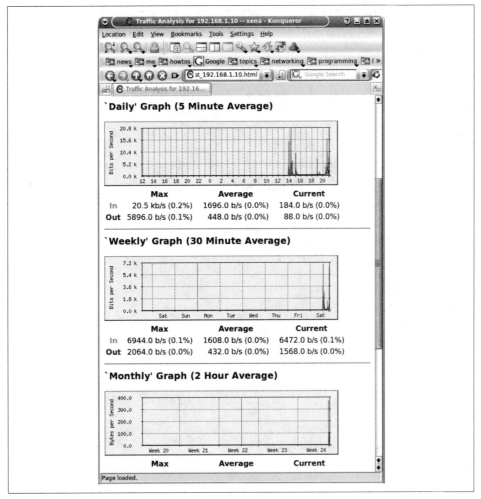

Figure 14-3. Detailed interface statistics

```
Rateup WARNING: /usr/bin/rateup Can't remove localhost_192.168.1.10.old updating log
file
Rateup WARNING: /usr/bin/rateup Can't rename localhost_192.168.1.10.log to localhost_
192.168.1.10.old updating log file
```

It's just complaining about routine business. Ignore it, and keep running the command until it doesn't emit any more error messages; three times usually does the job.

See Also

- man 1 cfgmaker
- man 1 mrtg-reference
- MRTG home page: *http://oss.oetiker.ch/mrtg/*

14.6   Configuring and Starting MRTG on Fedora

Problem

OK already, enough with the preliminaries. Your SNMP and HTTP daemons are installed and running, and you want to get going with MRTG and start making nice network graphs like everyone else. What do you do now?

Solution

First, we'll have MRTG monitor all the up network interfaces on our server.

Run this command to create the initial MRTG configuration file. `password` is what-ever SNMP community string you set:

```
# cfgmaker --output=/etc/mrtg/mrtg.cfg \
--global "workdir: /var/www/mrtg" -ifref=ip \
--global 'options[_]: growright,bits' \
password@localhost
```

Then, start it manually:

```
# mrtg /etc/mrtg/mrtg.cfg
----------------------------------------------------------------------
ERROR: Mrtg will most likely not work properly when the environment
       variable LANG is set to UTF-8. Please run mrtg in an environment
       where this is not the case. Try the following command to start:

       env LANG=C /usr/bin/mrtg /etc/mrtg.cfg
----------------------------------------------------------------------
```

So, do that:

```
# env LANG=C mrtg /etc/mrtg/mrtg.cfg
```

If your default is already `LANG=C`, then you won't see this message.

Run this command to create the HTML index file:

```
# indexmaker --output=/var/www/mrtg/index.html /etc/mrtg/mrtg.cfg
```

Now, point a web browser to localhost (*http://localhost/mrtg/*) and you should see nice graphs tracking all of your up interfaces, like in Figures 14-2 and 14-3 in the previous recipe. This shows that it is working correctly.

Discussion

Fedora installs a *crontab* for MRTG in */etc/cron.d/mrtg* that updates the graphs every five minutes, so you don't need to take any additional steps to keep it running.

See the Discussion in the previous recipe for explanations of the command options.

See Also

- man 1 cfgmaker
- man 1 mrtg-reference
- MRTG home page: *http://oss.oetiker.ch/mrtg/*

14.7 Monitoring Active CPU Load

Problem

You want to use MRTG to keep an eye on CPU performance. *cfgmaker* only sets up graphs for your network interfaces. Now what?

Solution

You'll need to edit *mrtg.cfg* by hand. Don't use *cfgmaker* anymore because it will overwrite your changes. This recipe monitors system, user, and nice values, and adds them up to give a snapshot of CPU load.

Add this line to the Global Config Options section:

```
# Global Config Options
LoadMIBs: /usr/share/snmp/mibs/UCD-SNMP-MIB.txt,/usr/share/snmp/mibs/TCP-MIB.txt
```

Then, add this section at the bottom of the file:

```
# monitor CPU load
#
Target[xena.cpu]: ssCpuRawUser.0&ssCpuRawUser.0:password@localhost + ssCpuRawSystem.
0&ssCpuRawSystem.0:password@localhost + ssCpuRawNice.0&ssCpuRawNice.0:
password@localhost
Title[xena.cpu]: Xena CPU Load
RouterUptime[xena.cpu]: password@127.0.0.1
PageTop[xena.cpu]: <H1>CPU System, User and Nice stats for Xena</H1>
MaxBytes[xena.cpu]: 100
ShortLegend[xena.cpu]: %
YLegend[xena.cpu]: CPU Usage
Legend1[xena.cpu]: Current CPU percentage load
LegendI[xena.cpu]: Used
LegendO[xena.cpu]:
Options[xena.cpu]: growright,nopercent
Unscaled[xena.cpu]: ymwd
```

While you're there, you might as well delete the entry for the loopback device, as you're not going to use it anyway. Now, run *mrtg* manually three times, or until it stops complaining, and mind your filepaths:

```
# env LANG=C mrtg /etc/mrtg.cfg
```

Then, generate a new *index.html* page:

```
# indexmaker --output=/var/www/mrtg/index.html /etc/mrtg.cfg
```

Now, you should see something like Figures 14-4 and 14-5.

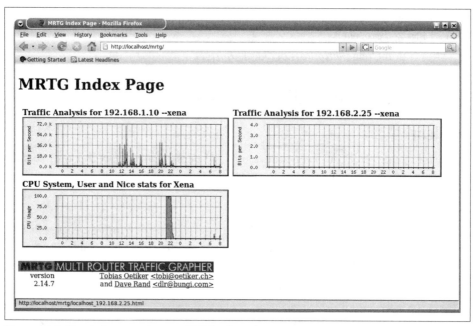

Figure 14-4. New index page showing CPU load graph

Discussion

These aren't very exciting graphs because they're on a test system with little activity. But, they do show what the entries in *mrtg.cfg* make the graphs look like. Let's take a tour of the configuration:

LoadMIBs

> You have to tell MRTG which MIB files from */usr/share/snmp/* to load. You'll see them cached in */var/www/mrtg/oid-mib-cache.txt*. Using the LoadMIBs option means you'll be able to use the symbolic names of the OIDs, rather than having to use their numbers.

Target[xena.cpu]: ssCpuRawUser.0&ssCpuRawUser.0:password@localhost...

> The syntax for this line is *Keyword[graph name]: value*. The Target keyword defines what you want monitored. The *value* is a list of OID pairs joined by the ampersand, &. The *graph name* is anything you want, and it must be unique. MRTG only knows how to measure pairs of values, so when you're plotting a single value, just repeat the target definition. Whitespace must surround each target definition. This example contains three target definitions, connected with the plus sign. The plus sign means "add these together."

Title

> This is the title of the detailed HTML page.

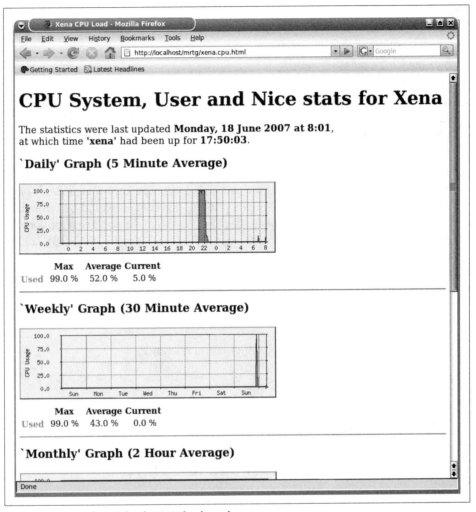

Figure 14-5. Detail page for the CPU load graph

RouterUptime

> Use this to display the system uptime on the detail page.

PageTop

> The headline of the detail page.

MaxBytes

> This is either a value in bytes, or it behaves as a percentage.

ShortLegend

> The units string used for Max, Average, and Current. The default is b/s, bits per second.

YLegend

The Y-axis, or vertical axis, which is for the label of the graph. If you make it too long, it will be silently ignored.

Legend1 *(and 2, 3, and 4)*

Strings for the color legends.

LegendI *(and 0)*

Input and output. Because the different values in this graph are added up to a single sum, and each OID pair is the same OID rather than two OIDs, we're only using LegendI.

Options

growright means expand the graph to the right, and nopercent means don't print percentage values. For our CPU graphs printing percentages would be redundant because we already have percentage displays. Without the nopercent option the graph legends it would display like this: *Used 65.0 % (65.0%) 35.0 % (35.0%) 6.0 % (6.0%).*

Unscaled

The default is scaled, which means MRTG will adjust the graph to make small data more visible. The unscaled option creates a fixed-size graph. ymwd represents year, month, week, day.

man 1 mrtg-reference is your primary configuration reference.

See Also

- man 1 mrtg-reference
- MRTG home page: *http://oss.oetiker.ch/mrtg/*

14.8 Monitoring CPU User and Idle Times

Problem

The previous recipe gives a useful snapshot of CPU activity over time, but you would like to see separate rather than aggregate values, such as idle time and user processes, or system and user processes, or perhaps one of these alone.

Solution

Try adding this to *mrtg.cfg*:

```
# monitor CPU user and idle loads
#
Target[xena2.cpu]: ssCpuRawUser.0&ssCpuRawIdle.0:password@localhost
RouterUptime[xena2.cpu]: password@localhost
MaxBytes[xena2.cpu]: 100
Title[xena2.cpu]: User and Idle CPU usage- Xena
```

```
PageTop[xena2.cpu]: <H1>User and CPU Load- Xena</H1>
ShortLegend[xena2.cpu]: %
YLegend[xena2.cpu]: CPU Usage
Legend1[xena2.cpu]: User CPU in % (Load)
Legend2[xena2.cpu]: Idle CPU in % (Load)
LegendI[xena2.cpu]:  User
LegendO[xena2.cpu]:  Idle
Options[xena2.cpu]: growright,nopercent
Unscaled[xena2.cpu]: ymwd
```

Make sure that LoadMIBs: /usr/local/share/snmp/mibs/UCD-SNMP-MIB.txt is in the Global Config Options section. Run these commands to load the changes:

```
# env LANG=C mrtg /etc/mrtg.cfg
# indexmaker --output=/var/www/mrtg/index.html /etc/mrtg.cfg
```

Mind your filepaths because they vary on different Linux distributions, and remember to run the first command until it quits emitting error messages, which should take no more than three tries.

So, point your web browser to localhost (*http://localhost/mrtg*), and admire your new graphs, which are now tracking two values:

```
        Max     Average  Current
User 9.0 %       8.0 %   6.0 %
Idle 92.0 %     79.0 %   93.0 %
```

Discussion

There are two important changes in this example from the previous recipe. One is the target line—note that the OID pair are two different OIDs. The other change is the graph name. Every graph name must be unique.

You can tweak this in a number of ways. Here are the four main CPU object variables:

ssCpuRawUser
> This tracks CPU usage by nonprivileged applications.

ssCpuRawNice
> Tracks the CPU usage of nonpriority applications.

ssCpuRawSystem
> CPU usage by privileged applications.

ssCpuRawIdle
> Measures idle time.

You may use these singly or in combination. To track single values, remember that you still need to specify an OID pair, so you use the same one twice:

```
Target[xena2.cpu]:ssCpuRawIdle.0&ssCpuRawIdle.0:password@localhost
```

And, remember to tweak your Legends and page titles accordingly.

See the Discussion in Recipe 14.7 for more information on configuration options, and man 1 mrtg-reference for detailed information.

See Also

- man 1 mrtg-reference
- MRTG home page: *http://oss.oetiker.ch/mrtg/*

14.9   Monitoring Physical Memory

Problem

You need to keep an eye on physical memory usage, and you want to track how much is free. How do you do this with MRTG?

Solution

Try this in *mrtg.cfg*:

```
# Monitoring Free Physical Memory
#
Target[xena.mem]: memAvailReal.0&memAvailReal.0:password@localhost
Title[xena.mem]: Free Memory In Bytes- Xena
PageTop[xena.mem]: <H1>Free Memory In Bytes- Xena</H1>
MaxBytes[xena.mem]: 512000
YLegend[xena.mem]: Free Memory in Bytes
ShortLegend[xena.mem]: bytes
LegendI[xena.mem]: Free Memory
LegendO[xena.mem]:
Legend1[xena.mem]: Free memory, not including swap, in bytes
options[xena.mem]: growright,gauge,nopercent
Unscaled[xena.mem]: ymwd
```

Don't forget to enter your total amount of system memory for the MaxBytes option.

Make sure that LoadMIBs: /usr/local/share/snmp/mibs/UCD-SNMP-MIB.txt is in the Global Config Options section. Run these commands to load the changes:

```
# env LANG=C mrtg /etc/mrtg.cfg
# indexmaker --output=/var/www/mrtg/index.html /etc/mrtg.cfg
```

Mind your filepaths, because they vary on different Linux distributions, and remember to run the first command until it quits emitting error messages, which should take no more than three tries.

Discussion

Use the free command to see how much RAM you have installed. This doesn't have be a precise number for the MaxBytes option because all it does is set the upper limit of what the graph will display, so you can round it up a bit.

Perhaps you would rather see a percentage than bytes. Do this by changing the target line, and then adjusting your legends:

```
Target[xena2.mem]: ( memAvailReal.0&memAvailReal.0:password@localhost ) * 100 / (
memTotalReal.0&memTotalReal.0:password@localhost )
RouterUptime[xena2.mem]: password@localhost
Title[xena2.mem]: Free Memory By Percentage- Xena
PageTop[xena2.mem]: <H1>Free Memory By Percentage- Xena</H1>
MaxBytes[xena2.mem]: 512000
YLegend[xena2.mem]: Memory %
ShortLegend[xena2.mem]: Percent
LegendI[xena2.mem]: Free
LegendO[xena2.mem]:
Legend1[xena2.mem]: % Free Memory
options[xena2.mem]: growright,gauge,nopercent
```

Remember that whitespace must surround each target definition.

This example does not use the Unscaled option because the amount of free memory was so small on my test system that it was barely visible. The MRTG default is scaled graphs, which adjusts the size of the graph to make the data more visible, so when you want this, all you do is leave off the unscaled option.

See Also

- man 1 mrtg-reference
- MRTG home page: *http://oss.oetiker.ch/mrtg/*

14.10 Monitoring Swap Space and Memory

Problem

You want MRTG to graph your physical memory and swap space, so you can see your total memory usage.

Solution

Try this in *mrtg.cfg*:

```
# Monitoring Memory and Swap Space

Target[xena.memswap]:memAvailReal.0&memAvailSwap.0:password@localhost
RouterUptime[xena.memswap]: password@localhost
Title[xena.memswap]: Free Memory and Swap - Xena
PageTop[xena.memswap]: <H1>Free Memory and Swap - Xena</H1>
MaxBytes[xena.memswap]: 650624
YLegend[xena.memswap]: total free memory
ShortLegend[xena.memswap]: bytes
LegendI[xena.memswap]: Free Memory
LegendO[xena.memswap]: Free Swap
Legend1[xena.memswap]: Free physical memory in bytes
```

```
Legend2[xena.memswap]: Free swap in bytes
options[xena.memswap]: growright,gauge,nopercent
Unscaled[xena.memswap]: ymwd
```

For MaxBytes, enter whichever is the larger value—swap or RAM.

Make sure that `LoadMIBs: /usr/local/share/snmp/mibs/UCD-SNMP-MIB.txt` is in the Global Config Options section. Run these commands to load the changes:

```
# env LANG=C mrtg /etc/mrtg.cfg
# indexmaker --output=/var/www/mrtg/index.html /etc/mrtg.cfg
```

Mind your filepaths because they vary on different Linux distributions, and remember to run the first command until it quits emitting error messages, which should take no more than three tries.

Discussion

Use the free command to see how much RAM and swap space your system has. This doesn't have be a precise number because all it does is set the upper limit of what the graph will display, so you can round it up a bit.

This is a useful graph to watch over time, so you can see if your installed RAM is adequate.

See Also

- man 1 mrtg-reference
- MRTG home page: *http://oss.oetiker.ch/mrtg/*

14.11 Monitoring Disk Usage

Problem

You want to keep an eye on some of your disk partitions and see how full they are getting.

Solution

First, you need to edit *snmpd.conf*, adding the partitions you wish to monitor:

```
## /etc/snmp/snmpd.conf
disk /var
disk /home
```

Then, restart *snmpd*:

```
# /etc/init.d/snmpd restart
```

Try this in *mrtg.cfg*:

```
# Monitor disk usage of /var and /home partitions
#
Target[server.disk]: dskPercent.1&dskPercent.2:password@localhost
```

```
Title[server.disk]: Disk Partition Usage
PageTop[server.disk]: <H1>Disk Partition Usage /var and /home</H1>
MaxBytes[server.disk]: 100
ShortLegend[server.disk]: % Y
Legend[server.disk]: % used
LegendI[server.disk]: /var
LegendO[server.disk]: /home
Options[server.disk]: gauge,growright,nopercent
Unscaled[server.disk]: ymwd
```

Make sure that `LoadMIBs: /usr/local/share/snmp/mibs/UCD-SNMP-MIB.txt` is in the Global Config Options section. Run these commands to load the changes:

```
# env LANG=C mrtg /etc/mrtg.cfg
# indexmaker --output=/var/www/mrtg/index.html /etc/mrtg.cfg
```

Mind your filepaths, because they vary on different Linux distributions, and remember to run the first command until it quits emitting error messages, which should take no more than three tries.

Discussion

This only works on disk partitions—you cannot select just any old directory.

Give MRTG an hour or so, then check your work with the `df -h` command:

```
$ df -h
Filesystem        Size  Used Avail Use% Mounted on
/dev/hda1          14G  2.3G   11G  17% /
/dev/hda3           5G  1.8G  3.2G  36% /usr
/dev/sda1          31G  6.5G   24G  22% /home
/dev/hda2         4.5G  603M  3.7G  14% /var
```

MRTG should agree with `df`. If it doesn't, MRTG is wrong.

There is a bit of trickiness with selecting your `dskPercent` OIDs. They follow the order they are listed in within *snmpd.conf*. Suppose you have four disk partitions listed like this:

```
disk /
disk /usr
disk /var
disk /home
```

Then, for */var* and */home*, you need to use `dskPercent.3` and `dskPercent.4`.

The computing world likes to cause confusion by numbering some things from zero, and some things from 1. Disk partitions on Linux start at 1.

See Also

- man 1 mrtg-reference
- man 1 df
- MRTG home page: *http://oss.oetiker.ch/mrtg/*

14.12 Monitoring TCP Connections

Problem

You're running a fairly busy web server, so you want to keep an eye on how many new TCP connections are hitting your server.

Solution

This example measures the number of new TCP connections per minute:

```
LoadMIBS: /usr/share/snmp/mibs/TCP-MIB.txt
#
# New TCP Connections per minute
#
Target[server.http]: tcpPassiveOpens.0&tcpActiveOpens.0:password@webserver1
RouterUptime[xena1.swap]: password@localhost
Title[server.http]: New TCP Connections- Webserver1
PageTop[server.http]: <h1>New TCP Connections per minute - Webserver1</h1>
MaxBytes[server.http]: 1000000000
ShortLegend[server.http]: c/s
YLegend[server.http]: Connections/Min
LegendI[server.http]: Incoming
LegendO[server.http]: Outgoing
Legend1[server.http]: New inbound connections
Legend2[server.http]: New outbound connections
Options[server.http]: growright,nopercent,perminute
```

Run these commands to load the changes:

```
# env LANG=C mrtg /etc/mrtg.cfg
# indexmaker --output=/var/www/mrtg/index.html /etc/mrtg.cfg
```

Mind your filepaths, because they vary on different Linux distributions, and remember to run the first command until it quits emitting error messages, which should take no more than three tries.

Discussion

This is a nice graph for keeping an eye on how hard visitors are pummeling your web server. tcpPassiveOpens.0 counts the incoming connections, and tcpActiveOpens.0 measures how many connections are being initiated by the server. Netstat shows the same data, but not in a pretty graph:

```
$ netstat -s | egrep '(passive|active)'
    211 active connections openings
    230581 passive connection openings
```

See Also

- man 1 mrtg-reference
- man 8 netstat
- MRTG home page: *http://oss.oetiker.ch/mrtg/*

14.13 Finding and Testing MIBs and OIDs

Problem

All of this MIB and OID stuff is a bit mysterious. How do you find them? How do you know what to use? How do you verify that you have the correct ones?

Solution

When you see an error like this from starting MRTG:

```
# env LANG=C mrtg /etc/mrtg.cfg
SNMP Error:
Received SNMP response with error code
  error status: noSuchName
  index 2 (OID: 1.3.6.1.4.1.2021.9.1.9.3)
[...]
```

It means either the OID does not exist, or you did not enter the correct file for the LoadMIBs option in *mrtg.cfg*. The first thing to do is query the numerical OID:

```
$ snmpwalk  -v 1 -c password localhost 1.3.6.1.4.1.2021.9.1.9.3
UCD-SNMP-MIB::dskPercent.3 = INTEGER: 22
```

This shows that you have the correct OID, so you need to correct your LoadMIBs entry. *snmpwalk* shows you the correct MIBs file. If you don't know what directory your MIBs files are in, the locate command will tell you:

```
$ locate UCD-SNMP-MIB
/usr/share/snmp/mibs/UCD-SNMP-MIB.txt
```

So, LoadMIBs needs to look like this:

```
LoadMIBs: /usr/share/snmp/mibs/UCD-SNMP-MIB.txt
```

Then, rerun mrtg, and you're in business.

This command lists all OIDs on your system:

```
$ snmpwalk -v 1 -c password localhost
```

There are thousands of them:

```
$ snmpwalk -v 1 -c password localhost | wc -l
1824
```

systemis actually a symbolic name; the real OID name is a number that you can see with the -On option:

```
$ snmpwalk -On -v 1 -c password localhost system
.1.3.6.1.2.1.1.1.0 = STRING: Linux xena 2.6.20-16-generic #2 SMP Thu Jun 7 20:19:32
UTC 2007 i686
.1.3.6.1.2.1.1.2.0 = OID: .1.3.6.1.4.1.8072.3.2.10
[...]
```

So, .1.3.6.1.2.1.1 is the same as system, and it has a hierarchy of OIDs under it. These two commands are the same:

```
$ snmpwalk -v 1 -c password localhost system
$ snmpwalk -v 1 -c password localhost .1.3.6.1.2.1.1
```

It's more common with commercial routers to use the OIDs in your MRTG configuration, rather than having the luxury of a symbolic name.

Discussion

How do you find out which ones you want in the first place? This is more complicated. You can dig up OIDs for some trial-and-error testing with the usual Linux search tools:

```
$ grep -ir tcp /usr/share/snmp/mibs/
/usr/share/snmp/mibs/TCP-MIB.txt:TCP-MIB DEFINITIONS ::= BEGIN
/usr/share/snmp/mibs/TCP-MIB.txt:tcpMIB MODULE-IDENTITY
/usr/share/snmp/mibs/TCP-MIB.txt: "The MIB module for managing TCP implementations.
/usr/share/snmp/mibs/TCP-MIB.txt:-- the TCP base variables group
[...]
```

You're probably better off looking for documentation specific to the devices and services you want to monitor, especially commercial routers such as Cisco, Juniper, NetGear, and so forth. In an ideal world, all vendors would make complete information available, and many vendors are good at keeping up-to-date information and helpful documentation on their web sites.

If you can't get what you need from the vendor, try these sites:

Alvestrand (http://www.alvestrand.no/objectid/)
    Everything you could ever want to know about MIBs and OIDs is here.

MIB Depot (http://www.mibdepot.com/index.shtml)
    This site is a good resource for vendor-specific information.

See Also

- Net-SNMP: *http://net-snmp.sourceforge.net*
- man snmpd.conf
- *Essential SNMP,* Second Edition, by Douglas Mauro and Kevin Schmidt (O'Reilly)

14.14 Testing Remote SNMP Queries

Problem

You want your MRTG server to monitor a number of remote devices, such as other servers or routers. How do you test to make sure that SNMP is going to work correctly? Because if SNMP queries fail, so will MRTG.

Solution

Test this with *snmpwalk* just like you did for localhost, substituting the hostname or IP address of the remote host, and using whatever OID you like, or no OID at all:

```
$ snmpwalk -v 2c -c password uberpc interfaces
```

What if you get the common and vexing "Timeout: No Response from uberpc" error message? This is the standard response to a lot of errors, such as:

- Wrong password (community string).
- Firewall is blocking port UDP 631.
- *tcpwrappers* is blocking port UDP 631.
- *snmpd* is listening to a different port.
- *snmpd* is not accepting queries from outside of localhost.

Port UDP 631 needs to be open on all SNMP hosts, and *snmpd* needs to be listening to 0.0.0.0:161, which you will see by running `netstat -untap`. On Debian, *snmpd* is restricted to localhost by default. You will see this with *netstat* and *ps*:

```
$ netstat -untap
udp    0    0   127.0.0.1:161      0.0.0.0:*
$ ps ax|grep snmpd
 9630 ?   S   0:01 /usr/sbin/snmpd -Lsd -Lf /dev/null -u snmp -I -smux -p /var/run/
snmpd.pid 127.0.0.1
```

This is controlled in */etc/default/snmpd* with this line:

```
SNMPDOPTS='-Lsd -Lf /dev/null -u snmp -I -smux -p /var/run/snmpd.pid 127.0.0.1'
```

Delete 127.0.0.1, restart *snmpd*, and you'll be fine. We're using *snmpd.conf* for access controls, so this is unnecessary.

This *iptables* rule allows traffic going to UDP port 631 to pass:

```
$ipt -A INPUT -p udp --dport 631 -j ACCEPT
```

Discussion

On mailing lists and forums, the most common suggestion for the "Timeout: No Response" error is to check *tcpwrappers* and make sure it is not blocking SNMP queries. This is rather unhelpful advice because modern Linux distributions don't use *tcpwrappers* very much. It's still installed on most stock installations, and it's easy enough to check—see if you have */etc/hosts.allow* or */etc/hosts.deny*, and if they are present, check to see if they are gumming up your SNMP queries. Chances are the files won't even exist on your system.

The most common causes are misconfiguring your SNMP access controls. See Recipe 14.2 or 14.3 to learn more about SNMP access controls.

See Also

- Chapter 3
- Net-SNMP: *http://net-snmp.sourceforge.net*
- man 1 snmpd.conf
- man 1 snmpwalk.conf

14.15 Monitoring Remote Hosts

Problem

All of this monitoring of your local system is OK, but what you really want to do is set up an MRTG server to monitor remote servers and routers. How do you do this?

Solution

The hosts you wish to monitor either need to have built-in SNMP agents, or they must have Net-snmp installed. Virtually all modern networking devices have built-in SNMP agents. Linux and Unix servers need Net-snmp.

For configuring your Linux hosts, follow Recipes 14.2, 14.3, and 14.14.

Then, in *mrtg.cfg*, you need to change the Target line to point to your remote host, like this:

```
Target[uberpc.disk]: dskPercent.2&dskPercent.3:password@uberpc
```

And of course, fiddle with the legends and page titles so you know what graph belongs to what.

Discussion

Be sure to review the SNMP Recipes to learn how to test and troubleshoot MRTG's SNMP queries, because if SNMP doesn't work, MRTG won't work.

You only need an SNMP agent on your remote hosts; they don't need an HTTP server or MRTG.

See Also

- Net-SNMP: *http://net-snmp.sourceforge.net*
- man 1 snmpd.conf
- man 1 snmpwalk.conf
- man 1 mrtg-reference
- MRTG home page: *http://oss.oetiker.ch/mrtg/*

14.16 Creating Multiple MRTG Index Pages

Problem

Your MRTG server is humming along happily, but you have a problem—your index page is growing out of control. How do you bring some organization to the MRTG index?

Solution

You might create separate index pages. You may choose to organize by hosts, service, or any way you want. In this recipe, we'll create a separate MRTG index page for the Linux server Uberpc, following these steps:

First, create a *mrtg-uberpc.cfg* file, and populate it with your chosen monitors. We're past the training wheels stage, so we won't bother with *cfgmaker*, but we will create the file from scratch. Be sure to specify the correct workdir:

```
workdir: /var/www/mrtg/uberpc
```

Then, create the */var/www/mrtg/uberpc* directory and the logfile directory:

```
# mkdir /var/www/mrtg/uberpc
# mkdir /var/log/mrtg/mrtg-uberpc.log
```

Next, run the two graph and index page creation commands:

```
# env LANG=C mrtg /etc/mrtg-uberpc.cfg
# indexmaker --output=/var/www/mrtg/uberpc/index.html /etc/mrtg-uberpc.cfg
```

Run env LANG=C mrtg /etc/mrtg-uberpc.cfg three times, until it stops emitting error messages.

Finally, add a new *cron* job for the new configuration in */etc/cron.d/mrtg*. This example copies the default Debian *cron* configuration for MRTG:

```
### xena
*/5 *  * * *   root    if [ -d /var/lock/mrtg ]; then if [ -x /usr/bin/mrtg ] && [ -
r /etc/mrtg.cfg ]; then env LANG=C /usr/bin/mrtg /etc/mrtg.cfg >> /var/log/mrtg/mrtg.
log 2>&1; fi else mkdir /var/lock/mrtg; fi

#### uberpc
*/5 *  * * *   root    if [ -d /var/lock/mrtg ]; then if [ -x /usr/bin/mrtg ] && [ -
r /etc/mrtg-uberpc.cfg ]; then env LANG=C /usr/bin/mrtg /etc/mrtg-uberpc.cfg >> /var/
log/mrtg/mrtg-uberpc.log 2>&1; fi else mkdir /var/lock/mrtg; fi
```

Finally, point your web browser to localhost (*http://localhost/mrtg/uberpc/*), and enjoy your new MRTG pages.

Discussion

Depending on how powerful your MRTG server is, running all those *cron* jobs will eventually bog it down. Running MRTG as a daemon is more efficient; see Recipe 14.17 for more information.

See Also

- man 1 mrtg-reference
- MRTG home page: *http://oss.oetiker.ch/mrtg/*

14.17 Running MRTG As a Daemon

Problem

You know that running MRTG from *cron* consumes more system resources because it loads and parses the configuration file or files every time it starts. So, you want to run it as a daemon. How do you do this?

Solution

It takes a number of steps, so roll up your sleeves and follow along:

Create a user and group just for running MRTG:

```
# groupadd mrtg
# useradd -d /dev/null -g mrtg -s /bin/false mrtg
```

Hunt down and change all files that the *mrtg* user must have write permissions for, and change them:

```
# chown -R mrtg:mrtg /var/www/mrtg
# chown -R mrtg:mrtg /var/log/mrtg/
```

Add these lines to the Global section of *mrtg.cfg*:

```
RunAsDaemon: Yes
Interval:    5
```

Delete all existing *cron* jobs, or just move them out of the way in case you want them back:

```
# mv /etc/cron.d/mrtg ../mrtg
```

Create a lockfile, and start MRTG from the command line:

```
# mkdir /var/lock/mrtg/
# chown -R mrtg:mrtg /var/lock/mrtg/
# env LANG=C mrtg --daemon --user=mrtg --group=mrtg /etc/mrtg.cfg
Daemonizing MRTG ...
```

If you have more than one configuration file, line 'em up:

```
# env LANG=C mrtg --daemon --user=mrtg --group=mrtg /etc/mrtg.cfg /etc/mrtg-uberpc.
cfg
```

Check with the *ps* command:

```
$ ps ax|grep mrtg
26324 ? Ss 0:00 /usr/bin/perl -w /usr/bin/mrtg --daemon --user=mrtg --group=mrtg /
etc/mrtg.cfg
```

And that shows we are successful!

To start it automatically at boot, you'll need a file in */etc/init.d*, and startup links on the runlevels you want to use. An *init* file can be as simple as this:

```
#!/bin/sh
## /etc/init.d/mrtg
# chkconfig 2345 90 30
#
mkdir /var/lock/mrtg/
chown -R mrtg:mrtg /var/lock/mrtg/
# this must be one unbroken line
env LANG=C mrtg --daemon --user=mrtg --group=mrtg /etc/mrtg.cfg \
/etc/mrtg-uberpc.cfg
```

Make it executable:

```
# chmod +x /etc/init.d/mrtg
```

Then, create your startup links on Debian with *update-rc.d*:

```
# update-rc.d mrtg start 90 2 3 4 5 . stop 30 0 1 6
```

Fedora uses *chkconfig*:

```
# chkconfig --add mrtg
```

Discussion

You really need a better *init* file than the example. Debian users can use */etc/init.d/ skeleton* as a model for creating new startup files.

This is a basic startup script that should work anywhere:

```
#! /bin/sh
## /etc/init.d/foo
#
# most apps need a lockfile
touch /var/lock/foo

# start 'er up
  case "$1" in
    start)
      echo "Starting script foo "
      echo "optional other things here"
      ;;
    stop)
```

```
        echo "Stopping script foo now"
        echo "optional other things here"
        ;;
    *)
    echo "Usage: /etc/init.d/foo {start|stop}"
    exit 1
    ;;
esac
exit 0
```

See Also

- man 1 mrtg-reference
- MRTG home page: *http://oss.oetiker.ch/mrtg/*

## CHAPTER 15

Getting Acquainted with IPv6

15.0 Introduction

IPv6 has far more to recommend it than merely providing a vastly larger pool of IP addresses. Here are some handy bullet-pointed highlights:

- Network autoconfiguration (say goodbye to DHCP)
- No more private address collisions
- Better multicast routing
- The newfangled anycast routing
- Network Address Translation (NAT) becomes an option, rather than a necessity
- Simplified, more efficient routing and smaller routing tables
- Genuine quality of service (QoS)
- Good-quality streaming media delivery

In short, it promises to make the life of the network administrator significantly easier, and to make a whole new generation of high-quality on-demand streaming audio and video services a reality.

In this chapter, you'll learn the basics of using IPv6: network addressing, autoconfiguration, network interface configuration, ad-hoc IPv6 LANs, and how to calculate IPv6 addresses without needing hundreds of fingers to count on.

IPv6 adoption is proceeding slowly in the U.S., but it is inevitable. It doesn't cost anything but a bit of time to get acquainted with it in your test lab. Linux has supported IPv6 since the later 2.1.x kernels, and most of the important Linux networking utilities now support IPv6.

Most of the pieces are in place: most networking hardware (e.g., switches, interfaces, routers) supports IPv6 now. Cameras, cell phones, PDAs, and all manner of devices now support IPv6. Growing numbers of Internet service providers offer native IPv6, and you can set up an IPv6-over-IPv4 tunnel that works over existing networks, which is good for practice and testing. Standards and protocols are pretty much hammered out and in place.

The two final pieces that are needed are first, application support (because networked applications must explicitly support IPv6), and second, service providers actually migrating to native IPv6. Some network engineers predict that the majority of ISPs will not get serious about it until the day they call up their Regional Internet Registry (RIR) to get more IPv4 addresses, and their RIR regretfully informs them that there aren't any more.

Barriers to Adoption

The barriers to faster IPv6 adoption are the usual suspects: cost, inertia, and lack of knowledge. The scarcity of IPv4 addresses means they are nice little revenue-generators because ISPs typically charge extra for static, routable addresses. This will change with IPv6—I will let the numbers speak for themselves. There are theoretically:

> 4,294,967,296

IPv4 addresses available because IPv4 uses a 32-bit address space. In contrast, there are theoretically:

> 340,282,366,920,938,463,463,374,607,431,768,211,456

addresses available under IPv6 because it is a 128-bit address space. In practice, because of reserved addresses and the way in which blocks of IPv4 addresses are allocated, the usable pool of IPv4 addresses is reported as 3,706,650,000, or about three-fourths of the theoretical total. The U.S. owns nearly 60 percent of these. (For details, see the "BGP Expert 2006 IPv4 Address Use Report" at *http://www.bgpexpert.com/addrspace2006.php.*)

The actual number of available IPv6 addresses is somewhat smaller than the theoretical number, but not enough to matter here on planet Earth. If we ever expand to a galaxy-wide Internet, then we'll need more addresses, but we'll cross that bridge when we come to it.

Interestingly, while the U.S. hogs the IPv4 address space, it lags considerably behind other countries in IPv6 adoption and affordable high-speed broadband. Many U.S. ISPs do dominate in one area: silly terms of service that forbid running servers, sharing your Internet connection, or supporting any operating system other than Microsoft Windows (which we know is ridiculous—favoring the most notoriously porous operating system, with all of its well-known security flaws and tens of thousands of Internet-clogging botnets is a policy direct from the planet Bizarro). Trying to control how many users share a single Internet connection is like charging per-user for tap water.

So, IPv6 uptake is more motivated in countries outside the U.S. Japan and the European Union lead in IPv6 adoption, and also in advanced broadband and wireless services.

IPv6 is not backward-compatible with IPv4. We're going to have IPv4 and IPv6 running side-by-side for some time, with all the added complexity and overhead that comes with that. But eventually, IPv4 is going to go away.

Anatomy of IPv6 Addresses

IPv6 addresses contain eight dotted quads totaling 128 bits, as this example of a global unicast address shows:

    2001:0db8:3c4d:0015:0000:0000:abcd:ef12

An IPv6 *global unicast* address is like a static, publicly routable unicast IPv4 address, such as 208.201.239.36 (one of *oreilly.com*'s addresses). These are globally unique addresses controlled by a central registrar. (For a list of regional registrars, see ICANN.org at *http://aso.icann.org/rirs/index.html*.)

In the IPv4 world, the provider's prefix can consume up to the first three dotted quads. *whois* shows us that the service provider's prefix eats up three-fourths of the *oreilly.com* address:

```
$ whois  208.201.239.36
[...]
SONIC.NET, INC. UU-208-201-224 (NET-208-201-224-0-1)
              208.201.224.0 - 208.201.255.255
```

If O'Reilly wants more addresses, it has to get them assigned from its upstream service provider. IPv4 addresses are doled out in a miserly fashion; a small customer might get lucky and get five, and a bigger customer can, with a bit of luck, get a larger number. It is unlikely that either one will receive enough to provision their whole organization, but either one will have to use nonroutable private addresses behind NAT. But, no matter how generous the service provider is, they can't come close to a typical IPv6 assignment, which is 2^{64} active hosts per subnet. Spelled out, that totals:

    18,446,744,073,709,551,616

That is a pool of globally unique, routable addresses just for you, times your number of subnets, which can be as many as 65,536. This should be sufficient to meet your needs.

Let's dissect our example IPv6 global unicast address:

```
2001:0db8:3c4d:0015:0000:0000:abcd:ef12
_____|___|_____ ___
global prefix subnet  Interface ID
```

Each quad is 16 bits. The global prefix is assigned by an ISP to its customers. Typically, this is /48 bits, as shown here, but it can vary; a large company might get /32, and a small company /56. This portion is not something you can arbitrarily change because it is assigned to you by your service provider. So, the network portion of the address is the first 64 bits, and the host portion is the remaining 64 bits. Even though it is a larger number, this is simpler than remembering all of those different IPv4 address classes and many ways to make subnets.

The next quad is for your own use for subnetting. With 16 bits to play with, this means you can have 65,536 subnets all for your very own.

The final 64 bits is the *interface ID*, or the network interface's address. This is often derived from the 48-bit MAC address of the network interface card, but this is not a requirement. Just like the subnet portion, you may use this however you want. So, under IPv6 you won't be a beggar any more, but truly the lord of your own domain.

IPv6 address types and ranges

These are the address ranges you'll be most concerned with. These are assigned by the Internet Assigned Numbers Authority (IANA) *http://www.iana.org/assignments/ipv6-address-space*. All the other addresses are reserved:

```
IPv6 Prefix   Allocation
-------------------------------
0000::/8      Reserved by IETF
2000::/3      Global Unicast
FC00::/7      Unique Local Unicast
FE80::/10     Link Local Unicast
FF00::/8      Multicast
```

These blocks are reserved for examples and documentation:

```
-------------------------------
3fff:ffff::/32
2001:0DB8::/32   EXAMPLENET-WF
```

The loopback address and IPv6 addresses with embedded IPv4 addresses come from the 0000::/8 address block. Your Linux system probably comes with IPv6 addressing already enabled:

```
$ ifconfig
eth0      Link encap:Ethernet  HWaddr 00:03:6D:00:83:CF
          inet addr:192.168.1.10  Bcast:192.168.1.255  Mask:255.255.255.0
          inet6 addr: fe80::203:6dff:fe00:83cf/64 Scope:Link
          UP BROADCAST RUNNING MULTICAST  MTU:1500  Metric:1
          [...]
```

```
lo          Link encap:Local Loopback
            inet addr:127.0.0.1  Mask:255.0.0.0
            inet6 addr: ::1/128 Scope:Host
            UP LOOPBACK RUNNING  MTU:16436  Metric:1
            [...]
```

Scope:Link, or the *Link Local Unicast* address for *eth0* means this is a private, non-routable IPv6 address that operates only within a single subnet. Link Local addresses are for easily throwing together ad-hoc networks, such as for conferences or meetings, and on most Linux distributions are created automatically.

Scope:Host for *lo* is the loopback address, which means packets from this address never leave the host.

Unique Local Unicast addresses are similar to Link Local Unicast addresses. They are meant to be routable locally, but not over the Internet. Link Local addresses may not always be unique, so you have a risk of address collisions; Unique Local Unicast addresses have a globally unique prefix, and are independent of any service provider, so they give you a unique private class of addresses to use internally.

Multicast in IPv6 is similar to the broadcast address in IPv4, with some useful differences. A packet sent to a multicast address is delivered to every interface in a defined group. So, it is targeted—only hosts who are members of the multicast group receive the multicast packets. Routers will not forward multicast packets unless there are members of the multicast groups to forward the packets to, which pretty much spells the end of broadcast storms. They always start with ff.

Where are these multicast groups defined? For a complete listing, see "IPv6 multicast addresses" at *http://www.iana.org/assignments/ipv6-multicast-addresses*.

An *anycast* address is a single address assigned to multiple nodes. A packet sent to an anycast address is then delivered to the first available node. This is a great way to provide both load-balancing and automatic failover. Several of the DNS *root* servers use a router-based anycast implementation. Anycast addresses can only be used as destination addresses, and not source addresses. Anycast addresses come from the unicast address space, so you can't tell from the prefix that they are anycast addresses.

You've probably seen 3FFE::/16 addresses in various How-tos. These were for the 6Bone test network that shut down in June 2006, so they don't work anymore.

Counting in Hexadecimal

IPv6 addresses are not dotted-decimal like IPv4, but base-16 numbers expressed in hexadecimal. So, you count like this:

```
0   1   2   3   4   5   6   7   8   9   A   B   C   D   E   F
10  11  12  13  14  15  16  17  18  19  1A  1B  1C  1D  1E  1F
20  21  22  23  24  25  26  27  28  29  2A  2B  2C  2D  2E  2F
```

When your lefthand digit gets to 9, you roll over to letters to keep going:

```
90  91  92  93  94  95  96  97  98  99  9A  9B  9C  9D  9E  9F
A0  A1  A2  A3  A4  A5  A6  A7  A8  A9  AA  AB  AC  AD  AE  AF
B0  B1  B2  B3  B4  B5  B6  B7  B8  B9  BA  BB  BC  BD  BE  BF
```

IP addresses start out as binary numbers. We use hexadecimal notation for convenience. Don't worry about managing these larger addresses because *ipv6calc* will do the calculating for you.

Mac and Windows IPv6 Support

Mac OS X has excellent IPv6 support, which should work out of the box.

Support for IPv6 in Microsoft Windows is a bit of a hodgepodge. Windows Vista, Windows Server 2008, Windows Server 2003, Windows XP with Service Pack 2, Windows XP with Service Pack 1, Windows XP Embedded SP1, and Windows CE .NET include native IPv6 support.

Windows 2000 admins can try the MS Tech Preview IPv6 stack. It's not intended for production systems, but for testing:

- tpipv6-001205-SP2-IE6.zip, SP2
- tpipv6-001205-SP3-IE6.zip, SP3
- tpipv6-001205-SP4-IE6.zip, SP4

Instructions are at *http://msdn.microsoft.com/downloads/sdks/platform/tpipv6/start.asp*.

Admins of Windows 95/98/ME and NT systems can try Trumpet Winsock v5.0.

For the least hassle and hair loss, you'll want the later Windows editions with native IPv6 suppport.

15.1   Testing Your Linux System for IPv6 Support

Problem

How do you know if your Linux system supports IPv6 and is ready to use it?

Solution

There are a few basic tests you can run to check your system for IPv6 readiness.

First, check kernel support:

```
$ cat /proc/net/if_inet6
00000000000000000000000000000001 01 80 10 80       lo
fe8000000000000002036dfffe0083cf 02 40 20 80     eth0
```

The file */proc/net/if_inet6* must exist, and this example shows two up interfaces with IPv6 addresses. You can also see if the IPv6 kernel module is loaded:

```
$ lsmod |grep -w 'ipv6'
ipv6        268960  12
```

Now, *ping6* localhost:

```
$ ping6 -c4 ::1
PING ::1(::1) 56 data bytes
64 bytes from ::1: icmp_seq=1 ttl=64 time=0.047 ms
64 bytes from ::1: icmp_seq=2 ttl=64 time=0.049 ms
64 bytes from ::1: icmp_seq=3 ttl=64 time=0.049 ms
64 bytes from ::1: icmp_seq=4 ttl=64 time=0.049 ms

--- ::1 ping statistics ---
4 packets transmitted, 4 received, 0% packet loss, time 3000ms
rtt min/avg/max/mdev = 0.047/0.048/0.049/0.007 ms
All systems are go for IPv6.
```

As the output says, you are good to go.

Discussion

All Linux distributions from this century should support IPv6 without needing any extra configuration. If yours doesn't, which would be very unusual, you'll need to use the documentation for your distribution to figure out what to do. Peter Bieringer's "Linux IPv6 HOWTO" (*http://tldp.org/HOWTO/Linux+IPv6-HOWTO/index.html*) should also be helpful.

See Also

- Peter Bieringer's "Linux IPv6 HOWTO":
    http://tldp.org/HOWTO/Linux+IPv6-HOWTO/index.html

15.2   Pinging Link Local IPv6 Hosts

Problem

You want to start with the basics—testing your IPv6 connectivity with *ping*. Can you even do this?

Solution

Of course you can, with the *ping6* command, which should be included in all modern Linux distributions. This is how you *ping6* localhost, and your Link Local addresses:

```
$ ping6 -c2 ::1
PING ::1(::1) 56 data bytes
64 bytes from ::1: icmp_seq=1 ttl=64 time=0.045 ms
64 bytes from ::1: icmp_seq=2 ttl=64 time=0.048 ms
```

```
--- ::1 ping statistics ---
2 packets transmitted, 2 received, 0% packet loss, time 1002ms
rtt min/avg/max/mdev = 0.045/0.046/0.048/0.007 ms
```

$ ping6 -c2 -I eth0 fe80::203:6dff:fe00:83cf
```
PING fe80::203:6dff:fe00:83cf(fe80::203:6dff:fe00:83cf) from fe80::203:6dff:fe00:83cf
eth0: 56 data bytes
64 bytes from fe80::203:6dff:fe00:83cf: icmp_seq=1 ttl=64 time=0.046 ms
64 bytes from fe80::203:6dff:fe00:83cf: icmp_seq=2 ttl=64 time=0.051 ms

--- fe80::203:6dff:fe00:83cf ping statistics ---
2 packets transmitted, 2 received, 0% packet loss, time 999ms
rtt min/avg/max/mdev = 0.046/0.048/0.051/0.007 ms
```

When you *ping6* the link local address, you must specify your network interface with the -I switch, even if you have only a single interface on your system. If you don't do this, you'll get a "connect: Invalid argument" error.

Now, how about *pinging* other hosts on your LAN? First, you must discover them by *pinging* the Link Local Multicast address:

$ ping6 -I eth1 ff02::1
```
PING ff02::1(ff02::1) from fe80::203:6dff:fe00:83cf eth0: 56 data bytes
64 bytes from fe80::203:6dff:fe00:83cf: icmp_seq=1 ttl=64 time=0.049 ms
64 bytes from fe80::214:2aff:fe54:67d6: icmp_seq=1 ttl=64 time=2.45 ms (DUP!)
64 bytes from fe80::20d:b9ff:fe05:25b4: icmp_seq=1 ttl=64 time=9.68 ms (DUP!)
[...]
```

Keep going until you see the same addresses repeating. *ping6* helps you by shouting (DUP!). Now you can *ping6* them:

$ ping6 -I eth0 fe80::214:2aff:fe54:67d6

Now you know that your IPv6 Link Local addresses work.

Discussion

How do you know what your Link Local address is? *ifconfig* tells you:

$ /sbin/ifconfig
```
eth0      Link encap:Ethernet  HWaddr 00:03:6D:00:83:CF
          inet addr:192.168.1.10  Bcast:192.168.1.255  Mask:255.255.255.0
          inet6 addr: fe80::203:6dff:fe00:83cf/64 Scope:Link
          UP BROADCAST RUNNING MULTICAST  MTU:1500  Metric:1
          [...]
```

See Also

- man 8 ping

15.3 Setting Unique Local Unicast Addresses on Interfaces

Problem

You don't want to use just the Link Local addresses, but you would like to know how to add and remove your own IPv6 addresses, and you want to experiment with Unique Local Unicast addresses, so you can test routing.

Solution

The *ip* command is the tool for this job. Use these commands to set some Unique Local Unicast addresses on two connected PCs:

```
root@xena:~# ip -6 addr add FC01::1/64 dev eth0
root@stinkpad:~# ip -6 addr add FC01::2/64 dev eth0
```

Now, you can *ping6* each other:

```
root@xena:~# ping6 FC01::2
PING FC01::2(fc01::2) 56 data bytes
64 bytes from fc01::2: icmp_seq=1 ttl=64 time=7.33 ms
```

```
root@stinkpad:~# ping6 FC01::1
$ ping6 FC01::1
PING FC01::3(fc01::1) 56 data bytes
64 bytes from fc01::1: icmp_seq=1 ttl=64 time=6.06 ms
```

And each host can *ping6* its own shiny new address. You don't need to specify the interface when you're *pinging* Unique Local Unicast addresses like you do for Link Local addresses.

These addresses are removed when you reboot, or you can use *ip*:

```
# ip -6 addr del FC01::1/64 dev eth0
```

Discussion

This is purely a technical exercise, and not useful for production systems. Unique Local Unicast addresses are supposed to be globally unique. How to achieve this without using a central registry? RFC 4193 "Unique Local IPv6 Unicast Addresses" offers some suggestions for methods for generating unique addresses, but they're intended for programmers to create nice address-generating utilities, not network administrators.

What you can do with this is simply increment the Interface ID portion of the address as you assign Unique Local Unicast addresses to additional hosts and use these for testing routing, name services, and other basic network functions.

Why bother with these, when you'll be able to get more global unicast addresses from your service provider than you'll ever be able to use? Because:

- They are independent of any service provider, so you can be just as arbitrary as you want.
- They have a well-known prefix to allow for easy filtering at border routers.
- If they accidentally leak outside your network, they shouldn't conflict with any other addresses.

The simple examples in this recipe demonstrate some shortcuts for expressing IPv6 addresses. FC01::1 is shorthand for FC01:0000:0000:0000:0000:0000:0000:0001. The required structure of the address looks like this:

```
| 7 bits |1|  40 bits  |  16 bits  |            64 bits            |
+--------+-+-----------+-----------+-------------------------------+
| Prefix |L| Global ID | Subnet ID |         Interface ID          |
+--------+-+-----------+-----------+-------------------------------+
```

IPv6 allows you to collapse quads full of zeros. FC01::1 could also be written as FC01:0:0:0:0:0:0:1. We'll discuss this more in Recipe 15.7.

See Also

- man 8 ping
- RFC 4193 "Unique Local IPv6 Unicast Addresses"

15.4   Using SSH with IPv6

Problem

Can you do remote administration with SSH using IPv6?

Solution

Of course you can, like this:

```
$ ssh fe80::214:2aff:fe54:67d6%eth0
carla@fe80::214:2aff:fe54:67d6%eth0's password:
Linux uberpc 2.6.20-15-generic #2 SMP Sun Apr 15 07:36:31 UTC 2007 i686
Last login: Wed Jun  6 18:51:46 2007 from xena.alrac.net
carla@uberpc:~$
```

Note that for Link Local addresses you must specify your network interface and preface it with the percent sign. You can log in as a different user this way:

```
$ ssh user@fe80::214:2aff:fe54:67d6%eth0
```

If you're using unicast addresses, you don't need to specify the interface:

```
$ ssh user@FC01::1
```

Copying files with *scp* is a pain because you have to enclose the address in brackets and then escape the brackets:

```
$ scp filename.txt \[FC01::2\]:
carla@fc01::2's password:
filename.txt
```

Discussion

This isn't all that useful in the real world because it's likely you'll be relying on DNS more than IPv6 addresses. But it is helpful for testing and troubleshooting.

If you have access controls set up on your SSH server, you may need to change some options to permit logins via IPv6:

AddressFamily
: The default is any. You may also use inet for IPv4, or inet6.

ListenAddress
: The default is any. If you are restricting access by IP addresses, you'll need to add the local IPv6 address.

See Also

- man 1 ssh
- man 5 sshd_config
- man 1 scp

15.5 Copying Files over IPv6 with scp

Problem

SSH works fine for logging in to remote PCs using IPv6 addresses, but when you try to copy files with *scp*, it doesn't work. You are rewarded with the unhelpful message:

```
ssh: fe80: Name or service not known
lost connection
```

Now what?

Solution

scp requires some strange syntax that you have to get just right, as this example shows:

```
$ scp filename carla@\[fe80::203:6dff:fe00:83cf%eth0\]:
```

The IPv6 address must be enclosed in brackets, which must then be escaped. If you're logging in as a different user, the username goes outside the braces. And you must specify the local interface with the percent sign for Link Local addresses, just like with OpenSSH.

Discussion

As this was written, neither the *scp* nor the OpenSSH manpages described the special IPv6 syntax, so you read it here first.

See Also

- man 1 ssh
- man 1 scp

15.6   Autoconfiguration with IPv6

Problem

You keep hearing about this wonderful autoconfiguration in IPv6. How do you do this?

Solution

Make it easy on yourself, and use the *radvd*, the router advertising daemon. This simple example */etc/radvd.conf* uses the addressing from Recipe 15.3:

```
##/etc/radvd.conf
interface eth0 {
        AdvSendAdvert on;
        MinRtrAdvInterval 3;
        MaxRtrAdvInterval 10;
        prefix FC00:0:0:1::/64 {
                AdvOnLink on;
                AdvAutonomous on;
                AdvRouterAddr on;
        };
};
```

Save your changes, and restart *radvd*:

```
# /etc/init.d/radvd restart
Restarting radvd: radvd.
```

radvd will advertise itself, and clients will automatically pick up new addresses, as the *ip* command will verify:

```
$ ip -6 addr show eth0
2: eth0: <BROADCAST,MULTICAST,UP,10000> mtu 1500 qlen 1000
    inet6 fc00::1:214:2aff:fe54:67d6/64 scope global dynamic
```

Discussion

radvd is meant to be simple, so that is really all there is to it. When you're playing around on your test network, you may use any IPv6 address range you want (see the Introduction for more information on these). Just keep in mind that the prefix is the first 64 bits, or the first four quads, and the host portion is also 64 bits. You leave the host portion blank in *radvd.conf* because the daemon will assign that part.

See Also

- man 8 radvd
- man 5 radvd.conf

15.7 Calculating IPv6 Addresses

Problem

Calculating IPv4 addresses was enough fun, and now you have these gigantic IPv6 addresses to manage. Is there a tool like *ipcalc* to help you make sure you get your addressing right?

Solution

Yes, there is—*ipv6calc*. It's easy to use, as the following examples show.

This command analyzes whatever address you give it, both IPv4 and IPv6:

```
$ ipv6calc --showinfo -m FC00:0:0:1::
No input type specified, try autodetection...found type: ipv6addr
No output type specified, try autodetection...found type: ipv6addr
IPV6=fc00:0000:0000:0001:0000:0000:0000:0000
TYPE=unicast,unique-local-unicast
SLA=0001
IPV6_REGISTRY=reserved
IID=0000:0000:0000:0000
EUI64_SCOPE=local
```

This example compresses an IPv6 address:

```
$ ipv6calc --addr_to_compressed fc00:0000:0000:0001:0000:0000:0000:0000
fc00:0:0:1::
```

This example partly uncompresses an IPv6 address:

```
$ ipv6calc --addr_to_uncompressed fc00:0:0:1::
fc00:0:0:1:0:0:0:0
```

This example spells it out completely:

```
$ ipv6calc --addr_to_fulluncompressed fc00:0:0:1::
fc00:0000:0000:0001:0000:0000:0000:0000
```

ipv6calc will figure out your DNS PTR records for you, so you can copy-and-paste them into your BIND zone files:

```
$ ipv6calc --out revnibbles.arpa fc00:0:0:1::
No input type specified, try autodetection...found type: ipv6addr
0.0.0.0.0.0.0.0.0.0.0.0.0.0.0.0.1.0.0.0.0.0.0.0.0.0.0.0.0.c.f.ip6.arpa.
```

You can convert IPv6 prefixes to IPv4, and the reverse:

```
$ ipv6calc -q --action conv6to4 --in ipv4 192.168.1.10 --out ipv6
2002:c0a8:10a::
$ ipv6calc -q --action conv6to4 --in ipv6 2002:c0a8:aeb:: --out ipv4
192.168.10.235
```

Discussion

Calculating subnets is easier in IPv6 because you only have a single field in the address to worry about, and even though there are several different address ranges (see the chapter Introduction for a table of address ranges and types), the structure of the addresses is the same for every one. The first 64 bits, or four quads, are always the network prefix and subnet. The last 64 bits are always the interface address.

You can test using IPv6 over the Internet by signing up with a 6to4 tunnel broker. These are service providers that provide special routing to carry IPv6 traffic over IPv4 networks. Your IPv4 address is converted to hexadecimal format, and embedded in your IPv6 tunnel prefix. 6to4 addresses always start with 2002:

```
2002:nnnn:nnnn::1
```

See Also

- man 8 ipv6calc

15.8   Using IPv6 over the Internet

Problem

All of this playing around on the LAN is OK, but you really want to do some serious Internet testing. Do you need a special ISP, or can you do it yourself?

Solution

You do need a special service provider. You have two options: an ISP that offers native IPv6 networking, which would be wonderful, or a broker that offers a 6to4 tunnel, which uses special routing that encapsulates IPv6 traffic inside of IPv4. ISPs and brokers give you a block of IPv6 addresses, just like a native IPv6 provider, and also offer DNS services. You may connect a single host, or set up a gateway for your LAN.

6to4 tunneling is transitional, and will eventually disappear in favor of native IPv6 networks. Here is a list of tunnel brokers, and doubtless a web search will find more:

- Hexago.com (*http://www.hexago.com*)
- SixXs.net (*https://noc.sixxs.net/*)
- Hurricane Electric (*http://www.tunnelbroker.net/*)
- BT Exact (*https://tb.ipv6.btexact.com/start.html*)
- AARNet IPv6 Migration Broker (*http://broker.aarnet.net.au/*)

Discussion

Each provider offers different tools for managing your service, so you'll need to follow their instructions for getting connected. Most of these offer free services, and it's a great way to get experience managing an IPv6 network.

See Also

- Deepspace6 (*http://www.deepspace6.net/*) is a good resource for Linux IPv6 admins

## CHAPTER 16

Setting Up Hands-Free Network Installations of New Systems

16.0   Introduction

Rolling out new Linux installations over the network and reimaging old ones is easy, once you have the necessary servers in place and have your clients set up to network-boot. It's a bit complicated on x86 hardware because the x86 platform was not originally designed for network booting, so even now, network booting x86 clients is rather hit-or-miss. Of course, Linux gives you a number of boot options, so you can make it work one way or another:

- Boot from a CD-ROM
- Boot from a USB flash drive
- Use PXE boot

Debian and Fedora Linux provide network-booting images for CD-ROM and USB devices. They also support Preboot Execution Environment (PXE) booting, which means you don't need a CD-ROM or USB drive—all you need is a network interface and a PC BIOS that support PXE booting, and a PXE boot server.

 If your BIOS or NIC do not support PXE booting, then go to the Etherboot project site (*http://www.etherboot.org*). Download a boot image, copy it to a floppy disk, configure the system to boot from the diskette, and you're good to go.

PXE Boot

If you're putting together a network with older gear, it might not support PXE boot; however, you might be able to to upgrade it without too much hassle. The first thing to check is the BIOS. Anything older than 2000 or so probably won't support PXE booting, but you might be able to flash-upgrade the BIOS and get support for PXE booting and other modern features.

Once the BIOS is squared away, check your network interface. Some network cards support PXE boot out of the box; this is the best and easiest way. Some have an empty socket designed to hold an add-on boot ROM chip.

Some just plain won't support PXE booting at all. You can purchase programmed ROM chips for around $18. You can also buy blank ROMs to put your own boot code on, which seems like a lot of work, but if that's what you want to do, then the Etherboot project (*http://www.etherboot.org*) will help you.

Or, again, avoid all this, and use an Etherboot diskette.

USB Boot

Booting from a USB drive, whether it's a large hard drive or a little USB pen drive, is also hit-or-miss. Newer machines should support it, though there are a few gotchas to look out for. Your USB drive must be plugged in before you power up the machine. Then, check your BIOS settings to make sure that all possible USB support options are enabled.

Next, check to see if it has a "boot to an alternate device" option; for example, on a newer Phoenix BIOS, you press F11 to get an alternate boot device menu. This saves the hassle of setting the boot order in the BIOS settings.

If there is not a specific "boot to USB flash drive" setting, try all available USB devices, such as USB-Zip or USB-HDD.

Installation

Once a client system is booted and on the network, the rest of the installation proceeds just as if you were using ordinary installation CDs or DVDs. Even better, you can set up customized automated installations so that once the installer is booted, and the client is connected to the installation server, you don't have to lift a finger.

16.1 Creating Network Installation Boot Media for Fedora Linux

Problem

Fedora Linux has gotten huge! Downloading the ISOs requires five CDs or a single DVD. BitTorrent or no, this is a huge download, and even the most compact installation requires packages from multiple disks. Can't you just install a minimal boot image on a CD or a USB stick, and then have the installer fetch the rest from a Fedora mirror?

Solution

You can indeed, and in fact have always been able to; however, it has not been well-publicized, so not many users know about it. You can copy a minimal boot image either to a CD or USB flash drive, boot the system, select a Fedora mirror, and then perform the installation completely over the Internet.

First, download the CD boot image or the USB media image, which you will find in the *os/* directory rather than the *iso/* directory of your chosen Fedora download mirror, as this example for Fedora 7 shows:

```
ftp://mirrors.kernel.org/fedora/releases/7/Fedora/i386/os/images
```

The CD boot image is *boot.iso*, and the USB media image is *diskboot.img*.

Use your favorite CD-writing program, like K3b, to create a boot CD from the *.iso* image.

Use *dd* to copy *diskboot.img* to your USB stick. Warning: this overwrites the whole device. Make sure your USB stick is unmounted first, and then transfer the boot image with this command, using the correct */dev* name for your own device:

```
# dd if=diskboot.img of=/dev/sdb
24576+0 records in
24576+0 records out
12582912 bytes (13 MB) copied, 3.99045 seconds, 3.2 MB/s
```

Mount it to verify that the files copied correctly. You should see something like this:

```
$ ls /media/disk
boot.msg     initrd.img    ldlinux.sys  param.msg   splash.jpg    vesamenu.c32
general.msg  isolinux.bin  options.msg  rescue.msg  syslinux.cfg  vmlinuz
```

Booting from removable media is controlled by your system's BIOS. When you try to boot from the CD or USB key, look for a "Press this key to select an alternate boot device" option. If your system does not have this option, you'll have to change boot options in your BIOS settings.

Discussion

Visit the Fedora mirrors page (*http://fedora.redhat.com/download/mirrors.html*) to find a mirror close to you.

Booting from a USB device is a relatively new-fangled feature, so don't be surprised if some of your PCs don't support it. It doesn't always work even on some systems that say they support booting from USB devices. So, don't make yourself crazy—if it's going to work, it will just work.

How do you know the *dev* name of your USB device? Try using the ls command:

```
$ ls -l /dev/disk/by-id/
[...]
lrwxrwxrwx 1 root root  9 2007-07-17 12:25 usb-LEXAR_JD_FIREFLY_106A6405142831060606-
0:0 -> ../../sdb
```

The lsscsi command should also identify it for you.

If you're wondering about using a 3.5" boot diskette, the answer is no. Fedora does not supply installation images for diskettes anymore because they're too small.

See Also

- man 1 dd
- The installation manual for your version of Fedora from Fedoraproject.org: *http://fedoraproject.org/*
- Always read the Release Notes before you start your installation

16.2 Network Installation of Fedora Using Network Boot Media

Problem

You created your Fedora boot CD or USB stick, and now you're ready to start your installation. What next?

Solution

Before you boot the installer, have a second Internet-connected computer handy. Or, first visit the Fedora mirrors page (*http://fedora.redhat.com/download/mirrors.html*), and write down some mirrors that are close to you. You'll need the complete file-path to the installation directory, for example:

```
ftp://mirrors.kernel.org/fedora/releases/7/Fedora/i386/os
```

Next, pop in your boot media, and boot up the system. Your first choice is to start the installer using either graphical mode or text mode. The main difference is you won't have a mouse in text mode. The graphical installer requires a minimum of 192 MB of RAM.

Go through the initial screens; there is nothing dramatic here, just the usual keyboard, language, and networking setup. The fun begins when you get to the "Installation Method" screen. Select either FTP or HTTP. Figure 16-1 shows the FTP screen.

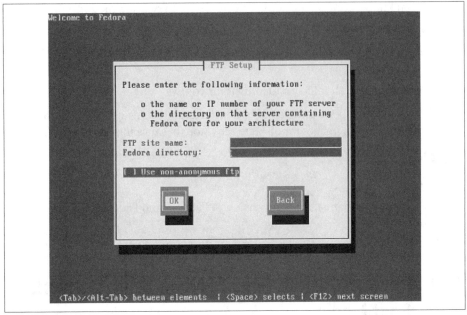

Figure 16-1. Selecting your FTP installation mirror

Entering the correct site name and Fedora directory is the same for FTP and HTTP. On the site name line, enter the top-level domain name, such as *ftp://mirrors.kernel. org*. On the Fedora Core directory line, enter the filepath, such as */fedora/releases/7/ Fedora/i386/os*, then hit OK. If you did it right, the next screen will say "Retrieving images/minstg2.img...." This is a 34 MB image, which you can see for yourself by poking around on the download mirror you selected.

Now, it's just like any other Fedora installation—you'll partition your drive, select packages, and do all the usual installation chores.

Discussion

You should run yum update immediately after installation to bring your system up to date.

This is a nice method for installing Fedora on a single PC, and for downloading and testing a new release. It's not suitable for mass customized rollouts, but we'll get to that in the next few recipes.

It doesn't matter if you select FTP or HTTP transfer; either one works fine. If you don't get your filepaths correct, Fedora's Anaconda installer will give you as many do-overs as you need until you get it right.

The installer image must fit in RAM, so only systems with more than 192 MB of RAM can use the graphical installer. Systems with less RAM will fall back to using the text-based installer automatically.

Fedora has a mediacheck feature for checking the integrity of installation CDs. Sometimes, it reports good CDs as being defective. To make it work correctly, boot the installer with the `linux ide=nodma` option.

If the installation fails partway through, try booting with `linux acpi=off`.

See Also

- Always read the Release Notes before you start your installation
- The Fedora mirrors page: *http://fedora.redhat.com/download/mirrors.html*
- The installation manual for your version of Fedora from Fedoraproject.org: *http://fedoraproject.org/*

16.3 Setting Up an HTTP-Based Fedora Installation Server

Problem

You want your own local Fedora installation server so you can plug-in and provision new systems with a minimum of fuss, and you prefer running an HTTP server.

Solution

First, download the Fedora DVD ISO. Visit fedoraproject.org (*http://fedoraproject.org/get-fedora.html*) to find a download site. If you use BitTorrent, it will verify file integrity for you; otherwise, be sure to compare the checksum manually when the download is finished:

```
$ sha1sum F-7-i386-DVD.iso
96b13dbbc9f3bc569ddad9745f64b9cdb43ea9ae  F-7-i386-DVD.iso
```

The correct checksum is posted in the same download directory as the ISO.

You may write the ISO to a DVD as a backup, but you won't need the DVD to operate your installation server, just the ISO.

Install the Lighttpd HTTP server to power your nice installation server. On Debian, install it with this command:

```
# aptitude install lighttpd lighttpd-doc
```

On Fedora:

```
# yum install lighttpd
```

You can store your Fedora ISO anywhere on this server, but you need to mount it in a web directory, such as */var/www/fedora*. Use the loopback device to mount it; for example:

```
# mount -o loop F-7-i386-DVD.iso /var/www/fedora
```

You should now see files in here, instead of a single giant file:

```
$ ls /var/www/fedora
Fedora        isolinux              RPM-GPG-KEY       RPM-GPG-KEY-fedora-test
fedora.css    README-BURNING-ISOS-en_US.txt  RPM-GPG-KEY-beta      RPM-GPG-KEY-rawhide
GPL           RELEASE-NOTES-en_US.html       RPM-GPG-KEY-fedora    stylesheet-images
images        repodata              RPM-GPG-KEY-fedora-rawhide  TRANS.TBL
```

Now, you can use the installation boot media we created in the previous recipes and install new systems from your own local Fedora installation server.

Discussion

This is a quick way to make a single copy of Fedora Linux available to your network, which should be a lot faster than an installation over the Internet, and kinder to the official download mirrors.

Make sure your Fedora directory is world-readable, but writable only by the owner. It's not necessary for *root* to own this directory, so you can make it owned by your HTTP user.

Your clients should run yum update immediately after installation to bring their systems up-to-date.

See Also

- Always read the Release Notes before you start your installation
- Lighttpd: *http://www.lighttpd.net/*
- The Fedora mirrors page: *http://fedora.redhat.com/download/mirrors.html*
- The installation manual for your version of Fedora from Fedoraproject.org: *http://fedoraproject.org/*

16.4 Setting Up an FTP-Based Fedora Installation Server

Problem

You want your own local Fedora installation server so you can plug-in and provision new systems with a minimum of fuss, and you prefer running an anonymous FTP server.

Solution

First, download the Fedora DVD ISO. Visit Fedoraproject.org (*http://fedoraproject. org/get-fedora.html*) to find a download site. If you use BitTorrent, it will verify file integrity for you; otherwise, be sure to compare the checksum manually when the download is finished:

```
$ sha1sum F-7-i386-DVD.iso
96b13dbbc9f3bc569ddad9745f64b9cdb43ea9ae  F-7-i386-DVD.iso
```

The correct checksum is posted in the same download directory as the ISO.

You may write the ISO to a DVD as a backup, but you won't need the DVD to operate your installation server, just the ISO.

Install *vsftpd*, the Very Secure FTP server, to power your nice installation server. On Debian, install it with this command:

```
# aptitude install vsftpd
```

On Fedora:

```
# yum install vsftpd
# chkconfig vsftpd on
```

Debian uses */etc/vsftpd.conf* and Fedora uses */etc/vsftpd/vsftpd.conf*. This configuration allows simple anonymous read-only access. Users may download files, but not upload:

```
##vsftpd.conf
listen=YES
anonymous_enable=YES
ftpd_banner=Welcome to your friendly Fedora installation server
#Debian users default directory
anon_root=/home/ftp/fedora
#Fedora users default directory
anon_root=/var/ftp/fedora
```

Debian users must create a directory to store their Fedora installation tree:

```
# mkdir /home/ftp/fedora
```

Fedora users do this:

```
# mkdir /var/ftp/fedora
```

You can store your Fedora ISO anywhere on this server, but you need to mount it in the *anon_root* directory. That is the default directory that users see when they connect to the server. Use the loopback device to mount it in this directory:

```
# mount -o loop F-7-i386-DVD.iso /var/ftp/fedora
```

You should see files in here, instead of a single giant ISO file:

```
$ ls /var/ftp/fedora
Fedora       isolinux     RPM-GPG-KEY      RPM-GPG-KEY-fedora-test
fedora.css   README-BURNING-ISOS-en_US.txt  RPM-GPG-KEY-beta      RPM-GPG-KEY-rawhide
```

```
   GPL        RELEASE-NOTES-en_US.html   RPM-GPG-KEY-fedora        stylesheet-images
   images     repodata                   RPM-GPG-KEY-fedora-rawhide  TRANS.TBL
```

Next, restart the server, which is the same command on both Debian and Fedora:

```
# /etc/init.d/vsftpd restart
```

Connect to the server with your favorite FTP client, and you're in business.

Now, you can use the installation boot media we created in the previous recipes and install new systems from your own local Fedora installation server.

Discussion

You can test your server with telnet:

```
$ telnet stinkpad 21
Trying 192.168.2.74...
Connected to stinkpad.alrac.net.
Escape character is '^]'.
220 Welcome to your friendly Fedora installation server
```

listen=YES

> Run *vsftpd* in daemon mode.

anonymous_enable=YES

> Allow anonymous logins. *ftp* and *anonymous* are recognised as anonymous logins.

ftpd_banner=

> Your message here.

anon_root=

> The default FTP data directory that will be displayed when users log in. This can go anywhere you want.

This is a quick way to make a single copy of Fedora Linux available to your network, which should be a lot faster than an installation over the Internet, and kinder to the official download mirrors.

Your clients should run yum update immediately after installation to bring their systems up-to-date.

See Also

- Always read the Release Notes before you start your installation
- man 5 vsftpd.conf
- The Fedora mirrors page: *http://fedora.redhat.com/download/mirrors.html*
- The manual for your version of Fedora from Fedoraproject.org:
    http://fedoraproject.org/

16.5 Creating a Customized Fedora Linux Installation

Problem

You want to create a customized version of Fedora Linux for multiple local installations. You want to select a standard set of packages, and then have an easy way to install it for new users.

Solution

Kickstart (Fedora's customization tool) and your own local installation server are just what you need. A Kickstart file is created automatically at installation, so you can see one at */root/anaconda-ks.cfg* on any Fedora system. This file answers all the questions asked by the installer, so all you do is point the installer to the Kickstart file and let it do the rest.

One way to create a Kickstart file is to perform a custom installation: select exactly the packages you want, set up partitioning and filesystems, and then use the automatically generated Kickstart file for new installations. This is also a great way to create an example file for reference.

Another way to is install the Kickstart configurator:

```
# yum install system-config-kickstart
```

This gives you a nice, easy-to-use graphical configurator, as Figure 16-2 shows.

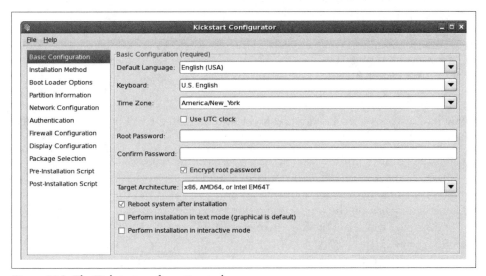

Figure 16-2. The Kickstart configuration tool

Just go through the tabs in order, and when you're finished, you'll have a *ks.cfg* file. You may use it as-is, or edit it manually to add further refinements.

Discussion

The Kickstart configurator has some limitations. You may select only package groups, not individual packages. You cannot configure Linux Volume Manager (LVM) with it. However, because it is a plaintext file, you can easily edit it to add any missing bits.

It has four sections: the `command` section and the `%packages` section, which are required and must be in that order, and the `%pre` and `%post` sections, which are not required, and do not have to be in any order.

Individual packages are listed under the `%packages` section of *ks.cfg*, like this:

```
%packages
@gnome-desktop
@graphical-internet
gimp
firefox
openoffice.org-writer
```

Package groups are prefaced with the ampersand; individual packages are not.

`%post` options are more common than `%pre` options. Both enable you to run any kind of script or command. After installation, I like to make sure that certain services are turned off for good, and that `yum update` runs to bring the system up-to-date:

```
%post
chkconfig isdn off
chkconfig pcmcia off
chkconfig bluetooth off
chkconfig portmap off
chkconfig apmd off
yum update
```

If you have ever installed Fedora, the Kickstart configurator will be familiar territory. There are a few potentially tricky bits, though:

- On the Partition Information screen, you have the option to specify the type of drive, either *sda* or *hda*. This could be useful on systems that have both. Or, if you have *sda* and *sdb*, for another example, you could put the *root* filesystem on one, and */home* on the other. If you don't specify a particular drive or partition, the installer will select the first drive in the BIOS order.

- Video configuration may need to be tweaked after installation because you have to select a color depth and resolution, such as $16 \times 1024 \times 768$. However, the installer will probe the graphics adapter and monitor, and install the drivers automatically.

- All kinds of ingenious admins have tried to figure out how to use Kickstart to assign ordinary user accounts. In my opinion, the easiest way is to add them manually after installation.

Complete Kickstart options are described in the Red Hat Enterprise Linux Installation Manual.

See Also

- Red Hat Enterprise Linux manuals:

    https://www.redhat.com/docs/manuals/enterprise/

16.6 Using a Kickstart File for a Hands-off Fedora Linux Installation

Problem

You have created your perfect *ks.cfg* file, and now you want to use it to control a new Fedora Linux installation.

Solution

You have several options:

- Store it on your installation server
- Store it on a 3.5" diskette
- Store it on a USB stick
- Store it on a CD-ROM

Installation server

This is the easiest way. Then, boot up the PC with a Fedora boot medium, such as a CD or USB stick, using this boot command:

```
linux ks=http://server/directory/ks.cfg
```

You may store several different Kickstart files this way, and specify which one to use:

```
linux ks=http://server.name.net/directory/devstation-ks.cfg
linux ks=http://server.name.net/directory/fileserver-ks.cfg
```

3.5" diskette

It must be in the top-level directory, and it must be named *ks.cfg*. Boot up the PC with a Fedora boot medium, using this boot command:

```
linux ks=floppy
```

If you want to use several different Kickstart files, such as workstation, web server, file server, and so on, you can specify the different filenames:

```
linux ks=floppy:/apache-ks.cfg
linux ks=floppy:/workstation-ks.cfg
```

Fedora no longer supports booting from a diskette, but you can still use them to hold Kickstart files.

USB stick

The filesystem must be *vfat* or *ext2*; I recommend *vfat* for the fewest hassles. Boot up the PC with a Fedora boot medium with this boot command, using your own */dev* name and filepath:

```
linux ks=hd:sda1:/websrv-ks.cfg
```

You may add a Kickstart file to your Fedora boot USB stick; first, copy the boot image, then copy your Kickstart file to the device. Use the same boot command as above.

CD-ROM

Kickstart files on a CD-ROM are booted with this command:

```
linux ks=cdrom:/directory/ks.cfg
```

Discussion

All kinds of ingenious admins have tried to figure out how to use Kickstart to assign ordinary user accounts. In my opinion, the easiest way is to add them manually after installation.

Assigning hostnames can be automated by configuring your DHCP server to assign hostnames by MAC address. In Dnsmasq, use a line like this:

```
dhcp-host=11:22:33:44:55:66,arnold
```

If you're using the ISC DHCP server, add lines like this to *dhcpd.conf*:

```
host mrhaney {
    hardware ethernet 08:00:07:26:c0:a5;
}
```

See Chapter 4 for some good recipes on configuring a Dnsmasq DHCP/DNS server.

See Also

- Red Hat Enterprise Linux manuals:

    https://www.redhat.com/docs/manuals/enterprise/

- Chapter 24, "Managing Name Resolution," in *Linux Cookbook*, by Carla Schroder (O'Reilly)

16.7 Fedora Network Installation via PXE Netboot

Problem

You want to netboot your installation, instead of using some sort of physical boot media. Your PCs have network interfaces that support netbooting or Etherboot diskettes, and you have configured the appropriate BIOS settings, so your clients are ready. You have your Fedora-based FTP or HTTP server all set up with a Fedora installation tree. What else do you need to do?

Solution

You need a DHCP server and a TFTP server. In this recipe, we'll put them all on the installation server.

Install these packages on your Fedora-based installation server:

```
# yum install tftp-server syslinux dhcp
```

Use this example *dhcpd.conf* with your own network addressing. *next-server* is the address of the TFTP server:

```
##dhcpd.conf
allow booting;
allow bootp;

subnet 192.168.1.0 netmask 255.255.255.0 {
        option subnet-mask 255.255.255.0;
        option broadcast-address 192.168.1.255;
        range dynamic-bootp 192.168.1.175 192.168.1.240;
        next-server 192.168.1.40;
        filename "pxelinux.0";
}
```

Next, copy the boot files *pxelinux.0*, *vmlinuz*, and *initrd.img* to the *tftpboot* directory. If you followed Recipe 16.3, *vmlinuz* and *initrd.img* are in */var/www/fedora*:

```
# cp /usr/lib/syslinux/pxelinux.0 /tftpboot
# cp /var/www/fedora/isolinux/vmlinuz /tftpboot
# cp /var/www/fedora/isolinux/initrd.img /tftpboot
```

If you set up an FTP-based installation server according to Recipe 16.4, your boot files are in */var/ftp/fedora*.

Create a minimal *tftpboot/pxelinux.cfg* file:

```
DEFAULT pxeboot
TIMEOUT 50
LABEL pxeboot
      KERNEL vmlinuz
      APPEND initrd=initrd.img
ONERROR LOCALBOOT 0
```

Now, start up everything. Go into */etc/xinetd.d./tftp* and change:

```
disable = yes
```

to:

```
disable = no
```

Then, run these commands:

```
# chkconfig xinetd on
# /etc/init.d/xinetd start
# chkconfig tftp on
```

Now, you can test it. Install the *tftp* client on a neighboring PC, and try to connect to the TFTP server:

```
$ tftp stinkpad
tftp> status
Connected to stinkpad.alrac.net.
Mode: netascii Verbose: off Tracing: off
Rexmt-interval: 5 seconds, Max-timeout: 25 seconds
```

Type a question mark, ?, to see a list of commands. This shows it's running and ready to go.

Power up a PXE-enabled client, which will automatically broadcast DHCPDISCOVER packets extended with PXE-specific options to port UDP 67, and within a few seconds, you should see the familiar Fedora installation screen.

Discussion

You may use any Linux distribution to power your installation server. You'll have different file locations and package names, but the contents of the configuration files will be the same.

The example *dhcpd.conf* contains just the options necessary to serve PXE clients. You may add them to your existing DHCP server configuration.

`ONERROR LOCALBOOT 0` in *pxelinux.cfg* means "boot to the local drive if the network boot fails."

You could try the *system-config-netboot* utility for configuring netbooting, if you prefer a graphical interface. It creates subdirectories under */tftpboot*, so you'll have some different file locations.

See Also

- Syslinux and PXELinux: *http//syslinux.zytor.com/pxe.php*
- `man 5 dhcpd.conf`
- `man 8 tftpd`

16.8   Network Installation of a Debian System

Debian Linux is the largest Linux distribution that exists, supporting more applications and hardware platforms than any other Linux distribution. Currently, a complete download requires 21 CDs or 3 DVDs. Of course, you don't need all those disks to do a basic installation, but it's still a big old beast. You prefer to boot with a small installation image, and then perform the rest of the installation over the network, rather than trying to download gigabytes of ISOs. How do you this?

Solution

Debian has long supported network installations. You can get boot images for CD-ROM and USB flash drive. It also supports PXE netbooting, which we'll get to in the next recipe. Visit Debian.org (*http://www.us.debian.org/distrib/netinst*) to download network installation images for CD-ROM.

You need dial-up, wired Ethernet, or a wireless interface with native Linux support. Don't even bother with a wireless interface that requires *ndiswrapper* to run on Linux; it won't work for the installer.

The *netinst* image contains the base Debian installation and weighs in at about 160 MB.

The *businesscard* image is about 32 MB, and has just the bare necessities for starting the installation.

The official file integrity checksums are posted on the download page. Always confirm the checksum before using the downloads:

```
$ sha1sum  debian-40r0-i386-businesscard.iso
641e67f6968ca08217f52f6fbe7dda1a8e6072ec  debian-40r0-i386-businesscard.iso
```

Use your favorite CD-writing software, such as K3b, to write your installation images to CD.

To create a bootable USB flash drive, you need at least a 256 MB drive. Then, download the *hd-media/boot.img.gz* file from your favorite Debian mirror. Make sure the drive is unmounted, and copy it to the drive with this command:

```
# zcat boot.img.gz > /dev/sda
```

How do you know the */dev* name of your USB device? Try using the ls command:

```
$ ls -l /dev/disk/by-id/
```

The lsscsi command should also tell the tale:

```
$ lsscsi
[2:0:0:0]    disk    LEXAR    JUMPDRIVE        1.10  /dev/sdb
```

To start the installation, boot your chosen media. You'll do the usual keyboard, language, and network settings, and then you'll have a drop-down list of Debian mirrors to choose from. After that, it's business as usual—select your packages, then go do something else while the operating system installs itself.

Discussion

This is a good way to perform a single installation, but not so good when you have several machines to install. For that, you should set up a local installation server, which we'll get to in the next recipe.

See Also

- Getting Debian: *http://www.debian.org/distrib/*
- Debian releases, manuals, and downloads: *http://www.debian.org/releases/*

16.9 Building a Complete Debian Mirror with apt-mirror

Problem

You want to provision your Debian hosts over the network from a local server, and you want a complete local mirror for this. How do you do this?

Solution

You need a Debian-based HTTP server to do this. There are two Debian applications for creating a local mirror: *apt-mirror*, which creates a complete mirror, and *apt-proxy*, which creates a partial mirror. In this recipe, we'll make a complete mirror with *apt-mirror*.

You will need anywhere from 40–120 GB of storage, according to which releases you want and how many CPU architectures. First, install *apt-mirror* in the usual Debian manner, plus Lighttpd:

```
# aptitude install apt-mirror lighttpd
```

Then, edit */etc/apt/mirror.list* to include your chosen repositories. You want to use Debian mirrors that are close to you, which you will find at the mirror list page (*http://www.debian.org/mirror/list*). They may not be geographically close, but you should run some *ping* and *tcptraceroute* tests to get an idea of which ones perform well. This example uses the mirror at *http://linux.csua.berkeley.edu/debian*:

```
## /etc/apt/mirror.list
############# config ##################
#
# set base_path    /var/spool/apt-mirror
# set mirror_path  $base_path/mirror
# set skel_path    $base_path/skel
# set var_path     $base_path/var
# set cleanscript $var_path/clean.sh
# set defaultarch
# set nthreads 20
set tilde 0
#
############# end config #############

# debian Etch (stable)
deb http://linux.csua.berkeley.edu/debian etch main contrib non-free
deb-src http://linux.csua.berkeley.edu/debian etch main contrib non-free
deb http://linux.csua.berkeley.edu/debian etch main/debian-installer
```

```
#debian Lenny (testing)
deb http://linux.csua.berkeley.edu/debian lenny main contrib non-free
deb-src http://linux.csua.berkeley.edu/debian lenny main contrib non-free
deb http://linux.csua.berkeley.edu/debian lenny main/debian-installer

#debian Sid (unstable)
deb http://linux.csua.berkeley.edu/debian sid main contrib non-free
deb-src http://linux.csua.berkeley.edu/debian sid main contrib non-free
deb http://linux.csua.berkeley.edu/debian sid main/debian-installer
```

Now, run this command to start downloading files:

```
# apt-mirror /etc/apt/mirror.list
Downloading 66 index files using 20 threads...
Begin time: Sun Jul 22 22:43:46 2007
[20]... [19]... [18]... [17]... [16]... [15]... 14]... [13]... [12]... [11]... [10]..
. [9]... [8]... [7]... [6]... [5]... [4]... [3]... [2]... [1]... [0]...
End time: Sun Jul 15 22:57:52 2007

Proceed indexes: [SSSSPPPPPPPP]

52.7 GiB will be downloaded into archive.
Downloading 81257 archive files using 20 threads...
Begin time: Sun Jul 15 22:58:37 2007
```

Packages download into */var/spool/apt-mirror/mirror/*, and this is obviously going to take some time, so you might as well find something else to do. Like configure Lighttpd. First, create a directory in your HTTP root:

```
# mkdir /var/www/debian
```

Then, link your package mirror to this directory:

```
# ln -s /var/spool/apt-mirror/mirror/linux.csua.berkeley.edu/debian \
  /var/www/debian
```

You could also set up a *cron* job to update the server every night. *apt-mirror* installs */etc/cron.d/apt-mirror*, so all you have to do is uncomment the command line:

```
0 1    * * *    apt-mirror    /usr/bin/apt-mirror > /var/spool/apt-mirror/var/cron.
log
```

This runs it every day at 1 a.m.

Discussion

The nice thing about having your own Debian mirror is that it's always current. Once the initial download is completed, subsequent downloads will be small.

It doesn't hurt to run apt-mirror /etc/apt/mirror.list a few times after the initial download is completed, just to be thorough.

Security updates are not cached on the server in this recipe, though you could do this if you wanted to. Some admins prefer to configure each client to download them directly to ensure they get fresh security updates.

You could also run *apt-mirror* on a different Linux distribution, such as Fedora or Slackware, or whatever you like. Download and install it from the source tarball, and then you'll have to create the directory structure and configure *cron* yourself.

See Also

- *apt-mirror* on SourceForge: *http://apt-mirror.sourceforge.net/*
- Debian releases, manuals, and downloads: *http://www.debian.org/releases/*

16.10 Building a Partial Debian Mirror with apt-proxy

Problem

While maintaining a local Debian mirror with *apt-mirror* doesn't sound too bad, you really don't need the whole works. Can't you just cache and share the packages that your local systems actually use?

Solution

You can, with *apt-proxy*. Install it on a server with at least 30 GB of free storage space:

```
# aptitude install apt-proxy
```

Then, configure */etc/apt-proxy/apt-proxy-v2.conf* to point to three different Debian mirrors:

```
address = 192.168.1.101
port = 9999
min_refresh_delay = 1s
debug = all:4 db:0
timeout = 15
cache_dir = /var/cache/apt-proxy
cleanup_freq = 1d
max_age = 120d
max_versions = 3
;; Backend servers
backends =
    http://us.debian.org/debian
    http://linux.csua.berkeley.edu/debian
    http://mirrors.geeks.org/debian
    http://debian.uchicago.edu/debian
```

Now, configure a client PC to point to your *apt-proxy* server:

```
## /etc/apt/sources.list
# debian Etch (stable)
deb http://192.168.1.75/debian etch main contrib non-free
deb-src http://192.168.1.75/debian etch main contrib non-free

deb http://security.debian.org/ etch/updates main contrib non-free
deb-src http://security.debian.org/debian-security etch/updates main \
contrib non-free
```

Run aptitude update on the client to initialize the server. If your server already has a good-sized package cache, you can import it into *apt-proxy* with this command:

```
# apt-proxy-import /var/cache/apt/archives
```

Now, every time a client computer installs new software, *apt-proxy* will cache it and serve additional requests from the cache. All you have to do in the way of maintenance is keep an eye on how much drive space *apt-proxy* is using.

Discussion

apt-proxy replicates the Debian mirror structure, and automatically purges old packages when newer versions become available. Using at least three different Debian mirrors for backend servers builds in failover; if one is not available, it automatically goes to the next one.

Visit the mirror list page (*http://www.debian.org/mirror/list*) to find available mirrors near you.

See Also

- man 8 apt-proxy
- man 5 apt-proxy.conf
- man 8 apt-proxy-import
- *apt-proxy* on SourceForge: *http://apt-proxy.sourceforge.net/*
- Debian releases, manuals, and downloads: *http://www.debian.org/releases/*

16.11 Configuring Client PCs to Use Your Local Debian Mirror

Problem

You made a nice local Debian mirror using *apt-mirror* or *apt-proxy*, and now you need to know how to configure your local Debian clients to use it.

Solution

Edit */etc/apt/sources.list* on your client computers to point to the address or hostname of your server:

```
## /etc/apt/sources.list
# debian Etch (stable)
deb http://192.168.1.75/debian etch main contrib non-free
deb-src http://192.168.1.75/debian etch main contrib non-free

deb http://security.debian.org/debian-security etch/updates main contrib non-free
deb-src http://security.debian.org/debian-security etch/updates main contrib non-free
```

This example is for a PC running Debian Etch. Of course you may configure your PCs to use whatever Debian release you prefer.

Run aptitude update on the clients to update their local package lists, and you're in business.

Discussion

This example has the client getting security updates directly from Debian.org, instead of from a local server cache. You may cache security updates on the server if you prefer. Some admins think it is safer and fresher to have the clients fetch their own security updates directly.

Debian's security updates are never mirrored, and are only available from *security. debian.org*.

See Also

- man 5 sources.list
- Debian releases, manuals, and downloads: *http://www.debian.org/releases/*

16.12 Setting Up a Debian PXE Netboot Server

Problem

You want a Debian boot server so you can perform network installations without an installation CD or USB flash device. Your PCs have network interfaces that support netbooting, or they have Etherboot diskettes, and you have configured the appropriate BIOS settings, so your clients are ready. You have your local Debian mirror all set up and ready to go.

What else do you need to do?

Solution

Your Debian mirror server needs to be PXE-netboot enabled. You'll need these packages:

```
# aptitude install tftpd-hpa dhcp3-server
```

Next, download *netboot/netboot.tar.gz* from your favorite Debian mirror into */var/lib/ tftpboot*, and unpack it there:

```
# wget http://debian.uchicago.edu/debian/dists/etch/main/installer-\
i386/current/images/netboot/netboot.tar.gz
# tar zxvf netboot.tar.gz
```

You must edit */etc/default/tftpd-hpa* to say:

```
RUN_DAEMON="yes"
```

And, you need a simple configuration in */etc/dhcp3/dhcpd.conf*:

```
##dhcpd.conf
allow booting;
allow bootp;

subnet 192.168.1.0 netmask 255.255.255.0 {
        option subnet-mask 255.255.255.0;
        option broadcast-address 192.168.1.255;
        range dynamic-bootp 192.168.1.175 192.168.1.240;
        next-server 192.168.1.40;
        filename "pxelinux.0";
}
```

Start up the new servers like this:

```
# /etc/init.d/dhcp3-server start
# /etc/init.d/tftpd-hpa start
```

Now, power up a PXE netboot-enabled client, and in a few moments, you should see the Debian installation menu:

```
- Boot Menu -
=============

etch_i386_install
etch_i386_linux
etch_i386_expert
etch_i386_rescue
```

Discussion

If you're running Dnsmasq instead of dhcpd, you need to add only a single line in *dnsmasq.conf* to enable netbooting:

```
dhcp-boot=pxelinux.0,cracker,192.168.1.40
```

Then, restart Dnsmasq:

```
# /etc/init.d/dnsmasq restart
```

If you're running some other Debian release than Etch, you'll need to use the *netboot.tar.gz* that is specific to that release.

See Also

- Debian releases, manuals, and downloads: *http://www.debian.org/releases/*

16.13 Installing New Systems from Your Local Debian Mirror

Problem

Your Debian mirror is all set up and ready to go to work, and your clients are all prepared: you have your CD-ROM or USB installation boot media (see Recipe 16.8) all set up and ready to go. How do you tell them to use your local Debian mirror?

Solution

Start up your systems with your installation boot media. Go through the usual keyboard, language, and network configuration screens. When you get to the Mirror Country screen, as Figure 16-3 shows, select "enter information manually." Then, enter the hostname of your server, like *cracker.alrac.net*; and then on the next screen, enter the archive directory, which is */debian/*. Continue the rest of the installation in the usual manner.

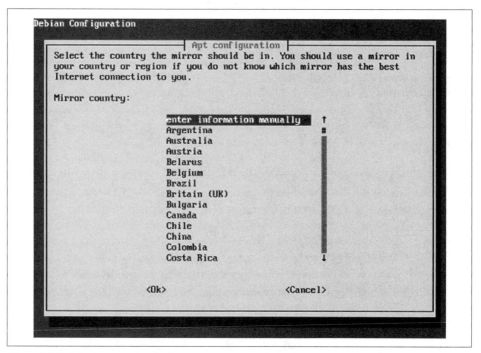

Figure 16-3. Selecting your local mirror

Discussion

This is all very nice and not that hard to set up, but you really want to know how to customize and automate your Debian installations. See the next recipe to learn how to do this with a *preseed* file.

See Also

- Debian releases, manuals, and downloads: *http://www.debian.org/releases/*

16.14 Automating Debian Installations with Preseed Files

Problem

You want a fairly simple way to automate network installation of new Debian PCs, and to create custom installations for different roles, such as web servers, workstations, file servers, and so forth.

Solution

Create a *preseed*, or preconfiguration file, that answers the installer questions, and does your package selections for you. First, study the example preseed file at *http://d-i.alioth.debian.org/manual/example-preseed.txt*. Then, create one from your own Debian system by running these two commands:

```
# debconf-get-selections --installer > preseed.txt
# debconf-get-selections >> file preseed.txt
```

Your own *preseed.txt* is going to look different from the *example-preseed.txt*; it's messier and has a lot more entries. You can't use your own *preseed.txt* as-is, but you can see exactly what was done on your system, and you can copy anything you want to duplicate to *example-preseed.txt*.

The *tasksel* command selects package groups. You can see a list of these:

```
$ tasksel --list-tasks
u desktop  Desktop environment
i web-server  Web server
u print-server  Print server
u dns-server  DNS server
[...]
```

u means uninstalled, and i means installed. Display individual packages with this command:

```
$ tasksel --task-packages desktop
twm
gimp-print
xresprobe
openoffice.org
[...]
```

Use *tasksel* to select package groups in your preseed file like this:

```
#tasksel tasksel/desktop multiselect kde-desktop, xfce-desktop
#tasksel tasksel/first multiselect standard, kde-desktop
```

This means when the desktop task is selected, install *kde-desktop* and *xfce-desktop* instead of the default selections. Individual packages are selected with *pkgsel*, like this:

```
d-i pkgsel/include string openvpn tftpd-hpa dnsmasq
```

I like to automate creating the *root* login, and disable the creation of a normal user account (because I do it later manually):

```
passwd passwd/root-password password $1$AiJg3$GHlS8/vqkSgBj9/1EKPUvO
passwd passwd/root-password-again password $1$AiJg3$GHlS8/vqkSgBj9/1EKPUvO
passwd passwd/make-user boolean false
```

Keeping cleartext passwords around is a bad idea, so you can encrypt them first with:

```
$ grub-md5-crypt
Password:
Retype password:
$1$AiJg3$GHlS8/vqkSgBj9/1EKPUvO
```

This command checks the format of your preseed file to make sure it is valid:

```
$ debconf-set-selections -c preseed.txt
```

After you have fine-tuned your preseed file and *debconf-set-selections* approves, how do you use it? With PXE netboot clients, copy your preseed file to */var/lib/tftpboot*. Then, edit the auto boot stanza in */var/lib/tftpboot/pxelinux.cfg/default* to point to the file:

```
LABEL auto
    kernel debian-installer/i386/linux
    append auto=true priority=critical vga=normal \
preseed/url=http://host/path/to/preseed.cfg \
initrd=debian-installer/i386/initrd.gz --
```

You can copy your preseed file to the top-level directory on your USB flash drive and then enter this boot command:

```
linux preseed/file=/dev/sdb/preseed.cfg debconf/priority=critical
```

Or, you can park your preseed file on a network server and then, for both CD and USB boot media, enter the URL:

```
linux preseed/url=http://servername/filename
```

Discussion

Debian's preseed files are not as easy as Fedora's Kickstart. But, it is one of the easier methods for creating customized Debian autoinstalls. See the Debian-Gnu Installation Guide (*http://d-i.alioth.debian.org/manual/en.i386/index.html*) for a detailed discussion of preseed and boot options.

See Also

- Debian releases, manuals, and downloads: *http://www.debian.org/releases/*

## CHAPTER 17

Linux Server Administration via Serial Console

17.0 Introduction

In these modern times, the hardworking admin might be tempted to turn her back on the Old Ways and indulge in increasingly exotic methods of interfacing with servers: Ethernet, USB, Firewire, Wireless, Infrared, KVM switches—next stop: direct neural implants.

There is one old-timer that still has a useful place in the network admininstrator's toolkit: the serial console. It's simple and cheap—you don't need to install drivers or expansion cards, it's just there. It's the lowest-level means of interfacing with your system. Configure your servers to accept serial logins, set up a laptop as a portable console, and you have an instant cheap rescue device when everything else fails.

Your portable serial console will also serve you well when you need it to connect to routers and switches.

When you're troubleshooting headless systems, it saves the hassle of hooking up a keyboard and monitor. You can capture kernel and logging messages that otherwise would be lost, reboot the system and get a boot menu, edit network settings and stop/start networking, restart or tweak SSH, and tweak network card settings.

I don't recommend it as your sole means of server administration—Ethernet is a lot faster. But, when nothing else works, the serial console will save the day.

There are a number of ways to make the physical connection. You can connect a hardware-controller modem, the kind old-timers fondly refer to as real modems, and do remote administration via dial-up. It couldn't be any simpler, just dial direct. This makes a nice inexpensive backup for Ethernet failures. Or, grab a null modem cable, connect to a laptop or a nearby workstation, and you have a directly connected serial console. (See Recipe 19.1 to learn about turning a laptop into a portable network diagnostic and repair tool.) You can turn any feeble old PC into a perfectly good serial console.

Users of x86 hardware, which is the majority of the Linux universe, must deal with the limitations of the x86 PC BIOS. Unlike real Unix hardware, it was not designed to support a serial console. This means you can't use the serial port to poke around in the BIOS to make changes or check the settings, and you don't see the Power On Self-Test (POST) messages. The Unix BIOS and bootloaders come with a lot of neat features not available in x86. They can do diskless netbooting, hard resets, reboots, suspend the boot process and then restart it, walk step-by-step through the boot process, and reconfigure the BIOS—all remotely. It's like having a little computer to jump-start and control the big computer.

There are some ways to get around these limitations. One is to purchase x86 server hardware with an advanced BIOS. For example, rackmount and blade units are usually equipped for serial port administration, and come with advanced management features, just like real Unix hardware. Another way is to purchase an expansion card like the PC Weasel. The PC Weasel is a PCI or ISA expansion card that emulates an attached video and keyboard, and presents a serial port for administration. At $250 to $350, it's not an inexpensive option, but when you consider that it's less hassle than a motherboard upgrade and comes with a great feature set, it looks like a pretty good deal.

A lot of data centers rely on commercial serial consoles such as those sold by Cyclades, Lantronix, and Digi, which fit nicely in racks, have up to 48 ports, and include all sorts of management software, remote logging and kernel message capture, and security features. (Don't be confused by all those RJ-45 ports—those are real, genuine serial RS-232 ports that use nice RJ-45 connectors.)

Or, you can build your own, using multiport serial expansion cards from vendors like Comtrol, Moxa, and Axxon. You can even add some management software—Conserver (*http://www.conserver.com*) is a great open source and free-of-cost console server. It includes excellent logging, SSL integration, user authentication, message broadcasting, spy mode, and system monitoring. This chapter covers how to set up an ordinary x86 PC as a headless server, and how to set up an ordinary x86 PC as a serial console. You could say this is Linux serial consoling on the cheap.

17.1 Preparing a Server for Serial Console Administration

Problem

You have an ordinary x86 server that you want to run headless, with serial console administration enabled, and you want to verify that all the pieces—hardware and software—are present. The serial console might or might not be your primary method of administering your server; regardless, you want to be sure that you can connect to it with a serial console.

Solution

First, check the BIOS for your server to see if it comes with serial console support already built-in. Most likely, a low-end PC won't, but higher-end and server-quality equipment might. If it does, follow the directions for your particular machine for setting it up for a serial console, and ignore the rest of this recipe.

If not, you'll need the following:

- Keyboard and monitor connected to the server until the serial connection is tested and ready.
- DB9 serial connector. If there is not one built-in to the motherboard, you can get a PCI serial port card inexpensively.
- *agetty* or *mgetty* utility.
- BIOS that allows the system to boot without an attached keyboard.
- Null-modem cable for direct connection to another PC.
- Kernel with console support built-in, not as a module.
- Hardware-controller modem if you want remote dial-in administration.
- Bootable rescue disk. (Always have one of these!)

Discussion

Serial port is one of those terms that covers a lot of ground. It means the physical connector, which on most PCs, is a male DB9 connector. It connects to a Universal Asynchronous Receiver-Transmitter (UART) chip on the motherboard. A serial port is also a logical device, */dev/ttyS**.

```
$ setserial -g /dev/ttyS[0123]
/dev/ttyS0, UART: 16550A, Port: 0x03f8, IRQ: 4
/dev/ttyS1: No such device
/dev/ttyS2, UART: unknown, Port: 0x03e8, IRQ: 4
/dev/ttyS3, UART: unknown, Port: 0x02e8, IRQ: 3
```

This shows that the system has only one serial port, */dev/ttyS0*. That is the only one with a UART value. You can get more information about it with the -a flag:

```
$ setserial -a /dev/ttyS0
/dev/ttyS0, Line 0, UART: 16550A, Port: 0x03f8, IRQ: 4
        Baud_base: 115200, close_delay: 50, divisor: 0
        closing_wait: 3000
        Flags: spd_normal skip_test
```

This shows a nice modern serial port that has a transfer rate of 115,200 baud. (Keep in mind this is the transfer rate between the UART chip and the PC—anything outside the PC is limited by cabling, network traffic, and other factors.)

You may be more familiar with COM1, COM2, COM3, and COM4 than */dev/ttyS1*, *dev/ttyS2*, and so forth. The ports and interrupts are the same no matter what you call it:

```
0x03f8  IRQ4  COM1  /dev/ttyS0
0x02f8  IRQ3  COM2  /dev/ttyS1
0x03e8  IRQ4  COM3  /dev/ttyS2
0x02e8  IRQ3  COM4  /dev/ttyS3
```

A *getty* ("get tty"—a holdover from the days of teletypes) is a program that manages logins over serial connections. It opens a serial device, such as a modem or virtual console, and waits for a connection. *getty* displays the login prompt, then hands off to the login program when a username is entered, and then quietly retires. There are all kinds of *gettys. mingetty* and *fgetty* support only local virtual consoles and have no serial support, so don't use them. It's OK if they are already present on the system because you'll use */etc/inittab* to control which one is used for serial console logins. *mgetty* is an excellent *getty* that also supports faxing and voicemail. *agetty*, *uugetty*, and plain old *getty* all work fine for serial consoling.

Most, but not all, PC BIOSes support booting without an attached keyboard. If yours doesn't, and a BIOS upgrade does not fix it, you'll need something like the PC Weasel to make it work. (See this chapter's Introduction for more information on hardware options.)

You can see what options your kernel has been compiled to support by looking at your */boot/config-** file. For example, on my Debian system, this is */boot/config-2.6.20-16*. This is a not a file that you edit; it is a record of how your kernel was built. Options are either built-in, =y, compiled as loadable modules, =m, or not included, like this example shows:

```
2.6.20-16
CONFIG_X86=y
CONFIG_X86_CPUID=m
# CONFIG_EMBEDDED is not set
```

Look for these lines to confirm console support, and remember you want it built-in, and not loadable modules:

```
#
# Serial drivers
#
CONFIG_SERIAL_8250=y
CONFIG_SERIAL_8250_CONSOLE=y
```

If it says CONFIG_SERIAL_8250=m or CONFIG_SERIAL_8250 is not set, then you'll need to rebuild the kernel. Look under Device Drivers → Character devices → Serial drivers in *menuconfig*.

Here are related configuration items to look for:

```
CONFIG_VT=y
CONFIG_VT_CONSOLE=y
CONFIG_HW_CONSOLE=y
CONFIG_SERIAL_NONSTANDARD=y
```

Most likely these will already be present.

Modems

Yes, I know that hardware-controller modems cost more than Winmodems/softmodems. Trust me, you want a good-quality hardware-controller modem on the server. If you can't afford new, try eBay and other secondhand outlets.

There are many advantages: you don't have to hassle with drivers, so it Just Works. The whole point of accessing a system via the serial line is to get the most low-level access you can, which you can't do if you have to hassle with drivers. An external modem has nice blinky lights that aid troubleshooting, and it's portable. Internal modems save space. An important feature to look for is retaining settings after a power outage, usually in nonvolatile RAM (NVRAM). Cheap modems lose their settings after a power cycle, so when you try to dial in, the modem does not respond.

I favor U.S. Robotics modems. Prices range from around $80 U.S. to $300. The following models (and all of their variants) work great with Linux:

- USR5686 56K External Faxmodem with V.92
- USR5610B 56K V.92 Performance Pro Modem
- USR3453 Courier 56K Business Modem with V.Everything and V.92
- USR5630 56K External Faxmodem with V.92
- USR5631 56K External Faxmodem with V.92
- USR0839 Sportster 33.6 External Faxmodem

For the purpose of Linux serial console administration, the lower-priced ones work fine, as all you're using are the most basic modem functions: answering the phone, keeping the data flowing, and then hanging up. The higher-end models, like the USR Courier, include useful security features such as callback, caller line identification, and authorized caller lists. These are useful in preventing attackers from ever getting as far as a login prompt.

See Also

- The manual for your motherboard
- The manpage for your *getty* program
- man 8 setserial
- man 1 tty
- man 4 tty
- Remote Serial Console HOWTO: *http://www.tldp.org/HOWTO/Remote-Serial-Console-HOWTO/*
- Chapter 10, "Patching, Customizing, and Upgrading Kernels," in *Linux Cookbook*, by Carla Schroder (O'Reilly)

17.2 Configuring a Headless Server with LILO

Problem

Your soon-to-be headless server now has all the pieces in place for running headless. Now, you need to know how to configure it to accept logins from a directly connected serial console, and you want to see a boot menu when you reboot from the console. You are using LILO as your bootloader.

Solution

First, edit */etc/inittab* to set the default runlevel so that the system boots into a text runlevel. If the server does not have X Windows installed, skip this step:

```
# The default runlevel.
id:3:initdefault:
```

Then, open up a serial port to accept logins. This also happens in */etc/inittab*:

```
# Example how to put a getty on a serial line (for a terminal)
#
T0:23:respawn:/sbin/getty -L ttyS0 9600 vt100
#T1:23:respawn:/sbin/getty -L ttyS1 9600 vt100
```

Uncomment the one you're going to connect to. (In this recipe, we'll use *ttyS0*.) The terminal emulation should already be vt100 or vt102; if it isn't, change it. Next, save your changes, and restart *init*:

```
# init q
```

Fedora Linux users must take two extra steps. First edit */etc/sysconfig/init* to disable ANSI colors, and disable the interactive startup with these lines:

```
BOOTUP=serial
PROMPT=no
```

Disable Kudzu because it will reset the serial port whenever it runs, and then you'll be disconnected. Edit */etc/sysconfig/kudzu*:

```
SAFE=yes
```

Now, edit the server bootloader to tell the kernel to make *ttyS0* (or whichever one you use) the default serial console. Use the following example as a model, substituting your own filepaths, kernels, and labels:

```
## /etc/lilo.conf
#Global section

boot=/dev/hda
map=/boot/map
install=menu
prompt
timeout=100
serial=0,9600n8
```

```
menu-title=" Webserver 1 "
default="CentOS 5-serial"

#boot stanzas

image=/boot/vmlinuz-2.6.18.ELsmp
        label="CentOS 5"
        initrd=/boot/initrd-2.6.18.ELsmp.img
        read-only
        root=LABEL=/

image=/boot/vmlinuz-2.6.18.EL
        label="CentOS 5- serial"
        initrd=/boot/initrd-vmlinuz-2.6.18.ELsmp.img
        read-only
        root=LABEL=/
        append="console=ttyS0,9600n8"
```

Disable any splash images by deleting or commenting out the line referring to them. Do not enable a boot message because it won't work.

Then, write the changes to the master boot record (MBR):

```
# /sbin/lilo -v
```

Reboot a few times to test. Don't disconnect the monitor and keyboard just yet—wait until you connect successfully from a remote serial console.

Discussion

The Fedora */etc/sysconfig/init* uses escape sequences to set colors, which can confuse your serial console, so it's best to disable colors entirely.

The `serial=0,9600n8` line tells your server to be ready to accept control from serial line *ttyS0*, initializes the serial port at a speed of 9600 baud, no parity, 8 bits.

`append="console=ttyS0,9600n8"` tells the kernel which serial port to use.

If you have more than one serial port, how do you know which one is *ttyS0*, and which one is *ttyS1*? If your motherboard manual doesn't tell you, you'll just have to use trial and error.

Use this line when you want to see boot messages on an attached monitor and the remote serial console:

```
append="console=tty0 console=ttyS0,9600n8"
```

The attached monitor will see only the boot menu, then will appear to hang until the login prompt comes up. The remote serial console will receive all boot messages, including output from the *init* system, and system log messages.

Remember that timeout is measured in tenths of second.

The `install` option has changed, starting with LILO version 22.3. It used to select the user interface from a file in *boot*; now, the user interface is an additional menu option. Your choices are `text`, `menu`, and `bmp`. `text` is strictly command-line. `menu` is a text-based boot menu, plus a command-line option. `bmp` is a big old graphical screen, which you definitely don't want over a serial line.

Booting to text mode still gives you the option to run X Windows when you want; simply run the `startx` command on the server to start up X Windows. You won't see an X session over the serial line—this only makes sense when you want an X session on an attached monitor, or you are running remote X clients from the server.

See Also

- `man 5 lilo.conf` explains all the options in */etc/lilo.conf*
- `man 5 inittab`
- `man 1 startx`
- Remote Serial Console HOWTO: *http://www.tldp.org/HOWTO/Remote-Serial-Console-HOWTO/*
- Chapter 7, "Starting and Stopping Linux," in *Linux Cookbook*, by Carla Schroder (O'Reilly) tells how to customize runlevels
- Chapter 12, "Managing the Bootloader and Multi-Booting," in *Linux Cookbook*
- Recipe 15.2, "Using Both X Windows and Consoles," in *Linux Cookbook*

17.3   Configuring a Headless Server with GRUB

Problem

Your soon-to-be headless server now has all the pieces in place for running headless. Now, you need to know how to configure it to accept logins from a directly connected serial console, and you want to see a boot menu when you reboot from the console. You are using GRUB as your bootloader.

Solution

First, edit */etc/inittab* to set the default runlevel so that the system boots into text mode (Debian users, please see Recipe 17.4 for more information):

```
# The default runlevel.
id:3:initdefault:
```

Then, open up a serial port to accept logins:

```
# Example how to put a getty on a serial line (for a terminal)
#
T0:23:respawn:/sbin/getty -L ttyS0 9600 vt100
#T1:23:respawn:/sbin/getty -L ttyS1 9600 vt100
```

Uncomment the one you're going to connect to. (In this recipe, we'll use *ttyS0*.) The terminal emulation should already be vt100 or vt102; if it isn't, change it. Then, save your changes and restart *init*:

```
# init q
```

Fedora Linux users must take two extra steps. First, edit */etc/sysconfig/init* to disable ANSI colors and disable the interactive startup with these lines:

```
BOOTUP=serial
PROMPT=no
```

Then, disable Kudzu because it will reset the serial port whenever it runs, and then you'll be disconnected. Edit */etc/sysconfig/kudzu*:

```
SAFE=yes
```

Now, edit */boot/grub/grub.conf* to tell the kernel to make *ttyS0* (or whichever one you use) the default system console. Use the following example as a model, substituting your own filepaths, kernels, and titles:

```
#/boot/grub/grub.conf
#Global section

default 1
timeout 10
serial --unit=0 --speed=9600 --word=8 --parity=no --stop=1
terminal --timeout=10 serial
#boot stanzas
title       Debian-Sarge
root        (hd0,0)
kernel      /boot/vmlinuz-2.6.20-16 root=/dev/hda2 ro
initrd      /boot/initrd.img-2.6.20-16

title       Debian-Sarge, serial
root        (hd0,0)
kernel      /boot/vmlinuz-2.6.20-16 root=/dev/hda2 ro console=ttyS0,9600n8
initrd      /boot/initrd.img-2.6.20-16
```

Disable any splash images by deleting or commenting out any lines referring to them. Reboot a few times to test. Don't disconnect the monitor and keyboard just yet—wait until you connect successfully from a remote serial console.

Discussion

GRUB counts from zero, so `default=1` makes the second boot stanza the default.

The `serial=0,9600n8` line tells your server to be ready to accept control from the serial line, and initializes the serial port.

`console=ttyS0,9600n8` on the kernel line tells the kernel which serial port to use.

The `--timeout=10` argument tells GRUB to default to the first device listed in the terminal line after 10 seconds.

If you have more than one serial port, how do you know which one is *ttyS0* and which one is *ttyS1*? If your motherboard manual doesn't tell you, you'll just have to use trial and error.

When you want to see boot messages on an attached monitor and the remote serial console, add the console option, like this:

```
#Global section
...
terminal --timeout=10 serial console

#boot stanzas
...
kernel    /boot/vmlinuz-2.6.11-ln.std root=/dev/hda2 ro console=tty0
console=ttyS0,9600n8
```

If you have an attached keyboard and monitor, and an attached remote serial console, you can strike a key on either one to make it the default. If you don't select one, it will default to the first device listed on the terminal line.

Booting to text mode still gives you the option to run X Windows when you want; simply run the startx command on the server to start up X Windows. You won't see an X session over the serial line—this only makes sense when you want an X session on an attached monitor, or you are running remote X clients from the server.

See Also

- man 8 grub
- man 1 startx
- Remote Serial Console HOWTO:

    http://www.tldp.org/HOWTO/Remote-Serial-Console-HOWTO/
- Chapter 7, "Starting and Stopping Linux," in *Linux Cookbook*, by Carla Schroder (O'Reilly) tells how to customize runlevels
- Chapter 12, "Managing the Bootloader and Multi-Booting," in *Linux Cookbook*
- Recipe 15.2, "Using Both X Windows and Consoles," in *Linux Cookbook*

17.4   Booting to Text Mode on Debian

Problem

Your Debian system boots X Windows automatically, probably with Gnome Display Manager (GDM), K Display Manager (KDM), or X Display Manager (XDM). But, Debian does not install with both text and graphical runlevels already configured like Red Hat; runlevels 2–5 by default are all the same. Because you chose a graphical login during installation, runlevels 2–5 all boot to a graphical login. How do you configure it to boot to a text-only session?

Solution

First, you need to know which display manager the system is using. Then, remove it from the appropriate runlevels. To see which one is running:

```
$ ps ax | grep dm
  537 |        S      0:00 /usr/bin/gdm
  544 |        S<     0:10 /usr/X11R6/bin/X :0 -dpi 100 -nolisten tcp vt7 -auth /var/
lib/gdm/A:0-PbCLdj
```

This tells us that GDM, the Gnome Display Manager, is running. First, remove it from all runlevels:

```
# update-rc.d -f gdm remove
update-rc.d: /etc/init.d/gdm exists during rc.d purge (continuing)
 Removing any system startup links for /etc/init.d/gdm ...
   /etc/rc0.d/K01gdm
   /etc/rc1.d/K01gdm
   /etc/rc2.d/S99gdm
   /etc/rc3.d/S99gdm
   /etc/rc4.d/S99gdm
   /etc/rc5.d/S99gdm
   /etc/rc6.d/K01gdm
```

Next, have GDM start on runlevel 5, and stop on all the others:

```
# update-rc.d gdm  start 99 5 . stop 01 0 1 2 3 4 6 .
 Adding system startup for /etc/init.d/gdm ...
   /etc/rc0.d/K01gdm -> ../init.d/gdm
   /etc/rc1.d/K01gdm -> ../init.d/gdm
   /etc/rc2.d/K01gdm -> ../init.d/gdm
   /etc/rc3.d/K01gdm -> ../init.d/gdm
   /etc/rc4.d/K01gdm -> ../init.d/gdm
   /etc/rc6.d/K01gdm -> ../init.d/gdm
   /etc/rc5.d/S99gdm -> ../init.d/gdm
```

Now, edit */etc/inittab* to set the default runlevel so that the system boots into text mode. Debian's default runlevel is 2, so why not stick with tradition:

```
# The default runlevel.
id:2:initdefault:
```

Now refer to Recipes 17.2 or 17.3 to finish setting up your server.

Discussion

Booting to text mode still gives you the option to run X Windows when you want; simply run the startx command on the server to start up X Windows. You won't see an X session over the serial line—this only makes sense when you want an X session on an attached monitor, or you are running remote X clients from the server.

update-rc.d is the Debian command for editing runlevels. The -f flag means "force removal of symlinks even if */etc/init.d/<name>* still exists." Runlevels are simply big batches of symlinks, which you can see in the */etc/rc*.d* directories. This preserves the

---

startup script in *etc/init.d*, which you definitely do not want to delete. If you're feeling nervous, run `update-rc.d -f -n <foo>` first to do a dry run, the `-n` switch meaning "not really."

See Also

- man 8 `update-rc.d`
- man 1 `startx`
- Remote Serial Console HOWTO:

    http://www.tldp.org/HOWTO/Remote-Serial-Console-HOWTO/

- Chapter 7, "Starting and Stopping Linux," in *Linux Cookbook*, by Carla Schroder (O'Reilly) tells how to customize runlevels
- Recipe 15.2, "Using Both X Windows and Consoles," in *Linux Cookbook*

17.5   Setting Up the Serial Console

Problem

You have a Linux laptop or workstation all ready to go into service as a serial console; all you need to know is how to configure it, and how to use the communications software. You want to connect directly to your headless server.

Solution

First, you need these things:

- A DB9 serial port. A lot of laptops don't have serial ports. An alternative is a USB-to-serial connector.
- Null modem cable.
- Minicom, the serial communications program.

Then, configure Minicom, connect the two systems, and you're done.

Start up Minicom with `-s` for Setup:

```
# minicom -s
------[configuration]-------
| Filenames and paths
| File transfer protocols
| Serial port setup
| Modem and dialing
| Screen and keyboard
| Save setup as dfl
| Save setup as..
| Exit
| Exit from Minicom
---------------------------
```

Select Serial port setup. From the following menu, select the letter of the option you want to change, then hit Return to get back to the "Change which setting?" screen:

```
-------------------------------------------
| A -    Serial Device     : /dev/ttyS0
| B - Lockfile Location    : /var/lock
| C -    Callin Program    :
| D -   Callout Program    :
| E -      Bps/Par/Bits    : 9600 8N1
| F - Hardware Flow Control : Yes
| G - Software Flow Control : No
|
|    Change which setting?
-------------------------------------------
```

From here, hit Return again to get back to the main menu. Next, select the Modem and dialing option, and make sure the Init string and Reset string settings are blank. Finally, select Save setup as dfl to make this the default, and then Exit from Minicom.

Now, take your nice new null-modem cable, and connect the two machines. Then, fire up Minicom:

```
# minicom
Welcome to minicom 2.1
OPTIONS: History Buffer, F-key Macros, Search History Buffer, I18n
Compiled on Nov 12 2003, 19:21:57
Press CTRL-A Z for help on special keys
headless login:
```

Login to your server, and you're in business. To exit, hit Ctrl-A, X.

Discussion

What can you do now? Anything that you can do from any Linux command shell. Now you can disconnect the keyboard and monitor from the server. Always turn computers off before connecting or disconnecting PS/2 keyboards and mice. I know, some folks say you don't have to turn off the power before removing PS/2 keyboards and mice. I say it's cheap insurance against possibly damaging your system; the PS/2 port was not designed to be hot-pluggable.

The default Bps value for option E - Bps/Par/Bits in the Minicom setup can be anything from 9600 to 115200, depending on your Linux distribution. The Bps setting, when you're connecting with a null modem cable, must be the same throughout all of your configurations—in the bootloader, /etc/inittab, and Minicom. 9600 is the safest. You can experiment with higher speeds: 38400 is the standard Linux console speed. If it doesn't work, try 19200.

The *setserial* command displays the speed of your UART:

```
$ setserial -g /dev/ttyS0
/dev/ttyS0, UART: 16550A, Port: 0x03f8, IRQ: 4
```

But, it's unlikely you'll successfully go higher than 38400. These are all the possible serial line speeds:

110 bps
300 bps
1200 bps
2400 bps
4800 bps
9600 bps
19,200 bps
38,400 bps
57,600 bps
115,200 bps

File permissions

File permissions can drive you a bit nuts. If the server won't let you log in as *root*, you need an entry in */etc/securetty* on the server:

```
# /etc/securetty: list of terminals on which root is allowed to login.
# See securetty(5) and login(1).
console
# for people with serial port consoles
ttyS0
```

If you cannot connect as an unprivileged user, it means */dev/ttyS0* is restricted to the *root* user. First, check permissions and ownership:

```
$ ls -al /dev/ttyS0
crw-rw---- 1 root dialout 4, 64 Sep  7 22:22 /dev/ttyS0
```

/dev/ttyS0 is owned by the *dialout* group, so all you need to do is add your authorized users to that group.

Some how-tos tell you to make */dev/ttyS0* mode 777, which from a security standpoint isn't a good idea. It's not much trouble to add users to groups, and it's a lot safer.

See Also

- man 5 securetty
- man 1 minicom
- Remote Serial Console HOWTO:
    http://www.tldp.org/HOWTO/Remote-Serial-Console-HOWTO/
- Chapter 8, "Managing Users and Groups," in *Linux Cookbook*, by Carla Schroder (O'Reilly)

17.6 Configuring Your Server for Dial-in Administration

Problem

You want to dial in from home or from other offsite locations, and perform remote administration on a server from your remote serial console. So, you need to set up your server for dial-in administration. You have a proper hardware-controller modem, either internal or external, installed and ready to go. You have enabled your server for serial administration. Now, all you need to know is how to configure the server's modem to answer the phone.

Solution

Use Minicom to set your modem to answer when you dial in. Your modem must be connected when you type in the commands.

This recipe uses the Hayes AT command set, which most modems use. Check your modem documentation to make sure. First, configure the basic modem settings, then enter the modem commands:

```
# minicom -s
-------[configuration]------
| Filenames and paths      |
| File transfer protocols  |
| Serial port setup        |
| Modem and dialing        |
| Screen and keyboard      |
| Save setup as dfl        |
| Save setup as..          |
| Exit                     |
| Exit from Minicom
```

Select Serial port setup, and enter everything as it's shown here (except the serial device, which must be the correct one for your system):

```
| A -    Serial Device    : /dev/ttyS0
| B - Lockfile Location   : /var/lock
| C -    Callin Program   :
| D -    Callout Program  :
| E -     Bps/Par/Bits    :115200 8N1
| F - Hardware Flow Control : Yes
| G - Software Flow Control : No
|
|    Change which setting?
```

When you're finished, return to the main menu, and select Save setup as dfl, then Exit. You'll see this:

```
Welcome to minicom 2.1
OPTIONS: History Buffer, F-key Macros, Search History Buffer, I18n
```

```
Compiled on Jan  1 2005, 19:46:57.

Press CTRL-A Z for help on special keys
```

Next, enter the following commands:

```
AT &F
OK
AT Z
OK
AT &C1 &D2 &K3 S0=2 M0
OK
AT E0 Q1 S2=255 &W
```

Then, hit Ctrl-A, Q for the final prompt:

```
------------------------
| Leave without reset| |
|     Yes       No    |
------------------------
```

Now, you can dial directly in to your server, and it will answer on the second ring. You'll get the same login as when you connect directly with a null modem cable.

Discussion

You can get away with cheap modems on whatever box you're dialing in from, but it pays to spend the money for a better one on the server.

Don't worry too much about Bps settings because modern modems auto-negotiate line speeds by themselves. You might try lower speeds if you have problems establishing a reliable connection.

How do you know what your serial port number is? The following command shows that the system has a single serial port, */dev/ttyS0*. You can tell which one it is because it's the one with a 16550A UART:

```
$ setserial -g /dev/ttyS[0123]
/dev/ttyS0, UART: 16550A, Port: 0x03f8, IRQ: 4
/dev/ttyS1: No such device
/dev/ttyS2, UART: unknown, Port: 0x03e8, IRQ: 4
/dev/ttyS3, UART: unknown, Port: 0x02e8, IRQ: 3
```

The modem commands are copied from Chapter 13 of the Remote Serial How-to. The complete set of Hayes AT commands is available from many Internet sources. It's a good idea to keep a hardcopy on hand, or to make sure your modem documentation is handy:

minicom -o -s
> Start Minicom without sending an initialization string to the modem, and open Minicom's setup menu.

AT

Attention, modem! I have new commands for you.

&F

Restore factory configuration.

Z

Reset to profile 1.

&C1

Data Carrier Detect (DCD) is on; be ready for data from the calling modem.

&D2

Data Terminal Ready (DTR); hang up when the calling modem has finished.

&K3

CTS/RTS handshaking, to prevent lost login characters.

S0=2

Answer incoming calls after two rings.

M0

Turn modem speaker off.

E0

Do not echo modem commands to the screen to prevent confusing the console.

Q1

Do not display modem responses to the screen.

S2=255

Disable modem command mode.

&W

Write changes to nonvolatile memory (NVRAM).

You should have a complete command listing with your modem documentation. Most modems use the Hayes AT command set, which you can easily find on the Internet.

If you want to hear your modem noises, change M0 to M1, which turns the speaker on during the handshaking only, then use L1, L2, or L3 to set the volume. L1 is the quietest, L3 the loudest.

See Also

- man 8 setserial
- man 1 minicom
- Remote Serial Console HOWTO:

    http://www.tldp.org/HOWTO/Remote-Serial-Console-HOWTO/
- The Serial HOWTO goes extremely in-depth into how serial ports work:

    http://www.tldp.org/HOWTO/Serial-HOWTO.html

17.7   Dialing In to the Server

Problem

Your server is all set up for remote serial administration over dial-up, so how do you dial in to it and get to work?

Solution

Use your good friend Minicom, your all-in-one serial communications program.

To dial out from your remote serial console machine, enter the phone number in Minicom's dialing directory, then hit the Dial command:

```
$ minicom
Initializing modem

Welcome to minicom 2.1

OPTIONS: History Buffer, F-key Macros, Search History Buffer, I18n
Compiled on Jan  1 2005, 19:46:57.

Press CTRL-A Z for help on special keys

AT S7=45 S0=0 L3 V1 X4 &c1 E1 Q0
OK
Ctrl-A, D
```

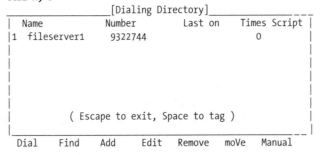

```
_____[Dialing Directory]_____ ___
|   Name           Number        Last on    Times Script |
|1  fileserver1     9322744                     0         |
|                                                         |
|                                                         |
|                                                         |
|                                                         |
|                                                         |
|           ( Escape to exit, Space to tag )              |
|_____| __ |
   Dial    Find    Add     Edit    Remove   moVe    Manual
```

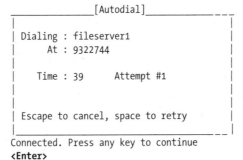

```
_____[Autodial]_____ ___
|                                         |
| Dialing : fileserver1                   |
|      At : 9322744                       |
|                                         |
|   Time : 39        Attempt #1           |
|                                         |
|                                         |
| Escape to cancel, space to retry        |
|_____| __ |
Connected. Press any key to continue
<Enter>
```

```
CONNECT 115200/V34/LAPM/V42BIS/33600:TX/33600:RX
fileserver1.carla.com ttyS0 login: carla
Password: ********
[carla@fileserver1:~]$
```

And there you are. To exit your remote session:

```
[carla@fileserver1:~]$ logout
```

Discussion

This makes a nice backup if your Internet service goes down, or your Ethernet fails, or if you need to reboot your server.

Don't worry too much about Bps settings, because modern modems auto-negotiate line speeds by themselves. You might try lower speeds if you have problems establishing a reliable connection. Use the Edit command in the dialing menu to try different line speeds.

See Also

- `man 1 minicom`
- Remote Serial Console HOWTO:

    http://www.tldp.org/HOWTO/Remote-Serial-Console-HOWTO/
- The Serial HOWTO goes extremely in-depth into how serial ports work:

    http://www.tldp.org/HOWTO/Serial-HOWTO.html

17.8   Adding Security

Problem

Because the serial line is a direct line to the kernel, bypassing firewalls and intrusion detectors, you want to set up some barriers against intruders, especially for dial-in administration.

Solution

Here are some ways to improve the security of a serial line:

- Direct all logging to a remote logging server.
- Use a higher-end modem with built-in security features such as automatic callbacks, caller line identification, and approved caller lists.
- Don't use a phone line with a publicly listed number.
- Disable the SysRq key with this line in */etc/sysctl.conf*: `kernel.sysrq = 0`.

- AT S2=255 disables the modem's command mode, but a remote attacker could possibly reset it to command mode, then input their own nefarious commands. A modem that uses DIP switches or jumpers to put it in and out of command mode is great for preventing this sort of attack.

Discussion

Your first line of defense is an obscure phone number. Security-through-obscurity has its place in your security architecture; don't make it easy for unsophisticated troublemakers. But this will not foil a war-dialer. If a war-dialer should target your network, it won't take long to discover which phone lines have modems on them. Then, to gain access, they'll need to get past the initial login. A cracker can cause you grief simply by repeatedly dialing the server's phone number—denial-of-service attacks are easy to launch and difficult to defend against. High-end modems like the U.S. Robotics Courier have security features that help against a persistent attacker, such as automatic callback and approved caller lists. You can't stop a cracker from dialing your number, but you can try to stop them from getting to a login prompt.

The SysRq key allows the user to send commands directly to the kernel. It is used primarily by kernel developers; otherwise, there is no good reason to leave it active. Check to see if support for it is compiled into your kernel. Look in your */boot/config-** file under Kernel hacking:

```
CONFIG_MAGIC_SYSRQ=y
```

This means it is. Another option is to rebuild the kernel and remove support for it; if you're not doing kernel hacking, there is no reason to have it available.

See Also

- Recipe 19.19
- Remote Serial Console HOWTO:

    http://www.tldp.org/HOWTO/Remote-Serial-Console-HOWTO/
- The Serial HOWTO goes extremely in-depth into how serial ports work:

    http://www.tldp.org/HOWTO/Serial-HOWTO.html

17.9 Configuring Logging

Problem

You want to direct kernel messages to your serial console and to a logfile so that you can follow along in real-time, and also have a logfile to study later. How do you do this?

Solution

Configure */etc/syslog.conf* to route your kernel messages where you want them to go:

```
kern.*    -/var/log/kern.log
kern.*    /dev/console
kern.*    @xena
```

This sends all kernel messages to three different locations. The first one is a local file, the second one is your serial console, and the third one is the remote logging server Xena.

There will be at least on default kern entry, so make sure you find and change or delete it if it doesn't suit your logging scheme.

Discussion

You may fine-tune your logging because *syslog* supports eight different severity levels:

```
debug, info, notice, warning, err, crit, alert, emerg
```

When you select one of these, you also get all the higher-priority messages as well. This example:

```
kern.crit    /dev/console
```

sends crit, alert, and emerg messages to the serial console.

You must restart *klogd* after changing this file. On Debian, use this command:

 # /etc/init.d/klogd restart

Fedora uses this command:

 # /etc/init.d/sysklogd restart

On Linux, the system logging daemon is actually two daemons: *sysklogd* and *klogd*. *klogd* is the kernel logging daemon. Debian gives each one its own *init* file; Fedora starts them both from the same file.

See Also

- man 5 syslog.conf
- Recipe 19.19

17.10 Uploading Files to the Server

Problem

You need to transfer some files to the server—perhaps a new NIC driver, or replacing a corrupted drive controller, or replacing a hopelessly messed-up *iptables* configuration. This is not Ethernet, so you can't use *scp*, or drag-'n'-drop in a file manager. What do you do?

Solution

Remember the olden days of Bulletin Board Services, and Xmodem, Ymodem, Zmodem, and Kermit file transfer protocols? Because you're using Minicom, you'll need one of these. Zmodem is the best choice, as it has built-in error correction, and is the most reliable.

First, install the *lrzsz* package on the server; this has the same package name for both RPM and Debian packages.

Then, log in to the server from the remote console with Minicom. Type this command on the server to tell it to wait to receive a file:

```
[server@remote:~]$ rz
rz waiting to receive.**|B0100000023be50
```

Then hit Alt-A, Z, and then S to bring up Minicom's file-sending menu. First, choose Zmodem protocol:

```
--[Upload]---
| zmodem    |
| ymodem    |
| xmodem    |
| kermit    |
| ascii     |
-------------
```

Then, select the file or files you want to upload:

```
---------[Select one or more files for upload]------
|Directory: /home/carla                            |
| [..]                                             |
| [.AbiSuite]                                       |
| [.cddb]                                          |
| [.cfagent]                                       |
| [.config]                                        |
| [.fonts]                                         |
|      ( Escape to exit, Space to tag )            |
||||||||||||||||||||||||||||||||||||||||||||||||||||
  [Goto]  [Prev]  [Show]  [Tag]  [Untag]  [Okay]
```

You don't have to navigate the menu if you already know the filename because you can type in the filenames by hitting "Okay" without tagging any files, which brings up this menu:

```
--------------------------------------
|No file selected - enter filename:  |
|>                                   |
--------------------------------------
```

To exit rz on the server, hit Ctrl-X. It might take a few tries.

Discussion

Files are transferred to the current working directory on the server, so be sure you're in the directory you want the files to land in.

See Also

- `man 1 rz`
- `man 1 minicom`

## CHAPTER 18

Running a Linux Dial-Up Server

18.0   Introduction

In these modern times, dial-up networking might seem a bit quaint. But it still has its place. Many parts of the world still have no access to affordable broadband. A dial-up server is an inexpensive way to provide remote administration access, and to set up a quick and cheap WAN. You may also share a dial-up Internet account; even though that sounds like a recipe for frustration, there are times when it works out. For example, two or three people who don't do a lot of heavy-duty Interneting could get by all right.

You should use a good-quality hardware-controller modem, ideally from a vendor that supports Linux. Messing with cheapie modem drivers on a server isn't worth the pain.

18.1   Configuring a Single Dial-Up Account with WvDial

Problem

You need to set up a dial-up Internet account on your Linux box, but you don't know what dialer or configuration utility to use. Or, you know about KPPP and Gnome-PPP, which are good utilities, but KPPP requires KDE libraries, Gnome-PPP requires Gnome libraries, and both require X Windows. You don't want to download all the baggage that comes with them; you just want a simple standalone dialer, or you want a command-line dialer.

Solution

The WvDial dial-up program runs from the command line, and runs on any Linux distribution. These are the steps to configure a single account:

- Make sure you have WvDial and *pppd* (point-to-point protocol daemon) installed
- Have your Internet account login information handy

Then, make sure that */etc/ppp/options* contains a basic set of options. You can copy this exactly:

```
asyncmap 0
crtscts
lock
hide-password
modem
proxyarp
lcp-echo-interval 30
lcp-echo-failure 4
noipx
```

As *root*, start up the WvDial configuration script, giving it the name of the configuration file, exactly as shown here:

```
# wvdialconf /etc/wvdial.conf
Scanning your serial ports for a modem.

ttyS0<*1>: ATQ0 V1 E1 -- OK
ttyS0<*1>: ATQ0 V1 E1 Z -- OK
ttyS0<*1>: ATQ0 V1 E1 S0=0 -- OK
[...]
Found a modem on /dev/ttyS0.
Modem configuration written to /etc/wvdial.conf.
ttyS0<Info>: Speed 115200; init "ATQ0 V1 E1 S0=0 &C1 &D2 +FCLASS=0"
```

This writes the modem defaults to */etc/wvdial.conf*. Now, open */etc/wvdial.conf*, and add your login information, using your own dial-up number, login, and password:

```
[Dialer Defaults]
Modem = /dev/ttyS0
Baud = 115200
Init1 = ATZ
Init2 = ATQ0 V1 E1 S0=0 &C1 &D2 +FCLASS=0
ISDN = 0
Modem Type = Analog Modem
Phone = 123-4567
Username = alrac
Password = passfoo
```

Save your changes, and try dialing in by running the wvdial command:

```
# wvdial
--> WvDial: Internet dialer version 1.54.0
--> Initializing modem.
--> Sending: ATZ
ATZ
OK
--> Sending: ATQ0 V1 E1 S0=0 &C1 &D2 +FCLASS=0
ATQ0 V1 E1 S0=0 &C1 &D2 +FCLASS=0
OK
--> Modem initialized.
--> Sending: ATDT9322744
--> Waiting for carrier.
ATDT9322744
CONNECT 115200
--> Carrier detected.  Starting PPP immediately.
--> Starting pppd at Thu March 13 13:54:09 2007
--> pid of pppd: 7754
--> Using interface ppp0
--> local  IP address 68.169.174.170
--> remote IP address 68.169.174.12
--> primary   DNS address 68.169.174.2
--> secondary DNS address 68.169.174.3
```

Test your connection by surfing the Web or *pinging* some reliable hosts:

```
$ ping -C2 yahoo.com
PING yahoo.com (216.109.112.135) 56(84) bytes of data.
64 bytes from w2.rc.vip.dcn.yahoo.com (216.109.112.135): icmp_seq=1 ttl=50 time=133
ms
64 bytes from w2.rc.vip.dcn.yahoo.com (216.109.112.135): icmp_seq=2 ttl=50 time=138
ms
```

There you go, all ready to web surf at the speed of dial-up.

Discussion

S0=0 tells the modem to answer the phone immediately, so delete this if you don't want to enable dial-in access. Or, change the value to 1, 2, 3, or 4 to answer on the first, second, etc. ring.

It is better to use */dev/ttyS** than */dev/modem*. On some Linux distributions, */dev/modem* is supposed to be a softlink to the modem, but it isn't always correct. It is better to name it explicitly.

Modern modems are good at auto-negotiating line speeds. 115200 is a safe default. If you have problems sustaining a connection, try lower speeds:

9,600 bps
19,200 bps
38,400 bps
57,600 bps

See man wvdial.conf to see what the default configuration values are.

See Also

- man 1 wvdial
- man 5 wvdial.conf
- WvDial: *http://open.nit.ca/wiki/?page=WvDial*

18.2 Configuring Multiple Accounts in WvDial

Problem

You have several dial-up accounts, so how do you configure WvDial to handle them?

Solution

Add different sections to your */etc/wvdial.conf*. This example divides it into a section containing global defaults, then three different dial-up accounts:

```
[Dialer Defaults]
Modem = /dev/ttyS3
Baud = 115200
Init1 = ATZ
Init2 = ATQ0 V1 E1 &C1 &D2 +FCLASS=0
ISDN = 0
Modem Type = Analog Modem
Dial Attempts = 10

[Dialer ISP1]
Stupid Mode = on
Phone = 1234567
Username = alrac
Password = secretfoo
Idle Seconds = 600

[Dialer ISP2]
Phone = 2345678
Username = foobear@isp1.net
Ask Password = yes
Idle Seconds = 200

[Dialer ISP2]
Stupid Mode = on
Phone = 3456789
Username = fredfoo@isp2.com
Password = fredsecret
```

Then, connect to the one you want by naming the Dialer section:

```
# wvdial ISP2
```

Discussion

Another way to do this is to put each account into a separate configuration file, then call the file with the --config option:

```
# wvdial --config /etc/wvdial-isp2
```

This gives you the flexibility to set up different configurations for different users; just remember to give them read permissions on the file.

Unprivileged users can have their own personal WvDial configurations, as long they have permissions on the necessary files. See the next recipe to learn how to do this.

See Also

- man 1 wvdial
- man 5 wvdial.conf
- WvDial: *http://open.nit.ca/wiki/?page=WvDial*

18.3 Configuring Dial-Up Permissions for Nonroot Users

Problem

You want your users to have dial-up privileges, but so far in this chapter, only the *root* user can use dial-up. How do you make dial-up available to nonprivileged users?

Solution

This takes a bit of tweaking permissions on a number of files:

> */etc/ppp/chap-secrets*
> */etc/ppp/pap-secrets*
> */dev/ttyS**
> */usr/sbin/pppd*
> */var/lock*

Some Linux distributions come with the *dialout* group for dial-up users. Others use *dip* or *uucp*. Make */etc/ppp/chap-secrets*, */etc/ppp/pap-secrets*, and */dev/ttyS** owned by the *dialout* group (or *dip*, or *uucp*, it doesn't matter as long as they are all in the same group):

```
# chown root:dialout /dev/ttyS3 /etc/ppp/chap-secrets \
  /etc/ppp/pap-secrets
```

Next, put your authorized users in the same group these files belong to:

```
dialout:x:20:alrac,foobear,fredfoo
```

Make sure that */etc/ppp/chap-secrets* and */etc/ppp/pap-secrets* are readable and writable only by the owner and group owner:

```
# chmod 0660 /etc/ppp/chap-secrets /etc/ppp/pap-secrets
```

Next, check the */var/lock* directory. It should be wide open to the world, and the sticky bit set:

```
$ ls -ld /var/lock
drwxrwxrwt  3 root root  4096 14. Okt 07:37 /var/lock
```

If it isn't, make it so:

```
# chmod 1777 /var/lock
```

pppd needs to be *suid*, as this shows:

```
$ ls -l /usr/sbin/pppd
-rwsr-xr--  1 root dip 232536 Dec 30  2004 /usr/sbin/pppd
```

If it isn't, make it so:

```
# chmod 4754 /usr/sbin/pppd
```

Discussion

If the group owner of any file is *root*, do not add users to the *root* group! Change the group owner to *dialout* (or whatever group you choose).

You'll see messages in your logfiles complaining that "Warning—secret file */etc/ppp/pap-secrets* has world and/or group access." Don't worry about them—just make sure they are not world-readable, and be careful who goes in the *dialout* group.

The little s in -rwsr-xr-- tells you */usr/sbin/pppd* is *suid* root. This means ordinary users get to run *pppd* with the necessary *root* privileges it needs to work. If you get "Cannot open device /dev/ttyS0- Device or resource busy" errors as an unprivileged user, chances are either */usr/sbin/pppd* is not *suid root*, or */var/lock* has incorrect permissions. *suid* opens a potential security hole, and should not be used casually; this is one of the few times where it is OK to use it.

See Also

- Chapters 8 and 9 of *Linux Cookbook*, by Carla Schroder (O'Reilly) for more information on file permissions, and user and group management.
- man 1 wvdial
- man 5 wvdial.conf
- man 8 pppd
- WvDial: *http://open.nit.ca/wiki/?page=WvDial*

18.4 Creating WvDial Accounts for Nonroot Users

Problem

You want your users to have their own private dial-up accounts, with the configuration file stored in their own home directories.

Solution

First, make sure all the necessary permissions and group ownerships are configured as in Recipe 18.3. Then, WvDial configuration for individual users is done just like in the first two recipes in this chapter, except the WvDial configuration file is stored in their home directories. Create the new configuration file as the user, with the `--config` option to specify the location of the user's personal configuration file:

```
$ wvdialconf --config ~/.wvdialrc
```

The file can have any name you like; using *.wvdialrc* creates a default that is called by using the `wvdial` command with no options. Multiple accounts are created by using Dialer sections, and called just like in the other recipes:

```
$ wvdial ISP2
```

If the file has a different name, it must be called with the `--config` option:

```
$ wvdial --config ~/dialup
```

If there are multiple Dialer sections in it, call them this way:

```
$ wvdialconf --config ~/dialup ISP1
```

Discussion

Some users like having a desktop icon to click on, instead of running a shell command. It is easy to make one; check the documentation for whatever desktop they are running, as each one is a little different.

For simple individual dial-up accounts, graphical utilities like KPPP and GnomePPP are nice for your users. But, you often still have to make manual edits to */etc/ppp/ options* or other *ppp* files. A common one is replacing the auth option in */etc/ppp/ options* with noauth. It shouldn't even be there, as virtually no commercial ISPs require two-way authentication. Most Linux distributions make noauth the default these days, thankfully.

See Also

- man 1 wvdial
- man 5 wvdial.conf
- man 8 pppd
- WvDial: *http://open.nit.ca/wiki/?page=WvDial*

18.5 Sharing a Dial-Up Internet Account

Problem

You have a small number of users who need to share a single dial-up Internet account. Maybe it's all you can afford, or it's all that's available, or maybe your needs are so minimal you don't need broadband. It could even be a fiendishly clever method for discouraging users from web surfing. You might have a mix of platforms on the client side—Linux, Mac, Windows. Your LAN is already set up and functioning. You want to use an old PC as your Internet gateway.

Solution

Use an old PC to act as your Internet gateway. Configure a dial-up account on this machine, then configure IP masquerading to direct all those Internet packets to all the hosts on your LAN.

You'll need the following:

- A modem on the dial-up server
- A program like WvDial, KPPP, or Gnome-PPP to configure dial-up networking on the server

First, connect the modem to the phone line, and set up your dial-up account. Do not connect the gateway box to the LAN yet. Get your dial-up account or accounts set up and working.

Then, run these *iptables* rules from the command line:

```
# modprobe iptable_nat
# iptables -t nat -A POSTROUTING -o ppp0 -j MASQUERADE
# echo "1" > /proc/sys/net/ipv4/ip_forward
```

Now, when the gateway machine is connected to the LAN, all users can share the connection. This provides no security whatsoever, and no persistence between reboots, so you need to add these rules to a proper *iptables* firewall script. Please see Chapter 3 to learn how to build a firewall.

Discussion

This is a great time to dig out that old AMD 586 box that lies under a layer of dust in your closet and put it to work. Don't use one of your user's PCs because this leads to frustration and woes. You can't control what the user does with it, and it must be on all the time. And, one of the reasons servers are more reliable than desktop PCs is they are not asked to do nearly as much, so you'll get better performance.

There are a lot of excellent specialized mini-Linux distributions made expressly to serve as firewalls and Internet gateways. Here is a list of some excellent ones to try that support dial-up networking:

- IPCop (*http://www.ipcop.org/*)
- FreeSCO (*http://www.freesco.org/*)
- Shorewall (*http://www.shorewall.net/*)

See Also

- man 8 iptables
- *Building Secure Servers with Linux*, by Michael D. Bauer (O'Reilly)

18.6   Setting Up Dial-on-Demand

Problem

You don't want to babysit a shared dial-up connection, or leave it on all the time; you want it to connect itself on demand, like when a user clicks on a web browser or checks email, and disconnect after a period of inactivity.

Solution

First, get WvDial and *ppp* working reliably, as we covered in the previous recipes.

Next, create a file called */etc/ppp/peers/demand* so that it looks like this, naming your own Dialer section, modem port, and user login:

```
noauth
name wvdial
usepeerdns
connect "/usr/bin/wvdial --chat ISP1"
/dev/ttyS2
115200
modem
crtscts
defaultroute
noipdefault
user alrac@isp.net
idle 300
persist
demand
logfd 6
```

Now, you can start up your new demand-dial server with the *pon* command, naming the configuration file you just created:

```
# pon demand
```

It will not dial up right away, but will wait for a user to initiate a link by trying to connect to the Internet. Test this by *pinging* some web sites, opening a web browser, or checking email. You can verify that the *pppd* daemon has started with *ps*:

```
$ ps ax | grep pppd
 6506 ?        Ss     0:00 /usr/sbin/pppd call demand
```

Shut down the link with *poff*:

```
# poff
```

Discussion

The */etc/ppp/peers/demand* file can be named anything you like.

pon means "pppd on" and *poff* means "pppd off."

The *demand* option prepares the *pppd* link; it configures the interface (*ppp0*), then stops short of connecting. Then, when packets start moving, such as checking email, *pppd* dials in and establishes the connection.

The persist option keeps the link open even when packets are no longer flowing over the link.

idle 300 means that the connection will close after 300 seconds of inactivity. You can set this to any value, or not use it at all if you want maximum availability.

You may do all of this with *ppp* alone, and not use WvDial. I like WvDial because it is easy to use. WvDial assumes that most modems understand the Hayes AT command set. *ppp* was created in the days when modem commands were not standard, so its structure and configuration are more complex.

See Also

- man 1 wvdial
- man 5 wvdial.conf
- man 8 pppd
- WvDial: *http://open.nit.ca/wiki/?page=WvDial*

18.7   Scheduling Dial-Up Availability with cron

Problem

You want to shut down dial-up activity completely during nights and weekends, as no one will be using it. Your modem bandwidth costs you money, or you don't want it accidentally running when no one is around just because someone left an IRC session or email client open.

Solution

A simple *cron* job will do the trick. If you are using demand dialing create a *crontab*, as *root*, using the name of your own */etc/ppp/peers/[foo]* file:

```
# crontab -e
00 6 * * 1-5 /usr/bin/pon demand
00 20 * * 1-5 /usr/bin/poff
```

Save the file without renaming it, and then exit the editor. This example starts dial-on-demand every morning at 6 a.m., and shuts it down every evening at 8 p.m. Verify your new rules with the -l (list) switch:

```
# crontab -l
00 6 * * 1-5 /usr/bin/pon filename
00 20 * * 1-5 /usr/bin/poff
```

Discussion

crontabs are user-specific, so when you want to create a system-wide *cron* job, you must do so as *root*. *crontab* opens the default editor as specified in your *~/.bashrc*. You may use any editor you like. In the example in the Solution, *crontab* opened the Vim editor. This is what the *~/.bashrc* entry that defines your default editor looks like:

```
EDITOR=vim
VISUAL=$EDITOR
export EDITOR VISUAL
```

crontab -e means "edit the current user's crontab."

This is what the fields in *crontab* mean:

```
field               allowed values
-----               --------------
minute              0-59
hour                0-23
day of month        1-31
month               1-12 (or names, see below)
day of week         0-7 (0 or 7 is Sun, or use names)
```

You may also use WvDial commands if your setup is like the first two recipes in this chapter, and you are not using demand dialing:

```
# crontab -e
00 6 * * 1-5 /usr/bin/wvdial filename
00 20 * * 1-5 kill `pidof wvdial`
```

This starts up WvDial at 6 a.m. and shuts it down at 8 p.m.

See Also

- man 5 crontab
- Recipe 6.15, "Setting Your Default Editor," in *Linux Cookbook*, by Carla Schroder (O'Reilly) to learn more about customizing the editor that *crontab* uses

18.8 Dialing over Voicemail Stutter Tones

Problem

When you have a message on your voicemail, the dial tone changes to a stutter tone. Your modem interprets this as no dial tone, and will not dial out.

Solution

Add or change this line in */etc/wvdial.conf*:

```
Abort on No Dialtone = no
```

This tells WvDial to dial no matter what, without checking for a dial tone.

Discussion

Hopefully, you are not in the sort of environment where phone cables are continually coming unplugged, which would make using this option a bit of a problem. You might want to turn up the modem speaker so you can hear it dialing out, just to keep an eye (OK, ear) on it, with these options added to the *Init2* line in */etc/wvdial.conf*:

```
M1 L3
```

M1 turns on the speaker for dialing and the handshake only. L1 is the lowest volume. L2, L3, and L4 are progressively louder.

See Also

- man 1 wvdial
- man 5 wvdial.conf
- man 8 pppd
- WvDial: *http://open.nit.ca/wiki/?page=WvDial*

18.9 Overriding Call Waiting

Problem

Your phone line has call waiting, so whenever you get a call when you are online it messes up your connection—you get disconnected, or your downloads get corrupted or interrupted.

Solution

Disable call waiting in */etc/wvdial.conf*. This option disables call waiting globally:

```
Dial Prefix = *70,
```

This disables it per phone number:

```
Phone = *70,1234567
```

You can add another comma or two to give it more time to take effect before dialing the number, if necessary.

Discussion

The V.92 modem standard allows for more options than merely disabling call waiting: ignore, disconnect, or place the Internet connection on hold and take the call. The last option requires using an ISP that supports this. You'll need a modem that supports these features to make them work.

See Also

- man 1 wvdial
- man 5 wvdial.conf
- man 8 pppd
- WvDial: *http://open.nit.ca/wiki/?page=WvDial*

18.10 Leaving the Password Out of the Configuration File

Problem

You don't want to leave your dial-up account password in the WvDial configuration file because it is stored in plaintext.

Solution

Add the Ask Password = yes option to your WvDial configuration file, like this:

```
[Dialer Defaults]
Modem = /dev/ttyS3
Baud = 115200
Init1 = ATZ
Init2 = ATQ0 V1 E1 &C1 &D2 +FCLASS=0
ISDN = 0
Modem Type = Analog Modem
Dial Attempts = 10

[Dialer ISP1]
Stupid Mode = on
Phone = 1234567
Username = alrac
Ask Password = yes
Idle Seconds = 600
```

Then, you'll be prompted for your password during login.

Discussion

This is not suitable for a dial-up server, unless you enjoy scampering to the server and entering a password every time someone needs to go online. It adds a bit of protection for users who do not have control over who uses their computers.

See Also

- man 1 wvdial
- man 5 wvdial.conf
- man 8 pppd
- WvDial: *http://open.nit.ca/wiki/?page=WvDial*

18.11 Creating a Separate pppd Logfile

Problem

All of your *pppd* messages are getting dumped into */var/log/messages*, and making a big mess, and you would rather have them going to a separate file.

Solution

Create your logfile:

```
# touch /var/log/ppp
```

Then, add the logfile option to */etc/ppp/options*:

```
logfile /var/log/ppp
```

Delete any references to *logfd*, as the two options are mutually exclusive.

Discussion

There is no downside to having separate logfiles for your services; it makes it a lot easier to find out what is happening on your system.

Customizing the standard Linux *syslog* is bit more difficult than it needs to be; see Chapter 19 to learn how to build a robust, easily customizable logging server with *syslog-ng*.

See Also

- man 8 pppd

Troubleshooting Networks

19.0 Introduction

Linux provides a host of software utilities for troubleshooting network problems. This chapter covers a number of excellent Linux utilities for pinpointing problems and seeing what's happening on your network. These are all intended to be quick and easy to use, rather than for ongoing monitoring. Check out Chapters 13 and 14 on Nagios and MRTG to learn how to set up monitoring and alerting.

Your workhorses are going to be *ping*, *tcpdump*, Wireshark, and *ngrep*. While *ping* is still the number one tool for checking connectivity, *tcpdump*, Wireshark, and *ngrep* all provide different and excellent ways to capture and read what's going over your wires. You can't count on applications to generate useful error messages when commands fail (or sometimes to generate any messages at all), but nothing is hidden from a packet sniffer. When you don't know if it's a hardware or software problem, run these first to narrow down the possibilities. Software problems are more common than hardware problems, so don't break out the hardware testers until you have eliminated software glitches. Of course, it never hurts to rule out the immediately obvious, such as a disconnected cable or a powered-down machine.

Practice running the various utilities in this chapter as often as you can on healthy systems. Then, you'll know what a healthy network looks like, and you'll develop elite skills that will come in handy when there are troubles.

Don't forget your logfiles. Most applications come with an option to crank up the logging levels to debug. Do this to collect as much data as possible, and then don't forget to turn the level back down to something sane so you don't fill your logfiles in record time.

Testing and Tracing Cabling

If you're into testing your own cabling, there are all kinds of interesting tools to help you. A basic multimeter should be your first purchase, along with an electrical outlet tester. These are inexpensive little yellow three-pronged gadgets with colored LEDs. Just plug one into an electrical outlet, and the LEDs will tell you if it is healthy or not.

Multimeters are useful for a lot of jobs, such as finding shorts and opens, testing for continuity and attenuation, and determining whether a wire is terminated correctly. They're also great for other jobs, such as testing power supplies and motherboards.

For installed cable, you'll need a special continuity tester that comes in two pieces—one for each end of the cable. Some of these also come with tone generators for tracing cables. If you crimp your own cables, you ought to invest in a good cable tester.

Tracking down cable problems inside walls—and tracing and identifying them—calls for a "fox and hound pair," which is a delightful name for a tone generator and amplifier pair. The fox connects to a cable and generates a tone, and then the hound sniffs out the tone to identify and trace the cable. The fox reads the tone through the wire's insulation, and even through drywall.

If you're not interested in being your own cable guru, find yourself a professional who understands analog wiring, digital wiring, and computer cabling, because these days, you're going to find all three jumbled together. Even when you are your own cabling guru, you'll still need an electrician and a telecom technician from time to time. Never try to be your own homegrown electrician—any wire that carries current should be touched only by a professional.

Spares for Testing

Don't forget hubs and switches in your bug hunts. Ordinary dumb hubs and switches are dirt cheap—keep a couple on hand for swapping with a suspect switch or hub. Keep extra patch cables, too. Using your handy network administrator laptop for portable testing is a fast way to figure out which side of a switch a problem is on, or even whether it's on the switch itself.

19.1 Building a Network Diagnostic and Repair Laptop

Problem

You want to set up an old laptop as a portable network diagnostic station. What should you have on it?

Solution

This is a fine and endlessly useful thing to have. It doesn't have to be a super-duper brand-new laptop; any one of reasonably recent vintage that supports USB 2.0 and Linux will do. It should have:

- Two wired Ethernet interfaces and one wireless
- Modem
- USB 2.0 ports
- Serial port
- Serial terminal

Most laptops don't have a serial port, so you can use a USB-to-serial adapter instead.

Another great thing to have is a PATA/SATA-to-USB 2.0 adapter for rescuing failing hard drives. This lets you plug in either 2.5" or 3.5" PATA or SATA hard drives, and then do a direct copy to save your data. Use the excellent GNU *ddrescue* utility for this. If your primary hard drive isn't big enough to hold the data, hook up a second one with another PATA/SATA-to-USB 2.0 adapter, or copy it over your network. Why not just copy it over the network in the first place? Because a failing drive is going to take the networking stack down along with everything else.

Install whatever Linux distribution you want, and these applications:

OpenSSH
Secure remote administration.

sshfs
Securely mount remote filesystems.

telnet
Insecurely login to servers; useful for several kinds of tests.

Nmap
Port scanner and network exploration.

tcptraceroute; traceroute
Show routes taken to other hosts.

tcpdump; Wireshark
Packet sniffers.

Netstat
Show listening and connected ports.

netstat-nat
Display NAT connections.

ping
Send ICMP ECHO_REQUEST to network hosts.

fping
> Send ICMP ECHO_REQUEST to multiple network hosts.

echoping
> Test that a server is listening.

ssmping
> Test multicast connectivity.

ngrep
> Packet sniffer that does plaintext and regular expression filtering, rather than filtering on hosts, protocols, and TCP flags.

etherwake
> Send Wake-on-LAN packets to WOL-compliant computers.

iptraf
> Console-based network statistics utility.

httping
> Ping-like program for http-requests.

iftop
> Display bandwidth usage on an interface.

iperf
> Measure TCP and UDP bandwidth performance.

host
> Find hostnames or IP addresses.

dig
> Query name servers.

arping
> Send ARP REQUEST to check for duplicate IP addresses, and to see if a host is up.

GNU ddrescue
> Excellent *dd*-type block copier for rescuing failing hard drives. GNU *ddrescue* is written by Antonio Diaz; don't confuse it with the older *dd-rescue*, authored by Kurt Garloff. That is also a good rescue utility, but the newer GNU *ddrescue* is faster and does a better job.

net-tools package; iproute2 package
> See the Introduction to Chapter 6 for additional information on the *net-tools* and *iproute2* packages.

Get these utilities for wireless troubleshooting:

Kismet
> 802.11b wireless network sniffer.

wireless-tools
> Userspace tools for Linux wireless extensions.

madwifi-tools
> Userspace tools for the Atheros Wireless driver.

hostapd
> Wireless authenticator.

aircrack-ng
> Crack and recover WEP/WPA passwords.

airsnort
> WLAN sniffer.

wpasupplicant
> Key negotiation with your WEP/WPA Authenticator.

Doubtless you will find others that you must have; just fling 'em in there and go to work.

Discussion

Don't forget to pay extra attention to security. Be sure to keep all of your packages updated, especially security updates, and be finicky with access controls. You can always run a firewall, but this often gets in the way, so your best strategy is to configure it as though you were always going to run it without a firewall. You shouldn't need to run any services anyway, except *sshd*, so a firewall isn't strictly necessary.

See Also

- Chapter 4
- Chapter 7
- Chapter 17

19.2 Testing Connectivity with ping

Problem

Some services or hosts on your network are not accessible, or have intermittent failures. You don't know if it's a physical problem, a problem with name services, routing, or what the heck. Where do you start?

Solution

Good old *ping* should always be your first stop. Use the -c switch to limit the number of *pings*; otherwise, it will run until you stop it with Ctrl-C:

```
$ ping localhost
PING xena.alrac.net (127.0.1.1) 56(84) bytes of data.
64 bytes from xena.alrac.net (127.0.1.1): icmp_seq=1 ttl=64 time=0.034 ms
64 bytes from xena.alrac.net (127.0.1.1): icmp_seq=2 ttl=64 time=0.037 ms
```

```
--- xena.alrac.net ping statistics ---
2 packets transmitted, 2 received, 0% packet loss, time 999ms
rtt min/avg/max/mdev = 0.034/0.035/0.037/0.006 ms
```

Pinging *localhost* first confirms that your network interface is up and operating. You can also *ping* your hostname and IP address to further confirm that local networking is operating correctly. Then, you can test other hosts:

```
$ ping -c10 uberpc
PING uberpc.alrac.net (192.168.1.76) 56(84) bytes of data.
64 bytes from uberpc.alrac.net (192.168.1.76): icmp_seq=1 ttl=64 time=5.49 ms
[...]

--- uberpc.alrac.net ping statistics ---
10 packets transmitted, 10 received, 0% packet loss, time 9031ms
rtt min/avg/max/mdev = 0.097/0.108/0.124/0.007 ms
```

The output from that simple command gives you several useful pieces of information, including that name resolution is working and you have a good, clean, fast connection.

This example shows a problem:

```
$ ping -c10 uberpc
ping: unknown host uberpc
```

This means you entered the wrong hostname, DNS is broken, routing is goofed up, or the remote host is not connected to the network. So, your next step is to *ping* the IP address:

```
$ ping -c10 192.168.1.76
PING 192.168.1.76 (192.168.1.76) 56(84) bytes of data.
From 192.168.1.10 icmp_seq=1 Destination Host Unreachable
[...]
From 192.168.1.10 icmp_seq=10 Destination Host Unreachable

--- 192.168.1.76 ping statistics ---
10 packets transmitted, 0 received, +9 errors, 100% packet loss, time 9011ms
, pipe 3
```

This shows that you entered the wrong IP address or the host is down, but you got as far as a router on the host's network. You know this because the router sent you the "Destination Host Unreachable" message.

If *pinging* the IP address had succeeded, then that would point to a DNS problem.

This is what it looks like when your own PC is not connected to the network:

```
$ ping  -c10 192.168.1.76
connect: Network is unreachable
```

This is what you see when the whole remote network is unreachable:

```
$ ping -c10 alrac.net
PING alrac.net(11.22.33.44) 56(84) bytes of data.
```

```
--- alrac.net ping statistics ---
10 packets transmitted, 0 received, 100% packet loss, time 10007ms
```

If the failure is intermittent, increase the number of *pings* to several hundred. It's a good idea to place a limit because we do go off and forget that it's running.

When the hosts that you are *pinging* are on the other side of your router or Internet gateway, run *ping* both from a workstation behind the router and then from the router itself.

On a multihomed host, use `ping -I <interface>` to specify which interface to use.

Discussion

Don't block `echo-request`, `echo-reply`, `time-exceeded`, or `destination-unreachable` *ping* messages. Some admins block all *ping* messages at their firewalls, and this is a mistake because many network functions require at least these four *ping* messages to operate correctly. See Chapter 3 to learn how to correctly configure your *iptables* firewall.

See Also

- man 8 ping
- IANA list of ICMP parameters:

    http://www.iana.org/assignments/icmp-parameters

19.3   Profiling Your Network with FPing and Nmap

Problem

You would like to like to discover all the hosts on your network, and you want to establish the baseline performance of your network with *ping*, so you have something for comparison when you're troubleshooting network performance problems. You could do it with *ping*, and perhaps write a clever script to automate *pinging* a whole subnet. But, isn't there already a way to do it with a single command?

Solution

FPing *pings* all the addresses in a range in sequence. This example *pings* a subnet once, reports which hosts are alive, queries DNS for the hostnames, and prints a summary:

```
$ fping -c1 -sdg 192.168.1.0/24
xena.alrac.net    : [0], 84 bytes, 0.04 ms (0.04 avg, 0% loss)
pyramid.alrac.net : [0], 84 bytes, 0.45 ms (0.45 avg, 0% loss)
uberpc.alrac.net  : [0], 84 bytes, 0.11 ms (0.11 avg, 0% loss)
ICMP Host Unreachable from 192.168.1.10 for ICMP Echo sent to 192.168.1.2
ICMP Host Unreachable from 192.168.1.10 for ICMP Echo sent to 192.168.1.3
ICMP Host Unreachable from 192.168.1.10 for ICMP Echo sent to 192.168.1.4
[...]
```

```
192.168.1.9        : xmt/rcv/%loss = 1/0/100%
xena.alrac.net     : xmt/rcv/%loss = 1/1/0%, min/avg/max = 0.04/0.04/0.04
192.168.1.11       : xmt/rcv/%loss = 1/0/100%
[...]
    128 targets
      3 alive
    126 unreachable
      0 unknown addresses

      0 timeouts (waiting for response)
    127 ICMP Echos sent
      3 ICMP Echo Replies received
    102 other ICMP received

  0.04 ms (min round trip time)
  1.02 ms (avg round trip time)
  2.58 ms (max round trip time)
        6.753 sec (elapsed real time)
```

It also reports which hosts are not alive, so you get a lot of output. Use this example to filter the output to show only up hosts and the summary:

```
$ fping -c1 -sdg 192.168.1.0/25 2>&1 | egrep -v "ICMP|xmt"
xena.alrac.net    : [0], 84 bytes, 0.06 ms (0.06 avg, 0% loss)
pyramid.alrac.net : [0], 84 bytes, 1.03 ms (1.03 avg, 0% loss)
uberpc.alrac.net  : [0], 84 bytes, 0.11 ms (0.11 avg, 0% loss)

    128 targets
      3 alive
    126 unreachable
      0 unknown addresses

      0 timeouts (waiting for response)

  0.06 ms (min round trip time)
  0.40 ms (avg round trip time)
  1.03 ms (max round trip time)
        6.720 sec (elapsed real time)
```

Use this example to append the results to a text file:

```
$ fping -c1 -sdg 192.168.1.0/24 2>&1 | egrep -v "ICMP|xmt" >> fpingtest
```

Run this several times at different times of day when your network is not having problems, and you'll have something to compare to when you are troubleshooting.

If all you want to do is to discover all the up hosts on your network, Nmap is faster and less verbose:

```
# nmap -sP 192.168.1.0/24
Starting Nmap 4.20 ( http://insecure.org ) at 2007-06-08 15:53 PDT
Host xena.alrac.net (192.168.1.10) appears to be up.
Host pyramid.alrac.net (192.168.1.50) appears to be up.
MAC Address: 00:0D:B9:05:25:B4 (PC Engines GmbH)
Host uberpc.alrac.net (192.168.1.76) appears to be up.
```

```
MAC Address: 00:14:2A:54:67:D6 (Elitegroup Computer System Co.)
Nmap finished: 256 IP addresses (3 hosts up) scanned in 4.879 seconds
```

If you run it as a non*root* user you won't see the MAC addresses.

You might want to use Nmap's operating system fingerprinting to see what your users are running, and what ports they're leaving open:

```
# nmap -sS -O 192.168.1.*
```

Nmap with no options scans your network for open ports on all hosts:

```
# nmap 192.168.1.*
```

Nmap output can also be redirected to a text file. Remember that > overwrites, and >> appends.

Discussion

FPing is good for occasional quick tests. If you want to track long-term activity try Smokeping. Smokeping charts *ping* statistics with RRDTool and makes pretty HTML graphs.

The -s switch for fping means print a summary at exit, -d means lookup hostnames, and -g specifies the address range to use. -c specifies how many times fping will run.

FPing sends most of its output to STDERR, so you can't *grep* it in the usual way. That's why you have to redirect it first with 2>&1, which means "make the standard error (file descriptor 2) go to the same place that the standard output (file descriptor 1) is going."

See Also

- man 8 fping
- man 1 grep
- Smokeping: *http://oss.oetiker.ch/smokeping/*

19.4   Finding Duplicate IP Addresses with arping

Problem

You want to know how to test an IP address on your LAN to see whether it is a duplicate.

Solution

Use *arping*, like this:

```
$ arping -D 192.168.1.76
ARPING 192.168.1.76 from 0.0.0.0 eth0
Unicast reply from 192.168.1.76 [00:14:2A:54:67:D6] for 192.168.1.76 [00:14:2A:54:67:
D6] 0.605ms
```

```
Sent 1 probes (1 broadcast(s))
Received 1 response(s)
```

Received 1 response(s) means that this address is already in use, and *arping* even gives you the MAC address. You may also test with a hostname:

```
$ arping -D uberpc
ARPING 192.168.1.76 from 0.0.0.0 eth0
Unicast reply from 192.168.1.76 [00:14:2A:54:67:D6] for 192.168.1.76 [00:14:2A:54:67:
D6] 0.590ms
Sent 1 probes (1 broadcast(s))
Received 1 response(s)
```

You should set a time limit or count limit, or *arping* will keep running when it gets no response. This example sets a time limit of 10 seconds:

```
$ arping -w10 -D 192.168.1.100
ARPING 192.168.1.100 from 0.0.0.0 eth0
Sent 11 probes (11 broadcast(s))
Received 0 response(s)
```

Use -c5 instead of -w10 to tell *arping* to run for five counts.

Discussion

Of course, you may use any value for -c and -w that you like.

This is a good test to run when you have mobile users with static IP addresses on their laptops that come and go a lot, or to use before assigning a static address to a new host. If you're having intermittent connectivity problems with a particular host, run *arping* to see if it has a duplicate address.

arping is also useful to see if a host is up when *ping* fails. Some folks like to block *ping*, which is not a good thing to do, so *arping* will work when *ping* is blocked.

Address Resolution Protocol (ARP) is used mainly to translate IP addresses to Ethernet MAC addresses. You can see this in action with *tcpdump*:

```
# tcpdump -pi eth0 arp
tcpdump: verbose output suppressed, use -v or -vv for full protocol decode
listening on eth0, link-type EN10MB (Ethernet), capture size 96 bytes
14:58:34.835461 arp who-has xena.alrac.net tell pyramid.alrac.net
14:58:34.839337 arp reply xena.alrac.net is-at 00:03:6d:00:83:cf (oui Unknown)
```

pyramid is the local name server, so it needs to keep track of the hosts on the LAN.

oui Unknown means the IEEE Organizational Unique Identifier is unknown. The first 24-bits of every MAC address are assigned to the manufacturer, and you can look them up at Standards.ieee.org (*http://standards.ieee.org/regauth/oui/index.shtml*). You can't just copy and paste because you have to enter the numbers separated by dashes, like this: 00-03-6d.

See Also

- man 8 arping

19.5   Testing HTTP Throughput and Latency with httping

Problem

As always, your users are complaining "the web site is too slow! We're dying here!" But it seems OK to you. Isn't there some way you can make some objective measurements without having to master some expensive, complicated analysis tool?

Solution

While sophisticated HTTP server analysis tools are nice, and there are dozens of them, sometimes you just want something quick and easy. *httping* is an excellent utility for measuring HTTP server throughput and latency, and because it's a tiny command-line tool, you can easily run it from multiple locations via SSH.

Its simplest invocation is to test latency:

```
$ httping -c4 -g http://www.oreilly.com
PING www.oreilly.com:80 (http://www.oreilly.com):
connected to www.oreilly.com:80, seq=0 time=177.37 ms
connected to www.oreilly.com:80, seq=1 time=170.28 ms
connected to www.oreilly.com:80, seq=2 time=165.71 ms
connected to www.oreilly.com:80, seq=3 time=179.51 ms
--- http://www.oreilly.com ping statistics ---
4 connects, 4 ok, 0.00% failed
round-trip min/avg/max = 165.7/173.2/179.5 ms
```

That's not too bad. This doesn't tell you how long it takes pages to load, only how long it takes the server to respond to a HEAD request, which means fetching only the page headers without the content. So, let's do a GET (-G) request, which fetches the whole page:

```
$ httping -c4 -Gg http://www.oreilly.com
PING www.oreilly.com:80 (http://www.oreilly.com):
connected to www.oreilly.com:80, seq=0 time=1553.78 ms
connected to www.oreilly.com:80, seq=1 time=2790.99 ms
connected to www.oreilly.com:80, seq=2 time=2067.32 ms
connected to www.oreilly.com:80, seq=3 time=2033.02 ms
--- http://www.oreilly.com ping statistics ---
4 connects, 4 ok, 0.00% failed
round-trip min/avg/max = 1553.8/2111.3/2791.0 ms
```

That slowed it down a bit!

The -r switch tells *httping* to resolve the hostname only once, to remove DNS latency from its measurements:

```
$ httping -c4 -Grg http://www.oreilly.com
```

You can test SSL-enabled sites with the -1 switch:

```
$ httping -c4 -lGg https://www.fictionalsslsite.org
```

To specify an alternate port, append it to the URL:

```
$ httping -c4 -Gg http://www.fictionalsslsite.org:8080
```

httping will report the roundtrip time with the -b switch in kilobytes per second (not kilobits):

```
$ httping -c4 -Gbg  http://www.fictionalsslsite.org
PING www.fictionalsslsite.org:80 (http://www.fictionalsslsite.org):
connected to www.fictionalsslsite.org:80, seq=0 time=2553.96 ms  43KB/s
```

Use the -s switch to display return codes. Put it all together, and this is what you get:

```
$ httping -c4 -Gsbrg http://www.oreilly.com
PING www.oreilly.com:80 (http://www.oreilly.com):
 75KB/sed to www.oreilly.com:80, seq=0 time=1567.91 ms 200 OK
 72KB/sed to www.oreilly.com:80, seq=1 time=1618.20 ms 200 OK
 18KB/sed to www.oreilly.com:80, seq=2 time=5869.12 ms 200 OK
 58KB/sed to www.oreilly.com:80, seq=3 time=1979.43 ms 200 OK
--- http://www.oreilly.com ping statistics ---
4 connects, 4 ok, 0.00% failed
round-trip min/avg/max = 1567.9/2758.7/5869.1 ms
Transfer speed: min/avg/max = 18/56/75 KB
```

You can test a local server by specifying the hostname and port instead of the URL:

```
$ httping -c4 -h xena -p 80
```

Discussion

Ubuntu Feisty ships with a buggy version of *httping*, so you may need to build it from sources to get SSL support and a few other features that seem to have fallen out.

Building from sources is easy; you'll need the OpenSSL development libraries, which on Debian are *libssl-devel*, and on Fedora are *openssl-devel*. Unpack the tarball and run:

```
# make all
# make install
```

That's all there is to it.

httping is also designed to be a Nagios plug-in. The command definition looks like this:

```
define command{
    command_name check_httping
    command_line /usr/bin/httping -N 2 -c 1 -h $HOSTADDRESS$
}
```

See Also

- man 1 httping
- *httping* home page: *http://www.vanheusden.com/httping/*

19.6 Using traceroute, tcptraceroute, and mtr to Pinpoint Network Problems

Problem

You're having problems reaching a particular host or network, and *ping* confirms there is a problem, but there are several routers between you and the problem, so you need to narrow it down further. How do you do this?

Solution

Use *traceroute*, *tcptraceroute*, or *mtr*.

traceroute is an old standby that works well on your local network. Here is a two-hop *traceroute* on a small LAN with at least two subnets:

```
$ traceroute mailserver1
traceroute to mailserver1.alrac.net (192.168.2.76), 30 hops max, 40 byte packets
 1 pyramid.alrac.net (192.168.1.45) 3.605 ms 6.902 ms 9.165 ms
 2 mailserver1.alrac.net (192.168.2.76)  3.010 ms  0.070 ms  0.068 ms
```

This shows you that it passes through a single router, *pyramid*. If you run *traceroute* on a single subnet, it should show only one hop, as no routing is involved:

```
$ traceroute uberpc
traceroute to uberpc.alrac.net (192.168.1.77), 30 hops max, 40 byte packets
 1  uberpc (192.168.1.77)  5.722 ms  0.075 ms  0.068 ms
```

traceroute may not work over the Internet because a lot of routers are programmed to ignore its UDP datagrams. If you see a lot of timeouts, try the -I option, which sends ICMP ECHO requests instead.

You could also try *tcptraceroute*, which sends TCP packets and is therefore nearly nonignorable:

```
$ tcptraceroute bratgrrl.com
Selected device eth0, address 192.168.1.10, port 49422 for outgoing packets
Tracing the path to bratgrrl.com (67.43.0.135) on TCP port 80 (www), 30 hops max
 1  192.168.1.50  6.498 ms  0.345 ms  0.334 ms
 2  gateway.foo.net (12.169.163.1)  23.381 ms  22.002 ms  23.047 ms
 3  router.foo.net (12.169.174.1)  23.285 ms  23.434 ms  22.804 ms
 4  12.100.100.201  54.091 ms  48.301 ms *
 5  12.101.6.101  101.154 ms  100.027 ms  110.753 ms
 6  tbr2.cgcil.ip.att.net (12.122.10.61)  104.155 ms  101.934 ms  101.387 ms
 7  tbr2.dtrmi.ip.att.net (12.122.10.133)  108.611 ms  105.148 ms  108.538 ms
 8  gar3.dtrmi.ip.att.net (12.123.139.141)  108.815 ms  116.832 ms  97.934 ms
```

```
 9  * * *
10  lw-core1-ge2.rtr.liquidweb.com (209.59.157.30)  116.363 ms  115.567 ms  149.428
ms
11  lw-dc1-dist1-ge1.rtr.liquidweb.com (209.59.157.2)  129.055 ms  137.067 ms  *
12  host6.miwebdns6.com (67.43.0.135) [open]  130.926 ms  122.942 ms  125.739 ms
```

An excellent utility that combines *ping* and *traceroute* is *mtr* (My Traceroute). Use this to capture combined latency, packet loss, and problem router statistics. Here is an example that runs *mtr* 100 times, organizes the data in a report format, and stores it in a text file:

```
$ mtr -r -c100 oreilly.com >> mtr.txt
```

The file looks like this:

```
HOST: xena                         Loss%   Snt   Last   Avg  Best  Wrst StDev
  1. pyramid.alrac.net             0.0%    100    0.4   0.5   0.3   6.8   0.7
  2. gateway.foo.net               0.0%    100   23.5  23.1  21.6  29.8   1.0
  3. router.foo.net                0.0%    100   23.4  24.4  21.9  78.9   5.9
  4. 12.222.222.201                1.0%    100   52.8  57.9  44.5 127.3  10.3
  5. 12.222.222.50                 4.0%    100   61.9  62.4  50.1 102.9   9.8
  6. gbr1.st6wa.ip.att.net         1.0%    100   61.4  76.2  46.2 307.8  48.8
  7. br1-a350s5.attga.ip.att.net   3.0%    100   57.2  60.0  44.4 107.1  11.6
  8. so0-3-0-2488M.scr1.SFO1.gblx  1.0%    100   73.9  83.4  64.0 265.9  27.6
  9. sonic-gw.customer.gblx.net    2.0%    100   72.6  79.9  69.3 119.5   7.5
 10. 0.ge-0-1-0.gw.sr.sonic.net    2.0%    100   71.5  78.2  67.6 142.2   9.3
 11. gig50.dist1-1.sr.sonic.net    0.0%    100   81.1  84.3  73.1 169.1  12.1
 12. ora-demarc.customer.sonic.ne  5.0%    100   69.1  82.9  69.1 144.6  10.2
 13. www.oreillynet.com            4.0%    100   75.4  81.0  69.8 119.1   7.0
```

This shows a reasonably clean run with low packet loss and low latency. When you're having problems, create a *cron* job to run *mtr* at regular intervals by using a command like this (using your own domain and filenames, of course):

```
$ mtr -r -c100 oreillynet.com >> mtr.txt && date >> mtr.txt
```

This stores the results of every *mtr* run in a single file, with the date and time at the end of each entry.

You can watch *mtr* in real time like this:

```
$ mtr -c100 oreillynet.com
```

You can skip DNS lookups with the -n switch.

Discussion

If any of these consistently get hung up at the same router, or if *mtr* consistently shows greater than 5 percent packet losses and long transit times on the same router, then it's safe to say that particular router has a problem. If it's a router that you control, then for gosh sakes fix it. If it isn't, use *dig* or *whois* to find out who it belongs to, and nicely report the trouble to them.

Save your records so they can see the numbers with their own eyes.

There are a lot of web sites that let you run various network tools, such as *ping* and *traceroute*, from their sites. This is a good way to get some additional information for comparison.

mtr can generate a lot of network traffic, so don't run it all the time.

tcptraceroute sends TCP SYN packets instead of UDP or ICMP ECHO packets. These are more likely to get through firewalls, and are not going to be ignored by routers. When the host responds, *tcptraceroute* sends TCP RST to close the connection, so the TCP three-way handshake is never completed. This is the same as the half-open (-sS) scan used by Nmap.

See Also

- man 8 traceroute
- man 1 tcptraceroute
- man 8 mtr

19.7 Using tcpdump to Capture and Analyze Traffic

Problem

You really need to see what's going over the wires, and you know that *tcpdump* is just the powerhouse packet sniffer you want. But, you don't know how to filter all those masses of traffic. How do you make it show only what you want to see?

Solution

tcpdump can filter your traffic as precisely as you like. Just follow these examples to learn the more commonly used filters.

You should routinely use the -p switch to prevent the interface from going into promiscuous mode because promiscuous mode is pretty much useless on switched networks.

Capture all traffic on a single host:

```
# tcpdump -pi eth0 host uberpc
```

Capture all traffic on more than one host:

```
# tcpdump -pi eth0 host uberpc and stinkpad and penguina
```

Capture all traffic on more than one host, except from a specified host:

```
# tcpdump -pi eth0 host uberpc and stinkpad and not penguina
```

Capture traffic going to a host:

```
# tcpdump -pi eth0 dst host uberpc
```

Capture traffic leaving a host:

```
# tcpdump -pi eth0 src host uberpc
```

Capture a single protocol:

```
# tcpdump -pi eth0 tcp
```

Capture more than one protocol:

```
# tcpdump -pi eth0 tcp or udp or icmp
```

Capture a specific port:

```
# tcpdump -pi eth0 port 110
```

Capture several ports:

```
# tcpdump -pi eth0 port 25 or port 80 or port 110
```

Capture a port range:

```
# tcpdump -pi eth0 portrange 3000-4000
```

Watch traffic leaving a port:

```
# tcpdump -pi eth0 src port 110
```

Watch traffic entering a port:

```
# tcpdump -pi eth0 dst port 110
```

Look for packets smaller than the specified size:

```
# tcpdump -pi eth0 less 512
```

Look for packets larger than the specified size:

```
# tcpdump -pi eth0 greater 512
```

Watch SSH connections from certain hosts:

```
# tcpdump -pi eth0 src host uberpc or stinkpad and dst port 22
```

Watch for traffic leaving one network and entering two other networks:

```
# tcpdump -pi eth0 src net 192.168.1.0/16 and dst net 10.0.0.0/8 or 172.16.0.0/16
```

The -X switch reads the data payload, but the default is to only read 68 bytes, so -s0 displays the whole data payload, as this example from an IRC conversation shows:

```
# tcpdump -X -s0 -pi eth0
10:40:14.683350 IP 192.168.1.10.35386 > 12.222.222.107.6667: P 1:65(64) ack 410 win
16022 <nop,nop,timestamp 1204830 3703450725>
        0x0000:  4500 0074 c43b 4000 4006 8157 c0a8 010a  E..t.;@.@..W....
        0x0010:  8cd3 a66b 8a3a 1a0b 420f ddd1 bb15 eb3b  ...k.:..B......;
        0x0020:  8018 3e96 4309 0000 0101 080a 0012 625e  ..>.C.........b^
        0x0030:  dcbe 2c65 5052 4956 4d53 4720 236c 696e  ..,ePRIVMSG.#lin
        0x0040:  7578 6368 6978 203a 746f 2062 6520 6120  uxchix.:to.be.a.
        0x0050:  7375 7065 722d 7365 6b72 6974 2073 7079  super-sekrit.spy
        0x0060:  2c20 7573 6520 7468 6520 2d73 2073 7769  ,.use.the.-s.swi
        0x0070:  7463 680a                                tch.
```

This particular incantation:

```
# tcpdump -pXi eth0 -w tcpdumpfile -s0 host stinkpad
```

captures all traffic passing through Stinkpad, including data payload, and stores it in the file *tcpdumpfile*. You can read this file with:

```
# tcpdump -r tcpdumpfile
```

Directing *tcpdump* output to a file lets you study it at leisure, or open it with Wireshark to read it in a prettier interface. The -w switch creates a file format that Wireshark can read. Figure 19-1 shows what it looks like in Wireshark.

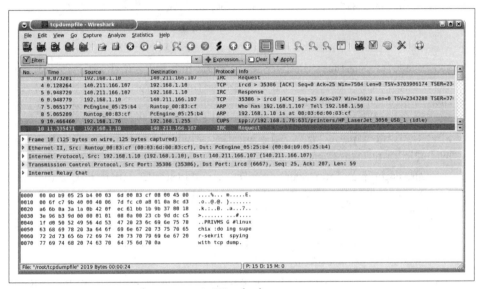

Figure 19-1. Examining tcpdump output in Wireshark

This command lets you see the live capture and store it in a file. This doesn't create a file that Wireshark can read, but it does create a text file that you can parse with your favorite text-searching utilities:

```
# tcpdump -pXi eth0 -s0 host stinkpad -l | tee tcpdumpfile
```

This is a good way to catch infected hosts that are sending out spam because nobody should be sending anything from port 25 except your official mail servers:

```
# tcpdump -pni eth0 dst port 25 and not src host mailserver1
```

The -n switch turns off name resolution.

Finally, you might want to use the -c switch to limit the number of packets captured:

```
# tcpdump -c 1000 -pXi eth0 -w tcpdumpfile -s0
```

Otherwise, it will run until you hit Ctrl-C.

Discussion

tcpdump should be your number one network troubleshooting tool because it shows you exactly what is happening over your wires. Don't guess—run *tcpdump*.

Let's dissect some typical *tcpdump* output, using an excerpt from checking mail:

```
# tcpdump -pi eth0
14:23:02.983415 IP xena.alrac.net.58154 > host6.foo.com.pop3s: S 3100965180:
3100965180(0) win 5840 <mss 1460,sackOK,timestamp 4546985 0,nop,wscale 2> (DF)
```

- 14:23:02.983415 is the timestamp, in *hh:mm:ss:fraction* format.

- xena.alrac.net.58154 is the originating host and port.

- host6.foo.com.pop3s is the destination host and port.

- S is the first part of the three-way TCP handshake (SYN, SYN, ACK).

- 3100965180:3100965180 is the byte sequence/range. The initial sequence number (ISN) is generated randomly. Then, sequence numbers for the rest of the bytes in the connection are incremented by 1 from the ISN. Because no data are exchanged at this stage, both numbers are the same.

- win 5840 is the window size, or the number of bytes of buffer space the host has available for receiving data.

- mss 1460 is the maximum segment size, or maximum IP datagram size that can be handled without using fragmentation. Both sides of the connection must agree on a value; if they are different, the lower value is used. This is called *path MTU (Maximum Transmission Unit) discovery*. MTU is the size of the total frame, which includes the MSS plus TCP/IP headers, and any other headers that are required by the sending protocol.

- sackOK means "selective acknowledgments," which allows the receiver to acknowledge packets out of sequence. Back in the olden days, packets could only be acknowledged in sequence. So, if the third packet out of a hundred packets received went missing, the host could only acknowledge the receipt of the first two packets, and the sender would have to resend all packets from number 3 through 1,000. sackOK allows only the missing packets to be resent.

- timestamp 4546985 0 measures the round-trip time. There are two fields: the Timestamp Value and the Timestamp Echo Reply. On the first exchange, the Echo Reply is set to 0. When the second host receives that packet, it transfers the timestamp from the old packet's Timestamp Value field to the new packet's Timestamp Echo Reply field. Then, it generates a new value for the Timestamp Value field. So, the Timestamp Value field contains the latest timestamp, while the Timestamp Echo Reply field contains the previous timestamp.

- nop, or "no operation," is just padding. TCP options must be multiples of 4 bytes, so nop is used to pad undersized fields.

- wscale 0 is a nifty hack to get around the original window size limitation of 65,535 bytes. wscale provides for a full gigabyte of buffer. Both sides of the connection must support this and agree; otherwise, the window size does not change.
- (DF) means "don't fragment."

Sometimes, you need the correct physical placement to capture the type of information you want. For example, if you want to catch infected hosts sending out spam, or want to watch traffic between networks, you'll need to run *tcpdump* on a router. Or, plug-in your handy network administrator laptop between the router and the switch, if you have dumb switches. Smart switches have network monitoring ports.

Plug-in your handy network administrator laptop between the Internet and your firewall to get an unfiltered view of what's trying to enter your network.

See Also

- man 8 tcpdump

19.8 Capturing TCP Flags with tcpdump

Problem

The syntax for *tcpdump* filters is pretty easy to understand, until you come to the part about filtering on specific TCP flags, like SYN, ACK, RST, and so forth. Then, it goes all bizarre. How do you know what to use?

Solution

The *tcpdump* manpage tells how to calculate the correct values for TCP flags. You are welcome to study it and learn how to figure them out from scratch. Or, you can copy them from here.

Capture all SYN packets:

```
# tcpdump 'tcp[13] & 2 != 0'
```

Capture all ACK packets:

```
# tcpdump 'tcp[13] & 16 != 0'
```

Capture all SYN-ACK packets:

```
# tcpdump 'tcp[13] = 18'
```

Capture all FIN packets:

```
# tcpdump 'tcp[13] & 1 != 0'
```

Capture all URG packets:

```
# tcpdump 'tcp[13] & 32 != 0'
```

Capture all PSH packets:

```
# tcpdump 'tcp[13] & 8 != 0'
```

Capture all RST packets:

```
# tcpdump 'tcp[13] & 4 != 0'
```

These may be combined with other filtering options such as ports, hosts, and networks, just like in the previous recipe.

Discussion

There are several scenarios where you'll want to look for certain TCP flags, such as when you're investigating suspicious activity, or having problems with misconfigured services sending the wrong responses. Another way to do this sort of filtering is to capture a lot of data with minimal filtering and dump it to a file with the -w switch, then examine the file in Wireshark. Then, you'll be able to filter the same set of data several different ways without having to get a new capture each time.

Using Wireshark to analyze and filter a *tcpdump* capture is probably the most flexible and powerful method available. Figure 19-2 shows my favorite feature, Follow TCP Stream. This lets you pluck out a single TCP stream from all the masses of data you've collected. Wireshark supports all the same filters as *tcpdump*, and has lots of nice graphical menus to help you put them together.

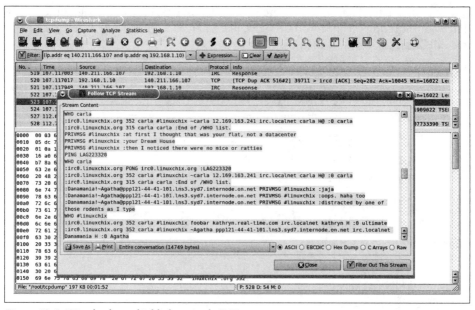

Figure 19-2. Wireshark can highlight a single TCP stream

You may prefer to use Wireshark in place of *tcpdump* entirely. If you're running any headless boxes or servers without X Windows, you'll still want to know how to use *tcpdump*.

See Also

- man 8 tcpdump
- Wireshark: *http://www.wireshark.org/*
- Wireshark's included Help pages

19.9 Measuring Throughput, Jitter, and Packet Loss with iperf

Problem

You want to measure throughput on your various network segments, and you want to collect jitter and datagram loss statistics. You might want these just as a routine part of periodically checking your network performance, or you're running a VoIP server like Asterisk, Trixbox, or PBXtra, so you need your network to be in extra-good shape to have good call quality.

Solution

Use *iperf*, which is a nifty utility for measuring TCP and UDP performance between two endpoints. It must be installed at both ends of the connection you're measuring; in this example, that is Xena and Penguina. We'll call Xena the server and Penguina the client. First, start *iperf* on Xena in server mode, then fire it up on Penguina. (The easy way is to do all this on Xena in two X terminals via SSH.)

```
carla@xena:~$ iperf -s
------------------------------------------------------------
Server listening on TCP port 5001
TCP window size: 85.3 KByte (default)
------------------------------------------------------------

terry@penguina:~$ iperf -c xena
------------------------------------------------------------
Client connecting to xena, TCP port 5001
TCP window size: 16.0 KByte (default)
------------------------------------------------------------
[  3] local 192.168.1.76 port 49215 connected with 192.168.1.10 port 5001
[  3]  0.0-10.0 sec    111 MBytes  92.6 Mbits/sec
```

And it's done. That's a good clean run, and as fast as you're going to see over Fast Ethernet.

You can conduct a bidirectional test that runs both ways at once:

```
terry@penguina:~$ iperf -c xena -d
------------------------------------------------------------
Server listening on TCP port 5001
TCP window size: 85.3 KByte (default)
------------------------------------------------------------
------------------------------------------------------------
Client connecting to xena, TCP port 5001
TCP window size: 56.4 KByte (default)
------------------------------------------------------------
[  5] local 192.168.1.76 port 59823 connected with 192.168.1.10 port 5001
[  4] local 192.168.1.76 port 5001 connected with 192.168.1.10 port 58665
[  5]  0.0-10.0 sec    109 MBytes   91.1 Mbits/sec
[  4]  0.0-10.0 sec   96.0 MBytes   80.5 Mbits/sec
```

Or, one way at a time:

```
$ terry@uberpc:~$ iperf -c xena -r
```

Compare the two to get an idea of how efficient your Ethernet duplexing is.

Troubleshooting multicasting can drive a network administrator to drink, but fortunately, *iperf* can help. You'll run *iperf* in server mode on all of your multicast hosts, and then test all of them at once from a single client:

```
admin@host1:~$ iperf -sB 239.0.0.1
admin@host2:~$ iperf -sB 239.0.0.1
admin@host3:~$ iperf -sB 239.0.0.1
carla@xena:~$ iperf -c 239.0.0.1
```

If you're using multicasting for video or audio streaming, you'll want to test with UDP instead of the default TCP, like this:

```
admin@host1:~$ iperf -sBu 239.0.0.1
admin@host2:~$ iperf -sBu 239.0.0.1
admin@host3:~$ iperf -sBu 239.0.0.1
carla@xena:~$ iperf -c 239.0.0.1 -ub 512k
```

Adjust the -b (bits per second) value to suit your own network, or use -m for megabits. Testing with UDP will generate a number of useful and interesting statistics. If the server is still running, stop it with Ctrl-C, then run this command:

```
carla@xena:~$ iperf -su
------------------------------------------------------------
Server listening on UDP port 5001
Receiving 1470 byte datagrams
UDP buffer size:   108 KByte (default)
------------------------------------------------------------
```

Then, start the client:

```
terry@penguina:~$ iperf -c xena -ub 100m
------------------------------------------------------------
Client connecting to xena, UDP port 5001
Sending 1470 byte datagrams
UDP buffer size:   108 KByte (default)
```

```
----------------------------------------------------------------
[  3] local 192.168.1.76 port 32774 connected with 192.168.1.10 port 5001
[  3]  0.0-10.0 sec    114 MBytes  95.7 Mbits/sec
[  3] Sent 81444 datagrams
[  3] Server Report:
[ ID] Interval    Transfer  Bandwidth        Jitter   Lost/Total     Datagrams
[  3]  0.0-10.0 sec 113 MBytes  94.9 Mbits/sec  0.242 ms  713/81443     (0.88%)
[  3]  0.0-10.0 sec  1 datagrams received out-of-order
```

Jitter and datagram loss are two important statistics for streaming media. Jitter over 200 ms is noticeable, like you're driving over a bumpy road, so the 0.242 ms in our test run is excellent. 0.88 percent datagram loss is also insignificant. Depending on the quality of your endpoints, VoIP can tolerate as much as 10 percent datagram loss, though ideally you don't want much over 3–4 percent.

The out-of-order value is also important to streaming media—obviously a bunch of UDP datagrams arriving randomly don't contribute to coherence.

You may adjust the size of the datagrams sent from the client to more closely reflect your real-world conditions. The default is 1,470 bytes, and voice traffic typically runs around 100–360 bytes per datagram (which you could find out for yourself with *tcpdump*). Set the size in *iperf* with the -1 switch. It looks a bit odd because the available values are kilobytes or megabytes per second only, so we have to use a fractional value:

```
terry@uberpc:~$ iperf -c xena -ub 100m -l .3K
----------------------------------------------------------------
Client connecting to xena, UDP port 5001
Sending 307 byte datagrams
UDP buffer size:    108 KByte (default)
----------------------------------------------------------------
[  3] local 192.168.1.76 port 32775 connected with 192.168.1.10 port 5001
[  3]  0.0-10.0 sec  98.2 MBytes  82.3 Mbits/sec
[  3] Sent 335247 datagrams
[  3] Server Report:
[ ID] Interval    Transfer  Bandwidth        Jitter   Lost/Total     Datagrams
[  3]  0.0-10.0 sec  96.9 MBytes  81.2 Mbits/sec  0.006 ms 4430/335246 (1.3%)
[  3]  0.0-10.0 sec  1 datagrams received out-of-order
```

Discussion

These same tests can be run over the Internet. *iperf* by default uses TCP/UDP port 5001. You can also specify which ports to use with the -p switch.

Link quality is becoming more important as we run more streaming services over packet-switched networks, and service providers are trying to meet these new needs. Talk to your ISP to see what they can do about link quality for your streaming services.

See Also

- man 1 iperf

19.10 Using ngrep for Advanced Packet Sniffing

Problem

You know and love both *tcpdump* and Wireshark, and are pretty good at finding the information you want. But sometimes, you still end up dumping the output to a text file and using *grep* to look for strings or regular expressions that *tcpdump* and Wireshark can't filter on. If only there were something like *tcpdump* and *grep* combined.

Solution

There is: *ngrep*, or "network grep." *ngrep* is a packet sniffer that is similar to *tcpdump*, with the added facility of being able to search on any text string or regular expression just like *grep*. Suppose you're snooping to see what your employees are saying about you on IRC. You want to get straight to the juicy stuff, so try this command:

```
# ngrep -qpd eth0 host ircserver -i carla
interface: eth0 (192.168.1.0/255.255.255.0)
match: carla
##
T 192.168.1.10:33116 -> 140.222.222.107:6667 [AP]
PRIVMSG #authors :that carla is truly wonderful and everyone loves her
##
T 192.168.1.32:39422 -> 140.222.222.107:6667 [AP]
PRIVMSG #authors :yes, carla is great, the world would be dust and ashes without her
```

It looks promising, and you want some more context, so you add the -A 5 switch to include the five lines that follow your match:

```
# ngrep -qpd eth0 -A5 host ircserver -i carla
T 192.168.1.10:33116 -> 140.222.222.107:6667 [AP]
PRIVMSG #authors :LOL thanks, I haven't laughed that hard in ages
##
T 192.168.1.32:39422 -> 140.222.222.107:6667 [AP]
PRIVMSG #authors :NP, it's a good thing the bossy little dope can't eavesdrop on us
```

ngrep uses the same protocol options as *tcpdump*. This example shows only POP3 traffic:

```
# ngrep -qpd eth0 '' tcp port 110
```

ngrep can tell the difference between Windows *pings* and Linux *pings*. Windows uses letters to fill out the payload, and Linux uses numbers, so you can tailor your search to see what OS certain *pings* are coming from:

```
# ngrep -qpd eth0 'abcd' icmp
interface: eth0 (192.168.1.0/255.255.255.0)
filter: (ip or ip6) and ( icmp )
match: abcd
#
I 192.168.1.77 -> 192.168.1.10 8:0
  ....abcdefghijklmnopqrstuvwabcdefghi
```

```
# ngrep -qpd eth0 '1234' icmp
interface: eth0 (192.168.1.0/255.255.255.0)
filter: (ip or ip6) and ( icmp )
match: 1234
#
I 192.168.1.76 -> 192.168.1.10 8:0
. .....F!s....
.................... !"#$%&'( )*+,-./01234567
```

That demonstrates how, if you can find something reasonably unique in the data payload, you can make some very fine-tuned searches. By default, *ngrep* displays the entire packet. The maximum size is 65,536 bytes; use the -S switch to view a smaller number of bytes. This example captures HTTP headers and views only the first 156 bytes:

```
# ngrep -qpd -S 156 '' tcp port 80
interface: eth0 (192.168.1.0/255.255.255.0)
filter: (ip or ip6) and ( tcp port 80 )

T 192.168.1.10:33812 -> 208.201.239.36:80 [AP]
  GET / HTTP/1.1..User-Agent: Mozilla/5.0 (compatible; Konqueror/3.5; Linux) KHTML/3.
5.6 (like Gecko) (Kubuntu)..Accept: te
  xt/html, image/jpeg, image/png, tex [...]
```

So, you can take a quick look at what web browsers your site visitors are using, without having to dig through logfiles or HTTP analyzers.

One of *ngrep*'s nicest features is the classic *grep* inversion match, -v, which means "don't match this." This example excludes any Session Initiation Protocol (SIP) INVITES requests on an Asterisk server:

```
# ngrep -qpd eth0 -vi invites port 5060
interface: eth0 (192.168.1.0/255.255.255.0)
filter: (ip or ip6) and ( port 5060 )
don't match: invites
```

Protocols and hosts are excluded with not statements:

```
# ngrep -qpd eth0 \(not port 22\)
interface: eth0 (192.168.1.0/255.255.255.0)
filter: (ip or ip6) and ( (not port 22) )
# ngrep -qpd eth0 \(not host irc.ircserver1.org\)
interface: eth0 (192.168.1.0/255.255.255.0)
filter: (ip or ip6) and ( (not host irc.ircserver1.org) )
```

The parentheses must be escaped, or the Bash shell will try to interpret them.

Discussion

q

This means quiet output. This displays headers and payload, and omits the hash marks that separate each packet.

p

This means turn off promiscuous mode, which you should do routinely because it doesn't really work on packet-switched networks anyway.

d

This means device, or your network interface. On a multihomed system, *ngrep* will use the lowest-numbered device by default.

i

This means case-insensitive.

S

This means display this number of bytes.

v

This means do not match this.

See Also

• man 8 ngrep

19.11 Using ntop for Colorful and Quick Network Monitoring

Problem

You like *tcpdump* and Wireshark just fine, but they're not easy to read, and don't give you nice visual snapshots of network activity. Isn't there some program that will monitor and collect network traffic data, and aggregate statistics, and make nice colorful charts so you can see at a glance what your network is doing? Such as established connections, protocols used, and traffic statistics? And that is quick and easy to set up?

Solution

You want *ntop*, which is a hybrid packet analyzer that monitors network protocols, and creates nice HTML charts and graphs. Debian users should install it this way:

```
# aptitude install ntop rrdtool graphviz
```

Fedora users will have to dig up an RPM (try *http://rpm.pbone.net/*), or build it from sources. You must have *libpcap* and GDBM installed, and some sort of HTTP server. (Lighttpd is an excellent lightweight HTTP server.) You should also install:

• RRDTool
• Graphviz
• OpenSSL
• ZLib
• GDChart
• GDLib
• LibPNG
• Ettercap

After installing *ntop*, start it with this command:

```
# /etc/init.d/ntop start
```

It will ask you for a password for the *admin* user. Then, open a web browser to *http://localhost:3000*. Give it a few minutes to collect some data, and you can help it along by checking email and web surfing. The pages will automatically refresh.

Everything is configurable via the web interface. You should visit Admin → Configure → Startup Options first to configure what you want monitored, such as the local machine only, the local subnet, or multiple subnets. Disable promiscuous mode. There are other configuration tabs that let you set up *ntop* pretty much any way you like.

Figures 19-3 and 19-4 give you an idea of what *ntop* looks like in action, allowing you to find out at glance who is engaged in monkey business.

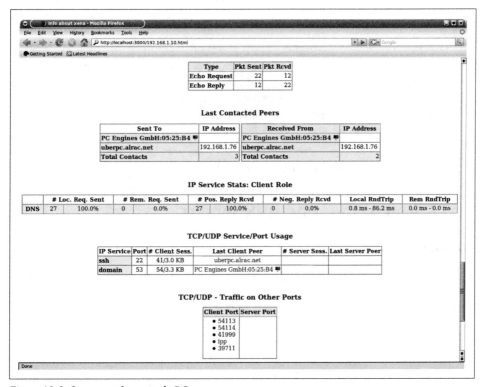

Figure 19-3. Summary for a single PC

Discussion

ntop doesn't have the power and customizability of heavier-duty network monitors, but it's great when you want something up and running quickly, and to generate some snapshots of network activity. The IP Local tab is especially interesting; this can help you find sneaky wireless access points, and lets you see at a glance which ports have been used. This can be an eye-opening; for example, if you're seeing activity on

---

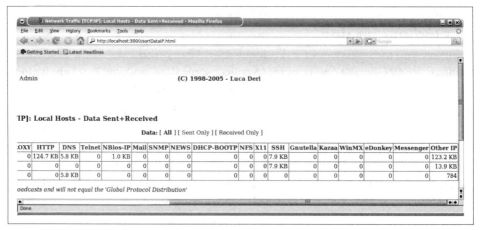

Figure 19-4. Summary of protocols for a subnet

port 110 (POP3) when you expect only port 995 (POP3s), you know you have an unsecured mail client running. Or, if you're seeing port 25 (SMTP) traffic when you're not running a mailserver, or it's on the wrong hosts, you might have some compromised PCs spewing forth spam. You'll see bandwidth usage at a glance, for homing in on bandwidth hogs, and a whole lot of other helpful data.

See Also

- *ntop* home page: *http://www.ntop.org/*

19.12 Troubleshooting DNS Servers

Problem

You're getting a lot of "unknown host" errors or timeouts, or mail bounces, or other signs of DNS problems. You can connect using the IP addresses, but not the hostnames. What do you do to track down the problem?

Solution

Use the *dig* and *host* commands to see what answers your DNS server is dishing out. Don't use *nslookup*; it has long been deprecated, and doesn't always work correctly anyway.

One of the biggest sources of trouble is having private and public authoritative name servers, or worse, a single server handling both jobs. So, you especially want to make sure that private name requests are not going out to the Internet. First, run the *host* command:

```
$ host uberpc
uberpc.alrac.net has address 192.168.1.76
```

```
$ host 192.168.1.76
76.1.168.192.in-addr.arpa domain name pointer uberpc.alrac.net.
```

This is good; the address is correct, and your reverse pointer is correctly configured. Now, run *dig* to see what server is being queried:

```
$ dig uberpc
; <<>> DiG 9.3.4 <<>> uberpc
;; global options:  printcmd
;; Got answer:
;; ->>HEADER<<- opcode: QUERY, status: NOERROR, id: 46745
;; flags: qr aa rd ra; QUERY: 1, ANSWER: 1, AUTHORITY: 0, ADDITIONAL: 0

;; QUESTION SECTION:
;uberpc.                        IN      A

;; ANSWER SECTION:
uberpc.                 0       IN      A       192.168.1.76

;; Query time: 42 msec
;; SERVER: 192.168.1.50#53(192.168.1.50)
;; WHEN: Sat Jul 14 23:17:02 2007
;; MSG SIZE  rcvd: 38
```

This shows the A record for Uberpc with a proper trailing dot, and that the server that is handling the request is 192.168.1.50, which presumably is your local caching resolver. On the other hand, this is what you do not want to see:

```
;; QUESTION SECTION:
;uberpc.alrac.net.                      IN      A

;; AUTHORITY SECTION:
alrac.net.              10800   IN      SOA     ns57.domaincontrol.com. dns.jomax.
net. 2007062900 28800 7200 604800 86400

;; Query time: 147 msec
;; SERVER: 192.168.1.50#53(192.168.1.50)
;; WHEN: Sat Jul 14 23:21:54 2007
;; MSG SIZE  rcvd: 100
```

Requests for private hostnames should not be wandering all over the Internet, so if you see this, you know your private name server is misconfigured.

You can query the remote nameserver you just found directly to double-check:

```
$ dig @ns57.domaincontrol.com alrac.net

; <<>> DiG 9.3.4 <<>> @ns57.domaincontrol.com alrac.net
; (1 server found)
;; global options:  printcmd
;; Got answer:
;; ->>HEADER<<- opcode: QUERY, status: NOERROR, id: 25896
;; flags: qr aa rd; QUERY: 1, ANSWER: 1, AUTHORITY: 2, ADDITIONAL: 0

;; QUESTION SECTION:
```

```
;alrac.net.                          IN      A

;; ANSWER SECTION:
alrac.net.               3600        IN      A        68.178.232.99

;; AUTHORITY SECTION:
alrac.net.               3600        IN      NS       ns57.domaincontrol.com.
alrac.net.               3600        IN      NS       ns58.domaincontrol.com.

;; Query time: 99 msec
;; SERVER: 208.109.14.50#53(208.109.14.50)
;; WHEN: Sat Jul 14 23:41:36 2007
;; MSG SIZE  rcvd: 98
```

Yep, someone out there has registered *alrac.net*, so if I want to use that domain name on my private network I need to make sure my DNS house is in order. Private domains should not be leaking out to the Internet anyway.

dig can retrieve most DNS record types by using the following options: a, any, mx, ns, soa, hinfo, axfr, txt, cname, naptr, rp, and srv. Use the -t switch to query specific record types, as this example for SRV records shows:

$ dig -t srv oreilly.com

To see the entire delegation path, use the +trace option:

$ dig -t oreilly.com +trace

This should be a short path from the authoritative *root* servers to your authoritative server. There should not be other authoritative servers, so if you see any, you need to investigate. This is a typical trace with the redundant output snipped:

```
$ dig -t a linuxchix.org  +trace
; <<>> DiG 9.3.4 <<>> -t a linuxchix.org +trace
;; global options:  printcmd
.                        299724  IN      NS       d.root-servers.net.

.;; Received 276 bytes from 192.168.1.50#53(192.168.1.50) in 36 ms

org.                     172800  IN      NS       TLD4.ULTRADNS.org.

;; Received 345 bytes from 128.8.10.90#53(d.root-servers.net) in 167 ms

linuxchix.org.           86400   IN      NS       ns0.linuxchix.org.

;; Received 153 bytes from 199.7.67.1#53(TLD4.ULTRADNS.org) in 92 ms

linuxchix.org.           86400   IN      A        140.211.166.107
linuxchix.org.           86400   IN      NS       ns0.linuxchix.org.
;; Received 130 bytes from 216.134.213.24#53(ns2.demandspace.com) in 137 ms
```

Following along with *tcpdump* as you run other tests is helpful:

 # tcpdump -pi eth0 port 53

And always check logfiles.

Discussion

Always check the ->>HEADER<<- line to see the status. When it says NOERROR, you have a successful query. When it says NXDOMAIN, that means it did not find a DNS record matching your query.

On your private LAN, you may use any arbitrary domain name and not have to register it. This is a perfectly good way to do local DNS for private hosts with no public services, and for private servers that serve only the LAN.

Misconfigured DNS servers are legion. If you must use BIND, please study Cricket Liu's books. Mr. Liu is the best BIND authority there is.

My recommended combination is Dnsmasq for a local caching resolver and private authoritative server, and Maradns for a public authoritative server.

Visit Internet Assigned Numbers Authority (*http://www.iana.org/*) for official and detailed information on how DNS is managed worldwide.

See Also

- man 1 dig
- man 1 host
- Chapter 4 for recipes on using the excellent Dnsmasq for both caching and authoritative local name services

19.13 Troubleshooting DNS Clients

Problem

Configuring DNS involves a number of seemingly random configuration files on Linux. What do you need to look for to make sure client configurations are good?

Solution

DHCP clients on Debian need only entries in */etc/network/interfaces*. Don't edit */etc/resolv.conf*. You may enter important hosts in */etc/hosts* as a fallback in case your DNS server goes down; just be careful to get it right because */etc/hosts* takes precedence over your DNS server.

On Fedora, each interface has its own configuration file, */etc/sysconfig/network-scripts/ifcfg-**. Again, don't edit */etc/resolv.conf* for DHCP clients, and you may use */etc/hosts* as a fallback.

Statically configured interfaces must have nameservers configured in */etc/resolv.conf*, and the correct gateway in the interface configuration file. You may use */etc/hosts* as a fallback.

On Windows and Mac clients, the same principles apply: don't configure conflicting static information on DHCP clients, and on statically configured clients, make sure you manually configure the correct gateway and DNS servers. And, just like Linux DHCP clients, you can serve up everything from your DHCP server.

Discussion

Make it easy on yourself—use your DHCP server to assign dynamic and static addresses, provide addresses for your network gateway and servers, and assign static routes. Then, the only client configuration you need is the usual DHCP configuration.

See Also

- Chapter 4 has several recipes on configuring DHCP and DNS with Dnsmasq
- Chapter 24, "Managing Name Resolution," in *Linux Cookbook*, by Carla Schroder (O'Reilly) has several recipes on configuring */etc/hosts* and using *dhcpd* for your DHCP server

19.14 Troubleshooting SMTP Servers

Problem

What are some tests you can run directly on your SMTP server to see if it is working correctly? You want to eliminate as many variables as you can, and talk directly to the server, if that's possible.

Solution

Good old *telnet* does the job. You also needthe *mailx* package installed, and Netstat.

First, run *telnet* on your SMTP server to see if you can talk to it. This example creates and sends a test message:

```
$ telnet localhost 25
Trying 127.0.0.1...
Connected to localhost.
Escape character is '^]'.
220 xena.alrac.net ESMTP Postfix (Ubuntu)
ehlo xena
250-xena.alrac.net
250-PIPELINING
250-SIZE 10240000
250-VRFY
250-ETRN
250-STARTTLS
250-ENHANCEDSTATUSCODES
250-8BITMIME
250 DSN
```

```
mail from: carla@testing.net
250 2.1.0 Ok
rcpt to: carla@xena
250 2.1.5 Ok
data
354 End data with <CR><LF>.<CR><LF>
Date: July 4, 2007
From: testcarla
Reply-to: testcarla@testing.net
Message-ID: one
Subject: SMTP testing
Hi Carla,
If you can read this, the SMTP server works.
.
250 2.0.0 Ok: queued as B2A033FBA
quit
221 2.0.0 Bye
Connection closed by foreign host.
```

Now, run mail to read your message:

```
$ mail
Mail version 8.1.2 01/15/2001.  Type ? for help.
"/var/mail/carla": 1 message 1 new
>N  1 testcarla@xena.al  Sun Jul 15 10:46   17/523   SMTP testing
& t
Message 1:
From carla@testing.net  Sun Jul 15 10:46:21 2007
X-Original-To: carla@xena.alrac.net
Date: July 4, 2007
From: testcarla@xena.alrac.net
Reply-to: testcarla@testing.net
Subject: SMTP testing
To: undisclosed-recipients:;

Hi Carla,
If you can read this, the SMTP server works.

& q
Saved 1 message in /home/carla/mbox
```

This shows you that your name services are working, and that the SMTP server is working. If you see this instead:

```
$ telnet localhost 25
Trying 127.0.0.1...
telnet: Unable to connect to remote host: Connection refused
```

That means the server is not running, which you can confirm with Netstat:

```
# netstat -pant|grep :25
```

If it returns nothing, your SMTP server is not running. This example shows a running Postfix server:

```
# netstat -pant|grep :25
tcp   0  127.0.0.1:25    0.0.0.0:*       LISTEN    8000/master
```

Once you get it running on localhost, you can test it remotely:

```
terry@uberpc:~$ telnet xena 25
Trying 192.168.1.10...
telnet: Unable to connect to remote host: Connection refused
```

Netstat already showed why you can't connect remotely—Postfix is only listening on localhost. So, you need to configure it to also listen on the LAN interface, which means you need two lines like this in *main.cf*:

```
mynetworks = 127.0.0.0/8, 192.168.1.0/24
inet_interfaces = 127.0.0.1, 192.168.1.10
```

Restart Postfix, and now Netstat should report this:

```
# netstat -pant|grep :25
tcp   0  0 192.168.1.10:25   0.0.0.0:*      LISTEN     8324/master
tcp   0  0 127.0.0.1:25      0.0.0.0:*      LISTEN     8324/master
```

Following along with *tcpdump* as you run your other tests is helpful:

```
# tcpdump -pi eth0 port 25
```

And, always check logfiles.

Discussion

Other SMTP servers are configured differently, so you'll need the documentation for your own server.

To exit a telnet session early, hit Ctrl-], then Q.

Why use *telnet*? Because it can talk directly to the server and find out quickly if the server is operating correctly. Bypassing intermediaries is always a good first step.

This recipe also shows you how easy it is to spoof mail headers, and how careful you must be with access controls. The SMTP protocol is completely insecure as spammers discovered many years ago, so make sure that you are not providing SMTP services to the world. As with all services, it's a two-pronged approach: careful configuration of the server's own access controls, and careful firewalling. You should also consider using *smtp-auth*, which requires your SMTP users to authenticate themselves to your server.

See Also

- Recipe 19.7
- Recipe 19.10
- Chapter 20, "Building a Postfix Mail Server," in *Linux Cookbook*, by Carla Schroder (O'Reilly)
- Chapter 21, "Managing Spam and Malware," in *Linux Cookbook*
- man 1 telnet

19.15 Troubleshooting a POP3, POP3s, or IMAP Server

Problem

What are some tests you can run directly on your POP3, POP3s, or IMAP server to see if it is working correctly? You want to eliminate as many variables as you can and talk directly to the server, if that's possible.

Solution

telnet and Netstat will do the job for you. Netstat shows you if it is running and listening to the correct ports and addresses, as this example shows for Dovecot:

```
# netstat -plunt | grep :110
tcp   0   0 :::110 :::*        LISTEN      4654/dovecot
```

This shows that Dovecot is open to all connections, so if you want to limit it to LAN connections, you'll need to fix its configuration. Then, Netstat will report this:

```
tcp   0   0 192.168.1.25:110 :::*       LISTEN      4654/dovecot
```

POP3s, which is POP3 over SSL, runs on TCP port 995.

IMAP runs on TCP port 143, and IMAP over SSL uses TCP port 993.

To test a POP3 server with *telnet*, you need to have a user account already set up on the server. Then, do this:

```
$ telnet localhost 110
Trying 127.0.0.1...
Connected to localhost.localdomain.
Escape character is '^]'.
+OK Hello there.
user carla
+OK Password required.
pass password
+OK logged in.
stat
+OK 2 1275
list
+OK
1 748
2 1028
3 922
.
```

This shows a successful login, and the list command shows there are three messages. At this point, you can quit, or enter retr 1, retr 2, or retr 3 to read your messages. quit closes the session.

Use the s_client command, which is part of OpenSSL, to test POP3s:

```
$ openssl s_client -connect localhost:995
```

This should spew forth bales of SSL certificate information so you can verify that it is indeed using your SSL certificate, and using the right one. Then, you can go ahead and run the usual POP3 commands:

```
+OK Hello there.
user carla
+OK Password required.
pass password
+OK logged in.
```

Once you have successfully connected directly on the server, try logging in from a remote PC:

```
$ telnet xena.alrac.net 110
$ openssl s_client -connect xena.alrac.net:995
```

IMAP can also be tested with *telnet* and openssl s_client:

```
$ telnet localhost 143
Trying 127.0.0.1...
Connected to localhost.localdomain.
Escape character is '^]'.
* OK [CAPABILITY IMAP4rev1 UIDPLUS CHILDREN NAMESPACE THREAD=ORDEREDSUBJECT
THREAD=REFERENCES SORT QUOTA IDLE ACL ACL2=UNION STARTTLS] Courier-IMAP ready.
a001 login carla password
a001 OK LOGIN Ok.
a002 examine inbox
* FLAGS (\Draft \Answered \Flagged \Deleted \Seen \Recent)
* OK [PERMANENTFLAGS ( )] No permanent flags permitted
* 0 EXISTS
* 0 RECENT
* OK [UIDVALIDITY 1085106842] Ok
* OK [MYRIGHTS "acdilrsw"] ACL
a002 OK [READ-ONLY] Ok
a003 logout
* BYE Courier-IMAP server shutting down
a003 OK LOGOUT completed
Connection closed by foreign host.

$ openssl s_client -connect localhost:993
[...]
```

Following along with *tcpdump* as you run your other tests is helpful:

```
# tcpdump -pi eth0 port 110
```

And always check logfiles.

Discussion

To exit a *telnet* session early, hit Ctrl-], then Q.

Why use *telnet*? Because it can talk directly to the server, and find out quickly if the server is operating correctly. Bypassing intermediaries is always a good first step.

Follow the previous recipe to send yourself some messages from your SMTP server and see if your POP3 server receives them. If they are on the same machine, and the POP3 server does not receive the messages, then you know you have a configuration problem. If they are on separate machines, then it could be either a connection problem, or a configuration problem. Always make sure your servers are operating correctly before looking for other problems.

Some admins think that operating behind a NAT firewall excuses them from paying close attention to access controls on their internal servers. This is not good thinking—always restrict your server access controls as narrowly as possible.

See Also

- RFC 1939 lists all POP3 commands
- RFC 3501 lists all IMAP commands
- Recipe 19.7
- Recipe 19.10
- Chapter 20, "Building a Postfix Mail Server," and Chapter 21, "Managing Spam and Malware," in *Linux Cookbook*, by Carla Schroder (O'Reilly)
- man 1 telnet

19.16 Creating SSL Keys for Your Syslog-ng Server on Debian

Problem

You want to set up a secure Syslog-ng server, and you know you need *stunnel* and OpenSSL to do this. Creating and managing OpenSSL certificates makes you break out in a rash—it's confusing, and it always takes you too long. Isn't there some kind soul who will show you the way? You're running Debian, or one of its descendants, or pretty much any Linux except Fedora or Red Hat.

Solution

Just follow along, and you'll be fine. What we're going to do is create an OpenSSL Certification Authority, and server and client encryption keys to use with *stunnel*. *stunnel* provides the transport for our Syslog-ng traffic, and OpenSSL does the encryption and authentication.

You should have OpenSSL already installed; if not, you know what to do.

We'll take this slowly because managing SSL certificates is confusing, and *stunnel* complicates matters by requiring a special keyfile format.

Although *stunnel* is going to use these certificates, I'm naming them "syslog-ng*" because they're for authenticating Syslog-ng traffic. We will create the Certificate Authority (CA) and public-/private-key pairs in the */etc/syslog-ng/* directory on the server. After they are created, I'll store them in */etc/syslog-ng/keys* on the server and the clients. Wherever you want to keep your stuff, first make sure that the directories exist.

Now, find your *CA.sh* script, which is part of OpenSSL, and edit these two lines:

```
DAYS="-days 3650"      # 10 years
CATOP=./syslog-ng-CA
```

The default lifetime of your new Certificate Authority (CA) is one year, so adjust this to suit. CATOP is the top-level directory of your new CA.

Now, edit *openssl.cnf* so that the top-level directory for the CA and number of default days agree with *CA.sh*:

```
[ CA_default ]
dir      = ./syslog-ng-CA   # Where everything is kept
[...]
default_days    = 3650   # how long to certify for
```

And, edit your personal information:

```
countryName_default          = US
stateOrProvinceName_default    = OR
0.organizationName_default     = Alrac's Fine Hooves
```

Make sure these lines are commented out:

```
[ req_attributes ]
#challengePassword             = A challenge password
#challengePassword_min        = 4
#challengePassword_max        = 20
#unstructuredName        = An optional company name
```

Now, let's change to the SSL certificate-creation directory:

 # cd /etc/syslog-ng

Create the new CA:

 # /usr/lib/ssl/misc/CA.sh -newca
```
CA certificate filename (or enter to create)
```

Hit Enter:

```
Making CA certificate ...
Generating a 1024 bit RSA private key
..++++++
............................++++++
writing new private key to './syslog-ng-CA/private/./cakey.pem'
```

Create a good strong passphrase, and don't lose it—you need it every time you create a new key pair:

```
Enter PEM pass phrase:
Verifying - Enter PEM pass phrase:
-----
You are about to be asked to enter information that will be incorporated
into your certificate request.
What you are about to enter is what is called a Distinguished Name or a DN.
There are quite a few fields but you can leave some blank
For some fields there will be a default value,
If you enter '.', the field will be left blank.
-----
Country Name (2 letter code) [US]:
State or Province Name (full name) [OR]:
Locality Name (eg, city) []:Portland
Organization Name (eg, company) [Alracs Fine Hooves]:
Organizational Unit Name (eg, section) []:HoofRanch
Common Name (eg, YOUR name) []:syslog-ng
Email Address []:alrac@hoofranch.net
```

You need the passphrase you just created:

```
Enter pass phrase for ./syslog-ng-CA/private/./cakey.pem:
Check that the request matches the signature
Signature ok
Certificate Details:
        Serial Number: 0 (0x0)
        Validity
            Not Before: Jul 16 19:05:29 2007 GMT
            Not After : Jul 15 19:05:29 2010 GMT
        Subject:
            countryName               = US
            stateOrProvinceName       = OR
            organizationName          = Alrac's Fine Hooves
            organizationalUnitName    = HoofRanch
```

Use the fully qualified domain name of your server for the common name, or clients
will emit complaints:

```
            commonName                = xena.alrac.net
            emailAddress              = alrac@hoofranch.net
        X509v3 extensions:
            X509v3 Basic Constraints:
                CA:FALSE
            Netscape Comment:
                OpenSSL Generated Certificate
            X509v3 Subject Key Identifier:
                27:F4:BE:F9:92:8A:2B:84:8F:C7:C8:88:B9:4E:8A:A7:D9:3F:FE:93
            X509v3 Authority Key Identifier:
                keyid:27:F4:BE:F9:92:8A:2B:84:8F:C7:C8:88:B9:4E:8A:A7:D9:3F:FE:93

Certificate is to be certified until Jul 15 19:05:29 2010 GMT (1095 days)

Write out database with 1 new entries
Data Base Updated
```

You should see */etc/syslog-ng/syslog-ng-CA* populated with a number of files and sub-directories.

Now, we will create the server and client key pairs. In this example, the server is Xena and the client is Uberpc. First, we create the signing requests:

```
# openssl req -new -nodes -out syslogserver-xena_req.pem -keyout \
  syslogserver-xena.pem
# openssl req -new -nodes -out uberpc_req.pem -keyout uberpc.pem
```

The next step is to sign the requests and create the new key pairs. First, the server:

```
# openssl ca -out syslogserver-xena_cert.pem -infiles \
syslogserver-xena_req.pem
Using configuration from /usr/lib/ssl/openssl.cnf
Enter pass phrase for ./syslog-ng-CA/private/cakey.pem:
Check that the request matches the signature
Signature ok
Certificate Details:
        Serial Number: 1 (0x1)
        Validity
            Not Before: Jul 16 19:27:01 2007 GMT
            Not After : Jul 13 19:27:01 2017 GMT
        Subject:
            countryName               = US
            stateOrProvinceName       = OR
            organizationName          = Alrac's Fine Hooves
            organizationalUnitName    = HoofRanch
            commonName                = xena.alrac.net
            emailAddress              = alrac@hoofranch.net
        X509v3 extensions:
            X509v3 Basic Constraints:
                CA:FALSE
            Netscape Comment:
                OpenSSL Generated Certificate
            X509v3 Subject Key Identifier:
                96:DE:84:A1:55:46:78:55:54:B1:4F:B7:E3:CE:EB:26:5A:90:7F:EA
            X509v3 Authority Key Identifier:
                keyid:27:F4:BE:F9:92:8A:2B:84:8F:C7:C8:88:B9:4E:8A:A7:D9:3F:FE:93

Certificate is to be certified until Jul 13 19:27:01 2017 GMT (3650 days)
Sign the certificate? [y/n]:y


1 out of 1 certificate requests certified, commit? [y/n]y
Write out database with 1 new entries
Data Base Updated
```

And then Uberpc:

```
# openssl ca -out uberpc_cert.pem -infiles uberpc_req.pem
```

OK, we're almost there. You should now have these files:

```
syslogserver-xena_cert.pem
syslogserver-xena_req.pem
```

```
syslogserver-xena.pem
uberpc_cert.pem
uberpc_req.pem
uberpc.pem
```

You can delete the *req.pem* files because they're not needed anymore. *uberpc.pem* and *syslogserver-xena.pem* are the private keys. Never ever share these. They are plaintext files, so you can open them and confirm that they say `-----BEGIN RSA PRIVATE KEY-----`.

Open *uberpc_cert.pem* and copy the public certificate, which is the bit between:

```
-----BEGIN CERTIFICATE-----
-----END CERTIFICATE-----
```

into a new file. You need to do this for every client—copy all of their public certificates into a single file on the Syslog-ng server, which in this recipe I call */etc/syslog-ng/clientkeys*.

Now, copy Uberpc's public certificate into *uberpc.pem*, like this:

```
-----BEGIN RSA PRIVATE KEY-----
[encoded key]
-----END RSA PRIVATE KEY-----
[empty line]
-----BEGIN CERTIFICATE-----
[encoded certificate]
-----END CERTIFICATE-----
[empty line]
```

Delete all of the plaintext certificate information. Then, do the same thing to the server's key pair, because *stunnel* is fussy about the format, and it must be done this way. So now, *syslogserver-xena.pem* and *uberpc.pem* contain their own public and private keys, and nothing else.

Now, you can copy Uberpc's keyfile into its permanent home:

```
# scp uberpc.pem root@uberpc:/etc/syslog-ng/keys/
```

If you have disabled *root* logins over SSH, I shall leave it to your own ingenuity to figure out how to transfer this file.

And do the same for the server:

```
root@xena:/etc/syslog-ng# scp syslogserver-xena.pem keys/
```

Finally, protect the private keys by changing them to mode 0400, or read-only by the owner:

```
# chmod 0400 uberpc.pem
# chmod 0400 syslogserver-xena.pem
```

For every new client, follow these steps:

```
# openssl req -new -nodes -out newclient_req.pem -keyout newclient.pem
# openssl ca -out newclient_cert.pem -infiles newclient_req.pem
```

- Concatenate the private and public key into a single file
- Copy the keyfile to the new client
- Adjust the permissions
- Copy the public certificate to the server

Well, that was a bit like work. But now you know how to do it.

Discussion

Of course, you have the option of not encrypting your Syslog-ng traffic; it will work fine without it. You know that it is trivially easy to sniff traffic on a network with commonly available tools, and any network with wireless access points is extra-vulnerable, so leaving it in the clear is risky.

I like to use the *CA.sh* script to create the Certificate Authority because it takes care of the gnarly job of creating all the necessary files. You can use it to create several different types of certificates, but it's almost as easy to use the *openssl* command, which has more flexibility. The *CA.pl* script does the same thing, except it's a Perl script instead of a Bash script.

This is what the options mean in the signing request:

req -new -nodes
> Create a new signing request for a private key, with no passphrase.

-out
> The *out* filename, or name of your new signing request. This can be anything you want, as long as you use the *.pem* extension.

-keyout
> The name of your new private key.

This is what the options mean when you sign the private keys:

ca -out
> Use your CA to sign a new private key, and give it the name of your choice.

-infiles
> Use this signing request, which must be an existing file.

There is often confusion over *keys* and *certificates*. A certificate binds a public key with a distinguished name. Certificates are signed with the issuer's private key, and each one is given a serial number. You can see all this in the example in this recipe, and in your own certificates. All kinds of encryptions and hashes are used to verify that a particular public key did indeed come from a particular CA.

If you trust the issuer, then presumably, you can trust all keys created from the same CA. Private CAs are perfect for jobs like this—we know who we are, so we don't need a third-party CA to vouch for us.

See Also

- man req
- man ca
- man openssl
- *Network Security with OpenSSL*, by John Viega et al. (O'Reilly)

19.17 Creating SSL Keys for Your Syslog-ng Server on Fedora

Problem

You want to set up a secure Syslog-ng server, and you know you need *stunnel* and OpenSSL to do this. OpenSSL on Fedora doesn't look like OpenSSL on any other Linux distribution—where is everything? No *CA.sh* or *CA.pl*, it uses the */etc/pki* directory, and it just looks all weird. What do you do?

Solution

Calm down, because Fedora has a nice Makefile for creating your Public Key Infrastructure (PKI) for *stunnel*. In fact, it is very easy. Change to its directory, and run it with no options to see what it does:

```
# cd /etc/pki/tls/certs
# make
This makefile allows you to create:
 o public/private key pairs
 o SSL certificate signing requests (CSRs)
 o Self-signed SSL test certificates
[...]
```

Create the server and one client certificate like this:

```
# make syslogserver-xena.pem
# make uberpc.pem
```

Use the fully qualified domain name of your server for the *common name*, or clients will emit complaints.

Open *uberpc.pem* and copy the public certificate, which is the bit between:

```
-----BEGIN CERTIFICATE-----
-----END CERTIFICATE-----
```

into a new file. You need to do this for every client—copy all of their public certificates into a single file on the Syslog-ng server, which in this recipe I call */etc/syslog-ng/ clientkeys*.

Now, you can copy Uberpc's keyfile into its permanent home:

```
# scp uberpc.pem root@uberpc:/etc/syslog-ng/keys/
```

If you have disabled *root* logins over SSH, I shall leave it to your own ingenuity to figure out how to copy this file.

And do the same for the server:

```
root@xena:/etc/syslog-ng# scp syslogserver-xena.pem keys/
```

Finally, protect the private keys by changing them to mode 0400, or read-only by the owner:

```
# chmod 0400 uberpc.pem
# chmod 0400 syslogserver-xena.pem
```

For every new client, follow these steps:

- Create a new, unique keyfile
- Copy the keyfile to the new client
- Adjust the permissions
- Copy the client's public certificate to the server

And that's all there is to it.

Discussion

Of course, you have the option of not encrypting your Syslog-ng traffic; it will work fine without it. You know that it is trivially easy to sniff traffic on a network with commonly available tools, and any network with wireless access points is extra-vulnerable, so leaving it in the clear is risky.

Fedora's keyfiles are created by the Makefile in the exactly correct format for *stunnel*, so you don't have to muck around like you do on Debian.

See Also

- man req
- man ca
- man openssl
- *Network Security with OpenSSL*, by John Viega et al. (O'Reilly)

19.18 Setting Up stunnel for Syslog-ng

Problem

You have your SSL infrastructure set up, and now you want to configure *stunnel* to use with your Syslog-ng server.

Solution

You'll need to install *stunnel* on the clients and server. Install it on Debian with this command:

```
# aptitude install stunnel4
```

On Fedora, use this command:

```
# yum install stunnel
```

Now, edit your server */etc/stunnel/stunnel.conf* file to look like this. The cert names come from the previous two recipes:

```
cert = /etc/syslog-ng/syslogserver-xena.pem
CAfile = /etc/syslog-ng/clientkeys
client = no
verify = 3
setgid = stunnel4
setuid = stunnel4

[syslog-ng]
#server address
accept = 192.168.1.50:5140
connect = 127.0.0.1:514
```

The *stunnel4* user and group are created by the Debian installer. If your system does not create an unprivileged user and group for *stunnel*, you should create them yourself:

```
# groupadd stunnel
# useradd -d /var/run/stunnel -m -g stunnel -s /bin/false stunnel
```

The *stunnel* client configuration file looks like this:

```
cert = /etc/syslog-ng/uberpc.pem
client = yes
verify = 3
setuid = stunnel4
setgid = stunnel4

[syslog-ng]
accept = 127.0.0.1:514
#server address
connect = 192.168.1.50:5140
```

Now, you're ready to move on to actually configuring Syslog-ng.

Discussion

This is as simple a setup as it is possible to use. By default, *stunnel* will listen on all interfaces, so if that is the behavior you want, it's not necessary to specify IP addresses. You do need to list which ports you want it to listen to, so check */etc/services* for open ports, and enter the ones you are using.

See Also

- man 8 stunnel

19.19 Building a Syslog Server

Problem

You want to have a central network logging server, but the mossy old Linux *syslog* isn't really up to the job. It's OK for host logging, but it's not as flexible as it could be, and its remote logging capability is not built-in—it's a bit of a hack job, really. You want a modern log server that is designed for network logging, has encryption, and that lets you fine-tune your settings.

You have your SSL certificates and *stunnel* all configured and ready to go, so now you want to set up Syslog-ng itself.

Solution

Install Syslog-ng on Debian with this command:

```
# aptitude install syslog-ng
```

And on Fedora with this command:

```
# yum install syslog-ng
```

These will automatically remove the old *syslog* and set up a default configuration that mimics a standard *syslog* installation.

You must install Syslog-ng, OpenSSL, and *stunnel* on all client hosts as well, so if you haven't done this yet, see the previous three recipes.

We don't want to make a lot of changes to the existing */etc/syslog-ng/syslog-ng.conf* file, so let's start with the options section on the Syslog-ng server:

```
options {
    sync (0);
    log_fifo_size (2048);
    time_reopen(10);
    time_reap(360);
    create_dirs (yes);
    perm (0640);
    dir_perm (0750);
    chain_hostnames(0);
    use_dns(no);
    use_fqdn(no);
    };
```

Add these lines to the source section to tell Syslog-ng to listen for messages via *stunnel*, and to give each remote host its own file in */var/log/hosts/*:

```
source stunnel {tcp(ip("127.0.0.1")port(514) max-connections(1));};
destination d_clients {file("/var/log/hosts/$HOST/$DATE_$FACILITY"); };
log {source(stunnel); destination(d_clients);};
```

Now, add the following to the *syslog-ng.conf* file on each client:

```
options
      {long_hostnames(off);
      sync(0);};

source s_local {unix-stream("/dev/log"); pipe("/proc/kmsg"); internal();};
destination stunnel {tcp("127.0.0.1" port(514));};
log { source(s_local); destination(stunnel); };
```

And now, the moment of truth—we start up *stunnel* and Syslog-ng:

```
# stunnel
# /etc/init.d/syslog-ng
```

Give it a test drive with the `logger` command on both the server and the client:

```
$ logger "this is a test!"
```

Look in */var/log/messages* to see a successful test:

```
Jul 14 21:46:32 xena logger: this is a test
```

Then, */var/log/hosts/* should have a new file created for the client, Uberpc, and Uberpc should have also logged the test message in its own */var/log/messages* file.

Discussion

That is a good setup that should suit most situtations because it nearly replicates the standard logging setup on the server. One difference is the client files are named with the hostname, date, and logging facility, so it's easy to find the file you want.

syslog-ng.conf has five sections:

options{}
: Global options. These can be overridden in any of the next four sections.

source{}
: Message sources, such as files, local sockets, or remote hosts.

destination{}
: Message destinations, such as files, local sockets, or remote hosts.

filter{}
: Filters are powerful and flexible; you can filter on any aspect of a log message, such as standard *syslogd* facility names (man 5 syslog.conf), log level, hostname, and arbitrary contents like words or number strings.

log{}
: Log statements connect the source, destination, and filter statements, and tell Syslog-ng what to do with them.

As you saw from our examples, you don't have to organize everything in this manner. I like to group the statements by task rather than the type of statement.

Source, destination, and filter statements have arbitrary names. For example, source s_local could be source local, or source fred, or anything. There is a convention of using s_ to indicate source statements and d_ for destination statements, but it's not required.

Debian comes with a startup file for *stunnel*; Fedora doesn't. So, Fedora users can create one using */etc/skel* as a model, or just drop it into */etc/rc.d/rc.local*.

What if things don't work? Well, this is a chapter on troubleshooting, so you might read backwards!

First, make sure that Syslog-ng is operating correctly locally, which you can check with the logger command.

stunnel's maximum logging level is debug = 7 (in *stunnel.conf*), and *stunnel* messages go into */var/log/daemon.log*. You might also try directing the log messages to the screen by starting it from the command line with these options:

```
# stunnel -f -D7
```

That keeps it in the foreground, so you'll see everything in real time.

Using a packet sniffer will show you the communications between the various players, so set *tcpdump* to watching your Syslog-ng ports to see what they're telling each other:

```
# tcpdump -pi eth0 -s0 port 514 or port 5140
```

See Also

- man 8 syslog-ng
- man 5 syslog-ng.conf
- man 1 logger
- The Syslog-ng Administrator Guide:

    http://www.balabit.com/dl/html/syslog-ng-admin-guide_en.html/index.html

Essential References

Computer networking is a deep and complex subject. Please refer to the references here for deeper study of the subjects covered in this book.

Andreasson, Oskar. "iptables and ipsysctl Tutorials." *http://iptables-tutorial. frozentux.net/*.

> Always start here to learn *iptables*. You'll see a lot of crazy iptables tutorials out there-stick with the master. This goes hand-in-hand with having an in-depth understanding of TCP/IP.

Barrett, Daniel J., et al. *SSH, The Secure Shell: The Definitive Guide*, Second Edition. Sebastopol, CA: O'Reilly Media, Inc., 2005.

> SSH is very flexible and capable, and it seems there is nothing you can't do with it. This books does a great job of covering all of it.

Bautts, Tony, et al. *Linux Network Administrator's Guide*, Third Edition. Sebastopol, CA: O'Reilly Media, Inc., 2005.

> This takes a more practical approach, and covers essential services like mail services, web services, name services, PPtP, and *iptables* firewalls.

Carter, Gerald. *LDAP System Administration*. Sebastopol, CA: O'Reilly Media, Inc., 2003.

> Spend the money. Buy the book. LDAP is complex and abstract, and you'll make yourself crazy trying to learn via the usual cheapskate channels online. You won't be sorry.

Hagen, Sylvia. *IPv6 Essentials*, Second Edition. Sebastopol, CA: O'Reilly Media, Inc., 2006.

> IPv6 is coming whether you want it to or not. Ms. Hagen has done a great job of teaching IPv6 fundamentals clearly and understandably. This is the background you'll need to understand implementing IPv6 in your networks.

Hall, Eric. *Internet Core Protocols: The Definitive Guide*. Sebastopol, CA: O'Reilly Media, Inc., 2000.

> As one reader review stated:
>
> > This book is not going to teach you how to program network software, and it's not going to teach you how to administer network servers. It goes into horrid detail on all the bits flying around on the network. And it does so incredibly well.
>
> Which it does—this book removes the mysteries of what happens when your bits go out across the wires.

Hosner, Charlie. "OpenVPN and the SSL VPN Revolution." *http://www.sans.org/ reading_room/whitepapers/vpns/*.

> A great paper that describes what a genuine Virtual Private Network (VPN) is, how OpenVPN is the best VPN of all, the problems with IPSec, and how the majority of pricey commercial SSL-based VPNs are not real VPNs, and not all that secure.

Hunt, Craig. *TCP/IP Network Administration*, Third Edition. Sebastopol, CA: O'Reilly Media, Inc., 2002.

> If you don't understand TCP/IP, you won't understand computer networking. This book is a great reference that covers essential theory as well as hands-on administration.

Krafft, Martin. *The Debian System: Concepts and Techniques*. San Francisco, CA: No Starch Press, 2005.

> This is a wonderful book for all Debian users and admins that fully explores all the riches and sophisticated power tools available to Debian users.

Mauro, Douglas, and Kevin Schmidt. *Essential SNMP*, Second Edition. Sebastopol, CA: O'Reilly Media, Inc., 2005.

> SNMP is the common language for network hardware and software, and the key to both monitoring and management. Once you figure out all those OIDs and MIBs and community strings and traps, the rest is easy.

Newham, Cameron. *Learning the bash Shell*, Third Edition. Sebastopol, CA: O'Reilly Media, Inc., 2005.

> Ace network admins need scripting skills, and this is the book to use to learn them.

Robbins, Arnold. *bash Quick Reference*. Sebastopol, CA: O'Reilly Media, Inc., 2006.

> A great, 72-page downloadable PDF that covers bash commands in detail; well-organized and with clear explanations.

Schroder, Carla. *Linux Cookbook*. Sebastopol, CA: O'Reilly Media, Inc., 2004.

My very own book for Linux system administrators and power users, designed to be a companion to *Linux Networking Cookbook*. It covers package management; running various servers such as mail, web, DNS, and DHCP; backup and recovery; system rescue; file and printer sharing on mixed networks; and more.

Siever, Ellen, et al. *Linux in a Nutshell*, Fifth Edition. Sebastopol, CA: O'Reilly Media, Inc., 2005.

A perennial classic, continually updated and containing all substantial user, programming, administration, and networking commands for the most common Linux distributions.

Stevens, Richard W., and Gary R. Wright. *TCP/IP Illustrated*, Volumes 1, 2, and 3. Boston, MA: Addison-Wesley, 2001.

If you really want to be the reigning TCP/IP Master of the Universe, these books are for you. Most admins wear out several copies of Volume 1. Clear, thorough, abundantly illustrated, and a pleasure to read.

Ts, Jay, et al. *Using Samba*, Third Edition. Sebastopol, CA: O'Reilly Media, Inc., 2007.

The official book of the Samba team, also available free online at *http://www. samba.org/*. It's especially valuable for understanding the weird stuff in Windows networking (which is pretty much all of it), and what you need to know to run Linux networks that have Windows hosts. Even if you can't migrate away from Windows desktops to nice solid Linux PCs, Windows clients on a Linux network makes all kinds of sense, and Samba is the key to making it all work.

Tyler, Chris. *Fedora Linux*. Sebastopol, CA: O'Reilly Media, Inc., 2006.

This book goes into useful detail on using different desktop environments, running Fedora on laptops, running servers, package management, RAID, SELinux, Xen, security, and data storage.

Viega, John, et al. *Network Security with OpenSSL*. Sebastopol, CA: O'Reilly Media, Inc., 2002.

This is targeted more at programmers than network administrators, but it's great at removing a lot of mystery from OpenSSL protocols and key management.

APPENDIX B
Glossary of Networking Terms

A

Active Directory

Microsoft's implementation of LDAP used in Windows environments. Active Directory is a directory service primarily used to provide authentication services for Windows computers, but can also be used to store any information about a network or organization in a central database designed to be quickly accessible. The data in Active Directory's database is held in one or more equal peer Domain Controllers, each of which holds a copy of all information within the Active Directory, and synchronizes changes made on one DC to all others. Compare this to pre-Windows 2000 Server systems, which used a Primary Domain Controller and multiple Backup Domain Controllers.

AGP—Accelerated Graphics Port

Originally, graphics cards didn't need any more bandwidth than a PCI slot could provide, but the more they developed, the more bandwidth they took from the PCI bus—eventually requiring a dedicated connection. The AGP slot was created specifically to cater to the bandwidth requirements of high performance graphics cards. Based on the architecture of a PCI slot, an AGP port is a dedicated single port, not just one slot of many on a shared bus. This means the AGP card gets all the bandwidth on that connection to itself, without having to share with anything else. Since the rise in popularity of PCIe slots (which can provide much higher bandwidth), fewer new motherboards are being released with AGP ports.

ATM—Asynchronous Transfer Mode

High-speed networking standard that supports both voice and data communications. ATM is normally used by ISPs on their private long-distance networks. ATM does not use routing like Ethernet. Instead, ATM switches establish point-to-point connections between endpoints, and data flows directly from source to destination. ATM uses fixed-sized cells of 53 bytes in length, rather than variable-length packets like Ethernet. ATM performance is usually expressed as OC (Optical Carrier) levels, written as "OC-xxx." Performance levels as high as 10 Gbps (OC-192) are theoretically possible, but it's more common to see 155 Mbps (OC-3) and 622 Mbps (OC-12).

B

Baud

The number of discrete signaling events that occur each second in a digitally modulated transmission. The term is named after Jean-Maurice-Emile Baudot, the inventor of the Baudot telegraph code. At slow rates, only one bit of information is encoded in each signalling event—in these cases, the baud is equivalent to the number of bits per second that are transmitted; for example, 300 baud means that 300 bits are transmitted each second (300 bps). It is possible to encode more than one bit in each signalling event, so that a 2400 baud connection may transfer 4 bits with each event, resulting in 9600 bps. At these higher speeds, data transmission rates are usually expressed in bits per second (bps) rather than baud.

BDC—Backup Domain Controller
See *Primary Domain Controller*.

BIOS—Basic Input/Output System

The BIOS in a PC is the code that runs when the computer is first turned on. It is stored in a form of memory on the motherboard, and when run will initialize and configure the hardware, load boot code for the operating system (usually from a hard disk), then transfer control to the operating system. Older operating systems would make use of the BIOS for I/O tasks, but current systems take full control of the machine, only using the BIOS for initialization and booting.

Bridging

Combining two network segments (for example, one segment connected to a wired Ethernet port and another connected wirelessly) as if they were one network. An Ethernet bridge does not use routing, but rather, relies on broadcasting to communicate between the two segments. So, this is a good way to share broadcast services, such as a Samba server, between two LAN segments, or to combine two LAN segments into one for easier administration and routing.

Bridging doesn't scale up well for larger LANs where the amount of broadcast traffic can become unwieldy. (Compare to *Routing*.)

Broadcasting

In the context of a computer network, broadcasting means sending packets that are designed to be received by all devices on a subnet. Broadcasting is limited to the broadcast domain, which includes only those computers able to talk to one another on a network directly, without going through a router.

C

Certificate or Public Key Certificate

A method used when implementing public-key cryptography across a large number of users or devices, where securely handling keys is impractical due to the large number of members. In normal public-key cryptography, you may want to allow others to send you encrypted secret messages, so you provide people with your public key. Anyone who wishes to contact you securely encrypts messages to you with your public key, which you decrypt with your private key.

This leaves open the possibility that an attacker may publish a public key of their own, claim it is yours, then intercept and read communication meant for you. In small webs of trust this may not be a problem, but across many thousands of users, it becomes more of an issue to keep track of who genuinely owns which public key.

To avoid this issue, each member in a large group may use a certificate instead of a plain public key. The certificate consists of their public key combined with their identity, signed by a third party who is trusted by all. In a Public Key Infrastructure, this third party will be a Certificate Authority. Now, anyone who wishes to send you an encrypted message can obtain your certificate, check to see that the trusted third party believes the key and the identity within it match, and with that verification complete, trust encrypted communication to you.

Self-signed certificates are used inside the LAN to authenticate local users and services; in that case, you do not need a third-party Certificate Authority because you can easily verify your own certificates.

CIDR—Classless Inter-Domain Routing

Introduced in 1993, CIDR removes the idea of classful networks by going to a resolution of bits for defining networks, indicated by a numerical suffix. The old Class A, B, and C networks corresponded to CIDR suffixes of /8, /16, or /24. Dividing IP addresses into CIDR blocks allows a resolution much finer than previous classful networks, which were wasteful of IP addresses. 192.168.0.0/16 corresponds to an old class B network, where 192.168 (the first 16 bits) define the network, and .0.0 up to .255.255 refer to hosts. Finer grained division of networks are possible, down to individual IP addresses, such as 192.168.100.2/32.

Codec

In the context of a VoIP network, a codec is an algorithm that encodes audio into digital form for transmission over the network, and can decode it back into audio for listening. Different codecs make different tradeoffs between high quality audio, bandwidth usage, and CPU cycles. If issues out of your control severely limit the bandwidth available, for example, you may be willing to use a more CPU-intensive codec that can compress audio into a smaller stream. In the wider sense of the term, other forms of data (such as video or pictures) can be encoded and decoded using other relevant codecs.

Community string

When devices communicate using SNMP, a piece of text known as a *community string* is included in every packet sent between a management station (an SNMP manager) and a device (an SNMP agent). It can be seen as a password defining the access an agent will allow a manager. A community string can be a read string or a read/write string—if a manager presents a read string, the agent will only allow the manager to read information, but if a read/write string is presented, an agent will allow that manager to read information and change the agent's settings.

Console

Console has many meanings. A Linux command-line session that is not running in X Windows is called a console session, or virtual console. Some Linux documentation refers to an attached keyboard and monitor as the console or the physical console. Console can refer to the logical device */dev/ttyS0*. Another way to think of the Linux console is as the location where kernel messages appear.

Circuit switching

In a circuit switching network, a dedicated circuit must be opened between users before they can communicate and, while the circuit is open, no other users may use that circuit or parts of it. A circuit may remain open without any information transmission, and still be unusable by others; it must be closed before its components are available to different users. (Compare this to *Packet switching*.)

CPE—Customer Premises Equipment

Any device at a subscriber's premises and connected to a telecommunications network on the customer side of a demarcation point (demarc). Equipment included may be for telephone communication, a cable Internet connection, DSL, or cable TV.

CSU/DSU—Channel Service Unit/Data Service Unit

Equipment used to connect a router to a T1 connection. The CSU provides the connection to the digital line, receiving and transmitting the signal required for communication, and the DSU converts the line frames as used on a T1 connection into frames useful for a LAN. In practice, the CSU and DSU are usually combined into the one box for connecting a LAN to a T1.

Collision domain

A segment of a network where packets can potentially collide if two or more computers send at the same time. Using a hub with multiple machines attached creates a collision domain, as the hub simply repeats the packet sent to the hub out to all other machines connected to it without regard for other network activity. Computers must sense the network to check it isn't busy before sending packets—even then packets might collide, which requires the packet be resent. Collisions waste time, and the more machines in a collision domain that are transmitting often, the more collisions occur. Using switches instead of hubs splits collision domains into smaller segments, and a 100 percent switched network has no collision domains.

D

Demarc—demarcation point

The point at which the wiring on a customer's premises meets that of telecommunications providers. A demarc can be as simple as a connection between internal and external telephone wires, or a box allowing connection of all forms of telecommunications, from telephone and cable, to fiber optic connections.

DHCP—Dynamic Host Configuration Protocol

DHCP is a protocol used between clients (network devices such as computers) and a DHCP server, so that the client can obtain a valid IP address and other information such as default gateway, subnet mask, and DNS servers, for the client to connect to the network.

DNS—Domain Name System

The system that provides information about domain names to users of the Internet. Essentially, a widespread distributed directory of information about the Internet. Publically available domain names must be globally unique and are managed via central registries. Domain names are matched to the IP addresses of specific hosts; these addresses must also be globally unique. The domain name system can take a domain name and return information about how to reach it (IP address); how to send mail to a user on it (mail exchange servers); and digging further, even information about the owner of the domain, when it was registered, and when it might expire.

Private domain names and addresses that are not accessible outside the LAN do not need to be unique, and do not have to be registered.

Domain (Windows)

A group of computers that share a central directory database that contains information about about users, their privileges, resources, and the privileges required to access those resources. A user who needs to use a computer within a domain has a single account that is unique across the domain. Implementing a domain provides several benefits, including centralized administration and a single login that authenticates access to potentially thousands of resources. For Windows NT domains, the directory was provided by a Primary Domain Controller, whereas Windows 2000 Server and later uses Active Directory.

DSL—Digital Subscriber Loop or Digital Subscriber Line

DSL is a family of technologies designed to provide high speed digital data transmission over the local loop of a telephone network (from exchange to customer premises). ADSL (Asynchronous DSL, where some bandwidth is sacrificed for voice compatibility, and download speed is many times higher than upload speed) is the most widely used DSL, and is designed to work with an existing voice service. SDSL (Synchronous DSL) and other faster forms of DSL require the line's entire bandwidth.

Dynamic address

A dynamic address refers to an IP address given out to a device on a network with no regard to matching a specific address to that device. When a client device (say a laptop plugged into a network) is given a dynamic address, it simply receives one from a pool of available addresses. It may or may not be allocated the same IP address as on previous connections; no attempt is made to do so, nor is an attempt made to give a specifically different one.

E

Encryption

A process by which information is changed from a meaningful usable form (called plaintext) into an encrypted form (called ciphertext), which is undecipherable except to those with the key to decrypt it. Encryption may apply to a single file on disk, to all data in packets over a network connection, or to an entire stream of data.

Ethernet, Fast Ethernet, Gigabit Ethernet

Ethernet refers to a family of related link-level protocols for sending data. Ethernet generally refers to the entire family, or sometimes just 10 megabit per second connections. Fast Ethernet is 100 megabits per second, and Gigabit Ethernet is 1,000 megabits (or one gigabit) per second Ethernet.

F

FQDN—Fully Qualified Domain Name

A complete domain name that unambiguously refers to an address in DNS. As an example, a host named *alrac* at *example.com* will have the FQDN of *alrac. example.com*.

Frame Relay

A point-to-point protocol that transmits traffic in variable-sized frames rather than TCP/IP packets, and that is used to connect branch offices or a customer to their ISP. Frame relay doesn't do any error correction; this is left up to the endpoints.

This used to be a lower-cost alternative to T-services, but these days is not as cost-competitive as it used to be, and is used mainly when high-speed DSL or T-services are not available.

FXS/FXO

"Foreign Exchange Station" and "Foreign Exchange Office." These are analog telephony terms. FXS is the interface the telco provides to its customers, such as the wall jack that the telephone plugs into. An analog telephone is an FXO device.

G

GRE—Generic Routing Encapsulation

A tunneling protocol that provides encapsulation of OSI layer 3 packets inside IP packets. GRE provides a virtual point-to-point link between machines at remote points on an IP network like the Internet. GRE is completely insecure, but it provides a fast and simple way to access a remote network.

GRUB—GNU GRUB or GRand Unified Bootloader

A multiboot bootloader for Linux and other operating systems. GNU GRUB is based on the GRand Unified Bootloader. When a computer is booted, GRUB executes and allows a user to make boot-time choices such as selecting different kernels or kernel options, then transfers control and options to a kernel to boot an operating system. Just one kernel may be installed, or multiple operating systems with multiple kernels. Most current, general-purpose Linux distributions use GRUB. GRUB features a rather powerful interactive interface, and unlike LILO, the master boot record on disk does not have to be overwritten for every configuration change. (See also *LILO*.)

H

Hub

An Ethernet hub is a networking device with multiple ports that connects many networking devices in a star topology. When a packet arrives in one of the hub's ports, the hub simply repeats that packet to all of its other ports so it is received by all computers connected to the hub, in the hope that the correct destination machine will receive the packet. Because every packet on every port in the hub is repeated back out its other ports, collisions occur frequently and slow down the network. (Contrast this with a *Switch*.)

I

IAX

The Inter-Asterisk eXchange protocol that is native to the Asterisk iPBX (Internet protocol-base Private Branch Exchange) and VoIP (Voice over IP) server. IAX can carry multiple audio and video data streams, which reduces IP overhead, and because it uses a single port, it is easy to get through firewalls.

Interface

In the context of networking, a name used in Linux operating systems to describe a network connection. The connection may directly correlate to a physical device, such as *eth0* (describing a specific ethernet port), or a virtual connection through another connection, such as *tun0* tunneled over another connection.

IOS—Internet Operating System

Used in most Cisco routers, IOS is a specific-purpose operating system designed for handling network tasks on Cisco networking hardware.

IP

Along with TCP, one of the most widely used and important protocols on the Internet. IP is the protocol involved in shipping a packet of information from one computer on a network to a remote machine potentially on the other side of the world. Routers pay attention to the IP address carried in an IP packet, and perform the magic required to shift the packet hop-by-hop to its final destination. IP provides no guarantees of reliability, so if packets are lost in transit, accidentally duplicated, arrive in the wrong order, or arrive corrupted, no effort is made to address the problem on the IP level—that is left to protocols a layer above, such as TCP. (If TCP detects a missing, corrupted, or out of order packet, it must request it be resent from the source.)

IP has two main flavors. First, is the widely popular and default IPv4 with its familiar 32-bit addressing (represented in dotted quad notation like 12.139.163.20), which gives a maximum of 4.3 billion addresses, not quite enough to give every human alive one IP address. Second, is IPv6, the successor to IPv4. With 128-bit addressing, IPv6 can provide enough addresses to give every human alive billions of IP addresses for every cell in their body. While a much larger address pool is one of the great features of IPv6, a few other extras are worth mentioning, such as multicast support by default, jumbograms (packets up to 4 GB in size), IPsec support by default, and stateless host auto-configuration.

IPsec—IP security

A set of protocols for encrypting, authenticating, and integrity checking packets at the level of IP streams. IPsec also includes protocols for cryptographic key establishment, and is widely used in some implementations of Virtual Private Networking (VPN). IPsec operates at the network layer below that of other Internet security systems (such as SSL), which can give extra flexibility with the tradeoff of more complexity. IPsec has two modes of operation: transport mode and tunnel mode. Transport mode is performed by each machine at the end of a connection, and only encrypts the payload of the IP packet, leaving the IP header as plaintext so it can be routed (although not by using NAT, which rewrites part of the packet, causing it to fail integrity checking). In tunnel mode, the entire packet is encrypted, and then encapsulated into a new IP packet to allow routing to function—using this method, secure traffic flow between two LANs can be provided by two nodes, one in each LAN.

ISDN—Integrated Services Digital Network

A digital network technology using ordinary telephone wires, ISDN is capable of delivering multiple channels of data, voice, video or fax over a single physical line. Channels on ISDN are either B (for Bearer, usually 64 Kbps channels that most data is transmitted on) or D (for the channel used to transmit control signals). Different ISDN services can provide varying numbers of channels, from a basic two B and one D, up to services with 30 B channels. In much of the world, ISDN has been supplanted by DSL.

K

Kerberos

An authentication protocol that allows users communicating over a network to prove their identity to one another securely. It not only allows a user to prove her identification to a server, for example, but allows the server to prove its identification to the user. Kerberos authentication uses symmetric key cryptography and a trusted third party, the Key Distribution Center (KDC). Each entity on the network has a secret key that is known only to itself and the KDC.

Authentication between two entities on the network is a complex process with many steps, but it can be summarized like this: a client wishes to access a server on the network, and communicates this wish to the KDC. The KDC and client communicate using the client's key (known only to the client and the KDC), and after some negotiation, the KDC returns multiple messages to the client, including one encrypted with the server's key that the client must send to the server to prove that the KDC has authenticated the client, and a session key specifically to be used for communication between the client and server. When the client presents the message encrypted with the server's key to the server, the server decrypts it and extracts the session key and other information identifying the client. This establishes a mutual trust, and the client and server can then communicate with each other using the session key to encrypt their messages.

KDC—Key Distribution Center

See *Kerberos*.

L

LAN—Local Area Network

LANs are networks based on a small physical area such as a residence, building, or college campus. They tend to consist of fast connections between systems (Gigabit Ethernet and Wi-Fi are common), and don't involve a paid network connection to the Internet as part of their structure, although one may be used to connect the LAN to the rest of the world.

LDAP—Lightweight Directory Access Protocol

A protocol for accessing information in and writing information to an LDAP directory. The directory itself is a database designed for very fast consistent reads, used for relatively static information like user data, passwords, security keys, customer data, etc. LDAP clients connect to an LDAP server and send requests—generally, a client can send multiple requests to the server and does not need to wait for responses in between, and the LDAP server can return responses in any order. Microsoft's Active Directory and Fedora Directory Server are two examples of heavyweight LDAP implementations.

LILO—LInux LOader

When a computer that has LILO installed is booted, the BIOS passes control to LILO from disk, and allows a user to make boot-time choices such as selecting different kernels or kernel options. Once an option is selected, LILO loads the relevant kernel and transfers control and options to it in order to boot an operating system. LILO has fallen out of favor among general Linux distributions, in favor of GRUB. (See also *GRUB*.)

M

Masquerading

IP Masquerading is a synonym for Network Address Translation (NAT).

MIB—Management Information Base

In the context of SNMP, it is a hierarchical structure that describes all the objects that an agent can be queried about or in some cases written to. The MIB for each agent contains the name, Object Identifier (OID), data type, and read or read/ write status of each object. Network equipment (agents) designed to be managed by SNMP must contain a MIB with objects relevant to the device's operation, and the manager for that agent must also know what can be sanely accessed on the agent. In reality, there is one MIB and the Internet Assigned Numbers Authority (IANA) manages the structure of it. Devices only implement a subset of the MIB tree with objects relevant to their operation.

Modem

From MOdulate/DEModulate, a modem is a device that encodes (by modulation of a carrier signal) digital data for transmission over an analog phone connection, and decodes a received analog signal back into a digital stream. Modems are best known for connecting two computers over the telephone system, but different forms of modems using other analog transmission mediums (such as radio) exist.

MPPE—Microsoft Point-to-Point Encryption

A protocol used to encrypt PPP and VPN connections. MPPE uses RSA's RC4 encryption using up to 128-bit session keys. Session keys are changed frequently for extra security, but due to keys being derived from information originally sent as plaintext, MPPE is not particularly robust encryption.

Multicast

IP Multicast is the process of sending a packet to multiple machines on a network. Contrast this with Unicast (sending to one host only) and with Broadcasting (sending to all hosts). Multicast only requires the source to send a packet once, no matter the number of receivers—it's the nodes within a network that replicates the packet as many times as needed. Movement and replication of the packet within the network to the correct hosts depends on the source sending to a group address, and having multiple receivers who have already announced to the network that they are part of that group. Nodes within the network (knowing who has joined the multicast group) can then intelligently forward the packet on, replicating it only when needed.

N

NAS—Network Access Server

A point of access to a network that guards access to that network. The NAS takes credentials from a client wishing to connect to the network, passes them to an authentication service of some kind, and then grants or denies the client access depending on the response from the authentication service. To perform as a NAS, a server does not require information about which clients are allowed access, although the authentication service used by the NAS may run on the same physical device. All the NAS must be able to do is prevent or allow a client access to the resources behind it.

NAT—Network Address Translation

A method used to allow a single public IP address to represent an entire private subnet, and to run public servers with private nonroutable addresses. A typical Internet connection may have one public IP address, and a LAN of 25 workstations, laptops, and servers behind it, protected by an *iptables* NAT firewall. The entire network will appear to the outside world as a single computer. Source NAT (SNAT) rewrites the source addresses of all outgoing packets to the firewall's address, and can retranslate the other way, too, when responses for machines inside the private network are received from the Internet. While having public routable IP addresses is desirable for public services, like web and mail servers, you can get by on the cheap without them and run public servers on private addresses. Destination NAT (DNAT) rewrites the destination address, which is the firewall address, to the real server addresses, then *iptables* forwards incoming traffic to these servers.

Netmask

Subnet Mask. (See also *Subnet*.)

NIC—Network Interface Card or Network Interface Controller

The hardware that allows a computer to connect to a network. It may consist of a card that plugs in to a computer motherboard, it could connect via USB port, or it could be integrated into the motherboard itself. It provides the physical connection that allows the computer to talk to the rest of the network. Most common is a connection to a TCP/IP network that may use cat5, wireless, or coax connections. NICs exist for other network types, including token ring and optical fiber.

NSS—Name Service Switch

A part of many Unix and related systems that defines how lookups for information relating to the environment of the machine are made. By default, most lookups for names such as user passwords, groups, hosts, and so on are done via files such as */etc/passwd* or */etc/hosts*. The Name Service Switch allows lookups using other databases to discover the same information, and defines the order in which those databases are accessed. It is through configuration of this switch that a Linux system can be used on a Windows domain, with the Winbind NSS module providing users and groups from a Windows domain.

NTP—Network Time Protocol

A protocol designed to allow computers on a network to synchronize their clocks, taking into account the variable latency on a packet switched network. Using NTP, it's possible for all computers on a network (like the Internet) to have clocks synchronized to within hundredths of a second. This is required for some network activities, such as Kerberos authentication, which in part relies upon accurate timestamps.

Null modem cable

A cable that allows a PC to connect directly to another PC via serial ports. Similar to a normal modem cable (except where receive/transmit lines would go straight through to transmit/receive pins on the modem), a Null modem cable swaps the lines inside the cable, allowing the two PCs to communicate using the same serial connection software and serial ports used to connect to a modem.

NVRAM—Non-Volatile Random Access Memory

Unlike the normal RAM inside a PC, NVRAM doesn't lose its contents when power is removed. Various forms of NVRAM generally come with disadvantages compared to normal RAM—it's often slower, requires more power to read, and many times more to write, and may wear out with the masses of writing that normal RAM requires. Different forms of NVRAM are most often used to store some settings within a device, where only occasional writes are required, but it can also serve as a silent replacement for a small hard drive. Flash memory is the most well-known form of NVRAM.

0

OID—Object IDentifier

Within the context of SNMP, a unique identifier referring to an object within a Management Information Base (MIB) used to store information and settings related to a network device. The OID is represented as a string of numbers separated by dots, and refers to an object's position in the tree structure of the MIB. For example, 1.3.4.16 would be a sibling of 1.3.4.1800, and both are children of 1.3.4. The object and the information it contains can be anything relevant to the device's operation, from the name of the device to the speed of fans, memory usage, bandwidth usage, or the number of hamster wheels in use.

OSPF—Open Shortest Path First

A link-state routing protocol, implemented by routers to dynamically adjust routing to changing network conditions. An OSPF router multicasts information to other routers when changes have occurred around its network, as well as routine updates every 30 minutes. From this information, each individual OSPF router builds a link-state database that contains a representation of the entire topology of the network in tree form, with the router itself at the *root*. When a router needs to forward a packet, it can use its copy of the link-state database to calculate the best path from the *root* (itself) to the destination on the tree, using a *path cost* as its routing metric (as opposed to RIP's hop count). In a practical sense, path cost is mainly determined by link speed over a given route, so a packet is forwarded toward the fastest of multiple routes. As a network grows larger, routers will spend more time and bandwidth talking to each other, which consumes valuable bandwidth just keeping the network together. OSPF addresses this issue by allowing the division of a network into areas. Areas must all be connected to a common backbone, and the routers inside each area only need to contain the topology for that area, with border routers communicating between different areas. (See also *RIP*.)

P

Packet filtering

Filtering by the attributes of a packet entering a device or network. Attributes may include the source or destination address for the device, the port, connection type, elements of the data payload, or any other number of detectable attributes of the packet.

Packet switching

A packet switched network breaks information to be transmitted into discrete packets, each of which is sent over a shared network used by multiple machines or users. Each individual packet contains information pertaining to its source and destination, and does not require a dedicated path to reach its destination; indeed, packets may travel between the same source and destination using different paths. Multiple users may transmit packets over the same connection at the same time, independently of one another. (Contrast with *Circuit switching*.)

PAM—Pluggable Authentication Modules

A system whereby applications that require authentication can use many kinds of authentication, all using the same API. An application only needs to know it is using PAM, and the relevant modules provide one of many kinds of authentication, transparently.

PBX—Private Branch eXchange

A PBX was originally a private telephone exchange that handled a business' own internal telephone requirements, so that an entire building's internal phone calls wouldn't need to use the costly public phone network. Now, a PBX is any system that handles in-house telephony, from manual exchanges to VOIP systems that route telephony over IP networks.

PCI—Peripheral Component Interconnect

The PCI Standard defines a 32- or 64-bit parallel bus for connecting devices to a computer motherboard. Peripherals connected via a PCI bus vary widely, including graphics cards, network cards, modems, disk controllers, and other I/O devices. The original PCI bus specification consisted of a 33 MHz 32-bit bus, and has been revised multiple times, culminating in PCI-X running up to 533 MHz with 64-bit signalling. PCIe (also called PCI Express) is a far faster interface that is physically and electrically very different to PCI, but retains software compatibility; i.e., an operating system written to talk to PCI devices won't be confused when it finds it's running on a PCIe system.

PDC—Primary Domain Controller

A server catering to Windows NT style domains that can give a user access to multiple resources on a network with the use of one login. NT Server domains have one Primary Domain Controller, and optionally multiple Backup Domain Controllers. While the Primary Domain Controller contains the database of accounts and privileges in a read/write form, each Backup Domain Controller gets a full backup of the database, but is read-only. If needed, a PDC can be removed and a BDC can be promoted to PDC. Under Linux, Samba can perform as a PDC. (Contrast to *Active Directory*, which supersedes NT-style domains.)

PKI—Public Key Infrastructure

A system that handles the work of creating public-key certificates containing identities tied to public keys and signed by a certificate authority (CA). The PKI can publish the public-key certificates to those who wish to communicate with the keys' owners, and verify that a certificate containing some public key and identity is genuine, so the public key can be trusted to belong to the owner described.

PPP—Point-to-Point Protocol

In its most common form, PPP is used to provide an OSI layer 2 (data link) between two nodes over a serial modem connection to allow TCP/IP to function and give a computer Internet access. Defined within PPP's specification is Link Control Protocol (LCP), which automatically configures the interfaces at each end of the PPP connection. PPP is also used as part of PPP over Ethernet (PPPoE) for some ADSL connections, and PPP over ATM (PPPoA) for some ADSL and Cable Internet connections.

PPTP—Point-to-Point Tunneling Protocol

A protocol used to create a VPN over an IP-based network such as the Internet. Network protocols on the original networks are sent over a regular PPP session using a Generic Routing Encapsulation (GRE) tunnel. A PPTP VPN can be encrypted using Microsoft Point to Point Encryption (MPPE), but the implementation isn't particularly secure in comparison to the SSL-based OpenVPN.

Q

QoS—Quality of Service

Any system whereby packets zipping around your network are handled in different ways according to their importance and need. Applications sending/receiving data don't all require the same performance from the network; VoIP may have strict requirements for low delay, high quality video may need consistent high throughput, an SSH session may require little bandwidth but must be highly responsive, and network warnings to on-call admins (you really do want to know when your most critical servers have something to complain about) absolutely must get through.

R

RAS/RRAS—Remote Access Service, Routing & Remote Access Service

RAS is Windows NT's Remote Access Service, which allows the sharing of network services over a dial-up connection. A remote user would dial in to a server, and then have the same access to the server's network as if they were connected to it physically.

RRAS is the equivalent to RAS in Windows 2000 Server and above, which not only provides dial-up remote access, but also a VPN server, IP Routing, and NAT.

RDP—Remote Desktop Protocol

The protocol used by client software to connect to a remote Windows computer running Microsoft Terminal Services, and to use that computer as if it were the local machine. Currently, the server software only runs on Windows, but clients are available for other operating systems, including Linux, Mac OS X, BSDs, and Solaris. RDP not only allows the remote machine to display graphics on the local screen, but applications on the remote can play audio and use serial ports, parallel ports, and printers on the local device.

Not all Windows computers can run an RDP service; notable exceptions are Windows XP Home Edition and Windows Vista Home Basic or Home Premium.

RFC—Request For Comments

Documents containing standards, technical, and organizational information about the Internet. An individual RFC is not necessarily a standard or even a proposed standard, but may be published to provide information about how other standards work in practice when applied to the Internet, to provide information on de facto adopted standards, or to convey new concepts related to the Internet. RFCs are serialized, and referred to by number; for example, RFC 4406 is a document covering an experimental protocol for email authentication. Anyone may publish a document to the Internet Engineering Task Force for inclusion as a possible RFC. The official source for RFCs is *http://www.rfc-editor.org/*.

RIP—Routing Information Protocol

A method by which routers within a network are able to adapt to changing network conditions (such as a downed router or suddenly congested links) by communicating to other routers. About every 30 seconds, a RIP-enabled router multicasts its routing table to any other connected routers, and can be triggered to do the same on certain events for quick response to sudden changes. As a distance-vector routing protocol, RIP uses the hop count of a destination to detect the most desirable path to route packets, but limits the number of hops to 15 to prevent routing loops. This creates a limit to the size of a network that can be supported by RIP, as anything more than 15 hops away appears not to exist to RIP routers. RIP benefits from simple configuration and low processing requirements, so for a relatively small LAN, RIP may be ideal. (See also *OSPF*.)

Routing

IP Routing is the process of path selection for packets traveling through an IP-based network. Compared to bridging, which automatically discovers the route that network traffic takes between multiple network segments, and does so via OSI Layer 2 (the data link layer), routing relies upon a coordinated OSI Layer 3 (network layer) network, and uses the IP addresses of packets to decide where to forward them. Routing is usually controlled by pre-constructed routing tables that define where a packet should go. Each router only needs to know where a packet should be sent on its next hop, and doesn't know nor care what happens afterward; the next hop plus one is the responsibility of the next router, and so on through the network until a packet reaches its destination.

S

SBC—Single Board Computer

A computer where everything needed to function is on a single board (mostly). A desktop computer can require a whole load of different boards and accessories to make it work. There's the motherboard, some RAM modules, a hard drive, a graphics card, a keyboard, and a mouse—and that's just for a basic system without including extra storage, exotic graphics setups, extra USB ports, or specialized sound and media cards. On the other hand are the single board computers with much more modest hardware. A fanless basic processor, RAM, flash RAM storage, multiple networking ports, and serial connections all on the one board is the norm. There may be some basic expansion available, but it's not necessary for most operations. The idea is that many specialized repetitive tasks like routing, firewalls, and some services can be handled by computers at about the speed of an early Pentium, and that's where these boards fit. Just cram it in a box, add power and an operating system to its flash RAM, and you're on your way.

Serial console

Any PC, laptop, or PDA that controls another machine via the serial port. Some folks think that only a real hardware serial terminal, like a Wyse terminal, can be called a console. Using an old PC for a serial console is a nice way to get a few more years' life out of an old machine.

SIP—Session Initiation Protocol

The SIP protocol is probably the most popular VoIP protocol in use now. Commercial VoIP providers like Vonage use SIP. SIP is not a multimedia protocol itself, but rather carries any type of audio or video stream, and it creates, modifies, and terminates sessions between at least two endpoints.

SLA—Service Level Agreement

A formal agreement that defines the level of service to be expected from a provider of those services. For example, with an Internet connection, an SLA may define the percentage of time a connection remains open and fully usable, the average time before the helpdesk answers their phones, or the average time taken for problems to be fixed. An SLA can also lay out billing reductions for the client or penalties for the provider if they fail to honor the level of service described.

Smurf

A Smurf attack is a form of Denial of Service attack that exploits the response of computers on a network to a broadcast ICMP echo request (a *ping*). The basic element of a Smurf attack is a single ICMP echo request carrying a faked source IP address, sent to a broadcast address. The routing device that receives the echo request then broadcasts the single request to all IP addresses covered by that broadcast address, and each one sends back an ICMP echo response directed to the faked source IP address. In this way, a single *ping* request from somewhere on the Internet can generate a much larger *ping* response to the faked source address (the victim). Floods of such pings can multiply the response hundreds-fold, and overwhelm the network connection or computer at the faked source IP.

SNMP—Simple Network Management Protocol

SNMP consists of managers (stations that oversee devices on a network) and agents (inside a network device itself) communicating through a simple language. Using SNMP, a manager is able to read information from an agent, or read and write information depending on the permissions it has to that agent. Information within agents is stored by objects within a Management Information Base (MIB), and those objects may contain a wide range of information about a device such as settings, usage statistics, performance data, or physical properties (e.g., temperature or fan speed).

SOHO—Small Office/Home Office

A term applying to a small business with up to about 10 users. Computing equipment labeled SOHO may be designed with some features typically for business use, but not necessarily capable of handling the requirements of large organizations with hundreds of users.

SRPM—Source RPM

A package for Red Hat-based Linux systems that contains source code and a spec file that lets the *rpm* utility compile and build an RPM package. The resulting RPM package can then be installed and managed like any other RPM.

SSH—Secure SHell

A protocol that allows the opening of a secure, encrypted channel between two computers with secure authentication. SSH is most often used to provide a secure shell to log in to a remote machine, but also supports file transfers, TCP, and X11 tunneling.

SSL/TLS—Secure Sockets Layer/Transport Layer Security

SSL and TLS are similar, related protocols for providing secure data transmission and authentication over networks, including the Internet. SSL was originally developed by Netscape in 1994, and was revised to become SSL 3.0 in 1996, which became the base of TLS. TLS 1.1 is the current version of the protocol. An SSL/TLS connection is started by a client requesting a secure connection to a server. The client and server decide on the strongest cipher and hash function they both share, and the server presents a digital certificate that can be checked by the client with the issuing certificate authority. Within the server's certificate is its public key, which the client uses to encrypt a random number to send to the server. If the connection is genuine, the server is able to decrypt the message and the server and client now have a matching secret random number that can be used to generate keys for data transfer. Now that this handshaking is complete, the server and client may communicate over a secure connection. The client may also present a digital certificate as part of the handshaking process, so that the server, too, can verify the client's identity.

State (packet filtering)

Filtering on the known state of a packet, identified by previous network activity. A single packet coming from a random machine on the Internet may be dropped by a firewall, or it may be accepted, depending on the known state. For example, a machine behind a firewall may request a web page from a web server. The web server then sends a response back, and the firewall allows the response because it knows a machine requested information from that server. The same response from the web server would be denied if there had been no original request passing through the firewall. While there was not necessarily any information within the packet that defined whether it was a valid response to be passed through, its state was derived by the firewall through previous activity between the two hosts.

Static address

A Static address is one meant to be matched to a particular computer, so that it always has the same address. Necessary when you have a server on a network, and must know a permanent IP address in order to use it. (Contrast with a *Dynamic address*.)

Subnet

In the context of an IP-based network, a subnet is a group of related IP addresses all beginning with the same binary network part, and ending in a unique binary sequence identifying the host within the subnet. An example might be the IP address 192.168.100.12 with subnet mask of 255.255.255.0. The first 24 bits of the address, shown by bits in the subnet mask, reveal which part is the network address (192.168.100.0), with the last 8 bits correspond to the hosts part (12 in this case). The entire subnet thus spans the address range 192.168.100.0 to 192.168.100.255. Dividing a network into subnets in this hierarchical sense keeps routing easy, as the IP addresses within a subnet can all be derived from the network address.

Switch

At first glance, a switch may look very similar to a hub, but it will act far more intelligently. Switches take note of the addresses of connected computers in order to send only data to the correct machine. For example, a packet arrives in a port on a switch, and is destined for one particular machine connected via another port. The switch has previously paid attention to which machines are connected to which port, and forwards the packet out only to the correct machine. An unmanaged switch has no configuration options, and simply connects to multiple network computers. A managed switch can be configured for various network fine tuning, such as limiting speed on certain ports, QoS, SNMP reporting/control, link aggregation, and so on. (Contrast with *Hub*.)

SYN/ACK—Synchronization/Acknowledgement

Part of opening a new TCP connection. When a client wishes to connect to a server on the Internet, it first sends a SYN packet to the server. The server responds back with a SYN-ACK (an acknowledgment), and the client returns a SYN-ACK-ACK (another acknowledgment). Both acknowledgments together indicate that the server can talk to the client, the client can talk to the server, and a TCP connection is now open for use between the two hosts.

T

TCAM—Ternary Content Addressable Memory

Unlike normal RAM in a computer where data is stored in many addresses and the RAM can only be queried for the contents at a given address, Content Addressable Memory (CAM) works in the other direction. CAM is provided with content, then searches its memory in order to return a list of addresses where the content was found. With RAM, a search requires software to repeatedly read from a memory address, compare the contents of memory to the content being searched for, then move on to the next address, repeating until the area of RAM to be searched is exhausted. With CAM, content can be provided, and the list of addresses containing that content is returned in one operation, which provides a phenomenal speedup for searching the contents of memory.

Ternary Content Addressable Memory takes this a step further. With normal CAM, the stored data is only in the form of bits—a word at an address may be 10011101, but TCAM may contain a third state of "don't care" or "X" in memory—so a word at an address could be 10011X01, which would match the search for 10011101 and 10011001. CAM and TCAM are often used in switches and routers to store MAC lookup tables and routing tables, respectively. A router may have a network address in memory, and when a packet arrives to be routed, its destination IP address can be searched for in TCAM, which will instantly return the address of a routing table entry for its destination address, stored with only the network part of the destination network as 1 or 0, and host part as X. CAM and TCAM are far more complex, expensive, and power-hungry memory-wise than normal RAM, but are necessary for applications like routing where a search through a routing table must be done thousands or millions of times per second.

TCP—Transmission Control Protocol

One of the central protocols essential to the function of the Internet, TCP allows applications to create connections that, once established, the applications can stream data across. TCP stacks in an operating system do the hard work of splitting the stream of data into segments with a sequence number, and sending them out over an IP-based network. At the remote end, the TCP stack acknowledges packets that have been received (so that missing packets can be resent) and reassembles received packets in the correct order to provide an in-order data stream to the remote application.

TLS/SSL—Transport Layer Security/Secure Sockets Layer

See *SSL/TLS*.

TTL—Time To Live

A TTL is a limit on how long a piece of information can exist before it should be discarded. One example is a DNS record. When first looked up by a caching DNS server, a domain's DNS records will be cached and the TTL will be recorded in seconds. Before the number of seconds has passed, any subsequent DNS lookups of that record will come from the cache. Once the TTL has passed, the cached record expires, and should be looked up again from an authoritative source. The time may also be a number of transmissions or hops on a network, for example performing a *traceroute* depends on a TTL being reduced by 1 on every hop. When a *traceroute* runs, a series of packets are sent towards a destination with increasing TTL values. With each hop, the TTL is reduced—when it reaches 0, the packet is considered expired, and an ICMP Time Exceeded packet is returned to the sender. The *traceroute* utility is able to record the origin of each ICMP packet returned as each successive longer TTL allows the packet to reach further through a network, then display the list of hosts a packet passes through to reach the destination.

U

UART—Universal Asynchronous Receiver/Transmitter

A UART is a device that performs a conversion between data in parallel form, such as bytes in memory, and a serial stream for transmission over a serial connection. *Universal* refers to the ability of the Asynchronous Receiver/Transmitter to operate at a number of different bit rates, depending on the need at the time.

V

VLAN—Virtual LAN

A method whereby multiple logical LAN segments are created on top of an existing physical LAN. An existing LAN segment may consist of 10 computers physically connected as a LAN. Along comes the concept of a VLAN, and it defines three of those computers as belonging to VLAN1, with the remaining seven on VLAN2. To software running on the machines in VLAN1, the entire LAN consists of just three computers, and the other seven (although physically connected as if they were part of the same LAN) are not seen. This logical subnetting reduces traffic on the network by providing smaller (and more numerous) broadcast domains, and subnets can be created without needing to rewire or relocate hardware physically. VLANs are implemented through the use of IEEE 802.1Q, which allows the tagging of Ethernet frames with information that identifies which VLAN they belong to.

VNC—Virtual Network Computing

VNC is a remote display system where a user can view or control the desktop environment of a remote computer that may be across the room, or on the other side of the world over the Internet. When controlling, communication goes both ways—keyboard and mouse events are sent from the viewer (the client) to the remote machine, and the remote (the server) provides updates of the screen display back to the client. VNC works on a framebuffer level, and does not require higher-level protocols to display windows, text, animation and so on—all screen updates are purely image based. A user may connect to a server, use its desktop for a time, then disconnect and move to another location. Upon reconnecting to the server, the user will see the exact desktop, down to the mouse pointer being in the same place.

There are many VNC implementations; you can control two PCs from a single keyboard and mouse, attach to an existing session, and mix-and-match operating systems.

VoIP—Voice over IP

Using packet-switched networks to transmit voice traffic instead of the traditional circuit-switched networks. Packet-switching allows the physical circuits to carry far more traffic.

VPN—Virtual Private Network

In its broadest sense, a network tunneled through another network. In the term's usage in this book, it is a tunnel used to connect trusted remote users (such as those on laptops working from home), or other remote networks (such as a branch office) into a LAN, so that the remote users may have full network access as if their computer were connected directly to the LAN. The connection is tunneled over the Internet, and the two endpoints authenticate to one another and encrypt communications. Think of it as a long, private Ethernet cable that extends over the Internet to your users in the field.

W

WAN—Wide Area Network

A Wide Area Network is a network that spans a large geographic area relative to a LAN. It will likely contain a paid network connection by a telecommunications provider, and cross legal (including national) boundaries. A school campus may consider its entire on-campus network to be a LAN (even if that supplies hundreds of buildings on the one site), and the connection to other campuses in different cities to be part of the WAN. On a different scale, a community wireless network may consider home computer networks of one or two machines to each be LANs, and the wireless network that connects them all across one part of a city to be their WAN. The Internet can be considered the largest of all WANs.

WAP—Wireless Access Point

The device that connects a wired LAN to a wireless network, and acts to move data between wireless devices and the wired LAN, or directly to the Internet. The WAP contains the antenna that transmits/receives wireless signals to/from any wireless-connected devices such as laptops, and is the device that implements the encryption required for good wireless security.

WEP—Wired Equivalent Privacy (or Wireless Encryption Protocol)

An encryption scheme used to secure wireless networks, part of the 802.11 standard. WEP is particularly weak protection, and vulnerable to an attacker within minutes using freely available tools such as AirSnort and WEPCrack. If your hardware only supports WEP, upgrade to something supporting WPA/WPA2. As of August 2003, Wi-Fi certification is not possible without WPA support.

Wi-Fi

Wi-Fi refers to standards (the 802.11 family) that define wireless networking most commonly used on LANs. While IEEE formally defines the 802.11 standards, testing and certification of products following the standard is performed by the Wi-Fi Alliance, an industry group formed to push the adoption of standard wireless networking. Only products tested by the Wi-Fi Alliance may carry the Wi-Fi trademark. Wi-Fi certification is a moving target that involves not just the wireless connection itself, but relevant technologies such as encryption, QoS, and power saving. As new wireless developments are ratified, the requirements for Wi-Fi certification change, too. One example is security; WPA2 certification is compulsory in order to obtain Wi-Fi certification as of 2006.

Winbind

A Name Service Switch (NSS) module that allows a Linux (and Unix/Unix-alike) system to join a Windows domain and obtain login information from the domain, instead of from the Linux system's local user database. Essentially, this means Windows domain users (NT or Active Directory) can appear and operate as Linux users on the Linux machine, and gain access to Windows domain services. Winbind is part of the Samba suite.

WINS—Windows Internet Name Service

WINS is Microsoft's name resolution service for NetBIOS computer names. A WINS server allows computers to register their NetBIOS names and IP addresses dynamically upon joining a network. A computer queries the WINS server by providing the NetBIOS name of a machine it is interested in, and the WINS server returns that machine's IP address. WINS is essentially to NetBIOS names as DNS is to domain names. Under Linux, Samba is perfectly capable of acting as a WINS server.

WPA/WPA2—Wi-Fi Protected Access

Encryption schemes used to secure wireless networks. There are two flavors of WPA: WPA and WPA2. WPA is an upgrade of WEP; both use RC4 stream encryption. It was designed to be a transitional protocol between WEP and WPA2. WPA is stronger than WEP, but not as strong as WPA2. WPA2 uses a new strong encryption protocol called Counter Mode with CBC-MAC Protocol (CCMP), which is based on Advanced Encryption Standard (AES).

Linux Kernel Building Reference

This is a quick guide to building a custom 2.6 kernel, patching the kernel, and adding loadable kernel modules. You'll find detailed recipes in *Linux Cookbook* (O'Reilly) in Chapter 10, "Patching, Customizing, and Upgrading Kernels," and Chapter 12, "Managing the Bootloader and Multi-Booting," which tells how to customize your GRUB or LILO boot menus for different kernels.

Why would you want to build a custom kernel? To add features or remove unnecessary features. On routers and firewalls, it adds a bit of security to use kernels that have had all the unnecessary features removed, and you can reduce the size considerably to fit on devices with limited storage.

Building a Custom Kernel

Many distributions have their own distribution-specific tools for building kernels. You don't need these for building vanilla kernels from *kernel.org*. But, it's a different story when you're using distribution-specific kernel sources. Red Hat and Fedora package theirs as source RPMs, so you can't just build the kernel, but must also build an RPM. Fear not, for this appendix reveals how. Red Hat/Fedora kernels are heavily patched, to the point that a vanilla kernel may not even work, so you need to know the Red Hat Way of customizing kernels.

Debian, on the other hand, does very little modification to Linux kernels. They remove any bits that don't meet their policies, and that's all. So, vanilla kernels work fine on Debian systems.

You'll need a build environment, kernel source code for your distribution, and at least 2 GB of free disk space. You can build a kernel on any system, then copy it to other systems. If you like to modify kernels a lot, you might set up an old PC as a dedicated kernel-building station. Then, you'll only have to maintain source trees and utilities on a single box.

Most documentation tells you to unpack kernel sources into */usr/src/linux*. Don't do this. As the kernel *README* says:

> Do NOT use the */usr/src/linux* area! This area has a (usually incomplete) set of kernel headers that are used by the library header files. They should match the library, and not get messed up by whatever the kernel-du-jour happens to be.

You may store binaries and source trees anywhere, and execute almost every step as an unprivileged user. Only the final steps require superuser privileges.

You may install as many kernels as you like, selecting the one you want to use at boot.

Prerequisites

You need a build environment and some helpful utilities. You should have the *lshw* and *lspci* commands installed in case you need to look up hardware information. Run the *update-pciids* command first to bring them up-to-date. Run `cat /proc/cpuinfo` to display your CPU specs.

Next, on Fedora, install these packages to get a basic build environment:

```
# yum groupinstall 'Development Tools'
# yum install qt-devel
```

On Debian, install these packages:

```
# aptitude install build-essential libqt3-mt-dev qt3-dev-tools
```

Building a Vanilla Kernel

Obtaining a kernel that has not been altered by distribution vendors is easy—go to *http://kernel.org/*, the mothership of the Linux kernel. Download and unpack it into a folder in your own home directory; for example *~/kernel*:

```
[carla@windbag:~/kernel]$ wget http://kernel.org/pub/linux/kernel/v2.6/linux-2.6.20.1
[carla@windbag:~/kernel]$ tar zxvf linux-2.6.20.1
```

This is about a 40 MB download that will unpack to about 240 MB.

Change to the top-level directory of your new source tree. All of the following commands will be run from here:

```
$ cd linux-2.6.20.1
```

Read the *Documentation/Changes* file to make sure you have the correct *gcc* version and other necessary utilities. Read the README for installation tips and other useful information.

Edit the new kernel makefile (*~/kernel/linux-2.6.20.1/Makefile*) to give a custom value to EXTRAVERSION, such as EXTRAVERSION =-test. Or, in the kernel configuration, enter your custom value in General Setup → Local version → append to kernel release.

Let's see what options the *make* command has:

```
$ make help
```

Even though this is a brand-new source tree, run a cleanup first:

```
$ make mrproper
```

At this point, you may copy your own custom *config* file to this directory, or just let *make* take care of it for you. If you don't provide one, it will use your */boot/config-** file. You can change everything anyway, so it doesn't matter all that much.

Now, run these commands:

```
$ make xconfig
$ make
$ su
# make modules_install
# mkinitrd -o /boot/initrd-linux-2.6.20.1
# cp linux-2.6.20.1/arch/i386/boot/bzImage /boot/vmlinuz-linux-2.6.20.1
# cp linux-2.6.20.1/System.map  /boot/System.map-linux-2.6.20.1
```

Save a copy of your new *config* file in a directory outside of the build tree. Add the new kernel to your GRUB bootloader menu:

```
# /boot/grub/menu.lst
title    new test kernel
root     (hd0,0)
kernel   /boot/vmlinuz-2.6.20.1 root=UUID=b099f554-db0b-45d4-843e-0d6a1c43ba44 ro
initrd   /boot/initrd-2.6.20.1
```

Where does the UUID come from? From running the *blkid* command:

```
$ blkid
/dev/sda1: UUID="b099f554-db0b-45d4-843e-0d6a1c43ba44" SEC_TYPE="ext2" TYPE="ext3"
/dev/hda1: UUID="1a5408ad-7d1d-4e24-b9db-d132d76e9e8e" SEC_TYPE="ext2" TYPE="ext3"
```

Remember that GRUB counts from zero, so hd0,0 means */dev/hda1*, or the first partition of the first block device. In this era of mixed PATA and SATA drives, this depends on the BIOS order of your hard drives, so you may need to dig around in your BIOS settings to see which drive the BIOS recognizes as the first, second, and so forth.

Reboot to your new kernel and enjoy. If it doesn't work, simply reboot to your old kernel, and try again.

You should use UUIDs to identify your block devices because */dev* names are no longer static, but at the mercy of *udev*. You need to create an *initrd* image because the */dev* directory is not populated until after boot, so there is no way to build the boot device into the kernel anymore.

Configuration Options

make xconfig is time-consuming, but very important. If you leave out anything important, some things won't work, or it might not boot at all. Every configuration item has a Help entry. The kernel source tree has reams of help in the *Documentation/* directory.

You have three options for each configuration item: leave it out, build it into the kernel, or build it as a loadable module. These things should be built-in to the kernel:

- Module support and *kmod*, for automatic module loading
- *a.out* binaries, ELF binaries, and MISC binaries
- VGA text console
- All filesystems you'll be using, such as ext2/3, ReiserFS, JFS, XFS, loopback, VFAT, NTFS, UDF, etc.

Any hardware support related to boot devices should be built into the kernel:

- IDE, ATA, and ATAPI block devices
- SCSI support (note that the 2.6 kernel does not need IDE-SCSI, so if you have no SCSI devices, you can omit this)
- USB support
- Any on-board controllers
- ACPI power management

These are fine to have as loadable modules:

- NIC drivers
- Netfilter/*iptables*
- USB drivers
- Sound card drivers
- PCI hotplug
- Video drivers

It doesn't matter if you prefer a large statically built kernel, or a lean kernel with lots of loadable modules. Don't obsess over building the leanest possible kernel because it doesn't matter—performance is the same either way. Just be sure to enable loadable module support so that you can add additional modules as needed; this is a lot quicker and easier than rebuilding a kernel. Your best chance of improving performance is to select support for your particular CPU, rather than generic i386.

Adding New Loadable Kernel Modules

Change to the directory that contains the build tree, like *~/kernel/linux-2.6.20.1*. Then, you'll need a good up-to-date *config* file. Copy it to the top level of your build tree, then run:

```
$ make oldconfig
```

This takes your existing configuration, and lets you add new features. As you go through the configuration, find the driver you need, and select it as a module. For example, the *tulip* module is a common driver for many Ethernet cards. Then, run these commands:

```
$ make dep
$ make modules
# make modules_install
# depmod -av
```

Load the module with *modprobe*:

```
# modprobe tulip
```

If you remembered to enable *kmod* in the kernel configuration, the kernel will try to find and load all necessary modules at boot. If it doesn't, add them to */etc/modules* (Debian) or */etc/modules.conf* (most other Linux distributions).

Vendor-supplied modules come with their own installation instructions. For example, Nvidia provides a script that does everything for you. Others have different methods, so it all depends on the vendor.

Patching a Kernel

If you wish to apply patches to your new kernel, this must be done before building it. The patch must be in the next-highest directory upstream from your build tree; for example:

```
$ ls ~/kernel
linux-2.6.20.1 patch-2.6.22.1.bz2
```

Now, change to the top level of your build tree, then unpack and apply the patch:

```
$ cd linux-2.6.20.1
$ bzip2 -dc ../patch-2.6.22.1.bz2 | patch -s -p1
```

Or, you can do a test-drive first with the --dry-run option:

```
$ bzip2 -dc ../patch-2.6.22.1.bz2 | patch -s -p1 --dry-run
```

Now, configure and build your kernel, and away you go.

Your kernel build tree includes a script to handle applying patches for you, in *scripts/ patch-kernel*. This is a great little script when you have several patches to apply because it automatically applies them in the correct order. Have all of your patches in the correct directory; then, from your top-level source directory, run this command:

```
[carla@windbag:~/kernel/linux-2.6.20.1]$ scripts/patch-kernel
```

Patches must be applied in order, and you must have all of them. For example, to use *patch-2.6.22.1-pre3.bz2*, you also need the first two in the series, unless you downloaded a kernel that already includes the first set of patches.

Customizing Fedora Kernels

Fedora patches kernels heavily; a vanilla kernel from *kernel.org* may or may not work. So, let's do this the 100 percent Fedora way.

Fedora supplies only source RPMs, so you'll have to customize your kernel and then package it into an RPM. Download your kernel SRPM from your favorite Fedora mirror, such as:

```
$ wget http://mirrors.kernel.org/fedora/core/development/source/SRPMS/kernel-2.6.21-
1.3194.fc7.src.rpm
```

Then, make sure you have all the build tools you need:

```
# yum install rpmdevtools
```

Now, set up a build tree in your home directory, and make sure to do this as yourself and not as the *root* user:

```
$ fedora-buildrpmtree
```

This creates an *rpmbuildtree* directory populated with *BUILD*, *RPMS*, *SOURCES*, *SPECS*, and *SRPMS* directories.

Now, install the source RPM. This will unpack files into your new *rpmbuildtree* directory:

```
$ rpm -ivh 2.6.21-1.3194.fc7.src.rpm
```

Ignore any warnings about "group kojibuilder does not exist."

Next, run the *%prep* stage of the RPM rebuild. Make the `--target` option match your CPU type:

```
$ rpmbuild -bp --target=i686 ~/rpmbuild/SPECS/kernel-2.6.spec
```

The kernel tarball has been extracted, and all the Fedora patches applied. Change to the source directory of your new build tree:

```
$ cd ~/rpmbuild/BUILD/kernel-2.6.21/linux-2.6.21-1.3194.i686/
```

Do housecleaning:

```
$ make mrproper
```

Now, let's get started with configuring the new kernel:

```
$ make xconfig
```

And, finally:

```
$ rpmbuild --target i686 -ba ~/rpmbuild/SPECS/kernel-2.6.spec
```

Again, make the --target option match your CPU type.

This builds the *kernel.rpm*, the *kernel-devel.rpm*, and rebuilds the *kernel.src.rpm* with your custom *config* included. The new binary kernel RPM is in *~/rpmbuild/RPMS/ i686/*. Grab your new *kernel.rpm*, and install it just like any other RPM:

```
# rpm -ivh kernel-2.6.21-1.3194.i686.rpm
```

Then, reboot and enjoy your new kernel.

Customizing Debian Kernels

Debian users can employ either vanilla kernels, or have the option to fetch official Debian kernel sources with *aptitude*. You should also install *kernel-package* and *fakeroot*:

```
# aptitude install linux-source-2.6.22 kernel-package fakeroot
```

This downloads the source tarball into */usr/src/*, so you need to move it to your personal kernel-building directory:

```
# mv /usr/src/linux-source-2.6.20.tar.bz2 ~/kernel
```

Remember that dpkg -L [package name] shows you all the installed files in a package if you can't find them.

Change to your ordinary user, change to your kernel directory, and unpack the tarball:

```
$ su carla
$ cd ~/kernel
$ tar zxvf linux-source-2.6.20.tar.bz2
```

Then, change to the top-level source directory, and start configuring your new kernel:

```
$ cd linux-source-2.6.20
$ make mrproper
$ make xconfig
```

When you're done slogging through configuration, run these commands:

```
$ make-kpkg clean
$ make-kpkg -rootcmd fakeroot -rev test.1 linux_image
```

This produces a *.deb* package named *linux-image-2.6.20_test.1_i686.deb*, which you can install in the usual way with *dpkg*:

```
# dpkg -i linux-image-2.6.20_test.1_i686.deb
```

This should put everything where it belongs and create a GRUB menu entry.

fakeroot fools the system into thinking you are the *root* user when you're not. It won't let you run commands that need genuine *root* privileges, but it's good enough for kernel-building.

Debian's binary kernel packages are named *linux-image-**, and the kernel source packages are named *linux-source-**. It has been this way since the 2.6.12 kernel; before then, they were called *kernel-image-** and *kernel-source-**. The new naming convention is in hopes of allowing other kernels to be used with Debian in addition to the Linux kernel.

See Also

- The Red Hat manuals also apply to Fedora; find them at:

  https://www.redhat.com/docs/manuals/enterprise/

- Fedora's own documentation is getting more thorough:

  http://docs.fedoraproject.org/

- The Debian Reference Manual has everything you need to know about Debian, including kernel building:

  http://www.debian.org/doc/manuals/reference/

Index

Numbers

32-bit Cardbus adapters, 10
3FFE::/16 addresses, 441
6Bone test network, 441
6to4 tunnels, 450

A

access keyword, 412
Active Directory, 566
    Active Directory domains, joining Linux
      hosts to, 319–323
    adding Poptop servers to, 298
AGP (Accelerated Graphics Port), 566
AllowGroups, 216
AllowUsers, 216
analog telephone adapters (ATA), 125
Andreasson, Oskar, 36
antenna diversity, turning off, 115
anycast addresses, 441
Apache, configuring for Nagios, 376–378
apt-cache command, 340
apt-mirror application, 468
apt-proxy application, 470
areas, 174
arping, 523
Asterisk, 123–127
    activation and making calls, 146–148
    applications, 141
    Asterisk.org, 128
    AsteriskNOW, 168–171
      installation and removal of packages
        on, 170

conferencing, 163
    conference types, 163
    monitoring conferences, 165
dialplans, 141
digital receptionists, creating, 151
extensions.conf, 137, 141
hold music, customizing, 161
IAX traffic, getting through NAT
    firewalls, 168
identifying unmet dependencies, 129
installation, versions 1.2 compared to
    1.4, 130
installing on Debian, 131
    apt-get, 131
    module-assistant utility, 131
invention of, 125
making calls, 136
message of the day maintenance, 156–158
MP3 files, playing, 161
parking calls, 159
PBX connection to analog lines, 148–151
phone calls, 138
phone extensions, adding to, 136–143
    local user accounts, setup, 136
production hardware and software, 124
recording custom prompts, 153–156
remote usage, 171
routing calls to groups of phones, 158
SIP traffic, getting through NAT
    firewalls, 166
sip.conf, 138
softphones, 143–145
source code installation, 127–131
    Linux build environment, 128

We'd like to hear your suggestions for improving our indexes. Send email to *index@oreilly.com*.

Asterisk (continued)
    starting and stopping, 132–135
        shutdown commands, 134
        startup files, 133
    supported IP telephony services, 123
    testing the server, 135
    test-lab hardware and software, 124
    transferring calls, 158
    voicemail broadcasts, 162
    voicemail.conf, 137, 142
ATM, 566
attributes, 334

B

bandwidth, 6
Bastille Linux, 43
bastion hosts, 37
Baud, 567
Bering uClibc, 43
Berkeley DB, 332
BGP (Border Gateway Protocol), 174
BGP Expert 2006 IPv4 Address Use
        Report, 438
BIOS (Basic Input/Output System), 567
boot
    Nagios, starting at, 390
    OpenVPN, boot startup
        configuration, 281
    PXE boot, 452
    time update at, 121
    USB boot, 453
boot.iso, 454
BOOTPROTO configuration option, 50
Border Gateway Protocol (see BGP)
bridging, 567
broadcasting, 567

C

ca.crt, 106
cable services, 2, 3
cabling, 11
    straight and crossover cables, 45
cachesize, 361
cache-size option, dnsmasq.conf, 118
Cardbus adapters, 10
Cat5, Cat5e, and Cat6 cabling, 11
CCMP (Counter Mode with CBC-MAC
        Protocol), 84
CentOS 5.0, 127
certificates, 568
    OpenVPN, revocation under, 282
CF (Compact Flash) cards, Pyramid Linux
        installation on, 17
cfgmaker command, 416
chains, 40

check_icmp, 392
Chicken of the VNC, 229
CIDR (Classless Inter-Domain Routing), 568
    notation, 178
        common netmasks, 176
circuit switching, 569
Classless Inter-Domain Routing (see CIDR)
code examples, xxi
codec, 568
collision domain, 569
com2sec keyword, 411
command-line operation of Quagga
        daemons, 195
community string, 411, 569
Compact Flash writers, 18
computer networks (see networks)
condrestart, 208, 313
conferencing, 163
consoles, 569
contexts, 141
continuity testers, 516
Counter Mode with CBC-MAC Protocol
        (CCMP), 84
CPE (customer premises equipment), 569
cron, scheduling dial-up availability with, 510
crontabs, 511
CSU/DSU (Channel Service Unit/Data Service
        Unit), 569

D

daemons file (Quagga), 188
DB_CONFIG file, 343
db_stat, 359
DD-WRT, 83
Debian, xx
    booting to text mode, 487
    kernel characteristics, 590
    kernels, customizing, 596
    MPPE support, kernel patches for, 291
    network installation of Pyramid
        Linux, 19–21
    network installs, 466
        automation with preseed files, 475
        building a mirror with apt-mirror, 468
        client PC configuration for your local
            mirror, 471
        new system installs from your local
            mirror, 474
        partial mirror with apt-proxy, 470
        PXE Netboot server setup, 472
    NIC configuration on, 45
    OpenLDAP installation on, 339
    RIP dynamic routing, using on, 187
    RIP implementation, 187–191
    Samba, supporting packages in, 308

security updates, 472
SSL key creation for Syslog
     services, 551–557
Debian Router, 43
default gateways, setting, 178–180
   for static hosts, 179
demarc, 570
demilitarized zones (DMZs), 37
DenyGroups, 216
DenyHosts, 216, 223
   cron versus daemon operation, 224
   options, 224
   startup file, creating, 225
Destination NAT (see DNAT)
Development Tools package, 128
DEVICE configuration option, 49
DHCP (Dynamic Host Configuration
     Protocol), 570
dhcpd.conf, 465
dialplans, 141
dial-up networking, 501
   call waiting, overriding, 512
   cron, scheduling dial-up availability
     with, 510
   dial-on-demand shared Internet
     dial-up, 509
   dial-up Internet account sharing, 508
   group ownership by root, 506
   separate pppd logfiles, creating, 514
   voicemail stutter tones, dialing over, 512
   WvDial, 502
     accounts for nonroot users,
       creating, 507
     leaving the password out of the
       configuration file, 513
     multiple accounts, configuring, 504
     permissions for nonroot users,
       configuring, 505
     single account configuration, 501–504
dial-up services, 4
dig command, 117
directory information tree (DIT), 333, 337
directory objects, 334
diskboot.img, 454
distance-vector routing algorithm, 173
distinguished names (see DNs)
DIT (directory information tree), 333, 337
Dixon, Jim, 126
DMZs (demilitarized zones), 37
dn2id.bdb, 359
DNAT (Destination NAT), 38
   directing traffic to private services, 70
DNs (distinguished names), 334
DNS (Domain Name System), 570
DNS cache management, Windows
     caches, 120

DNS clients, troubleshooting, 545
DNS servers, troubleshooting, 542–545
dnsmasq, 90, 96
   adding mail servers, 96
   cache flags, 119
   DNS cache management, 117–120
dnsmasq.conf, 91
   server representation in, 110
domain (Windows), 570
domain component, 335
dotted-quad netmask notation, 176, 178
dpkg command, 340
DSA keys, 211
DSL (Digital Subscriber Line), 2, 570
DSL services, 4
duplicate IP addresses, finding, 523
dynamic address, 571

E

EAP-TLS authentication, 101
ebtables, 89
EGP (Exterior Gateway Protocol), 174
encryption, 571
entries, 334
environment file (Quagga), 189
eq index type, 355
/etc/iftab, 46
/etc/network/interfaces, 46
Etherboot project, 453
Ethernet, 571
Ethernet bridges, 88–89, 107, 567
   OpenVPN servers, setting up to use, 284
   versus routing, 108
extensions, 141
extensions.conf, 137, 141
   calls, transferring, 158
Exterior Gateway Protocol (EGP), 174
exterior protocols, 174

F

Fast Ethernet, 571
Fedora
   customizing kernels, 595
   implementing RIP, 191
   ipcalc command version, 176
   kernel characteristics, 590
   LDAP installation on, 341
   mirrors page, 460
   MPPE support, kernel patches for, 294
   network installation of Pyramid
     linux, 21–24
   network installs
     boot media, creating, 453
     boot media, using, 455–457

Fedora *(continued)*
    customized installations,
      creating, 461–463
    FTP-based installation server
      setup, 458–460
    HTTP installation server setup, 457
    kickstart file installation, 463
    PXE Netboot, 464
    NIC configuration, 48–50
    OpenLDAP database, creating, 344–347
    Poptop pptpd, installing on, 293
    Samba, supporting packages in, 308
    SSL key creation for Syslog, 557–558
filter table, 41
firewall boxes, assembling network
    interfaces, 45
firewalls, 36–43
    DMZs, 37
    firewall boxes, assembling, 44
      cabling, 45
      required hardware, 44
    firewall init script, 60
    getting multiple SSH host keys past
      NAT, 68
    Internet sharing on dynamic WAN IP
      addresses, 51–55
    Internet sharing on static WAN IP
      addresses, 56
    iptables, 38, 40–42
      firewall setup on a server, 76–78
      firewall shutdown, 58
      logging configuration, 79
    manual activation and manual
      shutdown, 59
    need for, 39
    NIC configuration on Debian, 45
    public and private servers, 37
    public services on private IP addresses, 69
    remote SSH administration through NAT
      firewalls, 66
    remote SSH administration, configuration
      for, 65
    security of, 43
    single-host firewalls, setting up, 71–75
    specialized Linux distributions for, 42
    status, displaying, 57
    testing, 62–64
fox and hound pairs, 516
FPing, 521
FQDN (Fully Qualified Domain Name), 571
fractional T1 lines, 5
frame relay, 5, 571
FREE ciSCO, 42
Free World Dialup (FWD), 146

FreeNX, 228
    advantages, tunneling over Unix, 238
    custom desktop configuration, 242–244
    generating and managing SSH keys, 233
    managing FreeNX users, 239
    Nxclient (see Nxclient)
    running Linux from Solaris, Mac OS X, or
      Linux, 238
    running Linux from Windows, 233–237
    Session menu, 245
    source of older NoMachine clients, 237
    starting and stopping the server, 241
    troubleshooting, 247
    "Unable to create the X authorization
      cookie" message, 236
FreeRADIUS, 101
    clients, authenticating to, 106
    permissions, 103
    testing, 103
Fully Qualified Domain Name, 571
fw_flush script, 58
fw_nat script, 52, 56
FWD (Free World Dialup), 146
FXS/FXO, 571

G

Gast, Matthew, 84
gateway address assignment, 47
gateways, 2, 37, 178–180
    configuration definitions, 47
    default gateways, 270
    hardware options for Linux gateways, 7
    single-board computers, building
      on, 12–35
      required hardware, 13
      required software, 14
    (see also firewalls)
getty, 481
Gigabit Ethernet, 10, 571
Gnome remote desktop sharing, 230
GQ LDAP client, 334
GRE (Generic Routing Encapsulation), 572
group keyword, 412
GRUB (GRand Unified Bootloader), 572

H

Hardware Access Layer (HAL) blobs, 83
hardware IP phones (hardphones), 124
Heimdal Kerberos, 309
high-end enterprise routers, 7
Hosner, Charlie, 267
host keys, 207
    generating and copying, 211
    host-key authentication, 206, 209

hostapd, 84, 97–100
hostapd.conf, MAC address-based access
    control, 100
hostname command, 175
httping, 525
hub, 572
hubs versus switches, 8
HWADDR configuration option, 49

I

IAX (Inter-Asterisk eXchange), 572
ICMP, 39
id2entry.bdb, 359
IDE Compact Flash writers, 18
identity keys, 207
ifconfig -a, 46
ifrename, 46, 47
ifup and ifdown commands, 47, 93
ifup eth1 command, 54
Inter-Asterisk Exchange (IAX), 125
interface, 572
Internet, 1
Internet Assigned Numbers Authority
    (IANA), 440
Internet connection sharing
    NAT and, 182
    simplest configuration, 183–184
Internet gateways, 37
IOS (Internet Operating System), 573
IP, 39, 573
IP addresses
    Debian, assignment on, 46
    Fedora, assignment on, 48
    gateway address assignment, 49
    static addresses, setting from DHCP
      services, 93
ip command, 175, 445
    setting null routes in zebra.conf, 198
IP forwarding, 182
IP Masquerading, 575
IP Multicast, 575
IP phones, 124
IP routing, 581
IP telephony services, 123
IPADDR configuration option, 50
ipcalc command
    Fedora version, differences in, 176
    options, 178
ipcalc commsnd, 176
IPCop, 42
iperf, 535–537
iproute2 command, 178
IPSec, 266, 573

IPSec VPN, 288
iptables, 36, 38, 40–42, 59
    boot activation, 59
    built-in modules and implementation by
      differing kernels, 55
    chains, 40
    commands for displaying firewall
      status, 57
    configuration to allow Poptop VPN
      traffic, 300
    custom kernel modules, 41
    firewall testing, 63
    handling by different Linux
      distributions, 61
    Internet connection sharing over a dynamic
      WAN address, 52–55
    kernel level operation, 55
    logging configuration, 79
    mangle table, 41
    NAT table, 41
    policies and rules, 40
    running public services on private IP
      addresses, configuration, 69
    script for single-host firewalls, 71
    server firewalls, setting up, 76
    shared dial-up Internet accounts, rules
      for, 508
    simple Internet sharing script, 183
    tables in, 41
    TCP/IP headers and, 39
    turning off firewalls, 58
IPv4 private address ranges, 177
IPv6, 437–442
    addressing, 439–442
      address types and ranges, 440
      addresses, shortcuts for expressing, 446
      calculating addresses, 449
      global unicast addresses, 439
      hexadecimal format, 441
      interface ID, 440
      quantity of available addresses, 438
    autoconfiguration, 448
    barriers to adoption, 438
    copying files with scp, 447
    IPv4 compared to, 438
    Linux systems, testing for support of, 442
    Mac OS X, support in, 442
    Microsoft Windows, support in, 442
    pinging Link Local IPv6 hosts, 443–446
    SSH, using with, 446
    using over the Internet, 450
ipv6calc command, 449
ISDN (Integrated Services Digital
    Network), 573

ISPs (Internet Service Providers)
    cable services, 3
    choosing, 2
    dial-up services, 4
    DSL services, 4
    potential problems, 4
    private networks, 6
    regulated broadband services, 5
    service options, 3–7
    types of service, 2
iwlist, 113

J

J2ME VNC, 230
jumbo frames, 9

K

KDC (Key Distribution Center), 574
KDE remote desktop sharing, 230
Kerberos, 574
kernel building reference, 590–597
    custom kernels, 590
        adding new loadable kernel
            modules, 594
        configuration options, 593
        customizing Debian, 596
        customizing Fedora, 595
        patching, 594
        prerequisites, 591
        vanilla kernels, 591
Kickstart, 461
    hands-off Fedora installation, 463
known_hosts file, 210
Konqueror, 330
krdc command, 230
Kwlan, 100

L

L2TP/IPsec-based VPNs, 288
LANs (Local Area Networks), 574
    mixed Linux/Windows (see Samba)
latency, 6
LDAP (Lightweight Directory Access
        Protocol), 332–338, 574
    DB_CONFIG file, 343
    directory design considerations, 337
    directory information tree, 333
    directory structure, 333
    objectClass, 335
    OpenLDAP (see OpenLDAP)
    rootDSE, 336

ldapadd, 349
ldapmodify, 350
ldappasswd, 370
ldapsearch, 353
ldapwhoami, 370
LDIF (LDAP Data Interchange Format)
        file, 345
Lighttpd, 413
Lighttpd HTTP server, 457
Lightweight Directory Access Protocol (see
        LDAP)
LILO (LInux LOader), 575
Link Local address, finding with ifconfig, 444
Link Local Unicast address, 441
link-state algorithm, 174
LinNeighborhood, 331
Linux, xx
    installation over networks (see network
        installs)
    mini-distributions for firewalls and Internet
        gateways, 509
Linux PPTP VPN servers, 287–290
    connecting Linux clients to, 299
    Debian, installing Poptop on, 290
    Debian, patching for MPPE support, 291
    Fedora, patching for MPPE support, 294
    iptables configuration to allow Poptop
        VPN traffic, 300
    Linux requirements, 289
    monitoring, 301
    Poptop pptpd, installation on Fedora, 293
    Poptop server adding to Active
        Directory, 298
    PPTP security, 288
    standalone server setup, 295–298
    troubleshooting, 302–304
    Windows client update requirements, 288
LoadMIBs option, 420
local-ttl option, dnsmasq.conf, 118
locate command, 429
lrzsz package, 499

M

MAC addresses, 94
    finding, 46
Mac OS X, IPv6 support, 442
make menuselect, 129
mangle table, 41
Masquerading, 575
MDI/MDI-X (medium dependent
        interfaces), 9
meetme command, 165

meetme.conf, 165
Metrix.net, 13
mgetty, 481
MIB (Management Information Base), 575
MIB (Management Information Browser), 409
    MIB tree access controls, 411
Microsoft Windows
    ACLs and Windows filesystems, 247
    Active Directory, 566
        adding Poptop servers to, 298
        domains, joining Linux hosts
            to, 319–323
    DNS cache management, 120
    IPv6 support, 442
    Linux, connecting to with, 230–232
    MPPE, 575
    networking issues, 307
    remote desktop connections to, 228
    Samba, replacing NT4 domain controllers
        with, 305
    security, 38
    tunneling TightVNC to Linux, 262–264
    Windows machines, setting up as
        OpenVPN clients, 286
    Windows PPTP servers, connecting Linux
        clients to, 299
    WINS (Windows Internet Name
        Service), 588
    X-Lite softphone, 143
MIMO (multiple-input/output), 116
Minicom, 14, 495
    multiple profiles, configuring, 17
mirroring, 8
MIT Kerberos, 309
modems, 482, 575
MP3 files, playing on Asterisk, 161
MPPE (Microsoft Point-to-Point
        Encryption), 575
MPPE kernel module, building for
        Debian, 291
    building for Fedora, 294
MRTG (Multi-Router Traffic Graph), 408
    active CPU load, monitoring, 419–422
    cfgmaker command, 416
    configuration file, creating, 413
    CPU user and idle times, monitoring, 422
    Debian, configuring and starting
        on, 415–417
    disk usage, monitoring, 426
    Fedora, configuring and starting on, 418
    HTTP service configuration for, 413
    installing, 409
    MIBs and OIDs, finding and
        testing, 429–430

mrtg.cfg file, 416
    configuring to monitor CPU load, 419
    monitoring CPU user and idle
        times, 422
    options, 420
    multiple MRTG index pages, creating, 433
    physical memory, monitoring, 424
    remote hosts, monitoring, 432
    running as a daemon, 434–436
    SNMP, dependency on, 408
    snmpd, testing for operation, 410
    swap space and memory, monitoring, 425
    TCP connections, monitoring, 428
MSRC4 DSM plug-in, 229
mtr (My Traceroute) utility, 528
Multicast addressing, 441, 575
multimeters, 516
multiple-input/output (MIMO), 116
Multi-Router Traffic Graph (see MRTG)

N

Nagios, 371
    Apache, configuring for, 376–378
    CGI permissions, configuring for Nagios
        web access, 389
    configuration files, organizing, 378–380
    DNS and DHCP servers, monitoring, 403
    grouping related services with
        servicegroups, 402
    installing from source code, 372–376
    localhost monitoring
        configuration, 380–389
    mail servers, monitoring, 400–402
    remote administration with OpenSSH,
        setting up, 405
    remote administration with OpenSSL,
        setting up, 406
    speeding up with check_icmp, 392
    SSHD, monitoring, 393–396
    starting at boot, 390
    users, adding, 391
    web servers, monitoring, 397–399
name services, setting up, 90–92
naming context, 335
NAS (Network Access Server), 576
NAT (Network Address Translation), 38, 576
NAT table, 41
Nautilus, 330
ncache, 362
ndiswrapper, 51, 82
Netfilter FAQ, 36
Netgate.com, 13
NETMASK configuration option, 50

netmasks, 176
net-snmp, 409
netstat command, 52, 62, 64, 174, 549
netstat-nat command, 56
net-tools package, 174
Network Address Translation (NAT), 38, 576
network installs, 452
    Debian, 466
        automation with preseed files, 475
        building a mirror with apt-mirror, 468
        client PC configuration for your local
            mirror, 471
        new system installs from your local
            mirror, 474
        partial Debian mirrors with
            apt-proxy, 470
        PXE Netboot server setup, 472
    Fedora
        creating network install boot media
            for, 453
        customized installations,
            creating, 461–463
        FTP-based installation server
            setup, 458–460
        install using boot media, 455–457
        kickstart file installation, 463
        PXE Netboot, 464
        setting up an HTTP installation server
            for, 457
    ndiswrapper, problems with, 467
    PXE boot, 452
    USB boot, 453
network interfaces, 45
network restart command, 93
network troubleshooting, 515
    arping, finding duplicate IP addresses
        with, 523
    cabling, testing and tracing, 516
    DNS clients, 545
    DNS servers, 542–545
    FPing and Nmap, network profiling
        with, 521–523
    HTTP throughput and latency testing, 525
    measuring throughput and packet
        loss, 535–537
    network diagnostic and repair
        laptops, 516–519
    network monitoring with ntop, 540–542
    packet sniffing with ngrep, 538–540
    ping, 519
    POP3, POP3s, and IMAP servers, 549–551
    SMTP servers, 546–548
    spare equipment, 516
    SSL key creation for Syslog services on
        Debian, 551–557

    SSL key creation for Syslog services on
        Fedora, 557–558
    stunnel setup for Syslog-ng, 558
    Syslog servers, building, 560–562
    TCP flags, capturing with tcpdump, 533
    traceroute, tcptraceroute, and
        mtr, 527–529
    traffic, capturing and analyzing, 529–533
networking
    dial-up (see dial-up networking)
    Internet connection sharing between
        wireless and wired clients, 87
    Linux and Windows static DHCP client
        configuration, 94
    mail servers, adding to dnsmasq, 96
    networking commands, 174
    static IP addresses, setting from DHCP
        services, 93
networking restart command, 93
NetworkManager, 100, 107
networks, 1
    areas, 174
    bandwidth, latency, and throughput, 6
    Internet connections, 1
    mixed networks, integration of (see Samba)
    Nagios, monitoring with (see Nagios)
    troubleshooting (see network
        troubleshooting)
    wireless networking, 11
next hop, 180
next hop routers, 178
ngrep, 538–540
NICs (network interface cards), 10, 576
    configuration on Debian, 45
    Fedora, configuration on, 48–50
    identifying, 50
Nmap, 523
nmap, 62
nmap command, 63
nmbd, 312
NoMachine, 229
    source of older clients, 237
no-negcache option, dnsmasq.conf, 118
NSS (Name Service Switch), 577
ntop, 540–542
NTP (Network Time Protocol), 577
ntpdate, 121
null modem cable, 577
NVRAM (Non-Volatile Random Access
    Memory), 577
Nxclient
    creating additional Nxclient sessions, 244
    file and printer sharing, and
        multimedia, 246
    prevention of password saving in, 246
    watching users from a FreeNX server, 240

O

Object IDs (see OIDs)
objectClass, 335
objectClass definitions, 334
OIDs (Object Identifiers), 335, 336, 577
 LoadMIBs option and, 420
ONBOOT configuration option, 50
Open Shortest Path First (see OSPF)
OpenLDAP, 332
 access controls, refining, 366–369
 Berkeley DB configuration
  logging configuration and
   performance, 362
 Debian, installing on, 339
 directory backup and restoration, 364–366
 directory entries, correcting, 350–351
 directory management with graphical
  interfaces, 356–358
 directory searches, 352–354
 Fedora, creating a database on, 344–347
 Fedora, installing on, 341
 indexing the database, 354
  indexes and id2entry file size, 355
 logging configuration, 363–364
 passwords, changing, 370
 remote OpenLDAP servers, connecting
  to, 352
  -H option to commands, 352
 schemas, 335
 server testing and configuration, 341–344
 Sleepycat Berkeley DB
  configuration, 358–363
 users, adding to the directory, 348–349
OpenSSH, 205–207
 alternate ports, finding, 219
 client configuration files, using for easier
  logins, 218
 components, 205
 configuration syntax, checking, 218
 DenyHosts startup file, creating, 225
 encryption algorithms, 205
 hardening, 215
 host-key setup, 209
 identity key management, 214
 keys, 207
  fingerprints, changing, 217
  generating and copying, 211
  labeling with comments, 222
 passphrases, changing, 216
 passphrases, creating, 208
 public-key authentication for protection of
  passwords, 213
 remote command execution without a
  remote shell, 221
 servers and clients, 207

SSH attacks, foiling with DenyHosts, 223
sshfs, mounting remote filesystems
 with, 226
starting and stopping, 207
supported authentication schemes, 206
tunneling, 205
tunneling X Windows over SSH, 220
 (see also SSH)
OpenVPN, 265–267
 bridge mode server setup, 284
 certificates, revoking, 282
 client configuration, 267
 configuring to start at boot, 281
 connecting Windows clients, 286
 encryption process, 266
 encryption, testing with static keys, 272
 PKI, creating, 276–279
 remote Linux clients, connection with
  static keys, 274
 running as a nonprivileged user, 285
 server configuration for multiple
  clients, 279–281
 starting and testing, 270–272
  "Connection refused" message, 271
  --ifconfig option, 271
 TAP/TUN drivers and, 267
 test lab setup, 267–270
  IP addresses setting, 269
OpenWRT, 83
organizational units (OUs), 334
OSPF (Open Shortest Path First), 174,
 199–201, 578
 ospfd, monitoring, 202
 security enhancements, 201
OSXvnc, 229
OUs (organizational units), 334

P

packet filtering, 578
packet switching, 578
packets, 39
PalmVNC Palm OS client, 230
PAM (Pluggable Authentication
 Modules), 578
passphrase-less Authentication, 206
passphrases, 208
passwords, protection with public-key
 authentication, 213
PBX (Private Branch eXchange), 123, 579
PC Engines boards, 12
 WRAP boards, 87
PC Weasel, 479
PCI (Peripheral Component
 Interconnect), 579
PCI adapters for telephony, 125

PCI bus, 10
PCI-Express, 10
PDC (Primary Domain Controller), 579
permissions, dial-up for nonroot users, 505
ping, 515, 519
ping6 command, 443
pkgsel command, 476
PKI (Public Key Infrastructure), 266, 579
    OpenVPN, creating for, 276–279
PocketPC VNCServer, 230
PocketPC VNCViewer VNC client, 230
Point-to-Point Tunneling Protocol (see PPTP)
polarization diversity, 116
pool.ntp.org, 121
Poptop pptpd, 289
    Active Directory, adding to, 298
    Debian Linux, installing on, 290
    Fedora kernel patches for MPPE
        support, 294
    Fedora Linux, installing on, 293
    iptables firewalls, getting PPTP traffic
        through, 300
    PPTP servers, monitoring, 301
    PPTP servers, troubleshooting, 302–304
    setting up a standalone PPTP VPN
        server, 295
port 22, 208, 216
port trunking, 9
PPP (Point-to-Point Protocol), 579
PPTP (Point-to-Point Tunneling
        Protocol), 287, 580
    (see also Linux PPTP VPN servers)
pres index type, 355
preseed, 475
priorities, 141
Private Branch eXchange (PBX), 123
private key passphrases, changing, 216
Protocol 2, 216
proute2 package, 175
Public Key Certificates, 568
Public Key Infrastructure (PKI), 266
public-key authentication, 206
    sudo and, 214
PXE boot, 452
    Debian PXE Netboot server setup, 472
Pyramid Linux, 12, 14, 43
    adding software, 28–31
    booting, 24
    DHCP and DNS services, 90
    Fedora, network installation on, 21–24
    getting and installing the latest build, 28
    hardening, 27
    hardware drivers, adding, 32
    hostapd, 97–100
    installation on CF card, 17
    kernel customization, 33
    making the filesystem writable, 88
    network installation on Debian, 19–21
    Pyramid files, finding and editing, 26
    router hostname, changing, 114
    wireless access points, using for, 86

Q

QoS (Quality of Service), 9, 580
Quagga, 188–191
    command-line operation, 192
    command-line operation of daemons, 195
    configuration file comments, 189
    configuration files, 188
    included routing daemons, 190
    OSPF dynamic routing, 199–201
    remote login to Quagga daemons, 194
    startup file, 189

R

RADIUS servers, using for wireless
        authentication, 100–104
radiusd.conf, 103
radvd (router advertising daemon), 448
RAS (Remote Access Service), 580
rdesktop, 228
    compatible Microsoft operating
        systems, 232
    Linux, connecting to Microsoft
        Windows, 230–232
RDNs (Relative Distinguished Names), 334
RDP (Remote Desktop Protocol), 228, 580
RealVNC, 229
records, 334
Red Hat Linux, xx
regional registrars, 439
regulated broadband services, 5
RELATED,ESTABLISHED rules, 54
Relative Distinguished Names (RDNs), 334
remote administration, 204
Remote Desktop Protocol (RDP), 228
remote graphical desktops, 228
    built-in remote desktop sharing, KDE and
        Gnome, 230
    custom desktop configuration, 242–244
    displaying windows to multiple remote
        users, 254–256
    FreeNX (see FreeNX)
    Microsoft Windows, connecting to, 228
    Nxclient (see Nxclient)
    rdesktop, 228
        Linux, connecting to Microsoft
            Windows, 230–232
    tunneling x11vnc over SSH, 261
    VNC, 229
RFC (Request for Comment), 581

RFC 2132 numbers, 110
RHEL (Red Hat Enterprise Linux), xx
RIP (Routing Information Protocol), 173,
    188, 581
    Debian, configuration on, 187–191
    default logging level, 190
    dynamic routing on Debian, 187
    Fedora set up, 191
    security enhancements, 201
    versions, 190
RIPD, monitoring, 197
ripd.conf (Quagga), 188
ripd.conf file definitions, 189
rootdn, 339
rootDSE, 336
rootpw, 339
route command, 178, 269
routerboards, 12
routers, 2, 37
    commercial routers, 8
    enabling Internet connection
        sharing, 183–184
    enterprise routers, 7
    hardware choices, 173
    hostname, changing under Pyramid
        Linux, 114
    inexpensive options, 45
    Internet connection sharing between wired
        and wireless clients, 87
    simple local routers, setting up, 180
        private addressing schemes, 182
routes, blackholing with zebra, 198
routing, 581
    interior routing protocols, 173
    OSPF for dynamic routing, 199–201
    persistent static routes, configuring, 186
    RIP (see RIP)
    static routing, configuration across
        subnets, 185
    wireless routing between two LAN
        segments, 108–113
Routing Information Protocol (see RIP)
RRAS (Routing and Remote Access
    Service), 580
RSA keys, 211

S

Samba, 305
    compilation from source code, 310
    hardware requirements, 306
    Linux clients, command-line utilities for
        connecting, 326–329
    Linux clients, graphical programs for
        connecting, 330

    primary domain controller, using
        as, 313–317
    required software, 307
    starting and stopping, 312
    supporting Debian and Fedora
        packages, 308
    Windows 95/98/ME, joining to Samba
        domains, 323
    Windows NT/2000, connecting to Samba
        domains, 325
    Windows NT4 domain controllers,
        migrating from, 317–319
    Windows NT4 domain controllers,
        replacing with, 305
    Windows NT4, connecting to Samba
        domains, 324
    Windows XP, connnecting to Samba
        domains, 325
SBCs (single-board computers), 12, 581
    wireless access points, using for, 86
    (see also Soekris 4521 boards)
Scope:Link address, 441
scp, copying files over IPv6, 447
Secure Sockets Layer (see SSL)
Secure Sockets Layer-based Virtual Private
    Networks (see SSL VPNs)
security
    adding to RIP and OSPF, 201
    Debian security updates, 472
    firewalls (see firewalls)
    hardening Pyramid Linux, 27
    MAC addresses and, 94
    serial connections, 496
    wireless networking, 84
Sentry Firewall, 42
serial consoles, 478, 582
    commercial consoles, 479
    logging, configuring, 497
    networks, connecting to, 478
    security, improving, 496
    servers, dialing into, 495
    servers, file uploads to, 498
    servers, preparing for administration
        by, 479
        BIOS serial console support,
            checking, 480
        modems, 482
    setting up, 489–491
    x86 PC BIOS and, 479
    (see also servers, preparing for headless
        operation)
serial ports, 480
servers, preparing for headless operation, 479
    configuration for dial-in
        administration, 492–494
    GRUB, configuration with, 485–487

servers, preparing for headless operation
  (continued)
    LILO, configuration with, 483–485
    (see also serial consoles)
services file (Quagga), 189
set_cachesize, 361
single-board computers (see SBCs)
SIP (Session Initiation Protocol), 582
sip.conf, 138
SLA (Service Level Agreement), 582
slapadd, 365
slapcat, 364
slapd.conf, 337, 339, 342
    indexing options, 354
    security concerns, 346
slapindex, 355
Sleepycat Berkeley DB, 332, 340
    configuring, 358–363
        logging configuration and
            performance, 362
Smb4k, 330
smbclient, 328
smbd, 312
smbmnt, 329
smbmount and smbumount, 329
smbtree, 327
SMTP servers, troubleshooting, 546–548
Smurf attack, 582
SNAT (Source NAT), 38, 56
SNMP (Simple Network Management
        Protocol), 408, 582
    Debian, configuring on, 410–412
    Fedora, configuring on, 413
    MRTG and, 408
    snmpd, manual startup using
        chkconfig, 410
    snmpd, testing for operation, 410
    snmpd.conf, 410
    testing remote SNMP characters, 430
snmpwalk, 410
    remote snmp queries, testing, 431
    syntax, 412
Soekris 4521 boards, 12, 14–17
    comBIOS, updating, 34
    Minicom, loading to, 14
    netbooting, 19–24
        Debian, using, 19–21
        Fedora, using, 21–24
    Pyramid Linux files, finding and
        editing, 26
    Pyramid Linux kernel, customizing, 33
    Pyramid Linux, adding software to, 28
    Pyramid Linux, booting, 24
    Pyramid Linux, hardening, 27

Pyramid Linux, installing the latest
        build, 28
    serial port address configuration, 15
    serial terminal options, 16
Soekris routerboard series, 87
softphones (software phones), 143–145
software phones (softphones), ALSA
        soundsystem, 145
SOHO (Small Office/Home Office), 583
Source NAT (SNAT), 38, 56
spatial diversity, 116
speex-devel package, 130
Spencer, Mark, 125
SRPM (Source RPM), 583
SSH (Secure Shell), 39, 205, 583
    allowing remote SSH through NAT
        firewalls, 66
    default port, 208
        changing to a nonstandard port, 216
    firewall configuration for remote
        administration, 65
    FreeNX, key generation and management
        with, 233
    getting multiple host keys past NAT, 68
    IPv6 logins, options to permit, 447
    keys, labeling with comments, 222
    known_hosts file on clients, 210
    SSH-1 versus SSH-2, 216
    tunneling, 205
    tunneling x11vnc, 261
    (see also OpenSSH)
ssh-copy-id, 214
sshd -l command, 218
sshd_config, 215, 219
    syntax checking, 218
sshfs, mounting remote filesystems with, 226
ssh-keygen command, 215, 217
    -p switch, 217
SSL (Secure Sockets Layer), 265, 583
SSL VPNs, 265
state (packet filtering), 583
Static address, 584
stunnel, 551, 558
sub index type, 355
subnets, 584
    broadcast addresses, 177
    calculation with ipcalc, 176
subschemas, 336
sudo
    compared to su command, 222
    public-key authentication and, 214
suffix, 335
switch, 584

switches, 8
    management ports, 8
    MDI/MDI-X, 9
    serial ports, 9
SYN/ACK, 584
sysctl command, 55
Syslog servers, building, 560–562
SysRq, 497

T

T1 lines, 2
TAP/TUN drivers, 267
tasksel command, 475
tc command, 175
TCAM (Ternary Content Addressable
    Memory), 7, 173, 585
TCP (Transmission Control Protocol), 39,
    585
tcpdump, 529–533
    TCP flags, capturing with, 533
tcptraceroute, 527
telnet, 550
Ternary Content Addressable Memory (see
    TCAM)
throughput, 6
TightVNC, 229
    multiple concurrent users, 254
    tunneling between Linux and
        Windows, 262–264
time, updating at boot, 121
TLS (Transport Layer Security), 265, 583
traceroute, 527
Transport Layer Security (see TLS)
TTL (Time To Live), 586
tunnel brokers (6to4), 451
tunneling, 205
    X Windows over SSH, 220
    x11vnc over SSH, 261
Twinkle softphone, 143
TwinVNC, 230

U

UART (Universal Asynchronous
    Receiver/Transmitter), 586
UDP, 39
UIDs (user IDs), 334
UltraVNC, 229
Unique Local Unicast addresses, 441
USB 2.0 versus USB 1.1, 51
USB boot, 453
USB headsets, 145
user IDs (UIDs), 334
USERCTL configuration option, 50

V

vectors (RIP), 173
view keyword, 412
Vino, 230
Virtual Network Computing (see VNC)
VLAN (Virtual LAN), 586
VLANs, 9
VNC (Virtual Network Computing), 229, 587
    changing the Linux VNC server
        password, 256
    connecting to an existing X session, 259
    customizing remote desktops, 257
    displaying windows to multiple remote
        users, 254–256
    Microsoft Windows, controlling from
        Linux, 248–250
    remote desktop size, setting, 258
    tunneling TightVNC between Linux and
        Windows, 262–264
    using for remote Linux-to-Linux
        administration, 252
        port numbers, specifying, 253
    using to control Windows and Linux
        simultaneously, 250
    x11vnc, 230
        tunneling over SSH, 261
VNC server for MorphOS, 230
vncpasswd command, 256
voicemail broadcasts, 162
voicemail.conf, 137, 142
VoIP (Voice over Internet Protocol), 587
    VoIP services (see Asterisk)
Voyage Linux, 43
VPNs (Virtual Private Networks), 265, 587
    default gateways, 270
    IPSec VPN, 288
    Linux PPTP VPN servers (see Linux PPTP
        VPN servers)
vsftpd, 459
vtysh, 192

W

WAN (Wide Area Network), 587
WAP (Wireless Access Point), 588
WEP (Wired Equivalent Privacy), 11, 84, 588
wext driver, 99
whitelists, 223
Wi-Fi, 588
Wi-Fi Protected Access (WPA), 84
Win2VNC, 229
Winbind, 588
window manager startup commands, 244
Windows static DHCP clients,
    configuring, 94

Windows, Microsoft (see Microsoft Windows)
WindowsCE.NET server, 230
WINS (Windows Internet Name Service), 588
Wired Equivalent Privacy (WEP), 11, 84
wireless chipsets with Linux compatibility, 83
wireless networking, 11
    access points, 100
      building, 86
      inexpensive options, 45
      supported clients, 100
    authentication with RADIUS
      servers, 100–104
    binary blobs in the kernel, 83
    encryption and authentication, 84
    FreeRADIUS, authenticating clients
      to, 106
    hostnames, changing on Pyramid Linux
      routers, 114
    Internet connection sharing between wired
      and wireless clients, 87
    name services, setting up, 90–92
    probing wireless interface cards, 113
    routing between LAN segments, 108–113
    security, 84
    security risks of unsecured networks, 84
    shutting down one of two antennas, 115
    static IP addresses, setting from DHCP
      services, 93
    WPA2 security enhancements using
      Pyramid Linux, 97–100
Wistron CM9 mini-PCI interface, 83

wlanconfig, 113
WPA (Wi-Fi Protected Access), 84, 589
    support for Windows XP, 99
wpa_supplicant, 85
WPA2, 84, 589
    security enhancements using Pyramid
      Linux, 97–100
WPA-EAP, 84
WPA-Enterprise, 85
WPA-Personal, 84
WPA-PSK, 84
WRAP boards, 44
WvDial, 502
    (see also dial-up networking)
wvdial.conf, 504

X

x11vnc, 230
    tunneling over SSH, 261
x2vnc, 230, 250
X-Lite softphone, 143

Z

zebra, 188, 190
    blackholing routes, 198
zebra.conf, 188
    setting null routes in, 198
ztdummy module, 131

About the Author

Carla Schroder is a self-taught Linux and Windows sysadmin who laid hands on her first computer around her 37th birthday. Her first PC was a Macintosh LC II. Next came an IBM clone, a 386sx running MS-DOS 5, and Windows 3.1, with a 14" color display, which was adequate for many pleasant hours of *DOOM* play. Then, around 1997, she discovered Red Hat 5.0 and had a whole new world to explore.

Somewhere along the way she found herself doing freelance consulting for small businesses and home users, supporting both Linux and Windows users, and integrating Linux and Windows on the LAN. She is the author of *Linux Cookbook* (O'Reilly), and writes Linux how-tos for several computer publications.

Carla is living proof that you're never too old to try something new, computers are a heck of a lot of fun, and anyone can learn to do anything. Visit *http://tuxcomputing.com* for more Carla stuff.

Colophon

The image on the cover of *Linux Networking Cookbook* is a female blacksmith. While historically women worked more commonly as seamstresses and teachers, women blacksmiths have existed as far back as the Middle Ages. Though medieval women often stayed in to cook, bake bread, and sew, some were blacksmiths who made weapons to defend their homes and castles.

In spite of their history in the profession, the presence of women in the blacksmithing industry continued to surprise many. In 1741, author and bookshop owner William Hutton came across a blacksmith's shop while traveling the English countryside. At the shop, he witnessed "one or more females, stripped of their upper garments, and not overcharged with the lower, wielding the hammer with all the grace of the sex." It is thought that finding women—and not men—working as blacksmiths shocked Hutton, while the state of their dress remained an unimportant matter.

Controversy occasionally surrounded the idea of women working as blacksmiths. In 1895, Mrs. Hattie Graham sent in a proposal to the town hall of Sudbury, Massachusetts, to do business as a blacksmith in a shop owned by Miss Mary Heard. That a woman owned a blacksmith shop was not controversial, but a woman working as a blacksmith was. However, Graham's skilled work eventually won over those who had protested her early days of working at the shop.

Even in recent decades many people expressed astonishment at the fact that women previously worked as blacksmiths. Reportedly, tourists wandering through Colonial Williamsburg often asked if women were allowed to be blacksmiths, or wondered if the work was too physically demanding for them.

In the 21st century, blacksmithing has evolved into a profession of empowerment and artistic expression. In 2001, the documentary *Mama Wahunzi* (Swahili for "women blacksmiths") chronicled the lives of three women who learned to make their own wheelchairs and take control of their own mobility. In Africa, women blacksmiths work with women farmers in the design and maintenance of their tools. In the U.S., where it is estimated that 50 full-time female blacksmiths exist today, many blacksmiths produce public art, help restore architecture, and build modern furniture.

The cover image and chapter opening graphics are from *Dover's Women: A Pictorial Archive from 19th-Century Sources*. The cover font is Adobe ITC Garamond. The text font is Linotype Birka; the heading font is Adobe Myriad Condensed; and the code font is LucasFont's TheSans Mono Condensed.

70502

The O'Reilly Advantage

Stay Current and Save Money